Certified General
Accountants Association
of Canada

ADVANCED

CORPORATE

FINANCE

A PRACTICAL APPROACH

WAJEEH ELALI
MCGILL UNIVERSITY

THERESE TRAINOR
MCGILL UNIVERSITY

PEARSON

Addison
Wesley

Toronto

Library and Archives Canada Cataloguing in Publication

Elali, Wajeeh
  Advanced corporate finance: a practical approach / Wajeeh Elali, Therese Trainor.—1st ed.
  Includes index.
  ISBN 978-0-321-49407-8
  1. Corporations—Finance—Textbooks. 2. Business enterprises—Finance—Textbooks. I. Trainor, Therese, 1959-
II. Title.
HG4026.E43 2009   658.15   C2007-905883-3

ISBN-13: 978-0-321-49407-8
ISBN-10: 0-321-49407-5

Vice President, Editorial Director: Gary Bennett
Executive Editor: Samantha Scully
Marketing Manager: Leigh-Anne Graham
Developmental Editors: Helen Smith and Lisa Cicinelli
Production Editor: Imee Salumbides
Copy Editor: Tom Gamblin
Proofreader: Rodney Rawlings
Production Coordinator: Andrea Falkenberg
Composition: Integra
Permissions Research: Sandy Cooke
Art Director: Julia Hall
Cover Design: Kerrin Hands
Interior Design: Dave McKay
Cover Image: Getty Images

For permission to reproduce copyrighted material, the publisher gratefully acknowledges the copyright holders listed under exhibits, tables, and readings, which are considered an extension of this copyright page. The following sections and articles are printed courtesy of Gitman, *Principles of Managerial Finance*, Eleventh US Edition, pp. 16–19, 228, 269, 433–434, 462, 545, © 2006, 2003, 2000, 1997, 1994, 1991 Lawrence J. Gitman. Reproduced by permission of Pearson Education, Inc. All rights reserved: Corporate Governance section (pp. 23–24); Economic Value Added section (pp. 24–25); The Role of Ethics, Considering Ethics, and Ethics and Share Price (pp. 25–26); "Ethics at Hewlett-Packard" (pp. 27–28); the second paragraph under Moral Purposes and Limits of Business Activity (p. 28); the third and fourth paragraphs under Methods Used in Practice (p. 56); "Nonfinancial Considerations in Project Selection" (p. 57); "Warren Buffett versus California Earthquake Authority" (pp. 117–118); "What About Moral Risk?" (pp. 119–120); "Benefits of Two Classes" (p. 187); and "Adobe's Operating Leverage" (pp. 234–235).

2 3 4 5   12 11 10 09 08

Printed and bound in the United States of America.

PEARSON
Addison
Wesley

Brief Contents

Contents

Preface

Because of all the rapid and innovative changes that have occurred in the financial markets and financial technologies over the past decade, the practice of Corporate Finance has become more challenging and exciting than ever. This text is an attempt to convey our considerable enthusiasm for this dynamic and fascinating field. The text has been designed and developed for both practitioners and students alike, whether the latter are finance majors or non-majors. It is ideal for self-study, but given its direct style and focus on examples, it might also be used as a Web-based course.

Written in a relaxed, informal style, the text engages the reader as an active participant rather than as a passive information absorber. A proven learning system that integrates pedagogy with concepts and practical applications has been implemented, allowing the reader to concentrate on the techniques and practices required to make sound financial decisions in an increasingly competitive global business environment. Thus, this textbook serves as an easily accessible resource for readers at all levels who wish to gain a deeper understanding of the interesting and challenging world of corporate finance.

The text appeals to intuition as well as to basic principles whenever possible, because this approach facilitates understanding and promotes the effective implementation of the subject. In keeping with this practical approach, the text extensively uses mini-cases, numerical examples, conceptual questions, and articles concerning the practice of modern corporate finance. Self-evaluation problems and both qualitative and quantitative questions illustrate the application of the financial theories, thereby enabling readers to apply their knowledge to relatively complex, realistic financial situations.

The text is a self-contained resource. It assumes some familiarity with basic accounting and requires basic mathematical skills as well as an understanding of time-value-of-money concepts. However, these topics are also reviewed in chapters dedicated to these important fundamental concepts. Students or readers with differing career backgrounds and abilities will find the text accessible and easy to understand owing to the clear writing style and the regular use of examples. After studying this text, students will have the basic knowledge needed to advance in the subject and apply what they have learned.

This textbook is about corporate finance and, as such, it focuses on how companies invest in financial and real assets and how they raise the needed funds to pay for these investments. By design, the text does not serve as an encyclopedia on the topic. As the table of contents indicates, it has a total of 10 chapters that provide readers with a detailed overview of corporate finance. It focuses on financial tools and techniques without compromising the underlying theory. Use of the Web in financial analysis is encouraged so that Web-based content is introduced in several ways. The text also provides readings from leading financial journals and professional magazines.

Organization

The basic skills and knowledge presented in this book are as follows:

- **Chapters 1 and 2** focus on capital investment decisions under the assumption that the financing decisions have already been made.

- **Chapters 3, 4, and 5** assume that investment decisions have been made and expand upon the financing problems faced by a financial manager.

- **Chapter 6** considers investment and financing alternatives that have special features: project financing and leasing. This chapter describes the special tools and techniques that the financial manager needs to use to evaluate these investment decisions.

- **Chapter 7** provides a comprehensive analysis of treasury risk management. It complements the previous chapters on investment and financing. Prior to Chapter 7, the coverage of investing and financing decisions assumed a given level of risk and also assumed that diversification was the only way to manage this risk. This chapter highlights the basic knowledge and techniques used in actively managing risk.

- **Chapter 8** considers the features and the valuation techniques of futures and forwards derivative securities.

- **Chapter 9** studies the features and valuation techniques of options and swaps. It explains that investment projects undertaken by a firm and the securities used to raise funds often contain embedded options. These options are often ignored in the traditional techniques of analysis. A framework for estimating the values of these options is provided, taking the investment and financing decisions one step further in dealing with practical problems.

- **Chapter 10** explores the relationships between a firm's investment, financing, and risk management decisions. It introduces short-term financial planning and emphasizes the role of cash budgeting as the main tool for short-term financial management, addressing the relationship between the firm's liquidity and its long-term financing decisions. It then develops the long-term financial planning model as a tool to test the consistency of the firm's financial, operating, and investment decisions.

Chapter Elements

- **Chapter Overview** Each chapter begins with a general description of its contents.
- **Learning Objectives** A set of learning objectives at the beginning of each chapter enables the reader to focus their study.
- **Minicases** Practical minicases with questions and answers are presented throughout the book.
- **You Apply It** Other practical scenarios with questions and answers are given in selected chapters.
- **Readings** Selected articles intended to illustrate important concepts and practices are used throughout the book.
- **Key Terms** Boldfaced key terms defined within the text are alphabetically compiled at the end of each chapter.
- **Important Equations** A summary of key equations used throughout each chapter can be found in the end-of-chapter material.
- **Web Links** For additional reference, annotated Web links are listed at the end of each chapter.
- **Self-Test Questions** A set of five types of questions is given at the end of each chapter. Answers to these questions may be found on the Text Enrichment Site for this book (www.pearsoned.ca/elali).

Acknowledgments

This text was developed from CGA-Canada Lesson notes for their Advanced Finance course.

Writing a textbook is a lengthy and complicated process achievable only with the cooperation and effort of many people. The editors, the administrative support staff, and the publishing team at Pearson Education Canada and CGA-Canada deserve a tremendous amount of credit for the support and the work that went into putting this text together. All the many valuable comments and suggestions that we received helped us to improve the content, organization, discussions, and flow of the book. We would like to acknowledge our talented editors Samantha Scully and Lisa Cicinelli, as well as Susan Ferris from CGA-Canada, who made us persevere and who helped pull all the pieces of this project together, and Jennifer Trainor, our Webliographer. They all deserve special thanks. Sincere thanks also go to Tom Gamblin, Imee Salumbides, Gina Letourneau, and all the others who worked on the text. We particularly appreciated the team's ability to juggle deadlines with much grace and understanding. We highly appreciate your inspiration, the teamwork, and the organized effort that helped make this text a reality within a remarkably short time frame.

We believe this text will greatly benefit those who wish to engage in the world of corporate finance and use their expertise to advance in their careers. Good luck and best wishes!

Wajeeh Elali
Montreal, Quebec

Therese Trainor
Chateauguay, Quebec

Chapter 1
Basic Concepts

CHAPTER OVERVIEW

This introductory chapter reviews the fundamental concepts on which financial managers base their decisions. It also reviews the basics of capital budgeting techniques as tools for making capital investment decisions. These types of decisions represent some of the primary duties of the financial manager.

The chapter begins by describing the role of the financial market in allocating the wealth of individuals, businesses, and governments between current consumption and investments for future consumption. Section 1.1 explains that, under conditions of perfect and efficient markets, investors rank their investment opportunities in terms of the marginal rates of return. Only investment opportunities that have a marginal return greater than the opportunity cost of capital are considered. Investors invest and borrow to allocate the optimal amount of real assets, regardless of investment consumption desires. As a result, financial managers are able to separate investment decisions from financing decisions.

The appropriate allocation of capital by financial managers requires that financial markets be efficient. Section 1.2 explains briefly the conditions required for, and the implications of, market efficiency. Financial managers must understand market efficiency, the importance of arbitrage, and how historical information is reflected in the intrinsic value of a security.

Section 1.3 highlights the role of the financial manager as an agent for shareholders. In this role, the financial manager seeks to maximize shareholder wealth. You are reminded of the ethical and moral issues that you may face in your career as a financial manager. The goal is to alert you that moral and ethical considerations may, in the long run, be more important than a short-sighted pursuit of maximizing wealth.

Section 1.4 addresses the relationship between net present value and required return. In your introductory finance course, you studied the concepts of time value of money and their application to the present and future value of money. This topic serves as a brief reminder of their importance.

In Section 1.5, you review the basics of the capital budgeting process. The important steps in determining the desirability of a project are identifying and estimating incremental after-tax cash flows, determining the appropriate discount rate of the cash flows, calculating the net present value of the cash flows, and using other capital budgeting criteria if desirable. You are given the tools to account for the tax implications of capital investment and encouraged to study in detail the necessary adjustments.

Finally, you study various capital budgeting evaluation methods. Section 1.6 emphasizes that the net present value technique is the most appropriate for selecting desirable projects. A comparison between various techniques is provided to assist you in identifying situations where other methods may be useful.

Learning Objectives

After completing this chapter, you will be able to:

- Explain how the financial market helps individuals to transfer wealth from one period to another.

- Identify an individual's optimal investment strategy under certainty.

- Describe the nature of efficient financial markets and how arbitrage between market participants can lead to better pricing of securities.

- Explain the three levels of market efficiency and their consequences for the internal projects of firms.

- Describe the nature of the relationship between shareholders and managers and the ethical issues that may arise.

- Explain why management should select projects with a positive net present value.

- Explain how cash flows are estimated for capital budgeting purposes.

- Evaluate a project using the net present value technique.

- Evaluate economically dependent projects.

- Interpret the internal rate of return, average rate of return, profitability index, and payback of a project.

- Compare and contrast the net present value technique with other capital budgeting techniques.

This knowledge will provide you with the professional skills to:

- Evaluate investment strategies for individuals and organizations

- Understand the ethical implications in the relationships between shareholders and managers and to apply professional ethical standards to these situations.

- Develop financial forecasts and plans including looking at alternatives and assessing the tax implications.

HOW THIS CHAPTER RELATES TO OTHER CHAPTERS IN THIS BOOK

This first chapter presents the framework for understanding the finance environment. It requires an appreciation of basic finance concepts. This chapter serves as the foundation for all decision making in the remaining chapters.

The variables considered here will be examined in greater detail throughout the remainder of this book. For example, understanding the independence of the consumption and investment decisions allows for an exploration of portfolio risk and return. This leads to an investigation of capital budgeting under uncertainty, long-term financing issues, capital structure theory, and risk management. Each chapter in this book builds on the knowledge obtained in the previous one.

1.1 CONSUMPTION, INVESTMENT, AND FINANCIAL MARKETS

Transferring Wealth from One Period to Another

People generate and spend cash flows unevenly over time. For example, the typical Canadian starts generating significant cash flows immediately after entering employment. At this stage, the cash requirements to buy major assets such as a house or a car are greater than the available cash, leading the individual to become a net borrower. Cash flows from employment are used to repay the debt gradually. In the future, the individual will become a net investor. Cash flows from employment will continue until retirement. Beyond retirement, the person's main source of spending will be the wealth saved in prior years when income exceeded spending and was invested in anticipation of future needs.

The typical Canadian transfers wealth generated in prior years to future years for the purposes of spending. The financial market facilitates the process of wealth transfer from one period to the other. Deficit-spending individuals borrow by creating financial claims against their assets and sell these claims to surplus-spending individuals. These claims can be in the form of marketable securities, such as bonds, preferred shares, and common shares, or non-marketable securities, such as loans arranged privately between borrowers and lenders.

The financial market also determines the rate at which lending and borrowing take place. This rate of return is equal to the risk-free rate plus a risk premium. The **risk-free rate** is the rate that compensates lenders for:

- giving borrowers the right to use the lenders' money
- any expected losses to lenders that may occur because of changes in the money's purchasing power (inflation)

The premium added to compensate for the possible loss of purchasing power is approximately the inflation rate expected in the future. The risk-free rate does not compensate for past inflation. Instead, it attempts to compensate for future inflation.

The **risk premium** is the additional interest demanded by investors as compensation against several types of risk. **Default risk** refers to the possibility that some borrowers may not return the money fully or on time. **Liquidity risk** is the risk that lenders may need the money and demand it back when borrowers are not ready to return the money. **Reinvestment rate risk** is the risk that borrowers may return the money early when interest rates have dropped, so that the lender is forced to reinvest the money at a lower rate. The risk-free rate does not account for these risks.

Role of the Financial Market in Facilitating Wealth Transfer

Minicase 1-1 illustrates how people can borrow or lend in the financial market to consume their wealth in a pattern that is not necessarily similar to the pattern by which they receive their wealth. The information from this minicase will be used throughout this topic to illustrate concepts related to borrowing and lending in the financial market. The minicase assumes that markets are competitive and efficient.

An **efficient market** occurs when prices of securities traded regularly in the market fully reflect all publicly available information related to their valuation and adjust quickly to new information. In the absence of default risk and market uncertainty, a competitive and efficient financial market allows individuals to lend and borrow money at the same rate. A complete explanation of the conditions for efficiency is presented in Section 1.2.

MINICASE 1-1 TRADEOFFS BETWEEN PERIODS WHEN MARKETS ARE COMPETITIVE AND EFFICIENT

Marie just turned 21 years old and has exactly one year to finish college. Two days ago her parents handed her a cheque for $4,000, which can be cashed any time. They also gave her a $6,000 term deposit that yields 8% annually. The term deposit can be cashed one year from today with interest (interest at 8% is equal to $480).

Marie wonders whether she should borrow against the term deposit to buy a car now, or keep this money until she graduates from college and then take a long vacation to visit exotic places. Marie can either lend or borrow money at the current rate of 8%. She prepares Exhibit 1-1 to help herself visualize the alternatives.

Exhibit 1-1
Marie's Spending and Saving Choices

Choice #	Spending now (Period 1)	Investment or borrowing	Investment return or borrowing costs	Cash inflow one year later	Cash for spending (Period 2)
(1)	(2)	(3)	(4)	(5)	(6) = (3) + (4) + (5)
1	$10,000	$(6,000)	$(480)	$6,480	$ 0
2	8,000	(4,000)	(320)	6,480	2,160
3	7,000	(3,000)	(240)	6,480	3,240
4	6,000	(2,000)	(160)	6,480	4,320
5	5,000	(1,000)	(80)	6,480	5,400
6	4,000	0	0	6,480	6,480
7	3,000	1,000	80	6,480	7,560
8	2,000	2,000	160	6,480	8,640
9	1,000	3,000	240	6,480	9,720
10	0	4,000	320	6,480	10,800

Column 1 shows several examples of spending choices available to Marie. At one extreme, Marie can spend nothing (Choice #10). In this case, she will have an investment of $4,000 (Column 3), which can be invested in the market at 8%. In a year, this choice will yield Marie $320 (Column 4), which represents the 8% interest on the investment. Also, she expects $6,480 from the term deposit. In total, she can spend $10,800 at the beginning of the second year, the sum of the two cash flows expected at that time. The present value of $10,800 discounted at the 8% rate is $10,000.

Case Continued >

At the other extreme, Marie can spend as much as $10,000 (Choice #1) now. This amount represents the maximum amount of her spending and is equal to the present value of her new wealth, calculated as:

$$PV = C_0 + CF_1 \div (1 + r) = \$4,000 + \$6,480 \div 1.08$$
$$= \$10,000 \qquad \textbf{(Equation 1-1)}$$

where

PV = present value of Marie's wealth
C_0 = current cash flow ($4,000)
CF_1 = cash flow expected next year ($6,480)
r = lending and borrowing rate in the market (8%)

If Marie wants to spend $10,000 now, Column 3 shows that she must borrow $6,000 because her current cash position is only $4,000. Column 4 indicates the interest that Marie must repay at the beginning of Period 2. Given that she is expecting exactly the future value of the loan, nothing will be left for spending next year. The present value of her total spending over the two periods is $10,000.

Between the two extremes, Marie has an infinite number of choices. Other than spending $4,000 now and $6,480 a year from today, Marie can either invest or borrow to achieve her desired spending pattern. However, the present value of her current and future spending is always $10,000, regardless of the chosen spending pattern.

Exhibit 1-2 is a graphic representation of the information found in Exhibit 1-1. The horizontal axis $P_{10}W_1$ shows the spending alternatives Marie has for the first period. For example:

- P_3 represents Marie's choice to spend $7,000 this year and invest $3,000 ($10,000 – $7,000).

- P_6 represents spending $4,000 this year and investing $6,000.

- P_8 represents spending $2,000 this year and investing $8,000.

- P_{10} implies that she will not spend any part of her wealth this year but will invest the entire $10,000.

The vertical axis represents the wealth that will be spent during Period 2 corresponding to each alternative on $P_{10}W_1$. It shows the future value of the wealth invested for next year. For example:

- If Marie chooses to consume W_1 ($10,000) this year, she will not be able to save any wealth for next year. Her Period 2 consumption will be $0 ($P_{10}$ on the vertical axis).

- P_3 represents Marie's choice of spending $7,000 in Period 1 and investing $3,000 for Period 2. The interest earned from investing in the financial market gives Marie $3,240 ($3,000 × 1.08) for spending in Period 2 (F_3).

- If Marie chooses to spend $4,000 in Period 1, she will save $6,000 for next year ($P_6$). Her savings will be invested in the financial market at 8% to produce $6,480 ($F_6$) for spending in Period 2.

- P_8 represents a choice of spending $2,000 in Period 1 and investing $8,000 for Period 2. In this scenario, Marie's spending capacity for Period 2 is $8,640 ($8,000 × 1.08), indicated by F_8.

- The spending choice represented by P_6 and F_6 is the only choice that does not require Marie to borrow or lend in the first period. Her spending in Period 2 will

Case Continued >

Exhibit 1-2 Graphic Representation of Marie's Spending and Saving Choices

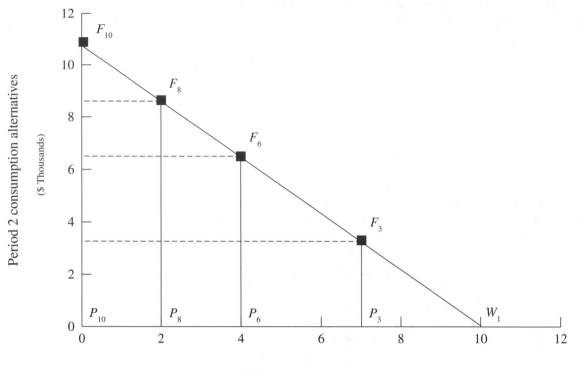

Period 1 consumption alternatives
($ Thousands)

P_i: spending choice, in thousands of dollars

F_i: amount of spending obtained from the financial market investment, in thousands of dollars

W_i: present value of wealth ($10,000)

where

$W_1 = \$10,000$	$F_8 = \$8,640$
$P_3 = \$7,000$	$F_6 = \$6,480$
$P_6 = \$4,000$	$F_3 = \$3,240$
$P_8 = \$2,000$	

equal her cash flow in Period 2 ($6,480), which is the future value of $6,000 (the term deposit), the portion of her current wealth saved for next year.

■ If Marie decides to spend $7,000 in Period 1 ($P_3$), her spending will be above her current cash flow. She has to borrow $3,000 ($7,000 – $4,000) against her future consumption. Consequently, her spending next year will be limited to the amount represented by F_3.

■ Any choice on segment P_6W_1 will require borrowing against next year's cash flows.

■ Any choice on segment $P_{10}P_6$ entails investing in Period 1 and spending in Period 2 an amount higher than $6,480. For example, P_8 represents spending $2,000 in Period 1 and investing $2,000 in addition to the amount currently invested ($6,000, the present value of the term deposit). F_8 shows that in this scenario, spending next year will be $8,640 ($8,000 × 1.08).

Impact of Interest Rate Levels on the Spending Pattern

Generally, the level of interest rates will affect the future value of wealth and the future spending power of individuals. Exhibit 1-3 shows this effect of market interest rates. It is a replication of Exhibit 1-2 with lines W_1Y_1 and W_1Y_2 added. Changes in the interest rate change the slope of the line. For example:

- The slope of line W_1Y_1 ($r = 0\%$) is -1.00.
- The slope of line W_1F_{10} ($r = 8\%$) is -1.08.
- The slope of line W_1Y_2 ($r = 16\%$) is -1.16.

Exhibit 1-3 Impact of Interest Rate Levels on Spending and Saving Choices

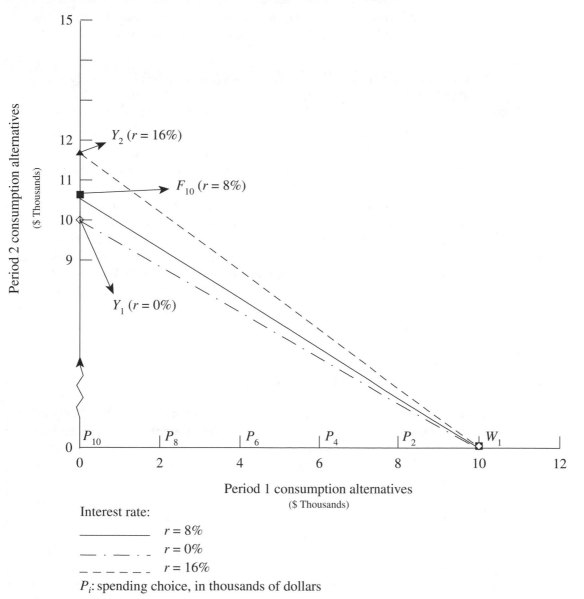

P_i: spending choice, in thousands of dollars

Generally, the slope of line W_1F_{10} is $-(1 + r)$, where r is the interest rate.

Exhibit 1-3 shows that for the same level of spending in year 1, spending next year under an 8% interest rate is less than spending under a 16% rate and higher than spending under 0% interest. However, the present value of the wealth, as represented by W_1 ($10,000), does not change, regardless of the interest rate level.

Including Real Assets as Investment Choices—the Investment Schedule

So far, it has been assumed that Marie's investment choices are limited to those available in the financial market where the investment rate of return is equal to the borrowing rate. Thus, the opportunity cost of using capital now as opposed to one year later is 8%. In Minicase 1-2, Marie is willing to invest in real assets as opposed to financial assets. The cash generated from these investments will fulfil her future consumption needs. An **investment schedule** is used to show available investment alternatives.

MINICASE 1-2 EXPANDING MARIE'S INVESTMENT CHOICES

After taking time to rethink her options, Marie comes up with a set of real asset investment alternatives. Three months ago, she was not able to find a reliable typing and printing service on campus to finish her term project on time. She thinks that an investment in such a business would be extremely profitable.

Using some of the concepts she has learned in accounting, finance, and marketing, she prepares the investment schedule shown in Exhibit 1-4. As a minimum investment, she needs $3,000 to open for business with limited capacity to service customers. Given that her service would be the only one on campus, she can charge high prices. She estimates that cash flow at the end of the year would be $12,000. However, Marie can increase capacity in incremental steps, where each increment will cost an additional $1,000. The total investment required and the estimated cash flows from investment under the various investment alternatives are displayed in Exhibit 1-4.

Exhibit 1-4
Marie's Investment Alternatives

Investment alternative	Total investment	Incremental investment	Year-end cash flow
1	$3,000	$3,000	$12,000
2	4,000	1,000	14,500
3	5,000	1,000	16,000
4	6,000	1,000	17,080
5	7,000	1,000	17,680
6	8,000	1,000	18,180
7	9,000	1,000	18,580
8	10,000	1,000	18,880

Case Continued >

Exhibit 1-5 Graphic Representation of Marie's Real Asset Investment Schedule

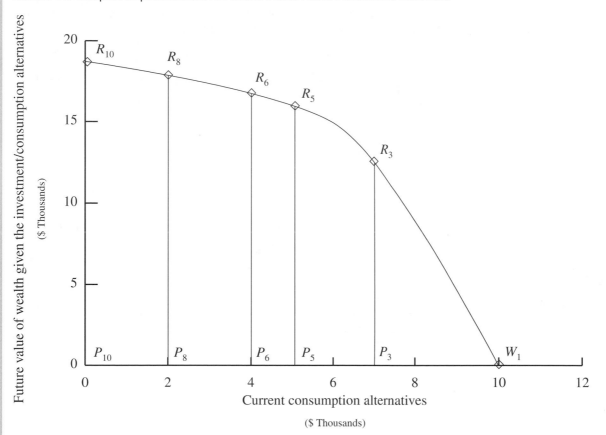

◇ investment schedule

P_i: current consumption choice, in thousands of dollars

R_i: level of spending obtained by investing in real assets, in thousands of dollars

where

$W_1 = \$10,000$	$P_6 = \$4,000$	$R_5 = \$16,000$	$R_{10} = \$18,880$
$P_3 = \$7,000$	$P_8 = \$2,000$	$R_6 = \$17,080$	
$P_5 = \$5,000$	$R_3 = \$12,000$	$R_8 = \$18,180$	

Exhibit 1-5 is a graphic representation of Marie's investment schedule. The horizontal axis represents the initial wealth that may be divided between investment in the project (the printing business) and current consumption. On this axis:

■ W_1 represents Marie's initial total wealth of $10,000.

■ P_3 represents the situation where Marie invests $3,000 in the printing business and allocates the balance of $7,000 for current consumption.

■ P_5 represents Marie's choice to invest $5,000 in the business and to allocate the balance of $5,000 to current consumption.

■ P_6 and P_8 represent respectively the choices of investing $6,000 or $8,000 in the business and allocating the balance to current consumption.

■ P_{10} represents Marie's choice to invest the entire $10,000 in the business and to allocate nothing to current consumption.

Case Continued >

The vertical axis represents the future value of the invested wealth for various investment alternatives at time 0. From Exhibit 1-4, if Marie's investment in the project is $3,000 ($P_3$), the year-end cash flow (R_3) will be $12,000. Similarly:

- R_5, R_6, R_8, and R_{10} are respectively $16,000, $17,080, $18,180, and $18,880.

Exhibit 1-5 shows a curved line that joins W_1, R_3, R_5, R_6, R_8, and R_{10}. This curved line represents Marie's real asset investment schedule.

Total Return and Marginal Return

The **total return** (as a percentage) over an investment horizon of one year is the growth rate of the initial investment. It is determined by the following formula:

$$\text{Total return} = \frac{CF_1}{C_0} - 1 \qquad \text{(Equation 1-2)}$$

where
  CF_1 = future cash flow to be received one year from today
  C_0 = cost of initial investment

The **marginal return** is defined as the return on the last dollar invested. It is determined by the following formula:

$$\text{Marginal return} = \frac{CF_{1_n} - CF_{1_{n-1}}}{C_{0_n} - C_{0_{n-1}}} - 1 \qquad \text{(Equation 1-3)}$$

where
  CF_{1_n} = total cash flows, alternative n
  $CF_{1_{n-1}}$ = total cash flows, alternative $n-1$
  C_{0_n} = capital invested, alternative n
  $C_{0_{n-1}}$ = capital invested, alternative $n-1$

MINICASE 1-3 DETERMINING TOTAL RETURN AND MARGINAL RETURN

Marie has prepared Exhibit 1-6 to determine total return and marginal return for her investment alternatives. The exhibit shows that she can invest a minimum of $3,000 (alternative 1) in the printing business. For this investment, her cash flow at the end of the year will be $12,000. This cash flow represents:

$$\text{Total return} = (\$12,000 \div \$3,000) - 1 = 300\%$$

If Marie invests an additional $1,000 (alternative 2) for a total investment of $4,000, her total cash inflow at the end of the year will be $14,500. Thus, her total return on the total amount invested will be 262.5%. Similarly, as she invests more and more in the business, her future cash flow increases and her total return on investment remains substantially higher than 8%, the rate in the financial market.

At the extreme, she can invest the entire $10,000, the present value of her current wealth, and her total return will be 88.80%. Based on this analysis, she decides to invest

Case Continued >

Exhibit 1-6
Total Return and Marginal Return for Marie's Investment Alternatives

Investment alternative	Total investment	Incremental investment	Year-end cash flow	Total return	Marginal return
1	$3,000	$3,000	$12,000	300.00%	300.00%
2	4,000	1,000	14,500	262.50	150.00
3	5,000	1,000	16,000	220.00	50.00
4	6,000	1,000	17,080	184.67	8.00
5	7,000	1,000	17,680	152.57	−40.00
6	8,000	1,000	18,180	127.25	−50.00
7	9,000	1,000	18,580	106.44	−60.00
8	10,000	1,000	18,880	88.80	−70.00

the entire present value of her wealth in the printing business. She arranges for a loan for $6,000 and gets the $10,000 ready for investment.

However, at the last minute, Marie decides to take another look at her alternatives. The more she thinks about it, the more she realizes that she made a mistake with her earlier analysis. The last column of Exhibit 1-6 calculates the marginal return. For example, if she invests only $3,000 in the business, the marginal return will be equal to the total return as the $3,000 are the last dollars invested in the business. Investment alternative 2 of Exhibit 1-6 shows that her return on the amount ($1,000) invested after the initial $3,000 will be:

Marginal return = [($14,500 − $12,000) ÷ ($4,000 − $3,000)] − 1 = 150%

This is the marginal return that occurs for investment alternative 2.

Marginal Return—The Appropriate Measure for Investment Purposes

The last column of Exhibit 1-6 shows that the marginal return decreases as the amount of invested capital increases. If the total investment equals $6,000, the marginal return equals 8%, the rate of return in the financial market. If the total investment equals $7,000, the marginal return drops to −40%, which is less than the market rate. Any additional investment beyond $7,000 also has a negative marginal return, implying that the additional investment will not be completely recovered.

The total return, however, continues to be positive because the cash flow from earlier investments offsets the losses on the additional capital. Based on the marginal return, Marie would be better off to limit her total investment to no more than $6,000, the point at which the marginal return is at least equal to 8%.

Exhibit 1-7 demonstrates the levels of cash flow expected next year under various scenarios of splitting the current wealth between the printing business and the financial market. The exhibit assumes that Marie decided to keep all her wealth and spend it next year. Suppose she decides to invest a portion of the $10,000 in the printing service and

Exhibit 1-7
Future Value of Marie's Investment Alternatives

Investment alternative	Amount invested in project	Cash flows from project	Amount invested in financial market at 8%	Cash flows from financial market	Total cash for spending next year
(1)	(2)	(3)	(4)	(5)	(6) = (3) + (5)
0	$ 0	$ 0	$10,000	$10,800	$10,800
1	3,000	12,000	7,000	7,560	19,560
2	4,000	14,500	6,000	6,480	20,980
3	5,000	16,000	5,000	5,400	21,400
4	6,000	17,080	4,000	4,320	21,400
5	7,000	17,680	3,000	3,240	20,920
6	8,000	18,180	2,000	2,160	20,340
7	9,000	18,580	1,000	1,080	19,660
8	10,000	18,880	0	0	18,880

Note: Shaded rows represent optimal investment strategies.

the other portion in the financial market at the 8% current rate. The objective is to find the optimal split that will maximize her future spending.

Column 6 of Exhibit 1-7 shows the future cash flow that Marie can expect under various alternatives of splitting the $10,000 between the financial market and the printing business. For example, investment alternative 0 shows the cash flow if she does not invest in the printing service. Investing her entire $10,000 in the financial market at 8% will give her $10,800.

Now consider investment alternative 1. Under this alternative, Marie invests $3,000 (Column 2) in the printing service and $7,000 (Column 4) in the financial market. One year later, she will receive $12,000 (Column 3) from the printing business plus $7,560 ($7,000 × 1.08) from the financial market (Column 5). Her total cash flow that year is $19,560 (Column 6).

Exhibit 1-7 shows that the **optimal investment strategy**, the aggregation of investments offering the highest net present value (NPV), is to invest either $5,000 or $6,000 in the printing service and to invest the remaining portion in the financial market. These two strategies dominate all other alternatives because each produces more future cash flow than the others. For example, if Marie chooses to invest $8,000 in the printing service and $2,000 in the financial market, this strategy will produce $20,340 for spending the following year. The optimal investment strategies will each produce a total of $21,400.

Marie should be indifferent, however, about choosing between the two optimal strategies because they produce the same results. The marginal return on the sixth $1,000 of investment in the printing business is exactly 8%, which is equal to the return in the financial market. Thus, Marie should be indifferent as to investing this $1,000 in the financial market or in the printing business. In this case, the optimal investment in real assets is the amount of capital that will produce a higher marginal return than that obtained in the financial market.

Independence of Investment and Financing Decisions

Perfect markets imply perfect competition, rational and well-informed investors and consumers, and prices that capture all external costs and benefits. On the other hand, efficient markets imply the existence of good information-processing mechanisms so that relevant information is embodied in security prices. In a perfect and efficient market, the optimal investment strategy should be independent of a person's consumption choices.

For example, suppose Marie needs to buy a car now and decides to start the printing business. As soon as the market realizes the project's value, she can borrow against the anticipated cash flow or sell the business. The current market price is equal to the present value of the future cash flow. The cash flow is $17,080 (alternative 4 of Exhibit 1-7) if Marie invests $6,000 in the business. What discount rate should be used to calculate its present value? When the business becomes well established, buyers should be satisfied with a return equal to the rate of return available in the financial market. This implies that the discount rate should be 8%. Therefore, the current present value of the business is $15,815 ($17,080 ÷ 1.08).

$$
\begin{aligned}
\text{Marie's current} \atop \text{total wealth} &= \text{initial} \atop \text{wealth} + \text{present value} \atop \text{of the business} - \text{investment} \atop \text{in the business} \\
&= \$10,000 + \$15,815 - \$6,000 \\
&= \$19,815
\end{aligned}
$$

$$
\text{Net present value} \atop \text{of the investment} \atop \text{opportunity} = \text{present value} \atop \text{of the business} - \text{investment} \atop \text{in the business}
$$

Thus, total wealth may be restated as:

Total wealth = initial wealth + NPV(investment opportunities)   **(Equation 1-4)**

Maximizing Wealth—Graphic Representation Exhibit 1-8 is a graphic representation of the previous explanation. The horizontal axis represents the initial wealth available for allocation between current consumption, investment in the business, and investment in the financial market. W_1 represents the initial total wealth of the investor, $10,000 in Marie's case. P_3, P_5, P_6, P_8, and P_{10} represent, respectively, Marie's choices to invest $3,000, $5,000, $6,000, $8,000, and the entire $10,000. In each case, she would allocate the balance to current consumption. Notice that the definitions of these points match the definitions provided with Exhibit 1-5. Similarly, the vertical axis represents the future value of the wealth under various investment alternatives taken at time 0.

Investing Exclusively in the Financial Market The straight line that joins W_1, F_3, F_5, F_6, F_8, and F_{10} represents future cash flows if the initial wealth is split between consumption today and investments in the financial market at the 8% rate. For example, F_3 represents $3,240, the amount of future cash flows expected from investing $3,000 in the financial market and leaving $7,000 for current consumption.

Investing Exclusively in Real Assets As demonstrated in Exhibit 1-5, the curved line that joins W_1, R_3, R_5, R_6, R_8, and R_{10} represents Marie's future cash flows if the initial wealth is split between consumption today and investments in the printing business. This curve is often called the investment schedule because it represents the cash flow

Exhibit 1-8 Investment Schedule and the Consumption Preferences Line

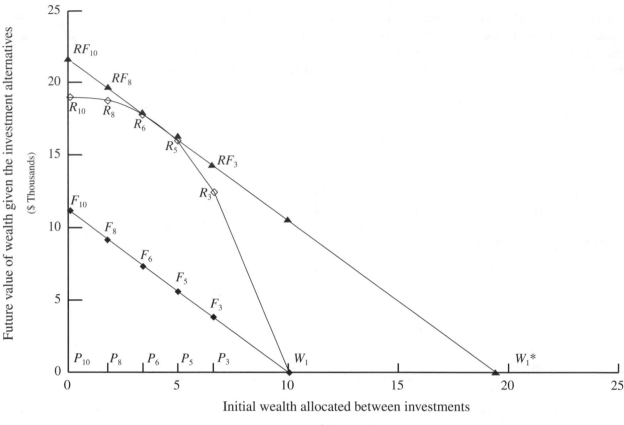

⬦ R_i: amount of spending obtained from investing exclusively in real assets

◆ F_i: amount of spending obtained from investing exclusively in the financial market

▲ RF_i: amount of spending from investment in a combination of real assets and financial market

    W_1^*: present value of future cash flows following the optimal investment strategy

where

W_1	=	\$10,000	R_5	=	\$16,000
P_3	=	\$7,000	R_6	=	\$17,080
P_5	=	\$5,000	R_8	=	\$18,180
P_6	=	\$4,000	R_{10}	=	\$18,880
P_8	=	\$2,000	RF_3	=	\$15,240
W_1^*	=	\$19,815	RF_8	=	\$19,240
R_3	=	\$12,000	RF_{10}	=	\$21,400

expected from the available investment alternatives. For example, R_3 represents \$12,000, the amount of future cash flows expected from investing \$3,000 in the printing business and leaving \$7,000 for current consumption.

Investment Schedule after Combining Real and Financial Investments

Exhibit 1-8 shows the line that joins W_1, R_3, R_5, R_6, RF_8, and RF_{10} and represents Marie's investment schedule if the initial wealth is distributed between current consumption, investing in the printing business, and investing in the financial market. While W_1, R_3, R_5, and R_6 are equal to the points illustrated in Exhibit 1-5, where Marie invested exclusively in real assets, RF_8 and RF_{10} are obtained by splitting the amount to be invested between real assets and the financial market. Therefore, they are labelled as RF, while the subscripts indicate the amount in thousands to be invested.

For example, the optimal investment strategies pointed out in Exhibit 1-7 suggest that Marie can invest up to $5,000 (or $6,000) in the printing business, invest another portion or none in the financial market at 8%, and allocate the remainder, if any, to current consumption. RF_8 represents a strategy of investing $5,000 in the printing business, $3,000 in the financial market, and allocating $2,000 to current consumption. Under this strategy, the investment in the printing business will produce $16,000, and the $3,000 at 8% in the financial market will produce $3,240. Thus, Marie's wealth after one year will be $19,240.

Comparing the Alternatives Exhibit 1-8 compares the alternatives. For example, consider P_8, which represents Marie's decision to allocate $2,000 for current consumption and $8,000 for investment. One choice is to invest the entire amount in the financial market at 8%. This means that she will have $8,640 ($8,000 × 1.08) for consumption in Period 2. This alternative is represented by F_8 in the exhibit. A second choice is to invest the entire $8,000 in the project (real assets). In this case, Marie's future wealth one year later will be $18,180, as indicated by alternative 6 in Exhibit 1-4. This future wealth is represented by R_8 in Exhibit 1-8.

However, Exhibit 1-7 shows that it is not optimal to invest the entire $8,000 in the printing business. A maximum of $5,000 (or $6,000) can be allocated to the business, and the remaining amount can be invested in the financial market. For example, Marie may invest $5,000 in the printing business and $3,000 in the financial market. In this case, Marie's wealth one year later will be $19,240. This wealth is represented by RF_8 in Exhibit 1-8.

R_5, R_6, RF_8, and RF_{10} form a straight line. This straight line occurs because optimally investing any amount beyond $5,000 will generate only 8% return, regardless of the amount. Thus, the slope of the line is -1.08, which is equal to the slope of line W_1F_{10}.

The straight line $RF_{10}R_5$ intersects the horizontal axis at point W_1^*. This point represents the present value of Marie's future cash flows if she follows the optimal investment strategy. Consequently, the new wealth that can be generated from investing the optimal amount in the printing business is represented by $W_1W_1^*$. This is the net present value of investing $5,000 in the printing business to generate $16,000 a year from today. Discounting $16,000 at 8% and subtracting the initial investment of $5,000 yields $9,815. W_1^* represents the new total wealth of $19,815 after the investment.

Consumption Preferences Line Exhibit 1-8 shows line $W_1^*RF_{10}$, which is often called the **consumption preferences line**. This line is a graphic representation of optimal investment strategies. It is obtained by drawing a line with a slope equal to $-(1 + r)$, where r is the rate of return in the financial market, and moving this line to a position where it will be tangent to the investment schedule. The point of tangency represents the optimal investment strategy. Any move away from the tangency position either is not feasible or reduces the net present value. For example, moving the line $W_1^*RF_{10}$ parallel to itself to the right beyond W_1^* is not feasible because it no longer intersects the given investment schedule. Any move to the left will decrease the distance between points W_1 and W_1^*, indicating a decrease in the present value.

In developing the consumption preferences line, it is assumed that Marie can borrow and lend at the same rate because in this example the market is perfect and efficient. The consumption preferences line would be different if the borrowing rate were higher than the lending rate.

When the lending rate is equal to the borrowing rate, the consumption preferences line is a straight line tangent to the investment opportunity set at the point where the marginal rate of return is equal to the opportunity cost of capital. The portion of the line to the left of the tangency point (left segment) represents situations where the investor lends money. The segment to the right of the tangency point (right segment) represents situations when the investor borrows money. The slope of the left segment is equal to $-(1 + r_L)$, where r_L is the lending rate. The slope of the right segment is equal to $-(1 + r_B)$, where r_B is the borrowing rate. When r_L equals r_B, the two slopes are equal and the straight line is obtained. If r_B is greater than r_L, the right segment will have a steeper slope. It will be tangent to the investment opportunity set at a point farther to the right from the initial tangency point. The resulting consumption preferences line would be similar to line $ABCD$ in Exhibit 1-9.

Exhibit 1-9 Consumption Preferences Line When the Borrowing Rate Is Higher Than the Lending Rate

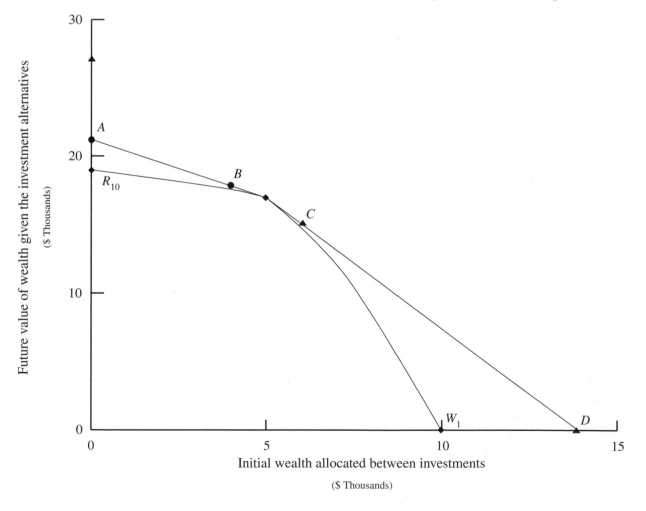

♦ Investment schedule

● Slope $= -(1 + r_L)$

▲ Slope $= -(1 + r_B)$

Consumption Choice Does Not Affect the Investment Decision In an environment where markets are efficient and perfect, an individual should always invest the optimal amount in real assets, regardless of consumption choice. To continue with Marie's example, she should invest $5,000 in the printing business. If her preference is to allocate $2,000 to current consumption and invest $8,000, she can invest the additional $3,000 in the financial market. This situation would be represented by point RF_8 on line W_1*RF_{10} in Exhibit 1-8.

Alternatively, if Marie decides to allocate $7,000 of her current wealth to current consumption and invest only $3,000, she should borrow an additional $2,000 to invest the optimal $5,000 in the printing business. This situation would be represented by point RF_3 on line W_1*RF_{10}. In either case, her net present value after making the investment would be $19,815.

Developing the Investment Schedule in Practice

With minor adjustments, the investment opportunity set faced by any individual, business, or government can be reduced to a schedule similar to Marie's. In Marie's case, constructing the schedule is a little easier because of the natural order of the choices. Investing the seventh $1,000 can be done only after investing the sixth.

In practice, investment projects are not likely to be ordered. The investor must rank available investment projects in terms of some performance measure. In Marie's case, the marginal return was used. For independent projects where partial investment is not possible (the investor can undertake the entire project or none), the marginal return is the appropriate measure.

Each project requires additional investment and promises future cash flows from which its return can be determined. This return is the marginal return on the incremental investments needed to undertake the project and must be used to rank the projects. The project with the highest marginal return should be ranked first, the one with the next highest marginal return should be ranked second, and so on. Projects with a return that falls short of the return available in the financial market should not be funded.

Conclusions

This section makes several important points:

- An investor who is facing an investment decision must rank the investment opportunities in terms of their marginal return.

- A project should be considered for investment as long as its marginal return is greater than the opportunity cost of money from the financial market.

- Investing or borrowing in the financial market enables an individual to allocate the optimal amount to invest in real assets, regardless of the individual's consumption preferences.

1.2 MARKET EFFICIENCY

The Canadian economy is based on the principle of free markets and private enterprise. To work effectively, the Canadian economy requires efficient capital markets. The theory of finance and its implications for decision making have been derived from the assumption of efficient markets. Unless otherwise indicated, the explanations and examples in this course assume market efficiency. It is therefore useful to reflect on this assumption and consider the circumstances from which conclusions about market efficiency are derived.

A market is said to be efficient when prices of securities traded regularly in the market fully reflect all publicly available information related to their valuation and adjust quickly to new information. In an efficient market, the price of a security is always equal or very close to its intrinsic value. The **market price** is the amount of money at which the security can be bought or sold in the market. The **intrinsic value** (or **economic value**) is determined by the present value of all expected future cash flows from the security.

How Information Affects Prices

The process by which information affects security prices can be demonstrated by the following example. Consider a situation where Car Power (CRPWR), a car parts designer and manufacturer, announces the discovery of a new technology for car engines. The new engine is cheaper to make and more efficient than currently available engines. As soon as the news becomes public, investors buy the shares of CRPWR to obtain a profit from the incremental increase in share price caused by the discovery. This type of price appreciation is caused by the increase in the net present value of the future cash flows expected from the discovery. Buying activity leads to higher demand for CRPWR shares while the supply is fixed. Investors who are eager to get a piece of the pie bid up the price.

The announcement may also affect the willingness of investors to buy shares of other companies involved in the production of traditional engines. The new technology will affect the future demand for their products and reduce the future cash flows to these firms. Investors sell the shares of these companies, and the selling pressure reduces their share prices. Similarly, the new technology may reduce the need for gasoline. Thus, oil prices around the world drop, leading investors to sell their shares in oil companies.

On the other hand, industries, such as the plastics industry, that use oil as a raw material to make other products benefit from the drop in oil prices because it means lower raw material costs. Following the news, alert investors buy shares of firms in these industries.

A drop in oil prices will also significantly affect the revenues of developing countries, which rely on oil production to finance their operations and service their foreign debt obligations. The drop in oil prices weakens the prospects of debt payment from these countries, leading investors to sell the shares of banks that have loans outstanding with these countries.

Consequently, the share prices of companies in the plastics industry rise, while the share prices of oil companies and banks that do business with countries relying on oil production for national revenues drop.

The process by which information is reflected in security prices is facilitated by the work of financial analysts. They continuously collect information regarding securities, evaluate the information, and determine its impact on intrinsic values. Once they arrive at what they believe to be the intrinsic value, they compare it to the market price. If there is a discrepancy between the two, they act to take advantage of this opportunity.

For example, if the market price is less than the intrinsic value, financial analysts buy the security and wait until the market realizes the value of the new information and adjusts the price. On the other hand, if the market price is higher than the intrinsic value, they sell the company's shares, which puts pressure on the share price and forces the share price and intrinsic value to be equal again. The work of financial analysts increases the efficiency of the market. The larger the number of financial analysts, the more likely it is that information is quickly reflected in security prices.

Forms of Market Efficiency

Market efficiency may be defined as weak, semi-strong, or strong.

Weak Form The **weak form of market efficiency** describes a market in which the historical price and volume data for securities contain no information that can be used to earn higher trading profits than would be obtained with a simple buy-and-hold strategy. This form of market efficiency implies that prices of securities already reflect all past information that has implications for their intrinsic values. Thus, the work of technical analysts who try to make profits by exploiting past information is useless. In terms of the CRPWR example, studying the pattern of price and volume data of CRPWR shares is not likely to lead to higher profits for traders than would be obtained from simply buying and holding the company's shares.

Semi-Strong Form The **semi-strong form of market efficiency** describes a market in which prices reflect all publicly available information, past and present. Only insiders, trading on short-run price changes, can earn a profit higher than what could be earned by using a naive buy-and-hold strategy. This form of market efficiency implies that financial analysts cannot increase profits by studying publicly known information, as this information is already reflected in security prices. For example, buying CRPWR shares after the announcement of the discovery of the new technology will be too late to benefit from the price rise.

Strong Form The **strong form of market efficiency** describes a market in which all securities prices quickly reflect all information available to investors. This form implies that no one can consistently earn a higher profit than what could be earned with a naive buy-and-hold strategy. Even insiders, who possess privileged information, are not likely to have valuable information that can consistently predict future security price movements. For example, CRPWR executives and engineers who designed the new technology are not likely to be able to exploit their privileged information to earn consistently superior profits on CRPWR shares.

A market cannot be strongly efficient without being semi-strongly efficient, and it cannot be semi-strongly efficient without being weakly efficient.

Conditions for Market Efficiency

A market is efficient if it is free from internal or external frictions that hinder trading. A market is **internally efficient** if it has depth, breadth, and resiliency:

- **Depth** requires the existence of many independent buyers and sellers who are ready to trade the security above and below the current quoted price.
- The market for a security has **breadth** if the outstanding orders for the security are numerous and coming from diverse and unrelated sources.
- The market has **resiliency** if a price change will activate a wave of new trading orders below and above the quoted price.

An internally efficient market has the following requirements, which are implicit in the previous conditions:

- There are no frictions to obstruct the entry and exit of traders.
- Securities are marketable and liquid and are available in convenient denominations.
- Securities can be easily transferred from one owner to the other with little or no transaction costs.

For Canadian securities listed on the major exchanges or trading in the money market, these requirements are almost satisfied. Even transaction costs are getting smaller because of the existence of discount brokerage firms and efforts by the exchanges to introduce automated trading. Many brokerage firms are experimenting with direct trading, which enables customers to place orders from their computers at home or work. To encourage direct trading, customers who trade directly receive further discounts on already deeply discounted commissions.

Low-cost online trading facilities have been developed to make full use of Internet technology. If you would like to know more about the type of services offered by such a facility, do a Google search for "e*trade canada."

A market is **externally efficient** if, given a set of information, the prices of securities in the market fully and immediately reflect that information. The following requirements are necessary for the external efficiency of a market:

- The market is internally efficient.
- Information is readily available to the public for evaluation.
- Transmittal of information is easy.
- There are many participants in the market, and no single participant can have a significant impact on prices of assets.
- Traders are protected by laws to ensure that only correct and relevant information is circulated.
- Regulations control price manipulations and require that security issuers disclose much information about themselves to the public.

In Canada, the requirements for external efficiency are almost satisfied for shares listed on the major exchanges. With the existence of many news agencies, newspapers, television, published books, and libraries, it is relatively easy to obtain accurate and timely information. More importantly, there are no significant time lags associated with news dissemination. National newspapers carry the same information nationwide, and with the advent of the Internet, investors can get accurate information hourly, or even more frequently.

The availability of information does not necessarily imply that all investors react in a similar manner to the same news. Market efficiency does not require similar reactions by all market participants. As long as there are many sellers and buyers in the market and single traders are not large enough to affect prices (if they are able to do so, regulations try to stop such practices), security prices move smoothly from one level to the other. **Continuous equilibrium** occurs if all security prices equal their intrinsic values. Continuous equilibrium exists if the information about one security is immediately reflected in its price, and the price of the security is immediately reflected in the prices of other securities.

Empirical Evidence on Market Efficiency

Much empirical research has been conducted to determine the degree of market efficiency. So far, no study has been able to show that markets are not weakly efficient. Yet there are several anomalies to this conclusion.

First, it is widely documented that the closing prices on Friday are mostly followed by lower closing prices on Monday. Hence, the average return over the weekend is negative. These results have been observed in Canadian, American, British, Australian, and Japanese markets. However, the studies conclude that the differences between prices are not enough to create any profit opportunities for retail investors who have to pay commissions.

Another anomaly is known as the **January effect**. Studies have found that Canadian shares, particularly those of small companies, tend to fall two to three percentage points late in December and rise early in January. Although this observation is well documented, research attempting to explain the phenomenon is ongoing. Similar results are reported by studies on American securities. Most studies conclude that investors cannot exploit these observations because **transaction costs**, the attendant costs of conducting securities transactions, would consume all the profits. Yet the existence of these anomalies may lead to the conclusion that markets are not weakly efficient. Nevertheless, Canadian markets are widely accepted to be weakly efficient, as scientific studies consistently show that past prices cannot be used to make profits above what can be made with a simple buy-and-hold strategy.

Similarly, studies conducted to test market efficiency have not rejected the semi-strongly efficient market hypothesis. They are not able to produce consistent evidence that public information is not already fully reflected in security prices. Indeed, many studies have found that the impact of important information releases such as dividend changes, merger announcements, and earnings reports are almost correctly anticipated by market analysts so that, in the majority of instances, information releases have little or no effect on share prices. The results of these studies indicate that market information travels instantly and prices reflect all available information immediately. Thus, news will affect prices immediately and no trends can be expected over any prolonged period.

Although the general consensus is that Canadian and American markets are semi-strongly efficient, the weight of the evidence suggests that markets in the two countries are not strongly efficient. Many studies conclude that insiders can earn abnormal profits if they trade on the basis of their privileged information. Regulations classify such practices as illegal and attempt to constrain the use of insider information for personal profits. Regulations require corporate officers to disclose their trades in securities on which they possess important information by virtue of their jobs.

As long as Canadian markets are semi-strongly efficient, models and conclusions can be derived assuming market efficiency. Indeed, the definition of market efficiency requires that prices fully reflect all publicly available information; however, nothing is said about privately held information. Therefore, unless otherwise specified, when the term "market efficiency" is used in this course, it implies the semi-strong form.

A conclusion on market efficiency should not be generalized across all markets and securities within a market. The studies previously cited were conducted on securities listed on the Toronto Stock Exchange (TSE) or the Montréal Exchange (ME). Therefore, the results cannot be generalized to other trading in Canada. Similarly, concluding that the TSE is an efficient market does not necessarily mean that all shares listed on the TSE are traded under circumstances that characterize efficient markets.

Implications of Market Efficiency

By analyzing the conditions under which market efficiency exists and reviewing evidence on the efficiency of Canadian markets, several useful implications of market efficiency become clear. The financial manager should understand the following implications:

- Efficient capital markets imply that investors quickly learn about the desirability and economic values of financial and real assets. Therefore, market participants allocate funds to the most desirable assets first. Combining this conclusion with the theory of optimal investment suggests that managers choose projects to maximize net present values. Firms that are successful in locating projects that accomplish this objective attract capital and increase shareholder wealth, while unsuccessful firms fade away through bankruptcy or mergers.

- Efficient capital markets imply that a security should have one price, even if it is trading simultaneously on several physically separated markets. **Arbitrage** describes the purchase of one security and the immediate or simultaneous sale of the same or a related security, the result being a risk-free profit. Arbitrage between market participants ensures the law of one price. For example, if a security were trading at C$10 on the TSE and at C$9 on the American Stock Exchange (ASE), market arbitragers would notice the difference and exploit it for immediate riskless profit. They would sell the same stock on the TSE for $10 and simultaneously buy it on the ASE for $9 for an immediate profit of $1. Selling on the TSE would put downward pressure on the TSE's price, while buying on the ASE would put upward pressure on the ASE's price. The trading activity would continue until the two prices become equal.

- The market price of a security continuously approximates its intrinsic value and reflects all available information on that security.

- The intrinsic value is determined by a firm's ability to generate cash from operations. Therefore, actions that seek to artificially increase earnings per share are ignored in the marketplace.

- Given that the intrinsic value of a security, and therefore its price, reflects current information available on the security, and that new information arrives randomly, future market (or stock price) trends are not predictable from past trends. Therefore, investors who rely on trading strategies based on historical market patterns should not earn superior returns.

- Given the assumptions of complete information and low transaction costs, investors will not reward management for activities that they can perform equally well themselves. For example, shareholders are not willing to reward management for using debt in the capital structure to magnify returns to shareholders. Shareholders can create their own homemade leverage (this process will be demonstrated in Chapter 3).

- Securities are purchased on the basis of their expected return and risk characteristics. Fads will not affect market trends or security prices for any prolonged period if investors' expectations are not met.

1.3 AGENCY ISSUES, ETHICAL CONSIDERATIONS, AND OTHER STAKEHOLDER ISSUES

The primary role of the financial manager, as agent to shareholders, is to make decisions designed to maximize shareholder wealth. Financial managers should make only those decisions that are consistent with the goal of maximizing shareholder wealth. The analysis in this book focuses on this goal.

Managers as Agents for Shareholders

Shareholders are the owners of the firm. In principle, they have the ultimate authority over decision making. In sole proprietorships and partnerships, owners often exercise this authority. They may hire financial managers to assist them in making decisions that will maximize the value of the business. In corporations where few shareholders hold shares, decision making is partially delegated to the managers, but shareholders exercise control over decision making.

In corporations where the shares are widely held, the authority over decision making is usually delegated to the managers. In other words, managers become agents who are responsible for making decisions in the best interests of shareholders, the principals.

In theory, the board of directors monitors managers' decisions. The board should be elected by shareholders and should have the legal responsibility to act in the best interests of shareholders. In practice, however, top management nominates directors, and shareholders are normally asked to approve or reject the nominations. Rejection rarely occurs.

There are practical problems with the expectation that managers will always act in the best interest of shareholders. In recent years, the financial pages of any large circulation newspaper have regularly contained articles about boards fighting take-over bids. It seems that the executives mentioned in these articles were more concerned about their own jobs or other issues and that no consideration had been given to the impact the fight would have on shareholder wealth.

Corporate Governance

The system used to direct and control a corporation is referred to as **corporate governance**. It defines the rights and responsibilities of the key corporate participants such as the shareholders, board of directors, officers and managers, and other stakeholders, and the rules and procedures for making corporate decisions. It also typically specifies the structure through which the company sets objectives, develops plans for achieving them, and establishes procedures for monitoring performance.

Individual versus Institutional Investors Clearly, the corporate board's first responsibility is to the shareholders. To better understand this responsibility it is helpful to differentiate between the two broad classes of owners—individuals and institutions. **Individual investors** are investors who buy relatively small quantities of shares so as to earn a return on idle funds, build a source of retirement income, or provide financial security. **Institutional investors** are investment professionals that are paid to manage other people's money. They hold and trade large quantities of securities for individuals, businesses, and governments. Institutional investors include banks, insurance companies, mutual funds, and pension funds, which invest large sums of money to earn competitive returns for their clients/plan participants.

Because they hold and trade large blocks of stock, institutional investors tend to have a much greater influence on corporate governance than do individual investors. Simply stated, because they own large amounts of common stock and have the resources to buy and sell large blocks of shares, institutional investors are able to maintain management's attention. If a large institutional investor sells or buys a sizable block of shares, the share price will likely be driven down or up, respectively. Clearly, these large investors speak in a much louder voice than does the individual investor.

The *Sarbanes-Oxley Act of 2002* Beginning in 2000, numerous corporate misdeeds were uncovered and disclosed by various regulatory bodies. The misdeeds derived from two main types of issues: 1) false disclosures in financial reporting and other information releases, and 2) undisclosed conflicts of interest between corporations and their analysts, auditors, and attorneys and between corporate directors, officers, and shareholders. In response to these fraudulent disclosures and conflicts of interest, in July 2002 Congress passed the *Sarbanes-Oxley Act of 2002* (commonly called **SOX**).

Sarbanes-Oxley focused on eliminating the many disclosure and conflict of interest problems that had surfaced. It did the following: established an oversight board to monitor the accounting industry; tightened audit regulations and controls; toughened penalties against executives who commit corporate fraud; strengthened accounting disclosure requirements and ethical guidelines for corporate officers; established corporate board structure and membership guidelines; established guidelines with regard to analyst conflicts of interest; mandated instant disclosure of stock sales by corporate executives; and increased securities regulation authority and budgets for auditors and investigators. Although it is too soon to know the full effect of SOX, most commentators believe it will be effective in eliminating fraudulent disclosures and conflicts of interest by corporations.

Economic Value Added

Under the principal–agent relationship, the manager's primary task in the firm is to make decisions with the overall objective of maximizing shareholder wealth. Any deviation from this task will lead to breach of contract between shareholders and managers. **Agency costs** are costs to an organization in the event that management violates the principal–agent relationship and commences decision making toward objectives other than maximizing shareholder wealth.

Economic value added (EVA) is a popular measure used by many firms to determine whether an investment—proposed or existing—positively contributes to the owners' wealth. EVA is calculated by subtracting the cost of funds used to finance an investment from its after-tax operating profits. Investments with positive EVAs increase shareholder value and those with negative EVAs reduce shareholder value. Clearly, only those investments with positive EVAs are desirable. For example, the EVA of an investment with after-tax operating profits of $410,000 and associated financing costs of $375,000 would be $35,000 (i.e., $410,000 − $375,000). Because this EVA is positive, the investment is expected to increase owner wealth and is therefore acceptable. Of course, in practice numerous accounting and financial issues would be involved in estimating both the after-tax operating profits attributable to the given investment and the cost of funds used to finance it.

The growing popularity of EVA is due to both its relative simplicity and its strong link to owner wealth maximization. Advocates of EVA believe it exhibits a strong link to share prices—positive EVAs are associated with increasing share prices, and vice versa. While EVA analysis is very popular in the United States, only a handful of companies in

Canada have attempted to implement the technique. Two of these companies are Domtar, the third largest manufacturer of business, printing and publishing, and technical and specialty paper in North America, and Alcan, the second largest aluminum company in the world. Coca-Cola is a long-time user of EVA. The former CEO of the company has stated: "You only get rich if you invest money at a higher rate of return than the cost of that money to you." This comment illustrates the simplicity of the concept.

Given that highly successful firms such as Coca-Cola use and widely tout the effectiveness of EVA in isolating investments that create shareholder value, it is surprising that more Canadian companies are not using the technique to help make investment decisions. While EVA is popular among some companies, it is important to note that it is simply a repackaged application of a standard investment decision-making technique called *net present value (NPV)*, which is described later in this chapter. What's important at this point is to recognize that useful tools, such as EVA, are available for operationalizing the owners' wealth maximization goal, particularly when making investment decisions.[1]

Ethical Considerations

Since the financial manager acts as an agent to shareholders, the manager's primary responsibility is to make decisions designed to maximize shareholder wealth. Assuming there is a perfect exchange of information between agent and principal, corporate managers will make only those decisions that are consistent with the goal of wealth maximization.

However, in a world where the agent knows more than the principal, the agent–principal relationship can be subject to much abuse from the agent. Agents may choose to act in their own self-interest rather than in the best interests of shareholders. For example, managers may pursue an unjustified acquisition or expansion to increase their power, prestige, and salaries. Also, managers may provide themselves with luxurious offices, company-paid vacations, and executive jets, which may not be needed for the effective management of the corporation.

The Role of Ethics In recent years, the ethics of actions taken by certain businesses have received major media attention. Examples include aircraft manufacturer Boeing Co.'s receiving billions of dollars of contracts with the Pentagon as a result of its questionable dealings with an Air Force acquisitions official, who later became a Boeing vice president and in 2004 was sentenced to nine months in prison for her actions; auditing firm KPMG's 2004 agreement to pay $115 million, one of the largest settlements ever paid by an auditing firm, to settle a shareholder lawsuit claiming they had failed in their audit work for Lernout & Hauspie Speech Products NV, a now-defunct Belgian maker of speech-recognition software; the late 2002 agreement by ten of Wall Street's largest firms to pay $1.4 billion to settle allegations by state and federal regulators that they provided misleading stock advice to investors for the benefit of their corporate investment banking clients; an agreement by financial services company American Express Co. in early 2002 to pay $31 million to settle a sex- and age-discrimination lawsuit filed on behalf of more than 4,000 women who said they were denied equal pay and promotions; and energy company Enron Corp.'s key executives indicating to employee-shareholders in mid-2001 that the firm's then-depressed stock price would soon recover while, at the same time, selling their own shares and, not long after, taking the firm into bankruptcy.

---

[1] For a good overview of EVA (including a video on the concept), see Stern Stewart & Co.'s Web site at www.sternstewart.com or Brian A. Schofield, "EVAluating Stocks," *Canadian Investment Review*, Spring, 2000; available at www.investmentreview.com/archives/spring00/stocks.html.

Clearly, these and similar actions have raised the question of **ethics**—standards of conduct or moral judgment. Today, the business community in general and the financial community in particular are developing and enforcing ethical standards. The goal of these ethical standards is to motivate business and market participants to adhere to both the letter and the spirit of laws and regulations concerned with business and professional practice. Most business leaders believe businesses actually strengthen their competitive positions by maintaining *high ethical standards*.

Considering Ethics Robert A. Cooke, a noted ethicist, suggests that the following questions be used to assess the ethical viability of a proposed action.[2]

1. Is the action arbitrary or capricious? Does it unfairly single out an individual or group?

2. Does the action violate the moral or legal rights of any individual or group?

3. Does the action conform to accepted moral standards?

4. Are there alternative courses of action that are less likely to cause actual or potential harm?

Clearly, considering such questions before taking an action can help to ensure its ethical viability. Specifically, Cooke suggests that the effects of a proposed decision should be evaluated from a number of perspectives before it is finalized:

1. Are the rights of any stakeholder being violated?

2. Does the firm have any overriding duties to any stakeholder?

3. Will the decision benefit any stakeholder to the detriment of another stakeholder?

4. If there is detriment to any stakeholder, how should it be remedied, if at all?

5. What is the relationship between shareholders and other stakeholders?

Today, an increasing number of firms are directly addressing the issue of ethics by establishing corporate ethics policies and requiring employee compliance with them. The article on page 27, for example, describes ethics concerns at Hewlett-Packard. A major impetus toward the development of corporate ethics policies has been the *Sarbanes-Oxley Act of 2002* described earlier. Frequently, employees are required to sign a formal pledge to uphold the firm's ethics policies. Such policies typically apply to employee actions in dealing with all corporate stakeholders, including the public. Many companies also require employees to participate in ethics seminars and training programs.

Ethics and Share Price An effective ethics program is believed to enhance corporate value and can produce a number of positive benefits. It can reduce potential litigation and judgment costs; maintain a positive corporate image; build shareholder confidence; and gain the loyalty, commitment, and respect of the firm's stakeholders. Such actions, by maintaining and enhancing cash flow and reducing perceived risk, can positively affect the firm's share price. Ethical behaviour is therefore viewed as necessary for achieving the firm's goal of owner wealth maximization.[3]

---

[2] Robert A. Cooke, "Business Ethics: A Perspective," in *Arthur Andersen Cases on Business Ethics* (Chicago: Arthur Andersen, September 1991), pp. 2 and 5.

[3] For an excellent discussion of this and related issues by a number of finance academics and practitioners who have given a lot of thought to financial ethics, see James S. Ang, "On Financial Ethics," *Financial Management* (Autumn 1993), pp. 32–59.

ETHICS AT HEWLETT-PACKARD

In 1939, long before anyone coined the expression "corporate social responsibility," Bill Hewlett and Dave Packard started a company, Hewlett-Packard, based on principles of fair dealing and respect. HP credits its ongoing commitment to "doing well by doing good" as a major reason why employees, suppliers, customers, and shareholders seek it out. HP is clear on its obligation to increase the market value of its common stock, yet it strives to maintain the integrity of each employee in every country in which it does business. HP's "Standards of Business Conduct" includes the following warning to employees, especially finance staffers (p. 1):

> *HP employees at every level must comply with these Standards, and associated policies and guidelines. Failure to do so is considered misconduct and may lead to termination of employment. In particular, all executive officers and senior financial officers, their staffs, and all managers and other employees contributing to HP's financial record-keeping must comply strictly with HP finance and accounting standards, policies, and guidelines.*

CEO Carly Fiorina, in her "CEO's Message" at the beginning of the "Standards of Business Conduct," states (p. iii): "Unethical or illegal business conduct on the part of HP is simply unacceptable and will not be tolerated."

Such a stance puts the company under the microscope. When HP began its publicity blitz to gain stockholder acceptance of its eventual merger with Compaq, Walter Hewlett, a member of both the board and the Hewlett family, filed suit alleging misstatement of financial facts and improper pressure of shareholder Deutsche Bank on the part of the HP management team. Although a Delaware judge dismissed the lawsuit, its mere existence underscored the fact that a company's ethics constantly face the scrutiny of the public and investors. HP's reputation was reaffirmed in 2003 when it was one of three companies awarded the Society of Financial Service Professionals' American Business Ethics Awards.

Maximizing shareholder wealth is what some call a "moral imperative," in that stockholders are owners who have property rights, and managers are stewards who are obliged to look out for owners' interests. Many times, doing what is right is consistent with maximizing the stock price. But what if integrity concerns cause a company to lose a contract or result in analysts reducing their rating of the stock from "buy" to "sell"? Despite the risk of such setbacks, the objective (maximizing shareholder wealth) holds, and company officers must pursue the objective within the ethical constraints. Those constraints occasionally limit the menu of actions from which managers may choose. Some critics have mistakenly assumed that the objective was the cause of unethical behaviour, ignoring the fact that *any* business goal might be cited as a factor pressuring individuals to be unethical.

American business professionals have tended to operate from within a strong moral foundation, based on early childhood moral development that takes place in families and religious institutions. This ethos does not prevent all ethical lapses, of course: After news of a major bond price manipulation episode broke, a Treasury Department official was quoted in the *Wall Street Journal* as saying the traders "broke lessons you learned in Sunday school in second grade." It's not surprising that chief financial officers declare that the number one personal attribute finance grads need is ethics—more than interpersonal skills, communication skills, decision-making ability, or computer skills. HP is aware of this, and has institutionalized it in its culture and policies.

There is much debate on whether managers are making decisions in pursuit of self-interest at the expense of shareholders' interests. Although it is difficult to establish the prevalence of such behaviour, many shareholder groups are trying to design new managerial contracts in attempts to limit such unethical behaviour.

From an ethical perspective, making wealth maximization paramount provides too narrow a view of managers' moral responsibilities. It misses significant ethical limitations on the means managers may adopt in order to pursue the interests of shareholders. Also, it implies that there is no other moral limit on what managers may do to advance shareholders' interests. For example, this view would allow deception, fraud, breaking promises, and even violent actions as long as shareholder wealth is maximized.

Moral Purposes and Limits of Business Activity

In addition to shareholders, there are others who have a morally significant stake in the actions of managers. These stakeholders include employees, customers, suppliers, the community where the business is located, and others. Therefore, in making their decisions, financial managers should be careful to observe the rights and well-being of stakeholders other than shareholders. Managers have moral and ethical obligations to avoid any decisions that may harm or endanger these stakeholders.

The stakeholder view does not alter the goal of maximizing shareholder wealth. Such a view is often considered part of the firm's "social responsibility." It is expected to provide long-run benefit to shareholders by maintaining positive stakeholder relationships. Such relationships should minimize stakeholder turnover, conflicts, and litigation. Clearly, the firm can better achieve its goal of shareholder wealth maximization by fostering cooperation with its other stakeholders, rather than conflict with them.

Minimalist Approach (Friedman: 1970) Milton Friedman offered a minimalist approach to business ethics in an article[4] in *The New York Times* of September 1970. He argues that the fiduciary relationship between managers (agents) and owners (principals) morally binds managers to serve the interests of the principals and not their own. The fiduciary duty of the manager originates from both the owner's property right to the business and the contract by which the manager is hired to perform the assigned duties.

This type of relationship gives each party of the contract special *positive* rights in respect of the other. The owner provides wages and benefits in exchange for the manager's labour. It is assumed that the owner has property rights to wages and benefits provided to the manager and that the manager has property rights to the provided labour.

---

[4] *The Social Responsibility of Business Is to Increase Its Profits*, September 13, 1970. © 1970 by The New York Times Co.

Friedman believes that limits on what owners can do with their property must be imposed by the legal system to ensure that immoral behaviour is not committed. Friedman places responsibility on the state to protect property rights. However, he advocates a libertarian or minimum state, which means government has the right to collect taxes to provide only for the police, the courts, and the army. In his model, the private sector should provide for other services such as social welfare, health care, and education. In such a state, the government must leave business alone, using only the minimum regulation necessary to secure a free market economy.

Profit Maximization Friedman argues that the manager has a positive duty to maximize owners' profits and a negative duty to respect the property rights of others. Thus, the manager's duty and fiduciary responsibility do not require the manager to undertake unethical activities to maximize profits. Similarly, the manager is not required to use force or fraud, because these actions are not consistent with the principle of protecting property rights.

Arguments in Support of the Minimum State At least two arguments can be advanced in support of Friedman's perspective. A practical argument suggests that profit-maximizing, property-rights-respecting activities produce the greatest amount of good with the smallest amount of resources. Friedman believes that the free market in a minimum state provides for the most efficient use of resources.

A philosophical argument suggests that, in a just, moral order, persons have sole exclusive property rights to themselves and to their own labour. Therefore, respect for property rights will exclude immoral behaviour.

Examples of Situations Requiring Ethical Judgment

There are many situations in which financial managers must exercise ethical judgment. Following are some common examples:

1. Many companies promote their products by promising to repair, service, or replace the product if it becomes necessary. These promises usually take the form of express or implied warranties. It is unethical to ignore such promises.

2. A firm's value can be derived from the possession of patents or copyrights that contain valuable ideas. Laws are created to protect these companies against illegal copying. Despite these laws, the media are full of examples in which a company sues another company for suspected illegal copying of patents or products. Copying has become a major issue in the area of computer software and in the use of electronic means for unauthorized transfer of data. Illegal copying may lead to temporary maximization of shareholder wealth because a business does not incur costs that are required to compensate owners of stolen ideas for their efforts. It is unethical to maximize wealth through such behaviour. Copying other people's ideas is illegal because the copyright law protects the expression of valuable ideas. Protection of copyright promotes the creation of valuable ideas that ultimately provide general benefits to the public.

3. Some companies try to maximize shareholder wealth through monopolistic practices such as price fixing or controlling supply and demand conditions. Such activities may create value to shareholders, but they are illegal and unethical.

4. Financial managers may engage in insider trading of the firm's securities for personal gain, or in market manipulation of the firm's securities for shareholders' gain. Both actions are wrong. For example, an executive who purchases shares based on insider information will deprive the seller of the price appreciation following the announcement of the information. On the other hand, an executive who manipulates the share price by providing incorrect information to the market will lead some buyers to pay higher prices for their purchases.

    It has been suggested that disclosure in the United States is better than in Canada, partly because shareholders can sue for damages related to inaccurate information.

    Another scenario that can be encountered occurs when market analysts and management meet in closed meetings. In these meetings, analysts become privy to information that is not yet public knowledge. This practice is criticized on the basis that such disclosure provides analysts with an unfair market advantage because they have information not available to other investors.

    The perception that there are disclosure problems in the financial markets in Canada affects the credibility of the Canadian capital market. Moreover, the existence of barriers to the transmittal of information makes Canadian markets less efficient.

    Penalties are one means by which the regulators can rectify the problems associated with disclosure. There are, however, loopholes that diminish the full impact of penalties. For example, professional advisors are often excluded from liability. More importantly, regulations often make compromises between opposing forces. To avoid frivolous suits from unhappy shareholders, regulators will often recommend sanctions rather than awarding compensation to injured shareholders. Yet sanctions are criticized as being ineffective deterrents.

5. Many companies are reporting record profits and, at the same time, announcing massive layoffs. Employee advocates and social welfare authorities are questioning the ethical and social responsibility of these companies. The companies are using the principle of maximizing shareholder wealth to defend their actions. However, the principle is derived on the assumption that shareholders are well diversified. Thus, they should be concerned only with nondiversifiable risk. The assumptions ignore the fact that employees are also stakeholders of the firm for which they work and that they are not well diversified. They have invested their human capital in the firm, and such an investment is rarely diversifiable. Is it ethical to maximize shareholder wealth without regard to the human capital invested in the firm? Can the financial manager quantify the value of the human capital?

These five situations exemplify the problems financial managers may face in demonstrating ethical behaviour within a corporation. These situations impose constraints on the behaviour of both the financial manager and the corporation. Although ethical behaviour may sometimes conflict with the principle of maximizing shareholder wealth in the immediate future, such behaviour ensures that the firm remains a going concern and assumes its corporate responsibility within society.

1.4 RELATIONSHIP BETWEEN NET PRESENT VALUE AND REQUIRED RETURN

As explained in Section 1.1, the investment of wealth in financial or real assets enables the transfer of wealth between periods to maximize investors' satisfaction. An investment entails investing surplus funds now with the expectation of receiving these funds later with compensation in the form of interest or a capital gain. Investors are compensated for the following reasons:

■ rent for lending their money

■ reward for taking the risk of loss of purchasing power

■ protection against uncertainty regarding the receipt of the expected cash flows

The rate of compensation evolves over time to maintain an equilibrium between lenders and borrowers in the financial market. Under conditions of certainty and financial market efficiency, the rate of compensation at any point in time should be the same for all investors and borrowers. Any investor with surplus funds should earn at least the equilibrium rate, and any borrower should be able to borrow by paying no more than the equilibrium rate.

Hence, an investor with funds to invest can invest them at the rate available in the financial market or invest in real assets. Using the funds to buy real assets entails forgoing the rate available in the financial market for the opportunity of receiving the cash flows promised by the real investment. The **opportunity cost of capital** is the return forgone by investing in real assets rather than investing in securities offered by the financial markets. Consequently, an investor should not invest in an asset unless it provides a return at least equal to the opportunity cost of capital. The following You Apply It minicase illustrates this concept. Try it.

YOU APPLY IT NET PRESENT VALUE AND RETURN ON INVESTMENT

Jill has $1,000 to invest. She can invest the money at 8%, guaranteed at the local bank. Her sister Sara offers to take the money now and return it a year from now plus $100. Sara is temporarily short on cash but is certain to fulfill her promise of repayment. For security, she offers Jill a signed cheque for $1,100 to be cashed a year from now.

Questions

Question 1: Should Jill accept Sara's offer?

Question 2: Jill buys Sara's $1,100 cheque, but immediately after finalizing the transaction she regrets giving up her money to Sara, as she would like to buy a bicycle right now. She meets a friend, Steve, who offers to buy her asset, Sara's cheque. What price should Jill demand for her asset if banks offer an 8% interest rate?

Question 3: Calculate and explain the difference between total return and the opportunity cost of capital.

Question 4: Jill paid $1,000 to buy Sara's cheque and immediately sold it to Steve for $1,018.52. What does the $18.52 represent?

Question 5: Why was Jill able to obtain the positive net present value?

You Apply It Continued >

Answers

Question 1: Should Jill accept Sara's offer?

Essentially, Jill must decide between paying $1,000 to buy Sara's cheque, which promises $1,100 one year from now, and investing with the bank to receive 8% on the invested amount. The cash flows to be received one year later from investing $1,000 with the bank are $1,080, which is less than the cash flows to be received from Sara's cheque. Jill should choose the investment that will maximize her future spending. Thus, Jill should buy Sara's cheque, which gives her an additional $20 for spending.

Question 2: Jill buys Sara's $1,100 cheque, but immediately after finalizing the transaction she regrets giving up her money to Sara, as she would like to buy a bicycle right now. She meets a friend, Steve, who offers to buy her asset, Sara's cheque. What price should Jill demand for her asset if banks offer an 8% interest rate?

The asset is offering $1,100 in cash flows a year from now. The opportunity cost of capital is 8% because this is the forgone return that financial markets offer if Jill invests in financial securities. How much money would be invested today at 8% to provide $1,100 in cash flows a year from now? The answer is:

$$\text{Investment} = \$1,100 \div 1.08 = \$1,018.52$$

Indeed, $1,018.52 is the present value of the cash flows discounted at the opportunity cost of capital. Steve should be willing to pay $1,018.52 for the asset because it will provide him with the rate that he will get on a similar investment. As the opportunity cost of capital is 8%, the $1,018.52 is the fair market price of the $1,100 in cash flows to be received one year from now.

Question 3: Calculate and explain the difference between total return and the opportunity cost of capital.

The total return for Jill is:

$$(\$1,100 \div \$1,000) - 1 = 10\%$$

The total return of 10% is greater than 8%, which represents the opportunity cost of capital. This is because of the positive net present value derived from the investment. It implies that investments with positive net present values will provide a return higher than the opportunity cost of capital.

Question 4: Jill paid $1,000 to buy Sara's cheque and immediately sold it to Steve for $1,018.52. What does the $18.52 represent?

The $18.52 represents Jill's immediate profit on this deal. It is equal to the fair market price of the asset (the price that Steve paid) minus the price Jill paid to acquire the asset. In financial terms, it is the present value of the cash flows discounted at the opportunity cost of capital minus the initial investment. It is equal to the net present value of Jill's investment. The $18.52 increases Jill's ability to consume because now she has $1,018.52 instead of $1,000.

Question 5: Why was Jill able to obtain the positive net present value?

There was a moment in which the market was not completely and perfectly efficient. A participant in the market, Sara, created this moment of inefficiency. She either is not fully aware how to price assets for a given set of information, does not

You Apply It Continued >

have access to the information, or faces barriers to enter the market (such as the embarrassing publicity that she is borrowing money). The situation presented an arbitrage opportunity for Jill and allowed her to make profits. Jill's actions and the actions of other market arbitragers ensure that prices of assets in the market only slightly and temporarily deviate from their fair market values.

Jill's situation emphasizes that the opportunity cost of capital is the rate to be used for discounting the future cash flows expected from an asset. The present value of the asset is calculated as:

$$PV = CF_1 \div (1 + k) \qquad \text{(Equation 1-5)}$$

where

PV = present value of the asset
k = cost of capital
CF_1 = one future cash flow to be received one year from today

The terms *discount rate, cost of capital, hurdle rate*, and *cost of funds* are often used interchangeably to denote the opportunity cost of funds. The present value of an asset, derived by discounting the future cash flows at the cost of capital, is the fair market price that should be paid for the asset. The difference between the present value of the future incremental operating cash inflows less the present value of all future incremental operating cash outflows, less the value of the initial investment, is the **net present value (NPV)** of the asset. As a result, Equation 1-5 is modified to obtain:

$$NPV = CF_1 \div (1 + k) - C_0 \qquad \text{(Equation 1-6)}$$

where

NPV = net present value of the asset acquisition
C_0 = cost of acquiring the asset

As indicated in the minicase, a positive NPV increases the investor's consumption capability. Therefore, investors should try to maximize the NPV of their investments.

The **internal rate of return (IRR)** from acquiring an asset is the rate that discounts the future cash flows to equate the acquisition price of the asset. That is, if IRR denotes the rate of return, it must satisfy:

$$CF_1 \div (1 + IRR) = C_0 \qquad \text{(Equation 1-7)}$$

The decision rules for the IRR technique are summarized as follows:

IRR < k: reject project
IRR = k: indifferent to accepting or rejecting project
IRR > k: accept project

While financial theory is developed under the assumption of market efficiency, it acknowledges and adjusts for the existence of risk. Under conditions of uncertainty, investors commit their funds hoping to receive future cash flows, but there is no guarantee that these expectations will materialize. In such an environment, it is no longer true that the return on investment should be equal to the cost of capital.

Investors expect a rate of return that is higher than the risk-free cost of capital. The premium is the expected compensation for their willingness to accept uncertainty.

Investors determine the desirability of their investments by comparing the expected rate of return with the risk-free cost of capital. The higher the perceived risk, the higher the expected rate of return demanded by investors who are willing to accept the risk. The term **risk-adjusted** is often added to the terms *discount rate*, *hurdle rate*, *cost of capital*, and *required rate* to indicate a rate that contains a premium to account for uncertainty. In Chapter 2, you will learn how uncertainty affects the investment decision.

1.5 ESTIMATING CASH FLOWS FOR CAPITAL BUDGETING PURPOSES

Overview

Section 1.1 pointed out that one of the primary responsibilities of the financial manager is the investment or capital budgeting decision. **Capital budgeting** is the process by which the financial manager decides whether to invest in specific capital assets or projects. In some situations, the process may entail acquiring assets that are completely new to the firm, such as land to establish a new business venture, plant for a new product, or equipment for a new process. In other situations, it may mean replacing an obsolete existing asset to maintain efficiency. Thus, capital budgeting is an important function of the financial manager and requires diverse skills. Often, it requires amounts of money ranging from small sums to replace minor equipment to large sums needed to start a new venture. Capital budgeting consumes a considerable amount of time in planning and implementation and includes many people from areas other than finance.

During the capital budgeting process, the financial manager will ask the following questions:

- What projects are good investment opportunities for the firm?
- From this group, which assets are the most desirable to acquire?
- Given the desirable group, how much should the firm invest in each of these assets?

Section 1.1 emphasized that the objective should be to ensure that the selected projects at least cover the opportunity cost of capital and that the funds are employed in the most productive manner to maximize shareholder wealth.

The purchase of capital assets entails spending cash now and perhaps in future periods in anticipation of cash in the future and over several years. One of the important tasks in the capital budgeting process is evaluating whether the proposed project is desirable from the shareholders' point of view. Expansion projects for manufacturing and processing firms generally require the acquisition of new assets for either initiating a production line or increasing the existing production capacity, whereas replacement projects involve the acquisition of a new asset to replace an older, less efficient asset. Section 1.3 emphasized that the primary concern of the financial manager is to find projects that will maximize shareholder wealth by generating positive net present values. In other words, the present value of the cash inflows from the project exceeds the present value of the cash outflows required by the project. Thus, the project evaluation process comprises several steps:

1. Identify and estimate incremental after-tax cash flows.
2. Determine the appropriate discount rate of the cash flows.

3. Calculate the net present value of the cash flows.

4. Use other capital budgeting criteria if desirable.

The rest of this chapter describes the first, third, and fourth steps in detail, assuming that the discount rate is given (step 2). In Chapter 2, you will learn how to determine the appropriate discount rate.

Identifying and Estimating the Incremental After-Tax Cash Flows

The financial manager's primary interest in any project stems from its ability to generate cash. Cash is important because it is used to purchase raw materials, settle wages, make interest and principal payments on debt, and pay dividends to shareholders. The following considerations are an important part of the process of analyzing cash flows.

■ *Identify and estimate the actual cash flows rather than accounting profits.* Often, the two are not the same. The larger the cash inflow is in relation to the cash outflow, the more valuable the project will be to shareholders. However, the timing of the cash inflow and outflow is important given the time value of money. The present value of a particular cash inflow will diminish as the timing of the inflow is extended in the future.

■ *Determine the marginal or incremental cash flows of a project.* This task implies that the relevant cash inflow from investing in a new project is measured by subtracting the current cash flows without the project from the cash flows expected after taking on the project. This treatment ensures that only the cash generated or consumed by the new project is attributed to the project and used in the evaluation process. Cash inflows or outflows that occur with or without the project are treated as irrelevant to the valuation of the project.

For example, any costs incurred prior to the decision to undertake a project are normally considered sunk costs and are irrelevant to the current decision. Research and development costs are sunk costs because they were incurred in the past and cannot be recovered. (Under certain circumstances, research and development costs may be recovered by selling the results of these efforts. In this case, the sale price is considered a cash outflow for evaluation purposes because it will be lost if the project is undertaken.)

Another example of how cash flows can be irrelevant to the valuation of a project is when a firm introduces a new product that reduces revenues from existing products. Suppose a firm sells one product that generates $20,000 in annual net cash inflow and introduces a new product that can generate $10,000 in annual net cash inflow. However, the introduction of the new product will decrease by $2,000 the annual net cash inflow from the existing product. In this case, the new product will generate $8,000 of incremental net cash inflow. The $8,000 is calculated as the total net cash inflow after the introduction of the new product minus the net cash inflows before introducing the product. Thus, if a new project is expected to reduce the cash flows from existing projects, the amount of the reduction should be subtracted from the net cash flows of the new project.

- *Measure the incremental cash flows on an after-tax basis.* A firm maximizes shareholder wealth if it measures only those cash flows of a project that affect shareholders directly. As a result, operating expenses, such as raw materials and wages, are deducted from operating revenues. In a similar manner, taxes paid to the government are a part of a firm's cost of doing business and are subtracted from a project's cash flows.

Classifying Incremental After-Tax Cash Flows The cash inflows and outflows considered in a capital budgeting decision can belong to one of three classes:

- initial investment outlay
- net cash benefits or savings from operations
- terminal cash flows

Initial Investment Outlay The initial investment outlay includes the cash needed to acquire the new equipment (or build the new plant), plus any costs associated with delivering, installing, or modifying the new equipment, less any salvage proceeds from the disposal of replaced equipment.

The cash flows of the initial investment outlay differ from the cash flows from operations because of tax treatment. The new equipment is capitalized and written off using capital cost allowances over the equipment's useful life, while operating costs are considered a tax deduction and are subtracted from operating profits. The treatment of operating costs is explained later in this chapter.

In situations where the new equipment (or plant) is replacing an old one, the initial investment outlay must be reduced by the net cash proceeds from the sale of the old equipment. If these proceeds are positive, they decrease the initial cash flows. If they are negative, such as when the company has to pay to dispose of the old equipment, they increase the initial investment outlay.

The sale of old equipment may have tax implications. Canada Revenue Agency requires the firm to reduce the **undepreciated capital cost (UCC)** for the asset class by the net proceeds from the sale of the equipment. If these net proceeds are higher than the UCC for the class plus the additions during the year, the difference must be reported as current income. This income gives rise to additional taxes. Consequently, the net proceeds from selling the equipment must be reduced by the size of the additional taxes.

The initial investment outlay also includes any additional working capital needed to buy raw material, finance accounts receivable, or satisfy other needs related to the new equipment. These items are likely to increase the initial investment outlay for new projects, but may decrease them under some circumstances. For example, in projects requiring equipment replacement, the new equipment may be more efficient than the older equipment, leading to lower working capital needs. In this case, the changes in working capital would be negative and would reduce the initial investment outlay. Only changes that occur at the beginning of the project are included as part of the initial investment outlay. Additional working capital needed (or no longer needed) in a future period is accounted for as a cash outflow (inflow) during that period.

Often, local, provincial, and federal governments provide investment incentives in the form of direct subsidies, interest-free loans, or tax credits to encourage investment. Such incentives affect initial investment outlay. The treatment of incentives depends on the type of incentive and the timing of the cash received from the incentive. For example, a direct cash subsidy at the beginning of the project decreases the initial investment outlay by the same amount. An interest-free loan is accounted for as a cash inflow at the time it is received plus a cash outflow at the time it is paid. Tax credits affect cash inflows at the time they are received.

Net Cash Benefits or Savings from Operations For capital budgeting purposes, the net cash flows received from an asset at the end of a period are calculated as the incremental change in operating revenues minus the incremental change in the operating costs, minus any taxes due on the net revenues, plus the tax shield from **capital cost allowance (CCA)**, plus or minus changes in the working capital and other adjustments. The taxes due on net revenues are calculated as:

$$\text{Tax rate} \times \left[\begin{array}{c} \text{incremental change in} \\ \text{operating revenues} \end{array} - \begin{array}{c} \text{incremental change in} \\ \text{operating expenses} \end{array} - \text{CCA} \right]$$

The CCA that can be claimed over the useful life can be calculated by creating a schedule, as suggested by Canada Revenue Agency publications. However, the procedure is cumbersome because it requires calculating CCA for all years that precede the target year.

Alternatively, you can use Equations 1-8 and 1-9. For the first year, CCA will be equal to half the capital cost (because of the half-year rule) of the asset multiplied by the CCA rate. The UCC at year end is equal to the acquisition capital cost minus CCA for the year. For the second year and beyond, the following formulas can be used to calculate CCA and the resulting UCC for any year i in the future.

$$CCA_i = C \times d \times (1 - d/2)(1 - d)^{i - 2} \qquad \textbf{(Equation 1-8)}$$

$$UCC_i = C \times (1 - d/2)(1 - d)^{i - 1} \qquad \textbf{(Equation 1-9)}$$

where
    C = initial capital cost
    d = capital cost allowance rate of the class
    i = year 2, 3, 4, . . .

Calculating the CCA per year, the depreciation per year of an asset's value for tax purposes, presents one of the complications of capital budgeting. In your introductory finance course and financial accounting courses, you learned how to determine the CCA allowed for deduction. Try the You Apply It minicase on page 38. It has been designed to remind you of these calculations. If after working through this minicase you do not have a good understanding of how to calculate CCA, it is recommended that you spend some time reviewing the calculation procedures in your previous courses.

Terminal Cash Flows The **terminal cash flows** from a project may include the net cash generated from the sale of the asset, tax effects from the termination of the project, and the release of net working capital. Of course, at the end of a project there may be expenses related to removal of the equipment and cleanup. Such costs are often deducted from the salvage value of the equipment.

Tax laws also complicate the calculations of cash that flows from the sale of an asset. For tax purposes, the sale of an asset can create either recaptured depreciation or a terminal loss if the asset class is terminated. **Recaptured depreciation** describes a situation in which an asset is sold for an amount greater than its UCC at the time of sale. As a result, recaptured depreciation is added to taxable income. A **terminal loss** occurs if an asset is sold, there are no other assets in the asset class, and the asset is sold for an amount less than its UCC at the time of sale. As a result, a terminal loss is deducted from taxable income. We illustrate these concepts by returning to the FPI scenario.

YOU APPLY IT ESTIMATING CCA FOR TAX PURPOSES

FPI Inc. is planning to buy a franchise to sell "Hot Hamburgers." The price of the franchise is $50,000, and its useful life is eight years. The incremental operating cash flows from the business are estimated to be $19,000 per year for the next eight years. The franchise will be the only asset in class 14. NOTE: Tax rules state that the maximum CCA per year for class 14 is equal to the minimum CCA using the straight-line method, or to the UCC at the end of the year, whichever is less.[5] The furniture, machinery, and refrigeration equipment belong to class 8; the CCA rate for this class is 20%. The half-year rule applies to class 8 assets but not to class 14 assets.

FPI Inc. also needs to buy:

- furniture $ 22,000
- machinery 20,000
- refrigeration equipment 8,000

The estimated useful life of these assets is eight years.

Questions

Question 1: Calculate the maximum CCA that can be claimed for class 14.

Question 2: Calculate UCC for year 5 and the maximum CCA that can be claimed in year 5 for the items other than the franchise.

Answers

Question 1: Calculate the maximum CCA that can be claimed for class 14.

Given that the franchise is the only asset in the class, CCA for class 14 will be a maximum of $6,250 per year for eight years.

$$\text{CCA per year} = \$50,000 \div 8 = \$6,250$$

Question 2: Calculate UCC for year 5 and the maximum CCA that can be claimed in year 5 for the items other than the franchise.

To calculate CCA for year 5:

$$\begin{aligned} CCA_5 &= \$50,000 \times 0.20 \times (1 - 0.10)(1 - 0.20)^{5-2} \\ &= \$4,608 \end{aligned}$$

To calculate UCC for year 5:

$$\begin{aligned} UCC_5 &= \$50,000 \times (1 - 0.10)(1 - 0.20)^{5-1} \\ &= \$18,432 \end{aligned}$$

Thus, the CCA and UCC for year 5 are respectively $4,608 and $18,432.

---

[5] For the purposes of this text, you will always be provided with the class to which an asset belongs, as well as the corresponding CCA rate.

FPI Inc. sells the furniture, machinery, and refrigeration equipment at the beginning of year 13 for $5,000. No other assets remain in class 8 after the sale. Assume that no other assets in class 8 were purchased in year 13.

Questions

Question 1: What is the tax effect of the sale on the cash flows in year 13?

Question 2: What is the tax effect if the salvage price is $2,000?

Answers

Question 1: What is the tax effect of the sale on the cash flows in year 13?

To determine the tax effect of the disposition of assets in class 8, you need to determine the UCC balance at the beginning of year 13. This balance is in fact the UCC balance at the end of year 12.

Using Equation 1-9, the UCC at the end of year 12 is calculated as follows:

$$UCC_{12} = \$50,000 \times (1 - 0.10)(1 - 0.20)^{12-1}$$
$$= \$3,865$$

The UCC balance at the beginning of year 13 is adjusted for any new acquisitions or any dispositions of assets in the asset class as follows:

UCC_{13} (beginning of year)	$3,865
Plus: Cost of new acquisitions	0
Minus: Proceeds of disposition	(5,000)
UCC (adjusted)	$(1,135)
Recapture of CCA taken into income at the end of year 13	$1,135

Question 2: What is the tax effect if the salvage price is $2,000?

The UCC balance at the beginning of year 13 is adjusted for any new acquisitions or any dispositions of assets in the asset class as follows[6]:

UCC_{13} (beginning of year)	$3,865
Plus: Cost of new acquisitions	0
Minus: Proceeds of disposition	(2,000)
UCC (adjusted)	$1,865
Terminal loss deducted from income at the end of year 13	$(1,865)

---

[6] No capital cost allowance can be claimed in year 13 if the asset class is being terminated. Thus, capital cost allowance can only be claimed when an asset class continues to exist.

Summary Cash flows relevant to capital budgeting may be calculated using general expressions such as:

$$\begin{array}{l}\text{Net initial} \\ \text{investment outlay}\end{array} = \begin{array}{l}\text{price of} \\ \text{the asset}\end{array} + \begin{array}{l}\text{shipping, installation,} \\ \text{and modification costs}\end{array} + \begin{array}{l}\text{increase in} \\ \text{working capital}\end{array}$$

$$- \begin{array}{l}\text{investment} \\ \text{incentives}\end{array} - \begin{array}{l}\text{salvage value} \\ \text{from old asset}\end{array} \qquad \textbf{(Equation 1-10)}$$

$$\begin{array}{l}\text{Operating cash flows at the} \\ \text{end of period } i \text{ (OCF}_i)\end{array} = \begin{array}{l}\text{incremental operating} \\ \text{revenues (IOR}_i)\end{array} - \begin{array}{l}\text{incremental operating} \\ \text{costs (IOC}_i)\end{array}$$

$$- \text{taxes } [T \times (\text{IOR}_i - \text{IOC}_i - \text{CCA}_i)] \quad \textbf{(Equation 1-11)}$$

where

OCF_i = operating cash flows at the end of period i

T = corporate tax rate

$$\begin{array}{l}\text{Expected cash flows} \\ \text{at end of period } i\end{array} = \text{OCF}_i - \begin{array}{l}\text{increases to working} \\ \text{capital } (\Delta W_i)\end{array} - \begin{array}{l}\text{other adjustments} \\ \text{(OA}_i)\end{array}$$

$$\textbf{(Equation 1-12)}$$

$$\text{Terminal cash flow} = \begin{array}{l}\text{net sale price} \\ \text{of the asset}\end{array} - \begin{array}{l}\text{taxes, if any,} \\ \text{on the proceeds}\end{array}$$

$$- \begin{array}{l}\text{removal and} \\ \text{clean-up costs}\end{array} + \begin{array}{l}\text{release of} \\ \text{working capital}\end{array} \quad \textbf{(Equation 1-13)}$$

Tax Shield Method of Estimating Operating Cash Flows

Calculating the CCA per year for capital budgeting purposes can be cumbersome because it requires using Equations 1-8 and 1-9 for every year involved. Fortunately, the process can be simplified without problems.

Equation 1-11 may be rewritten as:

$$\text{OCF}_i = \begin{array}{l}\text{incremental operating} \\ \text{revenues (IOR}_i)\end{array} - \begin{array}{l}\text{incremental operating} \\ \text{costs (IOC}_i)\end{array}$$

$$- \text{taxes } [T \times (\text{IOR}_i - \text{IOC}_i)]$$
$$+ (T \times \text{CCA}_i) \qquad \textbf{(Equation 1-14)}$$

This equation states that the cash flows from operations are equal to the net revenues minus operating costs, minus taxes on the incremental operating income (before deducting CCA), plus a tax refund to recognize that some of the taxed profits are indeed recoveries of the capital costs used to acquire the productive asset. Tax shields affect cash flows indirectly because they increase operating income through a reduction of taxes. The method used to calculate after-tax cash flows using tax shields is known as the **tax shield method**. The two methods of calculating the after-tax cash flows are mathematically equivalent. Exhibit 1-10 uses the first year of operations from the FPI Minicase to show that the two methods produce the same incremental after-tax cash flows, using a tax rate of 32%.

As the two methods of calculating the incremental after-tax cash flows from a project produce the same results, preference of one over the other is a matter of convenience. When the cash flows under consideration extend many years into the future, it

Exhibit 1-10
Tax Calculations in Estimating the Incremental Cash Flows[7]

Accounting method		Tax shield method	
Incremental operating income	$19,000	Incremental operating income	$19,000
Less CCA	$11,250	Less taxes at 32%	$6,080
Taxable income	$7,750	After-tax operating income	$12,920
Less taxes at 32%	$2,480		
Income after taxes	$5,270	Add tax shield on CCA at 32%	$11,250 × 0.32 = $3,600
Add CCA	$11,250		
Net incremental cash flows	$16,520	Net incremental cash flows	$12,920 + $3,600 = $16,520

is advantageous to use the tax shield method for the purpose of calculating the present value of the cash flows. In this case, it is easier to treat the tax shield separately from other cash flows. Equation 1-8 can be used to derive a formula for the present value of all the tax shields expected from an asset. The value of the tax shield is then added to the present value of the other cash flows to derive the total present value of the asset. This procedure is detailed in the next section.

1.6 CAPITAL BUDGETING EVALUATION CRITERIA
Net Present Value Technique

The financial manager is concerned with maximizing shareholder wealth. Every time the financial manager undertakes a project with a positive net present value, the firm's total value increases by the amount of the NPV. Accepting positive NPV projects is consistent with maximizing shareholder wealth. The financial manager must look for projects with positive NPV.

The NPV technique is a discounted cash flow method that comprises several steps. The financial manager must:

- consider all the incremental cash flows that are relevant to the decision and the timing of these cash flows
- determine the appropriate discount rate that represents the firm's cost of capital relevant to the expected cash flows
- discount the cash flows back to the time when the decision must be made
- determine the NPV

---

[7] CCA for the first year is $6,250 from class 14 and $5,000 from class 8. The half-year rule applies to class 8 but not to class 14 assets.

Using the expressions and notations introduced in Equations 1-10, 1-11, and 1-12, the present value of future incremental cash flows can be formulated as:

$$PV = \sum_{i=1}^{n} \frac{CF_i}{(1 + k)^i} + \frac{S_n}{(1 + k)^n} \qquad \text{(Equation 1-15)}$$

where

CF_i = expected cash flows at the end of period i
k = discount rate
S_n = salvage value of the project at the end of n periods

Equation 1-15 assumes that the tax shield derived from the CCA for period i is added to the cash flows CF_i. As indicated in the previous topic, if the useful life of the project is long, it is simpler to separate the tax shields from the other cash flows and calculate the present value of each cash stream separately. In this case, Equation 1-15 is replaced by:

$$PV = \sum_{i=1}^{n} \frac{F_i}{(1 + k)^i} + \frac{S_n}{(1 + k)^n} + PVTS \qquad \text{(Equation 1-16)}$$

where

F_i = cash flow during period i, excluding the tax shield
PVTS = present value of the tax shield

PVTS is calculated as:

$$PVTS = \left[\frac{C \times d \times T}{2(d + k)} \right] \left[\frac{2 + k}{1 + k} \right] \qquad \text{(Equation 1-17)}$$

where

C = capital cost paid to acquire the asset
d = capital cost allowance rate of the class to which the asset belongs

Equation 1-17 determines the value of the tax shield for an asset, assuming its useful life continues indefinitely, and adjusts this value for the half-year rule. In practice, assets do not continue indefinitely because the firm may decide to terminate the project and sell the assets. In the majority of cases in which a project is terminated, assets are sold but there are still other assets in the class for tax purposes. Canada Revenue Agency requires that the UCC_n balance of the asset class be reduced by the salvage value of the asset. Thus, Equation 1-17 is adjusted for the sale of the assets by reducing the tax shields that were expected to be claimed in future years. The present value of the tax shield lost in year n ($PVTSL_n$) is determined by Equation 1-18:

$$PVTSL_n = \left[\frac{S_n}{(1 + k)^n} \right] \left[\frac{d \times T}{d + k} \right] \qquad \text{(Equation 1-18)}$$

Thus, the present value of the project, as calculated in Equation 1-16, should be reduced by the tax shield loss $PVTSL_n$. Making these adjustments to Equation 1-16 yields:

$$PV = \sum_{i=1}^{n} \frac{F_i}{(1 + k)^i} + \frac{S_n}{(1 + k)^n}$$

$$+ \left[\frac{C \times d \times T}{2(d + k)} \right] \left[\frac{2 + k}{1 + k} \right] - \left[\frac{S_n}{(1 + k)^n} \right] \left[\frac{d \times T}{d + k} \right] \qquad \text{(Equation 1-19)}$$

Section 1.5 explained that the sale of assets can terminate a project and also close the asset class for tax purposes. As a result, there is either a terminal loss or recaptured depreciation. A terminal loss occurs if an asset is sold for an amount less than its undepreciated capital cost at the time of the sale. The terminal loss is subtracted from the taxable revenue of the firm, reducing the amount of taxes payable. On the other hand, recaptured depreciation occurs if a firm sells an asset for an amount greater than its undepreciated capital cost at the time of the sale. Recaptured capital cost allowance is added to the firm's taxable revenue and increases its taxes payable.

Remember that when a project has CCA from *different classes* of assets, Equations 1-17 and 1-18 must be used to calculate the $PVTS_n$ and $PVTSL_n$ generated by *each class*. The project's $PVTS_n$ and $PVTSL_n$ are the sum of the separate present values. This treatment is required because the capital cost allowance rate d changes from one class to the other. Similarly, when several CCA classes are involved, the last two terms in Equation 1-19 may have to be used more than once to calculate the additional tax breaks received or the additional taxes paid.

The NPV of the project is calculated as:

$$NPV = \sum_{i=1}^{n} \frac{F_i}{(1 + k)^i} + \frac{S_n}{(1 + k)^n} + \left[\frac{C \times d \times T}{2(d + k)}\right]\left[\frac{2 + k}{1 + k}\right]$$

$$- \left[\frac{S_n}{(1 + k)^n}\right]\left[\frac{d \times T}{d + k}\right] - C_0 \qquad \text{(Equation 1-20)}$$

where

C_0 = net initial investment outlay

Therefore, the project's NPV is determined from the difference between the present value of the cash flows discounted at the project's required rate of return and the initial cash outlay. Refer to Appendix A at the end of this chapter to see how we capture the effects of either a terminal loss or recaptured depreciation when a project is terminated and the asset class is closed.

The discount rate k used in calculating the net present value is the *opportunity cost* of taking the project. In other words, k is the return that can be earned by using the money in an alternative investment other than the project. The project must return at least k to be desirable because it is the rate that must be paid by the firm to raise the money required to undertake the project. If all else is equal, the higher the required rate k, the lower the NPV.

The discount rate can be used to explain the decision rule, which is to accept projects with positive or zero NPV. A zero NPV implies that the project will return enough cash flows to compensate the investor for the opportunity cost of funds. Thus, the investor should be indifferent between investing the money in the project or elsewhere. If the NPV is greater than zero, the investor is compensated for the opportunity cost of funds plus a bonus. The higher the NPV, the higher the bonus and the more desirable the project.

Notice that k appears in the denominators of the expressions on the right side of Equation 1-20 and determines the discounting factors for future cash flows. If all else is equal, the higher the discount rate k, the lower the present value of the cash flow. Thus, the discount rate plays an important role in determining the NPV.

Using Spreadsheets for Project Evaluation

The introduction of user-friendly spreadsheet programs makes project evaluations easier. Once a spreadsheet is developed to evaluate a project, the financial manager can quickly and accurately derive the NPV. The three major tasks in designing a spreadsheet for project evaluation are:

■ identifying the project's initial, operating, and terminal cash flows

■ generating the key outputs such as the incremental after-tax cash flows

■ generating the NPV of the project

Spreadsheets assist the financial manager in deriving the NPV under various scenarios of the input variables such as revenues and costs. You may find it convenient to use a spreadsheet to solve the practice minicases provided in the self-test section at the end of this chapter.

Alternative Valuation Techniques Used in Capital Budgeting

In addition to the NPV technique, other techniques may be used in investment analysis.

Internal Rate-of-Return Technique The internal rate of return (IRR) technique is a discounted cash flow method similar to the NPV method. Simply stated, the IRR is the discount rate k that makes the NPV equal to zero. Equivalently, the IRR is the level of k that makes the present value of future cash flows equal to the initial outlays. In Equation 1-19, which calculates the present value of future cash flows, the discount rate is k. Thus, the IRR is the level of k that will make the value derived by Equation 1-19 equal to C_0.

Keep in mind that the NPV is inversely related to the required rate of return k. Higher values of k will lead to lower NPVs and vice versa. Thus, the decision criteria for the IRR technique are stated in terms of the NPV decision criteria, as follows:

IRR < k; NPV < 0; reject project
IRR = k; NPV = 0; indifferent to rejecting or accepting project
IRR > k; NPV > 0; accept project

If the cost of capital for a project is less than (or equal to) the IRR, the NPV is positive (or zero) and the project is acceptable. If the IRR is less than the cost of capital, the project is not acceptable because its NPV is negative.

The IRR may be regarded as the yield from a project. It is the rate that must be earned in the financial market to make the investor indifferent between investing in the project and investing in the financial market. It is popular among practitioners as it is easy to understand and explain. Yet managers should be cautious when using the IRR for several reasons.

Sometimes, a project may have several internal rates of return. Generally, a project may have more than one IRR if it has a pattern of positive and negative net cash flows over its useful life. The maximum number of possible IRRs is the number of times the cash flows switch between negative and positive. When this occurs, the manager must decide which IRR is the relevant one to be used with the decision technique. While there is no simple approach to the decision, a simple solution to the entire problem would be to use the NPV technique.

The conflicts between the IRR and NPV techniques are related to assumptions regarding the reinvestment rate. IRR calculations assume the cash inflows from a project are reinvested at a rate equal to the IRR. In contrast, the NPV technique assumes the same cash flows are reinvested at a rate equal to the cost of capital. In a competitive financial market, it is rarely possible for a firm to consistently generate projects with rates of return higher than the firm's cost of capital. Therefore, the assumption that the IRR is the relevant reinvestment rate is not realistic over any prolonged period. The NPV technique should be used whenever possible to avoid any wrong decisions.

For example, consider a project that will cost $10,000 as an initial outlay. The project is expected to generate $26,000 in after-tax cash inflows in the first year and $16,500 in cash *outflows* in the second year. What is the internal rate of return of the project?

The problem can be solved by finding the IRR that satisfies:

$$\$10,000 = \$26,000 \div (1 + IRR) - \$16,500 \div (1 + IRR)^2$$

By simplifying, the solution to the problem can be reduced to solving the quadratic equation[8]:

$$10,000(1 + IRR)^2 - 26,000(1 + IRR) + 16,500 = 0$$

Simple calculations show that two IRRs, 10% and 50%, satisfy the equation. If the cost of capital is 20%, should the project be accepted or rejected? Assuming 20% cost of capital, the NPV of the project is $208. According to the NPV technique, the project must be accepted. If the IRR technique is used, the project will be rejected unless 50% is accepted to be the IRR.

Complications may also occur with the IRR technique when projects are mutually exclusive. Projects are said to be **mutually exclusive** when they cannot be undertaken simultaneously. For example, a firm may be planning to acquire a new machine and have three choices of suppliers. The three machines are mutually exclusive because the firm will choose just one machine from the three. The task is to choose the most profitable machine after taking into consideration maintenance costs, useful life, initial outlay, and operating costs.

Payback Technique The **payback period** is the time (usually in years) that it takes a project to pay back its initial cash outlays. Thus, the **payback technique** requires estimating a project's initial cash outflows and comparing them to the operating and terminal cash inflows. The decision technique is to accept any project with a payback period equal to or less than a target payback period.

---

[8] The general form of the quadratic equation is:

$$ax^2 + bx + c = 0$$

The equation has two roots and can be solved using the following quadratic formula:

$$x = \frac{-b \pm \sqrt{b^2 - 4ac}}{2a}$$

YOU APPLY IT CHOOSING BETWEEN MUTUALLY EXCLUSIVE PROJECTS

Tom, a mechanical engineer, is seeking help in determining his best alternative. He has two projects in mind and can pursue one or the other but not both, as either project will need his full time over five years to be successful. He can borrow money at 14%.

The first project is an innovative component that can be attached to seeding equipment to reduce wastage. The attachment will generate positive cash inflows over the next five years. These cash flows will gradually decline after the first year as other equipment manufacturers develop similar products.

The other project is to build new seeding equipment and to include the new part as a standard feature. The cash inflows from this alternative will be minor in the first year, but they are likely to increase gradually as time passes. Exhibit 1-11 provides data for the two projects.

Exhibit 1-11
Data for Mutually Exclusive Projects

End of year	Incremental after-tax cash inflows ($)					
	0	1	2	3	4	5
Alternative 1	(50,000)	21,000	18,000	16,000	14,000	13,000
Alternative 2	(50,000)	11,000	13,000	17,000	22,000	28,000

Question

Which project do you recommend and why?

Answer

Using a financial calculator we find alternative 1 has an IRR of 21.23%, while alternative 2 has an IRR of 19.92%. Therefore, the IRR technique will favour alternative 1 because it has the highest IRR.

In contrast, when the discount rate is 14%, alternative 1 has an NPV of $8,112, while alternative 2 has an NPV of $8,695. At a 14% discount rate, alternative 2 has the highest NPV. Therefore, according to the NPV technique, alternative 2 should be accepted.

The NPVs of the two projects under various discount rate scenarios are shown in Exhibit 1-12. Curve A_1BC_1 represents the NPV of alternative 1, while A_2BC_2 represents the NPV of alternative 2. The two curves intersect at point B, which corresponds to a discount rate of about 15.60%. This means that the two projects will have the same NPV if the discount rate is 15.60%. If the discount rate is less than 15.60%, alternative 2 dominates alternative 1 because its NPV would be higher than the NPV of alternative 1. If the discount rate is higher than 15.60%, the NPV technique will favour alternative 1. Thus, the NPV and the IRR techniques provide similar decisions if the cost of capital is higher than or equal to 15.60% and conflicting decisions if the cost of capital is lower than 15.60%.

You Apply It Continued >

Exhibit 1-12 NPVs of Alternatives 1 and 2 under Various Discount Rate Scenarios

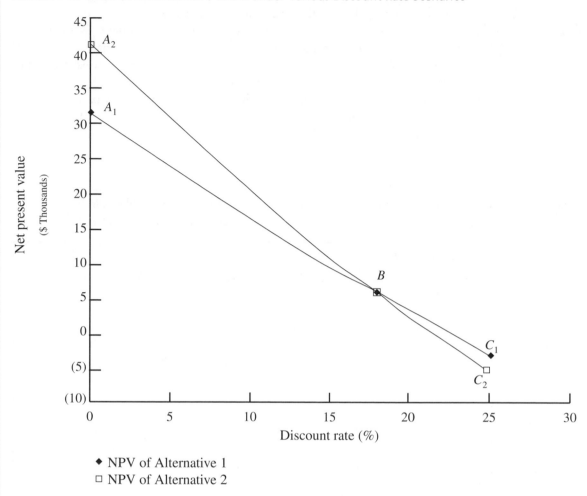

◆ NPV of Alternative 1
□ NPV of Alternative 2

For example, consider alternative 1 of Tom's minicase. The project's payback period is less than three years because the cash flows from the first three years ($55,000) are more than enough to cover the initial outlays of $50,000. That is:

$$(\$21{,}000 + \$18{,}000 + \$16{,}000) - \$50{,}000 > 0$$

Indeed, only $11,000 of the last $16,000 is needed to completely pay back the initial outlays. If the cash flows are generated evenly over the third year, the first two years plus only 68.75% ($11,000 ÷ $16,000) of the third year will be needed for the project to completely pay back its initial outlays. Thus, the payback period for the project is 2.6875 years.

Depending on the target payback period, the project will or will not be accepted. If the project's payback period is less than or equal to the target payback period, the project is acceptable. Otherwise the project will be rejected.

The technique is simple to understand and use, and it is easy to explain, which accounts for its popularity with managers. Often, managers can be heard saying that any project that takes more than three years to start generating profits is not a good project.

Essentially, these managers are describing a three-year payback period decision technique. Any cash flows received beyond three years are considered profits.

In addition to its simplicity, a practical value of the payback technique is its usefulness in providing a rough measure of the riskiness of a project. If all else is equal, short payback projects are less risky than long payback projects. For example, a cash flow expected after 20 years is much less certain than a cash flow expected over the next year. Moreover, short payback projects are more liquid than long payback projects. However, the payback method may be more useful in conjunction with other techniques such as NPV and IRR.

The payback period decision technique has major limitations. First, it fails to take into account the time value of money. As a correction to this limitation, some managers use the **discounted payback period**, which is similar to the payback period except that future cash flows are discounted as part of the evaluation. For example, consider alternative 1 from Tom's minicase. The discounted payback period is calculated in Exhibit 1-13. As indicated in the last row, the discounted payback period would be 3.8358 years.

Exhibit 1-13
Calculating the Discounted Payback Period for Alternative 1

End of year	0	1	2	3	4	5
			Cash inflows			
Alternative 1 ($)	(50,000)	21,000	18,000	16,000	14,000	13,000
Discount factor at 14%	1.0000	0.8772	0.7695	0.6750	0.5921	0.5194
Discounted cash flows ($)	(50,000)	18,421	13,851	10,800	8,289	6,752
Cumulative cash flows ($)	(50,000)	(31,579)	(17,728)	(6,928)	1,361	8,113

Payback period = 3 + 6,928 ÷ 8,289 = 3.8358 years

Second, the payback technique fails to account for cash flows after the payback period. It generally favours short-lived projects and projects with relatively higher cash flows in earlier years over other projects. For example, in Tom's Minicase, alternative 2 has a payback period of 3.4091 years ($50,000 − 11,000 − 13,000 − 17,000 − 0.4091 × 22,000 = 0) as opposed to 2.6875 years for alternative 1. A target payback period of three years will mean accepting alternative 1 and rejecting alternative 2. Yet if the cost of capital is 14%, alternative 2 is more desirable because it has the highest NPV. The reason is that alternative 2's cash flows are higher later in the project's life.

Finally, given that the payback technique ignores cash flows beyond the payback period, it is likely to reject projects that, if implemented, will increase the chances that a firm will accept future projects.

Profitability Index (PI) Technique The **profitability index (PI)** for a project is the present value of the incremental after-tax cash inflows divided by the PI initial investment outlay:

$$PI = PV \div C_0 \qquad \text{(Equation 1-21)}$$

The PI can be used as a decision technique. A project with a profitability index equal to or greater than 1 should be accepted. This technique emerges from the NPV technique, which states that a project must be accepted if the NPV is greater than or equal to zero.

If

$$NPV = 0$$

then

$$PV = C_0$$

and thus

$$PI = 1$$

If

$$NPV > 0$$

then

$$PV > C_0$$

and

$$PI > 1$$

The PI provides a measure of relative profitability and may be interpreted as the present value generated per dollar of investment. It gives the same results as the NPV technique when evaluating independent projects. Moreover, it is useful when the capital budget is limited and capital rationing forces the firm to select the best subset of projects from a large number of desirable projects. In this case, projects may be selected based on their profitability index. Yet the PI technique may lead to wrong decisions if used to choose between mutually exclusive projects. We have more to say on capital rationing in Chapter 2.

For example, consider projects A and B, which are mutually exclusive. Suppose that A has an NPV of $10,000 and a PI of 1.20. Project B has an NPV of $5,000 and a PI of 1.25. According to the PI technique, project B should be accepted and project A should be rejected. The NPV technique correctly suggests the opposite. Project A provides more value to the firm than project B. Therefore, it should be preferred over project B.

Average Rate of Return (ARR) on Book Value Technique

The **average rate of return on book value** measures the profitability of a proposed project as the ratio of the average annual incremental after-tax cash flows from operations to the average book value of the investment:

$$ARR = ACF \div I_a \qquad \textbf{(Equation 1-22)}$$

where

ACF = average annual incremental after-tax cash flows from operations over the life of the project

I_a = the firm's average book value of the investment in the project

The firm's average book value of the investment in the project represents an average of the historical cost less annual amortization expenses over the life of the project. As a rule, a project is acceptable if its average rate of return equals or exceeds a target return predetermined by management.

The ARR technique is not desirable as a capital budgeting decision-making tool because it ignores the time value of money. The major defect is that it averages cash flows between periods without regard to the time value of money. Moreover, companies often use accounting income rather than cash flows to measure investment returns.

Despite its shortfalls, some practitioners continue to use the ARR technique. Perhaps the reliance on accounting earnings to justify executive bonuses leads some managers to use the ARR method for project selection.

In practice, several other techniques such as return on assets (ROA), return on equity (ROE), and return on net assets (RONA) are used to measure corporate performance. However, these techniques are not proper for capital budgeting as they ignore the market opportunity costs of capital.

Comparison of Capital Budgeting Techniques

The techniques of NPV, IRR, and PI are time-adjusted approaches that take into account the time value of money. Therefore, they are superior to the other capital budgeting techniques. All three lead to the same accept/reject decisions if the projects under consideration are independent and there is only one IRR per project.

For example, when all future expected incremental cash flows from independent projects are positive, each project will have one IRR. In this case, if a project has a positive (or zero) NPV, it has an IRR greater than (or equal to) the cost of capital, and a PI greater than (or equal to) one. All three techniques recommend accepting the project. Similarly, if the NPV of a project is negative, the project's IRR is less than the cost of capital, and its profitability index is less than one. In this case, the recommendation is to reject the project.

However, the IRR and PI methods may lead to incorrect choices when projects are mutually exclusive. The NPV is superior to the other capital budgeting techniques because it is a direct measure of a project's contribution to shareholder wealth in dollars.

Estimating the Cash Flows of Economically Dependent Projects

Economic dependence of potential new projects complicates the capital budgeting process. It requires evaluating any possible combination of projects in addition to evaluating the projects on a stand-alone basis. For example, assume that a fabric manufacturer is considering building a clothing plant to manufacture women's or men's clothing. The two projects are economically dependent, as starting one line might make it easier to start the other. In this situation, the firm is faced with three capital budgeting calculations. First, the firm must evaluate each project separately, that is it must decide whether each line of clothing is desirable on its own. Then, it must evaluate the combination of the two projects by determining the desirability of starting the two lines simultaneously.

Economically dependent projects may also be physically dependent, when the acceptance of a project is conditional on the acceptance of another project. For example, the fabric manufacturer may be contemplating opening an outlet to sell some of the output from the clothing factory. Opening the retail outlet is contingent on whether a clothing factory is built. In this case, the decision is whether to invest in the clothing factory alone or to invest in the clothing factory plus the retail outlet. The capital budgeting evaluation process requires evaluating the clothing factory as a separate project and then the clothing factory plus a retail outlet as a joint project.

Economic dependence is not restricted to new projects. More often, a new project is economically dependent on the current operations of the firm and on existing projects. In this case, the proper procedure is to calculate the incremental cash flows from the new project by calculating the cash flows assuming that the project will be taken and subtracting the cash flows expected without the project. The net present value of the incremental cash flows determines the value of the new project and its desirability.

In conclusion, because economic dependence of projects complicates the capital budgeting process, it is desirable to formulate capital budgeting proposals so that they are economically independent. In this case, the incremental cash flows will be the cash flows from the project. Moreover, the net present value of the project is the exact amount that will be added to shareholder wealth as a consequence of undertaking the project.

The Savy Packaging Inc. minicase demonstrates the use of the NPV technique in determining the feasibility of economically dependent projects.

YOU APPLY IT DETERMINING THE FEASIBILITY OF ECONOMICALLY DEPENDENT PROJECTS

Savy Packaging, Inc. operates a canning plant that packages tuna. Over the past several years, management has increasingly found itself forced to turn away business because of capacity constraints. Ken, the financial manager of Savy Packaging, is studying the acquisition of a new canning machine. This machine will cost $350,000 and have a useful life of three years, after which it can be sold for $55,000. Ken forecasts that the machine will generate annual operating revenues of $350,000 and incur $100,000 in annual operating expenses over the useful life of the machine. The project requires an initial investment of $25,000 in working capital. However, net working capital will be recovered at the end of the three years. The firm's tax rate is 45%, its cost of capital is 16%, and the applicable CCA rate for the new canning machine is 30%. Assume that the asset class remains open after the sale of the canning machine.

Questions

Question 1: Determine the feasibility of the project by calculating the NPV.

Question 2: Suppose the canning machine can also be used to package local blueberries. The machine will require a one-time installation cost of $150,000 to put it in working order. The blueberry canning project will generate incremental annual operating revenues of $100,000 and incur incremental annual operating expenses of $75,000. The project will also require an additional investment in working capital of $5,000. All of the net working capital will be recovered at the end of the three years. Determine whether the project of canning tuna and blueberries is feasible by calculating the NPV.

You Apply It Continued >

Answers

Question 1: Determine the feasibility of the project by calculating the NPV.

Initial investment of the project

$$= \$350{,}000$$

Present value of net working capital

$$= \$25{,}000$$

Present value of the annual operating cash flows after tax

$$
\begin{aligned}
&= (\$350{,}000 - \$100{,}000) \times (1 - 0.45) \times \text{PVIFA}_{(16\%, \, 3 \text{ years})} \\
&= \$308{,}810
\end{aligned}
$$

Present value of tax shields

$$
\begin{aligned}
&= \left[\frac{\$350{,}000 \times 0.30 \times 0.45}{2(0.16 + 0.30)} \right] \left[\frac{2 + 0.16}{1 + 0.16} \right] - \left[\frac{\$55{,}000}{(1 + 0.16)^3} \right] \left[\frac{0.30 \times 0.45}{0.16 + 0.30} \right] \\
&= \$95{,}633 - \$10{,}341 \\
&= \$85{,}292
\end{aligned}
$$

Present value of the salvage value

$$
\begin{aligned}
&= \$55{,}000 \times \text{PVIF}_{(16\%, \, 3 \text{ years})} \\
&= \$35{,}236
\end{aligned}
$$

Present value of net working capital at the end of the project

$$
\begin{aligned}
&= \$25{,}000 \times \text{PVIF}_{(16\%, \, 3 \text{ years})} \\
&= \$16{,}016
\end{aligned}
$$

Net present value

$$
\begin{aligned}
&= \$308{,}810 + \$85{,}292 + \$35{,}236 + \$16{,}016 - \$350{,}000 - \$25{,}000 \\
&= \$70{,}354
\end{aligned}
$$

A positive NPV indicates that the project proposal is feasible.

Question 2: Suppose the canning machine can also be used to package local blueberries. The machine will require a one-time installation cost of $150,000 to put it in working order. The blueberry canning project will generate incremental annual operating revenues of $100,000 and incur incremental annual operating expenses of $75,000. The project will also require an additional investment in working capital of $5,000. All of the net working capital will be recovered at the end of the three years. Determine whether the project of canning tuna and blueberries is feasible by calculating the NPV.

Initial investment of the project

$$
\begin{aligned}
&= \$350{,}000 + \$150{,}000 \\
&= \$500{,}000
\end{aligned}
$$

You Apply It Continued >

Present value of net working capital

$$= \$30{,}000$$

Present value of the annual operating cash flows after tax

$$= (\$450{,}000 - \$175{,}000) \times (1 - 0.45) \times \text{PVIFA}_{(16\%, \, 3 \text{ years})}$$

$$= \$339{,}691$$

Present value of tax shields

$$= \left[\frac{\$500{,}000 \times 0.30 \times 0.45}{2(0.16 + 0.30)} \right] \left[\frac{2 + 0.16}{1 + 0.16} \right] - \left[\frac{\$55{,}000}{(1 + 0.16)^3} \right] \left[\frac{0.30 \times 0.45}{0.16 + 0.30} \right]$$

$$= \$136{,}619 - \$10{,}341$$

$$= \$126{,}278$$

Present value of the salvage value

$$= \$55{,}000 \times \text{PVIF}_{(16\%, \, 3 \text{ years})}$$

$$= \$35{,}236$$

Present value of net working capital at the end of the project

$$= \$30{,}000 \times \text{PVIF}_{(16\%, \, 3 \text{ years})}$$

$$= \$19{,}220$$

Net present value

$$= \$339{,}691 + \$126{,}278 + \$35{,}236 + \$19{,}220 - \$500{,}000 - \$30{,}000$$

$$= -\$9{,}575$$

A negative NPV indicates that the project is not feasible.

Dealing with Inflation

When inflationary expectations increase, creditors and shareholders demand higher rates of return on their investments. They add premiums to compensate themselves for the losses in purchasing power resulting from inflation. An increase in inflationary expectation increases the firm's opportunity cost of capital. Thus, the discount rate used for capital budgeting increases. If the cash flows from the project remain fixed, the present value of the project decreases.

However, as inflation increases, project revenues and expenses are likely to increase. It is difficult to generalize what happens to cash flows when inflationary expectations change. The present value of the project may be higher or lower depending on the circumstances. For example, if the increase in revenues is higher than the increase in costs, cash flows increase and the present value increases. On the other hand, if revenues increase by an amount less than the increase in costs, cash flows from the project drop and the present value is less.

There are two methods for dealing with inflation. The first method, called the **nominal method**, suggests that both the discount rate and the cash flows should be adjusted to reflect the impact of inflation.

The discount rate is adjusted by adding a premium to the discount rate to reflect the higher required rate of return of investors. Generally, the cost of capital, when properly calculated or observed from the market, includes a premium for inflation.

Cash flows are adjusted to estimate the nominal cash flows from the project. The financial manager must estimate the revenues and costs under the expected inflation rate.

The second method, called the **real method**, assumes that inflation will be zero over the life of the project. This method estimates the cash flows based on present-day dollars and uses the real (nominal less inflation adjustment) rate to discount the cash flows.

When markets are perfect and efficient, the two methods are equivalent and should produce the same results. In practice, the conditions of perfect and efficient markets may not be satisfied. For example, consider the case where inflation is expected to increase the costs of a firm by 10% over a particular year but because of competitive pressures the firm will not be able to increase prices to offset the rise in costs. In this case, the nominal method would be more accurate to use.

Taxes are another reason to prefer the nominal method to the real method. The real method assumes that inflation increases CCA deductions in the same way that it increases other costs and revenues. Thus, the cash flows increase at the same rate as inflation. However, existing accounting techniques and tax laws require using historical costs for CCA calculations. Therefore, the tax bill will be higher than the real method suggests.

Finally, the nominal method is preferable because it allows different inflation rates for revenues and expenses, and the financial manager can vary the rates from year to year.

Methods Used in Practice

In the article "Capital Budgeting," the authors Stan Paulo and Choon Gan demonstrate that firms often use a variety of capital budgeting techniques, some of which are not covered in this course. For example, some firms use the marginal and incremental revenues and costs as criteria for accepting or rejecting projects. The survey suggests, however, that the NPV and IRR techniques are the most frequently used criteria. Surprisingly, the survey reveals that despite its shortfalls, the payback method continues to be used by practitioners.

Capital Budgeting

Stan Paulo and Choon Gan of Lincoln University report on a survey of capital budgeting criteria used by New Zealand–listed companies.

The purpose of this summary is to report the empirical findings from a survey undertaken in May 1995 of the capital budgeting practices of all firms listed on the New Zealand Stock Exchange (NZSE). The main findings reveal a preference for the net present value criterion, even though the internal rate of return criterion has a higher incidence of use.

The payback period is used to a notable extent (see Table 1.1).

A complete survey was undertaken, a total of 130 questionnaires having been mailed to the financial managers of all firms listed on the NZSE. A total of 46 completed questionnaires were usable, representing a response rate of 35.6%. Twelve unusable responses were also received.

Table 1.1 Uses of Capital Budgeting Criteria

Criterion	Frequency of use (%)
Net present value (NPV)	29.5
Internal rate of return (IRR)	30.2
Payback period	21.3
Other	19.0

Main Findings

Objective function of capital budgeting criteria—Several different criteria are available to assist with valuing projects and allocating investment capital.

These are typically grouped as discounted cash flow (DCF) or non-DCF capital budgeting criteria, and consequently have different objective functions. Therefore, financial information is prepared and presented differently.

The differences in these objective functions were probed, and the results showed:

- Only four respondents answered these questions; one indicated differences existed in the objective functions, and three indicated no differences existed in the objective functions.

Respondents were also invited to describe and comment on the nature of differences in the objective functions of these capital budgeting criteria, but no responses were provided.

This lack of response is perhaps indicative of a disinclination or inability to comment on differences which have notable implications for capital budgeting, choice of criteria, and management of the capital budgeting process.

Use of capital budgeting criteria—The responses indicated that on average, uses of the criteria were as per Table 1.1.

From these findings, it is evident that use of the NPV criterion is very similar to that of IRR, and the popularity of the IRR criterion, given the difficulties of multiple internal rates of return and differences in the ranking of NPV and IRR, were not explained satisfactorily by respondents.

NPV was the preferred criterion for 62.5% of respondents and IRR was preferred by 31%.

Cash-flow determination—Empirical evidence showed that for non-DCF capital budgeting criteria (payback period), use of marginal and incremental revenues and costs scored an average of 3.4 on a 5-point Likert scale. This suggests a frequency of use greater than "sometimes" and less than "often."

Neither marginal nor incremental revenues or costs should be used when determining non-DCF cash flows. This suggests cash flows are being prepared incorrectly, which is consistent with the findings concerning inability (or disinclination) of respondents to motivate their preferences for different capital budgeting criteria on the basis of differences in objective functions.

Discount rates—The discount rate, or cost of capital, plays a pivotal role in all valuations when time value is taken into account.

Summary

In New Zealand–listed companies:

- A preference exists for using the net present value capital budgeting criterion.

- However, the internal rate of return criterion has a high incidence of use.

- The payback period criterion is used to a notable extent.

- Limited understanding of the differences in the objective functions of capital budgeting criteria exists.

- Imprecision in preparation and presentation of cash flows has arisen.

- Imprecision in use of the cost of capital exists.

Respondents were asked whether they used the same discount rate for the discounted payback period and NPV and IRR:

- The level of response was very low, only four respondents answering this question, three respondents indicated that they used the same discount rate, and one indicated that a different discount rate was used.

And in relation to whether the payback cut-off used for the discounted and non-discounted payback period was different:

- Only four respondents answered this question; two indicated that different cut-offs were used; two indicated that the same cut-off was used, and no explanations for the difference in payback cut-offs were received.

This survey suggests respondents experience difficulties with the role, function, use and determination of the discount rate, which is consistent with other research findings overseas.

Source: Stan Paulo and Choon Gan, published in *Chartered Accountants Journal*, March 1996, p. 71. Reprinted with permission.

The article's conclusions should be interpreted with caution because the sample size of the survey is not large enough to generalize the results. However, similar results can be found in surveys conducted with U.S. and Canadian business managers.

Evidence suggests that in spite of the theoretical superiority of NPV, financial managers prefer to use IRR.[9] The preference for IRR is due to the general disposition of businesspeople toward *rates of return* rather than *actual dollar returns*. Because interest rates, profitability, and so on are most often expressed as annual rates of return, the use of IRR makes sense to financial decision makers. They tend to find NPV less intuitive because it does not measure benefits *relative to the amount invested*. Because a variety of techniques are available for avoiding the pitfalls of the IRR, its widespread use does not imply a lack of sophistication on the part of financial decision makers. Clearly, corporate financial analysts are responsible for identifying and resolving problems with the IRR before the decision makers use it as a decision technique.

In addition, decision makers should keep in mind that nonfinancial considerations may be important elements in project selection, as discussed in the article "Nonfinancial Considerations in Project Selection."

---

[9] For example, see John R. Graham and Campbell R. Harvey, "The Theory and Practice of Corporate Finance: Evidence from the Field," *Journal of Financial Economics* (May/June 2001), pp. 187–243; Harold Bierman, Jr., "Capital Budgeting in 1992: A Survey," *Financial Management* (Autumn 1993), p. 24; and Lawrence J. Gitman and Charles E. Maxwell, "A Longitudinal Comparison of Capital Budgeting Techniques Used by Major U.S. Firms: 1986 versus 1976," *Journal of Applied Business Research* (Fall 1987), pp. 41–50, for discussions of evidence with respect to capital budgeting decision-making practices in major U.S. firms.

Nonfinancial Considerations in Project Selection

Corporate ethics codes are often faulted for being "window dressing"—that is, for having little or no effect on actual behaviour. Financial ethics expert John Dobson says day-to-day behaviour in the workplace "acculturates" employees—teaches them that the behaviour they see in the workplace is rational and acceptable in that environment. Dobson takes issue with the notion of "neoclassical economic theory," which states that people are "material opportunists who will readily jettison honesty and integrity in favour of guile and deceit whenever the latter are more likely to maximize some payoff function."

The good news is that professional ethical codes, such as those developed for chartered financial analysts, corporate treasury professionals, and certified financial planners, actually provide sound guidelines for behaviour. These codes, notes Dobson, are based on economically rational concepts such as honesty, integrity, and trustworthiness that guide the decision maker in attempting to increase shareholder wealth. Financial executives insist that there should be no separation between an individual's personal ethics and his or her business ethics. "It's a jungle out there" and "Business is business" are not excuses for engaging in unethical behaviour.

How do ethics codes apply to project selection and capital budgeting? Consider how Medtronics Inc. Vice-President Gary Ellis approaches one of the largest capital projects ever faced by a company—a merger or acquisition. No matter how financially attractive, an acquisition or other major project transaction does not get done if Medtronics officers are not comfortable with the other firm's management or organizational culture, as matched against Medtronics' mission statement and ethical code.

Another way to incorporate nonfinancial considerations into capital project evaluation is to take into account the likely effect of decisions on non-shareholder parties or stakeholders—employees, customers, the local community, and suppliers. A study by Omran, Atrill, and Pointon found that U.K. companies that had a stakeholder focus (explicit mention of stakeholders in the mission statement) fared no worse in various success measures than those with a narrowly defined shareholder focus. Even risk-adjusted common stock returns were no worse for these more broadly focused firms.

Sources: John Dobson, "Why Ethics Codes Don't Work," *Financial Analysts Journal* (November/December 2003), pp. 29–34; Frederick Militello and Michael Schwalberg, "Ethical Conduct: What Financial Executives Do to Lead," *Financial Executive* (January/ February 2003), pp. 49–51; Mohammed Omran, Peter Atrill, and John Pointon, "Shareholders versus Stakeholders: Corporate Mission Statements and Investor Returns," *Business Ethics: A European Review* (October 2002), pp. 318–326.

There are several explanations for the observation that the payback period evaluation criterion is used by practitioners:

- It is easy to understand and communicate.

- It may be used to eliminate some projects from further consideration. This technique may be desirable when a firm is studying the prospects of a large number of projects because the task of ranking them on the basis of NPV and IRR can become cumbersome.

- It provides a simple way to communicate the degree of riskiness of a project.

Nevertheless, the payback method is not a reliable approach to determine the economic feasibility of the investment or to assess risk.

Similarly, there are reasons for the use of the average rate of return on book value technique:

- It is simple to understand and communicate to a relatively unsophisticated audience.

- Traditionally, management compensation was often based on reported earnings and the average return on book value. In such cases, managers will use the average rate of return technique to pursue those projects that will have the greatest earnings to maximize their compensation. Clearly, there is an agency cost for having them do so.

Computer Activity: Evaluating Economically Dependent Projects

This computer illustration demonstrates how to determine whether to accept or to reject economically dependent projects using the following decision-making techniques: net present value and profitability index.

LEARNING OBJECTIVES

- Design and use a worksheet to calculate the NPV and PI of a project.
- Use a worksheet to calculate the NPV and PI of economically dependent projects.

Description

Cox Canada (CC) is a conglomerate that has interests in transportation and financial services. CC is considering acquiring a new automated system to sell tickets for an airport shuttle service from machines to be located in airports, shopping centres, and hotels. Following is a summary of the financial information for this project.

Automated System to Sell Shuttle Tickets	
Major costs:	
Computer system (hardware and software) (class 10, CCA rate: 30%)	$1,200,000
Computer installation	300,000
Dispensing machines (class 8, CCA rate: 20%)	500,000
Machine delivery and installation	200,000
Other factors:	
Rental fees, year 1	$40,000
Rental increases after year 1	3%/year
Project life expectancy	10 years
Salvage value of computer system	$200,000

Salvage value of dispensing machines	$150,000
Corporate tax rate	32%
Estimated cost of capital	14.5%
Operating costs:	
Year 1	$420,000
Increases after year 1	5%/year
Operating revenues:	
Year 1	$1,400,000
Increases after year 1	25,000/year

CC expects to have assets in these classes after 10 years. CC forecasts an increase in net working capital of about $100,000 during the first year. Thereafter, working capital will increase by $10,000 per year until the end of year 4. After year 4, no changes are expected in the amount of working capital.

CC is also interested in selling insurance services from these machines. In addition to the costs incurred to acquire the new automated system, the following list provides financial information for this project.

Upgrade to Sell Insurance from the Machines	
Major costs:	
Set-up to ready the dispensing machines	$150,000
Incremental cost to upgrade computer system to sell insurance	300,000
Incremental shipping and installation expenses	200,000
Incremental operating costs:	
Year 1	$145,000
Increases after year 1	4%/year
Incremental operating revenues:	
Year 1	$500,000
Increases after year 1	5%/year

Required

1. **a)** Calculate the initial investment for the project in which CC sells tickets for the airport shuttle.
    b) Calculate the present value of the incremental after-tax operating cash flows from the project assuming that CC only sells tickets for the airport shuttle.

c) Calculate the present value of the sum of the tax shields and terminal cash flows associated with the project assuming that CC only sells tickets for the airport shuttle.

d) Calculate the NPV and PI of the project assuming that CC only sells tickets for the airport shuttle.

2. **a)** Calculate the present value of the incremental after-tax operating cash flows from the project assuming that CC sells tickets for both the airport shuttle and insurance services.

    b) Calculate the NPV and PI of the project assuming that CC sells tickets for both the airport shuttle and insurance services.

3. Write a brief memo (no more than 350 words) to John Williams, the Vice-President of Finance, outlining your findings on the feasibility of these economically dependent projects. Include in your memo a table that summarizes important financial information from your worksheets.

Material Provided

FN2L1P1.xls   Excel

Following are the names of the sheet tabs and a brief description of each.

L1P1MEMO	A partially completed memo that you can use to write a summary of your findings on the feasibility of the new automated system to the Vice-President of Finance.
L1P1DATA	A worksheet containing a data table used to calculate NPV and PI for worksheets L1P1A and L1P1B.
L1P1A	A partially completed worksheet set up to calculate the NPV and PI of the project assuming the system operates on a stand-alone basis selling tickets for the airport shuttle service.
L1P1B	A partially completed worksheet set up to calculate the NPV and PI of the project assuming the system is shared between the airport shuttle services and insurance services.
L1P1MEMOS	A completed worksheet containing a sample memo to the Vice-President that summarizes the findings on the feasibility of the new automated system.
L1P1AS	The solution worksheet with completed NPV and PI for evaluating the project to sell tickets for the airport shuttle service.
L1P1BS	The solution worksheet with completed NPV and PI for evaluating the project to sell both tickets for the airport shuttle service and insurance services.

Procedure

Starting up:

1. Open the file FN2L1P1. Notice that it contains seven worksheets.

2. Click the L1P1MEMO sheet tab and study the layout of the partially completed worksheet, which you will use to write a summary of your findings. When writing your memo, include an exhibit to summarize important financial information on both economically dependent projects.

3. Click the L1P1DATA sheet tab and study the layout of the worksheet. Rows 5 to 23 contain the common data used to calculate the NPV and PI for sheet tabs L1P1A and L1P1B.

4. Click the L1P1A sheet tab and study the layout of the worksheet. Rows 4 to 39 are set up for you to calculate the NPV and the PI of the project.

5. Click the L1P1B sheet tab and study the layout of the worksheet. Rows 5 to 11 contain the additional data related to the airport shuttle and insurance services project. Rows 14 to 49 are set up for you to calculate the NPV and the PI of the project.

To complete part 1. a):

1. Click the L1P1A sheet tab and enter in cells C8 and C9 the necessary data to calculate the initial investment required for the project. (When constructing your formulas, reference the appropriate cells from the data table from the L1P1DATA worksheet.)

2. Enter in row 10, starting in column C, the working capital requirements for years 0 to 4.

3. In cell C11, enter the formulas to sum the initial investment (in year 0). Your answer should be –$2,300,000. Click the L1P1AS sheet tab and compare your result in cell C11 with the solution worksheet. Resolve any differences.

To complete part 1. b):

1. Enter in rows 15 to 20 the formulas to calculate the after-tax operating profit from the new system.

2. Enter in row 21 for each of years 1 to 10 the sum of the after-tax operating profit and the working capital requirements (row 10) for years 1 to 4.

3. Enter in cell C22 the formula required to calculate the present value of the operating cash flows. Your answer should be $3,242,189. Click the L1P1AS sheet tab and compare your result in cell C22 with the solution worksheet. Resolve any differences.

To complete part 1. c):

1. Enter in cell B26 the capital cost of the hardware. Cell C26 displays the present value of the tax shields resulting from the purchase of the computer system.

2. Enter in cell B27 the capital cost of the dispensing machines. Cell C27 displays the present value of the tax shields resulting from the purchase of the dispensing machines.

3. Enter in cell B28 the salvage value of the computer system. Cell C28 displays the present value of the system's salvage value, and cell C31 shows the present value of the lost tax shields resulting from the sale of the system.

4. Enter in cell B29 the salvage value of the dispensing machines. Cell C29 displays the present value of the dispensing machines' salvage value, and cell C32 shows the present value of the lost tax shields resulting from the sale of the dispensing machines.

5. Enter in cell B30 the amount of working capital to be recovered. Cell C30 displays the present value of the amount of working capital to be recovered in year 10.

6. Enter in cell C33 the formula to calculate the present value of the sum of the CCA tax shields and terminal cash flow. Your answer should be $532,929. Click the L1P1AS sheet tab and compare your result in cell C33 with the solution worksheet. Resolve any differences.

To complete part 1. d):

1. Enter in cell C37 the formula to calculate the NPV of the project. Your answer should be $1,475,117.

2. Enter in cell C39 the formula to calculate the PI of the project. Your answer should be 1.64.

To complete part 2. a):

1. Click the L1P1B sheet tab. Rows 5 to 11 provide additional data specific to the project of selling both airport shuttle and insurance services. Enter in rows 17 to 20 the formulas to calculate the total cash flows from selling both services. (When constructing your formulas, reference the appropriate cells from the data table as well as the data table from the L1P1DATA worksheet.)

2. In cell C21, enter the formula to sum the initial investment (in year 0). Your answer should be $2,950,000.00. Click the L1P1BS sheet tab and compare your result in cell C21 with the solution worksheet. Resolve any differences.

3. Enter in rows 24 to 31 the formulas to calculate the after-tax operating profit from the new system.

4. Enter in row 32 for each of years 1 to 10 the sum of the after-tax operating cash flows and the working capital requirements (row 20) for years 1 to 4.

5. Enter in C33 the formula required to calculate the present value of the operating cash flows. Your answer should be $4,735,785. Click the L1P1BS sheet tab and compare your result in cell C33 with the solution worksheet. Resolve any differences.

To complete part 2. b):

1. Enter in cell B37 the capital cost of the computer system. Cell C37 displays the present value of the tax shields resulting from the purchase of the system.

2. Enter in cell B38 the capital cost of the dispensing machines. Cell C38 displays the present value of the tax shields resulting from the purchase of the dispensing machines.

3. Enter in cell B39 the salvage value of the computer system. Cell C39 displays the present value of the system's salvage value, and cell C42 shows the present value of the lost tax shields resulting from the sale of the system.

4. Enter in cell B40 the salvage value of the dispensing machines. Cell C40 displays the present value of the dispensing machines' salvage value, and cell C43 shows the present value of the lost tax shields resulting from the sale of the dispensing machines.

5. Enter in cell B41 the amount of working capital to be recovered. Cell C41 displays the present value of the amount of working capital to be recovered in year 10.

6. Enter in cell C44 the formula to calculate the present value of the sum of the CCA tax shields and terminal cash flow.

7. Enter in cell C47 the formula to calculate the NPV of the project. Your answer should be $2,445,813. Click the L1P1BS sheet tab and compare your result in cell C47 with the solution worksheet. Resolve any differences.

8. Enter in cell C49 the formula to calculate the PI of the project. Your answer should be 1.83. Click the L1P1BS sheet tab and compare your result in cell C49 with the solution worksheet. Resolve any differences.

To complete part 3:
Click the L1P1MEMO sheet tab. Click anywhere in the body of the memo template and type your findings. Notice that the text wraps inside the text box. Create an exhibit outside the text box that summarizes important financial information from your worksheets.

Commentary

1. If CC only acquires the equipment to sell tickets for an airport shuttle system, the initial investment includes the purchase prices of both the computer system ($1,200,000) and the dispensing machines ($500,000) plus the shipping and installation costs. These costs include $300,000 for the computer system and $200,000 for the dispensing machines. In addition, the initial investment includes the initial increase in working capital of $100,000. The total initial investment is $2,300,000.

2. The first year's incremental revenue is $1,400,000. These revenues must be reduced by operating costs of $420,000 and rental fees of $40,000. Thus, the operating profit will be $940,000. If taxes at 32% are deducted, the first year's incremental after-tax operating profit equals $639,200, and the present value of operating after-tax cash flows is $3,242,189.

3. The various cash flow items required to calculate the present value of the tax shields and the terminal cash flows include:

- tax shields from computer system ($303,106)
- tax shields from the dispensing machines ($121,633)
- salvage value from computer system ($51,639)
- salvage value from the dispensing machines ($38,729)
- recovery of working capital ($36,147)
- lost tax shields from computer system (−$11,140)
- lost tax shields from the dispensing machines (−$7,185)

The sum of these cash flows is $532,929.

4. The NPV and PI for the project to acquire the automated system to sell tickets for the airport shuttle service are $1,475,117 and 1.64, respectively. Since the NPV is positive and the PI is above 1.00, CC should accept the project.

5. If CC acquires the equipment to sell tickets for an airport shuttle system and to sell insurance services, the initial investment becomes $2,950,000 ($300,000 of computer equipment, $200,000 of shipping and installation costs, and $150,000 of set-up costs in addition to the original $2,300,000).

6. The first year's incremental revenue is $1,900,000 ($1,400,000 + $500,000). These revenues must be reduced by operating costs of $565,000 ($420,000 + $145,000) and rental fees of $40,000. Thus, the pre-tax profit will be $1,295,000. If taxes at 32% are deducted, the first year's incremental after-tax operating profit is $880,600. The present value of operating after-tax cash flows is $4,735,785.

7. The NPV and PI of the project, assuming CC shares the system, are $2,445,813 and 1.83, respectively. Since the NPV is positive and the PI is greater than 1.00, CC should accept the project.

8. The memo to John Williams, Vice-President of Finance, should indicate that both projects are feasible. However, the project that sells airport shuttle and insurance services provides greater shareholder wealth. An exhibit providing information on NPV and PI should be included to support this conclusion. In addition, the memo should include a brief analysis of the cash flows generated by each project. The L1P1MEMOS worksheet contains an example of a memo that summarizes the findings of the analysis.

Conclusion

This computer illustration is an example of a capital budgeting decision on economically dependent projects. CC should acquire the automated system to sell both the airport shuttle tickets and insurance services. Each of the decision techniques, NPV ($2,445,813) and PI (1.83), indicate that the project to acquire an automated system to sell both the airport shuttle tickets and insurance services is better than the project to acquire an automated system to sell only tickets for the airport shuttle service.

CHAPTER SUMMARY

This introductory chapter has reviewed the fundamental concepts on which financial managers base their decisions. The concepts of present and future values, wealth maximization, and the optimal investment strategy are emphasized. In addition, the independence of investment and financing decisions is identified as a theoretical and practical issue. You learned about the role of the financial market in allocating the wealth of individuals, and the assumptions of market efficiency and perfect markets, as well as the implications of these assumptions. You are reminded of the ethical and moral issues that you may face in your career as a financial manager. Finally, you reviewed the basics of capital budgeting and examined various capital budgeting evaluation methods.

Key Terms

Important Equations

Present value of an asset discounted at the lending and borrowing rate

$$PV = C_0 + CF_1 \div (1 + r) \qquad \text{(Equation 1-1)}$$

where

PV = present value

C_0 = current cash flow

CF_1 = cash flow expected next year

r = lending and borrowing rate in the market

Total return

$$\text{Total return} = \frac{CF_1}{C_0} - 1 \qquad \text{(Equation 1-2)}$$

where

CF_1 = future cash flow to be received one year from today

C_0 = cost of initial investment

Marginal return

$$\text{Marginal return} = \frac{CF_{1_n} - CF_{1_{n-1}}}{C_{0_n} - C_{0_{n-1}}} - 1 \qquad \text{(Equation 1-3)}$$

where

CF_{1_n} = Total cash flows, alternative n

$CF_{1_{n-1}}$ = total cash flows, alternative $n - 1$

C_{0_n} = capital invested, alternative n

$C_{0_{n-1}}$ = capital invested, alternative $n - 1$

Total wealth of a business

Total wealth = initial wealth + NPV(investment opportunities)   **(Equation 1-4)**

Present value of an asset discounted at the cost of capital

$$PV = CF_1 \div (1 + k) \qquad \textbf{(Equation 1-5)}$$

where

PV = present value of the asset

k = cost of capital

CF_1 = one future cash flow to be received one year from today

Net present value

$$NPV = CF_1 \div (1 + k) - C_0 \qquad \textbf{(Equation 1-6)}$$

where

NPV = net present value of the asset acquisition

C_0 = cost of acquiring the asset

Internal rate of return

$$CF_1 \div (1 + IRR) = C_0 \qquad \textbf{(Equation 1-7)}$$

CCA for year i

$$CCA_i = C \times d \times (1 - d/2)(1 - d)^{i-2} \qquad \textbf{(Equation 1-8)}$$

UCC for year i

$$UCC_i = C \times (1 - d/2)(1 - d)^{i-1} \qquad \textbf{(Equation 1-9)}$$

where

C = initial capital cost

d = capital cost allowance rate of the class

i = year 2, 3, 4,...

Initial net cash outlay

$$\begin{array}{l} \text{Net initial} \\ \text{investment outlay} \end{array} = \begin{array}{l} \text{price of} \\ \text{the asset} \end{array} + \begin{array}{l} \text{shipping, installation,} \\ \text{and modification costs} \end{array} + \begin{array}{l} \text{increase in} \\ \text{working capital} \end{array}$$

$$- \begin{array}{l} \text{investment} \\ \text{incentives} \end{array} - \begin{array}{l} \text{salvage value} \\ \text{from old asset} \end{array} \qquad \textbf{(Equation 1-10)}$$

Operating cash flows at the end of period i

$$\begin{array}{l} \text{Operating cash flows at the} \\ \text{end of period } i \text{ (OCF}_i) \end{array} = \begin{array}{l} \text{incremental operating} \\ \text{revenues (IOR}_i) \end{array} - \begin{array}{l} \text{incremental operating} \\ \text{costs (IOC}_i) \end{array}$$

$$- \text{taxes } [T \times (IOR_i - IOC_i - CCA_i)] \qquad \textbf{(Equation 1-11)}$$

where

OCF_i = operating cash flows at the end of period i

T = corporate tax rate

Expected cash flows at the end of period i

$$\text{Expected cash flows at end of period } i = \text{OCF}_i - \text{increases to working capital } (\Delta W_i) - \text{other adjustments } (\text{OA}_i)$$

(Equation 1-12)

Terminal cash flow of the project at the end of n periods

$$\text{Terminal cash flow} = \text{net sale price of the asset} - \text{taxes, if any, on the proceeds} - \text{removal and clean-up costs} + \text{release of working capital}$$

(Equation 1-13)

Operating cash flows at the end of period i

$$\text{OCF}_i = \text{incremental operating revenues } (\text{IOR}_i) - \text{incremental operating costs } (\text{IOC}_i)$$
$$- \text{taxes } [T \times (\text{IOR}_i - \text{IOC}_i)]$$
$$+ (T \times \text{CCA}_i)$$

(Equation 1-14)

**Present value of future incremental cash flows
without tax shield formula method**

$$PV = \sum_{i=1}^{n} \frac{\text{CF}_i}{(1 + k)^i} + \frac{S_n}{(1 + k)^n}$$

(Equation 1-15)

where

CF_i = expected cash flows at the end of period i
k = discount rate
S_n = salvage value of the project at the end of n periods

**Present value of future incremental cash flows
separating out the present value of tax shields**

$$PV = \sum_{i=1}^{n} \frac{F_i}{(1 + k)^i} + \frac{S_n}{(1 + k)^n} + \text{PVTS}$$

(Equation 1-16)

where

F_i = cash flow during period i, excluding the tax shield
PVTS = present value of the tax shield

Present value of perpetual tax shields (half-year rule)

$$\text{PVTS} = \left[\frac{C \times d \times T}{2(d + k)} \right] \left[\frac{2 + k}{1 + k} \right]$$

(Equation 1-17)

where

C = capital cost paid to acquire the asset
d = capital cost allowance rate of the class to which the asset belongs

Present value of lost tax shields

$$\text{PVTSL}_n = \left[\frac{S_n}{(1 + k)^n} \right] \left[\frac{d \times T}{d + k} \right]$$

(Equation 1-18)

Present value of lost tax shields when terminating the asset class

$$\text{PVTSL}_n = \left[\frac{\text{UCC}_n}{(1 + k)^n}\right]\left[\frac{d \times T}{d + k}\right] \qquad \text{(Equation 1-18a)}$$

Present value of future incremental cash flows using the tax shield formula method

$$\text{PV} = \sum_{i=1}^{n}\frac{F_i}{(1 + k)^i} + \frac{S_n}{(1 + k)^n}$$

$$+ \left[\frac{C \times d \times T}{2(d + k)}\right]\left[\frac{2 + k}{1 + k}\right] - \left[\frac{S_n}{(1 + k)^n}\right]\left[\frac{d \times T}{d + k}\right] \quad \text{(Equation 1-19)}$$

Present value of cash flow when terminating the asset class

$$\text{PV} = \sum_{i=1}^{n}\frac{F_i}{(1 + k)^i} + \frac{S_n}{(1 + k)^n} + \left[\frac{C \times d \times T}{2(d + k)}\right]\left[\frac{2 + k}{1 + k}\right]$$

$$- \left[\frac{\text{UCC}_n}{(1 + k)^n}\right]\left[\frac{d \times T}{d + k}\right] + \left[\frac{(\text{UCC}_n - S_n)T}{(1 + k)^n}\right] \qquad \text{(Equation 1-19a)}$$

Net present value with the present value of tax shields

$$\text{NPV} = \sum_{i=1}^{n}\frac{F_i}{(1 + k)^i} + \frac{S_n}{(1 + k)^n} + \left[\frac{C \times d \times T}{2(d + k)}\right]\left[\frac{2 + k}{1 + k}\right]$$

$$- \left[\frac{S_n}{(1 + k)^n}\right]\left[\frac{d \times T}{d + k}\right] - C_0 \qquad \text{(Equation 1-20)}$$

where

C_0 = net initial investment outlay

Net present value when terminating the asset class

$$\text{NPV} = \sum_{i=1}^{n}\frac{F_i}{(1 + k)^i} + \frac{S_n}{(1 + k)^n} + \left[\frac{C \times d \times T}{2(d + k)}\right]\left[\frac{2 + k}{1 + k}\right]$$

$$- \left[\frac{\text{UCC}_n}{(1 + k)^n}\right]\left[\frac{d \times T}{d + k}\right] + \left[\frac{(\text{UCC}_n - S_n)T}{(1 + k)^n}\right] - C_0 \qquad \text{(Equation 1-20a)}$$

Profitability index

$$\text{PI} = \text{PV} \div C_0 \qquad \text{(Equation 1-21)}$$

Average rate of return on book value

$$\text{ARR} = \text{ACF} \div I_a \qquad \text{(Equation 1-22)}$$

where

ACF = average annual incremental after-tax cash flows from operations over the life of the project

I_a = the firm's average book value of the investment in the project

Web Links

The *Sarbanes-Oxley Act of 2002*

■ http://www.sarbanes-oxley-forum.com An interactive community portal designed to provide information to those seeking to comply with the requirements of the legislation. It acts as a guide by offering useful resources and tips in addition to providing an online forum, a FAQ section, and an experience sharing section.

Investopedia

■ http://www.investopedia.com/articles/03/082703.asp Investopedia is an "investing education" site, with articles, dictionary entries, and tutorials on finance and investing. Dictionary entries can be browsed by subject or alphabet or are searchable by keyword. Archived articles are arranged by subject, and tutorials can be viewed by knowledge level. The link above goes to an article entitled "Understanding the Time Value of Money."

Columbia Business School's PreMBA Finance Online Tutorial

■ http://ci.columbia.edu/ci/premba_test/c0332/s4/index.html Columbia's Business School's online tutorial offers an overview of time value of money and several mini case studies ("challenges") along with links to short videos and the full text of articles that are complementary to the subject. Terms throughout are hyperlinked to an online glossary.

Food and Agriculture Association of the United Nations

■ http://www.fao.org/docrep/W4343E/w4343e07.htm Chapter 6 of the extensive electronic document "Basic Finance for Marketers" discusses different types of investment projects, the economic evaluation of investment proposals, and various project valuation techniques, such as net present value and internal rate of return.

FinAid—Student's Guide to Financial Aid

■ http://www.finaid.org/loans/npv.phtml FinAid is a "how to" resource for students looking to secure financial aid. This section of the Web site gives a layman's overview of net present value as it relates specifically to student loans.

Understanding Net Present Value Analysis

■ http://tlc.uwaterloo.ca/projects/NPV/index.html An Industry Canada–funded project designed to address the problem of students not fully grasping net present value analysis in the lecture format. The goal for this site was to create a "learning tool that is centred on the needs of the learner," allowing the flexibility to follow the lesson step by step or to jump to various sections of the site as needed.

Analyzing Net Present Value and Internal Rate of Return

■ http://publib.boulder.ibm.com/infocenter/dmndhelp/v6rxmx/index.jsp?topic=/com.ibm.btools.help.modeler.doc/doc/tasks/analyzing/analyzingnpvirr.html This online simulation and analysis tool is provided by IBM as part of its Websphere Business Modeler.

Self-Test Questions

Qualitative Questions

Answer each of the following questions in point form:

1. How can an economic unit transfer wealth from one period to another to design its preferable consumption pattern?
2. What is an optimal investment strategy?
3. How is the optimal investment strategy determined?
4. How much of current wealth should be allocated to the optimal investment strategy?
5. What is the nature of efficient financial markets?
6. What are the three levels of market efficiency and their implications for the internal projects of firms?
7. What is meant by and what are the implications of the statement "managers are agents for shareholders"?
8. What are some of the ethical issues that may face a financial manager?
9. What process should be followed to evaluate projects for capital budgeting purposes?
10. What are some special issues typically encountered in project evaluation?
11. Is the IRR decision criterion equivalent to the NPV technique?
12. What are the qualifications of other capital budgeting decision criteria?

Qualitative Multiple Choice Questions

1. Which of the following statements correctly reflect current tax laws for a Canadian company?
   a) Terminal loss is written off as an expense only when a class of asset is liquidated.
   b) Allowable capital losses are written off against taxable capital gains.
   c) Flotation costs for new securities are amortized over five years.
      i) a only
      ii) a and b only
      iii) a and c only
      iv) b and c only
      v) a, b, and c

2. Which of the following indicators best reflect(s) the wealth of common shareholders?
   a) The retained earnings of the firm
   b) Dividend payments to common shareholders
   c) Market value of the common shares of a firm
      i) a only
      ii) b only
      iii) c only
      iv) b and c only
      v) a, b, and c

3. Which one of these statements does *not* apply to the optional investment strategy under perfect market conditions?
   i) The marginal rate of return on real assets equals the interest rate.
   ii) Financial side-effects *are* included in the investment decision.
   iii) The borrowing rate equals the lending rate.

iv) Investors may borrow to finance current consumption.

v) Investors may lend to enhance future consumption.

4. Which one of these transactions is *not* a financing decision?

i) Buying equipment on an installment plan

ii) Changing the debt/equity ratio

iii) Paying a dividend

iv) Paying an advance on supplies to be delivered in six months

v) Deciding to delay the implementation of a project

5. Which one of these items/expenditures is *not* taken into account to calculate the cash flows for a project?

i) Book value of spare machinery which has no alternative use but can be used in the project

ii) Installation costs for equipment

iii) Spare parts for equipment

iv) Working capital

v) Overheads caused by the project

6. Which of the following statements contradicts the strong form of efficient financial markets?

i) Insiders can earn abnormal profits by trading on the basis of their privileged information.

ii) Money managers are turning to mutual fund investments.

iii) A security tends to have one price even if it is trading simultaneously on several physically separated markets.

iv) Superficial changes in accounting methods cannot fool investors for long.

7. For the purposes of evaluating capital projects in an inflationary environment, what does the nominal method consist of?

i) Use of a nominal rate for cash flows expressed in current dollars

ii) Use of a nominal rate for cash flows expressed in constant dollars

iii) Use of a real rate for cash flows expressed in current dollars

iv) Use of a nominal rate regardless of whether cash flows are expressed in current or constant dollars

8. In order for a market to be externally efficient, it must be internally efficient. Which of the following is another requirement for *external* market efficiency?

i) There are no frictions to obstruct the entry and exit of investors.

ii) Securities are marketable and liquid.

iii) Securities can be easily transferred with little or no transaction costs.

iv) Information is readily available to the public for evaluation.

9. Which of the following will be true for an investment project that has a positive net present value?

i) The internal rate of return will be less than the opportunity cost of capital.

ii) The payback period will be equal to 3 years or less.

iii) The profitability index will be greater than 1.

iv) The cost of capital will equal the weighted cost of debt and equity financing.

10. According to the strong form of market efficiency, what information would security prices reflect?

i) Historical price and volume data

ii) All publicly available information, past and present

iii) All information available, including information available only to insiders who possess privileged information

iv) All current information

11. Which of the following policies should be used to reduce agency costs within a large, widely held public firm?

i) Stock splits should be used to regularly keep share prices in the most liquid range.

ii) Stocks and stock options should be used to compensate members of the board of directors.

iii) Bonuses for management should be based on a fixed percentage of the firm's capital investment budget.

iv) Decision-making authority for major capital investments should reside with the board of directors.

12. Why is net present value (NPV) superior to other capital budgeting techniques?

i) NPV can be positive when the profitability index (PI) is less than 1.

ii) NPV is the only approach that directly measures a project's contribution to shareholder wealth in dollars.

iii) NPV takes into account all cash flows up to the end of the payback period.

iv) NPV is the only time-adjusted approach that takes the time value of money into account.

13. Which of the following statements *best* describes the weak form of market efficiency?

i) Historical information about price and volume cannot be used to earn higher trading profits than would be obtained with a naive buy-and-hold strategy.

ii) Prices reflect all publicly available information, past and present.

iii) Prices quickly reflect all information available to investors, even to insiders.

iv) Present publicly available information can be used to earn abnormal profits as long as all investors are not equally informed.

14. When inflationary expectations *decrease*, which of the following statements is true?

i) The opportunity cost of capital for firms will remain unchanged.

ii) Project revenues and expenses are likely to increase.

iii) Under the real method of capital budgeting, the discount rate will decrease.

iv) Under the nominal method of capital budgeting, the discount rate will decrease.

15. ABC company has a weighted-average cost of capital of 12%. An investment project under consideration by ABC has an IRR of 13%, a PI of 1.1, an NPV of $90,000, a payback period of 3 years, and an accounting rate of return of 15%. Which of the following statements is true?

i) ABC should accept the project because the accounting rate of return exceeds 12%.

ii) ABC should reject the project because the IRR is above the weighted-average cost of capital.

iii) ABC should accept the project because the payback period is only 3 years.

iv) ABC should accept the project because it has a positive NPV.

16. Which of the following statements *best* describes the semi-strong form of market efficiency?

i) Historical information about price and volume cannot be used to earn higher trading profits than would be obtained with a naive buy-and-hold strategy.

ii) Prices reflect all publicly available information, past and present.

iii) Prices quickly reflect all information available to investors, even insiders.

iv) Present publicly available information can be used to earn abnormal profits as long as all investors are *not* equally informed.

17. Investment decisions may be different when using the internal rate of return (IRR) rule and when using the net present value (NPV) rule. Which of the following is the *main* reason for such differences?

   i) IRR assumes project cash flows are reinvested at a rate equal to the IRR, whereas NPV assumes they are reinvested at the cost of capital.

   ii) IRR assumes project cash flows are reinvested at the cost of capital until the project breaks even.

   iii) NPV does *not* assume project cash flows are reinvested, whereas IRR assumes they are invested at the IRR.

   iv) IRR assumes project cash flows are reinvested at a rate equal to the after-tax cost of debt.

18. Which of the following statements is correct for two mutually exclusive projects that have net present value profiles that intersect at a discount rate of 12%, as shown in the figure?

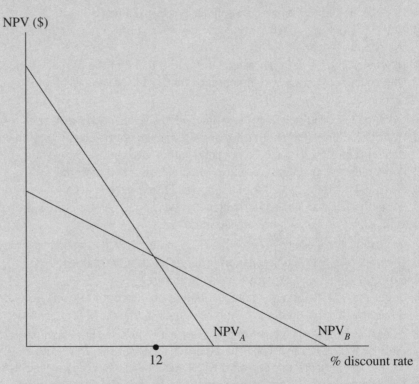

   i) Both project A and project B are acceptable at all discount rates above 12%.

   ii) Project A is always preferable to project B.

   iii) Project B has a higher internal rate of return than project A.

   iv) Project B is preferable to project A for all discount rates below 12%.

Quantitative Multiple Choice Questions

1. A new truck costs $40,000, qualifies for an investment tax credit of 20%, and replaces an existing truck which will be sold for a market value of $5,000. If the existing truck has a book value of $8,000 and both trucks belong to the same asset class, the incremental base for capital cost allowance calculation for the new truck is:

   i) $ 8,000

   ii) $27,000

iii) $32,000

iv) $35,000

v) $40,000

2. Given a desired return of 12%, the current price of a 10% perpetual bond, $1,000.00 par value, is:

  i) $ 120.00

  ii) $ 833.33

  iii) $1,000.00

  iv) $1,100.00

  v) $1,200.00

3. These details apply to a new project: equipment $10,000, installation of equipment $1,000, and inventory of spares $2,000. Also, the project will use a freezer which cost $5,000 to install 5 years ago, has no alternative use, and has zero market value. The initial investment in the new project is:

  i) $10,000

  ii) $11,000

  iii) $12,000

  iv) $13,000

  v) $18,000

4. A perpetual stock, par value $100, pays an annual dividend of $14.00. If investors desire a return of 12%, the current market price is:

  i) $ 7.00

  ii) $14.00

  iii) $58.33

  iv) $100.00

  v) $116.67

5. LaSalle Industries is considering a project that has the following cash flows:

Year	Cash flow
0	($10,000)
1	$4,000
2	$3,000
3	?
4	$2,000

    The project has a payback period of 2.5 years. The firm's cost of capital is 15%. What is the project's net present value?

  i) $835

  ii) $926

  iii) $1,055

  iv) $1,200

6. Some Company's cost of capital is 10%. Two mutually exclusive projects are under consideration and have the projected cash flows shown in the next table:

    Based *only* on the information given, what decision should be made?

Year	Project A	Project B
0	($150,000)	($140,000)
1	70,000	0
2	70,000	0
3	70,000	300,000

i) Project B, even though it has a longer discounted payback period.

ii) Either project, as they have the same AAR.

iii) Indifferent, because the projects have equal IRRs.

iv) Include both in the capital budget, since the present value sum of the cash inflows exceeds the initial investment in both cases.

v) Project A because its ratio of benefits to costs exceeds that of project B.

7. A $35,000 investment today promises to return $15,000 per year for the next 3 years. What is the approximate internal rate of return (IRR) on this investment?

i) 2.5%

ii) 3.5%

iii) 9.7%

iv) 14%

8. A company is evaluating a potential investment project. The appropriate risk-adjusted discount rate for the project is 12%. The project requires an initial investment outlay of $450,000 and will provide end-of-year cash flows of $200,000 each year for 3 years. What is the discounted payback period for this project?

i) 2.25 years

ii) 2.79 years

iii) 2.95 years

iv) 3.05 years

9. A company acquires an asset, owns it for 3 years, and then sells it at the end of year 3. The acquisition cost is $55,000 and the salvage value is $15,000. The CCA rate on an asset of this type is 15% and the company has a 35% tax rate and a 12% discount rate. What is the present value of tax shields from depreciation for this asset?

i) $ 8,618

ii) $ 8,046

iii) $7,778

iv) $7,205

10. A company has just purchased an asset for $222,000. The asset has an expected useful life of 14 years, is in a CCA class with a 25% CCA rate, and will be depreciated on a declining balance basis. There are many similar assets in use by the firm, and the CCA pool can be expected to always have a positive balance after the disposal of any particular asset in this class. The plan for this new asset is to keep it for 6 years and then to sell it for $70,000. If the company has a 45% tax rate and a 10% discount rate, what is the present value of the tax shields lost, due to the plan to salvage this asset?

i) $12,700

ii) $25,500

iii) $38,448

iv) $40,279

11. A company is considering investing in a project that has an initial cost of $200,000 and is expected to provide annual cash inflows of $48,000 per year for 5 years. The company is financed half with debt and half with equity and will maintain this same financing mix for the new project. The current cost of debt is 7% after tax and the current required return on equity is 14%. Which of the following statements is true about how the firm should assess the acceptability of this project?

   i) The project should be accepted because, using a discount rate of 7%, it has a positive net present value.

   ii) The project should be rejected because the weighted average cost of capital is 10.50% and the internal rate of return is less than 10.50%.

   iii) The project should be accepted because it has a payback period of only 5 years.

   iv) The project should be rejected because the internal rate of return is higher than the after-tax cost of debt.

12. Data for two mutually exclusive investment projects are provided below:

End of year	Project A's incremental after-tax cash inflows ($)	Project B's incremental after-tax cash inflows ($)
0	−200,000	−200,000
1	50,000	150,000
2	100,000	100,000
3	150,000	50,000

   a) If the firm has an opportunity cost of capital of 15%, then what is the profitability index (PI) for project A?

      i) 0.156

      ii) 1.0886

      iii) 2.33

      iv) 2.1772

   b) Project B is considered to be riskier than project A. Project B has an appropriate discount rate of 16%. Which of the following statements about projects A and B is true?

      i) Project B has a lower NPV because it has the same total cash inflows but a higher opportunity cost of funds.

      ii) Project A has a higher PI than project B.

      iii) Project B has a higher IRR than project A.

      iv) Project A has a shorter discounted payback period than project B.

13. XYZ Corp. is considering an investment proposal that will yield cash flows of $60,000 per year in years 1 through 4, $70,000 per year in years 5 through 9, and $80,000 in year 10. This investment costs $300,000 today. Assuming that cash flows occur evenly during the year, what is the payback period for this investment?

   i) 4.00 years

   ii) 4.35 years

   iii) 4.86 years

   iv) 5.23 years

Quantitative Problems

Problem 1

Average Incorporated has three projects available for assessment. Project Tiny and Project Huge are mutually exclusive. Project Medium is independent of both. Cash flows for the mutually exclusive projects are expected as follows:

Time	Cash flows Project Tiny	Cash flows Project Huge
0	−$150	−$425
1	55	150
2	55	150
3	55	150
4	55	150

The company uses a 12% cost of capital and plans to spend a maximum of $425 in new projects this year (the capital budget). You have been hired to assess the validity of these projects.

Draw the NPV profiles of the mutually exclusive projects. Make a recommendation to the company from the manager's viewpoint as well as the shareholder's. Be specific in your discussion.

Problem 2

Alast Corp. is considering purchasing a training program from a management consulting firm. Estimated initial costs of purchasing the appropriate DVD and electronic equipment are $250,000. Senior management feels that the training program will result in an annual increase in productivity. This translates into higher sales and lower costs. Specifically, current annual sales of $5,000,000 are expected to rise to $5,100,000 for each of the next 4 years. In 5 years' time, sales are expected to be $5,150,000, with this sales level sustained indefinitely.

The DVD and electronic equipment falls into class 9, with a CCA rate of 25%. Since it will be necessary to use the equipment for future training projects, the company has no plans to scrap or sell it.

The company currently has a marginal tax rate of 40% and an opportunity cost of capital of 12%. Using an NPV analysis, should the company install the new program?

Problem 3

Stanley Registers Inc. is considering the purchase of a new machine. This machine will reduce manufacturing costs by $6,000 annually. The new machine will be in CCA class 8 ($d = 20\%$). The firm expects to sell the machine at the end of its 5-year life for $10,000. The firm also expects to be able to reduce net working capital by $18,000 when the machine is installed. The firm's marginal tax rate is 40% and it uses a 12% cost of capital to evaluate projects of this nature. If the machine costs $60,000 what is the NPV of the project?

Cases

Case 1: Sudbury Foundries Ltd.

Sudbury Foundries Ltd. (SFL) is contemplating the replacement of an existing generator. The existing machine was purchased two years ago for $75,000 and belongs in Class 9 (with a 25% CCA rate). Currently, this machine can be sold for $50,000, and its salvage value 5 years from now is estimated at $6,000. The new generator will cost $120,000 and belongs to Class 9 as well. The new machine is estimated to have a salvage value of $15,000 in 5 years' time and is expected to generate the following cash savings before amortization and taxes (Case Exhibit 1-1).

Case Exhibit 1-1
Expected Cash Flows from New Machine

Year	Cash savings before amortization and taxes
1	$35,000
2	36,750
3	38,588
4	40,517
5	42,543

In addition, the new generator will require some additional space which is available at SFL but which is rented at $2,500 per year. The lease contract can be terminated without any penalty to SFL. Initially, additional working capital of $7,000 is required which is fully recoverable at the end of the fifth year. The firm's marginal tax rate is 30% and the firm's cost of capital is 15%.

Required

Note: In answering the following questions, assume that the new generator will be acquired and that all cash flows are at year end.

a) Identify the annual capital flows, calculate the annual net capital flows, and calculate the present value of the net capital flows. *State your assumptions.*

b) Calculate the annual after tax cash savings without taking amortization into consideration. Then calculate the present value of these after tax cash savings.

c) Calculate the incremental UCC and using the formula calculate the present value of the tax shield on CCA to infinity. *You may disregard the half-year rule.*

d) Calculate the net salvage value and the present value of the lost tax shield at year 5.

e) Calculate the net present value for the new generator. Should the new generator be acquired? Why?

Case 2: Digby Foods Ltd.

Jim Black, owner-manager of Digby Foods Ltd. (DFL), is reviewing a consultant's report on the profitability of a new product line for his firm. Recently, the firm's food technologist, Mary Stone, developed a "spicy" cod fish cake, and pilot marketing studies by DFL indicated a receptive market for this food item. Smart Consultants Ltd. was hired to assess the profitability of the project and recommended against the product line based largely on the data presented in Case Exhibit 1-2. The background information underlying the calculations (and available to the consultants) is summarized in Case Exhibit 1-2.

1. The project is expected to last for 5 years, since after that time competition from larger food processors will force DFL to abandon the market for some other venture. DFL proposes to add the product line as a division to its existing operations which are related to food processing.

Case Exhibit 1-2
Digby Food Ltd. Investment Analysis

	Year 0	Year 1	Year 2	Year 3	Year 4	Year 5
Capital outlay:						
Equipment	$500,000					
Freight	$20,000					
Installation	$10,000					
Building repairs	$50,000					
Total	$580,000					
Unit price	$5	$5	$5	$5	$5	$5
Unit fixed and variable cost	$3	$3	$3	$3	$3	$3
Unit sales		$130,000	$117,000	$105,300	$94,770	$85,293
Sales		$650,000	$585,000	$526,500	$473,850	$426,465
Cash operating expenses		$390,000	$351,000	$315,900	$284,310	$255,879
Capital cost allowance equipment		$62,500	$125,000	$78,125	$58,594	$43,945
Freight		$20,000				
Installation		$10,000				
Building repairs		$50,000				
Total operating expenses		$532,500	$476,000	$394,025	$342,904	$299,824
Interest		$24,000	$24,000	$24,000	$24,000	$24,000
Total		$556,500	$500,000	$418,025	$366,904	$323,824
Profit before tax		$93,500	$85,000	$108,475	$106,946	$102,641
Tax		$23,375	$21,250	$27,119	$26,737	$25,660
Profit after tax		$70,125	$63,750	$81,356	$80,210	$76,981
Add CCA		$62,500	$125,000	$78,125	$58,594	$43,945
Cash flow	−$580,000	$132,625	$188,750	$159,481	$138,804	$120,926

Discount rate = 12%

NPV   −$36,402

Decision: Drop the project

2. Equipment costs will be $500,000, freight $20,000, and installation $10,000. The equipment is subject to a CCA rate of 25%, and the half-year rule applies. Engineering estimates indicate that the salvage value of the equipment will approximate the UCC at the time of sale.

3. The facilities will be housed in an existing building which has no alternative use. However, repairs costing $50,000 will be incurred to upgrade the building. Buildings of this type attract a CCA rate of 10%, and salvage value approximates UCC at the time of sale. **Note:** Only the UCC of the repairs is salvageable.

4. Initial working capital for the project is estimated at $25,000, and year-end value of working capital at 10% of annual sales. **Note:** Investment in working capital is the difference between the year-end working capital balances.

5. The plant expects to operate at its full capacity of 130,000 units in the first year of operation but thereafter competition will reduce production by about 10% per year. Larger food processors will cut into DFL's sales to the point where the firm is expected to drop the product line. Unit price is currently estimated at $5.00 with an expected annual increase of 5%. The annual increase of 5% is net of expected inflation and price competition.

6. Currently, fixed and variable cash expenses are estimated at 60% of unit price with an expected annual increase of 4%.

7. Interest of $24,000 will be incurred on a term loan of $200,000 at 12%. These funds will be secured by the equipment, and the loan will be repaid at the end of 5 years.

8. The spicy cod fish cake will reduce sales of existing products of DFL by $15,000 in each of the next 5 years.

9. The food processing industry has an average project beta of 0.90, the risk-free rate is expected to be 8%, and the return on the TSX Index is estimated at 15.78%. These parameters are not expected to change significantly over the next 5 years.

Note: Using CAPM results in: $0.08 + (0.9)(0.1578 - 0.08) = 0.15$ average project cost of capital.

Jim has discussed the consultant's report with Mary and she is disappointed. She cannot forget the success that "spicy" Popeye Chicken had when it was introduced in the southern U.S.

Required

Mary has a feeling that the spicy cod fish cake has a future and has approached you to provide a critical review of the consultant's calculations in Case Exhibit 1-2. She knows very little about financial analysis and the evaluation of projects. Therefore, she requests that you review the calculations with a view to:

- Identifying procedures which are not correct, to explain why such procedures are wrong and to incorporate the correct calculations in Case Exhibit 1-2.

- Identifying procedures which are not included, to explain why such procedures should be included and to incorporate them into Case Exhibit 1-2.

- Making a recommendation on the project based on its NPV.

Case 3: Halifax Sea Service

From his window, Bill looked across the Halifax harbour and shook his head in disbelief. "How can I stand to lose over $1 million on an investment of $500,000?" he muttered to himself.

Bill Gillespie, President of Halifax Sea Service Ltd. (HSL), is considering the expansion of his firm's operations to service oil exploration activities off the coast of Nova Scotia. He is quite confident that he can lease adequate wharfside facilities along the Halifax waterfront and supply vessels to handle the offshore service. The most pressing and urgent requirement to commence operations is the need for two mobile cranes to load and unload supply vessels in Halifax. These cranes together cost $500,000 and can be installed relatively quickly. Bill plans to finance the acquisition through a bank loan carrying an interest rate of 10% per annum and repayable in 5 equal installments at the end of each of the next 5 years. In addition, funds will be needed for working capital for the offshore activities. Case Exhibit 1-3 shows the details of the capital requirements in Part A: Data table.

With this project on his mind, Bill leaves the office for a few days to talk with industry and government officials about the prospects of offshore oil production along the Nova Scotia coastline. In the meantime, he asks Rupert Steiner, the assistant bookkeeper at HSL, to put together a project report and to come up with a recommendation as to whether HSL should continue to have an interest in servicing offshore oil exploration activities. Rupert has at his

Case Exhibit 1-3
Halifax Sea Service Ltd.: Correct Project Evaluation

Part A: Data table	Year 0	Year 1	Year 2	Year 3	Year 4	Year 5
Cost of cranes	$500,000					
		$150,000	$105,000	$73,500	$51,450	$36,015
UCC	$500,000	$350,000	$245,000	$171,500	$120,050	$84,035
Loan:						
Principal outstanding	$500,000	$418,102	$328,014	$228,917	$119,911	$0
Annual payment		$131,898	$131,898	$131,898	$131,898	$131,898
Interest		$50,000	$41,810	$32,801	$22,892	$11,991
Principal repayment		$81,898	$90,088	$99,097	$109,006	$119,911
Total current assets	$100,000	$125,000	$130,000	$150,000	$135,000	$110,000
Part B: Cash flow computation						
Sales revenues		$750,000	$800,000	$850,000	$900,000	$850,000
Expected cash operating costs		$525,000	$560,000	$595,000	$630,000	$595,000
Interest expense		$50,000	$41,810	$32,801	$22,892	$11,991
Amortization (CCA)		$150,000	$105,000	$73,500	$51,450	$36,015
Earnings before taxes		$25,000	$93,190	$148,699	$195,658	$206,994
Taxes (25%)		$6,250	$23,298	$37,175	$48,915	$51,749
Earnings after taxes		$18,750	$69,893	$111,524	$146,744	$155,246
Less: principal repayment		$81,898	$90,088	$99,097	$109,006	$119,911
Cash flow from operations		−$63,148	−$20,196	$12,427	$37,738	$35,335
Part C: NPV calculations						
Cost of cranes	−$500,000					
Total current assets	−$100,000	−$125,000	−$130,000	−$150,000	−$135,000	−$110,000
Cash from operations		−$63,148	−$20,196	$12,427	$37,738	$35,335
Net cash flow	−$600,000	−$188,148	−$150,196	−$137,573	−$97,263	−$74,666
PV @ 10%	−$600,000	−$171,044	−$124,129	−$103,360	−$66,432	−$46,361
NPV	−$1,111,326					

disposal Bill's files and memos on the project and from these he extracts information to prepare the project report. Case Exhibit 1-3 represents the analytical portion of Rupert's project report. The cash flows from operations are shown in Part B and the NPV calculations in Part C. In Rupert's opinion, the project should be scrapped since it is expected (by his calculations) to lose over $1 million.

Bill does not want to believe Rupert's project report since he feels that the project is likely to be profitable. Accordingly, he approaches you and requests that you review the project report, conduct any additional investigation which you feel is necessary, and then adjust the report if required. You have the following additional information:

1. The two cranes have a useful life of 5 years and zero salvage value at the end of their useful lives. The UCC remaining at the end of year 5 will be amortized to infinity since there are other assets in the class.

2. Expected revenues are stated in constant (or today's) dollars and there are at least two problems with these estimates. First, the annual revenue estimates appear to be overstated by about $100,000; that is, the annual estimates are very optimistic. Secondly, the revenues have not accounted for inflation which is expected to be about 5% annually over the next 5 years.

3. Expected cash operating expenses are estimated at approximately 70% of expected revenue and this is reasonable for this line of business. These expenses include lease rentals for related facilities.

4. Traditionally, HSL was financed with 40% debt and 60% equity and this capital structure will prevail in the future. The marginal cost of debt for HSL is 10% and shareholders are looking for a return of about 20%. The firm's tax rate is 25%

Note: Using WACC: $(0.40)(0.10)(1 - 0.25) + (0.60)(0.20) = 0.15$ cost of capital.

5. The project under consideration has the same risk level as existing HSL projects.

Required

a) Review Case Exhibit 1-3 and identify the errors. For each error, state clearly why you think the report is wrong. Finally, for each error, state clearly the approach that you will take to correct it consistent with accepted financial theory and practice. No quantitative analysis is expected at this time. However, assume that Bill Gillespie, the reader of your report, knows very little about project analysis and that you need to provide a good discussion to secure his interest for the remainder of your report.

b) Following on from part a), you are now required to adjust the report. The errors which you identified should be corrected along the lines which you outlined in part a).

c) Will you recommend the project to Bill? Why, or why not?

APPENDIX A

1. To capture the effects of either a terminal loss or recaptured depreciation when a project is terminated and the asset class is terminated, the following adjustments are made to Equations 1-18 and 1-19.

   In Equation 1-18, which represents the present value of the lost tax shields, the undepreciated capital cost balance (UCC_n) of the asset class at the end of the year is substituted for the salvage value (S_n).

$$PVTSL_n = \left[\frac{UCC_n}{(1 + k)^n}\right]\left[\frac{d \times T}{d + k}\right] \qquad \textbf{(Equation 1-18a)}$$

   In Equation 1-19, the present value of future incremental cash flows is adjusted by the present value of the lost tax shields. Equation 1-19 is also adjusted by either the present value of the tax expense from recaptured depreciation or the present value of the tax savings from a terminal loss.

$$PV = \sum_{i=1}^{n}\frac{F_i}{(1 + k)^i} + \frac{S_n}{(1 + k)^n} + \left[\frac{C \times d \times T}{2(d + k)}\right]\left[\frac{2 + k}{1 + k}\right]$$

$$- \left[\frac{UCC_n}{(1 + k)^n}\right]\left[\frac{d \times T}{d + k}\right] + \left[\frac{(UCC_n - S_n)T}{(1 + k)^n}\right] \qquad \textbf{(Equation 1-19a)}$$

2. When terminating the asset class, Equations 1-18a and 1-19a are used to adjust the project's NPV. As a result, the following equation is used to calculate NPV:

$$NPV = \sum_{i=1}^{n}\frac{F_i}{(1 + k)^i} + \frac{S_n}{(1 + k)^n} + \left[\frac{C \times d \times T}{2(d + k)}\right]\left[\frac{2 + k}{1 + k}\right]$$

$$- \left[\frac{UCC_n}{(1 + k)^n}\right]\left[\frac{d \times T}{d + k}\right] + \left[\frac{(UCC_n - S_n)T}{(1 + k)^n}\right] - C_0 \qquad \textbf{(Equation 1-20a)}$$

Chapter 2
Capital Budgeting under Uncertainty

CHAPTER OVERVIEW

This chapter extends the capital budgeting concepts introduced in Chapter 1 to present a more realistic view of the uncertain environment in which decision making is performed. Financial managers often have to make decisions before they acquire complete knowledge of the outcomes. The degree of uncertainty regarding the impact of a decision on shareholder wealth and the welfare of other stakeholders varies from one decision to another. In this chapter, you learn how to deal with uncertainty and how to estimate the cost of capital for risky projects. You use portfolio theory to evaluate risk-return relationships. You are expected to be able to use some basic statistical tools, such as probabilities and mean-variance relationships, which are important to your understanding of the decision-making process under uncertainty. For example, in Section 2.1, you calculate the risk and expected return of a portfolio, and in Section 2.2, you determine the equation of the characteristic line from a simple regression.

This chapter covers the basics of portfolio theory, which is useful for decision making under uncertainty. The capital asset pricing model (CAPM) is introduced as the framework for evaluating risk-return relationships in a portfolio setting. The limitations of portfolio theory and the CAPM are presented to remind you of how they affect the pricing of assets. Despite these limitations, the CAPM remains a powerful tool. In this chapter, you learn the implications of the CAPM for project evaluation.

Section 2.1 illustrates how the relationship between returns on securities, as captured by the correlation coefficient, leads to diversification if these securities are combined in a portfolio. The section builds on this relationship to develop portfolio theory and to introduce the capital market line. An important conclusion of the topic is that under uncertainty, an efficient portfolio's return is a direct function of its risk as represented by the standard deviation.

Section 2.2 shows how the concepts of expected return, standard deviation, and correlation coefficient are used to develop the CAPM, which describes the relationship between the risk and return of a portfolio. You learn that, for well-diversified investors, only systematic risk should be used as a basis to price assets. Because the beta of a security is shown to be a good proxy for systematic risk, the CAPM states that a security's return is a linear function of the security's systematic risk.

In Section 2.3, you study the implications of the CAPM for capital budgeting. You learn that whenever a company or an investor is well diversified, a project's return can be determined by estimating the beta of the project and using the CAPM to estimate the required return. The analysis reminds you of the difficulties encountered in applying this process. It explains how to adjust the main approach or use alternative approaches to overcome the limitations. You learn the benefits of classifying projects in terms of their risk, how to estimate divisional costs of capital, and the difficulties in using betas of similar firms as proxies for project betas.

In Section 2.4, you learn why systematic risk, also called market risk, may not be the only relevant risk for project evaluation. In this case, total risk should be considered. You learn how the total risk of a project is estimated and used for capital budgeting.

Section 2.5 deals with another reality faced by financial managers. Firms face capital rationing because they are constrained by the amount of funds they have for capital projects. You learn how capital budgeting decisions are made under capital rationing.

Finally, Section 2.6 emphasizes that project evaluation is only one step in the capital budgeting process. The process includes idea generation, preparation of proposals, project evaluation, appropriation of funds, progress review, and performance evaluation.

Learning Objectives

After completing this chapter, you will be able to:

- Analyze a portfolio's risk and return using portfolio theory.

- Explain the importance of the correlation between the returns of two assets.

- Analyze a security's risk and return using the capital asset pricing model (CAPM).

- Analyze the risk-adjusted discount rates using the CAPM.

- Evaluate the discount rates for projects or divisions.

- Explain when a financial manager should focus on total risk.

- Identify and apply the methods of capital rationing.

- Describe the various steps of the capital budgeting process.

This knowledge will provide you with the professional skills to:

- Implement and advise on measures to mitigate risk.

- Identify, analyze, and advise on financial instruments to minimize the financial risk of the issuer, investor, or lender.

- Identify and analyze risk factors.

- Adapt performance measures, specifically project betas.

- Articulate the organization's resource requirements and implement a plan for resource allocation.

- Prepare and evaluate business cases or financial proposals.

- Develop and administer budgets.

- Advise on financing to meet organizational goals.

- Assess or design a financial risk management strategy.

- Develop financial forecasts and plans.

- Manage cash flow and working capital.

- Advise on the capital structure of the organization.

- Identify financial implications of operational strategy.

- Assess the value of a business.

- Evaluate and advise on growth strategies.

HOW THIS CHAPTER RELATES TO OTHER CHAPTERS IN THIS BOOK

Understanding the relationship between risk and return is paramount to understanding finance. Without this conceptual connection, the subject matter in this book's remaining chapters will have very little meaning. Because risk exists in the real world, every decision we make regarding our future contains it. Thus, any attempt to apply finance must necessarily involve a sound appreciation of risk.

Investors demand rewards, at least in part, due to the presence of risk. How much they require depends on the risk attributes of the investment. Whether they are investing long-term, as in Chapter 3, considering how the firm is financed, which is the subject of Chapter 4, or reflecting on the company's dividend policy, examined in Chapter 5, investors always factor risk into their decision-making process. In the same way, management must consider risk in its investment decisions. Although this chapter is the first to include risk in decision making, you will see that it remains a key issue in each of the chapters that follow.

2.1 BASICS OF PORTFOLIO THEORY

Recall that Chapter 1 emphasized that the required rate of return can be thought of as the opportunity cost of capital. In this chapter, we develop a model to determine the required rate without reference to an opportunity cost of capital. The required rate of return is expressed as the sum of the return on a risk-free asset plus an added return to compensate for the degree of risk of the asset. This concept is always presented under the assumption of capital market efficiency.

In this section we demonstrate that an asset's risk and return depend on how the asset's expected future cash flows co-vary with the overall cash flows from the portfolio of all investment opportunities available to the firm.

Expected Return and Standard Deviation in a Portfolio Setting

In Chapter 1, you learned that a company's cash flows provide more relevant information to investors than a company's earnings. Consequently, the return on either an investment or a project is measured as the amount of cash inflow compared to the amount of initial investment. Financial managers often use expected return to represent the average of possible returns for next year, weighted by their probabilities. In addition, the standard deviation is used to indicate the possible deviation of the actual outcome from the expected value. The expected value and standard deviation are calculated assuming that next year's returns will be distributed normally. Under this assumption, the expected value and standard deviation of returns will fully describe the behaviour of next year's returns. The question is—how accurate is it to use the expected value of returns to represent next year's returns?

In practice, investment decisions must be made before the outcomes are known. At the time of making a decision, an investment's statistical properties are described in terms of expected values, standard deviations, and the correlations between the investments. The **correlation coefficient** measures the degree of association between two variables.

For a combination of several investments, the procedure is to calculate the expected return and standard deviation of the portfolio. The actual returns on individual investments may be above or below their expected values, but the mean of the actual returns will be close to the expected return on the portfolio. Portfolio theory suggests that holding a sufficiently large number of investments with returns that are not perfectly positively correlated ensures that the realized mean of returns will be close to the expected return. Consequently, knowing the statistical properties of an investment is essential for decision making.

Equation 2-1a shows that the return on a portfolio is equal to the weighted average of the returns on the assets that make up the portfolio.

$$R_P = w_1 R_1 + w_2 R_2 + \ldots + w_n R_n \qquad \textbf{(Equation 2-1a)}$$

Equation 2-1a can be rewritten in more general terms:

$$R_P = \sum_{i=1}^{n} w_i R_i \qquad \textbf{(Equation 2-1b)}$$

where

R_P = portfolio return

$\sum_{i=1}^{n}$ = summation from $i = 1$ to n

$\quad i = 1, 2, \ldots, n$

$\quad n$ = number of securities in the portfolio

$\quad w_i$ = weight of return i, calculated as the ratio of the amount invested in security i divided by the total investment

$\quad R_i$ = return on security i

To calculate the expected return on a portfolio another way:

- use Equation 2-1b to calculate the return on the portfolio under various outcome scenarios and

- calculate the expected return on the portfolio, using:

$$E(R_P) = \sum_{i=1}^{n} P_i R_{Pi} \qquad \textbf{(Equation 2-2)}$$

where

$E(R_P)$ = expected portfolio return

$\quad i = 1, 2, \ldots, n$

$\quad n$ = number of possible outcomes

$\quad P_i$ = probability of outcome i

$\quad R_{Pi}$ = portfolio return associated with outcome i

The expected value is the weighted average of the possible values for R_{Pi}, with the weights being the probabilities P_i.

Similarly, the variance of the portfolio can be calculated using:

$$\sigma_P^2 = \sum_{i=1}^{n} P_i[R_{Pi} - E(R_P)]^2 \qquad \textbf{(Equation 2-3)}$$

where

σ_P^2 = variance of the portfolio

The term $[R_{Pi} - E(R_P)]$ measures how far outcome i is from the expected value. The term $[R_{Pi} - E(R_P)]^2$ is the squared deviation of outcome i from the mean. The variance is the weighted average of these squared deviations. The weights are the probabilities of occurrence.

MINICASE 2-1 COMBINING INVESTMENTS WITH NEGATIVE CORRELATION

Waseem is considering an investment in the securities of two companies. Prime Canyons Metal (PCM) is an integrated mining company with a primary focus on copper. Heavy Duty Batteries (HDB) is a manufacturer of batteries for household and industrial uses. The current share prices of PCM and HDB are $16 and $35 respectively. The correlation coefficient between the securities of the two companies is −0.966. Exhibit 2-1 shows how to calculate the expected returns on shares of PCM and HDB under three scenarios of copper prices.

Exhibit 2-1
Returns on Shares of PCM and HDB

Next year's price of copper relative to current price (1)	Probability (P_i) (2)	PCM's return (R_i) (3)	HDB's return (R_i) (4)	PCM $(P_i)(R_i)$ (5) = (2) × (3)	HDB $(P_i)(R_i)$ (6) = (2) × (4)
Higher	0.30	5.31%	3.57%	1.593	1.071
Same	0.40	3.75%	4.29%	1.500	1.716
Lower	0.30	2.81%	5.29%	0.843	1.587
			Expected returns	3.94%	4.37%
				$E(R_i)$	$E(R_i)$

Case Continued >

If Waseem buys 300 shares of each of the two companies, what are the expected return and standard deviation of his portfolio?

To determine the statistical properties of the return on Waseem's portfolio, it is necessary to determine the weights of the investments in his portfolio. The total investment is:

$$(300 \times \$16) + (300 \times \$35) = \$4,800 + \$10,500 = \$15,300$$

$$\text{PCM's weight} = 300 \times 16 \div 15,300 = 31.37\% \quad W_1$$

$$\text{HDB's weight} = 300 \times 35 \div 15,300 = 68.63\% \quad W_1$$

We now calculate the portfolio's expected return. Exhibit 2-2 shows the calculations and the results of this approach.

Exhibit 2-2
Portfolio's Return under Various Scenarios of Copper Prices

Next year's price of copper relative to current price	Probability (P_i)	PCM		HDB		Return on portfolio (R_{Pi})
		Return	Weight	Return	Weight	
(1)	(2)	(3)	(4)	(5)	(6)	(7) = [(3) × (4)] + [(5) × (6)]
Higher	0.30	5.31%	31.37%	3.57%	68.63%	4.12%
Same	0.40	3.75%	31.37%	4.29%	68.63%	4.12%
Lower	0.30	2.81%	31.37%	5.29%	68.63%	4.51%

Using Equation 2-2, the portfolio's expected return is calculated as: $E(R_P)$

$$E(R_P) = (4.12 \times 0.30) + (4.12 \times 0.40) + (4.51 \times 0.30) = 4.24\%$$

In a similar manner, the variance of the portfolio is calculated using Equation 2-3.

$$\sigma_P^2 = 0.30 \times (0.0412 - 0.0424)^2 + 0.40 \times (0.0412 - 0.0424)^2 + 0.30$$
$$\times (0.0451 - 0.0424)^2$$
$$= 0.0000032$$

The standard deviation is 0.18% (the square root of the variance).

Several observations can be made from these calculations:

■ Under any scenario of copper prices, the actual return on the portfolio will be only slightly different from the expected return on the portfolio.

■ This conclusion can be inferred from the small standard deviation, 0.18%, which indicates that the actual returns will be only slightly dispersed from the expected return.

■ The possible actual returns are concentrated around the expected return.

The third observation was made because the returns on the two securities that make up the portfolio are negatively correlated. This means that if the return on one is higher than its expected value, the other's return will be below its expected value. For example, under higher copper prices, PCM's return will be above its expected value while HDB's return will be below its expected value. Under lower copper prices, the opposite occurs. In general, the deviations from the mean will cancel each other out to bring a realized portfolio return almost equal to the expected return.

Another approach to determining the expected value of a portfolio is to calculate the weighted average of the expected values of the returns on the assets that make up the portfolio. The general formula for this approach is:

$$E(R_P) = \sum_{i=1}^{n} w_i E(R_i) \qquad \textbf{(Equation 2-4)}$$

where

$\qquad E(R_P)$ = expected portfolio return
$\qquad\quad w_i$ = weight of investment i in the portfolio
$\qquad\quad n$ = number of investments that make up the portfolio

Using this approach to calculate the yield on Waseem's portfolio gives us:

$$E(R_P) = (0.3137 \times 3.94\%) + (0.6863 \times 4.37\%) = 4.24\%$$

Similarly, the variance and standard deviation of a portfolio's return can be calculated using the standard deviations of returns on the individual investments making up the portfolio. The formula to calculate the variance for a two-investment portfolio is:

$$\sigma_P^2 = w_1^2 \sigma_1^2 + w_2^2 \sigma_2^2 + 2w_1 w_2 \rho_{12} \sigma_1 \sigma_2 \qquad \textbf{(Equation 2-5)}$$

where

$\qquad \sigma_P$ = standard deviation of portfolio return
$\qquad \sigma_1$ = standard deviation of investment 1
$\qquad \sigma_2$ = standard deviation of investment 2
$\qquad \rho_{12}$ = correlation coefficient of investments 1 and 2

Using this equation to calculate the variance of the return on Waseem's portfolio requires that σ_1, σ_2, and ρ_{12} be calculated. We compute them using the information in Exhibit 2-1 and basic statistical models. Doing so yields:

$$\sigma_1 = 0.98\%$$
$$\sigma_2 = 0.67\%$$
$$\rho_{12} = -0.966$$

Using these values in Equation 2-5 gives us:

$$\sigma_P^2 = (0.3137^2 \times 0.0098^2) + (0.6863^2 \times 0.0067^2)$$
$$+ (2 \times 0.3137 \times 0.6863 \times -0.966 \times 0.0098 \times 0.0067)$$
$$= 0.0000032$$

Thus, the standard deviation is 0.18%, as calculated using the previous method. Equation 2-5 can be generalized to the case where the portfolio has n securities, to obtain:

$$\sigma_P^2 = \sum_{i=1}^{n} \sum_{j=1}^{n} \rho_{ij} w_i w_j \sigma_i \sigma_j \qquad \textbf{(Equation 2-6)}$$

where

$\qquad \rho_{ij}$ = correlation coefficient between securities i and j

Equations 2-4 and 2-6 are convenient when the expected returns, standard deviations, and correlations are known or can be easily derived. Most of the time, the values of these statistical estimates are calculated from past data. These statistical estimates are used under the assumption that their values in the future will be the same.

The Impact of the Correlation Coefficient on Portfolio Risk

The best way to see the impact of correlation on risk is through a numeric illustration. However, making the necessary calculations by hand proves both time consuming and cumbersome. In the following You Apply It minicase, you will use a computer to illustrate how a correlation coefficient affects the degree of diversification in a portfolio. With our assistance, you will design and use a worksheet to determine the return and standard deviation of a portfolio for various combinations of portfolio weights and correlation coefficients; then select which combinations are best for Michelle.

YOU APPLY IT

Michelle would like to invest in a two-security portfolio, containing security X and one of securities Y_1, Y_2, Y_3, and Y_4. The securities Y_i, where $i = 1, \ldots, 4$, have the same expected returns and standard deviations, but they have different correlation coefficients with X. Exhibit 2-3 provides the data for these securities. Michelle considers herself to be a rational investor who would like to maximize expected return for a given risk or minimize risk for a given expected return. However, she is not sure what the correlation coefficient has to do with her investments.

Exhibit 2-3
Data for Securities X, Y_1, Y_2, Y_3, and Y_4

Stock	Expected return	Standard deviation	Correlation with security X
X	10%	12%	+1.0
Y_1	14%	18%	−1.0
Y_2	14%	18%	−0.25
Y_3	14%	18%	+0.25
Y_4	14%	18%	+1.0

Calculate the expected return and standard deviations for each portfolio combination of X and one of Y_1, Y_2, Y_3, and Y_4. Are some combinations better than others? Which choices are preferred by a rational investor?

You Apply It Continued >

Instructions

1. Open the file FN2L2P1.xls and click the L2P1 sheet tab.

Excel FN2L2P1.xls

2. Study the layout of the worksheet. Rows 6 to 10 contain the data for securities X, Y_1, Y_2, Y_3, and Y_4 from Exhibit 2-3.

   Rows 13 to 25 are set up for you to enter the required answers. Columns A and B contain the weights of securities X and Y_i for different portfolios. Column C is set up for you to calculate the expected return given the weights in columns A and B.

   Columns D to G are set up for you to calculate the standard deviation of the various portfolios given each combination of securities X and Y_i.

3. Enter in cell C15 the formula to calculate the expected return on the portfolio X and Y_1 given the weights in cells A15 and B15. Copy your formula down to cell C25. Keep in mind that Equation 2-4 determines the expected return on a portfolio.

4. Enter in cell D15 the formula to calculate the standard deviation of the portfolio combining securities X and Y_1 given the weights in cells A15 and B15 and the correlation coefficient in cell D7. Keep in mind that the standard deviation of a portfolio is the square root of its variance. The variance of a portfolio is described in Equation 2-5. Copy your formula down to cell D25.

5. Repeat step 4 for columns E to G for the appropriate weights and correlation coefficients.

6. Save a copy of your worksheet and print it.

7. Click the L2P1S sheet tab and compare your results from step 6 with the solution worksheet L2P1S. Correct any errors. Notice that cell D21 shows two securities that are perfectly negatively correlated (X and Y_1) and that the correlation coefficient is -1. In this case, the standard deviation of the portfolio is equal to zero when the weights are 60% for security X and 40% for security Y_1 (the highlighted combination). This means that the portfolio is risk-free.

Answer

Worksheet L2P1S shows how Michelle can choose between securities Y_1, Y_2, Y_3, and Y_4. More importantly, it shows the effect of the correlation coefficient on diversification. Given that Michelle is a rational investor, if she decides to invest 60% of her wealth in X and the rest in Y_1, Y_2, Y_3, or Y_4 (the highlighted combination), she will choose Y_1. Although choosing Y_1, Y_2, Y_3, or Y_4 would all give her the same expected return of 11.60%, the combination of X and Y_1 minimizes risk to zero. Keeping the weights fixed but moving across from Y_1 to Y_2 to Y_3 and to Y_4, the correlation coefficient increases toward 1 and the risk of the portfolio increases; however, the return does not change. This observation is consistent regardless of how the wealth is split between X and the alternatives Y_1, Y_2, Y_3, or Y_4.

Exhibit 2-4 shows graphically the relationship between the expected return and the standard deviation of the portfolio under the four scenarios of the correlation coefficient. Line G_1 shows the case $\rho_{XY_1} = -1$. A study of the points along line G_1 shows that a rational investor would never invest in security X alone (point A), because any combination of an investment in security X and security Y would provide a lower amount of risk

Exhibit 2-4 Relationship between the Correlation Coefficient and Diversification

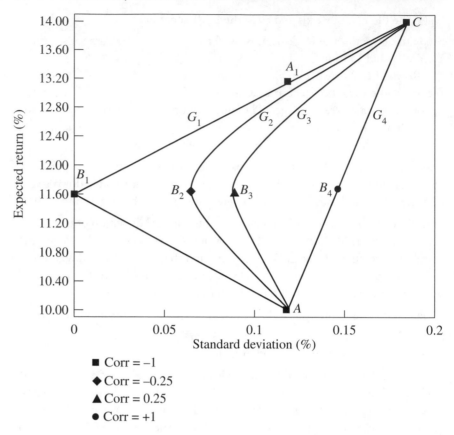

per unit of return (i.e., lower coefficient of variation). For example, Exhibit 2-4 shows that an investment of 20% in security X and 80% in security Y increases the expected rate of return by 3.2 percentage points (point A_1) for a given level of portfolio risk ($\sigma_P =$ 0.12%). Indeed, each point on line AB_1C represents a unique split of wealth between securities X and Y_1; however, the investment alternatives represented by segment B_1C dominate those represented by AB_1. Thus, the feasible set of choices for a rational investor is limited to segment B_1C.

The feasible choices on B_1C represent a linear relationship between risk and return. Point B_1 is a risk-free portfolio ($\sigma_P = 0\%$) and provides an expected rate of return of 11.60%. Moving toward point C, both the expected return and the risk increase. Given the linear relationship, a one-unit increase in risk leads to the same increase in expected return, regardless of the starting position on segment B_1C.

Similarly, curves G_2 ($\rho_{XY_2} = -0.25$) and G_3 ($\rho_{XY_3} = 0.25$) show that investments on segments AB_2 and AB_3 respectively are dominated by investments on segments B_2C and B_3C. These curves do not have a risk-free portfolio. Given that the correlation coefficient is not -1, there is no combination of these two securities that will eliminate risk completely. Finally, the risk-return relationships of investments on segments B_2C and B_3C are not linear. Moving from points B_2 and B_3 toward point C, the investor is compensated with a higher expected return for taking higher risk. Yet the compensation per unit of additional risk drops as point C is approached.

Line G_4 ($\rho_{XY_4} = +1$) shows that perfect positive correlation between two investments will not lead to the elimination of any possible portfolios. The choice between one combination of securities and another is a matter of risk preference. The investments on segment AC show a linear relationship between risk and return. An investor who takes higher risk will be compensated by higher expected return, regardless of the starting position.

If two investments are perfectly positively correlated, combining them does not provide diversification to the investor. If two investments are positively correlated, but not perfectly, combining them *does* provide diversification to the investor. As the correlation coefficient tends toward −1.00, the potential for diversification increases. In the extreme, if two investments are perfectly negatively correlated, combining them provides maximum diversification to the point where the investor can eliminate all risk.

Your results should show that for any combination of weights, the standard deviation (risk) of the portfolio increases as the correlation coefficient increases from −1 to +1. Moreover, if two securities are perfectly negatively correlated, that is, with a correlation coefficient of −1 (such as X and Y_1), the standard deviation of the portfolio is equal to 0 if the weights are 60% for security X and 40% for security Y_1. This means that the portfolio is risk-free.

Investment Opportunity Set

The conclusions from the You Apply It computer illustration imply that a rational investor should try to find investments that are perfectly negatively correlated and combine them to achieve maximum diversification. Unfortunately, in practice, it is not possible to find such investments. However, as long as investments are not perfectly positively correlated, partial diversification is possible.

The **investment opportunity set** is a selection of potential investments that represent, for individual investors, appropriate degrees of risk and efficiency. The **efficient set** of portfolios is the set of portfolios within the investment opportunity set that offers investors both maximum expected return for varying levels of risk and minimum risk for varying levels of expected return.

For example, Exhibit 2-4 shows that if Michelle decides to combine two investments, X and Y_3 ($\rho_{XY_3} = 0.25$), with a positive correlation, she will have an efficient set of portfolios on segment B_3C to choose from because all other portfolios on segment AB_3 are dominated by the alternatives on segment B_3C. From curve G_3, Michelle will choose one of these efficient alternatives as her preferable portfolio based on her risk tolerance.

Suppose Michelle decides to consider another investment security, S_1. Let P_{2j} denote a portfolio in the efficient set. In this case, Michelle must consider combining S_1 with every portfolio P_{2j} in the efficient set. Consider the first portfolio, P_{21}. Now she faces the decision of how to split her wealth between S_1 and P_{21}. She will follow the same procedure as with X and Y_3 to determine an efficient set of portfolios for S_1 and P_{21}. Similarly, she considers S_1 with P_{22}, another portfolio in the efficient set described by segment B_3C. The procedure terminates when she finds the efficient set P_{3j} that contains all efficient portfolios that can be formed from the three securities X, Y_3, and S_1.

Michelle may discover a fourth security, S_2. The process would be repeated to find the efficient set P_{4j} of the four securities. Indeed, the process will continue until she includes the last possible investment S_n in the portfolio. All possible combinations of the investments

Exhibit 2-5 Investment Opportunity Set

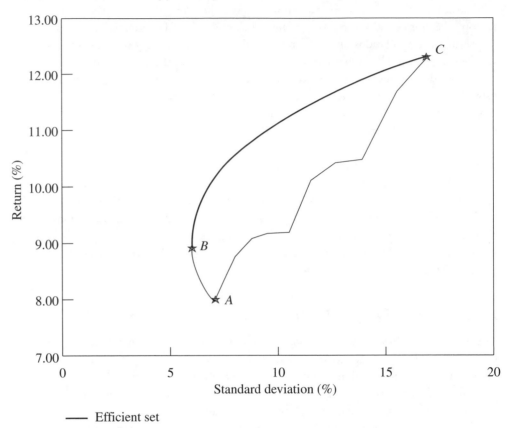

— Efficient set

X, Y_3, S_i, $i = 1, 2, \ldots, n$, will form the area enclosed within ABC in Exhibit 2-5. This area is a graphic representation of the investment opportunity set.

Several observations are in order:

- The efficient set of portfolios on the curved segment BC is determined for one investor. However, assuming that all investors are rational and have homogeneous expectations about investment returns (assign the same probability distributions to investment returns), the curved segment BC represents the efficient set from which all investors will choose.

- The assumption of homogeneous expectations does not necessarily mean that all investors will choose the same portfolio on the curved segment BC. The point beyond which the trade-off between risk and expected return is unacceptable for the investor determines an investor's preferred portfolio. For example, at B, the curved segment BC is steep, implying that a small increase in risk (a point slightly to the right of B) produces a substantial increase in return. At B, the reward for taking additional risk is high. However, in moving away from B toward C, the reward for taking additional risk becomes smaller and smaller. There is a point beyond which each investor concludes that the additional expected reward does not justify the additional risk. This point determines an investor's preferred portfolio. Since various investors have various tolerances for risk, every investor has a preferred position on the curved segment BC.

- The efficient set on segment BC is continuous, which means it is assumed that securities are infinitesimally divisible and there are no transaction costs or other frictions to constrain such divisibility.

- The efficient set is formed by including only those portfolios within the investment opportunity set that offer investors both maximum expected return for varying levels of risk and minimum risk for varying levels of expected return.

Including the Risk-Free Rate in the Investment Opportunity Set

The investment opportunity set depicted in Exhibit 2-5 was obtained by considering all combinations of risky assets available to investors. If the risk-free rate (which has a standard deviation of zero) is included, this asset will be shown on the vertical axis as point R_f. This point will be lower than the lowest point on the efficient set. Exhibit 2-6 shows the effect of adding the risk-free rate to the investment alternatives.

To illustrate, consider an investor, Paul, who selects portfolio B as his optimal investment without considering the risk-free asset. Portfolio B promises an expected return of R_B as compensation for the risk σ_B. If Paul is willing to invest part of his wealth in the risk-free asset and the other part in B, line R_fB represents the various ways he can split his wealth

Exhibit 2-6 Including the Risk-Free Asset in the Investment Portfolio

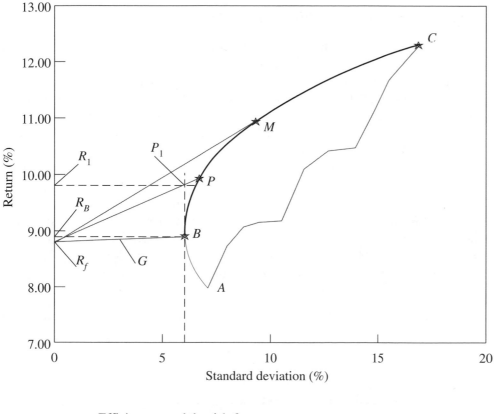

—— Efficient set and the risk-free asset

between the risk-free asset and portfolio B. For example, G is a point midway between R_f and B representing the situation where Paul spends half his wealth to buy the risk-free asset and the other half to buy portfolio B. Line R_fB represents all the combinations of risk and return available to Paul by combining the risk-free asset with the risky portfolio B.

If Paul is willing to combine the risk-free rate with portfolio P instead of B, line R_fP represents his new choices of risk and expected return. Because the investments on line R_fP show a higher expected return for the same risk than the investments on line R_fB, the investments on line R_fP are said to dominate the investments on line R_fB. For example, portfolio B is dominated by portfolio P_1 because the latter has a higher expected return for the same risk (R_1 is greater than R_B).

Ultimately, a rational investor will discover the set of investments represented by the segment R_fMC. The portion R_fM is a straight line drawn tangent to the efficient set of portfolios on segment BC at point M. The portion MC coincides with the efficient set. The segment dominates all other possible combinations between the risk-free asset and the efficient set of portfolios on segment BC. Thus, a rational investor would choose a portfolio on this segment by investing:

- in the risky portfolio M, or
- in any other portfolio on the curved segment MC, or
- exclusively in the risk-free asset, or
- part of his wealth in the risk-free asset and the remainder in the risky portfolio M.

Borrowing at the Risk-Free Rate

So far, it has been assumed that investors can lend at the risk-free rate. This next section assumes that they can borrow at the risk-free rate.

Exhibit 2-7 shows that when investors can borrow and lend at the risk-free rate, the straight segment ME will replace the curved segment MC to form the new efficient set of investments. For example, point D on segment ME represents a situation where an investor borrows at the risk-free rate and adds the borrowed money to his or her wealth to buy into the risky portfolio M. Assuming investors can borrow and lend unlimited amounts at the risk-free rate, line R_fME represents any desirable combination of expected return and risk.

This means that all investors who invest in risky assets will choose the risky portfolio M and no other. Because a security that is not in portfolio M will not be traded in the market, M is a portfolio that contains all securities in the market. That is, M is the market portfolio and the return is the weighted average of the returns on all securities in the market, with the weight of each security being the security's market value.

The expected value and standard deviation of the return to an investor i would be calculated, respectively, as follows:

$$E(R_{Pi}) = w_iR_f + (1 - w_i)E(R_M) \qquad \textbf{(Equation 2-7)}$$

$$\sigma_{Pi} = (1 - w_i)\sigma_M \qquad \textbf{(Equation 2-8)}$$

where
$E(R_{Pi})$ = expected return on portfolio i
σ_{Pi} = standard deviation of portfolio i

Exhibit 2-7 Capital Market Line

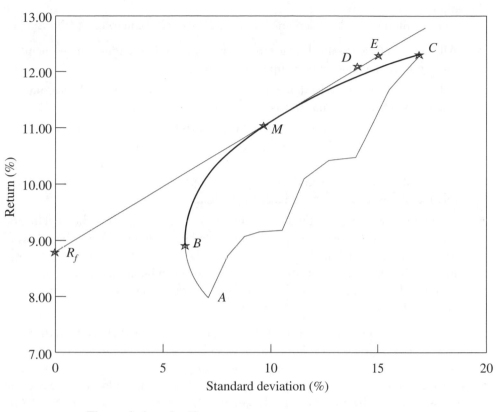

—— The capital market line

$E(R_M)$ = expected return on the market portfolio

w_i = portion of the investor's wealth invested in the risk-free asset

σ_M = standard deviation of the market portfolio

Equations 2-7 and 2-8 support the important conclusion that investors decide their financing arrangements separately from their investment decisions. Notice that the only term on the right side of the equations that has reference to investor i is the weight w_i. Investors do not select between investments on the basis of their risk characteristics. Instead, they invest in the market portfolio of risky assets, M, but decide carefully the portion of their wealth to be invested in the risky portfolio and the portion to be used to purchase the risk-free asset. Thus, the important decision is a financing decision.

Line $R_f ME$ is known as the **capital market line (CML)**. Investors obtain their preferred combination of risk and return on the CML by borrowing or lending and investing the balance in the market portfolio. Equations 2-7 and 2-8 can be combined to determine the relationship between a portfolio's risk and its expected return. This relationship is also known as the equation of the capital market line:

$$E(R_{Pi}) = R_f + \frac{\sigma_{Pi}}{\sigma_M}\,[E(R_M) - R_f]\qquad\textbf{(Equation 2-9)}$$

It can be derived by solving for w_i in Equation 2-8 and replacing the derived value in Equation 2-7.

The assumptions made in deriving Equation 2-9 can be summarized as follows:

- All investors have identical expectations. In planning their personal investments, they all have the same efficient frontier for risky assets.

- All investors are able to lend or borrow at the same risk-free rate R_f. This assumption enables borrowers and lenders to have the same R_f intercept.

- The first two assumptions imply that all investors find the same tangent portfolio (called M in Exhibit 2-7). However, because everyone wants to hold the same portfolio, the tangent portfolio must be the market portfolio. This market portfolio may be viewed as all securities in the market held in proportion to their market values relative to the value of the total market portfolio.

- Because investors differ in their risk preferences, different investors choose different portfolios. They choose combinations of the market portfolio (M) and the risk-free asset along the capital market line. The CML is a graphic presentation of possible investment strategies representing equally desirable combinations of expected return and risk. All portfolios along the CML are well diversified, but the risk is different for each.

Equation 2-9 shows that the expected return on any portfolio belonging to the CML should be at least equal to the risk-free rate plus a premium. The premium is proportional to the portfolio's standard deviation σ_{Pi} and increases as the standard deviation increases. Moreover, the term $[E(R_M) - R_f] \div \sigma_M$ can be considered the price per unit of risk as measured by the standard deviation. This term is the slope of the CML. For example, taking the two points R_f and M, the rise between these two points is $[E(R_M) - R_f]$, while the run is σ_M.

2.2 MEASURING THE RISK AND RETURN OF A SINGLE SECURITY

Portfolio theory suggests that investors should diversify their investments by spreading their savings among securities issued by a large number of firms in different industries. The rationale for diversification is that the risk of the portfolio can be averaged across a large number of individual assets. If one or two of these assets diminish in value, the gains from the others should compensate for the loss. However, what is the nature of the risk-return relationship for *individual* securities? This relationship is important for pricing single securities. To answer this question, it is necessary to first specify the type of risk.

Total Risk, Systematic Risk, and Unique Risk

Section 2.1 demonstrated that whenever two or more securities are combined, the portfolio's risk, as measured by the standard deviation, is less than the weighted average of the total risk of the individual securities. Thus, the contribution of a security to the overall risk of the portfolio is less than the security's risk taken individually. **Unsystematic risk** or **diversifiable risk** is the portion of total risk that can be eliminated by combining the security with others. In other words, unsystematic risk is unique to the security and is also known as **unique risk**. Factors that create this type of risk include management decisions, the firm's financial and operating leverage, strikes, raw material availability, competition, and other factors.

Despite the effectiveness of portfolios in diversifying risk, combining securities will not completely eliminate risk. Indeed, the previous topic showed that the risk of the market portfolio M could not be diversified, despite including all the securities. The risk of the market portfolio is the variation in security returns caused by factors that affect the market as a whole. The contribution of a security to the overall risk of the market portfolio is called the **systematic risk**, **non-diversifiable risk**, or **market risk** of the security. Factors such as interest rate changes, unexpected changes in the inflation rate, and changes in the general economic outlook affect all securities. Consequently, the variations of returns caused by such factors cannot be eliminated by diversification.

In summary:

■ A security's **total risk** (its standard deviation) can be divided between two components, systematic (or non-diversifiable) risk and unsystematic (or diversifiable) risk.

■ **Systematic**, **non-diversifiable**, or **market risk** is the part of the standard deviation that cannot be eliminated by combining the security with others in the market portfolio. It is created by factors that affect the prices or returns of stocks in general.

■ **Unsystematic**, **diversifiable**, or **unique risk** is the portion of total standard deviation that can be diversified by holding the security in a portfolio. It is created by factors that influence mainly the return or price of the individual security.

Now it is easier to answer the question about the type of risk. Assuming that a rational investor will always hold a diversified portfolio of assets, portfolio theory argues that systematic or market risk is more important and should be the only portion of total risk that concerns investors. The prices of securities should be based on their systematic risk.

Another question that must be answered is: Does an investor need to hold the market portfolio to be well diversified? The answer is no, as long as an investor does not wish to be completely diversified. Although an investor should hold a piece of the entire market to completely diversify unsystematic risk, empirical studies show that a fairly small number of securities, carefully selected from different industries and companies conducting business in diverse geographic locations, can diversify most of the risk. Some studies suggest that as few as 10 to 15 randomly selected securities can eliminate as much as 50% of the total risk of most individual securities. Of course, the higher the number of securities held in a portfolio, the lower the total risk of the portfolio. Yet, as the number of securities increases, adding a new security contributes less and less to diversification. The total risk line ABC in Exhibit 2-8 illustrates this principle of diminishing contribution to diversification. The line slowly approaches the market risk (systematic risk) line $A'B'C'$, which is the result of ideal diversification.

Exhibit 2-8 shows that every portfolio is exposed to market risk and unsystematic risk. The unsystematic risk drops as more securities in different industries are added to the portfolio. For example, a portfolio of five securities will have total risk represented by point A, but the distance between points A and A′ represents unsystematic risk. In contrast, a portfolio of 15 securities will have total risk represented by point B, but the unsystematic risk is represented by the distance between points B and B′.

Exhibit 2-8 Relationship between the Number of Randomly Selected Securities and Diversification

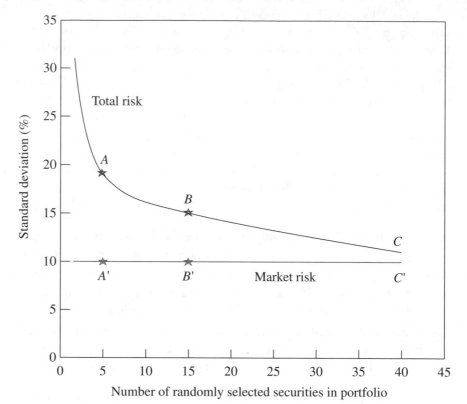

A Measure for Systematic Risk

Based on earlier conclusions in this topic, investors should only be compensated for the systematic portion of a security's risk. The capital market line (Exhibit 2-7) represents the relationship between the degree of risk of any portfolio on the line and its expected return. However, it does not estimate a fair return on a single security given the security's risk. As a result, a model is needed to estimate a given security's return based on its systematic risk.

Generally, the systematic risk of a security i is estimated by its beta, represented by the Greek letter β_i. Beta is a statistical measure of the volatility of a security's return in relation to market returns. Mathematically, it is defined as the covariance between the return on security i and the market returns divided by the variance of the market returns.

$$\beta_i = \frac{\text{Cov}(R_i, R_M)}{\sigma_M^2} = \frac{\rho_{iM} \times \sigma_i \times \sigma_M}{\sigma_M^2} \qquad \textbf{(Equation 2-10)}$$

where

$\text{Cov}(R_i, R_M)$ = covariance between return on security i and the market return R_M

In practice, the beta of a security is estimated by regression analysis of the security's returns on the market over several periods. Normally, a proxy to the overall market is used. In Canada, it is generally accepted to use the S&P/TSX Composite Index return as a proxy for the market return. The **S&P/TSX Composite Index** (known prior to May 2002 as the TSE300 Index) is an index made up of a selection of stocks from the Toronto Stock Exchange that meet certain minimum price, liquidity, and index weighting requirements. For more detail visit the Toronto Stock Exchange Web site provided in the Web Links section at the end of this chapter.

For the securities in the Index, the regression equation would be:

$$R_{i,t} = a_i + \beta_i R_{M,t} + e_{i,t} \qquad \textbf{(Equation 2-11)}$$

where

a_i = constant term
β_i = beta of the security
$e_{i,t}$ = error term

The terms a_i and β_i are determined by the regression based on historical data. The **characteristic line** is a graphic representation of Equation 2-11, which provides a given security's return based on the security's systematic risk. The slope of the characteristic line is beta (β_i), which has the following features:

■ A beta of less than 1 means that the security's premiums are expected to be less volatile than the premiums on the market portfolio. Therefore, its systematic risk is also less than the systematic risk of the average security in the market and its premium is less volatile than that of the average security.

■ A beta of more than 1 means that the security's premiums are expected to be more volatile than the premiums on the market portfolio. Therefore, its systematic risk is also more than the systematic risk of the average security in the market and its premium is more volatile than that of the average security.

■ A beta equal to 1 means that the security's premiums are expected to be as volatile as the premiums on the market portfolio. Its systematic risk is also equal to the systematic risk of the average security in the market.

The popularity of beta as a measure of the systematic risk of securities has prompted private companies to accumulate stock betas for sale to the public. In Canada, one such company is Canadian Polymetric Analysis (Toronto). In the United States, betas are readily available from Value Line Investment Survey and Merrill Lynch.

Betas can also be found on the Internet. Check the Web Links section at the end of this chapter for instructions on finding betas listed on the Yahoo! Finance Web page.

Calculating Coefficients of the Characteristic Line

Stock betas computed using regression analysis equal the slope of the characteristic line. The alpha is the x-intercept of the characteristic line. We use another computer illustration to demonstrate how to calculate the coefficients of the equation for the characteristic line, next. With our assistance, you will design and use a spreadsheet to compute the constant term a_i (alpha) and the slope β_i (beta) of the equation for the characteristic line. Try it by completing the following You Apply It minicase.

YOU APPLY IT ALPHA AND BETA

Although there are several ways of performing the regression to obtain the equation of the characteristic line, here you will use the premiums obtained from the market portfolio and security Z. The premium on the market portfolio $[E(R_M) - R_f]$ is determined as the difference between the market return $[E(R_M)]$ and the risk-free rate R_f. Hence, the regression equation takes the following form:

$$[R_{i,t} - R_{f,t}] = a_i + \beta_i[R_{M,t} - R_{f,t}] + e_{i,t} \qquad \textbf{(Equation 2-12)}$$

where

$$R_{i,t} - R_{f,t} = \text{excess return over risk-free rate } (R_f)$$
$$a_i = \text{constant term}$$
$$\beta_i = \text{beta of the security}$$
$$e_{i,t} = \text{error term}$$

Exhibit 2-9 shows monthly returns for the three-month Treasury bill (risk-free rate), the market portfolio, and security Z for the period beginning January 1992 and ending

Exhibit 2-9
Data for Calculating Security Z's Beta

Observation	Period	3-month Treasury bill	Market return	Security return	Observation	Period	3-month Treasury bill	Market return	Security return
1	01/31/92	11%	–2%	1%	31	07/31/94	10%	16%	29%
2	02/28/92	14%	0%	–2%	32	08/31/94	11%	17%	27%
3	03/31/92	15%	1%	4%	33	09/30/94	10%	16%	28%
4	04/30/92	16%	3%	–1%	34	10/31/94	9%	15%	26%
5	05/31/92	17%	6%	6%	35	11/30/94	8%	16%	26%
6	06/30/92	15%	8%	4%	36	12/31/94	8%	16%	25%
7	07/31/92	14%	9%	5%	37	01/31/95	9%	17%	24%
8	08/31/92	13%	11%	14%	38	02/28/95	9%	17%	23%
9	09/30/92	13%	12%	6%	39	03/31/95	8%	16%	26%
10	10/31/92	12%	14%	15%	40	04/30/95	7%	16%	27%
11	11/30/92	12%	15%	16%	41	05/31/95	7%	15%	28%
12	12/31/92	11%	16%	11%	42	06/30/95	7%	15%	27%
13	01/31/93	10%	13%	13%	43	07/31/95	9%	16%	27%
14	02/28/93	9%	14%	16%	44	08/31/95	10%	17%	26%
15	03/31/93	10%	15%	17%	45	09/30/95	10%	16%	23%
16	04/30/93	8%	15%	18%	46	10/31/95	9%	17%	24%
17	05/31/93	8%	16%	20%	47	11/30/95	9%	18%	21%
18	06/30/93	9%	17%	21%	48	12/31/95	8%	16%	20%
19	07/31/93	9%	16%	20%	49	01/31/96	9%	17%	19%
20	08/31/93	8%	15%	22%	50	02/28/96	8%	15%	18%
21	09/30/93	8%	15%	23%	51	03/31/96	7%	14%	16%
22	10/31/93	9%	14%	24%	52	04/30/96	6%	16%	14%
23	11/30/93	9%	14%	26%	53	05/31/96	5%	15%	14%
24	12/31/93	8%	16%	28%	54	06/30/96	4%	14%	13%
25	01/31/94	10%	16%	29%	55	07/31/96	4%	15%	12%
26	02/28/94	11%	17%	31%	56	08/31/96	3%	14%	13%
27	03/31/94	12%	18%	33%	57	09/30/96	5%	16%	15%
28	04/30/94	11%	16%	32%	58	10/31/96	4%	15%	14%
29	05/31/94	10%	17%	31%	59	11/30/96	3%	14%	16%
30	06/30/94	9%	16%	31%	60	12/31/96	4%	15%	16%

You Apply It Continued >

December 1996. You should note most professionals use monthly returns for five years in their beta estimates.

Using the data in Exhibit 2-9, compute the constant term a_i and the slope of the characteristic line β_i.

Instructions

1. Open file FN2L2P2.xls and click the L2P2 sheet tab. Study the layout of the worksheet. Rows 6 to 65 contain the data from Exhibit 2-9.

2. Enter in cell F6 the appropriate formula to calculate the market premium. Copy the formula down to cell F65.

3. Enter in cell G6 the appropriate formula to calculate the security premium. Copy the formula down to cell G65.

4. Choose Tools Data Analysis. If this option is not displayed in your Tools menu, click the How To tab and follow the "Use Excel" link listed under the "Use software in the course" section.

5. Choose Regression and click OK.

6. In the Input Y range text box, type the range **G6:G65** (the security premium). *Do not* press ENTER.

7. Click the Input X range text box and enter the range **F6:F65** (the market premium). *Do not* press ENTER.

8. Select New Worksheet Ply. Click OK. A new worksheet containing the regression results is displayed.

9. Print a copy of the new worksheet.

10. Compare your results with the results in worksheet L2P2S. They should be identical. If they are not, repeat the regression procedure from step 4.

 Excel FN2L2P2.xls

Answer

Cell B83 in worksheet L2P2S gives the value of the constant term (0.0374) and cell B84 gives the value of the X coefficient or the slope of the characteristic line (1.2797). Equation 2-12 can now be written as:

$$R_{Z,t} - R_{f,t} = 0.0374 + 1.2797[R_{M,t} - R_{f,t}] + e_{Z,t}$$

This equation means that for the periods under consideration, security Z's premiums were on average related to the market by the linear relationship:

$$R_Z - R_f = 0.0374 + 1.2797\,[R_M - R_f]$$

This relationship determines the characteristic line for security Z. It assumes that the random error is zero on average. Therefore, the straight line shown in Exhibit 2-10 approximates Z's expected premium. However, the actual premium in a period t deviates from the premium estimated by the characteristic line by a random error $e_{Z,t}$. The actual premium is represented by one of the points labelled "Actual premiums" in Exhibit 2-10, which most often do not belong to the line. The value of the random error e_Z of a point i will determine that point's position relative to the characteristic line. A point with an error term of −0.5% is located 0.5% below the line.

You Apply It Continued >

Exhibit 2-10 Characteristic Line for Security Z

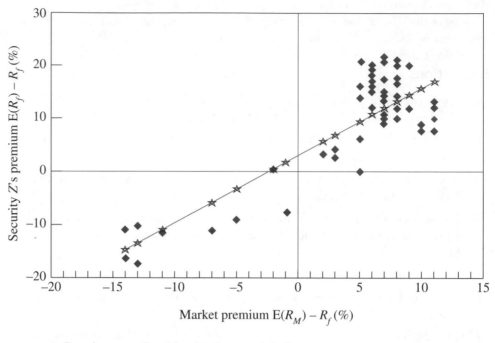

★ Premiums predicted by the characteristic line

◆ Actual premiums

Thus, the characteristic line of security Z shows the relationship between Z's expected premium and the market premium. If the market premium over the next period is expected to be 10%, Z's premium is expected to be 16.537% $[(0.10 \times 1.2797) + 0.0374 = 0.16537]$. On the other hand, if the market premium is expected to be −10%, Z's premium is expected to be −9.057% $[(-0.10 \times 1.2797) + 0.0374 = -0.09057]$. Of course, Z's actual premium would be different from 16.537% or −9.057% because of the random error $e_{Z,t}$. Yet the relationship in Equation 2-12 provides important information:

- The magnitude of Z's expected premium is generally more than the magnitude of the overall market premium. Given that investors are expected to be rewarded only for systematic risk, Z has more systematic risk than the market.

- A 1% change in the market premium means that Z's premium should change by 1.28%. Thus, Z's premium is more volatile than the market premium.

When the relationship of Equation 2-12 (or 2-11) has been completed, it is usual to substitute the estimates of beta and alpha back into the CAPM equation. (Since security Z has a positive alpha of 0.0374 (3.74%), it seems to be attractive, having a positive abnormal return.)

Thus,

$$E(R_z) - R_f = \alpha_z + \beta_Z [E(R_M) - R_f]$$

$$0.16537 = 0.0374 + 1.2797[0.10]$$

$$E(R_z) = R_f + \alpha_z + \beta_Z [E(R_M) - R_f]$$

You Apply It Continued >

$$0.16537 + ?? = ?? + 0.0374 + 1.2797[(0.10 + 0.0374) - 0.0374]$$

$$?? = \text{average 3-month Treasury bill return from exercise}$$

Now consider another security, Y, which has a beta of 1.

Excluding random error, if the market return over the next period is expected to be 10%, Y's return is expected to be 10%. On the other hand, if the market return is expected to be −10%, Y's return is expected to be −10%. Since Y's beta is the same as the market, its expected return should also be the same. Of course, Y's actual return would be different from the predicted values because of random error. Given that investors are expected to be rewarded only for systematic risk, Y has the same systematic risk as the market. In addition, a 1% change in the market return means a 1% change in Y's return. Thus, Y's return is as volatile as the market return.

In conclusion we can say that, because security Z's premiums are more volatile than the premiums on the market portfolio, security Z has more systematic risk than the market portfolio.

Capital Asset Pricing Model

In the previous section, Equation 2-9 showed that the expected return on any portfolio on the capital market line (CML) is a function of the risk-free rate plus a risk premium. The premium depends on:

- the spread between the expected market return and the risk-free rate, and
- the ratio of the portfolio's risk to the degree of risk of the market.

The question now is, can the CML be modified to develop a model to calculate the expected return on *individual securities*? The answer is provided through the contributions of several financial economists, particularly William F. Sharpe, John Lintner, and Jan Mossin. On the basis of the CML, they determined the relationship between a security's expected return and its systematic risk as:

$$E(R_i) = R_f + [E(R_M) - R_f]\beta_i \qquad \textbf{(Equation 2-13)}$$

where

$E(R_i)$ = expected return on security i
R_f = risk-free rate
$E(R_M)$ = expected return on the market portfolio
β_i = security i's beta

Equation 2-13 is known as the **capital asset pricing model (CAPM)**. It describes the relationship between a security's expected return and its systematic risk.

Equation 2-12 is used to calculate the beta of a security, which is then replaced in Equation 2-13 to calculate the security's expected rate of return. For example, it was determined in the alpha and beta You Apply It that security Z has a beta (calculated in Equation 2-12) of 1.28. This beta can then be used in Equation 2-13 to calculate security Z's expected rate of return under a given risk-free rate and expected market return.

Equation 2-13 indicates that the expected return on any security is equal to the risk-free rate plus a premium for risk. The premium is a multiple of the spread between the expected market return and the risk-free rate. As a proxy for the risk-free rate, the return on a Treasury bill is used. **Treasury bills** are short-term debt instruments issued by the federal government that mature within three months.

You can find Treasury bill rates for Canada (the Bank of Canada) or the United States (the Federal Reserve) by referring to the Web sites noted in the Web Links section.

The multiple is determined by the systematic risk of the security, as measured by the security's beta. Systematic risk is the only security-specific term on the right side of the equation. Thus, the systematic risk of the security is the only factor that determines the security's returns in the market.

Exhibit 2-11 is a graphic representation of the relationship between a security's expected return and its systematic risk. The line is often known as the **security market line (SML)**. Security M has a beta equal to 1, which means it has the same beta as the market. The return on this security should also be equal to the market return. Security A has a beta less than 1 (0.5); therefore, its return is expected to be less than the market return. In contrast, security C has a beta greater than 1 (1.75); thus, its return is expected to be greater than the market return.

Observe the difference between the SML and the CML (Exhibit 2-7). The CML shows the relationship between a portfolio's expected return and its standard deviation. In contrast, the SML depicts the relationship between the expected return on a single security and the security's systematic risk, its beta.

According to the CAPM, a security's expected return is a linear function of the security's systematic risk, as measured by beta. The higher a security's systematic risk, the more volatile the security's premium will be compared to the premium on the market portfolio. The market has a beta of 1. Therefore, any security that has the same risk as the market

Exhibit 2-11 Security Market Line

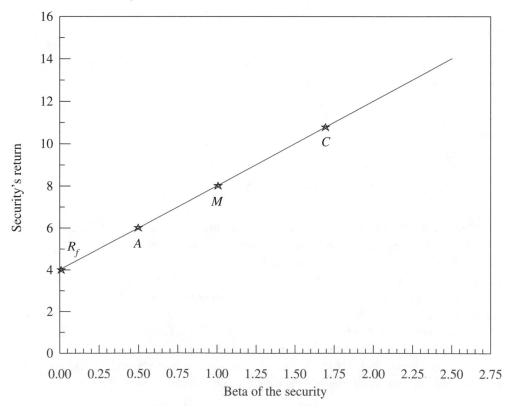

will have a beta of 1 and its premium will be as volatile as the premium of the market portfolio. A security that is less risky than the market will have a beta less than one and its premium will be less volatile than the premium of the market portfolio. A security that is more risky than the market will have a beta greater than one and its premium will be more volatile than the premium of the market portfolio.

The CAPM applies to portfolios in the same way as to individual securities. It is necessary to estimate the beta of a portfolio; then the beta can be used in Equation 2-13 to calculate the expected return on the portfolio. A useful characteristic of beta is that the beta of a portfolio can be calculated as a weighted average of the betas of the individual securities that make up the portfolio. The weight of security i is the portion of total wealth invested in security i. That is:

$$\beta_p = w_1\beta_1 + w_2\beta_2 + \ldots + w_n\beta_n \qquad \textbf{(Equation 2-14)}$$

where

β_p = beta of the portfolio of n securities

w_i = weight of security i in the portfolio, determined as the amount invested in i divided by the total value of the portfolio

β_i = beta of security i

$i = 1, 2, 3, \ldots, n$

Given the importance of the CAPM (Equation 2-13) and its wide applicability, it is important to remember the assumptions under which it is derived. Some of the assumptions do not hold in practice. Yet it is useful to accept them as relevant market assumptions in order to use the CAPM to assess the relationship between risk and expected return. It is a good idea to reflect on these assumptions before attempting to apply the CAPM.

The CAPM requires four assumptions in addition to those described in Section 2.1 as requirements for deriving the capital market line. These additional assumptions are:

- Investors choose between portfolios on the basis of expected return and variance (or standard deviation). This condition implies that portfolio returns are distributed normally.

- All investors have the same planning horizon and the same opinion about the distribution of portfolio (or security) returns. That is, all investors plan their investments over a single period of time.

- There are no frictions or impediments to the free flow of capital and information in the market. Transaction costs are zero, taxes are zero, and information is accessible to everyone in the marketplace.

- Because all investors are totally diversified, only systematic (or market) risk matters. Beta is a measure of the systematic risk of an individual security.

2.3 CAPITAL BUDGETING IN A PORTFOLIO FRAMEWORK

In Chapter 1, you studied capital budgeting in an environment where risk was the same for all projects. This allowed us to avoid its explicit consideration. In practice, the cash flows from a firm's projects should be evaluated in terms of their risk. The degree of risk of a project is defined as the probability that the actual cash flows will deviate from expected cash flows.

In this chapter, Sections 2.1 and 2.2 emphasized that the expected return on a highly risky asset should be higher than the expected return on a relatively less risky one. Thus, the capital budgeting process must take into consideration the degree of a project's risk before it can be evaluated for potential investment.

Accountants allocate funds on behalf of a company to investment projects such as plant expansion or the replacement of equipment. In order to diversify a company's risk, these allocations are usually spread over a series of projects instead of one single project. Analyzing the impact of the expected return and risk of each new project on the risk and return of existing projects is sound financial management.

We look at the capital budgeting problem of choosing between projects the same way investors choose between securities. In fact, the same diversification applies. Firms typically have many projects to choose from; each project may have a different level of risk. When sound projects are weakly correlated, combining them helps eliminate much of the individual project's risk. Thus, before management accepts or rejects a project they must account for the project's risk within the portfolio of other projects.

Additionally, there are arguments that support the relevance of total risk in capital budgeting. Many firms consider total risk in practice. In Section 2.4 we explain how total risk is estimated and incorporated into the capital budgeting process.

CAPM and Project Beta

The main thrust of portfolio theory is diversification. **Diversification** describes an investment strategy to reduce total risk whereby the investor acquires many securities from different industries with different risks. According to portfolio theory, a firm spreads its investments over a large number of projects so that the gains from some projects will offset the losses on others. The firm is guaranteed the average return, which is usually less risky than the return on individual projects. Portfolio theory also suggests that higher diversification can be achieved by choosing projects so that their correlations are as far as possible from being perfectly positive. Therefore, a project's systematic risk is the only risk that should concern a firm studying the possibility of investing in the project.

In perfect markets, this conclusion holds even if the firm is undertaking only one project. If the firm's shareholders are well diversified, the firm should be rewarded only for the systematic risk inherent in its operations. It is assumed that unsystematic risk is diversified away by shareholders in their own portfolios. In practice, there are problems with this argument, particularly because markets are not perfect and there are stakeholders other than the firm's shareholders.

If the systematic risk of a project is the only risk that should be rewarded in undertaking the project, the capital asset pricing model can be used to determine the appropriate risk-adjusted discount rate for the NPV analysis of the project. Section 2.2 indicated that the security market line suggests a linear relationship between expected returns and market risks for financial assets. This relationship also applies to individual projects. Project return can be calculated as:

$$E(R_i) = R_f + \beta_i[E(R_M) - R_f] \qquad \text{(Equation 2-15)}$$

where

$E(R_i)$ = expected return on project or asset i
R_f = risk-free rate

$$\beta_i = \text{beta of project or asset } i$$
$$E(R_M) = \text{expected return on the market portfolio}$$

The term $[E(R_M) - R_f]$ measures the difference between the expected return on the market portfolio and the risk-free rate. It represents the premium anticipated by investors for taking the risk of investing in the market portfolio. It is often called the **market risk premium** or the **market price of risk**. Historically, the long-term market risk premium has ranged from 5% to 7%. Financial managers can use this range to choose a market risk premium to be used in Equation 2-15. Moreover, practitioners and academics often use the current yield on three-month Treasury bills as an estimate of the risk-free rate. Thus, the important step in applying Equation 2-15 is determining the beta of the project, as the other parameters are easier to estimate.

The **project beta** measures the sensitivity of a project's expected return relative to the return on the market portfolio. The project beta can be used in Equation 2-15 to determine the required rate of return for a project. This rate captures the portfolio (or covariance) effects of a project. It is known as the **risk-adjusted discount rate** or the **risk-adjusted required rate** because it compensates the investor for committing the funds and accepting the risk to undertake the investment.

It must be emphasized that the risk-adjusted discount rate is useful in making capital budgeting decisions when the cash flows from a project are uncertain. When using the net present value rule, the risk-adjusted rate is the appropriate rate to discount the project's expected cash flows to obtain the risk-adjusted net present value. If the risk-adjusted NPV ≥ 0, accept the project. Conversely, if the risk-adjusted NPV < 0, reject the project.

MINICASE 2-2 ILLUSTRATING CAPM AND PROJECT BETA

Casual Wear (CW) is a small clothing distributor located in Calgary. The owner, Fred, is studying the possibility of opening a new outlet in Winnipeg. Fred would like to estimate an expected rate of return for this project. The risk-free rate is 7%.

CW's business is cyclical and sensitive to fluctuations in economic conditions. Fred believes the store in Winnipeg is likely to have the same pattern of cash flows as the Calgary outlet. The Calgary outlet has been valued at approximately $2,000,000. Exhibit 2-12 shows the population of cash flows that have been generated by the store since its opening.

Question 1: Estimate a beta for the proposed Winnipeg store assuming that it will be as risky as the Calgary store. Suppose the correlation coefficient is 0.9045

The first step is to calculate the return on the investment in the Calgary outlet. Exhibit 2-12 shows the cash flows generated from a store valued at $2,000,000. The return on the investment and the market return are provided in Exhibit 2-13.

Exhibit 2-12
Cash Flows ($ Thousands) of the Calgary Outlet

Year	20X8	20X7	20X6	20X5	20X4	20X3	20X2	20X1
CW cash flows	$210	$306	$244	$158	$164	$182	$220	$324

Case Continued >

Exhibit 2-13
Calgary Outlet and Market Returns

Year	20X8	20X7	20X6	20X5	20X4	20X3	20X2	20X1
CW return	10.5%	15.3%	12.2%	7.9%	8.2%	9.1%	11%	16.2%
Market return	11%	13%	11.5%	9%	9.2%	10%	9.6%	12%

The data in Exhibit 2-13 can now be used to estimate a beta for the Winnipeg store. The beta can be estimated by a characteristic analysis of CW's return on the market return and using the slope of the regression line as the beta. Another way is to use Equation 2-10. In this case, the data are used to calculate σ_M and the covariance between the market return and the return on the Calgary outlet.

Using the statistical standard deviation calculation for a finite population, the σ_M equals 1.3481% and σ_{CW} equals 2.9060%.[1]

The covariance between CW's return and the market return is:

$$\text{Cov}(R_i, R_M) = 0.9045 \times 1.3481 \times 2.9060 = 3.54$$

The beta of the Calgary outlet and the beta of the proposed Winnipeg store equal:

$$\beta_{CW} = \frac{3.54}{(1.3481)^2} = 1.95$$

Question 2: Use the CAPM to estimate the expected rate of return to Fred assuming the market return is expected to be 12%.

Equation 2-15 can be used to estimate the expected rate of return to Fred for the new store. The equation yields:

$$E(R_f) = 0.07 + (0.12 - 0.07) \times 1.95 = 16.8\%$$

The expected rate of return to Fred for the project is 16.8%.

Question 3: Fred estimates that the internal rate of return on this project is expected to be 11.3%. Should Fred invest in the project?

Because the IRR is less than the risk-adjusted required rate, Fred should not invest in the project.

---

[1] If data were sampled from a population, the probability of occurrence for each observation would be $\frac{1}{(n-1)}$. As a result, the variance of the sample is $s^2 = \frac{(R_1 - \bar{R})^2}{n-1} + \frac{(R_2 - \bar{R})^2}{n-1} + \ldots + \frac{(R_n - \bar{R})^2}{n-1}$.

When using the internal rate of return rule, the risk-adjusted rate should be used as the hurdle rate. If IRR $\geq$ the risk-adjusted rate, accept the project. On the other hand, if IRR $<$ the risk-adjusted rate, reject the project.

Practical Difficulties in Estimating Project Betas

There are a number of difficulties in estimating project betas in situations such as the one illustrated in Minicase 2-2.

- *Incomplete or unreliable data* present one difficulty. It may be impossible to derive the rates of return. The firm may not have compiled data on a suitable project, or the data may not be reliable. Moreover, the previous project may seem reasonably similar; yet it may be different enough to make the estimates unreliable.

■ Another problem encountered in practice is the *difficulty in estimating periodic returns*. The one-period return on the project is equal to the project cash flows at the end of the period divided by the market value of the project at the beginning of the period. How do you estimate the market value of the project on a periodic basis to make this calculation? With security investments there is a liquid secondary market, but no such market exists for projects.

■ There may be *no historical data*. In Minicase 2-2, a prior project existed that had similar circumstances and cash flows. In reality, most projects have no historical experience on which the financial manager can rely to estimate the beta of the project. For example, the manager may be analyzing a project to introduce a new product. In this case, the manager must estimate the expected cash flows and the correlation between the cash flows and the market return; these estimates are not likely to be reliable.

■ In addition to the uncertainties encountered with most projects, new products have particularly unpredictable outcomes. Project cash flows and market returns are influenced by an array of factors such as general economic conditions, project life, industry conditions, growth trends in cash flows, competition, and the pattern of expected cash flows over time. The *unpredictable outcome* and the possibility of large forecast errors casts doubt on the initial estimates of project betas.

■ Also, the analogy made between corporate investments and investments undertaken by individuals has weaknesses that cast doubt on the justification for using the CAPM in corporate decision making. One weakness is that projects have long economic lives and require multi-period analysis. The CAPM is a single-period model that assumes individuals seek to maximize their utility function over one period. Thus, the single discount rate obtained using the CAPM may not be constant from one period to the next. This type of fluctuation means that the discount rate for the project may not be constant over the life of the project. Therefore, CAPM *may not be suitable for multi-period analysis*.

■ Another problem with the CAPM is *the assumption about the relevant market portfolio to be used*. Generally, a broad market index, such as the S&P/TSX Composite Index, is used to approximate the market as required by the CAPM. The relevance of this approximation remains in doubt.

■ It is important to remember that *historical data may not predict future risk*. If the project beta is derived from historical data, it may not be a reliable predictor of future market risk. Many studies have shown that a firm's beta tends to converge to 1 over time. If a project's beta is estimated to be 1.7 based on historic data, the future beta may be only 1.6. In this case, using 1.7 overestimates the project's market risk and unduly penalizes the project. On the other hand, if a project's beta as estimated from historic data is 0.7, the future beta is likely to be 0.75. Using 0.7 to calculate the risk-adjusted return underestimates the degree of risk of the project and favours its acceptance.

Given all these difficulties with estimating the beta of a project, how can this approach be adjusted? Alternatively, what alternative approaches can be used to overcome these limitations?

Betas for Classes of Risky Projects

The problem of estimating a new project's beta if data are unavailable or unreliable can be solved by using the beta of the firm's common shares as a proxy for the project's beta. In certain circumstances, this approach may provide beta estimates that are better than those produced by direct estimates. For example, if the new project has the same risk as the firm's existing projects, then the firm's beta adjusted for debt proportion is a good proxy for project beta. This means that the new project and the firm's existing cash flows have the same chance that actual cash flows will deviate from expected cash flows.

In applying the NPV rule, the rate used to discount project cash flows is the firm's weighted average cost of capital. Remember, the **weighted average cost of capital (WACC)** is defined as the expected return on a portfolio of all the firm's securities and its retained earnings.

The firm's WACC can be used to calculate the NPV of a new project, assuming that the new project has the same risks as the firm's existing projects and the same capital structure as the firm. As you learned in Section 2.1, the capital market line indicates that the degree of risk of a particular portfolio depends on the degree to which the portfolio is financed by debt. Adjusting for financial leverage will be covered later in this section. The degree of risk of a company, as measured by the observed beta of the company, reflects business as well as financial risk factors.

The assumption that financial leverage occurs in all projects leads to the notion of risk classes. Many firms classify projects according to their risk. Projects that have the same risks as the existing projects of the firm are classified as average risk projects and their betas are equal to the beta of the company's own securities. In applying the NPV rule, the rate used to discount the cash flows of these projects is the firm's WACC.

Other projects are classified in terms of their own risk class or a class that has projects with similar risk characteristics. If the degree of risk of a class is considered to be higher than the degree of risk of the average class, the beta of this class will be higher than the beta of the firm's own shares. Thus, the rate used to discount the cash flows from projects in this class should be higher than the firm's WACC, which is charged to the average class. If the degree of risk of a class is less than that of the average group, both the beta and the discount rate should be lower as well.

Divisional Costs of Capital

Many firms with multiple divisions, products, or geographical markets also use risk classes. Conglomerate firms, whose divisions are likely to be in very different risk classes than the organization as a whole, often estimate divisional costs of capital for capital budgeting purposes. These divisional hurdle rates are estimated to reflect the required return to investors on the firm's portfolio of assets plus or minus an adjustment for the differential in financial leverage between the various divisions.

These types of firms treat the firm's overall beta as the weighted average of the betas of its divisions in which the weight of each division is the proportion of the firm's assets invested in the division. As shown in Equation 2-14, the beta of a portfolio is the weighted average of the betas of the individual securities making up the portfolio.

Using the Betas of Similar Firms as Proxies for Project Betas

Often a firm may attempt to develop a new product or service in response to competitive pressures. A widely-used method to estimate the new project's beta is based on the experience of a competitor. If a competitor exists and its main business has risks similar to those of the new project, the financial manager can estimate the project's beta from the competitor's beta. Of course, the beta of the proxy firm should be adjusted for financial leverage, as that firm's choice of leverage may not be the optimal choice for the new project's leverage.

If the competitor considered as a proxy has other projects unrelated to the new project, the process of estimating beta becomes complex and the resulting estimate is unreliable. The criteria for matching the proxy beta include:

- Asset life
- Growth
- Patterns of expected cash flows over time
- Characteristics of each component of the cash flows
- Relative contribution (or weights) to the firm's value (or portfolio of assets)

In practice, not all of these conditions are likely to be fully satisfied and the betas may be biased.

Adjusting Project Betas for Project Financial Leverage

Most firms use a combination of debt and equity in their capital structure. However, if a company finances its operations from all equity sources, such as common share offerings or retained earnings, the beta of the firm's common shares will reflect only the firm's business risk. An **unlevered firm** is a firm financed through means other than debt. In this case, the beta of the firm's common shares can be used as a proxy for the beta of projects with average risk. The cost of equity is used as the discount rate in the NPV analysis for the project.

Project betas must be adjusted for financial risk if a firm finances its assets through a combination of debt and equity. The beta of the firm's common shares reflects both business and financial risks. Financial risk relates to the additional variability in the firm's cash flows as the result of financial leverage. Debt financing increases the risk to shareholders because debt holders have senior claims on assets. The project beta reflects the business risk of the project and the beta of the firm's common shares reflects the business risk of the firm's portfolio of assets as well as the financial risk of debt financing.

Numerous studies have attempted to divide the beta of the firm's common shares between business and financial risks. These studies are based on the assumption that a firm's decision to use debt is independent from the business decision. A **levered firm** is one that is partially or wholly financed with debt. Thus, the difference between the betas of common shares from two firms that are undertaking the same business but with different capital structures should be attributed solely to differences in the capital structure.

Based on this assumption, the notion of an unlevered firm's beta (the beta of a firm financed with no debt) can be used to express a levered firm's beta, as:

$$\beta_L = \beta_U + (1 - T)(D/E)\beta_U \qquad \textbf{(Equation 2-16)}$$

where

β_L = beta of the levered firm
β_U = beta of the unlevered firm
T = corporate tax rate
D = market value of the firm's debt
E = market value of the firm's equity

The ratio D/E is the debt-to-equity ratio, which measures the firm's degree of financial leverage. The equation indicates that the levered firm's beta is always higher than the unlevered firm's beta and that the higher the financial leverage, the higher the levered firm's beta will be. The equation can be used as a basis to adjust project betas for financial leverage. Empirical studies show that firms use a similar adjustment process for calculating their hurdle rates.

Try adjusting a project's beta for leverage by completing the following You Apply It minicase.

YOU APPLY IT LEVERAGE AND PROJECT BETA

Refer back to the information provided about Casual Wear (CW) company in Minicase 2-2 on page 111. Now assume Fred has decided to open the new outlet in Winnipeg. Fred is encouraged because his banker has suggested a loan to supplement Fred's equity in buying the new outlet. The banker has reminded Fred that he can deduct interest payments for tax purposes. Fred's marginal tax rate is 42%. He used 70% debt in the Calgary store, but he would like to use 40% debt in the Winnipeg store. How should the new information affect Fred's expected rate of return for the new project?

Answer

The beta for the Winnipeg store was calculated earlier assuming it will be financed in the same way as the Calgary store. If the financial leverage changes, betas need to be adjusted using Equation 2-16. The first step is to determine the unlevered firm's beta. Solve for β_U as follows:

$$1.95 = \beta_U + (1 - 0.42)(0.70/0.30)\beta_U$$
$$1.95 = \beta_U + 1.3533\beta_U = 2.3533\beta_U$$
$$\beta_U = 0.8286$$

Equation 2-16 is used again to calculate the levered beta for the new outlet. This levered beta is:

$$\beta_L = 0.8286 + (1 - 0.42)(0.4/0.6) \times 0.8286 = 1.1490$$

The expected rate of return to Fred for the store is:

$$R_{CW} = 0.07 + (0.12 - 0.07) \times 1.149 = 12.75\%$$

Project Cost of Capital: Calculation Summary The following steps are generally completed to determine the cost of capital when calculating the NPV for a project that is in a different industry to the company evaluating the project and has a different leverage:

1. Identify a competitor that has business risks similar to those of the new project.

2. Estimate the competitor's beta.

3. Adjust the equity beta for financial leverage to obtain an estimate of the company's asset beta, which is the beta that the company would have if it were financed entirely through equity, that is, its unlevered beta.

4. Based on the financial leverage of the company that is considering the project, adjust the asset beta to obtain an estimate of the beta of equity for the project.

5. Use the CAPM to estimate the cost of equity for the project.

6. Calculate the WACC of the project using the target debt–equity ratio of the company that is considering the project.

2.4 MARKET RISK AND TOTAL RISK

Section 2.3 emphasized the role of portfolio theory in dealing with risk in project analysis. It was based on the assumption that the only relevant investment risk is the systematic (market) risk because investors hold only diversified portfolios of assets and because the market is efficient.

Although research shows the market is reasonably efficient for financial assets like stocks and bonds, it may not be very efficient for real corporate assets like real estate, machinery, and equipment. Failure to correctly measure total risk may result in poor decision making, for at least one party. Those who can identify such failures may profit from them. Consider Warren Buffett and the California Earthquake Authority in the following article.

WARREN BUFFETT VERSUS CALIFORNIA EARTHQUAKE AUTHORITY

Risk is an inherent component of business decisions. Risk may involve uncertainty concerning the project's future cash flows, political and exchange-rate risks, inflation, and other variables affecting the net present value of the investment decision. Another kind of risk may involve large volatility of cash flows, especially when potential gains from the project are quite small. Examples include the pricing of catastrophic insurance. Such projects require that insurers have deep pockets, and they usually command substantial risk premiums. To help diversify the catastrophic risk, the investment banker Morgan Stanley was asked to help the California Earthquake Authority (CEA). This public agency was created to insure California homeowners when most insurance companies left the state after the devastating Northridge earthquake of 1994.

The plan created by the CEA provided that, in the event of an earthquake, the first $4 billion of losses would be covered by contributions from participating insurance companies and premiums collected from policyholders. Reinsurance would then absorb the losses from $4 billion to $6 billion. The next $1 billion of losses would be covered by a line of credit to be repaid with proceeds from a bond offering. An additional $1.5 billion of risk would be underwritten in the capital markets. In case of devastating losses, $2 billion more would be paid by the participating insurance companies.

The CEA limited the insurance coverage to homeowners in an effort to keep insurance companies in a state where insurers have suffered huge losses because of fires, earthquakes, and mud slides. To raise additional funds and spread the risk, Morgan Stanley offered a plan to underwrite $1.5 billion of catastrophe (CAT) bonds to big institutional investors. Bondholders would earn 10 percent interest payments for four years, but if any earthquake were to cause more than $7 billion in losses to the state, bondholders could lose their principal. The California earthquake bonds were never issued, however, because a unit of Warren Buffett's Berkshire Hathaway stepped in at the last moment.

Berkshire Hathaway offered to reinsure the $1.5 billion of risk originally slated for the capital markets. The company was to receive almost $148 million per year in premiums for 4 years, an average premium rate of about 14 percent per year. (This was 40 percent more than what the capital markets were charging.) The probability that $1.5 billion in insurance would be needed was estimated by an independent consulting firm to be 1.27 percent per year. Had the proper capital budgeting techniques been implemented, the annual premiums should have been $19 million per year, and even less with discounted cash flows. (The original deal was later scaled back by a factor of 0.7 due to the fact that only 70 percent of eligible participants decided to buy insurance.) Nevertheless, "Berkshire got a pretty sweet deal," commented Mark Broido, marketing director of a Silicon Valley catastrophe risk management firm.

Source: Carolyn T. Geer and Ashlea Ebeling, "A Quack in the China Shop," *Forbes* (October 20, 1997).

In this section, we consider how total (systematic plus unsystematic) risk is estimated and incorporated into the capital budgeting process. We present arguments to support the view that under certain circumstances, total risk is the relevant measure of risk for capital budgeting.

Use of Total Risk for Project Analysis

Management is concerned with the total risk of the firm's projects for several reasons. Following are four important factors that support the use of total risk for project evaluation.

■ *High total risk can bring about insolvency and bankruptcy of the firm.* The CAPM establishes the importance of market risk under the assumption that markets are perfect. The assumption of perfect markets implies that transaction costs, including insolvency or bankruptcy costs, are negligible. It also implies that the sale of a firm's assets under distress is the same as selling them under normal circumstances.

In practice, however, a firm that goes bankrupt incurs substantial direct costs, such as lawyers' fees, or indirect costs, such as management time and loss of goodwill. Moreover, when a firm's assets are auctioned off under distress, they lose much of the value that they had when the firm was a going concern. The costs of bankruptcy are either directly or indirectly borne by shareholders.

The probability of defaulting on outstanding debt is a function of total firm risk. Shareholders are concerned with the probability of default on debt because bondholders can force the firm into bankruptcy or they may take over ownership of the firm's assets. For example, suppose that the market value of a firm's assets as a going concern is $100 million, while the total claims of bondholders are $60 million. If cash flows are not enough to service the debt, bondholders can force the firm into bankruptcy and cause the assets to be sold for $90 million, resulting in a loss to shareholders of $10 million. Thus, management should attempt to reduce total risk because a firm with high total risk may incur bankruptcy costs that decrease shareholder wealth.

- *Homemade diversification by individual investors may not be feasible.* Transaction costs may prohibit investors from proper diversification. Also, the firm's managers have more information about the firm's risk than do shareholders and this asymmetric information may prevent proper diversification at the investor level. In this case, the firm's managers should consider total risk and not only systematic risk.

- *Creditors value the stability of the firm in making their lending decisions.* Similarly, potential managers and employees take into consideration the firm's stability when they make employment decisions. If a firm is perceived to be unstable, it will have to pay more to attract creditors, managers, and employees. It will also have a hard time attracting good managers. Thus, its long-term profitability may suffer.

- *The firm has stakeholders other than shareholders.* As described in Chapter 1, the stakeholders of a firm include managers, workers, and the community in which the company operates. These stakeholders cannot diversify their investments in the firm. For example, managers and workers have invested their talents in the firm and such human capital cannot be diversified.

Using human capital introduces another source of risk: moral risk. The best way to diversify moral risk is through a solid and well-enforced code of conduct. Consider the impact one employee had on all the company's stakeholders in the following article.

WHAT ABOUT MORAL RISK?

The poster boy for "moral risk," exemplifying the devastating effects of unethical behaviour for a company's investors, has to be Nick Leeson. This 28-year-old trader violated his bank's investing rules while secretly placing huge bets on the direction of the Japanese stock market. When those bets proved to be wrong, the $1.24 billion losses resulted in the demise of the centuries-old Barings Bank. More than any other single episode in world financial history, Leeson's misdeeds proved the importance of character in the financial industry.

Forty-one percent of surveyed chief financial officers admit ethical problems in their organizations, and 48 percent of surveyed employees admit to engaging in unethical practices such as cheating on expense accounts or forging signatures. (The real numbers may actually be higher, as self-reported percentages are often low.) One of the main reasons cited for accounting fraud uncovered in recent years was the pressure to "hit the numbers" expected by some security analysts on Wall Street. In a 2004 survey, 47 percent of CFOs said that they felt pressure from CEOs to use aggressive accounting to "make the numbers work," according to *CFO* magazine. The good news was that the same *CFO* survey found the CFOs standing up to CEO pressure and improving ethical standards in their departments, thanks to the 2002 *Sarbanes-Oxley Act*.

What can be done to minimize moral risk? A first step is to build awareness through a code of ethics. Almost all *Fortune* 500 companies and about half of all companies have an ethics code spelling out general principles of right and wrong conduct. Companies such as Texas Instruments have gone into specifics, because ethical codes are often faulted for being vague and abstract.

Organizations also reveal their ethical commitment in other ways: Some companies are administering honesty tests prior to hiring new workers. Others talk about ethical values periodically and attempt to weed out employees who do not share those values before they can harm the company's reputation or culture. Still others include ethics in mid-level managers' required training (as at Procter & Gamble) or model ethics throughout top management and the board (termed "tone at the top," especially notable at Johnson & Johnson). Building on the whistle-blowing protection that is now mandated by the *Sarbanes-Oxley* legislation, some companies promote openness for employees who have ethics-related concerns. Another approach is to have a person designated as *ethics director,* as is now done at Boeing (as required by a key customer, the U.S. Air Force, following ethical problems at Boeing). Merck & Co. evaluates leaders' ethics in performance reviews.

The Leeson saga underscores the difficulty of dealing with the "moral hazard" problem, when the consequences of an individual's actions are largely borne by others. John Boatright argues in his book *Ethics in Finance* that the best antidote is to attract loyal, hardworking employees (although loyalty can be used as an excuse for doing wrong). Ethicists Scott Rae and Kenman L. Wong tell us that debating ethical issues is fruitless if we continue to ignore the character traits that empower people for moral behavior.

Source: Don Durfee, "It's Better (and Worse) Than You Think," *CFO* (May 2004), p. 29.

Measuring Total Risk for a Project

Several techniques enable financial managers to evaluate total risk on a project-by-project basis. These techniques include an approach that combines the net present value and payback techniques, sensitivity analysis, and simulation. Following are brief explanations of the first two techniques.

Combining the NPV and Payback Techniques In Chapter 1, the project payback period was defined as the length of time required to recover the net investment from a project. Because a project's cash inflows tend to be less certain as their time to receipt gets longer, applying a payback cut-off point helps to reduce uncertainty. Generally, firms combine the NPV technique with the payback technique to screen a project. For example, they will accept projects that have a positive NPV and satisfy a cut-off payback period.

Even when firms combine a cut-off payback period and a positive NPV to screen investment alternatives, the use of the payback period is not a good measure of project risk for several reasons. First, the cut-off payback period is determined without justification on the basis of variability of the project. Second, cash flows that are beyond the cut-off payback period are not necessarily less certain than earlier ones. For example, the cash flows of some projects may be more risky during their earlier years than in later years. *not too much time here.*

Sensitivity Analysis **Sensitivity analysis** is the process by which the financial manager studies the sensitivity of a project's net present value to changes in one of the variables used in determining the cash flows or the discount rate. The process requires that the financial manager define the relationship between the NPV and the variables that affect the NPV. Once the relationship is defined and established, preliminary estimates of the variables are needed. Most often, the manager starts with the expected value of a variable and calculates the NPV. Then the value of a variable is changed to determine its effects on the project's NPV.

For example, sensitivity analysis is used to estimate the NPV of a project in which a new product will be introduced. The analysis requires that the financial manager construct pro forma income statements for the project over several years. To construct pro forma income statements, the financial manager must obtain information on variables such as:

- General economic conditions
- Interest rates over several years
- Initial costs of equipment
- Total market size of the product
- The firm's market share
- Price ranges for the final product
- Fixed and variable costs of production

These forecasts are derived from several sources, both internal to the firm and external, including outside consultants and customer surveys.

Generally, forecasters provide their opinions in terms of most likely, pessimistic, and optimistic scenarios. In addition, any other likely scenario that might occur can be studied. The financial manager then calculates the NPV for each scenario. This means that the net present value is computed under different scenarios of any variable that cannot be estimated with certainty. Scenario analysis can also be used to determine the variability of the NPV to simultaneous changes in several variables.

It is often a good idea to draw sensitivity curves to summarize the results of the analysis. For example, a curve to depict the sensitivity of the NPV to changes in the price of the new product will plot the price on the horizontal axis and the NPV on the vertical axis. The steeper the curve, the more sensitive the NPV will be to the price.

In the Self-Test section at the end of this chapter, we have provided a sensitivity analysis computer activity. It allows you to precisely demonstrate how a project's net present value is affected by changes to its estimates. Make sure you try it.

Incorporating Total Risk into Project Evaluation

The financial manager should use the standard deviation of a project's net present value or the standard deviation of a project's return as a proxy for total risk whenever the project is the firm's only investment. This proxy would be appropriate if a new subsidiary is formed to run the new project.

In situations where a firm adds a new project to a portfolio of existing projects, simply adding the project's standard deviation to the portfolio's standard deviation cannot accurately capture the effect of the new project on the risk of the portfolio. A more accurate reflection of the effect must take into account the interaction of the new project with the existing projects. This is captured by the covariance. In such situations, the risk of the new portfolio must be recalculated using Equation 2-6.

If a new subsidiary has to make the choice between two new projects, the decision can be made on the basis of a project's total risk. In such a case, a subsidiary would choose the project that provides the minimum amount of risk for a given level of return or, conversely, the project that provides the maximum return for a given level of risk. In other words, the standard deviation is used to rank two or more projects in terms of their risk-return relationship. For example, consider the two projects A and B shown in Exhibit 2-14. These two projects have the same expected return, but project A has a lower standard deviation. Clearly, A is preferable to B as it is less risky. On the other hand, consider projects A and C. They have the same standard deviation, but project C is more desirable than A because it provides a higher expected return for the same level of risk.

Exhibit 2-14

Ranking Projects in Terms of the Relationship between their Expected Return and Total Risk

Project	Expected return E(R)	Standard deviation σ	Coefficient of variation (CV)	Rank using standard deviation	Rank using CV
(1)	(2)	(3)	(4) = (3) ÷ (2)	(5)	(6)
A	10.00%	6.25%	0.6250	2	3
B	10.00	8.50	0.8500	3	4
C	11.00	6.25	0.5682	1	1
D	15.45	9.00	0.5825	cannot determine	2

The application of these decision rules becomes more difficult if both the amounts of return and risk differ among projects being compared. The difficulty can be reduced by making the comparison using the coefficient of variation (CV). The CV is calculated as:

$$CV_i = \sigma_i \div E(R_i) \qquad \textbf{(Equation 2-17)}$$

where

CV_i = coefficient of variation for project i

σ_i = standard deviation of project i values

$E(R_i)$ = expected return on project i

The **coefficient of variation** measures the relative variation (or risk) in relation to the mean. A project with a low CV means that the variation per unit of the mean is low. In other words, the project's contribution to the firm's risk is low. Thus, a financial manager who uses the CV will choose the projects with the lowest CV first.

Now consider project D in Exhibit 2-14. This project has an expected return higher than the expected returns on A, B, or C. Also, D has a higher standard deviation than A, B, or C. In this case, the standard deviation cannot be used to rank these projects in terms of their risk-return relationship.

Exhibit 2-14 shows the CV for projects A, B, C, and D and the ranking of these projects on the basis of the CV. The CV ranking will preserve the relative ranking based on the standard deviation, while allowing the ranking of those projects that could not be ranked by standard deviation alone.

The CV rule is applied to rank projects on the basis of either return or net present value. In Exhibit 2-14, the projects are ranked in terms of the standard deviation per unit of the expected return. The CV rule can also be used if the expected NPVs of projects A, B, C, and D and the standard deviation of each project's NPV are given. In this case, however, the projects would be ranked in terms of the standard deviation per unit of the NPV.

It must be emphasized that the CV is a "rule-of-thumb" approach that trades off the standard deviation and expected return. It is not theoretically based because it may not represent the trade-off desired by the company or the individuals considering the investment. Despite this disadvantage, it is used in practice when this type of trade-off for total risk is necessary.

2.5 CAPITAL RATIONING

Capital rationing occurs when a firm does not invest in all its positive net present value projects because of a constraint imposed voluntarily or involuntarily on the total amount of funds to be used on capital projects. For example, a firm may decide that $20 million is the total budget to be spent in a particular year on new capital investments. Yet to undertake the projects identified as having positive NPVs may require $30 million. When such a capital constraint exists, the firm should select the combination of projects that maximizes the total NPV. This combination is called the **optimal set of projects**. In this section, you learn why firms face capital rationing and the procedures that can be used to determine the optimal set of projects.

Reasons for Capital Rationing

In a world of perfect and efficient markets, capital rationing should not occur. If a firm has a project with a positive NPV, it means that the return on the project exceeds the opportunity cost of capital. Because shareholders have perfect information, they know the value of the project and should provide funds to undertake it, as it will maximize their wealth. Thus, the firm should be able to obtain whatever funds are needed to undertake all positive NPV projects. In practice, markets are not necessarily perfect and efficient. Consequently, firms may face soft rationing and perhaps hard rationing.

Soft rationing refers to management's decision to limit the capital spending budget available for some or all divisions. This means that financial managers may face capital rationing even though their firms have enough funds to undertake all positive NPV projects. Information asymmetry between lower- and top-level managers will lead to such situations. Large firms often impose soft rationing to help them control the tendency of division managers to overstate the benefits of capital projects. Under perfect and efficient market assumptions, soft rationing is not justified because managers would not be able to overstate the potential of projects.

Hard rationing refers to a situation in which a firm is not able to finance all its positive NPV projects because of a lack of funds. In practice, many firms, particularly small and medium-sized ones, face hard rationing. The following market imperfections lead to hard rationing:

- *Information asymmetry* regarding the values of projects targeted by firms. Managers are likely to know more about the projects of a firm than current or potential investors in the firm. This information asymmetry leads investors to protect themselves against the risk that planned projects are not positive NPV projects. They demand a premium to cover this risk and the premium increases the firm's opportunity cost of capital. The present value of the project will be calculated based on the new discount rate, which is higher than the firm's cost of capital. Consequently, the project's NPV will be lower and may turn negative because of the higher discount rate.

- *Transaction costs.* Under perfect and efficient market assumptions, transaction costs are assumed to be negligible, but in practice, as a proportion of the funds raised, they can be substantial. For example, raising funds through the sale of bonds involves fixed costs regardless of the amount raised. A $250 million bond issue and a $20 million issue may both involve $1 million in flotation costs. Thus, the per-dollar cost of the $250 million issue will be 0.4%, whereas the per-dollar cost of the $20 million issue will be 5%. The larger the amount raised, the lower the per-dollar cost will be. Thus, firms may forgo small projects unless they promise returns high enough to compensate for their high opportunity cost of funds.

- *Transaction costs in the labour markets.* When a project is being evaluated for capital budgeting purposes, the financial manager is likely to assume that labour costs for the new project are the average of current costs. This assumption is reasonable when the new project is small compared to the size of the firm's current operations. However, when a capital investment means a large expansion for the firm, new managers and workers will be required. The transaction costs of hiring new personnel and the risk that new employees may not perform as well as the firm's experienced managers will make the required rate of return on the project much higher than the current opportunity cost of funds.

- *Agency problems.* Although a project may have a positive NPV because of its low systematic risk, it may not be desirable because of its high total risk. As explained in Section 2.2, systematic risk is used as the basis for determining a project's required rate of return. The higher the systematic risk, the higher the rate will be. For example, based on systematic risk, a firm's discount rate may be 15%, under which a project may have a positive NPV. However, managers may also be concerned with total risk. As projects approach the final stages of acceptance, managers may become risk averse and attempt to reduce the risk of bankruptcy. They will accept only projects that have significant positive NPVs and minimal total risk.

Despite capital rationing, which may preclude undertaking capital investments, a firm may still benefit from identifying positive NPV projects. For example, a firm may be able to sell some of the good ideas for profit. If markets were efficient, the firm would obtain a price equal to the NPV without having to invest in the project. Of course, markets are not perfect and many factors lead to a price less than the NPV of the project.

Another alternative that would enable the firm to capture some of the project's NPV is to form a joint venture with another firm. Each firm would invest less capital than the total amount required for the whole project. If markets were efficient, capital rationing would not be necessary and the firm would be able to capture all of the NPV of the project. In imperfect capital markets, firms, particularly small ones, should be willing to share some of the NPV in order to see the project proceed.

Incorporating Rationing into the Capital Budgeting Process

In almost all circumstances, the NPV rule is the best criterion for capital budgeting. However, under the constraint of limited resources, the procedure needs to be slightly modified. From the shareholders' perspective, the optimal capital budget is the one that maximizes the total NPV from investing the entire pool of funds available for capital investments. This objective can be achieved by choosing a group of projects that maximizes the NPV generated per dollar of initial investment.

When a firm is facing a single period capital constraint and a set of traditional independent projects (initial outlays occur in the first period and positive cash flows occur in later periods), a simple method that employs the profitability index can be used to choose the optimal capital budget.

Remember, the profitability index was defined in Chapter 1 as:

$$PI = PV \div C_0 = (NPV + C_0) \div C_0 \qquad \textbf{(Equation 2-18)}$$

where

PI = profitability index
PV = present value of the project[2]
C_0 = initial investment outlay in the project

The method comprises the following steps:

1. Calculate the PI for all the projects under consideration. Reject projects with a PI of less than 1 without further consideration. If the remaining projects can all be funded, the procedure stops here, as no capital rationing is required. If not, proceed with step 2.

2. Rank the projects in descending order of their PIs (highest PI first and lowest PI last).

3. Accept the first project and subtract its required initial outlays from the available budget. Accept the second project if its initial outlays are less than the remaining

---

[2] $PV = NPV + C_0$

budget. Accept the nth project if its initial outlays are less than the remaining budget after financing the first $n - 1$ accepted projects. The process stops when the remaining funds are less than the outlays needed for the next project.

One problem with this method is that projects cannot be partially accepted. A project is either entirely accepted or entirely rejected. The PI technique will only choose the optimal set of capital projects if the top ranked projects completely exhaust the budget. Consequently, the capital budget is not likely to be entirely spent.

In certain circumstances, this problem may lead to a sub-optimal capital budget. For example, suppose you have a total budget of $2.2 million and the independent projects listed in Exhibit 2-15.

Exhibit 2-15
Available Investment Projects

Project	Initial investment outlays ($ Millions)	PV ($ Millions)	PI	NPV ($ Millions)
(1)	(2)	(3)	(4) = (3) ÷ (2)	(5)
A	$0.70	$0.882	1.26	$0.182
B	2.00	2.500	1.25	0.500
C	0.80	0.912	1.14	0.112
D	0.60	0.678	1.13	0.078
A + C + D	2.10	2.472	1.18	0.372

According to the PI technique, project A must be accepted first because it has the highest PI of 1.26 and initial outlays of $0.7 million. The remaining budget forces you to stop short of accepting project B, which has a PI of 1.25 and requires $2 million as an initial investment. Ranking just behind B are projects C and D with PIs of 1.14 and 1.13, respectively. The budget has enough funds to undertake projects A, C, and D, while setting aside project B. The resulting NPV is indicated in the last row of Exhibit 2-15. However, comparing the combination A + C + D with project B on its own reveals that it is optimal to undertake project B alone because it will provide more NPV than the combination A + C + D. For this reason, project B should be preferred over the combination, even though it has a PI lower than project A.

This problem can be resolved with additional effort. It requires the financial manager to use a "brute force" method comprising three steps:

1. Label as feasible every combination of projects for which the overall fund requirements do not exceed the available budget.

2. Calculate the NPV that can be generated from investing in each feasible combination of projects.

3. Choose the feasible combination that has the highest total NPV.

Practise choosing amongst several investment projects when the capital budget is constrained. Try the following You Apply It minicase.

Montreal Textile Inc. (MTI) has identified several projects for possible investment. Exhibit 2-16 summarizes the results of evaluating these projects.

Exhibit 2-16
Investment Projects at MTI ($ millions)

Project	Initial investment outlays	NPV
A	$6.64	$2.18
B	3.65	1.40
C	1.79	1.25
D	0.97	1.35
E	1.43	0.54
F	2.32	1.66
G	3.45	0.76

MTI has allocated $16 million for capital investments during the coming year. Which projects should MTI invest in?

Answer

Exhibit 2-17 shows the analysis needed to come up with the set of projects that will maximize the NPV of investments given the budget constraint of $16 million. Panel A provides a starting point in which projects are ranked according to their PI. According to the PI technique, projects D, F, C, B, and E can be funded without going over budget. The total NPV generated from this group of investments will be $6.2 million.

Project A cannot be funded due to the constraint. The company will need an additional $0.8 million to undertake project A. Some firms may extend their budgets to accommodate projects such as A because failing to take A will keep a substantial amount of money underutilized. After all, A is a positive-NPV project and the amount remaining in the budget ($5.84 million) can at best be invested at the cost of capital.

Another strategy is shown in Panel B. A firm may set aside project A and move to the next positive NPV project until the entire budget is exhausted or the firm runs out of projects. This process will lead the firm to accept all the projects except A. Panel B shows that under this strategy the overall NPV is higher than the cumulative NPV shown in Panel A.

In reality, the process of obtaining the optimal mix of projects is much more cumbersome than is suggested by this minicase. It requires finding all the feasible combinations and their aggregate NPVs and choosing the combination with the maximum NPV (the "brute force" method). Panel C shows that the optimal strategy may require additional flexibility. It suggests that MTI should set aside projects E and G and undertake project A, even though A has a lower PI than E. The aggregate NPV that can be derived from the projects under the capital constraint will be maximized under this strategy.

You Apply It Continued >

Exhibit 2-17
Optimal Investment Choices at MTI

Panel A: Stopping if the budget cannot fund the next project

Project	Initial investment outlays ($ Millions)	NPV ($ Millions)	PI	Cumulative outlays ($ Millions)	Cumulative NPV ($ Millions)
D	$0.97	$1.35	2.392	$0.97	$1.35
F	2.32	1.66	1.716	3.29	3.01
C	1.79	1.25	1.698	5.08	4.26
B	3.65	1.40	1.384	8.73	5.66
E	1.43	0.54	1.378	10.16	6.20
A	6.64	2.18	1.328	16.80	8.38
G	3.45	0.76	1.220	20.25	9.14

Panel B: Accepting project G and leaving out project A

Project	Initial investment outlays ($ Millions)	NPV ($ Millions)	PI	Cumulative outlays ($ Millions)	Cumulative NPV ($ Millions)
D	$0.97	$1.35	2.392	$0.97	$1.35
F	2.32	1.66	1.716	3.29	3.01
C	1.79	1.25	1.698	5.08	4.26
B	3.65	1.40	1.384	8.73	5.66
E	1.43	0.54	1.378	10.16	6.20
G	3.45	0.76	1.220	13.61	6.96
A	6.64	2.18	1.328	20.25	9.14

Panel C: Accepting project A and rejecting projects E and G

Project	Initial investment outlays ($ Millions)	NPV ($ Millions)	PI	Cumulative outlays ($ Millions)	Cumulative NPV ($ Millions)
D	$0.97	$1.35	2.392	$0.97	$1.35
F	2.32	1.66	1.716	3.29	3.01
C	1.79	1.25	1.698	5.08	4.26
B	3.65	1.40	1.384	8.73	5.66
A	6.64	2.18	1.328	15.37	7.84
E	1.43	0.54	1.378	16.80	8.38
G	3.45	0.76	1.220	20.25	9.14

It must be emphasized that capital budgeting under rationing can be very complicated. For example, a large firm may have many interrelated projects where the cash flows from one project are dependent on the cash flows from several others. In these situations, the financial manager must use more sophisticated methods, such as linear programming, to choose the optimal set of projects. These methods can be quite involved depending on the complexity of the projects under consideration. For example, choosing the optimal set when projects have capital outlays that occur at the beginning of the project and over several periods in the future may require the use of integer or goal programming techniques. Such advanced analysis techniques are beyond the scope of this course; however, regardless of the techniques, the objective is always to maximize the net present value that can be generated from investing the entire pool of funds allocated for capital investment.

2.6 ANNUAL CAPITAL BUDGETING PROCESS

So far, we have focused on the capital budgeting process: the estimation of cash flows, risk assessment of cash flows, and net present value estimations. It is important to understand that the process by which projects are approved for investment is much larger and more complex than our focus has been thus far. In this section we consider how the evaluation process is related to other stages in the capital budgeting process.

The capital budgeting process is an important area of responsibility of the financial manager. Often, it involves large sums of money and consumes considerable time for planning and implementation. Given the many factors that must be considered in the process and the many ways these factors can affect each other, the capital budgeting process rarely produces accurate estimations. Yet the outcomes from projects will likely affect most stakeholders: shareholders, creditors, executives, managers, employees, and the public.

Since capital budgeting is an ongoing process, each project must go through several steps before it is approved for investment. We consider each, next.

New Project Ideas

The generation of ideas that can evolve into projects is important to firms because new projects can contribute to the maximization of shareholder wealth. Unfortunately, there is no formal process to ensure the creation of valuable new ideas. Nevertheless, the financial manager must stress the importance of new ideas and ensure that they are given serious consideration.

New project ideas can come from various sources:

■ Line employees and their managers may identify projects that will lead to additional efficiency, for example equipment replacement, floor space layout changes, and new processes.

■ Marketing personnel and managers who deal directly with customers may discover new product ideas from their contacts. Often, customers express their needs to customer representatives. The marketing manager may then consult with the engineering and production departments to assess the feasibility of the project.

■ Division managers are positioned to take a broader view of the firm's business and can initiate ideas for projects that would not be visible to lower level employees, such as merging two units, developing a new unit, or eliminating an old one.

■ Senior level managers generate ideas for new business ventures, targets for mergers and acquisitions, strategic alliances, and ways to improve profitability and/or increase revenues.

Idea generation should not be confined to any group of individuals within an organization, but should be encouraged and rewarded at all levels.

Most of the time, division managers screen projects emerging from the floor or the field in terms of their feasibility and attractiveness. Similarly, higher-level managers may screen projects advancing upward until they reach the top. This bottom-up process may lead managers at all levels to eliminate projects that may present threats to their own welfare. Therefore, it is advisable for firms to have an independent committee to study all proposals, no matter how they are judged at various stages. Larger companies that rely on innovation to keep their competitive edge may have separate departments (a research and development group, for example) to study new project ideas and provide their own.

Preparation of Proposals

Proposals for new projects vary in complexity depending on the amount of funds they require and their impact on the firm. For example, replacing old equipment is less complicated than starting a new division that would require new equipment, and a new division would be less complicated than merging with another firm. Most firms use standard forms for simple projects; as a project gets more complex, additional requirements arise. For example, a proposal to start a new product line may require supplying forecasts prepared by economic consultants. Large firms generally classify projects into categories according to their degree of complexity and the depth to which they must be studied. Exhibit 2-18 presents some common categories.

The ultimate result of proposal preparation is a detailed description of the possible cash inflows and outflows from the project. These descriptions are often made in general terms such as "sales can increase by 12% over existing levels" or "costs can be cut by 25%." The details of the calculations are often left to the evaluation stage of the capital budgeting process.

Evaluation of Proposals

Projects that survive the proposal preparation stage are then evaluated. The objective of evaluation is to identify positive-NPV projects. At this stage, detailed cash flow estimates are prepared, the degree of risk of these cash flows is considered, and the NPVs of the projects are estimated under various scenarios of cash flows. The result of the evaluation process is a list of positive-NPV projects.

Generation of Capital Budgets

A project that survives the evaluation process will have a positive NPV, maximize shareholder wealth, and be desirable from an investment point of view. However, in practice, certain factors may force a firm to abandon or postpone some positive-NPV projects. The generation of the capital budget requires consideration of such factors as capital

**Exhibit 2-18
Project Categories and Major Issues in the Preparation
of Proposals**

Project category	Types of analysis performed in the preparation of proposals
Compliance*	Compare the efficiency of alternatives that meet the requirements and choose the option that minimizes the NPV of the cost.
Maintenance	Compare the costs of the alternatives and choose the one that minimizes the NPV of the cost.
Replacement	Compare alternatives, including the option of postponing.
Capacity expansion	Compare expanding existing facilities or adding a new one. Forecast demand and competitor strategies. Cash flow projections are less certain than for replacement projects.
New product	Requires long lead-time and analysis by outside consultants. Cash flows are highly uncertain. Analysis may entail considering managerial options such as later expansion, introduction of other products, and entering new markets.
Business acquisition	Requires thorough analysis by consultants. Analysis concentrates on synergies between the two businesses and emerging opportunities. Justification for the company not starting its own project may also be required.
International expansion or acquisition	Requires additional analysis compared to similar domestic projects, for example, analysis of foreign exchange implications, domestic capacity building as opposed to options abroad, and strategic alliance alternatives.

* Compliance projects include pollution control, occupational safety, and other projects required to meet regulations.

rationing, pressures from competition, market forces, and other issues that might justify postponing or eliminating otherwise good projects. The capital budget contains a list of all projects recommended for funding along with the amount recommended for each project.

Typically, the capital budget breaks down the total budget by the various divisions or business units and by new projects and projects from prior years. It is also useful to indicate projects that will require funds in future years for completion. Indeed, some firms forecast future capital expenditures (e.g., over five years). Generally, the chief financial officer manages the review and approval process of the final budget. Other senior managers must also review and approve the budget before it is presented to the firm's board of directors for final approval.

Periodic Review of Progress

Capital budgeting is a dynamic process that includes procedures for periodic review of progress. The objective of the reviews is to identify projects that should be discontinued and liquidated and projects that should be given additional attention and resources.

The frequency of the reviews depends on the degree of project complexity and overall costs. The higher the complexity and costs of a project, the more frequent the reviews should be.

Generally, the capital budgeting manager, in consultation with the project manager, determines the stages at which periodic reviews should be conducted. However, many projects are undertaken in incremental steps. The end of each step is a natural review point prior to approval of the next step.

For example, a project to introduce a new product may require a sequence of several separate capital budgeting decisions:

- Approval is required to fund research that may result in a product idea.

- Funds may be required to develop a product with the desirable characteristics.

- The firm must conduct market research to determine whether a production plan can be justified.

- Funds will be needed for plant and equipment purchases and for marketing the product.

At each review and approval stage, the project manager justifies the request based on new cash inflow and outflow estimates and NPV calculations. The approval involves various levels of the firm and enforces the review process. The result is automatic: unsuccessful projects are cancelled and firm costs are lowered.

Post-Completion Audits

The capital budgeting process should include a system to review the costs of projects immediately after they are completed. The objective is to compare the actual expenditures with the approved budgets. Any discrepancies must be discussed with the project manager, and records must be kept for future reference.

In addition, audits must be conducted at various periods after completion. The purpose is to compare the actual cash flows and benefits of a project with those claimed at the time of project initiation. Again, a discussion of the reasons for any major discrepancies must be recorded for future reference.

Post-completion audits can help create incentives to avoid underestimating costs or overstating cash flow for individual projects. They also help reduce conflict of interest between shareholders and managers, provide a good basis for performance evaluation of managers, and improve the firm's ability to judge the costs and benefits of projects in general over longer time periods.

CHAPTER SUMMARY

In this chapter you have learned how to deal with uncertainty when making capital budgeting decisions and how to estimate the discount rate for risky projects. The capital asset pricing model (CAPM) was reviewed as it is the proper framework for evaluating the risk-return relationships within a portfolio setting. This chapter highlighted the practical implications of the CAPM for capital budgeting, along with its limitations. You studied the role of total risk in investment analysis and the impact of capital rationing on capital investments. Furthermore, other issues related to project analysis such as idea generation, preparation of proposals, project evaluation, appropriations of funds, progress review, and performance evaluation were considered.

Key Terms

Important Equations

Return of a portfolio based on the weighted average of the asset returns in the portfolio

$$R_P = w_1 R_1 + w_2 R_2 + \ldots + w_n R_n \qquad \text{(Equation 2-1a)}$$

$$R_P = \sum_{i=1}^{n} w_i R_i \qquad \text{(Equation 2-1b)}$$

where

R_P = portfolio return

$\sum_{i=1}^{n}$ = summation from $i = 1$ to n

$i = 1, 2, \ldots, n$

n = number of securities in the portfolio

w_i = weight of return i, calculated as the ratio of the amount invested in security i divided by the total investment

R_i = return on security i

Expected return on a portfolio using probabilities of states of economy

$$E(R_P) = \sum_{i=1}^{n} P_i R_{Pi} \qquad \text{(Equation 2-2)}$$

where

$E(R_P)$ = expected portfolio return

$i = 1, 2, \ldots, n$

n = number of possible outcomes

P_i = probability of outcome i

R_{Pi} = portfolio return associated with outcome i

Note: This equation can also be used to compute the expected return on individual stocks or assets.

Variance of portfolio

$$\sigma_P{}^2 = \sum_{i=1}^{n} P_i [R_{Pi} - E(R_P)]^2 \qquad \text{(Equation 2-3)}$$

where

$\sigma_P{}^2$ = variance of the portfolio

Note: This equation can also be used to compute the variance of individual stocks or assets.

Expected return on a portfolio using a weighted average of expected returns

$$E(R_P) = \sum_{i=1}^{n} w_i E(R_i) \qquad \text{(Equation 2-4)}$$

where

$E(R_P)$ = expected portfolio return

w_i = weight of investment i in the portfolio

n = number of investments that make up the portfolio

Variance of a two-asset portfolio

$$\sigma_P{}^2 = w_1{}^2\sigma_1{}^2 + w_2{}^2\sigma_2{}^2 + 2w_1w_2\rho_{12}\sigma_1\sigma_2 \qquad \text{(Equation 2-5)}$$

where

σ_P = standard deviation of portfolio return
σ_1 = standard deviation of investment 1
σ_2 = standard deviation of investment 2
ρ_{12} = correlation coefficient of investments 1 and 2

General equation for the variance of a two-asset portfolio

$$\sigma_P{}^2 = \sum_{i=1}^{n}\sum_{j=1}^{n}\rho_{ij}w_iw_j\sigma_i\sigma_j \qquad \text{(Equation 2-6)}$$

where

ρ_{ij} = correlation coefficient between securities i and j

Expected return on a portfolio containing risk-free assets and the market portfolio

$$E(R_{P_i}) = w_iR_f + (1 - w_i)E(R_M) \qquad \text{(Equation 2-7)}$$

where

$E(R_{P_i})$ = expected return on portfolio i
$E(R_M)$ = expected return on the market portfolio
w_i = portion of the investor's wealth invested in the risk-free asset

Standard deviation of a portfolio containing risk-free assets and the market portfolio

$$\sigma_{P_i} = (1 - w_i)\sigma_M \qquad \text{(Equation 2-8)}$$

where

σ_{P_i} = standard deviation of portfolio i
w_i = portion of the investor's wealth invested in the risk-free asset
σ_M = standard deviation of the market portfolio

Capital market line

$$E(R_{P_i}) = R_f + \frac{\sigma_{P_i}}{\sigma_M}[E(R_M) - R_f] \qquad \text{(Equation 2-9)}$$

Beta of an asset

$$\beta_i = \frac{\text{Cov}(R_i, R_M)}{\sigma_M{}^2} = \frac{\rho_{iM} \times \sigma_i \times \sigma_M}{\sigma_M{}^2} \qquad \text{(Equation 2-10)}$$

where

$\text{Cov}(R_i, R_M)$ = covariance between return on security i and the market return R_M

Regression equation for a total security return to estimate beta

$$R_{i,t} = a_i + \beta_iR_{M,t} + e_{i,t} \qquad \text{(Equation 2-11)}$$

where

a_i = constant term
β_i = beta of the security
$e_{i,t}$ = error term

Regression equation for a security premium to estimate beta

$$[R_{i,t} - R_{f,t}] = a_i + \beta_i[R_{M,t} - R_{f,t}] + e_{i,t}$$ (Equation 2-12)

where

$R_{i,t} - R_{f,t}$ = excess return over risk-free rate (R_f)
a_i = constant term
β_i = beta of the security
$e_{i,t}$ = error term

Equation for the capital asset pricing model

$$E(R_i) = R_f + [E(R_M) - R_f]\beta_i$$ (Equation 2-13)

where

$E(R_i)$ = expected return on security i
R_f = risk-free rate
$E(R_M)$ = expected return on the market portfolio
β_i = security i's beta

Portfolio beta calculated as a weighted average

$$\beta_p = w_1\beta_1 + w_2\beta_2 + \ldots + w_n\beta_n$$ (Equation 2-14)

where

β_p = beta of the portfolio of n securities
w_i = weight of security i in the portfolio, determined as the amount invested in i divided by the total value of the portfolio
β_i = beta of security i
i = 1, 2, 3, . . . , n

Security market line for a project (also called CAPM)

$$E(R_i) = R_f + \beta_i[E(R_M) - R_f]$$ (Equation 2-15)

where

$E(R_i)$ = expected return on project or asset i
R_f = risk-free rate
β_i = beta of project or asset i
$E(R_M)$ = expected return on the market portfolio

Beta for a levered firm

$$\beta_L = \beta_U + (1 - T)(D/E)\beta_U$$ (Equation 2-16)

where

β_L = beta of the levered firm
β_U = beta of the unlevered firm
T = corporate tax rate
D = market value of the firm's debt
E = market value of the firm's equity

Coefficient of variation

$$CV_i = \sigma_i \div E(R_i)$$ (Equation 2-17)

where

CV_i = coefficient of variation of project i
σ_i = standard deviation of project i values
$E(R_i)$ = expected return on project i

Profitability index

$$PI = PV \div C_0 = (NPV + C_0) \div C_0 \qquad \text{(Equation 2-18)}$$

where

$\quad$ PI $=$ profitability index

PV $=$ present value of the project

C_0 $=$ initial investment outlay in the project

Web Links

Betas

■ http://finance.yahoo.com Enter the company's stock ticker symbol or click "Symbol Lookup" and enter the first few letters of the company name. Click on "Key Statistics" under the company's profile to see its beta, along with other information under Stock Price History.

Federal Reserve

■ http://www.federalreserve.gov/ The Fed's Web site contains breaking news, policy information, statistical releases, and a searchable and browsable subject index.

Financial Management Training Centre Courses

■ http://exinfmvs.securesites.net/training/ Free, downloadable "short" courses on various financial management topics. Course 3 is about "Capital Budgeting Analysis."

Investopedia

■ http://www.investopedia.com A Web site for investor education owned by Forbes Media. Contains links to stock simulators, quotes, over 1,000 articles, and a searchable and browsable dictionary of thousands of financial terms, acronyms, and "buzz words."

Canadian Stock Market Indices

■ Toronto Stock Exchange (TSX) http://www.tsx.com

■ TSX Venture Exchange http://ww.tsxventure.com

■ NASDAQ Canada http://www.nasdaq-canada.com

■ Montréal Exchange http://www.m-x.ca/accueil_en.php

■ Canada's New Stock Exchange (CNQ) http://www.cnq.ca

U.S. Stock Market Indices

■ New York Stock Exchange (NYSE) http://www.nyse.com

■ American Stock Exchange (AMEX) http://www.amex.com

■ NASDAQ http://www.nasdaq.com

■ Chicago Stock Exchange (CHX) http://www.chx.com

■ Philadelphia Stock Exchange (PHLX) http://www.phlx.com

Canadian Treasury Bill Rates

■ http://www.bank-banque-canada.ca To access a ten-year history of selected rates from the Bank of Canada homepage, click on Rates and Statistics, Interest Rates, then Treasury Bills.

U.S. Treasury Bill Rates

■ http://www.ustreas.gov/ To access daily Treasury bill rates from the U.S. Department of the Treasury, click on Interest Rate Statistics under the "Direct Links" menu.

Self-Test Questions

Qualitative Questions

Answer each of the following questions in point form:

1. Why should one be concerned with the correlation between the cash flows of a new project and those of the existing assets of a firm?

2. How is diversification accomplished?

3. What is the capital market line (CML)?

4. What is the security market line (SML)?

5. How would the CAPM be used to calculate the cost of equity?

6. What are the main problems in using the CAPM to determine risk-adjusted discount rates for projects?

7. How is a project beta estimated?

8. How are the discount rates for projects or divisions calculated?

9. Why would a financial manager be concerned with total risk?

10. How can a financial manager estimate total risk?

11. What is capital rationing?

12. What are the main purposes of the annual capital budgeting process?

13. Your employer, THEM Inc., is a multi-divisional firm that is financed with both debt and equity. At a recent meeting of head office finance personnel, an issue was raised about how to evaluate new investment project proposals. The firm currently uses divisional hurdle rates to estimate the present value of proposed projects, depending on which line of business and hence in which division it will be undertaken. A new project is now being considered that is unique to the firm. There is no comparable project within any of the existing divisions. A further complication is that the project will be 100% equity financed, whereas all existing lines of business routinely employ some debt in their project financing.

Required

Prepare a brief report explaining how the capital asset pricing model (CAPM) can be used to assess the value of a unique new project for THEM. In your report, include a definition of "project beta" and describe how it might be calculated in practice. Also describe how the amount of debt financing affects the project beta.

Qualitative Multiple Choice Questions

1. Which of the following terms is another name for the unsystematic risk of a security?

   i) Security beta   **iii)** Diversifiable risk

   ii) Market risk   **iv)** Total risk

2. Which of the following statements correctly describes the characteristic line for a security?

   i) The relationship between the return on the security and the security's total risk
   ii) A line with a slope equal to the security's beta
   iii) The relationship between the return on the security and the security's unsystematic risk
   iv) A line with a slope equal to 1

3. In order to maximize shareholder wealth when investment funds are limited and investment projects are mutually exclusive, which of the following projects should firms select?

   i) The project that has the highest coefficient of variation
   ii) The project that has the highest net present value
   iii) The project that has the highest profitability index
   iv) The project that has the highest payback period

4. Which of the following statements *best* describes the unsystematic risk of a security?

   i) The unique risk that can be eliminated by diversification
   ii) The market risk created by factors that affect the prices or returns of stocks in general
   iii) The uncertainty regarding a firm's operating income before interest and taxes
   iv) The variability of operating earnings due to fixed operating costs

For Questions 5, 6, and 7, refer to Exhibit 2-7, repeated below, showing the efficient set of portfolios and the capital market line.

Exhibit 2-7 Capital Market Line

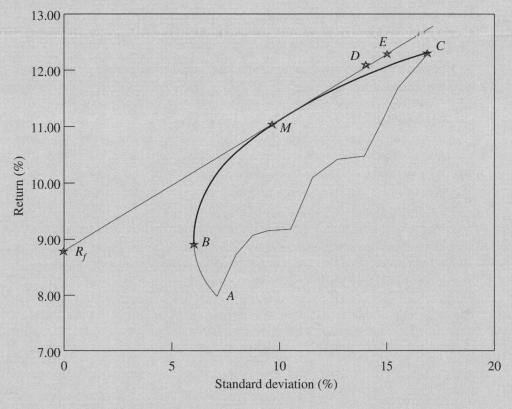

—— The capital market line

5. Which of the following statements *best* describes the point *M* on the capital market line?

   i) *M* is the most desirable portfolio for all investors because it is the tangency point between the capital market line and the efficient set.

   ii) *M* is the only portfolio on the capital market line that is not efficient.

   iii) *M* is a portfolio of all securities in the market held in proportion to their market values, relative to the value of the total market portfolio.

   iv) The portfolio *M* earns an average return because it includes risk-free securities and all risky securities in the market.

6. Identify which of the following statements is *false*.

   i) The line R_fMDE is the security market line (SML).

   ii) The curve *BMC* is the efficient set of portfolios without loans or borrowing.

   iii) The point *M* is the market portfolio of risky assets.

   iv) Portfolios on the line R_fMDE, such as portfolio *D*, can be attained by combining an investment in portfolio *M* with borrowing or lending at the rate R_f.

7. Which of the following statements about the line R_fMDE is true?

   i) Line R_fMDE is the security market line (SML).

   ii) All investors will prefer to invest in the portfolio of risky assets, *M*, in combination with borrowing or lending the risk-free asset, and this is how they achieve points on the line R_fMDE.

   iii) All investors will prefer the points *B* or *C* to point *M* when selecting a portfolio of risky assets, so they will not invest on the line R_fMDE if given a choice.

   iv) Point *D* on the line R_fMDE is a combination of lending at the risk-free rate and investing in portfolio *M*.

8. Which of the following statements about systematic risk is true?

   i) Systematic risk is the portion of total risk that can be eliminated through diversification.

   ii) Systematic risk is created by factors that influence mainly the return or price of the individual security.

   iii) Systematic risk is the contribution of a security to the overall risk of the market portfolio.

   iv) Systematic risk can be divided into two components: the unique risk of the firm and the market risk of the security.

9. Which of the following statements about the beta of an equity security is true?

   i) Beta is the slope of the characteristic line.

   ii) Beta is a measure of the total risk of a security.

   iii) A beta of greater than 1 means that the security's premiums are expected to be less volatile than the premiums on the market portfolio.

   iv) A beta of less than 1 means that the security's premiums are expected to be more volatile than the premiums on the market portfolio.

10. Transaction costs and asymmetric information may prevent individual investors from achieving proper diversification in their portfolios. For this reason, what should a firm's managers consider for project evaluation in addition to the market risk?

   i) The unsystematic risk

   ii) The systematic risk

   iii) Beta

   iv) The total risk

11. ABC Corp. is considering investing in a project whose risk is greater than the current risk of the firm. What should ABC's decision maker do?

   i) Increase the internal rate of return (IRR) of the project to reflect the risk increase

   ii) Reject the project, as its acceptance would increase the risk of the firm

   iii) Ignore the risk differential if the project to be accepted would comprise only a small fraction of the total assets of the firm

   iv) Increase the cost of capital used to evaluate the project to reflect the higher risk of the project

Questions 12 and 13 are based on the exhibit below.

12. Portfolio expected return and standard deviation are shown for different combinations of investments in two securities. The four lines in the exhibit are each drawn for different assumed correlation coefficients, for the relationship between the returns of the two securities. Which of the following statements is the *best* interpretation of this exhibit?

   i) Segment G_4 shows an increasing relationship between risk and return, where there is perfect negative correlation between security returns.

   ii) On curve G_2, all investments are equally desirable

   iii) On line G_1, perfect negative correlation between security returns creates an opportunity for the investor to eliminate portfolio risk completely.

   iv) As the correlation coefficient increases, the standard deviation of the portfolio decreases, for any combination of investments in the two securities.

Relationship between the Correlation Coefficient and Diversification

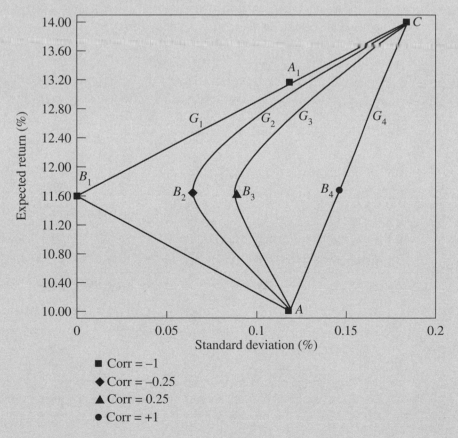

13. Which of the following statements *best* describes the relationship between a correlation coefficient and diversification?

    i) Investments on segments AB_1, AB_2, and AB_3 dominate the investments on segments B_1C, B_2C, and B_3C. They will be preferred by all rational investors.

    ii) The feasible choices on B_1C include a risk-free alternative, B_1, which occurs because the correlation coefficient is –1.

    iii) The feasible choices on AC include a risk-free alternative, A, which occurs because the correlation coefficient is +1.

    iv) On the segment B_2C, a 1-unit increase in risk leads to the same increase in expected return, regardless of the starting position.

Quantitative Multiple Choice Questions

Use the following information to answer Questions 1 and 2:

    Two securities are available. Alpha company shares are selling at $20 each, and Zeta company shares are selling at $50 each. The correlation coefficient between the securities of the two companies is 0.65. The expected returns and standard deviation of returns for the two securities are given below:

Company	Expected return	Standard deviation
Alpha	0.18	0.3
Zeta	0.28	0.4

1. If you purchase 100 shares of each company, what will the expected return on your portfolio be, rounded to the nearest 1%?

    i) 20%

    ii) 25%

    iii) 30%

    iv) 35%

2. What will be the standard deviation of expected returns on your portfolio comprising 100 shares of each company, rounded to the nearest half of 1%?

    i) 28.0%

    ii) 33.5%

    iii) 35.0%

    iv) 53.0%

3. A new subsidiary of a firm has to select a project from among four mutually exclusive projects with the risk and return characteristics in the table below. Which of the following statements *best* describes how this selection should be made?

Project	Expected return	Standard deviation
A	23%	12%
B	15%	7.69%
C	18%	8.23%
D	20%	10.67%

    i) Project *A* should be selected because it has the highest expected return at 23%.

    ii) Project *B* should be selected because it has a standard deviation of only 7.69%.

iii) Project C should be selected because it has the lowest coefficient of variation, which measures the risk per unit of return.

iv) Project D should be selected because it has the highest coefficient of variation, which measures the expected return per unit of risk.

4. The returns on shares of Campbell company are highly correlated with market returns, with a correlation of 0.85. The standard deviation of returns on the market portfolio is 10% and the standard deviation of returns on shares of Campbell company is 15%. What is the beta for Campbell shares, approximately?

   i) 0.57

   ii) 0.85

   iii) 1.15

   iv) 1.28

5. An investor owns 1,000 shares of BXO shares and 500 shares of MBA stock. BXO shares are currently selling for $23 each and have a beta of 1.4. MBA shares are currently selling for $55 each and have a beta of 1.2. What is the beta of the portfolio of shares owned by this investor?

   i) 1.20

   ii) 1.23

   iii) 1.29

   iv) 1.33

6. What is the beta of an equally weighted five-stock portfolio composed of the following stocks?

Stock	Beta
M	0.5
N	1
O	1.25
P	1.5
Q	1.8

   i) 1.05

   ii) 1.21

   iii) 1.23

   iv) 1.25

7. Truro Corp. is experiencing tight capital rationing and has decided not to invest more than $800,000 this year. It has the following three unrelated projects, which will all last 4 years. The firm uses a 14% discount rate. Which projects should be selected?

Project	Cost ($)	Annual cash flows ($)
D	600,000	200,000
E	400,000	198,000
F	250,000	133,000

   i) D and E

   ii) E and F

   iii) F and D

   iv) D, E, and F

8. An investment portfolio has 35% invested in stock ONE and the remainder invested in stock TWO. While the standard deviations of ONE and TWO are 15% and 22%, respectively, their correlation coefficient is –0.2. What is the portfolio's standard deviation?

   i) 2.02%

   ii) 13.60%

   iii) 14.21%

   iv) 16.19%

9. Springfield Corp. has $25 million in assets and $10 million of debt. If its beta is currently 1.45 and its income tax rate is 35%, what is its unlevered beta?

   i) 1.00

   ii) 1.01

   iii) 1.15

   iv) 1.18

10. Moncton Corp. has $33 million in assets of which 75% is equity financed. If its unlevered beta is 1.05 and its tax rate is 40%, what is Moncton Corp.'s levered beta?

   i) 1.05

   ii) 1.21

   iii) 1.26

   iv) 1.50

Quantitative Problems

Problem 1

The stock of company W has a beta of 1.7 and an expected rate of return of 23.5%. The stock of company X has a beta of 0.8. The current risk-free rate of return is 9.6%. You have invested a total of $20,000 in the two stocks, and the beta of your portfolio is 1.2. Assume that the CAPM holds. Calculate the expected rate of return on the portfolio.

Calculate the percentage and dollar value invested in each of the two stocks within the portfolio.

Problem 2

The following information is available for stocks Marc and Unik:

"State" of economy	Probability of "state"	E(R) for "state" of stock Marc	E(R) for "state" of stock Unik
Bear market*	20%	8%	–25%
Normal	55%	47%	16%
Bull market*	25%	23%	58%
*A bear market occurs when the economy is weak; a bull market when it is strong.			

On average, the stock market has been providing a market risk premium of 12%, while Treasury bills are yielding 4%.

a) Which of the two stocks carries the greatest systematic or market risk?

b) Which of the two stocks carries the greatest total risk?

c) Which one has the greatest unsystematic or unique risk?

Problem 3

An investment manager is holding the following portfolio:

Stock	Amount invested	Beta
1	$300	0.6
2	300	1.0
3	500	1.4
4	500	1.8

Treasury bills have been yielding 5% and the portfolio's expected return right now is 14.10%.

The manager would like to sell all of her holdings of Stock 1 and use the proceeds to purchase more shares of Stock 4. What would be the portfolio's expected rate of return following this change?

Problem 4

Quebec Mining, an all-equity firm, is considering the formation of a new division that will increase the assets of the firm by 50%. Quebec Mining currently has a required rate of return of 18%. Recently, Treasury bonds have yielded 7%, and the market risk premium has been around 5%. If Quebec Mining wants to reduce its required rate of return to 16%, what is the maximum beta coefficient the new division could have?

Problem 5

The following is an investment portfolio made up of three securities:

Security	Value of holdings	Expected return	Beta
A	$40,000	13%	1.4
B	$80,000	14%	1.0
C	$80,000	15%	1.1

Assume that the risk-free rate of interest is 5% and that the expected return on the market portfolio of risky assets is 14%.

Required

a) Calculate the portfolio expected return and the portfolio beta.
b) According to the security market line (SML), which, if any, of the securities in this portfolio is earning an expected return greater than what is required for its risk level? Is the portfolio overall earning an expected return greater than what is required for its risk level? Explain what your results imply about whether the three securities and the portfolio are good investments.
c) Explain the meaning of beta and how to interpret a beta greater than 1.
d) Identify *three* problems that might be experienced when trying to estimate the beta of an investment project in practice.
e) Explain the difference between the capital asset pricing model (CAPM) (or the security market line [SML]) and the capital market line (CML).

Cases

Case 1: Phelps Corp.

Thanks to a successful acquisition, Phelps Corp. has more than doubled in size (both assets and sales) over the past two years. Management at Phelps is stretched to the limit.

The annual capital budgeting process has begun and several attractive projects are under consideration. Management believes it can support at most three additional projects, with total capital outlays up to $3,000,000. All of the available projects are independent, with the exception of projects A and B, which are mutually exclusive. The projects are described in Case Exhibit 2-1.

Required

a) Explain the difference between hard and soft capital rationing. Give at least two examples of each.

b) Calculate the profitability index (PI) for each project. Explain how PI differs from NPV.

c) Prepare a brief report stating which projects Phelps Corp. should undertake and explaining why. Refer to all underlying calculations and capital budgeting criteria that you used to come to your conclusion.

Case Exhibit 2-1
Phelps Corp. Project Proposals

Project	Initial investment outlay	Expected NPV
A	$1,000,000	$270,000
B	1,280,000	330,000
C	460,000	176,000
D	500,000	198,000
E	800,000	330,000

Case 2: Consolidated Company

Consolidated Company is contemplating two investment projects.

■ Project A has an expected return of 16% and a standard deviation of returns of 12%. Project A is in the same line of business as this firm's other activities and has a beta of 1.7.

■ Project B is in a different line of business, which has returns that are not highly correlated with the returns of the firm's other business activities or of project A. The correlation coefficient of returns on project A and project B is only 0.88. The two projects are independent of one another and the firm can undertake them in any combination. The risk-free rate of interest is 5%.

As a project analyst, you have collected the information shown in Case Exhibit 2-2 on project B.

Case Exhibit 2-2
Market Data and Data for Project B

State of economy	Probability	Project B returns	Market returns
Bad	0.3	3%	6%
Fair	0.4	9%	7%
Good	0.3	17%	8%

Required

a) Calculate the expected return on the market and on project B.

b) Calculate the standard deviation for project B's expected return and for the market's expected return.

c) Calculate the beta of project B.

d) Calculate the coefficient of variation (CV) of projects A and B.

e) According to the capital asset pricing model (CAPM), which of project A and B is (are) acceptable and what actions would you recommend that the firm take with regard to these two projects? Write a summary in report format.

Case 3: GHI Corp.

GHI Corp. has identified the following three projects with initial outlays and after-tax cash flows, presented in Case Exhibit 2-3. All these projects are independent, not divisible, and in the firm's regular line of business. The firm has a beta of 1. The expected return on Canadian Treasury bills is 4% and the TSX stock market index is expected to increase by 12% in the coming year.

Case Exhibit 2-3
Outlays and After-Tax Cash Flows of GHI Corp. Projects

Year	Project 1	Project 2	Project 3
0	$(100,000)	$(200,000)	$(100,000)
1	70,000	130,000	75,000
2	70,000	130,000	60,000

Required

a) Identify the possible investment opportunities by combining these projects, and summarize the initial outlay and after-tax cash flows for each project combination.

b) Given a capital budget of $300,000, select the best investment opportunity and explain your decision criteria.

Case 4: Manitou Inc.

Manitou Inc. is an all-equity company. Its management has identified the following three capital projects.

Case Exhibit 2-4
Outlays and After-Tax Cash Flows of Manitou Inc. Projects

Projects	Initial investment outlay	5-year after-tax cash flows
A	−$400	$120
B	−$575	$180
C	−$370	$120

These projects have different requirements and risks: Project A requires the firm to purchase more equipment to expand its production, Project B requires new equipment to replace existing equipment, and Project C would enable the firm to produce a brand-new product line. Although Manitou has a beta of 1.6, it also determines the following risk classes of projects.

Projects	Beta
New product	2.2
Capacity expansion	1.54
Replacement	1
Maintenance	0.53

It is expected that the return on Canadian Treasury bills will be 5% in the coming year and that the TSX stock market index will increase by 13%.

Required

a) Compute the IRR for each project. Explain why it is essential in evaluating projects of very different risks to apply a discount rate appropriate to each category in evaluating these projects. What will be the consequence if Manitou Inc. fails to adjust the discount rate that is unique to a project? Use the three projects identified to illustrate your explanations.

b) Explain how Manitou Inc. can estimate betas for its new projects.

Computer Activity: Sensitivity Analysis

This computer illustration demonstrates the use of sensitivity analysis in investment decisions to study how changes in the values of the input variables affect a project's net present value.

LEARNING OBJECTIVES

■ Design and use a worksheet to calculate the NPV of an expansion project.

■ Design and use a worksheet to perform a sensitivity analysis of the effect of changes in values of an input variable on a project's NPV.

Description

Kate and James Clark are planning to start a part-time business. Kate has experience in marketing and James is an expert in the processing of jams. They have decided to manufacture a new line of country-style strawberry jam. Although the basic product is the same for both wholesale and retail markets, the marketing and packaging strategies are different. Their marketing strategy includes selling their product directly to retail customers in the local farmer's market and selling their product wholesale to the main food stores and chains across Canada. The Clarks are planning to sell the business after 10 years.

After a preliminary market survey, Kate's market research has revealed the following conclusions:

Wholesale price	$1.50/jar
Retail price	$2.25/jar
Wholesale market demand in year 1	40,000 jars
Increase in wholesale demand over 10 years	5%/year
Retail market demand in year 1	9,000 jars
Increase in retail demand over 10 years	4%/year

James's research on business costs has generated the following data:

Cost of empty jars	$0.15
Cost of ingredients per jar	$0.80
Increase in costs over 10 years	3%/year
Handling (packaging and delivery)	$2,000/year
Insurance	$500/year
Farmer's market stall rental	$1,500/year
Custom-designed jam processor (class 8, 20% CCA rate) (includes shipping and installation)	$105,000
Salvage value after 10 years	$10,000
Working capital requirement	$4,000
Cost of capital	12%
Tax rate	40%

For tax purposes, assume that the asset class will be kept open after the business is sold.

Required

1. Calculate the NPV of the project.

    a) Perform a sensitivity analysis to show how the distribution of NPVs changes if wholesale demand does not meet demand expectations of 40,000 units.

    b) Repeat the sensitivity analysis to show how the distribution of NPVs changes if retail demand does not meet demand expectations of 9,000 units.

2. Perform a sensitivity analysis to show how the distribution of NPVs changes if variable costs per jar increase.

3. As a consultant to the Clarks, write a brief memo (350 words or less) summarizing your findings on how NPV is affected by changes in either demand or variable cost estimates. Include a table summarizing important financial information to support your findings.

Material Provided

The file FN2L2P3.xls contains seven worksheets:

L2P3MEMO	A partially completed memo that you can use to summarize your findings.
L2P3	A partially completed worksheet that you can use to calculate the NPV of the project.
L2P3MEMOS	A completed worksheet containing a sample memo that summarizes the findings on how sensitive NPV is to changes in demand and variable cost estimates.
L2P3S	A completed worksheet containing the solution for the NPV of the project.
L2P3SWHOLESALE	A sensitivity analysis on wholesale demand as required in part 2. a).
L2P3SRETAIL	A sensitivity analysis on retail demand as required in part 2. b).
L2P3SVARIABLE	A sensitivity analysis on variable cost as required in part 3.

Procedure

To complete part 1:

1. Open the file FN2L2P3.

2. Click the sheet tab L2P3. Study the layout of the worksheet. Rows 5 to 20 contain the data related to the calculation of the project's NPV. Rows 22 to 49 are set up for you to calculate the NPV of the project. Some of the formulas have already been entered for your convenience.

3. Enter in row 29, beginning in column D and copying to column M, the formulas to calculate wholesale demand for each year of the project.

4. Enter in row 30, beginning in column D and copying to column M, the formulas to calculate retail demand for each year of the project.

5. Enter in row 34, beginning in column D and copying to column M, the formulas to calculate the variable costs for each year of the project.

6. Enter in cell C41 the formula to calculate the present value (PV) of the operating cash flows.

7. Enter in cell B43 the capital cost of the jam processor. Cell C43 displays the PV of the CCA tax shields.

8. Enter in cell C46 the formula to calculate the PV of the amount of working capital to be received in year 10.

9. Enter in cell B47 the salvage value of the jam processor in year 10. Cells C47 and C48 display the PV of the salvage value and the lost tax shields.

10. Enter in cell C49 the formula to calculate the project's NPV.

11. Save a copy of your worksheet. If you did not obtain an NPV of $17,449, print a copy of your worksheet and compare your results with the solution worksheet L2P3S (click the sheet tab L2P3S to display the solution).

To complete part 2. a):
Wholesale demand sensitivity analysis

1. Display your completed worksheet from part 1 or the solution sheet L2P3S.

2. Choose Tools Scenarios Add.

3. In the Scenario name text box, type **–3.33%**. *Do not* press ENTER.

4. If you are using L2P3S, you will get the error message "Scenario names must be unique." Delete the existing scenario names by highlighting each and clicking Delete. Now repeat step 3 and continue with the procedure.

5. Select the Changing cells text box and enter **D6**. This is the cell address for the value of the wholesale demand. Click OK.

6. In the text box for Scenario Values, enter the new value for wholesale demand. This value should be **38668**, corresponding to a decrease in demand of –3.33%. Click OK.

7. Repeat steps 2 to 5 to create the following three additional scenarios:

Scenario name	Changing cells	Scenario values
–6.67%	D6	37332
–10.00%	D6	36000
–16.67%	D6	33332

8. Once you have added the final scenario, the Scenario Manager box should be displayed. Select Summary.

9. Select Scenario Summary and enter **C49** in the Result Cells text box. This is the value of the NPV for different levels of wholesale demand in the first year of the project. Click OK.

10. A Scenario Summary worksheet is created. Your results should resemble Exhibit 2-19. Click the sheet tab and rename it L2P3WHOLESALE.

11. Print a copy of L2P3WHOLESALE.

Exhibit 2-19
Sensitivity of NPV to Year 1 Wholesale Demand

	Wholesale demand	
Percentage decrease	Resulting demand	NPV
0.00%	40,000	$17,449
3.33	38,668	15,125
6.67	37,332	12,795
10.00	36,000	10,472
16.67	33,332	5,819

To complete part 2. b):

The same procedure can be used to do a sensitivity analysis of the first year's retail demand, after deleting the scenarios entered for part 2. a). The changing cell in this case is D9 instead of D6. The results of this analysis appear in Exhibit 2-20 and in the L2P3SRETAIL solution sheet in file FN2L2P3.xls.

Exhibit 2-20
Sensitivity of NPV to Year 1 Retail Demand

| | Retail demand | |
Percentage decrease	Resulting demand	NPV
0.00%	9,000	$17,449
3.33	8,700	16,058
6.67	8,400	14,668
10.00	8,100	13,278
16.67	7,500	10,498

To complete part 3:

To complete the variable cost sensitivity analysis, repeat the procedure that was used for the sensitivity analysis of the first year's wholesale demand, after deleting the scenarios entered for part 2. b). The changing cell in this case is D11 instead of D6. The results of this analysis appear in Exhibit 2-21 and in the L2P3SVARIABLE solution sheet in file FN2L2P3.xls.

Exhibit 2-21
Sensitivity of NPV to Changes in the Forecast of Variable Costs

| | Variable costs/jar | |
Percentage increase	Variable costs of jam per jar	NPV
0.00%	$0.95	$17,449
3.33	0.98	10,735
6.67	1.01	4,022
10.00	1.05	(4,930)
16.67	1.11	(18,356)

COMMENTARY

The solution sheet L2P3SWHOLESALE shows the sensitivity of NPV to the year 1 wholesale demand. For example, if the demand is 3.33% less than forecast, which implies that the starting demand is 38,668 (cell E8) rather than 40,000 units (cell D8), the NPV will drop to $15,125 (cell E10), a drop of 13.32%.

The solution sheet L2P3SRETAIL shows the sensitivity of NPV to retail demand. For example, if the demand is 3.33% less than forecast, which implies that the starting demand is 8,700 units (cell E8) rather than 9,000 units (cell D8), the NPV will drop to $16,058 (cell E10), a drop of 8.0%. Thus, NPV is more sensitive to changes in wholesale demand than to changes in retail demand.

The solution sheet L2P3SVARIABLE shows the sensitivity of the NPV to the first year's forecast of variable costs. The scenario analysis shows that if variable costs are 3.33% higher than forecast, which implies a variable cost of $0.98 (cell E8) rather than $0.95 (cell D8), the NPV will drop to $10,735 (cell E10), a decrease of 38.5%. The breakeven point for variable costs is approximately $1.03.

As a consultant to Kate and James Clark, you should indicate in your memo that the project to manufacture strawberry jam is feasible. You should also indicate that the project's NPV is more sensitive to variable costs than either wholesale or retail demand. Include an exhibit illustrating the effects of percentage changes in wholesale demand, retail demand, and variable costs on the project's NPV. Also include a brief analysis of the effects of each variable on the project's NPV in order to emphasize the extent of the adverse effect. The worksheet L2P3MEMOS provides an example of a memo that summarizes the findings of the analysis.

CONCLUSION

Sensitivity analysis has been used in this computer illustration to demonstrate how the distribution of a project's NPVs is affected by changes in each input variable, one at a time. In this project, a change in variable costs demonstrates greater adverse effects on the distribution of NPVs than changes in either wholesale or retail demand.

Chapter 3
Long-Term Sources of Funds

CHAPTER OVERVIEW

This chapter describes the basic features of the securities most commonly used by firms to raise medium- or long-term financing. To meet their needs for medium- and long-term funds, firms borrow from banks and issue bonds, preferred shares, and common shares. Knowledge of the features and characteristics of these instruments is important for the financial manager, who is responsible for designing and issuing securities. The attributes of securities affect their valuation in the market and the ability of the firm to sell them. Knowing these attributes will enable the financial manager to identify the method of financing that will minimize the cost of funds to the firm.

Any businessperson should be aware of the major financing alternatives available to firms. Section 3.1 describes the characteristics and features of term loans from banks. Generally, term loans are used for medium- or long-term financing, or as temporary arrangements until the economic environment or the firm's situation permits it to issue more permanent securities such as bonds, preferred shares, or common shares. Remember that the finance perspective on determining cost differs from the accounting perspective. In finance, the concern is the effective annual interest cost, which accounts for compounding in future periods. In accounting, interest is measured, recorded, and reported on a time basis. It is reported as an expense of the period during which the borrowed amount is unpaid.

Section 3.2 covers the various types of bonds and bond provisions. Bonds are more permanent than bank loans but less permanent than preferred shares. They are debt obligations that require the issuer to pay the holder fixed contractual cash payments at specified dates. Given the long-term nature of the fixed payments associated with bonds and the dynamic nature of market interest rates, a firm may find it advantageous to refinance a bond issue.

In Section 3.3, you learn the conditions under which bond refinancing is advantageous. From the finance perspective, the goal is to determine whether a particular bond issue should be refinanced. Once again, the accounting perspective differs from the finance perspective because accountants are more interested in knowing when debt is extinguished and how to classify the gain or loss on debt extinguishment.

The types and features of preferred shares are analyzed in Section 3.4. Similarly to bonds, preferred shares make fixed dividend payments to shareholders and these dividends determine the value of the preferred shares. Preferred shares can be refinanced to decrease the cost of capital to the firm. In Section 3.5, you learn the basic model by which preferred shares can be valued, the conditions under which refinancing is advantageous, and how to perform analysis to determine whether or not a preferred issue should be refinanced.

The general features of common shares and issues that concern shareholders are described in Section 3.6. Common shareholders are the owners of the firm. They are entitled to vote in the election of members to the board of directors and on important issues. Also, they are entitled to any residual profits from the firm's operations.

Finally, Section 3.7 describes the processes by which common shares are issued and sold to investors. Although the explanations are intended for common-share issues, they also apply to bond and preferred-share issues.

Learning Objectives

After completing this chapter, you will be able to:

- Describe the most common types of bank loans and calculate the effective annual rates on these loans.

- Summarize the factors to be concerned with when choosing a financial institution.

- Identify and explain the various types of bonds and bond provisions.

- Analyze the refunding of a bond issue.

- Identify the types and features of preferred shares.

- Analyze the refinancing of a preferred-share issue.

- Identify and explain the rights associated with common-share ownership.

- Explain the process used to issue corporate securities.

- Compare and contrast public issues and private placements.

- Explain how rights are used to raise equity capital.

This knowledge will provide you with the professional skills to:

- Give counsel on financing to meet the organization's goals.

- Identify, analyze, and advise on financial instruments to minimize the financial risk of the issuer, investor, or lender.

- Give an opinion on the capital structure of the organization to maximize the organization's value.

- Evaluate and advise on the implications of an organization's access to resources.

- Identify the financial implications of operational strategies.

HOW THIS CHAPTER RELATES TO OTHER CHAPTERS IN THIS BOOK

Much of this chapter is descriptive. You will find the information set out here valuable throughout the remaining chapters, particularly Chapters 4, 5, and 6. In Chapter 4 we continue the discussion of financing alternatives by examining capital structure theory. In Chapter 5 we look at the impact of financing alternatives by considering a firm's dividend policy. In Chapter 6 we revisit the investment decision, but from a different perspective than the NPV technique of Chapter 1; Chapter 6 allows the investment decision to interact with the financing decision.

Overall, the information you will find in this chapter is practical. It will help you to value securities and decide the financing alternative most suitable for a firm's particular needs. Although this chapter describes the features and characteristics of bank loans, bonds, preferred shares, and common shares in general terms, in practice lenders and borrowers often design more sophisticated financing instruments. Therefore, you may find real-world loan and bond issues with characteristics that vary considerably from the ones described in this book.

You should further note that the material here is presented from the issuer's perspective. It is geared toward the financial manager whose job it is to raise long-term funds by negotiating loans with banks or issuing bonds, preferred shares, or common shares. These arguments may not be applicable to the investment manager, whose primary job is to buy securities for investment purposes, or for the commercial lender, whose job is to make decisions to invest money for a financial institution.

3.1 BANK FINANCING

Loans from commercial banks are an important source of financing for firms, especially for small and medium-sized firms. The majority of bank loans are short term. However, banks also grant intermediate- and long-term loans, with maturities ranging from one to as long as 25 years.

For their short-term, day-to-day requirements, firms normally use revolving lines of credit. A **revolving line of credit** is a variant on a straight loan. The firm negotiates a line of credit, at a predetermined interest rate, and the lender advances funds as required to cover the firm's cash outlays. As the firm deposits its cash receipts in its bank account, they are applied to reduce the outstanding loan balance whenever there are funds available to do so. This inflow/outflow, fluctuating nature of the loan balance explains why this type of line of credit is called "revolving." The firm only pays interest on the portion of the line of credit that it uses, plus a commitment fee for the portion it does not use. While this makes it more expensive than a straight loan, it gives the firm guaranteed access to additional borrowings at a predetermined interest rate.

A **promissory note** is a written promise that commits the borrower to pay the lender a specified sum of money either on demand or at a fixed future date, with or without interest. A bank loan is created when a promissory note is negotiated between a borrower and a lender, as funds are needed. The promissory note often specifies the amount borrowed, the interest rate, the repayment schedule (in a lump sum or instalments), any collateral offered as security, and any other terms of the loan.

Term Loans from Banks

A **term loan** is a loan for a specified amount to be repaid over a specified period of time. Term loans are often used to finance capital equipment or plant, or to provide permanent working capital. They are preferable to other forms of financing when the cost of issuing bonds or other securities is too high. They are also used when cash is needed temporarily until cash flows from operations are sufficient to repay the loan.

An **instalment loan** is a type of term loan that specifies that the borrower will pay equal periodic payments (often monthly, quarterly, or yearly). These instalment payments include the accrued interest on the outstanding balance plus a portion of the principal. The principal portion is calculated so that the entire loan will be gradually repaid as instalments are made. The last instalment reduces the balance to zero.

A popular form of instalment loan is a mortgage. This type of loan is secured by the property that is financed by the loan and is amortized over equal instalments. Another form of instalment loan requires equal periodic principal payments to amortize the loan over the agreed term. Such a loan is called a **level principal repayment loan**. The interest portion of the periodic payment is determined as the interest on the outstanding balance over the instalment period. Under this arrangement, the monthly payments decrease with time as the outstanding balance gradually declines with principal payments.

For example, consider a $10,000 loan at 6% to be amortized over five years with annual payments. Under a mortgage arrangement, the annual payment would be $2,373.96, which includes principal repayment and interest. Exhibit 3-1 shows the mortgage amortization schedule.

Exhibit 3-1
Mortgage Amortization Schedule

Starting balance	Annual payment	Interest payment	Principal payment
$10,000.00	$2,373.96	$600.00	$1,773.96
8,226.04	2,373.96	493.56	1,880.40
6,345.64	2,373.96	380.74	1,993.22
4,352.42	2,373.96	261.15	2,112.81
2,239.61	2,373.96	134.35	2,239.61

For a level principal repayment loan, the principal repayment per year would be $2,000. The total annual instalment would also include the interest on the outstanding balance incurred during the period. Exhibit 3-2 shows the amortization schedule for the level principal repayment loan.

Exhibit 3-2
Level Principal Repayment Amortization Schedule

Starting balance	Principal repayment	Interest payment	Total payment
$10,000	$2,000	$600	$2,600
8,000	2,000	480	2,480
6,000	2,000	360	2,360
4,000	2,000	240	2,240
2,000	2,000	120	2,120

When the principal portion of an instalment is less than the amount needed to amortize the loan over the agreed term, the balance remaining at the end of the term is known as a **balloon payment**. The borrower usually pays this amount with the last instalment or negotiates a new term loan to amortize the remaining amount to zero. Such loans are known as **balloon loans**.

In some instances, instalments may only pay the interest on the loan, with no allowance for principal repayment. In this case, the entire principal will be due at the end of the loan term. This type of loan is called a **bullet loan**.

Term loans are generally granted on the ability of the firm to generate cash flows. The lender relies on the long-term profitability of the firm for repayment. Lenders prefer instalment loans to balloon or bullet loans because they reduce the risk that the borrower will not have enough cash to repay the loan at maturity.

Term loans are often secured by capital assets or by the equipment purchased from the proceeds of the loan. Gradual repayment of the principal is desired to ensure that the economic value of the collateral does not fall below the outstanding balance of the loan.

Borrowers are normally required to meet certain financial requirements related to working capital, new debt issues, and dividend payments. Borrowers may be restricted from taking actions that may affect the ability of the firm to repay the loan. Such provisions are often listed as covenants attached to the loan agreement. **Covenants** are provisions placed by the lender on the borrower in order to protect the lender against possible default of a loan. Any violation of these covenants will make the loan immediately due and give the lender the right to call the loan.

Consider the article entitled "Loose Lending?" on page 160. Its author, Lyn Perlmuth, indicates that the supply of funds available from banks can be affected by both market factors and regulations. During periods of tight money conditions, regulators try to encourage banks to be more aggressive in their lending practices. Regulators express concern when banks unjustifiably withhold credit from worthy customers, as this may hurt the economy.

During periods of good credit conditions, banks become aggressive in their lending practices. Aggressive lending practices also concern regulators. In this case, the concern is the stability of the banking system. Granting loans with relaxed covenants or extending credit to borrowers of questionable credit quality may lead to high rates of default by borrowers, may weaken the financial positions of banks, and may undermine the confidence of depositors. Reflect upon what happened in the summer of 2007. A drop in the housing market led to significant losses in the stock market and a gloomy outlook for the overall economy. When house prices dropped it became apparent that many borrowers were over-extended. By the fall of 2007, previously generous lending practices looked like they might result in a global credit crunch.

The article shows that the lending practices of banks vary from one firm to another depending on the creditworthiness of the firm and the circumstances in the market. When market conditions are tight, banks prefer lending to mature companies that have assets that can be used for collateral. However, as market conditions become easier, mature companies, which are sophisticated and more aggressive, shift to raising money directly from the market by selling their own securities. Consequently, banks shift their attention to smaller companies. Because these companies do not have the kind of assets that bankers consider as collateral, banks become willing to make unsecured loans. The article also shows that lenders can be innovative if the demand for loans warrants flexibility. For example, banks are willing to make loans with relaxed restrictions.

Loose Lending?

Lyn Perlmuth

Now that banks have rediscovered the lost art of making loans, regulators are nervous that they'll abandon credit standards.

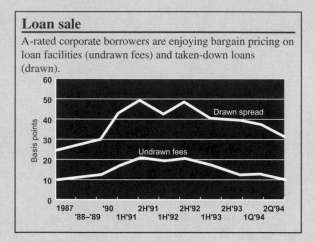

Loan sale

A-rated corporate borrowers are enjoying bargain pricing on loan facilities (undrawn fees) and taken-down loans (drawn).

Banks are lending again—at lower pricing levels and with looser covenants. Moreover, a significant number of these more relaxed loans are in the risky, leveraged category.

The trend, a reversal of tight lending policies that drew flak from regulators in recent years, has the same folks fretting again, for the opposite reason. Concerned about a repeat of the loan debacles of the 1980s, Federal Reserve Board chairman Alan Greenspan and Comptroller of the Currency Eugene Ludwig have chastised banks for a perceived weakening in credit standards and urged them to avoid drifting into loose lending policies.

Pricing of both investment-grade and below-investment-grade credits would seem to support the regulators' fears. Spurred on by the recovering economy and corporations' growing need for capital, banks have been eager to lend, creating a highly competitive loan market. . . . Even as rising interest rates have been deterring corporations from issuing fixed-rate debt, banks have been offering them sweet loan terms reminiscent of the late '80s.

All-in pricing (the interest rate and the fees) on new loans drawn down from credit facilities by single-A-rated corporations averaged 31 basis points in this year's [1994] second quarter, according to New York–based Loan Pricing Corp. That's close to the favourable spreads of 1990. And the 11 basis points banks charged such borrowers on committed but undrawn funds in the second quarter of this year mirrored the fees for 1989–90. Pricing for drawn-down loans on non-leveraged credits for double-B borrowers slipped to 1 basis point below that charged in 1990.

Not surprisingly, as the cost of capital declined across all rating categories, the volume of new corporate loans rose dramatically from January 1 through September 30 of this year. Most notably, leveraged loans syndicated during the first three quarters totaled $56.3 billion—more than twice the volume for all of 1993.

Hard data on the easing of loan covenants is unavailable, but bankers themselves report that the restrictions embedded in loan agreements have been relaxed significantly. Indeed, in loans for some strong investment-grade companies, such as Pepsico, covenants have disappeared altogether.

Since word of borrower-friendly deals has spread, a number of companies have gone back to their banks demanding more attractive terms. In October Tacoma, Washington's First Healthcare was able to slash pricing and ease covenants on a $360 million facility set up a year earlier, saving the nursing home subsidiary of Hillhaven Corp. $1.7 million a year at its current outstanding balances, says treasurer Robert Schneider.

First Healthcare, whose parent's subordinated debt is rated below investment grade by Moody's Investors Service (B2) and by Standard & Poor's Corp. (B–), wangled a highly favorable loan amendment. The pricing on its $85 million revolver, based on a grid tied to leverage, was chopped from LIBOR plus 2% to LIBOR plus 1.375%. On its term loan, which was increased to $165 million from $145 million, the rate declined from LIBOR plus 2.125% to LIBOR plus 1.375%. Even nicer, the commitment fee on unused balances plunged from 50 basis points to 37.5.

The revised covenants allow First Healthcare more flexibility to make acquisitions and lay out capital without obtaining approval from the bank group, led by Morgan Guaranty Trust Co. and Chemical Bank.

Whether rumblings from the regulators will cause bankers to tighten their lending practices is an open question. Some contend the market may be starting to tap on the brakes. "On the general matter of pricing and structure of loans we're beginning to see signs of a bottoming out," says James Lee, senior managing director in charge of structured finance at Chemical. In the meantime, corporate borrowers are lining up to take advantage of a bargain loan sale not seen since, well, the '80s.

Source: *Institutional Investor Magazine,* December 1994.

Advantages of Term Loans

Term loans provide several advantages to both the lender and borrower over other forms of financing for a firm.

Advantages to the Lender

- Term loans offer security to lenders because they are often backed by capital assets such as buildings and equipment. They can be structured so that the cash flows from the asset coincide with the interest and repayment schedule of the loan.

- Term loans do not have to be registered with provincial securities commissions as is required for bond issues.

- Issue costs are much lower for term loans, especially when the loan amount is small.

Advantages to the Borrower

- Loan provisions can be worked out more quickly than the provisions for more complex instruments such as a bond issue. Consequently, the borrower can obtain the cash more quickly.

- Term loan provisions are more flexible than bond provisions.

- Any changes in the term loan contract can be negotiated more easily and it can be tailored to the borrower's needs.

The article "Loose Lending?" demonstrates some of the advantages of using a term loan. According to the article, First Healthcare was able to renegotiate the rate and the covenants on its loan agreements. The revised covenants allowed First Healthcare more flexibility to make acquisitions and lay out capital without obtaining approval from the current lender.

Cost of Bank Loans

The costs of bank financing include costs of maintaining a compensating balance and direct interest costs.

COMPENSATING BALANCE

A **compensating balance** is the average minimum cash balance that a borrower is required to keep on deposit with the lending institution. For example, if a compensating balance is 8% of the amount of the loan and the principal amount is $50,000, the borrower is required to keep $4,000 on deposit with the lender. The effect of the compensating balance is a higher effective interest rate on the loan. To illustrate, suppose the contractual interest rate on a $50,000 loan is 10%. The borrower is obligated to pay $5,000 per year, although the amount that can be used for the purposes of the loan is only $46,000. Thus, the effective interest rate of the loan is $5,000 ÷ $46,000 = 10.87%. If all else is equal, a loan with a compensating balance generally has a higher effective interest rate than a similar loan without a compensating balance.

Banks often use a compensating balance to forge a longer-term relationship between the borrower and the lender. The cost of a compensating balance can be used to offset the cost of other banking services such as the processing of payroll and demand deposit transactions. For example, a bank might accommodate a borrower by lowering the nominal interest rate on a loan and adding a compensating balance requirement to make up the rate differential.

Direct Interest Costs The interest costs of loans vary for different types of borrowers and for all borrowers over time. In general, interest costs depend on economic conditions. Direct interest costs for a particular borrower depend on the risk of the borrower, the term to maturity, and the size of the loan. The **prime rate** is the interest rate that banks charge their most favoured and creditworthy clients. Banks try to compete with the corporate paper rate and they may be willing to match market rates even if these rates are lower than the prime rate. For smaller borrowers, rates generally range from prime to 2.5% above prime. Rates are often fixed but can be floating or adjustable. These rates may be set as a fixed percentage above the prime rate or some other publicly known rate.

The direct interest costs of a loan may not reflect the effective interest rate on the loan due to the many ways in which interest on bank loans can be quoted. Canadian regulations require lenders to disclose the effective interest rate to borrowers. The **nominal interest rate** is the stated or contracted interest rate on a bank loan. Nevertheless, financial managers should be aware of the various ways of calculating effective rates on bank loans.

The nominal interest rate is quoted on an annual interest basis. The interest calculation is based on the outstanding balance and the interest is paid at the end of the year. For example, consider a simple interest loan of $50,000, which requires the borrower to pay $5,000 at the end of each year over which it is outstanding. The effective rate on this loan is the same as the nominal interest rate, which is 10%. The **effective annual rate (EAR)** is equal to the amount of annual interest divided by the amount of the outstanding balance. Thus, the effective interest rate on an annual interest basis is:

$$\text{Effective annual rate} = \frac{\text{amount of annual interest}}{\text{outstanding balance}} \quad \textbf{(Equation 3-1)}$$

Often, the effective annual interest rate is quoted on an annual basis but the borrower has to pay the interest on the outstanding balance more than once a year. In such cases, the number of compounding periods is separately specified. If not specified, it should be set equal to the number of interest payments per year. The effective annual rate is then calculated as:

$$EAR = \left(1 + \frac{k_{nom}}{m}\right)^m - 1.0 \qquad \textbf{(Equation 3-2)}$$

where
$\quad EAR = $ effective annual rate
$\quad k_{nom} = $ nominal or stated interest rate
$\quad m = $ number of compounding periods per year

The effective annual rate is higher than the nominal rate because loan payments are being made on a more frequent basis than the annual payment. For example, consider the case of a term loan for which interest payments are made quarterly. If the nominal rate is 10%, the effective annual rate will be:

$$EAR = \left(1 + \frac{0.10}{4}\right)^4 - 1.0 = 0.1038 \text{ or } 10.38\%$$

It must be emphasized that Equation 3-2 assumes that the frequency at which interest is compounded per year is equal to the number of payments per year, which may not always be the case. Canadian mortgage rates are often quoted on a yearly basis, for example 8%, compounded semi-annually. This means that the compounding frequency for the mortgage is 2. Yet the mortgage payments are made monthly, that is, 12 per year. In this case, the effective annual rate is calculated as:

$$EAR = \left(1 + \frac{0.08}{2}\right)^2 - 1 = 0.0816 \text{ or } 8.16\%$$

As explained earlier in this section, Canadian financial institutions are required to reveal the true rates to customers. In practice, the frequency of compounding per year is assumed to be equal to the frequency of payments per year unless the compounding frequency is clearly stated. Therefore, when the compounding frequency of mortgage rates is different from the number of payments, the mortgage rate always specifies the compounding frequency. For the rest of this book, the number of payments will be used as an indicator of the compounding frequency unless otherwise stated.

Types of Interest Costs

Interest costs can be calculated on a simple or discount basis.

Simple Interest Loans with Compensating Balance
Compensating balances increase the effective interest rate on bank loans because part of the loan is charged interest without being used. For loans with terms of one or more years, the effective annual rate is calculated as:

$$EAR = \frac{k_{nom}}{1.0 - CB} \qquad \textbf{(Equation 3-3)}$$

where
$\quad CB = $ compensating balance as a percentage of the total loan amount

The borrower has to borrow more than its fund requirement in order to have a compensating balance amount. The denominator of Equation 3-3 represents the percentage of the loan's face value actually used by the borrower. The face value of the loan needed to obtain a given amount of funds may be determined by:

$$\text{Face value} = \frac{\text{funds needed}}{1.0 - CB} \qquad \textbf{(Equation 3-4)}$$

For example, suppose the funds required are $50,000 and the interest is 10%, with a 20% compensating balance for a period of one year. The effective annual rate is:

$$\text{EAR} = \frac{0.10}{1.0 - 0.20} = 0.125 \text{ or } 12.5\%$$

The face value of the loan is:

$$\text{Face value} = \frac{\$50,000}{1.0 - 0.20} = \$62,500$$

For loans with more frequent periodic payments than on an annual basis and for which the compounding frequency is not separately specified, the effective annual rate is calculated as:

$$\text{EAR} = \left[1 + \frac{\dfrac{k_{nom}}{m}}{1.0 - CB} \right]^m - 1.0 \qquad \textbf{(Equation 3-5)}$$

where CB is as defined in Equation 3-3. For example, if loan payments are made quarterly and the compounding frequency is not separately specified, the effective annual rate is:

$$\text{EAR} = \left[1 + \frac{\dfrac{0.10}{4}}{1.0 - 0.2} \right]^4 - 1.0 = 0.131 \text{ or } 13.1\%$$

Discount Interest Loans With **discount interest loans**, the bank deducts the interest from the loan amount in advance. Hence, the effective annual rate of interest on the amount actually used is higher than the nominal rate. For example, consider a one-year term loan for $10,000 with a nominal rate of 10% deducted up front. The borrower will receive $9,000 as the proceeds from the loan. The effective annual rate on this loan is:

$$\text{EAR} = \frac{\text{interest}}{\text{face value} - \text{interest}} \qquad \textbf{(Equation 3-6)}$$

or equivalently:

$$\text{EAR} = \frac{k_{nom}}{1.0 - k_{nom}} \qquad \textbf{(Equation 3-7)}$$

In this example:

$$EAR = \frac{0.1}{1.0 - 0.1} = 0.1111 \text{ or } 11.11\%$$

This treatment is required because the borrower will have the privilege of using the amount of $9,000, while the interest payment is $1,000. Thus, the effective annual interest rate is above the nominal 10% rate. In this example, 11.11% is often referred to as the **non-discounted equivalent rate**. It is the rate that will make a one-year, $10,000 loan at 10% with interest paid up front equivalent to a one-year, $9,000 loan at 11.11% with interest paid at year end. The loans are equivalent because either loan will provide the borrower with a $9,000 cash inflow at the beginning of the year and require a $10,000 cash outflow at the end of the year.

The effective annual rate on a discounted loan is equal to the non-discounted equivalent if the payments are made once a year. For loans with more frequent periodic payments than once a year, the effective annual rate can be obtained as follows:

1. Obtain the non-discounted equivalent rate for one compounding period.

2. Compound the non-discounted equivalent rate for the appropriate number of periods.

This process yields:

$$EAR = \left[1 + \frac{\dfrac{k_{nom}}{m}}{1.0 - \dfrac{k_{nom}}{m}} \right]^m - 1.0 \qquad \textbf{(Equation 3-8)}$$

If in the previous example the compounding period is six months, the effective annual rate can be calculated as:

$$EAR = \left[1 + \frac{\dfrac{0.1}{2}}{1.0 - \dfrac{0.1}{2}} \right]^2 - 1.0 = 0.1080 \text{ or } 10.8\%$$

In general terms, the face value of a discount interest loan is:

$$\text{Face value} = \frac{\text{funds needed}}{1 - \dfrac{k_{nom}}{m}} \qquad \textbf{(Equation 3-9)}$$

Continuing with the previous example, if the borrower requires $10,000 up front and the bank offers a 10% discount interest loan with a compounding period of six months, the face value of the loan needed will be:

$$\text{Face value} = \frac{\$10,000}{1 - \dfrac{0.10}{2}} = \frac{\$10,000}{0.95} = \$10,526$$

Discount Interest Loans with Compensating Balance When the bank deducts interest up front and requires the borrower to maintain a compensating balance, the effective annual interest rate must be adjusted for both. For loans with terms of one year or a multiple of years, the effective annual rate, where payments are on an annual basis, is calculated as:

$$EAR = \frac{k_{nom}}{1.0 - k_{nom} - CB} \qquad \text{(Equation 3-10)}$$

The face value of the loan needed to obtain the desired funds is determined by:

$$Face\ value = \frac{funds\ needed}{1.0 - k_{nom} - CB} \qquad \text{(Equation 3-11)}$$

Suppose in the previous example the interest is paid up front and the bank requires a 20% compensating balance. Then:

$$EAR = \frac{0.1}{1.0 - 0.1 - 0.2} = 0.1429\ or\ 14.29\%$$

The face value of the loan is:

$$Face\ value = \frac{\$10,000}{1.0 - 0.1 - 0.2} = \$14,286$$

Choosing a Financial Institution

When selecting a financial institution as a potential source of funds, borrowers should be particularly concerned with the following factors:

- *Lending practices.* Financial institutions have different policies toward risk. Some follow relatively conservative lending practices while others are creative. The bank's policy reflects the attitudes of the bank's officers and the characteristics of the bank's deposit liabilities. For example, the credit risk of a borrower may not be acceptable to a small financial institution. Yet a large financial institution may accept the risk because the large number of loans may help in reducing the overall risks of a group of marginal accounts (portfolio diversification effect).

- *Willingness and capacity to provide advice and counsel.* Some loan officers are active in counselling their clients. This service is particularly important in the initial and formative years of a firm.

- *Loyalty to its customers.* The willingness of a financial institution to support its clients during difficult economic times is similar to an option obtained by a borrower that may be used in the future to obtain additional funds.

- *Lender's stability.* The higher a lender's degree of stability, the more willing it will be to help customers during difficult times. A lending institution is considered to be stable if it is well capitalized, has stable sources of funds, enjoys a high reputation in the financial market, and has an established record of good financial performance. A borrower who cannot independently determine a financial institution's stability may inspect the lender's rating, provided by the credit rating agencies. You will learn more about credit rating agencies later in this chapter.

- *Industry specialization.* The degree to which a financial institution specializes in lending to an industry affects the ability of customers in the industry to obtain loans from the financial institution. For example, larger financial institutions have separate departments specializing in different kinds of loans. Specialization in specific lines such as agriculture, oil and gas, and high technology products can help the borrower obtain more creative cooperation and active support from the lender.

■ *Other support services.* Services such as the provision of foreign exchange accounts and transactions, international trade services, and electronic fund transfers can be valuable for small as well as large firms.

Visit Air Canada's Web site, found in the Web Links section at the end of this chapter, to view the many different types of loan arrangements it uses.

3.2 BONDS

A **bond** is a debt contract between the borrower and the lender. The borrower receives a fixed amount, the principal, at time 0 and promises to pay the interest periodically and the principal at maturity. A bond normally carries a face value of $1,000 (the principal). The maturity of long-term bonds is usually about 20 to 30 years. Yet companies may be willing to issue bonds with shorter terms to maturity, such as 10 years or less, if they believe that current interest rates are temporarily high and likely to drop in the near future.

Public utilities and other capital-intensive industries rely heavily on long-term debt to finance their operations. Manufacturing companies are also heavy users of long-term debt but to varying degrees. Large firms normally enter capital markets at least once every two years to re-fund old debt or to finance new projects. These firms often have a continuous need for new funds. They use revolving lines of credit to finance projects until the borrowed amount becomes large and warrants a new debt issue. A plan of issuing bonds only to raise large amounts of debt will save costs over the long run. Because the fixed cost per issue of bonds is almost the same for large or small issues, the fixed cost per dollar will be lower for larger issues.

The **bond indenture**, also called the **deed of trust**, is the formal agreement between the issuer of a bond and the bondholders. The indenture covers the terms of the bond issue and the features that affect the market value of the debt. It also covers the terms that affect the future flexibility of the issuer in issuing new debt, retiring old debt, or changing the terms of the agreement. Bond indentures contain such features and provisions as:

■ amount of the issue

■ type of bond

■ property pledged, if any

■ protective covenants, including requirements to maintain specified levels of working capital and other important ratios, restrictions on future dividend payments, and limitations on new debt issues or leases

■ provision for a sinking fund

■ redemption rights or call privileges

■ extendibility and retractability

■ convertibility

■ warrant privileges

Securities commissions approve indentures to ensure all material information is revealed to the public. Approval certifies that no information is missing but makes no judgment regarding the quality of the bond or the required yield. In addition, regulations require that a trustee be appointed to ensure that the issuing company adheres to the terms of the indenture. The issuer pays the fees for the trustee services. To view an example of an indenture, visit the Bell Canada Enterprises Web site listed in the Web Links section at the end of this chapter.

An **offering memorandum** provides detailed information on a bond indenture and is part of the package used by investors in making decisions. It includes information such as the coupon rate, provisions related to voting rights, and any special provisions that relate to the bond issue.

Types of Bonds

Bonds can be classified as secured or unsecured depending on the collateral arrangement. **Secured bonds** are backed by a pledge of specific assets. **Unsecured bonds** are backed only by the earning power of the borrower and a claim against residual assets.

For examples of secured bonds, review the Rogers Communications Annual Report. Instructions can be found in the Web Links section at the end of this chapter.

Mortgage Bonds Secured bonds are specifically guaranteed by certain assets. An example of a secured bond is a mortgage bond. A mortgage is a legal document containing an agreement pledging land, buildings, or equipment as security for a loan. The mortgage entitles the lender to take ownership of the pledged properties if the borrower fails to repay the principal or the interest when due. The lender holds the mortgage until the loan is repaid, at which time the mortgage is cancelled or destroyed. It is not exercised unless the borrower fails to satisfy the terms of the loan.

Mortgage bonds are similar to mortgages, which are used to finance home purchases. In the case of a mortgage bond, a mortgage against a corporation's property is deposited with a trustee, usually a trust company, which sees that the terms of the loan contract are followed. The amount of the loan is divided into portions, usually $1,000 or multiples thereof, and each investor receives a bond as evidence of proportionate participation in the loan to the company. The same percentage of ownership is used to settle any claims under the terms of the mortgage. There are many types of mortgage bonds.

First Mortgage Bonds Sometimes, a company's asset may be mortgaged twice to secure two bond issues. **First mortgage bonds** (sometimes called **senior mortgage bonds**) are bonds that rank ahead of any other bonds secured by the same asset. They constitute a first charge on the asset. In case of liquidation, the interest and principal of first mortgage bonds are paid from the sale of the mortgaged asset. If cash from liquidation is not enough, the first mortgage holders become general creditors with rights equal to the rights of other creditors with regards to the balance owed to them after receipt of the liquidation proceeds. If cash from liquidation is more than the claims of the first mortgage bonds, the additional cash is distributed to other creditors.

Second Mortgage Bonds Second mortgage bonds, also called **junior mortgage bonds**, are junior in priority to the claims of first or senior mortgage bonds. In case of liquidation, once the rights of first mortgage holders are satisfied, second mortgage holders have first claims against the remaining cash from liquidation of the mortgaged asset. If no cash or insufficient cash is left, second mortgage holders become general creditors with claims against the assets of the firm for the balance owed to them after receipt of any available cash.

Debentures **Debentures** are unsecured bonds. The only protection to the buyer of these bonds is the good faith of the issuer. They are the direct obligation of the issuing company but do not have a specific claim or an assignment on any particular asset or property. In liquidation, a debenture ranks behind secured bonds. The quality of debentures depends on the creditworthiness of the issuer and its ability to repay from general revenues. Thus, debentures are issued mainly by large and financially strong corporations that have established credit records.

Subordinated Debentures **Subordinated debentures** are debentures that are junior to other securities issued by the company. In case of liquidation or reorganization, the claims of subordinated debentures are considered only after the claims of regular debenture holders and other types of debt, including bank loans.

Debentures with Warrants A **warrant** is a certificate giving the holder the right to purchase additional securities at a stipulated price within a specified time limit. An example of a warrant is a certificate that gives the holder the right to buy five shares of Bell Canada Enterprises at $45 per share any time over the next 5 years. Warrants may be attached to debentures, preferred shares and common shares to make them more attractive to investors.

In the article that follows, entitled "U.S. Investors Hungry for Euro Hybrids," the author, Danielle Robinson, describes the environment in which debentures with warrants are issued. As you read, note the following:

- Warrants are attractive to investors as long as investors expect higher yields because of the equity characteristic of warrants.

- Attaching warrants to debentures seems to increase the acceptability of low-grade bonds, also known as junk bonds, as investors hope for high returns on the warrants.

- The market for securities with warrants is dominated by institutional investors who are more sophisticated than individual investors and are willing to accept risk for the prospects of high returns.

- Given the attractiveness of the equity characteristic of warrants, issuers can raise funds at reasonable coupon rates despite their low credit rating.

Perpetual Bonds **Perpetual bonds** are bonds that have no maturity. The issuer is under no obligation to retire the issue and the holder will receive interest payments forever. The bonds can be sold in the market.

Domestic, Foreign, and Eurobonds **Domestic bonds** are denominated in the currency of the issuer's country and sold in the issuer's domestic market. For example, the Canadian dollar–denominated bonds issued by Bell Canada Enterprises (BCE) and sold in Canada are domestic bonds.

Foreign bonds are issued in a country other than the country of the issuer. They are denominated in the currency of the foreign country in which they are issued. A Bell Canada bond denominated in Swiss francs, issued and sold in Switzerland, is called a foreign bond.

U.S. Investors Hungry
for Euro Hybrids

Danielle Robinson

High-yield investors in the U.S. have seen returns in their domestic market fall sharply. To ensure continued inflows to their funds they need a new source of high-yield paper. U.K. and European companies in search of hybrid or mezzanine financing will find a ready market in the U.S.

The thirst for strong double-digit returns among U.S. high-yield fund managers sparked a rash of junk bond deals with warrants in the fourth quarter of 1993. Some bankers believe that the increased acceptance by fund managers of bond-with-warrant deals will open the way for U.K. and European issuers to tap the private placement or even public high-yield market more aggressively with their own cum-warrant deals.

To date, only a handful of U.K. and European companies have launched such issues into the U.S. private placement market. In these cases, the warrants, although detachable, are usually retained by the investors in the bonds for the life of the issue and are not traded separately. The warrants are exercisable into ordinary shares and are sterling-denominated.

However, some firms, Wertheim Schroder among them, are beginning to see an increase in demand for these types of securities, especially given the increasing willingness of U.S. investors to extend their analysis beyond American markets.

The ability to execute such U.K. deals was exemplified in September last year when Wertheim managed to place $75 million worth of senior notes with warrants attached for the U.K. aggregates company Bardon Group, which is a weak triple-B and whose financial performance, given its exposure to the construction industry, has suffered during the recession. The Bardon warrants, for 3.5% of the company's shares, had coverage of 20% of the offering, and the strike price equated to a premium of 25%. Although they were detachable, the deal was sold to private investors who are holding the notes to maturity, and so neither the notes nor the warrants have traded.

The deal was split evenly into three tranches to give the company debt-payment relief in the earlier years of the deal and to satisfy investor appetite for different maturities. All three tranches had warrants attached. Tranche A was a five-year bullet priced to yield Treasuries plus 160 basis points; tranche B comprised eight-year notes with a seven-year average life priced at Treasuries plus 175pb; and tranche C was an issue of nine-year notes with an eight-year average life priced at Treasuries plus 190bp. By attaching warrants, Bardon Group managed not only to cut the cost of its issue but also to increase its equity base.

The deal, says Stephen Schechter, managing director at Wertheim Schroder in New York, "saved them well over 100bp compared with the cost of issuing straight notes."

Schechter adds that the deal, with the warrant exercise price struck well out of the money, means that the hybrid debt/equity does not dilute the company's shareholder base in the early years.

A Play on Sector Recovery

Although the deal was tough to place, given the poor recent performance of Bardon during the recession, it was taken up by a total of five U.S. private placement investors, who were confident that the deal would provide them with a play on the perceived upside for the U.K. construction industry.

In many cases, the U.S. market is more receptive to such issues than Europe, says Schechter. "There is no real efficient private placement market in the U.K. and the point is that credits that are not single-A or better struggle to enter the U.K. market. U.S. institutions, however, have the manpower and analysis skills to understand triple-B transactions. Also, remember that U.S. institutions tend to keep the warrants until maturity. In Europe they will normally sell them once they are in the money, so there is a different philosophy of the holder."

The Bardon deal has a special currency feature that enhances its attractiveness to U.S. investors. The investor can exercise the warrants using either cash or notes. If notes are used, the exchange rate is $1.50/£1, a rate that was fixed at the pricing of the notes. If the dollar weakens to, say, $1.75/£1, using the notes to exercise the warrants results in a lower exercise price and would be preferable to using cash. If the exchange rate goes to, say, $1.25/£1, however, using cash to exercise the warrants would result in a lower exercise price.

Schechter expects the market to grow this year (1994) for non-U.S. bond-with-warrant deals, especially for marginal credits wanting to raise funds at the cheapest possible price to retire higher-costing debt.

Although investment-grade deals are targeted at a different group of investors, the fact that the domestic junk bond with warrant market has suddenly taken off has increased the likelihood of emerging-market and lesser credits — say, BB-rated U.K. and European companies — tapping the U.S. high-yield investors with cum-warrant deals.

At the time of going to press, nearly 20 corporates, most particularly U.S. casino companies, had raised about $1 billion in the fourth quarter of 1993 in the junk bond market by offering investors bonds with warrants, a tool that has not been popular since the mid-1980s. The instrument was a favourite of defunct junk bond house Drexel Burnham Lambert, which used it to make hard-to-sell issues more attractive, distributing the warrants to favoured clients and employees.

Mutual Fund Interest

This time round the warrants are held by junk-bond mutual funds, which buy them in a bid to boost their returns; at the time of going to press in late December these were at 16.7% per year. The mutual funds have been impressed with deals such as that of Hollywood Casino Corp., a Dallas-based venture, which raised $90 million with the issue of 14% senior notes with warrants before its initial public offering in May. Since the IPO, the units (the senior notes with warrants) have more than doubled. Another deal, by Grand Casinos in Minneapolis, issued warrants for 13% of its stock; the stock doubled in price and investors received a 28-fold return on the warrants.

Normally, junk bond funds do not buy stock and would sell the warrants, but with these deals the high-yield fund manager is often looking to do better in terms of return on the warrant portion of the deal than the bond, and the bulk of the price-talk will focus on the warrants. U.S. mutual funds also like debt-with-warrant deals, because many of them are not allowed to have direct equity stakes, in the same way that corporate high-yield paper itself is seen by more conventional fixed-income investors as an equity substitute.

Source: *Corporate Finance*, January 1994.

Eurobonds are denominated in a currency foreign to the country in which they are sold. A Bell Canada bond denominated in U.S. dollars and sold in the United Kingdom is an example of a Eurobond.

The market for Eurobonds is known as the Euromarket, and the market for all international bonds is known as the international bond market. Eurobonds can be issued in a number of different currencies. The Euromarket is outside any domestic jurisdiction and is regulated by the International Securities Market Association (ISMA).

Strip Bonds Strip bonds (also known as **zero coupon bonds**) do not promise any cash flows to the owner until maturity, when the face value is paid back to the owner. Thus, they do not make periodic coupon payments.

In Canada, corporations issue few strip bonds. Yet investment dealers are active in creating these bonds to satisfy the demand from investors who find attractive features in strip bonds. An investment dealer can create a strip bond by acquiring a block of existing high quality bonds (usually Government of Canada bonds) and then separating the individual interest coupons from the underlying principal of the bond. The coupons and the principal are then sold separately at significant discounts to their face values.

Consider the following example showing how a strip bond is created:

An investment dealer has 20 bonds. Each bond has a face value of $1,000, a maturity of 5 years, and a coupon rate of 10% paid semi-annually. Each bond promises 10 coupon payments and will pay $50 every 6 months. The 20 bonds will pay $1,000 ($50 × 20) every 6 months.

The cash stream expected from the 20 bonds grouped together can be divided into 30 strip bonds with a $1,000 face value for each strip:

- The face values ($1,000 each) of the 20 bonds at maturity are 20 strips. Each of these strips has a maturity of 5 years.

- The first set of coupon payments, one coupon payment of $50 from each of the 20 original bonds, will mature 6 months from today. This set will make another strip with a face value of $1,000. This strip will have a maturity of 6 months.

- Similarly, sets 2, 3, 4, 5, 6, 7, 8, 9, and 10 of coupon payments will each make a strip with a face value of $1,000. The maturities of these strips are respectively 1, 1½, 2, 2½, 3, 3½, 4, 4½, and 5 years.

Holders of strip bonds do not receive interest payments. Strips are purchased at a discount from the face value to provide the return for investors. The size of the discount determines the return.

Bond Provisions

Corporate bond indentures may contain several options and provisions. The most common of these include the sinking fund, call provision, extension or retraction, and conversion. We examine each next.

Sinking- or Purchase-Fund Provision Corporate bonds can be retired by either a sinking fund or a purchase fund. Most corporate debt carries a sinking-fund provision. A **sinking fund** is money set aside by the bond issuer to provide for the repayment of all or part of a debt issue before maturity. This requirement is similar to the principal portion of a regular mortgage payment, except that the sinking fund is more flexible. The sinking fund allows the issuer the convenience of paying off part of the issue early, thus reducing the balloon refinancing risk of some issues.

Normally, a trust company is appointed trustee to administer a sinking fund. At a fixed date each year, the borrower must pay the required amount to the trustee. Usually, a specified set of bonds is retired by the provisions of the sinking fund. For example, bonds may be assigned serial numbers and every year a set of bonds carrying specified numbers are called for redemption. Alternatively, bonds may be chosen randomly for redemption. For example, every year a lottery may be held to decide which numbers will be retired. The bonds associated with the chosen numbers are then called for redemption.

A **purchase fund** is set up to retire, through purchases in the market, a specified amount of outstanding bonds or debentures only if purchases can be made at or below a stipulated price. A purchase fund accomplishes the same objectives as a sinking fund with minor differences:

- A purchase fund normally retires less of a bond issue than a sinking fund.
- There are no provisions for calling bonds as in the case of a sinking fund.
- A purchase fund normally has fewer mandatory provisions.

Sometimes, an issuer may be given the option to purchase bonds in the open market to satisfy the sinking-fund provisions. This method of purchase is more attractive to the issuer if the bond's market price is less than the face value. This occurs when the market rate for similar bonds is greater than the coupon rate.

Sinking funds and purchase funds reduce the investor's risk. As the bond issue is retired gradually, the risk of default is reduced. Moreover, the purchase-fund requirement adds liquidity to the bond issue as some bonds are purchased when the price falls below a given level. This action provides price support to the bonds and prevents their price from dropping significantly below face value.

Call Provision A **call provision** enables a bond issuer to reserve the right to pay off the entire bond issue before maturity. Consequently, bonds with call provisions are known as **callable** or **redeemable bonds**. Callable bonds are issued with a provision that allows the issuer to redeem partially or pay off the entire bond issue before the maturity date.

Most callable bonds have a period prior to the first call date during which they cannot be called. In this case, the call provision is referred to as a deferred call. For example, Air Canada had perpetual debt, which was denominated in Japanese yen. It was not callable until 2004. Had it not been called in 2004, it could not be called again until 2009. In any case, the issuer agrees to 30 or more days' notice when the bond is called or redeemed. The call provision also specifies the amount that will be paid to the bondholders if the bond is called. Generally, this amount is greater than the face value. This extra amount is known as a **call premium** and is typically set as a fraction of one year's interest. The fraction may be determined as the ratio of the years remaining to maturity to the original maturity. In other words, the call premium may be calculated as:

$$\text{Call premium} = C_y \times N_r \div N \qquad \textbf{(Equation 3-12)}$$

where

C_y = annual coupon
N_r = number of years remaining to maturity
N = number of years of original maturity

For example, if a bond is called after the first year, the call premium is $(N - 1) \div N$ of the coupon. As the maturity approaches, the call premium declines at a constant rate of $C_y \div N$ per year. Thus, if a bond has 20 years to maturity, a coupon of \$100 per year, and is called at the end of the fifth year, the call premium will be \$75 (100 $\times$ $^{15}\!/_{20}$). The investor receives the face value plus the \$100 in coupon payment plus \$75 in call premium.

Issuers include a call provision to take advantage of lower interest rates in the future. For example, if current rates are 9% and a company is expecting rates to drop to 8%, it may include a call provision in a bond issue to take advantage of the expected drop in rates. If rates drop to 8%, it may be advantageous to recall the bonds, pay the call premium, and refund the issue at the new lower rate. This process is known as bond refinancing. Section 3.3 will demonstrate the process by which management can analyze the profitability of bond refinancing.

A call provision may be included to retire all or a portion of the debt early. For example, a firm may be expecting cash flow in the future, which will not be used immediately for investment projects. In this case, the cash can be used to retire some of the debt issue to eliminate interest charges. This strategy is especially advisable when the rate at which the money was borrowed (the coupon rate) is higher than the rate at which additional funds can be invested.

A call provision remains the option of the issuer and will not be exercised unless it is advantageous to the issuer. This fact explains why firms are willing to pay a premium to call outstanding bond issues.

Extension and Retraction Provision Extension and retraction provisions are options of the holders of both bonds and preferred shares. They reduce the holder's risk of interest rate changes. Issuers include extension or retraction provisions to lower the investor's required rate of return on both bonds and preferred shares.

Bonds with an extension provision, called **extendible bonds**, are issued with a short term to maturity, typically five years, plus an option for the holder to exchange the debt for an identical amount of longer-term debt at the same or a slightly higher interest rate. Extendible bonds protect the holder against interest rate drops. If the interest rate drops, the holder cannot reinvest the funds at the rate obtained on the original bond. Thus, the investor will exercise the option of extending.

Bonds with a retraction provision, called **retractable bonds**, are issued with a long term to maturity plus an option for the holder to redeem the bond at par several years sooner (i.e., the holder can retract the term of the bond). Retractable bonds protect the investor in case of a rise in interest rates. For example, suppose a bond was originally issued to yield 9%. If rates rise, the interest that can be earned in the market will be higher than the rate currently received from the bond. If the holder sells the bond in the market, the sale price will be less than the face value. If the bond is retractable, the investor can retract it to obtain the face value instead of selling the bond and receiving less than the face value. If rates increase, the investor will not exercise an option of extending but will instead cash in the bonds and reinvest the funds in new bonds at higher rates.

Conversion Provision Bonds with a conversion provision, called **convertible bonds**, are similar to regular bonds except that they carry the additional option of being exchanged for common shares. They are similar to regular bonds in that they carry a fixed coupon rate to be paid periodically, a date of maturity, and a face value. Convertible bonds offer possibilities of capital appreciation through the right to convert the bonds into common shares at the holder's option. The conversion is usually done at a stated price indicated in the bond inden-ture. Investors are often given a window of time during which conversion can be done. Convertibles are usually callable at a small premium and after reasonable notice.

Some convertibles have a forced conversion clause built into them through a call or redemption provision. A company can call bonds for redemption at a stipulated price if its common shares trade at or above a specified price for a specified number of consecu-tive trading days. The price will be much lower than the level at which the convertible debt is trading because of the price rise of the common share, thus forcing conversion. Companies try to force conversion to improve their debt–equity ratio and to open the door for new debt financing.

Bond Ratings

Bond ratings are assessments of the possible risk of default prepared by independent pri-vate companies that specialize in bond rating, known as bond rating agencies. The ratings depend on several factors that are perceived to affect the ability of the issuer to make the promised interest and principal payments in full and on time. Ratings do not take factors such as pricing or market risk into consideration, and they are expected to be used by bond purchasers as only one part of their investment process. Every rating is based on quantitative and qualitative considerations that are relevant for the borrowing entity. Important ratios considered in the ranking process include the firm's debt to asset ratio, times interest earned, the ratio of earnings to fixed obligations, and current ratios.

In Canada, there are two well-known rating agencies—the Dominion Bond Rating Service (DBRS) and Standard & Poor's. In the United States, two well-known bond-rating services are Moody's Investors Service (MIS) and Standard & Poor's (S&P) Corporation. Visit this chapter's Web Links section for these bond raters' addresses.

The purpose of the ratings is to help investors to decide the values of bonds in the market. As notations differ from one agency to another, Exhibit 3-3 shows the notations used by MIS, S&P, and DBRS. The highest-rated bonds, such as AAA, yield the lowest interest rates at any given time. As the rating drops below the AAA level, the yield increases to compensate buyers for additional risk.

Exhibit 3-3
Bond Ratings Used by MIS, S&P Corporation, and DBRS

MIS	S&P	DBRS	Meaning
Aaa	AAA	AAA	Highest credit quality
Aa	AA	AA	Superior credit quality
A	A	A	Satisfactory credit quality
Baa	BBB	BBB	Adequate credit quality
Ba	BB	BB	Speculative
B	B	B	Highly speculative
Caa	CCC/CC	CCC/CC/C	Very highly speculative, danger of default
Ca	C		Clearly speculative, danger of default
C	D	D	In default

Source: Dominion Bond Rating Service.

Companies that are financially weak often issue bonds carrying high yields to raise funds. Such bonds are known as junk bonds because of their low credit ratings. Normally, bonds with ratings of BB (or Ba for Moody's) and lower are considered junk bonds and typically pay more than 3 percentage points above AAA rated bonds. Canadian laws prohibit institutional investors such as insurance companies, banks, and pension plans from investing in junk bonds.

Advantages and Disadvantages of Long-Term Debt Financing

The major advantages to the issuer of long-term debt are the deductibility of interest payments for tax purposes, the ability to magnify profits through financial leverage, and the ability of current common shareholders to maintain their control over the firm. The disadvantages are the additional risk resulting from the higher financial leverage and the restrictions that might be imposed on the firm by lenders.

3.3 BOND REFINANCING

Reasons for Bond Refinancing

Bond refinancing is the process by which a company retires an outstanding bond issue from the proceeds of a new issue. The process is also known as **bond refunding**. The two terms may be used interchangeably.

Corporations conduct bond refinancing for two main reasons. First, a firm may refinance bonds to eliminate restrictive covenants. These covenants are often imposed to prevent the borrower from taking actions that might endanger the position of the lender by diluting the security of their bond holdings. They are intended to make the loan safer to the lender. The borrower may have agreed to these covenants at a time when they were not binding. However, as the borrower's financial condition improves, covenants may deprive the borrower of valuable investment options and strategies. This issue is demonstrated in the article "Loose Lending?" on page 160, which indicates that First Healthcare had binding covenants that were relaxed after negotiating with the lender. First Healthcare needed to remove the restrictions to open the possibility for new investments. Firms do not often have the flexibility to renegotiate the terms of bonds. Thus, bond refinancing is sometimes conducted to eliminate restrictive covenants.

Second, a firm may refinance bonds when the current rates at which it can borrow are lower than the coupon rate paid to its outstanding bondholders. There are many reasons for this difference. For example, the existing bonds may have been issued at a time when the firm's financial situation was weak. Consequently, the firm had to pay high coupon rates to attract lenders. Now the firm's situation has improved. As a result, the rate of return required by investors to buy the firm's bonds has dropped. The firm can issue bonds that promise coupon rates lower than the rates promised by outstanding bonds.

Bond Refinancing Analysis

The decision to refinance a bond issue should be treated as a project that compares the costs and benefits of replacing the current bond issue with a new bond issue. Refinancing entails eliminating the series of current cash flows required to service the existing bond issue and replacing it with a new series to service the new issue. Because the net cash flows of either alternative are indeed net outflows, the company must choose the lower outflow. The comparison must be done on a present value basis. Therefore, if the present value of the current stream is higher than the present value of the replacement, refinancing will increase the value to shareholders and should take place. Otherwise, refinancing will decrease the value to shareholders and should not take place.

The analysis of a bond refinancing comprises four steps:

1. Determine the net investment required to refinance the old issue. This step includes several components:
   - Cost of retiring the old issue (referred to as the "call premium"): This cost consists of the cash flows required to pay the call premium (not tax deductible).
   - Net flotation costs: Flotation costs incurred when issuing securities include an underwriter's fee and issuing expenses. The underwriter's fee is the spread or difference between the price the issuer receives and the offer price. Examples of issuing expenses include commissions, printing and engraving expenses, SEC registration costs, taxes, and legal, accounting, and trustee fees. According to Canadian tax laws, flotation costs can be divided equally across the years to maturity of the bonds or over 5 years, whichever is less, and deducted from income as expenses. Thus, when analyzing the refinancing of a bond issue, the after-tax net flotation costs are equal to the cash costs of flotation minus the present value of the tax shield from deducting flotation costs as expenses over the allowable years.
   - Net additional interest expenses that may be incurred during the bond overlap period: This period occurs because corporations would like to obtain the funds from the new issue before calling the old bonds in order to be sure of having the needed financing.
   - The proceeds from the new issue can always be invested in short-term securities during the overlap period, thus reducing the actual expense of overlap. To facilitate the calculation for the interest expense during the overlap period, assume that the underwriter remits the full proceeds.
2. Determine the incremental after-tax interest savings from refinancing.
3. Determine the present value of the after-tax interest savings from refinancing.
4. Determine the net present value of the refinancing. If the net present value is positive, refinancing should be undertaken. Otherwise, it is not justifiable to refinance a bond issue.

In a refinancing analysis, all cash flows should be discounted at the after-tax cost of new debt because the cash flows in a refinancing are known with certainty and do not present the firm with any additional risk other than the firm's default risk.

Remember that effective rates for the appropriate discounting period need to be used. For example, bond returns (yield-to-maturity) in North America are generally quoted as a stated rate per year, compounded semi-annually, while preferred-share yields are quoted as a stated rate per year, compounded quarterly. In both cases, the effective annual rate must be calculated before proceeding with the net present value analysis. We take you step by step through the refunding analysis in Minicase 3-1, which demonstrates the process of evaluating a bond refinancing decision.

MINICASE 3-1 REFINANCING A BOND ISSUE

Medical Equipment Inc. (MEI) is a fast-growing company. It has an outstanding callable bond issue that was issued 5 years ago and has 15 years remaining to maturity. At the time of issue, the company was not well known and interest rates were high. Consequently, MEI had to pay 12% in coupon payments to ensure the sale of $100 million of bonds at face value. Also, MEI was forced to accept a covenant that prohibits the firm from issuing any new debt. The proceeds were used to develop and market new equipment.

Since the initial issue, conditions have changed. The general level of interest rates has dropped. Also, MEI has been successful in developing new product ideas and has become famous. The only constraint is the lack of capital funds. Lenders are knocking at the company's doors to provide new financing, but the restrictive covenant imposed with the first bond issue prohibits new financing. The company is therefore eager to refinance the old issue. MEI's tax rate is 38% and the Treasury bill rate is 6%. Exhibit 3-4 provides a summary of other information available on the company.

Exhibit 3-4
Bond Refinancing at MEI

Bond	Old issue	Planned issue
Face value	$100 million	$100 million
Remaining or planned maturity	15 years	15 years
Likely overlap period	1 month	1 month
Coupon rate	12%, paid semi-annually	10%, paid semi-annually
Call premium/flotation costs	75% of the coupon rate	2% of the total face value

Assume for tax purposes that flotation costs include the underwriter's fee and the firm's issuing expenses, and that the investment banker does not withhold the underwriter's fee so that interest received during the overlap period is based on the gross proceeds of the new issue.

Should MEI go ahead and refinance the old issue?

Step 1: Determine the net investment required to refinance the old issue.

The net investment required to refinance the issue is equal to the call premium of the old issue, plus the net flotation cost of the new issue, plus the interest cost of the overlap period. That is:

$$\frac{\text{Net}}{\text{Investment}} = \frac{\text{call}}{\text{premium}} + \frac{\text{net flotation}}{\text{cost}} + \frac{\text{net additional interest expenses}}{\text{during the overlap period}}$$

- Call premium: $0.75 \times \$100,000,000 \times 0.12 = \$9,000,000$

- Net flotation cost: Flotation costs are $2 million (0.02 × $100 million), to be amortized over 5 years, given that maturity is 15 years. Thus, the firm can claim an annual flotation cost of $400,000 ($2 million ÷ 5) over the next 5 years. Each year

Case Continued >

the firm will realize tax savings equal to $152,000 (0.38 × $400,000). These future tax savings form an annuity, the present value of which can be obtained by discounting at the effective after-tax rate on new debt. The after-tax rate on new debt is 6.2% [10%(1 − 0.38)]. Thus, the effective annual rate is:

$$(1 + 0.031)^2 − 1 = 6.2961\%$$

The present value of the future tax savings is $635,155 ($152,000 × $PVIFA_{5,\,6.2961\%}$). Net flotation cost: $2,000,000 − $635,155 = $1,364,845.

■ Net additional interest expenses during the overlap period:

$$\$100,000,000 \times [(0.12 − 0.06) \div 12] \times (1 − 0.38) = \$6,000,000 \div 12 \times 0.62$$
$$= \$310,000$$

The 12% is the cost of the old debt issue and the 6% is the interest that can be earned on the short-term securities purchased with the funds raised.

Thus, the net investment is:

$$\$9,000,000 + \$1,364,845 + \$310,000 = \$10,674,845$$

Step 2: Determine the incremental after-tax interest savings from refinancing. Semi-annual interest on the old issue

$$= \$100,000,000 \times 0.12 \times (1 − 0.38) \div 2$$
$$= \$3,720,000$$

Semi-annual interest on the new issue

$$= \$100,000,000 \times 0.10 \times (1 − 0.38) \div 2$$
$$= \$3,100,000$$

Therefore, incremental semi-annual after-tax interest savings = $620,000.
Step 3: Calculate the present value of semi-annual interest savings. Present value of semi-annual interest savings

$$= \$620,000 \left(PVIFA_{30,\frac{6.2\%}{2}} \right) = \$620,000(19.3495)$$
$$= \$11,996,683$$

The present value of the semi-annual interest savings extends over 30 periods (15 × 2) and is discounted at the semi-annual after-tax cost of the new issue, 3.1%.

Step 4: Calculate the net present value of refinancing and determine whether or not to refinance.

The present value of interest savings minus the net investment for refinancing is:

$$\$11,996,683 − \$10,674,845 = \$1,321,838$$

Given that the present value of the interest savings outweighs the present value of the refinancing costs, MEI should go ahead with its refinancing plans.

This process, however, does not consider the value to MEI of refinancing to eliminate restrictive protective covenants that constrain its ability to issue new debt. The value of eliminating these covenants may justify refinancing a bond issue even if the net present value based solely on interest savings is not positive.

Generally, the net present value of refinancing is equal to:

$$\begin{array}{c} \text{NPV of} \\ \text{refinancing} \end{array} = \begin{array}{c} \text{NPV} \\ \text{based on} \\ \text{interest savings} \end{array} + \begin{array}{c} \text{present value} \\ \text{of eliminating} \\ \text{restrictive covenants} \end{array} \qquad \textbf{(Equation 3-13)}$$

Unfortunately, there is no standard procedure for estimating the value of eliminating restrictive covenants. However, one method is to calculate the present value of all future projects that can be undertaken by eliminating the covenants. For example, if MEI has a project that cannot be funded because of the covenant but if funded will generate $4 million in net present value, the value of eliminating the covenant can be estimated as $4 million. In this case, the value of eliminating the restrictive covenants adds further value to the refinancing of the old bond issue and the firm should go ahead with its refinancing plans.

3.4 PREFERRED SHARES

Preferred shares have some characteristics of equity, as they entitle owners to periodic dividend payments and have no specified maturity date. They also combine some characteristics of debt, as the payments are specified in the firm's charter and do not change in amount over time. In the case of liquidation, the claims of preferred shareholders are senior to common shareholders' claims but subordinate to creditors' claims.

Types of Preferred Shares

Many different kinds of preferred shares exist. We describe the most common types of preferred shares, next.

Straight Preferred Shares **Straight preferred shares** rank in priority ahead of common shares and behind debt in their claim to assets and earnings. They have a fixed dividend rate and trade in the market on a yield basis. Unlike common shares, straight preferred shares have no voting privileges and no potential for appreciation. Normally, they have no maturity.

Generally, a preferred share has a face value assigned by the issuer that is typically equal to the initial sale price. The preferred dividend is specified by the company's charter as a stated amount. For example, the annual dividend may be specified as $2.50 per share, paid quarterly. Alternatively, the dividend may be stated as a percentage of the face value. Preferred dividends are normally paid quarterly after approval from the board of directors.

Cumulative Preferred Shares **Cumulative preferred shares** require that unpaid dividends on such shares accumulate until the company is able to make full payment. Dividends to common shareholders are discontinued until all dividends in arrears are paid to preferred shareholders. In contrast, non-cumulative preferred shares entitle the shareholder to the payment of dividends in any year only when approved by the board of directors and declared by the company.

Convertible Preferred Shares **Convertible preferred shares** are similar to convertible bonds in that they enable the holder to convert the preferred shares into some other class of shares (usually common) at a predetermined price. The conversion must occur within a stated period of time. The price of the preferred shares is generally set at a modest premium (10% to 15%) above their conversion value in order to discourage an early conversion. Most convertible preferred shares are redeemable, forcing conversion to the underlying shares when the market price of the preferred shares rises above the redemption price. No commission is charged on conversion. These shares give the holder a more secure position than the common shareholder's as well as a chance of capital appreciation if the market price of the common shares rises sufficiently.

Retractable Preferred Shares **Retractable preferred shares** are similar to retractable bonds. A preferred shareholder can retract the shares at maturity by tendering the shares to the issuer for redemption. Some shares do not retract automatically. Hence, they become straight preferred shares if not retracted when the **election period**—the specified time within which preferred shares can be redeemed—expires.

Variable- or Floating-Rate Preferred Shares **Variable- or floating-rate preferred shares** pay dividends that fluctuate to reflect changes in interest rates. If interest rates rise, so do dividend payments. If interest rates drop, dividends also drop. Typically, the rate is tied to the prime rate, certificate of deposit rate, Treasury bill rate, or some other publicly known rate.

Preferred Shares with Warrants **Preferred shares with warrants** entitle the holder to purchase common shares of the issuer at a stated price without commission. Including warrants as part of a preferred-share issue increases its attractiveness because it enables buyers to participate in the appreciation of the common shares. Normally, the two securities are sold together as a unit.

Participating Preferred Shares **Participating preferred shares** entitle shareholders to share in the earnings of the company over and above their specified dividend rate.

Callable or Redeemable Preferred Shares **Callable or redeemable preferred shares** give the issuer the right to call the shares for redemption. Generally, the issuer pays a small premium above the face value per share as compensation to the holder of the redeemed shares.

Preferred-Share Provisions

Preferred shares may have the following provisions: voting rights, purchase or sinking funds, and protective covenants. We examine each in turn.

Voting Rights Under normal circumstances, preferred shareholders have no voting rights. However, if the firm does not pay a stated number of preferred dividends, it is common practice to assign voting privileges to the preferred shareholders. Moreover, preferred shareholders are usually given a vote on matters affecting the quality of their security.

Purchase- or Sinking-Fund Provision Similarly to bond issues, preferred shares may be issued with a purchase-fund or sinking-fund provision. With a purchase-fund provision, the company agrees to retire, through purchases in the open market, a specified number of preferred shares that are available at or below a stipulated price each year.

Under a sinking-fund provision, the company sets aside annually a stipulated percentage of net earnings or a fixed sum to gradually retire the preferred issue over a specified number of years. Money from the sinking fund is used to purchase the shares in the open market for redemption. If market purchases are unsuccessful in retiring the required number of shares, the remainder is called by a lottery for purchase by the sinking fund. Shareholders whose securities are called receive a fixed price per share, usually the par or stated value per share, plus accrued dividends, unpaid dividends, and a stated call premium.

Protective Covenants Preferred shares are usually issued with protective covenants. **Protective covenants**, also known as **protective provisions**, help in safeguarding the position of the preferred shareholders against any actions that may dilute the dividends of the security. Protective covenants make the issue more attractive to investors in comparison to similar issues without covenants. Some common covenants are:

- A working-capital maintenance clause requiring the company to maintain its viable financial position. For example, it prevents the company from seriously weakening its short-term cash position if dividends are paid on common shares.

- Restrictions on issuing further preferred shares to make sure the firm is not burdened by additional fixed obligations.

- A restriction on the sale of assets to guarantee that the preferred shareholders' capital is not weakened by asset disposal.

- A restriction on changing the terms of the preferred issue.

While debtholders' rights are found in the trust deed or indenture, preferred shareholders' rights are found in the charter of the company. Each issue of preferred shares is unique in its features.

Advantages and Disadvantages of Preferred-Share Financing

Compared to debt, preferred shares are usually more expensive for a firm because dividend payments are not a tax-deductible expense. For example, consider a firm that has a marginal tax rate of 35%, a bond issue paying 10% in annual coupon payments, and a preferred-share issue paying 10% in annual dividend payments. Given that the interest payments are deductible from income for tax purposes, the after-tax cost of debt is $(1 - 0.35) \times 10\%$, or 6.5%. The after-tax cost of preferred shares is still 10%.

Despite this disadvantage, corporations continue to issue preferred shares. Tax laws provide an incentive for institutional investors to invest in preferred shares. Dividends are not taxable if received from a taxable Canadian corporation, while interest income is taxable as regular income. Therefore, if all else is equal, a taxable Canadian company will prefer dividends to interest income. Moreover, individual investors pay a reduced tax rate on dividend income. These tax-induced preferences for dividends, as opposed to interest income, create investor demand for preferred shares. Sometimes, this demand allows a company to issue preferred shares that pay lower rates than the company's debt, although preferred shares are considered by investors to be riskier than debt.

Preferred shares are less risky to the issuer than bonds. They do not create the urgency that a debt issue creates. A firm has much more flexibility in deciding whether to declare a preferred dividend, while interest and principal repayment of debt are non-discretionary. Failure to make interest payments constitutes an act of default, while failure to pay preferred dividends has no legal consequences for the issuer. Straight preferred shares offer the advantage of avoiding the dilution of equity that results from a new issue of common shares.

Utilities and other capital-intensive companies are the most active in issuing preferred shares. Issuers opt for preferred-share financing over debt or common equity for several reasons:

- Issuers may be restricted in the amount of additional debt they can issue, preventing them from raising funds through such means.

- Common-share prices may be depressed and additional offerings may lead to dilution of per-share earnings.

- Companies with low marginal tax rates, because of high capital cost allowances or for other reasons, lose the tax advantage in issuing bonds as opposed to preferred shares. As previously indicated, these companies may be able to issue preferred shares at a lower yield than the yield on bonds.

3.5 PREFERRED-SHARE REFINANCING

Because preferred shares are similar to bonds in that they promise the holder fixed periodic payments over a predetermined period (or forever), analyzing the profitability of refinancing preferred shares is similar to analyzing the profitability of refinancing bonds. There are, however, major differences between preferred shares and bonds. These must be considered in the refinancing analysis of preferred shares:

- Preferred-share dividends are not tax deductible to the firm. In contrast, the other costs of retiring the preferred-share issue and the costs of selling a new issue are deductible, with the exception of the call premium costs.

- Preferred-share dividends are generally payable quarterly. Consequently, the present value of the cash savings from refinancing should be calculated and discounted on a quarterly basis.

- It is important to consider in the analysis any other outcome from refinancing that will affect the firm's refinancing decision. For example, if the preferred shares are refinanced with a debt issue or a common-share issue, the resulting changes to the capital structure will affect the firm's value. Also, refinancing may lead to the elimination of restrictive covenants that impose conditions on the ability of the firm to raise additional financing.

- Preferred shares often carry no voting rights unless the firm defaults on its dividend payments. In contrast, common shares normally carry voting privileges. Refinancing a preferred-share issue with a common-share issue may dilute the voting power of current shareholders.

Test your understanding of refinancing. Attempt the You Apply It minicase that follows.

Super Communications Corporation (SCC) has outstanding Series B cumulative pre-ferred shares. The shares were issued 10 years ago and have no maturity. They have a deferred-call option that becomes effective in one month.

Shares outstanding	2,000,000
Face value	$50
Quarterly dividend	$1.25
Call premium plus accumulated dividends	5%
SCC tax rate	40%
Risk-free rate	6%

Current interest levels and the recent upgrade in SCC's credit rating will enable the firm to refinance the share issue on more favourable terms. The firm's investment banker indicates that the firm can sell new preferred shares at $50 per share if quarterly dividends are $1.10. However, flotation costs are likely to be 8% of the total proceeds from the issue. SCC is likely to issue the new shares at least one month prior to paying off and retiring the old issue.

Should SCC refinance the preferred-share issue? Assume for tax purposes that flota-tion costs include the underwriter's fee and the firm's issuing expenses, and that the investment banker does not withhold the underwriter's fee, so that interest received dur-ing the overlap period is based on the gross proceeds of the new issue.

Answer

Step 1: Determine the net investment required to refinance the old issue.

The net investment needed to refinance the issue is equal to the call premium of the old issue, plus the net flotation cost of the new issue, plus the dividend cost of the overlap period. That is:

$$\text{Net investment} = \text{call premium} + \text{net flotation cost} + \text{net additional interest expenses during the overlap period}$$

- Call premium:

$$0.05 \times \$100,000,000 = \$5,000,000$$

- Net flotation cost: Flotation costs are $8 million (0.08 × 2,000,000 × $50), to be amortized over 5 years given that the shares will be perpetual. Thus, the firm can claim an annual flotation cost of $1.6 million ($8 million ÷ 5) over the next 5 years, which will result in an annual tax saving of $640,000 (0.40 × $1.6 million). These future tax savings form an annuity, the present value of which can be obtained by discounting at the rate of the new issue.

Given that the new issue will pay $1.10 quarterly and the net proceeds per share will be $50, the quarterly cost of the new issue will be:

$$\$1.10 \div \$50 = 2.2\%$$

You Apply It Continued >

The annual cost of the new funds will be:

$$(1 + 0.022)^4 - 1 = 9.09\%$$

Thus, the present value of the $640,000 tax savings over the next 5 years is:

$$\$640,000 \times \text{PVIFA}_{(5,\ 9.09\%)} = \$640,000 \times 3.8806 = \$2,483,584$$

Net flotation cost:

$$\$8,000,000 - \$2,483,584 = \$5,516,416$$

■ Net additional dividends during the overlap period:

$$2,000,000 \times \$1.25 \div 3 - [(1 - 0.4) \times 2,000,000 \times 50 \times 0.06 \div 12]$$
$$= \$533,333$$

The cost of the old preferred share dividend is a quarterly concept and is divided by three to determine the cost of the dividends for one month. The proceeds of the new preferred shares are invested at 6%, annual percentage rate, for one month, before tax.

Thus, the net investment is:

$$\$5,000,000 + \$5,516,416 + \$533,333 = \$11,049,749$$

Step 2: Determine the incremental quarterly dividend savings from refinancing.

Quarterly dividend on the new issue
$$= \$1.10 \times 2,000,000$$
$$= \$2,200,000$$

Quarterly dividend on the old issue
$$= \$1.25 \times 2,000,000$$
$$= \$2,500,000$$

Net savings per quarter
$$= \$300,000$$

Step 3: Calculate the present value of the quarterly dividend savings.

The savings are perpetual and should be discounted at the quarterly cost of the new issue (2.2%). Thus, the present value of the quarterly dividend savings is:

$$\$300,000 \div 0.022 = \$13,636,364$$

Step 4: Calculate the net present value of refinancing and determine whether or not to refinance.

Present value of dividend savings minus the net investment needed for refinancing is:

$$\$13,636,364 - \$11,049,749 = \$2,586,615$$

Because the present value of the refinancing costs is less than the present value of the dividend savings from refinancing, SCC should go ahead with its refinancing plans.

3.6 COMMON SHARES

Rights of Common Shareholders

Common shareholders are the owners of the company. As owners, they are entitled to any cash flows earned by the company above interest to bondholders and dividends to preferred shareholders. These cash flows are paid to common shareholders as dividends on their holdings or accumulated as retained earnings, which increase the share value.

The rights to residual cash flows expose common shareholders to substantial variability in their wealth. The residual cash flows will be relatively large during years of good profits and relatively low, sometimes negative, during years of poor profits. Remember, share values are directly affected by the firm's expected dividend payments—the cash flows shareholders expect to receive. As dividends are paid from the residual cash flows, the market price of the shares rises and falls depending on whether cash flows are high or low.

The market prices of common shares are more affected by market conditions than are bond or preferred-share prices. Because common shares are considered to be riskier investments than bonds and preferred shares, they should promise higher returns than bonds or preferred shares.

In the event of liquidation, the claims of government, employees, secured and unsecured creditors, and owners of bonds and preferred shares take priority over the claims of common shareholders. In return, common shares have more potential for capital appreciation, which is not available to other capital contributors.

Voting Rights As owners of the company, common shareholders normally have the right to vote on the selection of directors and on important matters. In principle, this right gives shareholders the ability to influence important decisions and to control the corporation.

Chapter 1 stated that in practice voting rights have little value for some shareholders, while for other shareholders voting rights are important. Some corporations have special provisions in their charters designed to preserve a desirable control structure. Bombardier Inc. founders managed to maintain control of the business by using two classes of shares, as demonstrated in the following article "Benefits of Two Classes."

Pre-emptive Rights Acknowledging that voting rights are important for some shareholders, some firms give their shareholders the right to preserve their proportions of ownership and control through **pre-emptive rights**. These rights give existing shareholders the privilege of buying from any new share issue an amount proportionate to their current degree of ownership.

Voting Scheme There are typically two methods of voting used to elect directors of corporations. **Non-cumulative voting**, also known as **majority voting**, requires one vote per share for each director up for election. This method does not leave much room for minority shareholders to affect the election of directors.

In contrast, **cumulative voting** is designed to enable minority shareholders to have a voice in the control of the company by permitting shareholders to cast their available votes for one candidate or many candidates at their discretion. For example, assume that four directors are up for election. A shareholder owning 100 shares of a company would dispose of 400 votes (100 × 4). The shareholder could use all 400 votes for one director, use 100 votes for each of the four directors to be elected, or choose any combination of

BENEFITS OF TWO CLASSES

One of the key characteristics of common shares is that one share equals one vote. Therefore, a shareholder owning 50,000 common shares of a company where 1 million common shares are outstanding owns 5% of the company and is entitled to 5% of the votes. (This shareholder is also entitled to 5% of the earnings available for common shareholders.) In Canada, however, there are a large number of companies with two classes of common shares: one class with superior voting privileges, one with subordinate. For the company's founders, this situation is highly attractive. By selling subordinate voting shares, the founders enjoy the advantage of raising financing using common shares without the disadvantage of losing control.

For example, Bombardier, a company based in Montreal with operations around the world, is a leading manufacturer of aircraft, rail transportation equipment, and motorized recreational products.[1] For the fiscal year ended January 31, 2002, the company had sales of over $21.6 billion and assets of $27.8 billion. The company has two classes of common shares. As of January 31, 2002, there were 342.4 million Class A shares and over 1 billion Class B shares outstanding. The total capital provided by the Class A shareholders was $47.4 million; the B provided $849 million. The A shares have 10 votes each; the B, one. For the common shares in total, there was a total of 4,453,234,222 votes. The Bombardier family, the offspring of Armand Bombardier, the company's founder, owned 81.9% or 280.4 million Class A shares. Therefore, the Bombardiers owned 20.4% of the total number of shares but had 63% of the votes, while only providing 4.3% of the common-share financing.

The opportunity to be able to sell subordinate voting shares has greatly benefited the Bombardier family. They have been able to retain majority control of the company while providing a minority of the common equity financing. The Bombardier family members, however, have not been the only ones to benefit from this arrangement—the subordinate shareholders have also profited. Consider that on January 31, 1993, the subordinate shares were trading on the TSX for $1.45 per share. During the 2002 fiscal year, the shares traded as high as $24.65 (implying an annual gain of 37%) and closed the fiscal year at $14.70 (an annualized gain of 29.4%). Obviously, allowing the founding owners control can benefit all shareholders.

---

[1] Bombardier, Inc., *2002 Annual Report and Management Proxy Circular*, May 3, 2002.

---

the 400 votes. Under such a scheme, minority shareholders can elect a chosen set of directors if they carefully concentrate their votes.

The number of shares required to guarantee the election of a desired number of directors is given by:

$$N = \left[\frac{d \times S}{D + 1} \right] + 1 \qquad \text{(Equation 3-14)}$$

where

N = number of shares required to elect a desired number of directors
d = number of directors the minority shareholders seek to elect
S = total number of shares outstanding
D = total number of directors to be elected

Test your skill. Try the You Apply It minicase that follows.

YOU APPLY IT CUMULATIVE VOTING AND COMMON SHARES

ABC Company has 1,000 voting shares outstanding and uses cumulative voting. The company has to elect 7 directors, but a minority group of shareholders wants to elect at least 2 particular directors.

Questions

Question 1: How many shares must the minority group have to ensure the election of the desired directors?

Question 2: How many votes will the minority group have?

Question 3: If the minority wants to elect two directors, how many votes are needed per director?

Question 4: What is the maximum number of directors the majority group can elect?

Answers

Question 1: How many shares must the minority group have to ensure the election of the desired directors?

$$\left[\frac{2 \times 1,000}{7 + 1} \right] + 1 = 250 + 1 = 251$$

Thus, the number of shares the minority group needs to elect two directors is 251.

Question 2: How many votes will the minority group have?

As there are 7 directors to be elected, the minority votes will be:

$$251 \times 7 = 1,757$$

Question 3: If the minority wants to elect two directors, how many votes are needed per director?

The number of votes per director will be:

$$\frac{1,757}{2} = 878.50$$

Question 4: What is the maximum number of directors the majority group can elect?

If the majority group wants to elect 6 directors, the number of votes per director will be:

$$\frac{(1,000 - 251) \times 7}{6} = 873.83$$

As this number is less than 878.50, the majority group cannot elect 6 directors. The maximum the group can elect is 5 directors

$$\frac{(1,000 - 251) \times 7}{5} = 1,048.6$$

using up to 1,048.6 votes for each.

Different Classes of Common Shares

As with Bombardier Inc., companies may issue more than one class of common shares. A second class may be created to raise equity capital without diluting the control of current shareholders. In practice, different companies have different classes of common shares and each class has different rights.

Restricted shares are shares that do not entitle shareholders to full voting rights; however, shareholders maintain their rights to participate to an unlimited degree in the earnings of the company and in its assets on liquidation. Generally, there are three categories of restricted shares:

- *Non-voting shares* do not have voting rights except perhaps in certain limited circumstances.

- *Subordinate voting shares* have fewer voting rights compared to other common shares. In this case, two or more classes of common shares exist and one class has greater voting rights on a per-share basis than the subordinate voting class. Bombardier Inc. subordinated one class of voting shares to the other.

- *Restricted voting shares* are limited in their voting rights to a certain percentage. For example, only 75% of shares can be voted by a person, company, or group.

Common-Share Financing: Advantages and Disadvantages

There are several advantages to common-share financing compared to other forms of long-term financing:

- Unlike debt, there are no required periodic cash payments associated with common shares. The company pays dividends only if earnings and cash flows are sufficient. Some firms choose to pay constant or slightly increasing dividends over time, but there is no obligation to pay these dividends. More importantly, forgoing payment does not constitute failure and does not lead to bankruptcy. The reasons for the various dividend policies observed in practice are explained in Chapter 5.

- Common shares never mature and they do not have to be repaid. They are a permanent source of capital, which reduces their risk to the issuer.

- Common-share financing improves the firm's debt-to-equity ratio. The increased amount of equity enables the firm to use more debt in the future. Firms restricted by covenants from issuing more debt or preferred shares can issue common shares to finance expansions and new projects. Moreover, common-share financing is desirable when a firm has more debt than is optimal, as additional equity decreases the weighted average cost of capital. In Chapter 4, we discuss the optimal capital structure and its relationship to the cost of capital.

Common-share financing also has several disadvantages:

- Common shareholders have voting privileges; hence, current shareholders lose some control when a company issues new common shares. Pre-emptive rights can be used to maintain a desired degree of control by an existing shareholder, but very few shares are currently issued with these rights.

- The cost of underwriting and distributing new common shares generally exceeds the cost of issuing preferred shares or debt.

- Investors demand higher returns on common shares than on debt or preferred shares. Therefore, if a firm has more equity than is required for the optimal capital structure, its weighted average cost of capital is higher.

- Dividends are not tax deductible for the firm, while interest paid to bondholders is a deductible expense. Consequently, one dollar in dividend payments is more expensive to the issuer than one dollar of interest payments.

3.7 ISSUING SECURITIES

The financial manager plays an important role in raising funds through the sale of securities to the public. In this section we analyze the major issues related to this process.

The sale of common shares is affected by general market conditions. Firms normally rush to sell shares during a rising market and try to time their sales when the market peaks. During these periods, the demand for new shares is particularly strong.

Private and Public Share Issues

One of the important decisions in raising funds through bonds, preferred shares, or common shares is whether to sell the securities through a private placement or a public offering.

A **public offering** is a sale of securities to the general public. Securities laws require the issuer to register the issue with provincial securities commissions. The issuer is required to publish a prospectus to provide information about itself and the securities to be sold and to distribute the prospectus to all potential buyers. Approval of registration by a securities commission certifies that all information relevant to the issue is included in the prospectus and that the information is accurate. Approval does not imply any conclusion regarding the merits of the security or the fairness of the sale price. Once approved, the shares can be traded freely in the market. Generally, most common-share issues and a portion of bonds and preferred shares are sold in public offerings.

In contrast, in a **private placement**, the issue is sold to a group of institutional investors such as insurance companies, pension plans, or mutual funds. The issuer is not required to publish and distribute a prospectus. Securities commissions consider such investors to be sophisticated enough to request and obtain the information provided by a prospectus before buying the securities. Thus, an issue sold in a private placement cannot be freely traded in the market. The majority of bonds and preferred shares are sold through private placements. However, very few common shares are sold in this fashion.

Private placements offer several advantages to the issuer:

- The flotation costs of a private placement are generally less than those of a public placement of similar size. Private placements do not have to pay the costs of registration, printing and distribution of prospectuses, or credit rating fees. Moreover, in a private placement, there are no selling expenses, management fees, or underwriting fees, because the deal is negotiated directly with investors.

- Private issues can be finalized more rapidly than a public offering. Registration and approval of a prospectus take time unless the security qualifies for a

prompt offering prospectus (POP). This is a short prospectus approved by the Ontario Securities Commission (OSC) for large corporations that file regular annual and interim financial statements with the OSC for at least 12 months and comply with the continuous disclosure requirements, regardless of whether they are issuing new securities.

■ Private placements provide more flexibility in issue size than public offerings. While the flotation costs of small public issues are prohibitively high, in private placements most of the transaction costs are eliminated through direct negotiations between investors and issuers, which makes small issues economically feasible.

■ Private placements provide greater flexibility regarding the terms of the issue. Because institutional investors are more sophisticated than general investors, it is easier to raise funds even though the arrangements for the security issue may be complex. Also, dealing exclusively with institutional investors makes it much easier to change the terms of an issue should the need arise.

Despite the lower flotation and administrative costs, private placements are generally more expensive than a public offering. Because privately sold securities lack liquidity, investors are likely to demand higher yields. Thus, they will buy the securities at deeper discounts than what might be obtained in a public offering. Private investors are also likely to demand tighter covenants on the issuer. Complying with tighter constraints creates additional costs, which increase the costs of funds from private placements.

Role of the Investment Banker

Public offerings generally involve one or more investment bankers and normally a syndicate of bankers. The **investment banker** serves as an intermediary between the issuer and the purchasers of the securities, providing advice regarding the type and terms of the securities to be issued and the market in which the securities are to be sold (private or public, foreign or domestic).

In public offerings, the investment banker assists in preparing documentation including the prospectus, securing approval from the securities commissions, and distributing the prospectus to potential investors. The investment banker also assists in setting the offering price.

In private placements, the investment banker assists in preparing the offering memorandum, which describes the proposed terms and provides information regarding the issuer. The investment banker also assists in negotiating the sale price.

Compensation to the Investment Banker Compensation to the investment banker or syndicate represents a significant portion of the issuer's cost. In a public offering, the underwriting group often charges a gross underwriting spread that ranges from 4% to 12% of the aggregate sale price of the issue. The **underwriting spread** is the difference between the sale and purchase price. The spread may be divided between three components:

■ The *management fee* covers assistance for designing the issue, preparing the documents and managing the offering process. This portion makes up 12% to 18% of the gross underwriting spread.

- The *underwriting fee* compensates the syndicate for taking the underwriting risk. This portion consumes 15% to 25% of the gross underwriting spread.
- The *selling fee* compensates the group for its marketing and selling efforts. It ranges from 57% to 73% of the gross underwriting spread.

Underwritten Offerings

Share issues are often underwritten by a syndicate of investment bankers. The issuer selects a securities firm to act as the lead investment banker and underwriter. After accepting the job, the lead underwriter invites others to participate in the underwriting and selling of the security. The underwriting group or syndicate offers to buy the entire issue at a guaranteed price for subsequent sale at a higher price.

Under this agreement, the underwriting group bears the risk that the security will not sell in the market as expected. For example, the group may agree to purchase a share issue for $10 per share, hoping to sell it later at $11 per share. Immediately after the agreement, the market may turn down, making it difficult for the underwriting group to sell the shares as expected. The group may be forced to sell the shares at a loss.

Generally, the syndicate has 30 days (or some other agreed period) during which it agrees not to sell any shares to the public at a price below the offering price. The lead underwriter is allowed to buy shares if the market price falls below the offering price. This action supports the price against any downward pressure. After the 30-day period, members of the selling syndicate can sell any remaining shares at the market price.

Negotiated Offerings

A **negotiated offering** is a sale of a security whereby the issuer negotiates the offering price and gross underwriting margin with the underwriting syndicate. Sometimes, companies may put the shares up for bidding and invite securities firms to submit bids to purchase the entire issue for resale to the public. This process is known as a **competitive offering**. The securities dealer assumes all the risk of the issue. In practice, securities dealers usually sell in advance parts or all of the issue to institutional investors. The remaining shares, if any, are usually sold quickly in the market. Also, given the risk of competitive offerings, only well-established firms and firms that qualify for prompt offering prospectuses can sell their shares under these arrangements.

Offerings on a Best-Efforts Basis

When an offer is not underwritten, the investment banker or syndicate will undertake to sell the issue on a best-efforts basis. Under a **best-efforts underwriting** arrangement, securities dealers do not purchase shares for sale, but they use their best efforts to sell the issue on behalf of the issuer at the highest possible price. Alternatively, the syndicate may buy the issue with a put option. The put gives the syndicate the right to return shares to the issuer when the market price drops significantly from the offering price prior to the sale of the entire issue. In this case, the issue will likely be withdrawn from the market. Normally, private placements, issues of less-known companies, and small issues are sold on a best-efforts basis or with put options.

Rights Offerings

Companies often offer common shares directly to their current shareholders through a **rights offering**. Under this type of offering, the company distributes certificates to its current shareholders, giving them the rights to subscribe to additional shares of the company at a specified price. Many companies specify in their charters that all share offerings of a particular class should be made exclusively through rights offerings. The pre-emptive right is a provision inherent in the ownership of common shares that enable current shareholders to maintain their control of the company. Unless stated otherwise, you should assume that a rights offering gives each existing shareholder one right for every share held. In practice this is often the case. The formulas provided in this book reflect this assumption.

In a rights offering, there are four important dates:

- The **announcement date** on which the company announces the rights offering.

- The **record date** on which the company distributes to its current shareholders of record one right for each common share held. A shareholder becomes a shareholder of record three business days after purchasing common shares.

- The **ex-rights date**, set two business days before the record date.

- The **expiration date** on which the right expires. The right can be exercised up to this date. The time to expiration is usually short, ranging from 15 to 45 days, because the company needs the proceeds from the sale of new shares.

Each right carries a subscription or exercise price. The time between the announcement date and the ex-rights date is known as the **rights-on period**. During this period, selling a share includes selling the right associated with this share. On the ex-rights date and after, the share will trade ex-rights and the right will trade as a separate security.

Rights are essentially call options on newly issued shares. Consequently, each right carries a non-negative market value. This value depends on many factors such as:

- exercise price
- price of the underlying share
- time to expiration
- variance of the underlying share price
- level of the risk-free rate

In particular, the lower the exercise price in relation to the market price, the more valuable the right will be to the holder. Issuers usually set the exercise price low enough to encourage holders to exercise their rights or to sell them in the market. Moreover, shareholders can purchase additional rights from other shareholders who wish to sell their rights. Companies sometimes issue over-subscription privileges whereby shareholders can over-subscribe to an issue. Any shares that are not subscribed under the regular rights offering are distributed to the over-subscribers on a pro rata basis.

The market value of a call option consists of time value and intrinsic value (we cover options in more detail in Chapter 7). The *time value* of a right is usually negligible, as the time to expiration is short. Thus, the value of a right is often approximated by its *intrinsic value*, which is determined by the difference between the market price of the underlying share and the exercise price.

The theoretical value of a right during the rights-on period is different from its theoretical value during the ex-rights period. During the rights-on period, the theoretical value can be approximated by:

$$R_{on} = \frac{P_{on} - E}{N + 1}$$

(Equation 3-15)

where

R_{on} = theoretical value of the right during the rights-on period
P_{on} = market price of the underlying share during the rights-on period
E = exercise price
N = number of rights required to purchase one new share (note that adding one to the denominator is required because the market price of the share includes the value of one right)

In contrast, the theoretical value of a right during the ex-rights period can be approximated by:

$$R_{ex} = \frac{P_{ex} - E}{N}$$

(Equation 3-16)

where

R_{ex} = theoretical value of a right during the ex-rights period
P_{ex} = market price of the underlying share during the ex-rights period

Equations 3-15 and 3-16 refer to the theoretical value of a right during the rights-on and the ex-rights periods. In practice, the actual value of a right will differ from its theoretical value because of transaction costs and shifts in supply that will push the market price above or below the theoretical value. For the purposes of this book, use the theoretical value formulas and ignore other factors. Attempt the You Apply It mini-case that follows.

YOU APPLY IT VALUATION OF A RIGHT

Mountain Gem and Jewellery (MGJ) has just announced a rights offering. The current common share price is $23. The rights entitle the holders to purchase MGJ shares at $20 per share for every 5 rights.

Questions

Question 1: What is the theoretical value of a right during the rights-on period?

Question 2: What is the theoretical value of a right during the ex-rights period if the share price ex-rights is $22.50?

Question 3: Suppose Stella, a shareholder of MGJ, owned 1,000 shares in MGJ before the rights offering. Stella has no money to purchase new shares. Will she lose or gain after the rights offering, and by how much?

You Apply It Continued >

Answers

Question 1: What is the theoretical value of a right during the rights-on period?

$$R_{on} = \frac{23 - 20}{5 + 1} = \$0.50$$

Question 2: What is the theoretical value of a right during the ex-rights period if the share price ex-rights is $22.50?

$$R_{ex} = \frac{\$22.50 - \$20.00}{5} = \$0.50$$

The share price during the ex-rights period is assumed to be less than the share price during the rights-on period by the value of the right. This is expected because the right will be traded separately from the share after the ex-rights date. With no change in the fundamental value of the underlying share, the share price during the ex-rights period will be less than the share price during the rights-on period by exactly the value of the right.

Question 3: Suppose Stella, a shareholder of MGJ, owned 1,000 shares in MGJ before the rights offering. Stella has no money to purchase new shares. Will she lose or gain after the rights offering, and by how much?

There are two scenarios for this question. If Stella ignores the rights and lets them expire, she will lose $500 because the market value of her shares ex-rights will be only $22,500 ($22.5 × 1,000). If, instead, she sells her rights in the market, she will receive $500 ($0.50 per right for 1,000 rights). The sale price offsets the loss on the shares.

Thus, the total value of Stella's wealth of $23,000 in MGJ is preserved. Stella's wealth is the same before and after the rights offering if she sells her rights in the market. Of course, this assumes there are zero transaction costs. In reality, investors must pay a transaction fee to exercise their rights. However, this fee is usually kept quite low to encourage investors to exercise.

It is important to understand that the pricing of rights in the market preserves the value to shareholders. As demonstrated by Question 3 of the You Apply It minicase above, in the absence of a fundamental change in the value of the share, the shareholder's wealth will not change as the share moves from the rights-on period to the ex-rights period.

CHAPTER SUMMARY

Chapter 3 describes the basic features and general characteristics of term loans from banks, bonds, preferred shares, and common shares. These are the securities most commonly used by firms to raise medium- or long-term financing. This chapter explains the conditions and circumstances under which the refinancing of either bonds or preferred shares is advantageous. The analytical framework by which the financial manager can determine whether or not a particular issue should be refinanced is also covered. Finally, this chapter teaches you about the processes by which securities are issued.

Key Terms

announcement date, page 193

balloon loan, page 159

balloon payment, page 158

best-efforts underwriting, page 192

bond, page 167

bond indenture, page 167

bond rating, page 175

bond refinancing, page 176

bond refunding, page 176

bullet loan, page 159

call premium, page 173

call provision, page 173

callable or redeemable bond, page 173

callable or redeemable preferred shares, page 181

compensating balance, page 162

competitive offering, page 192

convertible bond, page 174

convertible preferred shares, page 180

covenant, page 159

cumulative preferred shares, page 180

cumulative voting, page 186

debenture, page 169

deed of trust, page 167

discount interest loan, page 164

domestic bond, page 169

effective annual rate (EAR), page 162

election period, page 181

Eurobond, page 172

expiration date, page 193

ex-rights date, page 193

extendible bond, page 174

Important Equations

Effective annual rate for annual interest payments

$$\text{Effective annual rate} = \frac{\text{amount of annual interest}}{\text{outstanding balance}} \quad \text{(Equation 3-1)}$$

Effective annual rate for interest payments more frequent than an annual basis

$$EAR = \left(1 + \frac{k_{nom}}{m}\right)^{m} - 1.0 \quad \text{(Equation 3-2)}$$

where

    EAR = effective annual rate
    k_{nom} = nominal or stated interest rate
    m = number of compounding periods per year

Effective annual rate for simple interest loans with a compensating balance (annual interest payments)

$$EAR = \frac{k_{nom}}{1.0 - CB} \quad \text{(Equation 3-3)}$$

where

    CB = compensating balance as a percentage of the total loan amount

Face value needed to obtain the desired funds for a simple interest loan

$$\text{Face value} = \frac{\text{funds needed}}{1.0 - CB} \quad \text{(Equation 3-4)}$$

Effective annual rate for simple interest loans with a compensating balance for interest payments more frequent than an annual basis

$$EAR = \left[1 + \frac{\dfrac{k_{nom}}{m}}{1.0 - CB}\right]^{m} - 1.0 \quad \text{(Equation 3-5)}$$

Effective annual rate (non-discounted equivalent rate) for discounted annual interest payments

$$EAR = \frac{\text{interest}}{\text{face value} - \text{interest}} \quad \text{(Equation 3-6)}$$

or equivalently:

$$EAR = \frac{k_{nom}}{1.0 - k_{nom}} \quad \text{(Equation 3-7)}$$

Effective annual rate for discount interest loans for interest payments more frequent than an annual basis

$$\text{EAR} = \left[1 + \frac{\dfrac{k_{nom}}{m}}{1.0 - \dfrac{k_{nom}}{m}} \right]^m - 1.0 \qquad \textbf{(Equation 3-8)}$$

Face value needed to obtain the desired funds for a discount interest loan

$$\text{Face value} = \frac{\text{funds needed}}{1 - \dfrac{k_{nom}}{m}} \qquad \textbf{(Equation 3-9)}$$

Effective annual rate for loans with compensating balances that have terms of one year or a multiple of years and annual interest payments

$$\text{EAR} = \frac{k_{nom}}{1.0 - k_{nom} - \text{CB}} \qquad \textbf{(Equation 3-10)}$$

Face value needed to obtain the desired funds for a discount interest loan with compensating balance (annual interest payments)

$$\text{Face value} = \frac{\text{funds needed}}{1.0 - k_{nom} - \text{CB}} \qquad \textbf{(Equation 3-11)}$$

Value of a call premium

$$\text{Call premium} = C_y \times N_r \div N \qquad \textbf{(Equation 3-12)}$$

where

C_y = annual coupon
N_r = number of years remaining to maturity
N = number of years of original maturity

Net present value of bond refinancing

$$\begin{matrix} \text{NPV of} \\ \text{refinancing} \end{matrix} = \begin{matrix} \text{NPV} \\ \text{based on} \\ \text{interest savings} \end{matrix} + \begin{matrix} \text{present value} \\ \text{of eliminating} \\ \text{restrictive covenants} \end{matrix} \qquad \textbf{(Equation 3-13)}$$

Number of shares required to elect a desired number of directors

$$N = \left[\frac{d \times S}{D + 1} \right] + 1 \qquad \textbf{(Equation 3-14)}$$

where

N = number of shares required to elect a desired number of directors
d = number of directors the minority shareholders seek to elect
S = total number of shares outstanding
D = total number of directors to be elected

Theoretical value of a right during the rights-on period

$$R_{on} = \frac{P_{on} - E}{N + 1}$$

(Equation 3-15)

where

R_{on} = theoretical value of the right during the rights-on period
P_{on} = market price of the underlying share during the rights-on period
E = exercise price
N = number of rights required to purchase one new share

Theoretical value of a right during the ex-rights period

$$R_{ex} = \frac{P_{ex} - E}{N}$$

(Equation 3-16)

where

R_{ex} = theoretical value of a right during the ex-rights period
P_{ex} = market price of the underlying share during the ex-rights period

Web Links

Air Canada Consolidated Financial Statements

■ http://www.aircanada.com/en/home.html Go to "About Air Canada" at the bottom of the screen, then click on Investor Relations and finally Financial Reports to get the Annual Report. In its Table of Contents, look for the Consolidated Financial Statements to see the debt and equity sections of the Balance Sheet and corresponding notes describing the financing characteristics.

Bell Canada Enterprises

■ http://www.bce.ca/en/ To see copies of bond indentures, click on "Investors" and then "Bonds & Preferreds." Choose a security from the drop-down list. Then click on "Download the pricing supplement" to see the indenture for that security.

Bond Rating Services

■ **Standard & Poor's** http://www.standardandpoors.com

■ **Moody's Investors Service (MIS)** http://www.moodys.com

■ **Fitch Ratings** http://www.fitchinv.com/

■ **Dominion Bond Rating Service (DBRS)** http://www.dbrs.com/intnlweb/

■ **A.M. Best Ratings** http://www.ambest.com/

Investing in Bonds

■ http://www.investinginbonds.com/ "Bond Basics," a glossary of terms, headline news, and commentary from The Bond Market Association, the trade association representing the global bond industry.

National Bank's Financial Learning Centre

■ http://info.nbf.ca Under "Learning Centre" on the homepage, select "Investment Selector" to access information about preferred shares, bonds, and other investments by level of risk.

Reuters Financial News

■ http://www.reuters.com/home Reuters provides news to media outlets all around the world with the bulk of their business in financial news services and analysis. Click "Investing" to access a series of detailed submenus on a variety of investment topics.

Rogers Communications Bond Information

■ http://www.shoprogers.com To see the many different types of bond issues Rogers has outstanding, go to "For Business," then "Investor Relations," and finally "Bond Information." Under Investor Relations you may also obtain additional information on the company's bonds by searching the Annual Report using the term "bonds."

Securities Industry and Financial Markets Association (SIFMA)

■ http://www.sifma.org/ Includes links to Bonds Markets news bulletins and research, including statistical tables and a variety of research reports.

U.S. Treasury Bonds Rates

■ http://finance.yahoo.com/bonds Provides links to rates, summaries of the market, current news, and headlines, as well as a bonds "primer" containing a glossary of terms and types of bonds.

Self-Test Questions

Qualitative Questions

Answer each of the following questions in point form:

1. Why would corporations use term loans to finance their operations?
2. What are the various characteristics of term loans?
3. What are the popular types of bonds?
4. What are the ways in which bonds are partially or fully redeemed prior to maturity?
5. What are the dividend features of preferred shares?
6. What are the advantages and disadvantages of preferred-share financing?
7. What are the typical features of common shares?
8. What are the advantages and disadvantages of common share financing?
9. Why do corporations issue common shares using a private placement?
10. What is the role of the investment banker in public offerings?
11. What are some features of rights offerings?

Qualitative Multiple Choice Questions

1. Everything else being equal, which of the following combinations of term loan features will provide the lowest effective annual interest rate?
   i) Simple interest loans, annual compounding, and no compensating balance
   ii) Discount interest loans, quarterly compounding, and no compensating balance
   iii) Simple interest loans, monthly compounding, and a compensating balance
   iv) Discount interest loans, monthly compounding, and a compensating balance

2. Which of the following statements correctly describes Eurobonds?
   i) Bonds denominated in a currency foreign to the country in which they are sold
   ii) Bonds that do not promise any cash flows to the owner until maturity, when the face value is paid back to the owner
   iii) Bonds that have no maturity
   iv) Bonds issued in a country other than the country of the issuer, denominated in the currency of the foreign country in which they are issued

3. If a company has different classes of common shares, what restrictions are there on shareholders who purchase the "restricted voting shares" of the firm?
   i) These shareholders have no voting rights except in certain limited circumstances.
   ii) These shareholders have no voting rights.
   iii) These shareholders do not share in the regular dividends paid to other common shareholders.
   iv) These shareholders are limited in their voting rights to a certain percentage, so that the maximum percentage of shares that can be voted by a person, company, or group is specified.

4. When a firm borrows from a bank that requires a compensating balance, what is the effect of this requirement?
   i) To make more funds available for use by the borrowing firm to compensate for high bank service charges
   ii) To reduce the percentage of borrowing costs to compensate the borrower for not fully funding the investment project
   iii) To increase up-front service charges to compensate for charging below-market interest rates on loans
   iv) To increase borrowing costs

5. The investment banker or syndicate charges an underwriting spread for issuing securities. Which of the following *best* describes the costs to the issuer?
   i) Management fee plus underwriting fee
   ii) Underwriting fee plus selling fee
   iii) Management fee plus selling fee
   iv) Management fee plus underwriting fee plus selling fee

6. Everything else being equal, which type of loan will have the highest effective annual interest cost for the borrowing firm?
   i) A 5% simple interest loan with interest paid every 3 months
   ii) A 10% simple interest loan with interest paid once a year
   iii) A 5% discount loan with interest paid once a year
   iv) A 10% discount loan with interest paid every 3 months

7. A company issues additional common shares via a rights offering. Under which of the following conditions will the rights be more valuable?

   i) If the exercise price is higher in relation to the market price of the shares

   ii) If the rights have less time to expiry

   iii) If the underlying share price is less variable

   iv) If the risk-free rate is higher

8. Participating preferred shares entitle owners to privileges including which of the following?

   i) The right to convert their shares into common shares under certain terms and conditions

   ii) The right to participate in voting for the members of the board of directors

   iii) The right to dividends that fluctuate with market interest rates

   iv) The right to share in the earnings of the company over and above their specified dividend rate

9. Which of the following statements about foreign bonds is true?

   i) Foreign bonds are issued in a country other than the country of the issuer and are denominated in the currency of the foreign country in which they are issued.

   ii) Foreign bonds are issued in a country other than the country of the issuer and are denominated in the currency of the country where the issuing company is domiciled.

   iii) Foreign bonds are issued in the borrower's domestic market and are denominated in a currency of a different country.

   iv) Foreign bonds are denominated in a currency foreign to the country in which they are issued and can be issued by foreign or domestic firms.

10. Which of the following statements about a bond purchase-fund provision is true?

    i) A purchase fund is money set aside by the bond issuer to provide for the repayment of all or part of a debt issue before maturity.

    ii) A purchase fund is set up to retire, through purchases in the market, a specified amount of outstanding bonds or debentures only if purchases can be made at or below a stipulated price.

    iii) A purchase fund normally retires more of a bond issue than a sinking fund.

    iv) Purchase funds normally have provisions for calling bonds, as do sinking funds.

11. Why is the pre-emptive right important to shareholders?

    i) Because it allows management to sell additional shares below the current market price

    ii) Because it protects the current shareholders' degree of ownership

    iii) Because it is guaranteed by law in many provinces

    iv) Because it will result in higher dividends per share

Quantitative Multiple Choice Questions

Use the information provided below to answer Questions 1 and 2.

A company has 5 million outstanding preferred shares with a market value of $45 per share. The shares pay a quarterly dividend of $1.20, and this dividend was paid yesterday. The shares were issued 5 years ago and have no maturity, but the company has an opportunity to call the shares if it pays a call premium of 3%, plus accumulated dividends. If new preferred shares are issued at this time at a price of $45 per share, the quarterly dividend would be $1.35. The old issue would remain outstanding for 2 months after the new preferred shares were sold, and interest could be earned on the proceeds of the new issue at a rate of 5% per annum. The corporate tax rate is 35%.

1. What is the amount the company must pay in additional dividends during the overlap period, net of any interest earned during this period?
   i) $4,000,000
   ii) $2,781,250
   iii) $2,125,000
   iv) $1,125,000

2. What is the call premium?
   i) $1,500,000
   ii) $5,000,000
   iii) $4,387,500
   iv) $6,750,000

3. A company has 10,000 voting shares outstanding. The company has to elect 10 directors, but a minority group of shareholders wants to elect at least 4 particular directors. If voting is cumulative, how many shares must the minority shareholders own in order to ensure the election of the desired directors?
   i) 1,000 shares
   ii) 1,111 shares
   iii) 3,637 shares
   iv) 4,445 shares

4. A firm needs to borrow $500,000 from a bank. The annual interest rate is 10% with a 7% compensating balance for a period of 1 year. Loan payments are to be made annually. The loan is to be charged discount interest. What will be the face value of the loan?
   i) $500,000
   ii) $537,634
   iii) $555,556
   iv) $602,410

5. A firm borrows $500,000 from a bank. Interest is 10% with a 7% compensating balance for a period of 1 year. Loan payments are to be made quarterly. What is the effective annual rate of interest on the loan?
   i) 10%
   ii) 10.38%
   iii) 1.77%
   iv) 11.19%

6. AlbertEd Corp. plans a rights offering to raise $5 million. There are 10 million shares outstanding. The exercise price will be $50 per share. The value of a right is $2. What is the current rights-on share price?
   i) $252
   ii) $250
   iii) $220
   iv) $200

Quantitative Problems

Problem 1

Sueng-Soo has $115,000 cash and 10,000 shares of Westol Inc. stock in her portfolio. She has just been notified that Westol will issue additional common shares via a rights offering. Every shareholder will get 1 right for each share held. The current share price is $50 and the rights entitle the holders to purchase Westol shares at $46 per share for every 4 rights. The shares are now trading rights-on. Westol now has 80,000 shares outstanding and the company has to elect 8 directors at its upcoming annual meeting. There are 2 candidates that Sueng-Soo would like to elect to serve on the board. The meeting will occur in a few months' time, after the rights offering is completed.

Required

a) Calculate the value of a right during the rights-on period.

b) Sueng-Soo can exercise her rights, or sell them to other investors. How will each of these two options affect the following?

  i) the amount she has invested in Westol

  ii) the number of shares she owns

  iii) her overall wealth

  iv) her percentage of ownership

c) If Westol has cumulative voting, how many shares must Sueng-Soo own to elect two board members? Show your calculation. Explain how Sueng-Soo can obtain the required number of shares.

Problem 2

Halifont Corp. has an issue of preferred shares outstanding with a $100 million face value and quarterly dividends of 3%, based on a rate of 12% per annum. The shares were issued 10 years ago, and the financial strategy at that time called for a redemption of the shares after 20 years. However, the issue is redeemable now, on the 10-year anniversary date. Interest rates have now declined to the point where Halifont can float a bond issue maturing in 10 years, with a semi-annual coupon rate of just 5%. Hence, the firm is contemplating redeeming the preferred shares 10 years earlier than originally planned and replacing the financing with the proceeds of a bond issue.

If the new bonds are issued so that the preferred shares can be redeemed, Halifont must pay flotation costs of 2% of face value, and this amount would be deductible for tax purposes over a 5-year period. Halifont has sufficient cash available to pay these flotation costs. Halifont has a tax rate of 40%.

In order to ensure a smooth transition from preferred share financing to bond financing, a 2-month overlap period is needed. New bonds will be issued 2 months prior to the preferred share redemption. During the overlap months, bond issue proceeds can be invested at a rate of 4% per year.

Required

Calculate the net present value (NPV) of the opportunity to refinance the preferred shares using the bond issue, and state whether Halifont should proceed and why. As a simplifying assumption, use a discount rate of 1.5% per quarter to calculate the present value of the dividends saved if the preferred shares are redeemed. For the remainder of your calculations, use the effective (after-tax) interest rate on the new bond issue.

Problem 3

Your company requires $100,000 of financing to support a higher balance of accounts receivable, arising from more relaxed credit terms that will be offered to customers. You have met with bank officers at three different banks and received the following proposals:

1. Bank ALB offers a term loan at an interest rate of 7%, compounded monthly.
2. Bank BCC offers a discount interest term loan at an interest rate of 7%, compounded semi-annually.
3. Bank NFL offers a discount interest term loan at an interest rate of 6%, compounded annually, and a compensating balance of 10%.

Required

Prepare a report that compares these three financing alternatives, and recommend which is preferred. For each alternative, describe the meaning of the loan terms to the borrower. Conclude by indicating which proposal you would choose on the basis of the effective annual interest rate and the face value.

Problem 4

NOVA Corporation has an outstanding issue of preferred shares with a dividend yield of 9% per annum (2.25% per quarter). Current yields on comparable new issues are lower at 7% per annum (1.75% per quarter). As a consequence, the NOVA preferred shares are now selling at a premium over their face value. These shares have a deferred call option that becomes effective 1 month from now, and NOVA is considering refinancing the issue. NOVA has a corporate tax rate of 40% and the risk-free rate of interest is 5%. Information about the current issue and the proposed new issue is provided below.

NOVA Corporation Preferred Shares	
Current issue	
Preferred shares outstanding	2,000,000
Face value	$100
Quarterly dividend	$2.25
Call premium plus accumulated dividends (per share)	$6.00
Proposed new issue	
Preferred shares outstanding	2,000,000
Face value	$100
Estimated market price	$100
Quarterly dividend	$1.75
Flotation costs	$1,000,000

Required

a) Identify *two* differences between preferred shares and common shares.
b) Identify *two* differences between preferred shares and debt.
c) Calculate the net present value (NPV) of refinancing the outstanding preferred share issue for NOVA Corporation, assuming no overlap period. Is the refinancing worthwhile?
d) If NOVA Corporation calls its existing issue, how does this affect the current preferred shareholders? Do these shareholders have any recourse if they are disadvantaged by the call? Explain.

Cases

Case 1: SASK

Saskapeg Corp. (SASK) has an outstanding public bond issue with $20 million of face value, and in 2 months' time the bond issue will have 5 years to maturity. The coupon rate on the issue is 10% per annum. Coupons are paid semi-annually at 5%. The issue can be called at a premium of 1% of the total face value. Assume that this premium includes any flotation costs and that the premium is not tax deductible. The tax rate for SASK is 35%.

The company is considering refinancing the outstanding bond issue with one of two alternatives. Alternative 1 is a new public bond issue, with 5 years to maturity. Interest rates have declined, and the new coupon rate is only 7% per annum, payable annually. It would take 2 months to issue the new debt, and no overlap interest period is needed, as the company has ample cash on hand should any problems arise.

Alternative 2 is a bank term loan. A term loan is available, requiring a 2% compensating balance, at an annual interest rate of only 4.6%. Interest is payable quarterly, with payments based on 1.15% of face value. The loan could be arranged to coincide exactly with the timing of the bond refunding, in 2 months, so that no overlap interest period is needed. Assume that SASK requires the full use of $20 million of funds during the loan period.

Required

a) Calculate, at the financing date, the net present value (NPV) of refinancing the existing public bond issue 2 months from now using the new public bond issue. Identify and briefly explain your choice of discount rate for this analysis. If refinancing the public bond issue were the only alternative, should SASK proceed with it?

b) Identify at least *two* advantages of financing using a bank term loan rather than using a public bond issue, for *each* of the lender and the borrower.

c) **i)** Explain what a compensating balance on a term loan is, and explain how it affects the effective cost of financing and the amount borrowed.

   ii) Under the term loan alternative, calculate both the effective after-tax cost of financing and the amount SASK would borrow.

d) Compare the effective after-tax cost of financing for each of the two alternatives. Explain whether the term loan seems to be a favourable alternative for SASK.

Case 2: Mrs. Finacco

A wealthy shareholder, Mrs. Finacco, owns 40% of the 12 million outstanding common shares of Vanreal Corp., and she wants to increase her influence over corporate decisions. Currently, Vanreal has an outstanding bond issue with the characteristics outlined in Case Exhibit 3-1 on page 208. The issue becomes callable shortly. Mrs. Finacco is concerned that Vanreal has too much debt in its capital structure—a view not shared by many of the members of the board of directors. She views the upcoming chance to call the bond issue as an opportunity to address her concerns. Summary financial information for Vanreal is presented in Case Exhibit 3-2.

There are three potential financing strategies that Vanreal could follow. It could continue with the existing bond issue, it could call the issue and refinance with bank debt, or it could call the issue and refinance with new common equity that would be raised via a rights issue. Details of the bank debt and rights issue alternatives are presented in Case Exhibit 3-3. Vanreal has a tax rate of 40% and a weighted average cost of capital of 15%.

Required

a) **i)** If Vanreal has cumulative voting and 10 members on its board, how many members can Mrs. Finacco currently vote into office?

   ii) How many additional shares would she need in order to elect 6 board members, if that is the number that she feels will result in her successfully influencing the board to reduce financial leverage?

   iii) At current share prices, what will the additional shares cost?

   iv) What percentage of the company will she own after purchasing the additional shares?

b) Assuming that the alternative is bank debt, recommend whether the outstanding bond issue should be refunded. Explain briefly. Select an appropriate method of evaluating this choice, and explain how your analysis results in an appropriate financing decision.

c) **i)** How many rights will be needed to purchase each new share if the firm proceeds with raising equity via a rights offering?

   ii) What is the value of one right in the proposed rights offering?

   iii) What will the ex-rights share price be?

d) Under the rights issue, determine the new capital structure of the firm as follows:

   i) Calculate the amounts of debt and equity outstanding, as well as the debt-to-equity ratio, both before and after the rights offering.

   ii) Calculate the old and new levels of earnings and earnings per share. Show your calculations.

e) Mrs. Finacco wishes to maintain her new, higher ownership level after the rights offering, so that she can continue to elect 6 board members. How many shares will she end up owning? What will be the value of her overall investment in Vanreal?

Case Exhibit 3-1
Characteristics of Outstanding Bond Issue of Vanreal Corp.

Date issued	January 1, 2003
Face value	$20 million
Coupon rate	10%
Periodic interest payments	Annual end-of-year payments of interest only
Maturity	January 1, 2018
When callable	After January 1, 2008
Call premium	3% of face value

Case Exhibit 3-2
Summary Financial Information for Vanreal Corp.

Outstanding debt:

Bank debt	$10,000,000—7% interest
Public debt issue	$20,000,000—as described in Exhibit 1
Outstanding common shares:	Number of shares: 12 million
	Market value per share: $5.45
Expected EBIT:	$21,500,000

Case Exhibit 3-3
Details of Bank Debt and Rights Issue Alternatives for Vanreal Corp.

Bank debt features:	$20 million of debt
	8% annual interest
	Annual end-of-year interest-only payments
	10 years to maturity
Rights issue features:	1 right will be issued for every share held
	Subscription price = $4.45 per share purchased
	Issue to raise $20 million of equity financing

Case 3: Dorval Inc.

Dorval Inc. has established its capital budget for the coming year at $50 million and expects to finance $20 million with retained earnings. The target capital structure is 40% debt and 60% equity, so the remaining $30 million is to be funded with $18 million of equity and an additional $12 million of debt.

Dorval currently has 8,000,000 outstanding common shares with a market price of $60 each. The shares are widely held. Insiders to the firm own 2,000,000 of the shares, and the remaining shares are owned by a large number of shareholders, none of whom individually controls more than 1,000,000 shares. To raise the required additional outside equity, Dorval will offer additional shares to current shareholders in a rights offering. Each right will entitle holders to purchase shares at $50 per share.

To raise the additional debt, Dorval is considering issuing $32 million of debt and using part of the proceeds to retire an existing debt issue. The existing issue is publicly held by many individual bondholders. Information about the existing issue and the proposed new issue is presented in Case Exhibit 3-4.

Case Exhibit 3-4
Dorval Inc. Debt Arrangements

	Existing debt	Proposed new issue
Face value	$20 million	Up to $32 million
Maturity	5 years remaining	10 years
Coupon rate	9%, paid semi-annually	7%, paid semi-annually
Call premium	60% of the coupon rate	Not callable
Flotation costs	Fully amortized	3% of face value

Required

Provide an assessment of the financing plans for Dorval. Analyze all of the costs associated with the proposed new financial arrangements for the firm and for its shareholders and debtholders. Assume there are no overlap interest costs or revenues and that Dorval has a corporate tax rate of 40%.

a) Dorval will give 1 right to each holder of 1 share. How many rights will be needed to purchase 1 new share? Determine the value of each right. Determine the number of shares outstanding after the rights issue, and their market value.

b) For an owner of 50,000 shares, determine the number of shares owned, the shares' percentage of ownership, and the value of the owner's investment in the firm or as cash, if the owner:

  i) exercises the rights

  ii) sells the rights

c) Evaluate the consequences to Dorval of refinancing its existing $10 million outstanding of debt. Calculate the present value of the costs and benefits of the refinancing, from the perspective of the company. Also separately calculate the present value of the flotation costs associated with raising the additional $12 million of debt beyond that needed to refund the existing issue.

d) If Dorval calls in the outstanding bonds, what impact does this have on a bondholder who currently owns bonds with $100,000 of face value? Is this bondholder protected in any way against the refunding, if it is not in his/her interests? Explain.

Chapter 4
Capital Structure

CHAPTER OVERVIEW

In this chapter, you study the theory proposed to justify the differences in capital structure between firms. Section 4.1 introduces two main views. According to the traditional view, the introduction of a moderate amount of debt into a firm's capital structure lowers the weighted average cost of capital. As the proportion of debt increases significantly, the costs of debt and equity rise sharply, suggesting the existence of an optimal capital structure. In contrast, the perfect-market view argues that the capital structure decision does not affect the value of a firm if it is operating in an environment where transaction costs and taxes are nil, information is readily available, and there are no bankruptcy costs. This view also argues that even though debt is cheaper than equity, financial leverage increases the risk to common shareholders. The weighted average cost of capital is constant because the advantage of cheaper debt is offset by the higher cost of equity.

Section 4.2 illustrates how corporate taxes influence the value of a firm when it uses debt financing. The topic points out that interest on corporate debt is deductible from income before taxes. Thus, interest payments on debt provide a tax shield and the firm's value increases by the present value of the interest tax shield.

Section 4.3 introduces personal taxes as a factor in the determination of capital structure. Personal taxes favour capital gains and dividend income over interest income, while corporate taxes favour interest income over capital gains and dividend income. Consequently, the tax shield provided by corporate interest payments is partially cancelled by the higher personal tax rate on interest income.

In Section 4.4, you learn how financial leverage decisions are affected by bankruptcy costs. The inclusion of debt in the capital structure increases the probability of bankruptcy. Both direct and indirect costs are incurred when a firm is under threat of bankruptcy. The magnitude of the expected bankruptcy costs depends on the degree of financial leverage. Consequently, the existence of bankruptcy costs prohibits a firm from using debt excessively in its capital structure.

Other factors influence the capital structure decision. Section 4.5 considers the impact of the following factors: business risk, agency costs, signalling and asymmetric information, and managerial preference.

Finally, in Section 4.6 you learn how financial managers use leverage-indifference EBIT analysis and industry averages to determine an initial estimate of what the firm's capital structure should be. The initial estimate is then adjusted to reflect the influence of factors such as the firm's degree of financial flexibility, the effects of financing on control, the firm's growth rate and profitability, and managerial preference.

Learning Objectives

After completing this chapter, you will be able to:

- Explain why methods of financing should not influence the value of a firm under perfect market conditions.

- Illustrate how corporate taxes encourage the use of debt financing.

- Explain the relationship between the present value of the interest tax shield and the value of a levered firm.

- Explain and demonstrate the impact of personal taxes on the decision to use debt financing.

- Explain the effect of bankruptcy costs on the value of a levered firm.

- Identify and explain other factors that limit the amount of debt financing.

- Calculate the leverage-indifference level of earnings before interest and taxes.

- Analyze the influence of industry averages, debt rating agencies, and other factors on the capital structure decision.

This knowledge will provide you with the professional skills to:

- Identify financial risk strategies and challenges in the organization's environment.

- Identify and analyze risk factors.

- Advise on the capital structure of the organization to maximize the organization's value.

- Evaluate tax implications of proposed and completed transactions.

- Analyze and advise on tax planning issues.

- Apply professional ethical standards.

- Advise on financing alternatives to meet the organization's goals.

- Prepare or evaluate financial proposals.

HOW THIS CHAPTER RELATES TO OTHER CHAPTERS IN THIS BOOK

Chapter 3 considered various financing alternatives. Chapter 4 attempts to answer the question "How much debt should be used?" It continues exploring the capital structure question. Although the initial discussion here is theoretical, its focus quickly changes to one of application. Chapter 4 presents both qualitative and quantitative arguments to help managers understand the impact of financing choices—the subject matter of the remaining chapters in this book.

Chapters 1 and 2 explained that the cost of capital is a major factor in choosing a firm's investment projects. The higher this cost, the lower the net present value of any project under consideration. We measure the cost of capital as the weighted average cost of funds from all relevant sources, where the weight of a source is the proportion of funds raised from that source.

The firm's investment policy and financing decisions are directly linked together. Financial structure is reflected in the cost of money. The suitability of a project is dependent on the cost of money. Thus establishing one impacts the other. Since the capital structure determines the cost of capital, the best structure will be one that minimizes the weighted average cost of capital. Doing so increases a project's value.

The content of this chapter is implicit in all the other chapters. The knowledge here may be carried both forward and back; we considered investments and financing in earlier chapters and continue to do so in those remaining.

4.1 CAPITAL STRUCTURE THEORY

Capital structure refers to the proportions of funds raised from different financing sources. Because we can generally classify funds as either debt or equity, the term "capital structure" is often used to indicate the mix of debt and equity in a firm's financing. The use of debt in the capital structure is often referred to as *financial leverage*. We call the ratio of debt to total firm value the *debt ratio* and the ratio of debt to equity the *leverage ratio*.

In practice, most corporations use debt for part of their financing. Debt ratios for nonfinancial firms operating under normal conditions typically range from 0% if the firm is financed entirely with equity to 75% if the corporation has a large percentage of debt financing. Even higher debt ratios exist, for example, if a company has been formed as a result of a leveraged buyout, where equity makes up about 10% of total capitalization. Also, a firm's capital base may deteriorate as a result of several years of losses and the firm's debt ratio may approach 100%.

In this section, you learn the theory proposed to explain why firms choose one capital structure over another in the observed range. You also learn about financial risk, an important concept that plays a central role in capital structure theory.

Financial Risk

Financial risk is the additional risk placed on common shareholders as a result of using debt (or preferred-share) financing in the firm's capital structure. Technically, financial risk can be defined as total risk to the shareholders of the levered firm minus total risk to the shareholders of the unlevered firm. Total risk is measured by the standard deviation of the return on equity (ROE). In this case, ROE is defined as net income divided by common equity. This definition of financial risk uses the marginal risk concept to measure total shareholder risk after leverage in comparison with total risk before leverage. Formally, this definition can be stated as:

$$\text{Financial risk} = \sigma_L - \sigma_U \qquad \textbf{(Equation 4-1)}$$

where
σ_L = total risk to shareholders of the levered firm
σ_U = total risk to shareholders of the unlevered firm

Keep in mind that the use of the standard deviation as a measure of risk ignores the effects of diversification. Therefore, Equation 4-1 is useful in practice whenever total risk is an appropriate measure of the firm's risk. You will use it in the You Apply It minicase below, to demonstrate the impact of leverage on risk.

When a firm does not have debt in its capital structure, total assets equal total equity. The return on equity of an unlevered firm is equal to the after-tax return on assets. Therefore, σ_U is often called **business risk** or **asset risk** because it measures the total risk generated by the nature of the firm's assets and business. In contrast, when the firm uses debt, σ_L is greater than σ_U, and the difference is a measure of financial risk.

The more long-term debt in the capital structure, the greater the financial leverage of the firm will be. Shareholders benefit from financial leverage as long as the return on borrowed money exceeds the interest costs of acquiring the money. Also, leverage implies that the firm is required to make interest and principal payments, regardless of the firm's actual cash flows. If such payments are not made on time and as specified by the debt contract, the lender may force the firm into liquidation. Thus, leverage ultimately increases **default risk**.

In addition to default risk, financial leverage tends to magnify the effects on earnings per share from changes in sales levels. Interest payments on debt are fixed costs. During periods of high earnings, financial leverage causes the return to shareholders to be higher than the required rate on the debt. In contrast, the return to shareholders is lower than the required return on debt during periods of low earnings. Thus, financial leverage increases the variation of earnings around the mean and increases the total risk of the firm.

Demonstrate the impact of financial leverage on common share risk by completing the You Apply It minicase below. You should note that the information supplied here will also be used in the four minicases following this one.

YOU APPLY IT DEMONSTRATING FINANCIAL RISK

Creative Components Enterprises (CCE) expects its earnings before interest and taxes (EBIT) to fluctuate with the economy according to the distribution presented in Exhibit 4-1. This earnings distribution is expected to continue in perpetuity. The company has 1 million shares outstanding and no debt in its capital structure. It pays all earnings in dividends and shareholders require a 12% return. The firm pays no taxes.

Exhibit 4-1
Distribution of CCE's Earnings with No Debt and No Taxes

| | State of the economy | | | |
	Bad	Fair	Good	Very good
Probability	0.25	0.25	0.25	0.25
EBIT ($ millions)	$2.20	$3.80	$4.80	$6.00
Earnings per share	$2.20	$3.80	$4.80	$6.00
Return if share price is $35	6.29%	10.86%	13.71%	17.14%

Questions

Question 1: What are the expected earnings per share and the standard deviation of per-share earnings? What is its market value?

You Apply It Continued >

Question 2: The firm is planning to sell $22.05 million in bonds at 10% interest. The firm's goal is to use the proceeds to buy 630,000 of its own shares at the market price of $35 per share. What will the distribution of earnings per share be after issuing the bonds and buying the shares?

Question 3: Given your answer to Question 2, what are the expected earnings per share and the standard deviation of per-share earnings after the debt issue? **Note:** before proceeding, we suggest you first check your answers against those in Exhibit 4-2 contained in the answer to Question 2, below.

Question 4: Because the risk of earnings per share is higher, the required rate of return to common shareholders should also be higher. What would the expected return and the standard deviation of return to shareholders be if the share price remains at $35 and the expected earnings per share are $5.39?

Answers

Question 1: What are the expected earnings per share and the standard deviation of per-share earnings? What is its market value?

The expected earnings per share are:

$$(0.25 \times 2.20) + (0.25 \times 3.80) + (0.25 \times 4.80) + (0.25 \times 6.00) = \$4.20$$

The variance of per-share earnings is:

$$0.25 \times (2.20 - 4.20)^2 + 0.25 \times (3.80 - 4.20)^2 + 0.25 \times (4.80 - 4.20)^2$$
$$+ 0.25 \times (6.00 - 4.20)^2$$
$$- (0.25 \times 4) + (0.25 \times 0.16) + (0.25 \times 0.36) + (0.25 \times 3.24)$$
$$= 1.94$$

Thus, the standard deviation is equal to $1.39 ($\sigma = \sqrt{1.94}$).

Because each share is expected to yield $4.20 in dividends in perpetuity, capitalizing these dividends at 12% yields a price of $35 per share ($4.20 ÷ 0.12). Thus, the firm's market value should be $35 million ($35 × 1,000,000).

The standard deviation of the expected return is 4%. This standard deviation is determined by dividing the standard deviation of earnings by the per-share price of $35.

Question 2: The firm is planning to sell $22.05 million in bonds at 10% interest. The firm's goal is to use the proceeds to buy 630,000 of its own shares at the market price of $35 per share. What will the distribution of earnings per share be after issuing the bonds and buying the shares?

The number of shares remaining after the repurchase will be 370,000 (1,000,000 − 630,000). Exhibit 4-2 shows the distribution of earnings after including $22.05 million of debt in the firm's capital structure.

Question 3: Exhibit 4-2 provides the distribution of CCE's earnings per share. What are the expected earnings per share and the standard deviation of per-share earnings after the debt issue?

You Apply It Continued >

Exhibit 4-2
Distribution of CCE's Earnings with Debt and No Taxes

| | State of the economy | | | |
	Bad	Fair	Good	Very good
Probability	0.25	0.25	0.25	0.25
EBIT ($ millions)	$2.200	$3.800	$4.800	$6.000
Interest ($ millions)	$2.205	$2.205	$2.205	$2.205
Net earnings ($ millions)	($0.005)	$1.595	$2.595	$3.795
Earnings per share	($0.01)	$4.31	$7.01	$10.26
Return if share price remains $35	(0.03%)	12.31%	20.03%	29.31%

EPS INVEST ≈

The expected earnings per share are:

$$(0.25 \times -0.01) + (0.25 \times 4.31) + (0.25 \times 7.01) + (0.25 \times 10.26)$$
$$= \$5.3925$$
$$= \$5.39 \text{ (rounded to the nearest cent)}$$

The variance of per-share earning is:

$$0.25 \times (-0.01 - 5.3925)^2 + 0.25 \times (4.31 - 5.3925)^2 + 0.25$$
$$\times (7.01 - 5.3925)^2 + 0.25 \times (10.26 - 5.3925)^2$$
$$= (0.25 \times 29.187) + (0.25 \times 1.1718) + (0.25 \times 2.6163)$$
$$+ (0.25 \times 23.6926)$$
$$= 14.1669$$

Thus, the standard deviation is equal to $3.76 ($\sigma = \sqrt{14.1670}$).

Question 4: Because the risk of earnings per share is higher, the required rate of return to common shareholders should also be higher. What would the expected return and the standard deviation of return to shareholders be if the share price remains at $35 and the expected earnings per share are $5.39?

Let R be the expected return at which the new share price is equal to the original price of $35 per share. Then R can be obtained by:

$$R = \frac{\$5.39}{\$35.00} = 15.40\%$$

Thus, if the required rate of return to shareholders is less than 15.40%, the value per share of the remaining shares will be higher because of leverage.

If the share price remains at $35, the standard deviation of expected return is equal to 10.74% ($3.76 ÷ $35). This is much higher than the 4% standard deviation of expected return when the firm was without leverage.

In conclusion, leverage results in higher expected earnings per share than if there is no leverage. In addition, the variability of earnings around the mean will be much higher when the firm uses debt in its capital structure. More importantly, if a firm uses debt and the state of the economy turns out to be bad, the firm's earnings before interest may be less than the cash required to pay the interest on the debt. In this case, debtholders may force the firm into bankruptcy, which will decrease shareholder value. Given the higher risk, it is natural that the remaining shareholders will demand a higher return for their investment.

Traditional View

The **traditional view of capital structure** proposes that under perfect market conditions and in the absence of taxes, a large proportion of debt in the capital structure is desirable. Proponents argue that debtholders are entitled to receive interest and principal payments, as specified by the bond indenture, as long as the firm's cash flows are above debt service requirements. Therefore, debtholders are not affected by fluctuations in the firm's cash flows unless the firm is bankrupt. In contrast, shareholders are subject to the risk that the cash flows may not permit the firm to pay dividends as expected. The inability to pay dividends depresses share price and produces losses to shareholders, while debtholders can receive their interest as promised.

Debtholders are generally in a more secure position than common shareholders because of their priority in claiming cash from the firm's profits. Consequently, the cost of debt is normally less than the cost of funds from common shares. The weighted average cost of capital will drop when the firm adds debt to its capital structure, as long as the debt does not exceed a critical level.

Exhibit 4-3 shows the proposed relationship between the debt ratio and the weighted average cost of capital. It indicates that a U-shaped cost of capital curve exists. In other words, as debt increases, both debt and equity costs begin to rise because of the increase in financial risk. As debt reaches a critical level, the advantages of cheaper debt are outweighed by the higher costs of equity. Thus, the weighted average cost of capital starts to increase with additional debt financing beyond the critical level W^*.

Exhibit 4-3 Relationship between the Debt Ratio, WACC, Cost of Equity, and Cost of Debt in the Absence of Corporate Taxes

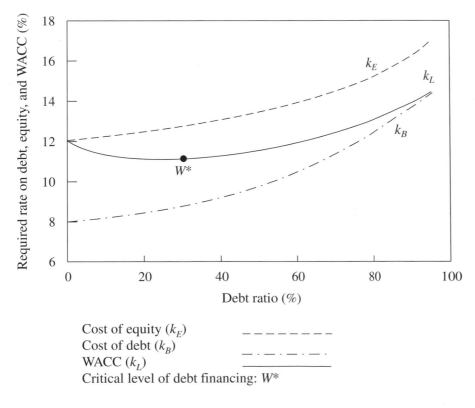

Cost of equity (k_E)   – – – – – – – –
Cost of debt (k_B)   – · — · — · — ·
WACC (k_L)   ————————
Critical level of debt financing: W^*

Proponents of the traditional view of capital structure argue that below the critical level W^*, the use of moderate levels of debt will decrease the firm's cost of capital. Beyond the critical level W^*, the use of debt increases the firm's cost of capital. From low debt levels, the firm's value will increase until it hits a peak that coincides with the critical level W^*. Beyond the critical level W^*, the value of the firm decreases as financial leverage increases.

Perfect-Market View

Chapter 1 showed that in the absence of risk and under the assumptions of perfect markets, a project should be undertaken if its return is more than the opportunity cost of capital. In other words, the financing decision is independent of the investment decision. A firm cannot affect the value of its assets by using innovative financing techniques.

In a seminal 1958 article, F. Modigliani and M.H. Miller (M&M) addressed the capital structure issue.[1] They showed that under conditions of uncertainty, the capital structure is irrelevant if markets are efficient and perfect. Their conclusion has been summarized in what is known as "Proposition I": As long as investors have homogeneous expectations regarding the future earnings of firms and there are no transaction costs or taxes, a firm's choice of financing sources should not affect the value of its assets.

M&M proposed that a firm's business risk can be measured by the standard deviation of the earnings before interest and taxes (EBIT). Firms with the same degree of business risk are grouped into homogeneous risk classes. Within a given risk class, firms are expected to provide equivalent returns. Thus, the expected operating income of these firms should be capitalized at the same risk-adjusted discount rate, regardless of whether the firm is levered or not. The discount rate is the weighted average cost of capital for the firm. Given that leverage will not affect the firm's business risk, the discount rate of the levered firm is equal to the discount rate of the unlevered firm and the value of the firm is therefore independent of leverage.

Proposition I can be formalized as:

$$V = \frac{\text{EBIT}}{k_L} = \frac{\text{EBIT}}{k_U} \qquad \text{(Equation 4-2)}$$

where

$\qquad V$ = value of the firm

$\quad \text{EBIT}$ = perpetual earnings before interest and taxes

$\qquad k_L$ = risk-adjusted discount rate for the levered firm

$\qquad k_U$ = risk-adjusted discount rate for the unlevered firm

Equation 4-2 will hold only if k_L is equal to k_U. The discount rates are consistent with the firm's business risk. Because leverage does not affect business risk, the two rates are equal and the value of a firm is independent of its leverage.

---

[1] Franco Modigliani and Merton H. Miller, "The Cost of Capital, Corporation Finance, and the Theory of Investment," *American Economic Review*, Volume 48, June 1958, pp. 261–297.

Essentially, Equation 4-2 is an application of the perpetuity valuation model. This model applies if EBIT is constant and is discounted by the risk-adjusted discount rate. This relationship shows that firm value is directly related to EBIT. Thus, for a given discount rate k, firm value increases (decreases) if EBIT increases (decreases). In contrast, firm value is inversely related to the risk-adjusted discount rate. For a given EBIT, firm value increases (decreases) if the discount rate decreases (increases).

M&M further explained that the use of debt increases the risk to a firm's shareholders. The cost of equity to a levered firm is equal to the cost of equity to an unlevered firm plus a risk premium, which is a function of increasing leverage. Formally, the cost of equity is given by:

$$k_E = k_U + (k_U - k_B)\left(\frac{D}{E}\right) \qquad \textbf{(Equation 4-3)}$$

where

$\quad k_E$ = cost of equity of the levered firm
$\quad k_U$ = cost of equity of the unlevered firm
$\quad k_B$ = before-tax cost of debt
$\quad D$ = market value of the firm's debt
$\quad E$ = market value of the firm's equity

This result is known as "Proposition II."

Determining the cost of equity, as suggested by Equation 4-3, implies that the weighted average cost of capital k_U to the firm is constant because the effect of cheaper debt is neutralized by the higher cost of equity. For example, the weighted average cost of capital of a firm with equity E and debt D is equal to:

$$k_L = k_B\left[\frac{D}{E+D}\right] + \left[k_U + (k_U - k_B)\left(\frac{D}{E}\right)\right]\left[\frac{E}{E+D}\right] \qquad \textbf{(Equation 4-4)}$$

Simplifying, $k_L = k_U$, regardless of the magnitude of financial leverage. Thus, the value of the firm is independent of leverage. The operating cash flows of the unlevered firm should be capitalized at the weighted average cost of capital of the unlevered firm. The advantages of cheaper debt are neutralized by an increase in the cost of equity.

The leverage ratio, D/E, measures the amount of debt as a percentage of equity. In contrast, the debt ratio, $D/(D + E)$, measures the portion of total assets financed with debt. It is important to remember that the leverage ratio is used in Equation 4-3 to calculate the cost of the levered firm's equity, while the debt ratio is used in Equation 4-4 to calculate the weighted average cost of capital.

Homemade Leverage

M&M's assumptions that markets are perfect and efficient are critical to the conclusion that financial leverage should not increase the value of the firm. As you learned in Chapter 2, in perfect and efficient capital markets information is free, investors can borrow or lend at the same rate, and all investors should invest in the same risky portfolio. However, they can use **homemade leverage**, the practice of lending or borrowing to establish their preferred expected return and risk. For example, an investor can create homemade leverage by borrowing money and investing it in more shares of the company to obtain dividend revenue. An investor can also unlever an investment by selling shares and investing the proceeds in debt to obtain interest revenue. These investors are not willing to pay for services that they can perform on their own.

Let's revisit the company CCE from the You Apply It minicase above. We will supply additional information to demonstrate homemade leverage.

MINICASE 4-1 DEMONSTRATING HOMEMADE LEVERAGE

Creative Components Enterprises (CCE) decides not to issue the bonds to buy 630,000 of its own shares at a market price of $35 per share. Kathy owns 10,000 CCE shares and is willing to take the additional risk presented by the proposed leverage for the sake of the possible additional return. She decides to create her own homemade leverage. She borrows $595,945 at 10% to buy 17,027 additional shares of CCE.

Question 1: How did Kathy determine the number of additional shares to buy?

Under the proposed debt issue, the company would have been left with 370,000 outstanding shares out of 1 million. Thus, the capital structure after the proposed debt issue would have been 37% equity and 63% debt. Because Kathy already has $350,000 invested in CCE, she must borrow enough to make this amount only 37% of the total investment. Her total investment should be:

$$\$350,000 \div 0.37 = \$945,945$$

The amount to be borrowed is:

$$\$945,945 - \$350,000 = \$595,945$$

Thus, the number of shares to buy is 17,027 ($595,945 ÷ $35).

Question 2: Given the information in Exhibit 4-4, what is the distribution of Kathy's return for the various states of economy after borrowing $595,945 and buying an additional 17,027 shares?

The last row of Exhibit 4-4 shows the distribution of Kathy's returns after using 63% debt in her investment.

Exhibit 4-4
Distribution of Kathy's Returns with Debt and No Taxes

| | State of the economy | | | |
	Bad	Fair	Good	Very good
Probability	0.25	0.25	0.25	0.25
EBIT (per share)	$2.20	$3.80	$4.80	$6.00
Kathy's total earnings	$59,459.40	$102,702.60	$129,729.60	$162,162.00
Interest at 10%	$59,594.50	$59,594.50	$59,594.50	$59,594.50
Kathy's earnings after interest	($135.10)	$43,108.10	$70,135.10	$102,567.50
Kathy's return	(0.04%)	12.32%	20.04%	29.31%

Case Continued >

Question 3: How would Kathy's return after leveraging her investment compare to her return had the firm issued the bonds and purchased the shares?

Comparing the last row of Exhibit 4-2 with the last row of Exhibit 4-4 shows that the distribution of Kathy's returns would be the same whether the firm leverages equity with a debt issue or Kathy leverages her investment with borrowing. The discrepancy between the two sets of returns is attributed to rounding error.

In conclusion, leverage increases expected return, and the variability of return around the mean will be much higher when the firm uses debt in its capital structure. More importantly, investors can create the same expected return and risk combination by borrowing on their own and leveraging their investments. Investors can borrow and lever the returns from the unlevered firm so that the return distributions are identical to those of the levered firm. Assuming that capital markets are perfect and efficient, investors should be indifferent between buying shares in a financially levered company and buying shares in an identical but unlevered company.

4.2 IMPACT OF CORPORATE TAXES

The models described in the previous topic did not consider taxes. In general, corporate income is subject to taxes. Furthermore, interest payments to debtholders are considered to be a business expense for the firm. These payments are tax deductible in that they are paid from income before calculating taxes. In contrast, dividend payments to shareholders are not tax deductible. This preferential tax treatment for interest payments makes debt financing cheaper for a firm than common share financing, despite the efficiency of the capital market. The use of moderate levels of debt in a firm's capital structure decreases the weighted average cost of capital and increases the value of the firm.

In 1963, Modigliani and Miller presented a model of firm value in which the impact of corporate taxes was considered.[2] They pointed out that although the capital market is efficient, the preferential tax treatment of interest could make the capital structure important in determining the firm's value.

Let's revisit the company CCE from the You Apply It minicase and Minicase 4-1 above. We will supply additional information to demonstrate the impact of corporate taxes.

MINICASE 4-2 IMPACT OF CORPORATE TAXES

Question 1: Given the information in Exhibit 4-5, what would the distribution of CCE's earnings be for the various states of the economy, if the firm pays 40% taxes and does not use debt in its capital structure?

Exhibit 4-5 shows the taxes payable under the various states of the economy. Deducting these taxes from the operating earnings yields the cash flow to shareholders because there is no debt in the capital structure.

Case Continued >

---

[2] Franco Modigliani and Merton H. Miller, "Corporate Income Taxes and the Cost of Capital: A Correction," *American Economic Review*, Volume 53, June 1963, pp. 433–443.

Question 2: What are the expected after-tax earnings available to shareholders?

The expected after-tax earnings are:

$$(0.25 \times 1.32) + (0.25 \times 2.28) + (0.25 \times 2.88) + (0.25 \times 3.60) = \$2.52 \text{ million}$$

Question 3: What is the value of the firm if the required rate of return remains at 12%?

Given that shareholders receive $2.52 million in dividends in perpetuity, capitalizing these dividends at 12% yields a market value for the firm equal to $21 million.

Question 4: The firm decides to sell bonds and use the proceeds to buy back 630,000 outstanding shares. Because the value of the firm is $21 million and the firm has 1 million shares outstanding, the price per share should be $21. Thus, the firm has to raise $13.23 million (630,000 × $21). The rate at which the debt can be raised is 10%.

What is the distribution of after-tax earnings available to shareholders for the various states of economy if the firm issues debt and buys back the shares? What is the cash distribution to all security holders?

Exhibit 4-6 shows the distribution of earnings after interest and taxes. Notice how interest is deducted from income before calculating taxes. Consequently, the tax bill

Case Continued >

decreases under all states of the economy and the combined cash disbursement to bond and common shareholders increases.

Question 5: What is CCE's expected net income?

The expected net income is:

$$(0.25 \times 0.5262) + (0.25 \times 1.4862) + (0.25 \times 2.0862) + (0.25 \times 2.8062)$$
$$= \$1.7262 \text{ million}$$

Question 6: What are the expected disbursements to all security holders and how do they compare to the disbursements when the firm is unlevered?

The expected disbursements to all security holders are equal to the expected disbursements to bondholders plus the expected disbursements to shareholders. They are equal to:

$$\$1.323 + \$1.7262 = \$3.0492 \text{ million}$$

The cash disbursements to all security holders of the levered firm are higher than the cash disbursements when the firm is unlevered. The levered firm distributes \$0.5292 million (0.40 × \$1.323 million) more to security holders as a result of tax savings.

Question 7: What is the firm's value after leverage?

The unlevered firm's value is \$21 million. After leverage, the firm distributes an additional \$0.5292 million to security holders. This additional amount should be capitalized at the rate of return required by bondholders, as these cash benefits accrue to shareholders whenever interest payments are made. Thus, the savings from leverage are as risky as the interest payments to debtholders. The value of these savings to shareholders is:

$$\$0.5292 \div 0.10 = \$5.292 \text{ million}$$

The total value of the firm can now be calculated as the value without leverage plus the value of the additional cash flow created from leverage. The firm's value after leverage is, therefore, \$26.292 million (\$21 million + \$5.292 million).

The amount of the annual tax savings is equal to the annual interest payments multiplied by the tax rate. Therefore, if the amount of debt in the capital structure is denoted by D, the coupon rate on the debt is r, and the corporate tax rate is denoted by T_C, the annual tax savings are rDT_C. As shown in Equation 4-5, the capitalization of interest tax savings at the required rate of debtholders yields the present value of the interest tax savings:

$$\text{PV(interest tax savings)} = T_C D \qquad \textbf{(Equation 4-5)}$$

where

T_C = corporate tax rate
D = amount of debt

In conclusion, leverage *decreases* the expected tax payments by the firm. These interest tax savings accrue to the firm and increase the cash inflows to shareholders. Capitalizing these interest tax savings at the rate of return required by bondholders produces the present value of the interest tax savings ($T_C D$), which is the value that the firm can capture by using debt in its capital structure.

Modifying the M&M Propositions

M&M are generally credited with the conclusion that the use of debt adds value to a firm if the interest payments on debt are tax deductible and corporate dividends are not. Their earlier results regarding the impact of financial leverage on the firm should therefore be modified to include the impact of corporate taxes.

With corporate taxes added, M&M's propositions need to be modified as follows.

Proposition I The value of an unlevered firm is the firm's perpetual after-tax operating income divided by its cost of capital. The value of a levered firm is equal to the value of an unlevered firm plus the value of the tax savings created because of the deductibility of interest as a business expense. Formally, these values can be calculated as shown in Equations 4-6 and 4-7:

$$V_U = \frac{\text{EBIT}(1 - T_C)}{k_U} \qquad \text{(Equation 4-6)}$$

$$V_L = V_U + T_C D \qquad \text{(Equation 4-7)}$$

where

V_U = unlevered firm's value
V_L = levered firm's value
T_C = corporate tax rate
D = amount of debt

Proposition II The cost of equity to a levered firm is equal to the cost of equity to an unlevered firm plus a risk premium. The risk premium is equal to the product of the spread between the cost of unlevered equity and the cost of debt, the leverage ratio (debt divided by equity), and the proportion $(1 - T_C)$. Formally, this gives:

$$k_E = k_U + [k_U - k_B]\left[\frac{D}{E}\right][1 - T_C] \qquad \text{(Equation 4-8)}$$

where

k_E = cost of equity of the levered firm
k_B = before-tax cost of debt
k_U = cost of equity to the unlevered firm after taxes

There are two important differences between these propositions and those of the no-tax case:

- In the presence of corporate taxes, the value of the firm increases as debt is added to the capital structure. The greater the debt usage, the higher the value of the firm will be.

- The cost of equity to the levered firm increases less rapidly than when there are no corporate taxes. As you learned in your introductory finance course, the weighted average cost of capital (k_L) is calculated as:

$$k_L = \left(\frac{D}{V}\right)k_B(1 - T_C) + \left(\frac{E}{V}\right)k_E \qquad \text{(Equation 4-9)}$$

where

k_L = weighted average cost of capital
V = value of the firm, which equals debt plus equity

Exhibit 4-7 Relationship between the Debt Ratio, WACC, Cost of Equit, and Cost of Debt in the Presence of Corporate Taxes

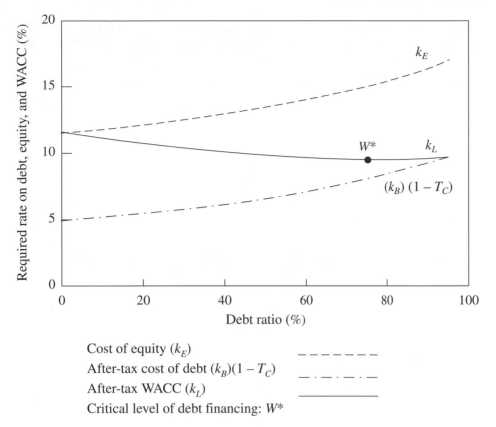

Cost of equity (k_E) $\quad$ — — — — — —
After-tax cost of debt (k_B)($1 - T_C$) $\quad$ — . — . — . —
After-tax WACC (k_L) $\quad$ ————————
Critical level of debt financing: W^*

If no debt is used, D is zero and WACC equals k_E. In this case, k_E will be equal to k_U because the leverage ratio is zero. If D is greater than zero, the portion of WACC contributed by equity capital decreases from 100%, to be replaced by debt capital, which costs less than equity. As long as the marginal increase in the cost of the remaining equity is outweighed by the marginal decrease caused by the introduction of debt, WACC for the levered firm is lower than for the unlevered firm.

Exhibit 4-7 shows the impact of corporate taxes on the firm's weighted average cost of capital. Notice how the value of the tax shield lowers the after-tax cost of debt and increases the optimal level of debt financing.

The differences between the M&M propositions after introducing corporate taxes and the same propositions before introducing taxes are caused by the tax deductibility of interest payments on debt financing. M&M's model with corporate taxes leads to the conclusion that firms should use almost 100% debt. However, in practice, this does not occur. This means that other factors affecting the capital structure decision must be considered.

4.3 IMPACT OF PERSONAL TAXES

The perfect-market assumptions considered so far include the assumption that personal taxes are negligible. In practice, this is not true. Investors pay taxes on interest, dividend, and capital gains income from investments. More importantly, the rate at which interest income is taxed is higher than the rate at which capital gains and dividends are taxed.

Tax Treatment of Interest, Dividends, and Capital Gains

In Canada, interest income is taxed as regular income to investors. In contrast, dividend and capital gains income is tax-favoured. Dividends from taxable Canadian corporations received by a Canadian taxpayer who is not a corporation are subject to a gross up and a dividend tax credit. Since 2006 the amount now depends on whether or not dividends are eligible. Eligibility is determined by the payer of the dividends. Eligible dividends are grossed up by 145% and receive a tax credit of 18.9655% while other-than-eligible dividends are grossed up by 125% and receive a 13.33% tax credit. Since October 18, 2000, only 50% of net capital gains are taxed at the rate of regular income.

For more information on personal taxation, visit the Canada Revenue Agency Web site listed in the Web Links section at the end of this chapter.

We demonstrate the impact of the preferential tax treatment of dividends and capital gains in the following minicase:

MINICASE 4-3 IMPACT OF TAX TREATMENT

Claude is in the 29% federal tax rate and the 60% provincial tax rate. Suppose he is expecting $1,000 in interest income, $1,000 in capital gains, and $1,000 in other than eligible dividends. What is Claude's marginal tax rate (his tax rate on the last dollar of income) from each of these sources?

■ The tax rate on the last dollar of interest income is:

$$0.29 \times (1 + 0.60) = 46.4\%$$

■ The tax rate on the last dollar of capital gains income is:

$$0.50 \times 0.29 \times (1 + 0.60) = 23.2\%$$

■ The tax rate on the last dollar of dividend income is calculated in Exhibit 4-8 as 31.3%. **Note:** the gross-up and tax credit rates are based on the other than eligible

Exhibit 4-8
Claude's Tax Bill on the Last Dollar of Dividend Income

Dividends	$1,000.00
Gross-up at 25%	250.00
Taxable dividends	1,250.00
Federal taxes at 29%	362.50
Dividend tax credit (13.33% of taxable dividends)	166.62
Federal taxes	195.88
Provincial taxes at 60%	117.53
Total taxes paid	313.41
Tax rate	31.34%

Case Continued >

rates given by the Canada Revenue Agency. Therefore, Claude's tax rate on capital gains is less than the tax rate on dividends and the dividends' tax rate is in turn less than the tax rate on interest income.

The preferential tax treatment of dividend and capital gains income creates an investor bias against interest income. Investors with high tax rates favour investments that offer dividend or capital gains income and are willing to pay relatively more for these securities. In contrast, tax-exempt investors favour interest income.

When corporate borrowers sell securities to raise funds, they try to provide the market with securities that have characteristics desired by the target buyers and fund suppliers. For example, preferred and common shares have characteristics desired by investors with high tax rates, while bonds match the desires of tax-exempt investors. Thus, you can expect to see debt and equity capital in the capital structure of firms. Also, the personal income tax structure will influence management's decision on capital structure.

Miller Model of Firm Value

In a 1997 article entitled "Debt and Taxes," Miller presented a model for firm value that includes both corporate and personal taxes.[3] According to this model, individuals favour dividend and capital gains income over interest income because of their different tax treatment. Thus, investors force corporations to issue shares as part of their capitalization. Personal taxes partially explain why firms do not have 100% debt financing despite the corporate tax effects.

To demonstrate the effects of personal taxes, we use the information from Minicase 4-1.

MINICASE 4-4 EFFECTS OF PERSONAL TAXES

Question 1: What is the value of CCE if the firm does not use debt in its capital structure and the personal tax rate on the income paid to shareholders is 20%?

Exhibit 4-9 shows the distribution of income to shareholders after taxes. The expected earnings to shareholders after taxes are $2.016 million. If the after-tax required

Exhibit 4-9
Distribution of Earnings to CCE Shareholders after Corporate and Individual Taxes ($ Millions)

	State of the economy			
	Bad	**Fair**	**Good**	**Very good**
Probability	0.25	0.25	0.25	0.25
EBIT	$2.200	$3.800	$4.800	$6.000
Corporate taxes	$0.880	$1.520	$1.920	$2.400
Earnings after corporate taxes	$1.320	$2.280	$2.880	$3.600
Personal taxes	$0.264	$0.456	$0.576	$0.720
Net earnings to shareholders	$1.056	$1.824	$2.304	$2.880

Case Continued >

---

[3] Merton H. Miller, "Debt and Taxes," *Journal of Finance*, Volume 32, May 1997, pp. 261–275.

rate to shareholders is 12%, the firm's value is $16.8 million. Given that the firm has 1 million shares outstanding, the price per share is $16.80.

Question 2: CCE sells bonds at 10% and uses the proceeds to buy back some of its outstanding shares. The firm raises $10.584 million and buys back 630,000 shares at the price of $16.80 per share. The personal tax rate on interest income is 52%. What is the value of the firm?

Exhibit 4-10 shows the distribution of earnings to CCE shareholders after corporate and individual taxes. The expected earnings are $1.507968 million.

Exhibit 4-10
Distribution of Earnings to CCE Shareholders after Corporate and Individual Taxes ($ Millions)

| | State of the economy | | | |
	Bad	**Fair**	**Good**	**Very good**
Probability	0.25	0.25	0.25	0.25
EBIT	$2.200000	$3.800000	$4.800000	$6.000000
Interest	$1.058400	$1.058400	$1.058400	$1.058400
Net earnings	$1.141600	$2.741600	$3.741600	$4.941600
Corporate taxes	$0.456640	$1.096640	$1.496640	$1.976640
Earnings after corporate taxes	$0.684960	$1.644960	$2.244960	$2.964960
Personal taxes	$0.136992	$0.328992	$0.448992	$0.592992
Net earnings to shareholders	$0.547968	$1.315968	$1.795968	$2.371968

It is necessary to discount the expected earnings at the required rate to the shareholders of the levered firm. In the absence of personal taxes, Equation 4-8 can be used to calculate the required rate. In the presence of personal taxes, Equation 4-3 can be used on condition that K_U and the cost of debt are calculated after corporate and individual taxes. You are given K_U equal to 12%. The cost of debt after tax can be calculated as 4.8% [= 10% × (1 − 0.52)]. Using Equation 4-3 yields:

$$k_L = 0.12 + (0.12 - 0.048)(10.584 \div 6.216) = 24.26\%$$

Capitalizing the expected earnings of $1.507968 million yields $6.216 million. Adding $10.584 million, the value of debt, produces $16.8 million, the value of the levered firm, which is equal to the value of the unlevered firm.

Minicase 4-4 above shows that the existence of corporate and individual taxes may have no effect on a firm's value, regardless of whether the firm uses debt in its capital structure. In Minicase 4-4, however, the tax rates were purposely chosen to satisfy:

$$1 - T_D = (1 - T_C)(1 - T_S) \qquad \textbf{(Equation 4-10)}$$

where

T_D = tax rate on interest income
T_C = corporate tax rate
T_S = personal tax rate on income from shares

The non-effect of taxes on the value of the firm, as demonstrated in Minicase 4-4, occurred as a result of choosing the tax rates to satisfy Equation 4-10. Equation 4-10 implies that taxes are irrelevant to the capital structure decision if the tax rate on income from shares is lower than the tax rate on interest income by a margin that accounts for the corporate tax rate. Under this condition, an investor would be indifferent between buying bonds or shares if they have the same risk-return relationship.

If the left-hand side of Equation 4-10 is greater than the right-hand side, the investor will prefer to invest in bonds rather than in shares. In this case, it is optimal to have bonds in the capital structure of the firm. In contrast, if the left-hand side is less than the right-hand side, the investor will prefer to receive income in the form of dividends and capital gains. In this case, the firm is better off raising all its capital in the form of equity.

With the existence of personal and corporate taxes, the unlevered firm's value is given by:

$$V_U = \frac{EBIT(1 - T_C)(1 - T_S)}{k_U}$$ **(Equation 4-11)**

where

V_U = value of the unlevered firm
EBIT = earnings before interest and taxes
T_C = corporate tax rate
T_S = personal tax rate on income from shares
k_U = cost of equity of the unlevered firm

The return from shares consists of dividends and capital gains. Thus, T_S is the weighted average of the effective tax rates on dividends and capital gains. Equation 4-11 shows how personal taxes lower disposable income and lower the value of the unlevered firm.

Notice that in Equation 4-6, the factor $(1 - T_C)$ reduces the value of the unlevered firm. Now observe that the factor $(1 - T_S)$ reduces the value of the unlevered firm by an even greater amount.

Value of the Levered Firm and Personal Taxes The value of the levered firm also decreases because of personal taxes. This effect can be demonstrated by developing a formula to calculate the levered firm's value while considering personal taxes.

The annual cash flows from a levered firm consist of net cash flows to shareholders and net cash flows to bondholders. Let CF_L denote the net cash flows to shareholders plus the net cash flows to bondholders. Formally, these cash flows can be represented as:

$$CF_L = EBIT(1 - T_C)(1 - T_S) - I(1 - T_C)(1 - T_S)$$
$$+ I(1 - T_D)$$ **(Equation 4-12)**

where

CF_L = cash flows from a levered firm
EBIT = earnings before interest and taxes
I = annual payments to debtholders
T_C = corporate tax rate
T_S = personal tax rate on income from shares
T_D = personal tax rate on income from debt

The cash flows to a levered firm are equal to the after-tax cash flow of an all-equity firm plus the cash flows from the effect of leverage. Therefore, the value of the levered firm is equal to the sum of the values of these cash flows discounted at the appropriate discount rates. This yields:

$$V_L = V_U + \left[1 - \frac{(1 - T_C)(1 - T_S)}{(1 - T_D)}\right]D \qquad \text{(Equation 4-13)}$$

where

V_L = value of the levered firm
V_U = value of the unlevered firm
D = market value of debt

In conclusion, the value of a levered firm is obtained by discounting the cash flows derived from the firm at the appropriate rates.

The Miller model generalizes the previous M&M models. For example, if all taxes are ignored, $T_C = T_S = T_D = 0$ and the model reduces to the original M&M model without taxes (Equation 4-2). If only personal taxes are ignored, $T_S = T_D = 0$ and the model reduces to the M&M model with corporate taxes (Equation 4-7).

Conclusions from the Miller Model Corporate income tax law favours debt financing over equity financing because interest is tax deductible while dividends are not. Personal income tax law favours equity securities because income from shares is taxed at a lower effective rate than interest. Consequently, the net effect of taxes depends on the relative corporate or personal tax rates. Empirical evidence shows that the addition of personal taxes lowers but does not eliminate the value of debt financing to the firm.

4.4 EFFECT OF BANKRUPTCY COSTS

If a firm's cash flows from operations do not meet payments of interest or principal in full and on time, creditors may take actions that can force the firm into **bankruptcy**. The higher the percentage of debt in the capital structure of a firm, the higher is the probability of bankruptcy. As reported by Statistics Canada, there were 6,756 business bankruptcies reported in Canada in 2006. This compares to 10,026 business bankruptcies reported in 1999. Although Statistics Canada is reporting fewer firms bankrupting, the average size of the financial loss resulting from bankruptcy is on the rise. For more information, refer to the Web Links section at the end of this chapter.

So far, this chapter has assumed that bankruptcy-related costs are zero. Yet when both direct and indirect costs are considered, the costs of bankruptcy can be substantial. Given that these costs are incurred only if the firm has debt in its capital structure, the costs of bankruptcy are essentially costs of financial leverage. Ignoring these costs ultimately leads to overestimating the optimal degree of financial leverage.

Direct Bankruptcy Costs

Direct costs of bankruptcy are the result of default or actual bankruptcy. They include notification costs, court costs, lawyers' fees, and the loss from the forced sale of assets below market prices or the deterioration of property through negligence or lack of maintenance.

Indirect Bankruptcy Costs

Indirect costs are incurred when a firm is under threat of bankruptcy.

Defence Costs **Defence costs** are the costs of actions taken by managers in an attempt to ward off bankruptcy. They include waste of managerial time and perhaps direct costs to shareholders. For example, managers may adopt a course of non-optimal managerial action to keep the firm alive and avoid losing their jobs. Such actions undoubtedly reduce the firm's value in the long run and often fail to prevent bankruptcy.

Costs of Customer and Supplier Actions Indirect costs may be incurred because of actions by suppliers, customers, and capital providers. As soon as they learn that a firm is in financial distress, customers may take their business to the competition to avoid receiving poor product and service quality from the financially distressed firm. Consequently, sales and profits drop and the firm's value drops as well.

Similarly, suppliers are reluctant to grant normal credit terms to a financially distressed firm. The costs of searching for new suppliers or getting credit elsewhere under conditions of distress can be substantial and can lead to a lower value for the firm.

Costs of Creditors' Actions Indirect costs may also be incurred as a result of creditors' actions. On learning of the precarious financial condition of a firm, creditors may demand earlier payment of their debt, more collateral, or more restrictive covenants, or may require a higher yield on the debt.

Costs of Shareholders' Actions Finally, shareholders may sell the shares they hold in order to reduce their losses. These actions generally have a multiplier effect and may ultimately lead the firm into bankruptcy.

In general, the costs of bankruptcy are incurred only if there is a real threat of such an event occurring. Therefore, when a firm is not in a serious bankruptcy position, analyzing the impact of bankruptcy costs on the firm's capital structure decision entails estimating the present value of the expected bankruptcy-related costs [PV(BC)]. These costs can then be considered in M&M's Proposition I.

When bankruptcy costs are considered, Proposition I becomes:

$$V_L = V_U + T_C D - \text{PV(BC)} \qquad \textbf{(Equation 4-14)}$$

where

$$V_L = \text{value of the levered firm}$$
$$V_U = \text{value of the unlevered firm}$$
$$T_C = \text{corporate tax rate}$$
$$D = \text{market value of the firm's debt}$$
$$\text{PV(BC)} = \text{present value of the expected bankruptcy-related costs}$$

Generally, the probability of financial distress and the magnitude of bankruptcy costs increase as more debt is used in the capital structure. Therefore, the magnitude of the expected bankruptcy costs depends on the degree of financial leverage.

Equation 4-14 shows that estimating the optimal degree of financial leverage entails finding the optimal trade-off between the tax benefits and the bankruptcy costs of debt. When the degree of financial leverage is low, the probability of bankruptcy is small and the PV(BC) is negligible. As the degree of financial leverage increases, the probability of

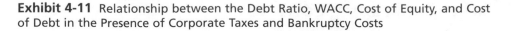

Exhibit 4-11 Relationship between the Debt Ratio, WACC, Cost of Equity, and Cost of Debt in the Presence of Corporate Taxes and Bankruptcy Costs

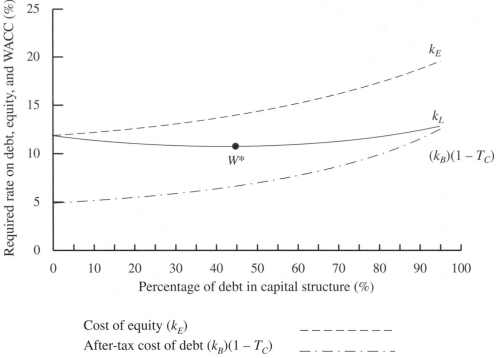

Cost of equity (k_E) — — — — — — —

After-tax cost of debt ($k_B)(1 - T_C$) — · — · — · — · ·

WACC (k_L) _____

Critical level of debt financing: W^*

bankruptcy increases and PV(BC) becomes significant. At some point short of 100% debt financing, the present value of the marginal bankruptcy costs will exactly equal the marginal tax benefits of debt. This point determines the firm's optimal capital structure. The **optimal capital structure** is a combination of long-term sources of financing that maximizes firm value and minimizes the weighted average cost of capital (WACC). Increasing financial leverage beyond this point decreases the firm's value.

Exhibit 4-11 plots the WACC of the levered firm in the presence of corporate taxes and bankruptcy costs against the percentage of debt in the firm's capital structure. The exhibit shows that the firm's WACC drops until leverage reaches the optimal level, beyond which additional leverage increases WACC.

Equation 4-14 estimates the optimal capital structure by balancing the tax shield benefits of leverage against the financial distress costs. However, bankruptcy-related costs are difficult to estimate. Thus, in practice it is difficult, if not impossible, to identify point W^* (the optimal WACC) with any precision. Yet several observations can be made about this model, which trades off the benefits of leverage against the financial distress costs.

■ Firms with higher business risk are likely to borrow less than firms with lower business risk. Firms with high business risk experience higher variability of expected returns on their assets and hence have a greater probability of bankruptcy at any debt level.

- Firms with predominantly tangible assets are likely to borrow more than firms with predominantly intangible assets because intangible assets are likely to lose most of their value when financial distress occurs. *Tangible assets* are physical assets, such as cash, real estate, and machinery. *Intangible assets* are non-physical assets that represent an advantage in the marketplace, such as copyright, trademark, and goodwill.

- Firms in higher tax brackets can benefit most from tax shields and hence should borrow more than firms in lower tax brackets. On the other hand, firms with relatively large investments in plant and equipment can claim large capital cost allowances that shelter income from taxes. Thus, these firms have lower leverage ratios than firms that cannot use capital cost allowances to shelter income.

4.5 OTHER INFLUENCES ON CAPITAL STRUCTURE

As explained previously in this chapter, capital structure theory suggests that there is an optimal level of debt financing that increases share price and minimizes the weighted average cost of capital. Although it is difficult to determine the optimal capital structure with precision, it is possible to identify factors that influence it. Financial managers should learn how these factors interact so they can establish a target capital structure for their firms. Some factors are related to a firm's industry, while others are unique to the individual firm.

Business Risk

Business risk is defined as the uncertainty regarding a firm's operating income before interest and taxes. It represents the degree of risk of the firm's operations when no debt is used. Business risk depends on several factors that vary from one firm to another and from industry to industry. These factors are:

- demand variability
- sales price variability
- input cost variability
- competitive factors
- exposure to product liability suits
- operating leverage

While the first five factors are mostly beyond the control of an individual firm, operating leverage is usually a matter of choice. **Operating leverage** is the extent to which a company's costs are fixed (rent, insurance, executive salaries) as opposed to variable (materials, direct labour). When a firm has high fixed operating costs, a change in sales is magnified into a big change in earnings before interest and taxes.

The **degree of operating leverage** is defined as the percentage change in earnings before interest and taxes divided by the percentage change in sales. It measures the sensitivity of a firm's profits to changes in sales volume. Formally, the degree of operating leverage (DOL) may be written as:

$$DOL = \frac{\frac{\Delta EBIT}{EBIT}}{\frac{\Delta Sales}{Sales}}$$

(Equation 4-15)

where

DOL = degree of operating leverage
EBIT = earnings before interest and taxes
Δ = change in the variable

Equation 4-15 is important because it implies that DOL measures the percentage change in EBIT for a 1% change in sales. It also emphasizes that DOL is a function of the sales level at which it is measured. That is, DOL at one sales level is different from DOL at a different level.

The following article demonstrates the impact DOL had on Adobe Systems' EBIT.

ADOBE'S OPERATING LEVERAGE

Adobe Systems, the second largest PC software company in the United States, dominates the markets for graphic design, imaging, dynamic media, and authoring-tool software. Web site designers prefer its Photoshop and Illustrator software applications, and Adobe's Acrobat software has become a standard for sharing documents online.

Despite a sales slowdown in 2001–2002, the company continued to meet its earnings targets. Its ability to manage discretionary expenses helped to keep its bottom line strong. As a software company, Adobe has an additional advantage: *operating leverage,* the use of fixed operating costs to magnify the effects of changes in sales on earnings before interest and taxes (EBIT).

Adobe and its peers in the software industry incur the bulk of their costs early in a product's life cycle, during the research and development (R&D) and initial marketing stages. The up-front development costs are fixed, regardless of how many copies of a program the company sells, and subsequent production costs are practically zero. The economies of scale are huge. Indeed, once a company sells enough copies to cover its fixed costs, incremental dollars go primarily to profit.

As demonstrated in the table below, operating leverage magnified the *increase* in Adobe's EBIT in 2000 and 2003 while magnifying the *decrease* in EBIT in 2001 and 2002. A 2.8% drop in 2001 sales resulted in an EBIT reduction of 7.3%. In 2002, an additional drop in sales of 5.3% resulted in a 24.1% decrease in EBIT. In 2003, a modest increase in sales—just over 11%—turned into a 32% increase in EBIT. Because the company has no long-term debt in its capital structure, its total leverage is derived only from fixed operating costs. (It's important to remember that this example represents only 4 years of data and that Adobe's degree of operating leverage may change in the future.)

The table below demonstrates the impact of operating leverage on Adobe Systems in fiscal years (FYs) 2000–2003.

Item	FY1999	FY2000	FY2001	FY2002	FY2003
Sales revenue (millions)	$1,015	$1,266	$1,230	$1,165	$1,295
EBIT (millions)	$260	$408	$378	$287	$379
(1) Percent change in sales		24.7%	−2.8%	−5.3%	11.2%
(2) Percent change in EBIT		56.9%	−7.3%	−24.1%	32.0%
DOL [(2) ÷ (1)]		2.3	2.6	4.5	2.9

Sources: Adapted from Zeke Ashton, "The Software Advantage," *Motley Fool* (March 31, 2000); and "Operating Leverage Helps Adobe," *Motley Fool* (March 16, 2001), both downloaded from www.motley.fool.com; updated using data from Adobe's 2003 *Annual Report*.

Attempt the DOL computation. Try the following You Apply It minicase.

YOU APPLY IT DEGREE OF OPERATING LEVERAGE

Total Shine Products (TSP) is a manufacturer of small lighting fixtures. TSP has 10 million shares outstanding with a total market value of $145 million. The forecast income statement of TSP and two other possible scenarios of the income statement are shown in Exhibit 4-12. The company's tax rate is 40%.

Exhibit 4-12
Forecast Income Statements of TSP ($ Millions Except Per-Share Figures)

	Forecast	Scenario 1	Scenario 2
Sales	$150.00	$100.00	$200.00
Variable costs	48.75	32.50	65.00
Fixed costs	60.00	60.00	60.00
EBIT	41.25	7.50	75.00
Interest	21.00	21.00	21.00
EBT	20.25	(13.50)	54.00
Taxes	8.10	(5.40)*	21.60
Net income	12.15	(8.10)	32.40
Earnings per share	1.215	(0.810)	3.240

* The negative tax bill recognizes the deduction arising from the loss carryback and carryforward provision of the *Income Tax Act*.

Questions

Question 1: What is DOL when sales are $150 million (base case) and change to $200 million?

Question 2: What is DOL when sales are $100 million (base case) and change to $150 million?

You Apply It Continued >

Question 3: What is DOL when sales are $150 million (base case) and change to $100 million? Comment on this result.

Answers

Question 1: What is DOL when sales are $150 million (base case) and change to $200 million?

$$\text{DOL at \$150 million} = \frac{\dfrac{75.00 - 41.25}{41.25}}{\dfrac{200 - 150}{150}} = 2.45 \text{ times}$$

A DOL of 2.45 at $150 million sales implies that a 1% increase in sales over a sales level of $150 million will increase earnings before interest and taxes by 2.45%.

Question 2: What is DOL when sales are $100 million (base case) and change to $150 million?

$$\text{DOL at \$100 million} = \frac{\dfrac{41.25 - 7.50}{7.50}}{\dfrac{150 - 100}{100}} = 9 \text{ times}$$

A DOL of 9 at $100 million sales implies that a 1% increase in sales over a sales level of $100 million will increase earnings before interest and taxes by 9%.

Question 3: What is DOL when sales are $150 million (base case) and change to $100 million? Comment on this result.

$$\text{DOL at \$150 million} = \frac{\dfrac{7.50 - 41.25}{41.25}}{\dfrac{100 - 150}{150}} = 2.45 \text{ times}$$

The DOL at a point of sales is the same regardless of whether it is measured when sales increase or decrease.

Equation 4-15 can be simplified to a more practical formula for the degree of operating leverage:

$$\text{DOL} = \frac{\text{contribution margin}}{\text{EBIT}} = \frac{(P - V)Q}{(P - V)Q - \text{FC}} \quad \textbf{(Equation 4-16)}$$

where
DOL = degree of operating leverage
P = price per unit
V = variable cost per unit
Q = amount of sales in units Q
FC = fixed operating charges, which include fixed costs, lease payments, and other costs that do not change with the level of sales but do not include any financing charges

Equation 4-16 can be expressed in terms of total sales and total variable costs as:

$$DOL = \frac{PQ - VQ}{PQ - VQ - FC} = \frac{\text{sales} - \text{variable costs}}{\text{sales} - \text{variable costs} - FC} \quad \textbf{(Equation 4-17)}$$

The break-even sales level is the sales level Q that makes the contribution margin equal to FC. At the break-even point, DOL is very large (infinite) because a positive number is being divided by 0. Practically, it means that a firm at the break-even point will increase EBIT by a large percentage if sales increase by 1%. EBIT increases from 0 to a positive number.

Use the information provided for Total Shine Products previously and apply it to answer the questions given below:

YOU APPLY IT DEGREE OF OPERATING LEVERAGE (CONTINUED)

Questions

Question 1: Given that variable costs are $48.75 million and fixed costs are $60 million, what is the DOL of Total Shine Products from above when the sales level changes from $150 million (base case) to $200 million?

Question 2: Given that variable costs are $32.5 million and fixed costs are $60 million, what is the DOL of Total Shine Products from above when the sales level is $100 million (base case) and changes to $150 million?

Answer

Question 1: Given that variable costs are $48.75 million and fixed costs are $60 million, what is the DOL of Total Shine Products when the sales level changes from $150 million (base case) to $200 million?

Equation 4-16 or 4-17 can be used to calculate DOL as:

$$DOL = \frac{150 - 48.75}{150 - 48.75 - 60} = 2.45 \text{ times}$$

Question 2: Given that variable costs are $32.5 million and fixed costs are $60 million, what is the DOL of Total Shine Products when the sales level is $100 million (base case) and changes to $150 million?

Equation 4-16 or 4-17 can be used to calculate DOL as:

$$DOL = \frac{100 - 32.50}{100 - 32.50 - 60} = 9 \text{ times}$$

The results from Equation 4-16 or 4-17 are the same as the results from Equation 4-15.

A few observations are useful at this point:

- The operating leverage changes from one base sales level to another.
- DOL is largest at the break-even point.
- At a sales level below the break-even point, DOL is negative. For example, DOL might be equal to −3. In this case, a 1% increase in sales reduces losses by 3% or a 1% decrease in sales increases losses by 3%.

In a totally automated company, costs are virtually all fixed. Once sales exceed the break-even point, a $1 increase in sales increases operating income by $1. In contrast, a company with costs that are largely variable will show a relatively lower increase in operating income when production and sales increase. As costs and production increase together, an increase in sales increases operating profits by almost the same percentage. At the extreme, when fixed charges are zero, DOL is 1, meaning that a 1% increase in sales will increase EBIT by 1%.

The important point to remember is that operating leverage increases the degree of risk of cash flows from sales. Financial leverage increases risk further as it magnifies the profits and losses to shareholders. Consequently, a firm with a high degree of operating leverage is likely to operate with a low degree of financial leverage to avoid magnifying risk beyond the level desired by shareholders. Generally, managers consider the operating risk of the firm when they decide the degree of financial leverage.

Agency Costs

When debt is used in the capital structure of a firm, shareholders can be considered as agents for debtholders. As explained in Chapter 3, debtholders have no voting rights whereas shareholders do. Consequently, shareholders are in a position to affect managers' decisions through their choice of directors. Yet shareholders may undertake actions that are detrimental to the interests of debtholders. For example, they may choose to increase financial leverage. This action would reduce the protection provided to debtholders. Alternatively, shareholders may decide to undertake extremely risky projects. The profits of these projects accrue to shareholders, but the risk borne by debtholders is higher without additional compensation.

In either case, debtholders incur agency costs as wealth is transferred from debtholders to shareholders. For example, suppose the cash flows to a firm and the value of a firm are fixed. The value of a firm can be found by summing the values of debt D and equity E ($V = D + E$). If the manager's actions make the debt less valuable, D drops. As V is fixed, E rises by the amount of the drop in D. Therefore, shareholders gain at the expense of debtholders.

Debtholders may demand a high interest rate on the debt to compensate for any potential agency costs. Alternatively, they may impose restrictions on the firm's actions to minimize agency costs. These restrictions take the form of protective covenants attached to the bond indenture. Monitoring the firm's compliance with covenants is expensive and the more restrictive the covenants are, the more expensive the monitoring process will be. Monitoring costs are often borne by shareholders as direct cash payments to the trustee, who holds the bond indenture and ensures that the firm is complying with the provisions of the indenture. Shareholders may also pay indirect monitoring costs, such as loss of managerial time and efficiency.

When a firm uses a small amount of debt in the capital structure, the agency costs are minor. As the percentage of debt increases, so do agency costs. As the debt reaches a high level, agency costs increase rapidly until they form a serious constraint on issuing additional debt.

Signalling and Asymmetric Information

Signalling represents the process of conveying information through a firm's actions. It affects the nature of returns to shareholders and the degree to which they are positive or negative. The issue of new securities to the public is considered by researchers such as Ross (1977) as a **signalling event**[4] because raising new funds in the market provides information regarding the future projects planned by the firm. Empirical evidence suggests that the signals provided by changes in the capital structure should be taken seriously because the firm could incur substantial bankruptcy costs if the expected cash flows do not materialize.

Generally, empirical evidence indicates that new equity offerings yield negative returns to shareholders, while actions that increase leverage produce positive share returns. These observations may be interpreted as follows. A new common-share issue decreases leverage and the benefits associated with it. Moreover, it signals that the firm is not confident that it can support the current level of debt. Shareholders expect a share price decline and are willing to sell the share at discounted prices. Thus, they suffer negative returns on their holdings.

In contrast, additional borrowing increases the benefits of leverage, such as tax breaks. A firm that increases leverage indicates that it is confident in servicing the new debt without the risk of bankruptcy. In other words, projects financed with the new funds from debt have large expected net present values that accrue to existing shareholders.

The involvement of shareholders in the financing of a new project is a signalling event that conveys information about the shareholders' opinion of the investment opportunity. For example, when a firm has projects with low expected net present values, its current shareholders will be indifferent about bringing in other shareholders to share in the firm's profits. The proportion of current shareholders investing in these projects will not be very high. These statements assume that shareholders possess **asymmetric information**— information not available to other investors.

Another asymmetric information problem arises when shareholders possess more accurate information than the general public. If the firm's share price is higher than its intrinsic value, the firm's current shareholders will prefer to issue new equity. The new shareholders bear some of the future decline in the share price once the market realizes that the firm is overvalued. On the other hand, if the market price of the firm is less than its intrinsic value, current shareholders will prefer to raise new funds through debt issues. This choice guarantees that the future appreciation in the share price is captured by current shareholders rather than by outsiders when the market realizes the true value of the firm.

These arguments can be generalized as follows. If current shareholders or their agents possess information not available to the market and the firm has investment projects with positive expected net present values, a pattern of financing can be predicted for the firm. The first preference of the firm is to finance the new projects with internally generated funds. If these funds are inadequate, the firm will prefer to make up the difference with a new debt issue. If funds from debt sources fall short of financing the new projects, the firm will prefer to raise additional funds through debt–equity combinations such as convertible debt or debt with warrants. Last to be considered for raising funds is an equity issue. This order by which various sources of funds are selected is often called the **pecking order theory** of capital structure (Meyers, 1984).[5]

The arguments in this section have implications for the efficient market hypothesis, which was explained in Chapter 1. These arguments implicitly assume that markets are not strongly efficient. Otherwise, shareholders or their agents would not be able to exploit information unavailable to the market. However, the arguments still hold under the conditions of a semi-strongly efficient market.

---

[4] Stephen A. Ross, "The Determination of Financial Structure: The Incentive Signalling Approach," *Bell Journal of Economics*, Volume 8, Spring 1977, pp. 23–40.

[5] Stewart C. Meyers, "The Capital Structure Puzzle," *Journal of Finance*, Volume 39, July 1984, pp. 575–592.

Ethical Response to Asymmetrical Information An interesting ethical issue arises from these arguments. Because management and shareholders are more informed than the market, is it ethical for them to exploit that information to increase the wealth of current shareholders at the expense of incoming shareholders? The answer is no. Although it is tempting to argue that exploiting information for the benefit of shareholders is a sound business practice, it must be emphasized that the use of privileged information for personal or shareholder gains is highly unethical.

The ethical action in this case is to fully release the information to the public. If the information is positive, the firm's shares rise and existing shareholders benefit. If the news is bad, share prices drop and the firm's existing shareholders suffer the loss.

Managerial Preference

Managerial preference regarding risk has a major impact on the capital structure of a firm. While managerial preference does not alter the optimal capital structure, managers usually influence the choice. Some managers are risk averse and choose low-risk structures, whereas other managers choose unusually risky capital structures that match their preferences. When the market realizes that a firm's capital structure is sub-optimal, it will penalize the firm.

Consider the following article by George G. Triantis. It suggests that the managerial decision-making process is not dominated by shareholder voting and that many other forces are involved. A wide range of other forms of leverage should be considered along with their interaction within a broadly conceived corporate governance system. Debt imposes on the issuer an obligation to make a series of fixed payments that are not discretionary. The inclusion of debt in a firm's capital structure imposes discipline on managers, which affects their decision making.

This article should help you understand how debt financing and security design affect decision making by management. As you read it, consider the situations it presents to understand how debt and debtholders influence the firm's decision-making process. The analysis shows how debt priority, governance, and bankruptcy affect managers' decision-making process. It also explains how security design can be used to influence the capital structure decision. As you read this section of the article, try to identify the various financial features and governance rights that a manager must combine in security design to maximize the value of the firm.

Debt Financing, Corporate Decision Making, and Security Design

George G. Triantis[1]

I. Introduction

The scope of the term *corporate governance* varies a great deal. In its narrowest sense, it concerns the mechanisms that shareholders use to discipline their managers. As owners, shareholders hold decision-making authority in the corporation. Shareholders delegate this power to the board of directors and the firm's management. From this perspective,

---

[1] Professor of Law, University of Virginia.

the goal of corporate governance is to ensure that managers act as perfect agents of their principals, the firm's shareholders.

It is clear, however, that managers are subject to influence from many sources other than shareholder voting, proxy battles, hostile takeovers, and the like. Indeed, the study of corporate governance arguably should encompass all factors that affect the decision-making of managers. In competitive product and factor markets, virtually all of the firm's transactions or relationships affect its prospects for survival and hence managerial incentives. Accordingly, they should properly be included in the decision-making model of the corporation. The decisions of the firm are affected by the threat of a customer taking its business elsewhere, a supplier that cuts off deliveries, a key employee who resigns, or a bank that calls its loan. These factors may have as much or more of an impact than threatened or actual shareholder action. Therefore, if the purpose of the study of corporate governance is to explain why and how managers make the decisions that they do and how these decisions might be made more efficient, we must not be preoccupied with the role of shareholders. Rather, we should consider a wide range of other forms of leverage over the decisions of the firm and their interaction within a broadly conceived corporate governance system.

In this article, I review several respects in which debt and debtholders influence the decision-making process in a firm. The principal feature that distinguishes debt from equity is that debt imposes on the issuer a fixed obligation to make a series of payments to the debtholder. The fact that these payments are fixed and not discretionary imposes a discipline on managers that affects their decisions. In addition, the structure of the debt of a firm is typically hierarchical; classes of debtholders enjoy different priorities upon the dissolution or liquidation of the firm. Some classes of creditors may have across-the-board, debtor-based priority over others; for example, senior creditors are entitled to be paid in full on dissolution or liquidation before junior or subordinated creditors receive anything. Alternatively, a creditor may have asset-specific priority by virtue of a security interest in an asset or group of firm assets. The ability of the debtor to grant either debtor-based or asset-based priority to some creditors affects the investment incentives of the firm.

Firms often agree to a variety of affirmative and restrictive covenants in their debt contracts. The violation of any covenant is an event of default and triggers the acceleration of the maturity of the debt and the enforcement right of the lender. Debt covenants therefore constrain the firm's decision space and, if they are violated, may trigger the more active intervention of the lender in the firm's decisions. Later in this article, I discuss briefly the effect of debtholder monitoring, enforcement and intervention on the decisions of the borrower. In the final section of this article, I comment on the erosion of the traditional distinction between debt and equity by the design of financial instruments that combine features of equity and debt. It may well be that the distinction has lost its analytic utility and a new taxonomy should be adopted to describe the financial and governance characteristics of financial instruments.

II. The Discipline of Debt Obligations

A debt investor purchases the right to receive a series of payments at specified future dates. If the firm fails to meet a scheduled payment, the debtholder is typically entitled to accelerate the maturity of future payments and force the firm to surrender assets which may be sold to satisfy the debt. In contrast, an equityholder is entitled to the residue after the claims of debtholders and creditors are satisfied in full. The equityholder may receive dividends, but these are paid at the discretion of the firm's management and only to the extent allowed by law and the firm's contracts with its debtholders.

The fixed obligations of debt are a source of discipline on managers that requires minimal monitoring. First, as Michael Jensen has suggested, debt forces managers to pay out free cash flow to the firm's investors.[2] Without the existence of periodic payment obligations, managers have the incentive to accumulate cash and liquid assets. The resulting pool of funds gives the managers greater discretion and power over future decisions. This discretion is potentially costly in the following respects. The financial reserves are often held in the form of cash or low-yield, liquid securities. This problem is especially acute in mature industries (e.g., chemicals, tobacco, steel, and tires) that generate significant cash flows that cannot be profitably reinvested in opportunities available to these firms. Moreover, the pool of liquid reserves provides managers with a buffer against financial downturns and an internal source from which they may finance new projects. The result is that managers are insulated somewhat from competitive pressures in product markets and are not subject to the periodic scrutiny of capital markets. The existence of periodic fixed-debt obligations forces managers to disgorge the cash flow and put it in the hands of investors who can invest it profitably. Dividends or share repurchases have the same effect.[3] However, debt is a more reliable mechanism because the consequences of missing a scheduled debt repayment are typically far more immediate than those that follow a reduction in dividends or a decision not to repurchase stock.

Second, the existence of fixed obligations may provide incentives that lead to greater managerial effort.[4] The firm's investments must produce sufficient cash flow to meet the periodic repayment obligations. Otherwise, the exercise of enforcement rights by debtholders may lead to the liquidation of the firm. Thus, the issuance of debt sets challenging goals for periodic cash flows. The firm's managers accept these goals as their personal goals (with greater or lesser degrees of commitment, as I explain below). These goals provide direction for managerial action and promote effort and persistence in the pursuit of the goal.[5]

Three core predictions of goal-setting theory have been the subject of considerable empirical testing and lend support to the professed motivational virtue of corporate debt. First, specific goals are more effective in motivating higher performance than general goals, such as to do one's best. In this sense, debt is preferable to equity because it encourages the manager to set specific cash flow goals. This prescription is reinforced by the second prediction: proximal goals have a greater positive effect on performance than distal goals. The periodic payment obligations may give rise to more immediate goals than the pressure to maximize the value of equity over a longer time horizon.

---

[2] "Agency Costs of Free Cash Flow, Corporate Finance and Takeovers" (1986), 76 *American Econ. Rev.* 323. In addition, see M.C. Jensen, "Eclipse of the Public Corporation" (1989), 67 *Harv. Bus. Rev.* 61.

[3] F.H. Easterbrook, "Two Agency Cost Explanations for Dividends" (1984), 74 *Amer. Econ. Rev.* 650.

[4] "[A]fter a firm promises to pay out most of its cash flow to holders of debt, it is eternally skating on thin ice. Managers (at least top managers) realize that deficiencies in their own efforts could cause the firms to fail." F.H. Easterbrook, "High-Yield Debt as an Incentive Device" (1991), 11 *Int'l Rev. of Law and Econ.* 183 at p. 186.

[5] For a general explanation of the links between goal setting, effort, and performance, and a review of the empirical work in this area, see E.A. Locke & G.P. Latham, *A Theory of Goal Setting & Task Performance* (Englewood Cliffs, New Jersey Prentice-Hall, 1990). The authors explain in detail the core predictions that I summarize here.

The third core prediction is that, as a general matter, more difficult goals tend to motivate higher levels of effort and performance than easier goals. The mix of debt and equity in a firm's capital structure can therefore be adjusted to provide challenging, specific, and periodic goals for its manager. However, the link between goal level and performance motivation is not sufficiently direct to warrant an irrebutable inference that managers can be motivated to achieve greater cash flows simply through the higher goals that are implicitly assigned when the firm issues a greater proportion of debt. The direction and magnitude of the effect of goal level on performance is moderated by the manager's commitment to the goal implicitly assigned by the level of fixed obligations, as well as the manager's sense of the likely effectiveness of her performance.[6] For example, as a firm sets higher goals for cash flow production, the probability of meeting those goals falls. Without a compensating increase in the manager's personal gratification from achieving those goals, her commitment may well fall off. Some empirical studies have shown that commitment can decline as the goal becomes more difficult and the individual's perceived chances of reaching it declines. If the manager's commitment in fact does not decrease, a different problem may impair performance. A commitment to a very difficult goal may create pressure on the actor leading to emotional states—notably stress and anxiety—that can be detrimental to performance. Therefore, while debt may set challenging goals that improve managerial effort and performance, increases in leverage beyond an optimal point are likely to impair performance.[7]

Third, Jensen also observed that debt is a powerful agent for change. In particular, he argued that an increase in a firm's debt-equity ratio, caused by a leveraged buyout, forces managers to rethink their strategies and induces directors to reconsider the organization and composition of their management teams.[8] However, beyond a certain point, leveraging may be counterproductive in this respect as well. On the one hand, if managers feel that they can just meet the implicit goals, they may be discouraged from taking even profitable risks or experimenting with new strategies. On the other hand, if the managers sense that they will not be able to meet the obligations, leveraging may produce the opposite effect.[9] Locke and Latham make a more general observation to this effect:[10] Specific, hard goals may push individuals with hard goals into a less than systematic "scramble" to find a strategy that will get immediate results, whereas those with easy goals, do-your-best goals, or learning goals are more likely, or at least equally likely, to take the time to use a more careful, systematic approach.

---

[6] The concept of self-efficacy is a central component in the social-cognitive theories developed by Albert Bandura. Bandura defines self-efficacy as one's judgment of "how well one can execute courses of action required to deal with prospective situations": See *Social Foundations of Thought and Action: A Social Cognitive Theory* (Englewood Cliffs, New Jersey, Prentice-Hall, 1986).

[7] G.G. Triantis, "A Discussion of the Motivational Properties of Debt" (Sept. 1993), Can. Law and Econ. Assoc. Conference Papers.

[8] "Overleveraging creates the crisis atmosphere managers require to slash unsound investment programs, shrink overhead, and dispose of assets that are more valuable outside the company. The proceeds generated by these overdue restructurings can then be used to reduce debt to more sustainable levels, creating a leaner, more efficient and competitive organization. . . . In other circumstances, the violation of debt covenants creates a board-level crisis that brings new actors onto the scene, motivates a fresh review of top management and strategy, and accelerates response." Jensen, *supra*, footnote 2, at p. 67.

[9] In this respect, the point of insolvency is a knife's edge separating risk averse and risk preferring managerial behavior. See S. Rose-Ackerman, "Risk Taking and Ruin: Bankruptcy and Investment Choice" (1991), 20 *J. of Legal Studies* 277.

[10] *Supra*, footnote 5, at p. 105.

III. Debt Priorities

The fixed claims against a corporation are typically arranged as a hierarchy. A creditor with higher priority is entitled to be paid in full before a debtholder of lower priority gets paid anything in a dissolution or liquidation of the corporation. The priority of a claim may be either debtor-based (e.g., senior, junior, or subordinated debt) or asset-based through the use of security interest. Recent scholarship has suggested that the priority structure of a firm's debt affects its investment decisions.[11] The following two examples illustrate the efficient and inefficient effects of priority debt on investment incentives.

Suppose Firm has assets in place worth 50, unsecured liabilities of 80, and no free cash. The firm has an opportunity to invest in a profitable project that requires an investment of 20 and yields a payoff of 25. Firm will not be able to finance the new project by issuing new equity because the debtholders would capture the full payoff of the profitable project, including the investment of the new equityholders. Firms would also not be able to raise the necessary funds by borrowing on an unsecured basis. The new lenders would have to share the payoff from the project with the existing creditors. This problem is referred to in the literature as debt overhang or underinvestment, since the firm's insolvency and consequent inability to raise funds may cause it to underinvest in low-risk, profitable projects. However, if the new investor is given priority over existing lenders, it will be paid first out of the payoff from the project and therefore would finance the profitable investment. The existing unsecured creditors would share in the project's payoff after the new priority lender has been repaid in full.

Suppose now that the project is risky and has a negative net present value. It yields a payoff of 35 in one state of the world and nothing in the other state of the world. The states are equally likely to materialize. Although the project is unprofitable on an expected-value basis, it offers a 50 percent chance that the firm may regain solvency. Therefore, both the managers and the existing shareholders want to find some way to raise the funds to exploit this project. Firm would be unable to finance this project by issuing either new equity or new unsecured debt. A new lender would be willing to fund the project if it were given priority over existing liabilities because it would thereby be guaranteed repayment in full, even if the bad state materializes. This financing arrangement harms existing unsecured creditors because they bear the expected loss from the project. This problem is referred to as the overinvestment in risky, unprofitable projects.

The incentives created by the issuance of priority debt are most pronounced and demonstrable in an insolvent firm. These incentives exist also in a solvent firm, provided that there is some possibility of insolvency.[12] However, the severity of the underinvestment and overinvestment problems varies inversely with the firm's solvency. Priority financing simply reduces the cost of new capital and thereby increases the tendency of the firm to invest in new projects. As such, it is a double-edged sword that mitigates underinvestment and aggravates overinvestment. There is little way of knowing, particularly ahead of time, whether priority debt financing will be used by the firm to finance low-risk, profitable investment opportunities that would otherwise be forgone or to fund high-risk, negative net present

---

[11] See Rene M. Stulz and Herb Johnson, "An Analysis of Secured Debt" (1985), 14 *J. Fin. Econ.* 501; Robert Gertner and David Scharfstein, "A Theory of Workouts and the Effects of Reorganization Law" (1991), 46 *J. Finance* 1189; G.G. Triantis. "A Theory of the Regulation of Debtor-in-Possession Financing" (1993), 46 *Vanderbilt Law Rev.* 901; G.G. Triantis, "A Free-Cash-Flow Theory of Secured Debt and Creditor Priorities" (1994), 80 *Va. Law Rev.* 2155; H. Kanda & S. Levmore. "Explaining Creditor Priorities" (1994), 80 *Va. Law Rev.* 2103.

[12] Triantis (1994), *supra*, footnote 11, at pp. 2161–63.

value projects which the firm would have otherwise been unable to exploit.[13] It appears, however, that the dilemma may be solved and incentives may be optimized if the new lender is given priority only in the value of the new project. This solution explains the existence of asset-based priority and is reflected in the priority structure in the law of secured transactions. The general rule is that a secured creditor (who files in the appropriate public registry) can prevent its debtor from granting a more senior security interest in the same collateral to a subsequent creditor. An exception is made for the purchase money security interest. A creditor who finances the purchase of assets in which she takes a security interest (the purchase money security creditor) may enjoy priority over the earlier secured party, but only with respect to the value from such assets. With respect to the other assets of the debtor, the purchase money security creditor ranks behind the earlier secured financer. This combination approximates the type of project financing referred to above.[14]

IV. Governance Levers of Debtholders

The role of the debtholders in the mechanisms described thus far has been essentially passive. The obligation of the borrower to make periodic payments forces the payout of free cash, creates incentive for managerial effort, and provides a stimulus for change. The priority given to new debt over existing claims increases the tendency of the firm to invest in new projects. Yet holders of debt, particularly banks and finance companies, do more than screen their borrowers, receive fixed payments, and enforce their debt when payments are missed. Borrowers make a variety of other promises or covenants to these lenders. For instance, the debtor may covenant to restrict its distributions to shareholders and compensation to management, to insure its premises, to maintain a specified minimum asset-to-debt ratio, or not to sell key assets without the consent of the lender. These affirmative or restrictive covenants constrain the decision space available to management. The violation of a covenant is typically an event of default that triggers the acceleration and enforcement rights of the debtholder. Debt covenants are well recognized in the literature as mechanisms by which the firm bonds its commitment not to engage in behavior that benefits managers or shareholders at the expense of creditors.[15] These covenants are effective only to the extent that the lender monitors their compliance. In turn, to the extent that the firm is deterred from engaging in actions that harm its creditors, other creditors benefit from the monitoring of the lender who walks the beat on their behalf.[16]

While covenants are well understood as bonding mechanisms, they are much less appreciated for the role they play in triggering lender activism.[17] They serve as trip wires for the lender's right to accelerate and enforce (exit) or to intervene in the borrower's

---

[13] In bankruptcy, the court is authorized to make this determination in approving debtor-in-possession financing. See Triantis (1993), *supra*, footnote 11.

[14] See H. Kanda & S. Levmore, *supra*, footnote 11; G.G. Triantis (1994), *supra*, footnote 11.

[15] C.W. Smith, Jr. & Jerold Warner, "On Financial Contracting: An Analysis of Bond Covenants" (1979), 7 *J. of Fin. Econ.* 117.

[16] R.E. Scott, "A Relational Theory of Secured Financing" (1986), 86 *Columbia Law Rev.* 901 at p. 931; G.G. Triantis, "Secured Debt under Conditions of Imperfect Information" (1992), 21 *J. of Legal Studies* 225, at pp. 242–43.

[17] The discussion that follows is based on G.G. Triantis & R.J. Daniels, "An Interactive Model of Corporate Governance: Redefining the Role of Debt" (1995), 83 *California Law Rev.* 601.

decisions (exercise voice).[18] This function is perhaps most apparent in covenants that impose financial ratio tests on the borrower and are supported by periodic reporting requirements. The covenants in lending agreements with banks or finance companies are usually designed to be tripped well before the borrower either misses a payment or becomes insolvent. As a result, the lender has the opportunity to act when the firm is in financial difficulty, but before it becomes insolvent.

When a covenant is violated, the lender may use the threat of acceleration to influence the decisions of the borrower: for example, to discontinue a product line, to sell a division unrelated to the core business of the firm, or to replace a manager. The lender's voice in this respect may be as direct and effective as the voice of a shareholder who threatens to vote to replace incumbent directors. The lender's exercise of voice is regulated, however. If the lender uses its exit threat to improve the value of its exit option by, for instance, taking new or additional security interests in the debtor's assets, the courts may use doctrines of lender liability, equitable subordination, and preferential transfers to reverse the advantage.[19] Lender voice may carry a more subtle bias in favour of conservative measures that contain losses rather than maximize firm value. As a general rule, however, the courts do not interfere in these less blatant cases of lender influence unless the lender is found to have held absolute dominion or control over the affairs of the debtor.

The role of lender exit in corporate governance is less direct and clear than that of lender voice. In many cases, the exit of the lender communicates information about the debtor to other stakeholders. In order for this information to be useful, it must signal some problem in the corporation and must appear at a time when corrective action may still be taken. A variety of contractual and legal rules that constrain the lender's ability to exit may be explained as mechanisms that enhance the informational value of exit. In this vein, the window of time during which a lender may exit is defined, at one end, by the triggering of an event of default and, at the other, by the borrower's insolvency. The event of default is triggered by a covenant violation, which provides at least some evidence that the insolvency risk of the borrower has risen to a threshold level of concern. But a lender who delays enforcing its debt until the debtor becomes insolvent runs the risk that its enforcement rights will be stayed in bankruptcy. In addition, while the debt of a secured creditor may be satisfied prior to bankruptcy, an unsecured lender who is paid by an insolvent debtor on the eve of bankruptcy may be forced to surrender its recovery under preference rules. The implicit policy behind preference rules is that lender exit should be permitted only when it occurs early enough to prompt useful intervention by other stakeholders of the corporation. Through such rules, the advantages of an interactivity in corporate governance are enhanced.

Finally, bankruptcy itself provides an important mechanism for correcting managerial problems. Insolvency is a financial condition that should not be viewed as an illness in itself, but rather a deliberately set litmus paper that signals the presence of fundamental economic problems. The debt load of a firm may be set in order to cause insolvency when the firm's managers are failing to deploy its assets in their most profitable use. Thus, if the

---

[18] The choice between exit and voice options has been used to describe responses to unsatisfactory states of affairs in a variety of political and economic contexts; see A.O. Hirschman. *Exit, Voice and Loyalty—Responses to Decline in Firms, Organizations and States* (Cambridge, Massachusetts. Harvard University Press. 1970).

[19] For a review of these doctrines and their role in corporate governance, see Triantis and Daniels, *supra*, footnote 17.

firm becomes insolvent, it is a sign that its assets may not be optimally deployed. A variety of mechanisms may be available to correct this inefficiency: for example, a successful takeover of another firm in the industry or by a corporate raider, a shareholder vote to replace the board of directors, the intervention of an active lender. If these mechanisms fail and creditors seek to exit the firm en masse, bankruptcy is available as a collective procedure for transferring the assets of the firm to one or more third parties who will earn a return by redeploying the assets in a more profitable manner. Thus, while bankruptcy is traditionally seen as a way of resolving financial distress while preserving the going concern value of the firm, it should be analyzed as a process for correcting the inefficient deployment of assets in order to enhance the value of the firm.[20]

V. Hybrid Financial Instruments[21]

As a result of the dynamic process of financial engineering, the financing decision facing the firm is no longer usefully described as a choice between debt and equity, but as a question of security design. The firm must decide what combination of various building blocks will yield the most value to its investors as a group. The available *financial* features include periodic payment obligations, liquidation priority in bad times, and the entitlement to share in residue in good times. The *governance* building blocks include voting rights, the right to enforce fiduciary obligations, and the right to enforce fixed claims against firm assets or to trigger bankruptcy proceedings. Conventional debt and equity instruments are simply specific combinations of these features. Conventional debt is a fixed claim to a series of payments from the borrower, a priority over equity in liquidation, but no right to share in the residue in good times. Debtholders have the right to enforce their fixed claims, but no right to vote or enforce fiduciary duties of directors. Conventional equity carries a right to share in the residue of firm value, but no fixed claim and no priority in liquidation. Equityholders can vote and enforce management's fiduciary obligations, but have no right to seize firm assets prior to dissolution.

However, not all debt and equity issues have these characteristics: for example, some debt issues do not impose periodic payment obligations on the issuer. These include zero-coupon bonds or payment-in-kind bonds. To take another example, convertible debt provides the combination of a liquidation priority in bad times and a share of the residue in good times. A similar combination is achieved through redeemable common stock that the holder may put to the corporation in return for debt (puttable stock). Convertible debt and puttable stock are typically distinguished on the basis that the former gives an option for downstream conversion while the latter provides an option for upstream conversion. The distinction seems important because corporate law regards upstream conversion with suspicion. Some corporate statutes still do not allow it and all prohibit conversion from equity to debt when the issuer is insolvent. The distinction drawn between convertible debt and puttable stock based on the direction of conversion rights is misleading, however. The financial payoffs of any convertible debt may be replicated in a puttable stock, and vice versa. The meaningful difference lies in the governance rights held by the respective investors until conversion. This difference is significant because, as a general rule, option rights are not exercised until their

---

[20] For a more complete discussion, see G.G. Triantis. "The Interplay Between Liquidation and Reorganization in Bankruptcy: The Role of Screens, Gatekeepers, and Guillotines" (1996), 16 *Int'l Rev. of Law and Econ.*, forthcoming.

[21] The discussion that follows is a summary of A.J. Triantis & G.G. Triantis, "Conversion Rights and the Design of Financial Contracts" (1994), 72 *Washington Univ. Law Quarterly* 1231.

maturity. Until this time, the puttable common stockholder might be able to vote and enforce fiduciary duties, while the convertible debtholder can do neither. The convertible debtholder has leverage over the firm's management only through the mechanisms identified in the previous section as traditionally associated with debt. These governance levers appear only after the occurrence of an event of default specified in the debt contract.

Ultimately, therefore, we are left with a question of security design that is informed neither by concepts of debt or equity nor by the related notion of conversion. The issuer's objective is to combine financial and governance rights in a way that maximizes the value of the firm. Therefore, suppose that an investor receives the combination of financial features described in the previous paragraph: liquidation priority in bad times and participation in residue in good times. Should that investor be given significant governance participation? An investor holding this financial claim has a preference for risk taking by the corporation that exceeds that of either creditors or shareholders of the firm when the conversion option is at or close to the money, when the stock price is around the conversion price of the puttable stock or the convertible debt, as the case may be. Thus, an issuer should be cautious in combining financial and governance features in a single instrument. As stockbrokers, owners of puttable shares generally have the right to vote or to enforce fiduciary duties at all times. In contrast, the governance levers of convertible debtholders do not arise until the firm is in some kind of default under the debt contract, at which time the conversion option is less likely to be near the money. This governance feature, rather than any difference in financial characteristics, explains the relative popularity of convertible debt over puttable shares.

VI. Conclusion

It should be apparent that the decisions of managers are influenced by forces from various directions and that rights to vote and to enforce fiduciary duties do not dominate the process. The task for future research is to examine and compare these forces and to determine the optimal packages of financial claims and governance levers that should be issued by any given firm. In thinking about optimal packaging, the traditional distinction between debt and equity may be of limited analytical utility and should therefore be replaced by a more finely-tuned taxonomy of financial and governance building blocks.

Source: George G. Triantis, *Canadian Business Law Journal*, Vol. 26, 1995–1996, pp. 93–105.

4.6 SELECTING CAPITAL STRUCTURE IN PRACTICE

The process of setting the target capital structure requires a considerable degree of managerial judgment. This section begins by describing a tool that managers use to assess the effect of financial leverage from capital structure on shareholders' earnings: leverage-indifference EBIT level analysis. The section continues with other factors that influence the capital structure, including industry averages, the opinions of rating and lending agencies, and the firm's ability to service its debt obligations.

Leverage-Indifference EBIT Level

One of the main results of financial leverage is that it magnifies shareholders' earnings during periods when the return on assets is high and it depresses earnings or magnifies losses when the return on assets is low. This result is observed because interest on debt is mostly fixed, regardless of whether a firm's profits are high or low.

If the return on assets is higher than the cost of debt, the difference between the two will accumulate to magnify shareholders' return. If the return on assets is lower than the cost of debt, the difference will reduce the return to shareholders below the return to debtholders and may result in negative returns to shareholders.

If the return on assets is equal to the interest cost of debt, the return to shareholders will also be equal to the return on assets and to the interest cost of debt. The EBIT level at which the returns are equal is known as the **leverage-indifference EBIT level**.

The best way to demonstrate how to determine the leverage indifference EBIT level is through a numeric illustration. However, making the necessary calculations by hand sometimes proves both time consuming and cumbersome. In the following Computer Activity, we use a spreadsheet to illustrate the distribution of expected EBIT levels under four states of economy for a levered firm. The activity demonstrates how to determine the leverage indifference EBIT level, which causes the return on equity to equal the interest cost of debt. In addition, it outlines shareholders' risk and return for the expected EBIT levels. *With our assistance*, you will design and use this worksheet to calculate shareholders' risk and return for the expected EBIT level.

Computer Activity

Description

Heavy Duty Fabrics (HDF) has $1 million of assets financed with 50% debt that pays a 10% coupon rate. HDF has 50% equity. Because of substantial tax credits, the firm is not expected to pay taxes in the near future. As a result, the benefit of tax shields generated from interest payments is eliminated. Exhibit 4-13 provides the financial manager's best estimate of how the firm's EBITs will react under four states of the economy. Exhibit 4-14 shows the EBIT levels for a very bad economy as a function of return on assets.

Exhibit 4-13
Estimate of Growth Factors for EBIT Levels under Four States of the Economy

| | State of economy | | | |
	Very bad	**Fair**	**Good**	**Very good**
Probability	0.25	0.25	0.25	0.25
EBIT growth factor	1.0000 ×	1.2857 ×	1.5714 ×	1.8571 ×

Exhibit 4-14
EBIT Levels for a Very Bad Economy as a Function of Return on Assets

Scenarios	A	B	C
EBIT level in a very bad economy ($)	85,000	70,000	55,000

Required

a) Calculate the expected EBIT levels for each of the three scenarios in Exhibit 4-14.

b) Determine the leverage indifference EBIT level.

c) Write a brief memo to Janet White, the Controller, explaining how shareholders' risk and return is affected by the various EBIT levels.

Instructions

To complete parts a) and b):
Scenario A

FN2L4P1.xls Excel

1. Open the file FN2L4P1.xls and study the layout of worksheet L4P1. Rows 5 to 8 contain the data table, cell E10 is provided for you to enter the EBIT levels for a very bad economy from Exhibit 4-14, and rows 12 to 24 contain the calculation table for shareholders' risk and return.

2. Enter in cell E10 the value for the EBIT level in a very bad economy for scenario A.

3. Enter in row 16, starting in column B, the formulas to calculate EBIT. The formula should incorporate the growth factor from Exhibit 4-13 (pre-entered in row 15) and the estimated EBIT level for the very bad state of economy.

4. Enter in row 17 the formulas to calculate interest.

5. Enter in row 18 the formulas to calculate earnings.

6. Enter in cell E19 the formula to calculate the expected EBIT.

7. Enter in cell E20 the formula to calculate the expected earnings.

8. Enter in cell E21 the formula to calculate the expected return on assets, using expected EBIT as numerator.

9. Enter in cell E22 the formula to calculate the expected return on equity.

10. Enter in cell E23 the formula to calculate the standard deviation of the return on equity.

11. Enter in cell E24 the formula to calculate the coefficient of variation for the return on equity.

12. Save a copy of your worksheet and print it.

13. Compare your results with answer sheet L4P1AS. Correct any errors.

Scenarios B and C

14. Repeat steps 2 to 13 for scenarios B and C, checking your answers against sheets L4P1BS and L4P1CS. You can now determine the leverage indifference EBIT level.

To complete part c):
Click the L4P1MEMO sheet tab. Click anywhere in the body of the memo template and type your findings.

Commentary

a) Exhibit 4-15 summarizes the expected EBIT levels required to obtain returns on assets of 12%, 10%, and 8%. Worksheets L4P1AS, L4P1BS, and L4P1CS show the expected EBIT levels for returns on assets of 12%, 10%, and 8%, respectively.

Exhibit 4-15
Expected EBIT Levels Required to Calculate Returns on Assets

Scenarios	A	B	C
Return on assets	12%	10%	8%
Expected EBIT level	$121,427	$99,999	$78,570
EBIT level in a very bad economy	$85,000	$70,000	$55,000

b) Exhibit 4-16 shows that at the expected EBIT level of $99,999 the return on assets equals the interest cost on debt and the return on equity. The EBIT level at which all returns are equal is known as the leverage-indifference EBIT level. Remember that the indifference level for ROA and ROE is determined in terms of book values. Financial theory suggests that market value is more appropriate when calculating the leverage-indifference EBIT level.

Exhibit 4-16
Leverage-Indifference EBIT Level Required to Calculate Return on Assets and Return on Equity

Leverage-indifference EBIT level	Return on assets	Return on equity	Interest cost
$99,999	10%	10%	10%

c) The memo to Janet White, the Controller, should indicate that an increase in the level of expected EBIT increases both the return on equity and shareholders' risk, as described by the standard deviation on the return on equity. Include an exhibit to show that as the expected EBIT level increases from $78,570 to $121,427, the return on equity increases from 6% to 14%. In addition, the increase in expected EBIT level from $78,570 to $121,427 increases the standard deviation on the return on equity from 3.51% to 5.43%. The memo should indicate that the leverage-indifference EBIT level occurs at the expected EBIT level of $99,999, which is the level where return on assets equals return on equity. It should also indicate that the coefficient of variation is lower at the level of expected EBIT of $121,427 than at the expected EBIT level of $99,999. By using financial leverage, management is signalling its confidence to shareholders that the firm's expected EBIT level is likely to be higher than the leverage-indifference EBIT level.

Conclusion

This computer illustration demonstrates that as the expected EBIT levels increase in a leveraged firm, the levels of return on assets increase correspondingly. The coefficient of

> variation decreases with increasing levels of expected EBITs. Hence, the decreasing trend of risk per unit of return at expected EBIT levels above the indifference level supports management's decision to use debt. Also, the illustration has determined that the leverage-indifference EBIT level of $99,999 represents the level at which all returns are equal.

Next, we demonstrate the effect of leverage on the return on equity using Minicase 4-5, below. You should note that the information supplied here will also be used in the three mini-cases following this one.

MINICASE 4-5 EFFECT OF LEVERAGE ON THE RETURN ON EQUITY

Precise Gauges Incorporated (PGI) is a medium-sized company specializing in manufacturing gauges for a variety of industrial applications. The company's most recent balance sheet is provided in Exhibit 4-17 and a forecast of the income statement under four scenarios of the state of the economy is provided in Exhibit 4-18. The firm pays out 100% of earnings in dividends and is expected to have the same distribution of EBIT in perpetuity. Current shareholders capitalize expected earnings per share at 12.5%.

Exhibit 4-17
Precise Gauges Incorporated Balance Sheet December 31, 20X1 ($ Millions)

Assets			Liabilities		
Current assets			**Current liabilities**		
Cash	$	10	Accounts payable	$	6
Temporary investments		12	Accruals		4
Accounts receivable		20	Notes payable		14
Inventories		38			24
		80			
			Long-term liabilities		
Capital assets			Bonds		30
Equipment		95			
Plant		40	**Shareholders' equity**		
		135	Common shares		175
Patents		14			
Total assets		$229	Total liabilities and shareholders' equity		$229

Question 1: What is PGI's leverage-indifference EBIT level?

An issue that must be resolved before answering this question is whether to use book value or market value of equity in the calculations. Financial theory suggests that the use

Case Continued >

Exhibit 4-18
Forecast Income Statements ($ Millions Except Per-Share Figures)

| | State of the economy | | | |
	Very bad	Fair	Good	Very good
Probability	0.25	0.25	0.25	0.25
EBIT	$15.00	$25.00	$49.80	$75.00
Interest at 10%	$ 4.40	$ 4.40	$ 4.40	$ 4.40
EBT	$10.60	$20.60	$45.40	$70.60
Taxes at 40%	$ 4.24	$ 8.24	$18.16	$28.24
Net income	$ 6.36	$12.36	$27.24	$42.36
Shares outstanding	7.50	7.50	7.50	7.50
Earnings per share	$ 0.848	$ 1.648	$ 3.632	$ 5.648

of market value is more relevant. Therefore, the first step is to calculate the total market value of equity.

The expected earnings per share are $2.944. Capitalizing these earnings at 12.5% yields $23.55 per share. As a result, the total market value of equity is $176.625 million (7,500,000 × $23.55).

The total value of liabilities is $54 million. Thus, the total market value of the firm is $230.625 million ($176.625 million + $54 million). However, as only $44 million of liabilities are expected to be serviced by interest payments, the total market value of liabilities and shareholders' equity that is expected to be compensated is $220.625 million. Therefore, PGI's indifference EBIT level is $22.0625 million ($220.625 million × 0.10), given that the interest cost of debt is 10%. As long as EBIT is greater than this level, leverage magnifies the return to shareholders. If EBIT is less than $22.0625 million, leverage depresses the return to shareholders.

Question 2: What is the return on equity if the state of the economy turns out to be very bad or fair?

If the state of the economy is very bad, earnings per share will be $0.848, while the share price is $23.55. The return on equity in this case is 3.60% ($0.848 ÷ $23.55). If the state of the economy is fair, earnings per share will be $1.648. Given a share price of $23.55, the return on equity will be 7.00% ($1.648 ÷ $23.55).

Question 3: Suppose the firm sells 1,868,365 common shares at $23.55 per share for total proceeds of $44 million. The money is used to retire the $30 million of 10% bonds plus the notes payable. What will the earnings per share and the return to shareholders be if the state of the economy is very bad or fair? Comment on the results.

Exhibit 4-19 shows the earnings per share and the return to shareholders if the state of the economy is very bad or fair.

Exhibit 4-20 summarizes the return on equity before and after retiring the debt under two states of the economy, very bad and fair. Notice how leverage magnifies return on equity when EBIT is $25 million (greater than the indifference level of $22.0625 million). On the other hand, when EBIT is $15 million (less than $22.0625 million), leverage depresses share value.

Case Continued >

Exhibit 4-19
Forecast Income Statements after Retiring $44 Million of Debt ($ Millions Except Per-Share Figures)

| | State of the economy | |
	Very bad	Fair
Probability	0.25	0.25
EBIT	$15.00	$25.00
Taxes at 40%	$6.00	$10.00
Net income	$9.00	$15.00
Shares outstanding	9,368,365	9,368,365
Earnings per share	$0.961	$1.601
Return on equity	4.08%	6.80%

Exhibit 4-20
Comparison of Returns on Equity with and without Leverage When EBIT Is below and above the Indifference Level

| | State of the economy | |
	Very bad	Fair
EBIT ($ millions)	$15	$25
Return on equity without leverage	4.08%	6.80%
Return on equity with leverage	3.60%	7.00%

Question 4: The "very bad" scenario occurs and EBIT turns out to be $3 million instead of $15 million. For tax purposes, the firm cannot claim this year's losses, if any, against profits from prior or future years. This fact implies that taxes are zero if EBIT is negative. What are the earnings per share and the return on equity:

a) without leverage?

b) with leverage?

Comment on the results.

a) Without leverage, the firm's EBT is $3 million.

$$\text{Net income} = \$3,000,000 \times (1 - 0.4) = \$1,800,000$$
$$\text{Earnings per share} = \$1,800,000 \div 9,368,355 = \$0.19$$
$$\text{Return on equity} = \$0.19 \div \$23.55 = 0.81\%$$

b) With leverage, the firm's EBT is:

$$\text{EBT} = \$3,000,000 - \$4,400,000 = -\$1,400,000$$
$$\text{Earnings per share} = -\$1,400,000 \div 7,500,000 = -\$0.19$$
$$\text{Return on equity} = -\$0.19 \div \$23.55 = -0.81\%$$

Case Continued >

The results emphasize the earlier conclusion that whenever EBIT is lower than the indifference level, financial leverage will make a bad situation worse by further depressing the earnings per share and return on equity. In this case, financial leverage turned a small operating profit into a loss to shareholders.

Leverage-Indifference EBIT Level for Preferred Shares So far, you have considered the debt/common equity leverage-indifference EBIT level. In practice, preferred share financing may provide some leverage to common shareholders. As you learned in Chapter 3, preferred-share financing is similar to debt financing except that the dividend payments are paid from after-tax income. Thus, leverage indifference can occur between debt and common equity and between preferred-share equity and common equity.

Similarly to the debt/common equity leverage-indifference EBIT level, the preferred equity/common equity leverage-indifference EBIT level can be defined in terms of the return on assets. It is the EBIT level at which the return on assets is equal to the before-tax cost of preferred shares. If the EBIT is greater than the indifference level, the preferred-share financing magnifies the return on equity. Otherwise, preferred-share financing depresses the return on equity.

The preferred equity/common equity leverage-indifference EBIT level can be obtained in two steps:

1. Calculate the before-tax cost of preferred shares by dividing the yield on preferred shares by $(1 - T_C)$.

2. Multiply the before-tax cost of preferred shares by the amount of total preferred shares and common equity for which dividends will be paid.

Demonstrate the indifference level for two financing alternatives by completing the You Apply It minicase that follows.

YOU APPLY IT PREFERRED-SHARES LEVERAGE-INDIFFERENCE EBIT LEVEL

PGI from Minicase 4-5 is not comfortable with the current amount of $44 million in bonds and notes payable on which it is paying 10% in coupon payments. It is considering a change in capital structure whereby the firm will be left with only $10 million in liabilities. Suppose PGI has $220.625 million in interest-bearing liabilities and common equity. The firm's corporate tax rate is 40%.

PGI is considering two alternatives to replace $44 million in bonds and notes payable:

Exhibit 4-21
Alternatives for Replacing PGI Debt Financing

	Alternative 1	Alternative 2
Share type	Preferred shares	Common shares
Quantity issued	440,000	1,868,365
Face value	$100	$23.55
Dividend yield	8%	—

You Apply It Continued >

Required

What is the EBIT level at which the firm will be indifferent in its choice between the two financing alternatives?

Answer

If PGI replaces the debt with preferred shares, the total liabilities for which dividends will be paid will be $220.625 million.

The before-tax cost of the preferred shares is:

$$0.08 \div (1 - 0.4) = 13.33\%$$

Therefore, preferred equity/common equity leverage-indifference EBIT is:

$$13.33\% \times \$220,625,000 = \$29,409,313$$

If the firm's EBIT level is greater than the indifference level of $29.409 million, the return on equity is magnified by preferred-share financing. Otherwise, preferred-share financing depresses the return on equity.

Formula Approach to Calculating Leverage-Indifference EBIT Levels

Equation 4-18 is a general formula that can be used to calculate leverage-indifference EBIT levels:

$$\frac{(\text{EBIT}^* - I_1)(1 - T_C) - \text{PD}_1}{S_1} = \frac{(\text{EBIT}^* - I_2)(1 - T_C) - \text{PD}_2}{S_2}$$

(Equation 4-18)

where

EBIT^* = indifference EBIT level

I = interest payments under each alternative

T_C = corporate tax rate

PD = preferred dividends under each alternative

S = number of common shares outstanding under each alternative

In principle, this equation can be used to find the indifference EBIT level between any two combinations of financing alternatives that include debt, preferred shares, and common equity. However, assuming that the interest cost of debt and the dividend yield on preferred shares are constant for the levels of debt or preferred financing under consideration, an indifference level between the two does not exist. One of them will be preferable to the other. In this case, you compare the after-tax interest cost of debt with the yield on preferred shares. If the after-tax interest cost of debt is less than the dividend yield, debt financing is preferable. Otherwise, preferred financing is preferable over debt financing.

Therefore, when it is reasonable to assume that the interest cost of debt and the dividend yield on preferred shares are constant, Equation 4-18 can be useful to compare common-equity financing with debt financing and preferred-share financing with common-equity financing. To illustrate this comparison, try the following You Apply It minicase.

COMPARING COMMON-SHARE
FINANCING WITH DEBT FINANCING
AND PREFERRED-SHARE FINANCING WITH
COMMON-SHARE FINANCING

Required

Question 1: From the previous You Apply It minicase, PGI can sell 1,019,108 common shares at $23.55 per share for total proceeds of $24 million. The money will be used to retire $24 million of the $44 million bonds and notes payable. What is the EBIT level that makes the firm indifferent in its choice between its current capital structure and the one resulting from refinancing?

Question 2: Why is the answer to Minicase 4-5 above the same as the answer to Question 1 of this minicase?

Question 3: From the previous You Apply It minicase, PGI can sell 240,000 preferred shares at $100 per share for total proceeds of $24 million. The shares will be sold at face value, as PGI will provide an 8% dividend yield. The money will be used to retire $24 million out of the $44 million bonds and notes payable. As long as PGI's debt or preferred shares do not exceed $100, the required rates on these funds are constant. Should PGI refinance the $24 million of debt?

Question 4: PGI is considering two alternatives to replace $44 million in bonds and notes payable, as set out in Exhibit 4-21 on page 255.

Use Equation 4-18 to determine the EBIT level at which the firm will be indifferent in its choice between these two financing alternatives.

Answers

Question 1: From the previous You Apply It minicase, PGI can sell 1,019,108 common shares at $23.55 per share for total proceeds of $24 million. The money will be used to retire $24 million of the $44 million bonds and notes payable. What is the EBIT level that makes the firm indifferent in its choice between its current capital structure and the one resulting from refinancing?

Using Equation 4-18 to calculate the indifference EBIT level yields:

$$\frac{(\text{EBIT}^* - \$4,400,000)(1 - 0.40)}{7,500,000} = \frac{(\text{EBIT}^* - 2,000,000)(1 - 0.40)}{7,500,000 + 1,019,108}$$

Solving for EBIT* yields $22,062,505.

Question 2: Why is the answer to Minicase 4-5 the same as the answer to Question 1 of this minicase?

Earlier in this section, the indifference EBIT level was defined as the EBIT at which the return on assets is equal to the interest cost of debt. Therefore, unless the interest cost of debt changes from one debt level to another, the indifference EBIT level is the same regardless of whether PGI has $44 million or $20 million of debt in its capital structure. This result implies that the EBIT indifference analysis provides the level of

You Apply It Continued >

EBIT beyond which shareholders benefit from leverage, but it does not tell the financial manager the *optimal level* of debt financing.

In practice, however, when a firm lowers the total amount of debt, it may be able to refinance the remaining debt at a lower cost. Debtholders may be willing to accept a lower yield because of the lower risk level. In this case, the EBIT indifference level is lower when the firm has less debt.

Question 3: From the previous You Apply It minicase, PGI can sell 240,000 preferred shares at $100 per share for total proceeds of $24 million. The shares will be sold at face value, as PGI will provide an 8% dividend yield. The money will be used to retire $24 million out of the $44 million bonds and notes payable. As long as PGI's debt or preferred shares do not exceed $100, the required rates on these funds are constant. Should PGI refinance the $24 million of debt?

The after-tax interest cost of the debt is 6% [10% × (1 − 0.40)]. The dividend yield on the preferred shares is 8%. Therefore, it is better for shareholders if the firm keeps the debt.

Using Equation 4-18 to calculate the indifference EBIT level between the two alternatives yields:

$$\frac{(\text{EBIT}^* - \$4,400,000)(1 - 0.40)}{7,500,000}$$

$$= \frac{(\text{EBIT}^* - \$2,000,000)(1 - 0.40) - (\$24,000,000 \times 0.08)}{7,500,000}$$

The equation has no solution, implying that no indifference EBIT exists.

Question 4: PGI is considering two alternatives to replace $44 million in bonds and notes payable, as set out in Exhibit 4-21 above. Use Equation 4-18 to determine the EBIT level at which the firm will be indifferent in its choice between these two financing alternatives.

$$\frac{\text{EBIT}^*(1 - 0.40)}{7,500,000 + 1,868,365} = \frac{\text{EBIT}^*(1 - 0.40) - \$44,000,000 \times 0.08}{7,500,000}$$

Solving this equation yields an EBIT* equal to $29,416,667. It should, however, give the same answer as the one obtained for Question 1 in the previous You Apply It minicase. The difference is due to the rounding in the previous You Apply It minicase of the before-tax cost of the preferred shares to 13.33%, while the actual cost is 13.333333 . . . %.

As stated in the introduction to this section, the manager's decision on capital structure is influenced by factors such as industry averages, the opinions of rating and lending agencies, and the firm's ability to service its debt obligations. The importance of these factors depends on the firm's situation at the time of the decision.

Industry Averages

The process of determining the optimal capital structure that minimizes the weighted average cost of capital is complex. Consequently, managers tend to follow the example of others to resolve their problems. Generally, industry conditions may permit high financial leverage or they may dictate low financial leverage. This situation leads to **industry norms**, where the degrees of financial leverage of firms in an industry tend to cluster in a narrow band around the mean for the industry.

For example, empirical studies show that industries characterized by stable cash flows tend to have high levels of financial leverage. Utility companies such as telephone, electric, and heating gas companies are known to have high leverage. Other studies have found that the level of financial leverage of an industry is negatively related to the frequency of bankruptcies among firms in the industry.

Managers often consider the average debt utilization for firms in their industry. As firms in the same industry are likely to face the same business risks, it is not surprising that their leverage ratios tend to cluster in a narrow range around the average. The industry average is considered to be a relevant measure because it indicates the industry's ability to service its debt obligations for the given level of business risk.

Market or Book Value Whether to use market or book values of equity and debt is a serious issue in practice, where book values sometimes vary significantly from market values. Financial theory suggests the use of market value rather than book value.

Another issue that arises in practice is whether to include accounts payable, accruals, and notes payable in calculating the leverage ratios. Theoretically, these liabilities should be included with debt. Although they are short term in nature, they are often recurrent in a way that makes them permanent on the balance sheet.

We revisit Minicase 4-5 to illustrate changes in the capital structure and answer the following questions:

Question 1: Given the following information, what is the debt to firm value ratio of PGI?

Market value of equity	$ 176,625,000
Market value of current liabilities	24,000,000
Market value of bonds	30,000,000

Using the market value of equity and including short-term liabilities with debt, the debt-to-firm-value ratio is $54 ÷ $230.625 = 23.41%.

Question 2: Other companies in the firm's industry rely on debt more heavily than PGI. Excluding PGI, there are five companies with 75% market share. On average, these firms use 47% debt financing. If PGI decides to follow the industry norm, how much additional debt should it have? PGI would alter its capital structure by issuing debt at 10% yield to repurchase shares at the market price.

PGI's current market value of equity is $176.625 million and the market value of debt is $54 million, for a total market value of $230.625 million. In order to match the industry norm with a 47% debt-to-market-value ratio, PGI should have approximately $108.394 million in debt. Thus, PGI should raise an additional $54.394 million ($108.394 − $54) in debt.

However, these calculations are only approximations. As shown in Equation 4-7, the levered firm's value is equal to the unlevered firm's value plus the present value of the tax shield. Thus, increasing debt by $54.394 million increases the firm's value by the amount of the new tax shield. As a result, the new debt-to-total-value ratio is still less than the industry average of 47%.

The amount of additional debt, D_N, required to satisfy the debt-to-total-value ratio of 47% can be calculated by modifying Equation 4-7 slightly:

$$V_N = V_C + T_C D_N \qquad \text{(Equation 4-19)}$$

where

V_N = firm value after the new debt issue
V_C = current market value of the firm
T_C = corporate tax rate
D_N = amount of required additional debt

This equation indicates that the new debt increases the market value of the firm by the amount of the new tax shield.

V_N and D_N must satisfy:

$$V_N \times 0.47 = D_N + 54$$
$$V_N = \$230.625 \text{ million} + (0.40 \times D_N)$$

Solving these simultaneous equations for V_N and D_N yields:

$$V_N = \$257.42 \text{ million}$$
$$D_N = \$66.987 \text{ million}$$

Therefore, the amount of additional debt required is $66.987 million.

Question 3: Assuming the market is perfect and efficient, what is the market value per share after announcing the restructuring plans?

If the market were perfect and efficient at the time of the announcement of the capital restructuring plans, every current shareholder would expect to obtain a fair portion of the increase in the firm's market value. Unless the share price reflects the increase, no shareholder would sell shares. Therefore, the increase in the firm's value should be equally distributed among currently outstanding shares.

Before repurchasing any shares from the market, the firm has 7.5 million shares outstanding. The increase in the total market value of the firm is:

$$\text{new market value} - \text{initial value}$$
$$= \$257.42 \text{ million} - \$230.625 \text{ million}$$
$$= \$26.795 \text{ million}$$

This amount is distributed between 7.5 million shares. Therefore, the increase in the price per share should be $3.57. The new market price per share should be:

$$\$3.57 + \$23.55 = \$27.12$$

Question 4: How many shares remain outstanding after completing the restructuring plans?

The number of shares to be repurchased can be calculated as:

$$\frac{\text{amount of}}{\text{debt issued}} \div \frac{\text{market price}}{\text{per share}}$$
$$= \$66,987,000 \div \$27.12$$
$$= 2,470,022 \text{ shares}$$

The current number of outstanding shares is 7.5 million. Thus:

$$\begin{array}{c}\text{current number of} \\ \text{outstanding shares}\end{array} - \begin{array}{c}\text{number of shares to} \\ \text{be repurchased}\end{array}$$

$$= 7,500,000 - 2,470,022$$
$$= 5,029,978 \text{ shares}$$

Rating and Lending Agencies

Managers often consult lending agencies on whether they should issue debt or equity. Lenders provide objective outside opinions that are important in determining financial structures. They generally focus on the risk of default and consider various ratios to make their conclusions regarding the appropriateness for the firm of issuing debt or equity. Moreover, they assist the firm in setting the coupon rate on bonds to ensure that the bonds sell at par value.

Similarly, managers are influenced by the opinions of credit-rating agencies. Generally, the higher the credit rating assigned to a bond issue, the lower the coupon rate on the debt and the cost of capital will be. Companies try to keep a high credit rating to satisfy creditors and minimize the cost of capital. If the rating drops below a certain level, the bond issue may become hard to sell in the market. For example, if an issue is given the equivalent of BBB rating (Dominion Bond Rating Service) or better, it is labelled as investment grade. If the rating is below BBB, it is labelled as speculative grade. Many institutions such as pension plans and insurance companies are prohibited from investing in speculative-grade bonds. The market for such securities becomes thin and the required rate rises significantly when the rating drops below BBB.

Lending agencies and bond-rating services use ratio analysis to evaluate the credit-worthiness of debt issuers. This analysis aims to assess the default risk of issuers and the likelihood that they may have problems in paying the interest obligations and/or repaying the principal. Exhibit 4-22 shows the levels of a select group of ratios required to give a firm a credit rating by Standard & Poor's.

In practice, firms choose several key ratios and use them to estimate debt capacity. These ratios are calculated under various scenarios of the capital structure and the states of the economy. The resulting ratios are then compared to industry ratios and benchmarks established by credit agencies. The firm can then choose the capital structure that will result in ratios desirable by the firm to achieve a target credit rating. You will learn more about ratio analysis in Chapter 10.

Other Factors

In practice, a financial manager's decision on capital structure involves many factors that cannot be easily quantified. Yet these issues must be considered in order to identify the capital structure that will maximize shareholder wealth. The rest of this section deals with some of these factors.

Degree of Financial Flexibility   **Financial flexibility** refers to a firm's ability to raise funds quickly at reasonable costs. The firm's degree of financial flexibility influences its choice of capital structure.

Exhibit 4-22
Key Industrial Financial Ratios, Long-Term Debt

Three-year (2002 to 2004) medians	AAA	AA	A	BBB	BB	B	CCC
EBIT interest coverage (×)	23.8	19.5	8.0	4.7	2.5	1.2	0.4
EBITDA interest coverage (×)	25.5	24.6	10.2	6.5	3.5	1.9	0.9
FFO/total debt (%)	203.3	79.9	48.0	35.9	22.4	11.5	5.0
Free operating cash flow/total debt (%)	127.6	44.5	25.0	17.3	8.3	2.8	(2.1)
Total debt/EBITDA (×)	0.4	0.9	1.6	2.2	3.5	5.3	7.9
Return on capital (%)	27.6	27.0	17.5	13.4	11.3	8.7	3.2
Total debt/total debt + equity (%)	12.4	28.3	37.5	42.5	53.7	75.9	113.5

Source: *Standard & Poor's Corporate Ratings Criteria 2006,* Copyright 2005. Reproduced with permission of Standard & Poor's, a division of The McGraw-Hill Companies, Inc.

In practice, firms that are operating at an optimal capital structure do not lack flexibility. They are able to raise small amounts of additional funds without having to pay yields substantially higher than the yields on their existing debt. Generally, the market tolerates minor excess borrowing without penalizing the borrower with higher required yields. However, once the firm passes the optimal level of debt, its difficulty in raising additional funds through debt increases significantly. Consequently, some firms purposely use less debt than optimal in order to maintain immediate access to relatively low-cost debt. This flexibility can be modelled as an option or a combination of options with positive values. As long as the level of debt is less than optimal, the value of flexibility to the firm is positive. Thus, in setting the optimal capital structure, the firm must consider the trade-off between the benefits of additional debt financing and the value of the flexibility option.

Control The choice of financing generally affects control. If a majority of shareholders of a firm have a desirable level of voting control, there could be a tendency to use more debt financing instead of a new share issue. Conversely, excessive use of debt coupled with an economic downturn could lead to excessive influence by creditors. In general, control conditions do not necessarily suggest the use of debt or equity, but the effects of the capital structure on control should certainly be considered.

Asset Growth The growth rate of a firm affects its choice of financing alternatives. Firms with high growth rates need lots of capital and the flexibility of tapping financial markets on a regular basis to finance new projects. Moreover, they need to keep all internally generated funds to finance new projects. Consequently, fast-growing firms tend to raise funds through the sale of new shares to keep a careful balance between debt and equity financing and to maintain ready access to financial markets.

High Regular Cash Flows Firms that have high regular cash flows often have very low debt ratios. Such firms do not need to sell much debt, as they obtain most of their financing through retained earnings.

A high level of retained earnings does not necessarily mean high cash flows and less need for financing. Many firms report a high level of retained earnings while they face a shortage of cash. This is particularly the case for small, rapidly growing firms, whose internally generated funds fall short of satisfying the cash needs for expansion and growth.

The following article by Franklin J. Chu considers how firm use these factors to determine capital structure. It provides a practical perspective on many of the issues considered in this chapter. The article explains why the capital structure varies between industries and why capital structure is a crucial variable for success or failure in a volatile environment. It reviews the major events that affected the financial market during the period from 1960 to 1993 and summarizes the lessons that can be learned. It suggests that financial markets are always changing and that financial decision making is not static. It also notes that financial markets are undergoing increased internationalization.

OPTIMAL CAPITAL STRUCTURE REVISITED

FRANKLIN J. CHU

Over a decade ago, this author published an article in *The Bankers Magazine* describing the concerns and challenges of those who were engaged in the practical problems of raising capital for corporations. Back in the early 1980s, we bore witness to a veritable revolution in corporate finance and financial technology that tested such theories as optimal capital structure, the cost of capital, and the volatility of business and financial cycles. Already, the pace of change and the accelerating complexity in corporate finance were reflected in the proliferation of new types of securities devised by corporations, and the acceptance of these new instruments by the market.

During this period, there were several distinct trends that underscored the theme that a company's targeted optimal capital structure requires ongoing monitoring and must change to better reflect the evolving conditions of both the underlying business and the financial markets. First, there developed a much more sophisticated layering of capitalization. Instead of simply debt and equity, there were often several layers of debt and several layers of equity. Second, the individual layers themselves often contained convertibility, adjustability, or contingency provisions that provided for the change of debt into equity, the extension of debt securities, or the adjustment of required current payments. Finally, we witnessed a massive number of corporate recapitalizations in the 1980s that substituted debt for equity. This trend subsequently reversed itself in the 1990s with the rapid retirement of debt by new equity issuances. All these developments were the result of sustained volatility in business cycles and securities markets, and corporations' corresponding desires to balance numerous simultaneous objectives (e.g., current required interest payments, equity dilution, the market's valuation of its securities, and future financial flexibility).

The result of these events is that corporations and financiers no longer think in terms of an optimal capital structure per se, but strive to create a "flexible capitalization" that takes maximum advantage of a firm's evolving financial requirements and the windows of opportunity offered by the securities markets.

The highly visible globalization of both financial and corporate markets has also added an exciting new dimension to corporate finance. Bankers, investors, and corporations have become increasingly knowledgeable concerning the relative attractiveness and limitations of alternative capital markets other than their own primary domestic market. The comparative differences between various markets extend to more than currency rates or interest rates, and include taxation, accounting convention, debt maturities and covenants, and relative levels of acceptance risk. This increasingly prevalent international context provides an opportunity for issuers to take advantage of significant cross-border arbitrage opportunities in which properly structured financings can enable issuers to raise funds at lower costs, on more attractive terms, or with greater future flexibility than they could otherwise achieve in a conventional format. In part, these financing alternatives have been made possible because of the enormous growth of the global swaps and derivatives markets. On the one hand, these have enhanced the ability of companies to use "synthetic" instruments to capture fluctuating arbitrage disparities between currencies, products and markets; on the other hand, they allow investors to separate and quantify various classes of risk.

A Brief Financial History

In the two decades before 1980, the financial markets experienced tumultuous structural changes that foreshadowed many of the events that shaped the current generation of borrowers, lenders, and investors during the 1980s. Unfortunately, since the careers of most participants in the financial services industry rarely last beyond one business cycle, the collective institutional memory of the financial markets rarely extends beyond 1980. It is, therefore, instructive to review some of the lessons recent financial history has taught us, especially in the credit sector.

During the five-year period of 1963–1968, the Dow Jones rose more than 50%. At the same time, billions of dollars of below-investment grade debt were used to finance the acquisitions that formed major conglomerates such as Loew's, LTV, and Gulf & Western. More than 200 convertible bond issues and bonds with other forms of equity participation, such as warrants, were sold. Many of these bonds were issued by airlines such as TWA, American, and United and aerospace companies such as Lockheed and Grumman which, collectively, financed these industries into the forefront of global market leadership.

Beginning in 1969, the collapse of high-technology IPOs and the resulting 35% to 50% loss of stock value suffered by many retail investors ignited an extended period of turmoil and panic on Wall Street. In 1970, Penn Central filed for bankruptcy and many investors believed that such companies as Lockheed, Chrysler, and LTV were headed for the same fate. The bonds of these companies traded as low as 15 cents on the dollar, even though no other major bankruptcies of this magnitude were to occur during this time. The elimination of the gold standard in 1971 further contributed to the rising volatility of the bond market. The steady rise in inflation and tax rates propped up the returns on property commodities and other tangible assets, relative to the return on securities. As investors liquidated securities en masse to purchase tangible assets, stock and bond prices collapsed.

By the end of 1974, the financial markets were in complete disarray. The Dow Jones had peaked in 1973 at 1052 and would not reach this level again for the balance of the decade. Excessive real-estate speculation and overbuilding depressed property values and caused the banks, heavily burdened by non-performing REIT loans, to curtail their lending activities. At this point, the principal value of corporate debt exceeded the stock market value of corporate equities by an astounding $20 billion. With the banks refusing to lend to all but the most stellar creditors, the prices of bonds for companies like Con Ed and Singer fell to 20 cents on the dollar. Amidst this gloom, a few legendary financiers such as Jimmy Ling at LTV, Henry Singleton at Teledyne, and Charles Tandy at Tandy Corporation launched debt-for-debt exchanges to extend debt maturities or debt-for-equity swaps to take advantage of depressed equity prices. These were the earliest forms of capital restructuring that eventually resulted in dramatically enhanced stock prices and market capitalizations for the underlying companies.

In the transition period of 1975–1979, investor confidence slowly returned as the stock market recovered from the depths of the 1974 panic. With long-term rates at a relatively low 7%, middle-market industrial companies who had limited access to the bank market supplemented what long-term debt capital was made available by insurance companies in the private placement market with new issues of high-yield debt in the public markets. By 1978, virtually every major investment banking firm was underwriting and trading below-investment-grade debt. These funds were used by corporate borrowers for growth and liquidity rather than for acquisitions. However, stock prices remained depressed as investors, mindful of their catastrophic experiences in 1974, continued to be disillusioned with equities. Nervous investors were eager to put their money at work in fixed-income instruments that provided relatively good current income as well as some form of hedge against inflation.

The Advent of the Modern Era

In the 1980s, the advent of commodity disinflation reduced the returns of holding real assets, forcing investors to shift out of tangible assets into financial assets. The result was dramatic commodity and property deflation, accompanied by soaring prices for bonds and stock market values. The net effect for business was a sharp drop in the real cost of capital for corporations. In part as a result of this trend, by 1980 corporate borrowers had obtained greater access to financial markets than ever before. Dramatic financial innovations led to new financial instruments that fuelled the growth of new sources of credit such as the high-yield bond market, the private placement market, and the wholesale securitization of assets. Credit growth was also fuelled by unrestrained lending by the nation's financial institutions. A merger wave during the second half of the decade led to a pervasive financial restructuring of business balance sheets in the United States. Spurred by generally undervalued equity prices and a tax code that favored debt financing, equity was liquidated and replaced by debt.

In the mid-1980s, even though the general market was rising, most stocks were priced at significant discounts to replacement value and even to book value. The ratio of stock prices to underlying value made it cheaper to buy assets than to build them. This was the engine propelling the dramatic rise of acquisitions activity. In the beginning of the 1980s, former bluechip companies such as International Harvester, Chrysler, and Montgomery Ward were perceived to be in profound trouble, and their debt joined the ranks of junk bonds. With interest rates high, the government and mortgage portfolios of most financial institutions had market values far below their original cost.

In volatile and uncertain markets, the demand for high-yield bonds rose steadily, paving the way for many of the spectacular financings and corporate restructurings of the decade. The pioneering $1.9 billion leveraged buyout of Metromedia in 1984 was the largest financing ever done in the public markets. It was soon followed by such classic hostile takeovers as the financings of National Can by Nelson Peltz and Revlon by Ronald Perelman. Even as stock market values rose inexorably to a level approximating replacement value, the leveraged buyouts of major corporations continued unabated, climaxing in 1989 with the gargantuan $25 billion LBO of RJR Nabisco. Within months, a series of major junk bond–financed bankruptcies were filed, and banks cut off most new lending activities. By the beginning of 1990, a lingering recession and a credit crunch signalled the end of an exuberant decade of leverage and dealmaking. In 1990 and 1991 alone, more than 20 companies, each with liabilities of more than $1 billion, entered bankruptcy, propelled by excess leverage, increasing global competition, deregulation, and a lingering recession.

Lessons from an Era of Debt

A leveraged capital structure is appropriate when the acquiror is buying underpriced assets. It is sheer lunacy, however, to use debt to acquire overpriced assets, particularly when the cost of capital is in double digits. By 1990, most U.S. businesses had worked very hard to become more efficient. Therefore, an acquiror could no longer easily create value by improving operations. Many of the high-profile bankruptcies of recent years such as Federated Department Stores and Macy's involved viable businesses that just had the wrong capital structures. In most instances, the individual businesses survived but the equity investors and the subordinated creditors lost most of their investment.

In a volatile environment like the present, capital structure is a crucial variable influencing the success or failure of a business enterprise. Equity, bank debt, subordinated debt, convertible debt, and preferred stock are all part of the equation. The capital structure that was right in 1990 is not necessarily right for today. During the 1990s, most leveraged companies rushed to go public or sell stock to repay debt, because the rising equity markets placed a valuation on businesses at least equal to the private resale value of these enterprises, and investors worried about the danger of leveraged balance sheets. The time for leverage had passed, and the time for deleveraging had arrived. The strategic choices for corporations were not just between pure debt and equity, but also included the many permutations of hybrid and synthetic securities that are designed to produce a predictable fixed-income return. These include features that reduce volatility, such as floating-rate securities, securities with puts, and securities with other protective contingencies (e.g., convertible securities that allow investors to participate in some of the upside enjoyed by equity owners via conversion into stock or a total return tied to some predetermined index).

Companies should vary their capital structures as their businesses change and in accordance with the financial markets' preference for debt and equity, or as interest rates fluctuate. Certain industries such as computers and commodities should not have leveraged capital structures, because their entire inventories can be rendered obsolete overnight or the price structure of the industry can change precipitously. Other industries (e.g., airlines and aerospace companies) need to adjust their capital structures constantly. During the early 1990s, as long-term rates declined to their lowest levels in 20 years, there was an unprecedented issuance of corporate debt securities that allowed businesses to lock in at very favorable rates. There was also a renaissance in the high-yield debt market as hundreds of companies refinanced 12% to 15% debt with 8% to 11% debt.

Integration of Theory and Practice

Companies ideally seek a capital structure that simultaneously maximizes the value of the company and its share price and minimizes its weighted average cost of capital. Firms also seek to liquefy their balance sheets and develop new sources of capital. In the case of increasingly profitable firms, adding debt to the capital structure lowers the weighted average cost of capital and increases the value of the firm. However, as leverage is increased, so is the probability of financial distress. During periods of tight money, firms with high debt ratios may have difficulty raising funds on acceptable terms, if at all. This restrains the freedom of management to make decisions that are in the long-term best interests of shareholders. High levels of leverage may hinder a firm from undertaking attractive investments to remain competitive, or force it to sell assets or issue equity at highly unfavorable times. At the extreme, the firm could face bankruptcy. In a period of extreme financial distress, many managements realize too late that, at high levels of leverage, the present value of the expected costs of financial distress far exceeds the present value of financial leverage. These companies had reached the state at which the value of the firm decreases with increasing leverage.

Contrary to conventional wisdom, sometimes the stock price of a company will rise when it issues equity. This is because, at certain points in the financial cycle, equity is valued at a higher multiple of future earnings and is thus a more valued currency. This is especially true when the proceeds of equity are used to repay or refinance high-cost debt whose overhanging presence simultaneously depresses the overall value of the enterprise and the existing equity investment. Re-equitization—the flip side of debt restructuring and bankruptcy—has been an important theme in the capital markets in the 1990s. Since 1991, U.S. corporations have issued substantially more stock than they retired. This trend represents a dramatic shift in the replenishment of corporate America's equity base, which had been eroded during the 1980s through leveraged buyouts and other exchanges of equity for debt.

During the past 15 years, many examples have been seen of the diverging fates of companies that use leverage prudently and those that use it recklessly. Companies that judiciously raised debt and equity capital to diversify the revenue base, make strategic acquisitions, or rationalize their capital structure have positioned themselves to achieve relatively high levels of return on equity and to improve their credit ratings over time. In contrast, those who used leverage for speculation or financial arbitrage have sometimes seen their paper companies crumble. The reality of the capital markets is that managers of diverse companies are all in the same essential business—deploying scarce capital to its best use. In competing with other capital-hungry businesses, companies that cannot generate competitive returns on capital from their underlying businesses find it increasingly difficult to raise funds in the capital markets on acceptable terms. If the situation is allowed to continue, the company may be shut off from the credit markets completely. Analogously, negative judgments on the past performance and future prospects of a company will drive that company's stock price so low that issuing equity to fund corporate activities will have a highly punitive effect on existing shareholders. In the extreme, equity prices can be forced so far below underlying asset values that the corporation becomes easy prey for either financial investors or aggressive industrial competitors. A company's ability to access funds in the capital markets is predicated on confidence in and credibility of management to lead the business through changing markets.

In the final analysis, the capital structure decision rests heavily on the manager's business judgment and risk profile, and on management's ability to make the ongoing optimal trade-offs between maximizing the long-term value of the firm and minimizing the cost of capital. The plethora of financial instruments now available to corporations to use to implement these judgments provides more practical alternatives than ever before, but also makes the decisions more difficult. The essential lesson that many corporations have learned is that as long as business cycles and securities markets move unpredictably, the concept of a flexible capitalization is the ultimate response to uncertainty.

Source: "Optimal Capital Structure Revisited" by Franklin J. Chu, published in *The Banker,* Sept./Oct. 1996, pp. 9–13. Reproduced with permission of *The Banker.*

CHAPTER SUMMARY

This chapter dealt with the theory of capital structure, focusing on the traditional view, the perfect-market view, the impact of corporate and personal taxes, and the effect of bankruptcy costs. It also analyzed other factors that influence the capital structure decision, such as business risk, the nature of capital assets, differential tax brackets, agency costs, industry characteristics, signalling implications, and the preference of managers. You applied the theory by using the leverage-indifference EBIT analysis along with consulting industry averages to estimate the firm's target capital structure.

Key Terms

asymmetric information,   page 239

bankruptcy,   page 230

business or asset risk,   page 214

business risk,   page 233

default risk,   page 214

defence costs,   page 231

degree of operating leverage,   page 233

direct costs of bankruptcy,   page 230

financial flexibility,   page 261

financial risk,   page 213

homemade leverage,   page 219

industry norms,   page 259

leverage-indifference EBIT level,   page 249

operating leverage,   page 233

optimal capital structure,   page 232

pecking order theory,   page 239

signalling,   page 238

signalling event,   page 239

traditional view of capital structure,   page 217

Important Equations

Financial risk

$$\text{Financial risk} = \sigma_L - \sigma_U \qquad \text{(Equation 4-1)}$$

where

σ_L = total risk to shareholders of the levered firm
σ_U = total risk to shareholders of the unlevered firm

Value of a firm in the absence of corporate taxes

$$V = \frac{\text{EBIT}}{k_L} = \frac{\text{EBIT}}{k_U} \qquad \text{(Equation 4-2)}$$

where

V = value of the firm
EBIT = perpetual earnings before interest and taxes

k_L = risk-adjusted discount rate for the levered firm

k_U = risk-adjusted discount rate for the unlevered firm

Cost of equity for a levered firm in the absence of corporate taxes

$$k_E = k_U + (k_U - k_B)\left(\frac{D}{E}\right) \qquad \text{(Equation 4-3)}$$

where

k_E = cost of equity of the levered firm

k_U = cost of equity of the unlevered firm

k_B = before-tax cost of debt

D = market value of the firm's debt

E = market value of the firm's equity

Weighted average cost of capital for a levered firm in the absence of corporate taxes

$$k_L = k_B\left[\frac{D}{E + D}\right] + \left[k_U + (k_U - k_B)\left(\frac{D}{E}\right)\right]\left[\frac{E}{E + D}\right] \qquad \text{(Equation 4-4)}$$

Present value of interest tax savings

$$\text{PV(interest tax savings)} = T_C D \qquad \text{(Equation 4-5)}$$

where

T_C = corporate tax rate

D = amount of debt

Value of an unlevered firm in the presence of corporate taxes

$$V_U = \frac{\text{EBIT}(1 - T_C)}{k_U} \qquad \text{(Equation 4-6)}$$

Value of a levered firm in the presence of corporate taxes

$$V_L = V_U + T_C D \qquad \text{(Equation 4-7)}$$

where

V_U = unlevered firm's value

V_L = levered firm's value

T_C = corporate tax rate

D = amount of debt

Cost of equity for a levered firm in the presence of corporate taxes

$$k_E = k_U + [k_U - k_B]\left[\frac{D}{E}\right][1 - T_C] \qquad \text{(Equation 4-8)}$$

where

k_E = cost of equity of the levered firm

k_B = before-tax cost of debt

k_U = cost of equity to the unlevered firm after taxes

Weighted average cost of capital

$$k_L = \left(\frac{D}{V}\right)k_B(1 - T_C) + \left(\frac{E}{V}\right)k_E \qquad \text{(Equation 4-9)}$$

where

k_L = weighted average cost of capital

V = value of the firm, which equals debt plus equity

Tax parity between tax rate on interest income, corporate tax rate, and personal tax rate on income from shares

$$1 - T_D = (1 - T_C)(1 - T_S)$$ (Equation 4-10)

where

T_D = tax rate on interest income

T_C = corporate tax rate

T_S = personal tax rate on income from shares

Value of an unlevered firm in the presence of personal and corporate taxes

$$V_U = \frac{\text{EBIT}(1 - T_C)(1 - T_S)}{k_U}$$ (Equation 4-11)

where

V_U = value of the unlevered firm

EBIT = earnings before interest and taxes

T_C = corporate tax rate

T_S = personal tax rate on income from shares

k_U = cost of equity of the unlevered firm

Cash flows from a levered firm

$$\text{CF}_L = \text{EBIT}(1 - T_C)(1 - T_S) - I(1 - T_C)(1 - T_S) + I(1 - T_D)$$ (Equation 4-12)

where

CF_L = cash flows from a levered firm

EBIT = earnings before interest and taxes

I = annual payments to debtholders

T_C = corporate tax rate

T_S = personal tax rate on income from shares

T_D = personal tax rate on income from debt

Value of a levered firm in the presence of personal and corporate taxes

$$V_L = V_U + \left[1 - \frac{(1 - T_C)(1 - T_S)}{(1 - T_D)}\right]D$$ (Equation 4-13)

where

V_L = value of the levered firm

V_U = value of the unlevered firm

D = market value of debt

Value of a levered firm in the presence of bankruptcy costs

$$V_L = V_U + T_C D - \text{PV(BC)}$$ (Equation 4-14)

where

V_L = value of the levered firm
V_U = value of the unlevered firm
T_C = corporate tax rate
D = market value of the firm's debt
PV(BC) = present value of the expected bankruptcy-related costs

Degree of operating leverage as a function of sales level

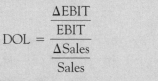

$$DOL = \frac{\frac{\Delta EBIT}{EBIT}}{\frac{\Delta Sales}{Sales}}$$ (Equation 4-15)

where

DOL = degree of operating leverage
EBIT = earnings before interest and taxes
Δ = change in the variable

Degree of operating leverage as a function of a contribution margin

$$DOL = \frac{\text{contribution margin}}{EBIT} = \frac{(P - V)Q}{(P - V)Q - FC}$$ (Equation 4-16)

where

DOL = degree of operating leverage
P = price per unit
V = variable cost per unit
Q = amount of sales in units Q
FC = fixed operating charges, which include fixed costs, lease payments, and other costs that do not change with the level of sales but do not include any financing charges

Degree of operating leverage as a function of variable costs

$$DOL = \frac{PQ - VQ}{PQ - VQ - FC} = \frac{\text{sales} - \text{variable costs}}{\text{sales} - \text{variable costs} - FC}$$ (Equation 4-17)

Leverage indifference EBIT level

$$\frac{(EBIT^* - I_1)(1 - T_C) - PD_1}{S_1} = \frac{(EBIT^* - I_2)(1 - T_C) - PD_2}{S_2}$$ (Equation 4-18)

where

EBIT* = indifference EBIT level
I = interest payments under each alternative
T_C = corporate tax rate
PD = preferred dividends under each alternative
S = number of common shares outstanding under each alternative

Firm value after a new debt issue

$$V_N = V_C + T_C D_N$$ (Equation 4-19)

where

V_N = firm value after the new debt issue
V_C = current market value of the firm
T_C = corporate tax rate
D_N = amount of required additional debt

Web Links

Bankruptcy Statistics

■ http://strategis.ic.gc.ca/epic/site/bsf-osb.nsf/vwapj/06AnnualSTATS.pdf/$FILE/06AnnualSTATS.pdf Office of the Superintendent of Bankruptcy Canada's Annual Statistic Report for 2006.

■ http://www.statcan.ca/Daily/English/061012/d061012c.htm Statistics Canada, "Trends in Business Bankruptcies 1980–2005," *The Daily*, October 12, 2006.

Bond Rating Services

■ **Standard & Poor's** http://www.standardandpoors.com

■ **Moody's Investors Service (MIS)** http://www.moodys.com

■ **Fitch Ratings** http://www.fitchinv.com/

■ **Dominion Bond Rating Service (DBRS)** http://www.dbrs.com/intnlweb/

■ **A.M. Best Ratings** http://www.ambest.com/

Canada Revenue Agency

■ http://www.cra.gc.ca Canada Revenue Agency administers tax laws as well as the various tax benefit programs and incentives on behalf of the Government of Canada. This Web site contains links to their publications, online tax forms and filing, and a number of business functions such as GST/HST information and business registration.

Damodaran Online

■ http://pages.stern.nyu.edu/~adamodar/New_Home_Page/home.htm Professor Aswath Damodaran is a Professor of Finance and David Margolis Teaching Fellow at the Stern School of Business at New York University. Included on this Web site are links to data sets, notes, research, publications, and Web casts, as well as problems and a downloadable PDF file of solutions on corporate finance-related topics, investments, valuation, and portfolio management.

Federal Reserve Economic Research

■ http://www.frbsf.org/publications/fedinprint/index.html A searchable database with links to full text of articles and working papers on a variety of economic research topics.

Forbes Favourites: Investing

■ http://www.forbes.com/bow/b2c/favorite.jhtml?id=7 Links to Forbes' "Best of the Web": a selection of international Web sites on a variety of investing subtopics such as Financial Portals, Fund Selection, Stock Valuation Tools.

Strategis

■ http://strategis.ic.gc.ca/ Contains news, company directories, analysis, statistics, and other business and consumer information related to starting a business, exploring new markets, or keeping up to date with the latest industry research.

Self-Test Questions

Qualitative Questions

Answer each of the following questions in point form:

1. According to the traditional view, what effect does financial leverage have on the weighted average cost of capital?
2. What is financial risk?
3. According to the perfect-market view, what impact does financial leverage have on a firm's value and the weighted average cost of capital?
4. How does the presence of corporate taxes influence the value of a firm with debt financing?
5. What effect do personal taxes have on the present value of the interest tax shield?
6. What is the relationship between financial leverage and bankruptcy costs?
7. What effect do bankruptcy costs have on firm value and the optimal degree of financial leverage?
8. What general conclusions can financial managers draw on when setting the capital structures of their firms? (Ignore factors related to corporate and personal taxes as well as bankruptcy costs.)
9. What are the other influences on the capital structure decision?
10. What factors affect the selection of the optimal capital structure in practice?

Qualitative Multiple Choice Questions

1. Which of the following is an indirect cost of bankruptcy?
   i) Legal fees
   ii) Loss from forced asset sales at below market prices
   iii) Deterioration of property due to negligence
   iv) Costs of management actions to ward off bankruptcy, including waste of management time

2. According to capital structure theory, in the presence of both corporate and personal taxes, which of the following interpretations of the formula below is correct?

$$1 - T_D = (1 - T_C)(1 - T_S)$$

where
   T_D = tax rate on interest income
   T_C = corporate tax rate
   T_S = personal tax rate on income from shares

   i) When this equality holds, firms should not use debt in their capital structures.
   ii) When the left-hand side is less than the right-hand side, investors prefer bonds, so it is optimal for firms to include bonds in their capital structure.

iii) When the left-hand side is less than the right-hand side, investors prefer dividends and capital gains, so firms should use all equity financing.

iv) When this equality holds, firms should have 100% debt financing.

3. According to the traditional view of capital structure, which of the following *best* describes the optimal debt level for firms?

i) Zero debt

ii) 100% debt

iii) A high percentage of debt, but below 100%

iv) A very low proportion of debt financing (below 15%)

4. Which of the following statements applies to financial risk?

i) Financial risk to the shareholders can be defined as total risk to the shareholders of the levered firm minus total risk of the unlevered firm.

ii) A firm with high financial leverage is likely to have high business risk because the two offset each other.

iii) Financial risk is the total risk generated by the nature of the firm's assets and business.

iv) Shareholders benefit from financial leverage as long as the interest costs of acquiring money exceed the return on borrowed money.

5. Which of the following statements *best* describes the significance of Exhibit 4-3, repeated below?

i) The point W^* represents the optimal capital budget of the firm.

ii) The intercept 12% represents the risk-free rate of interest.

Exhibit 4-3 Relationship between the Debt Ratio, WACC, Cost of Equity, and Cost of Debt in the Absence of Corporate Taxes

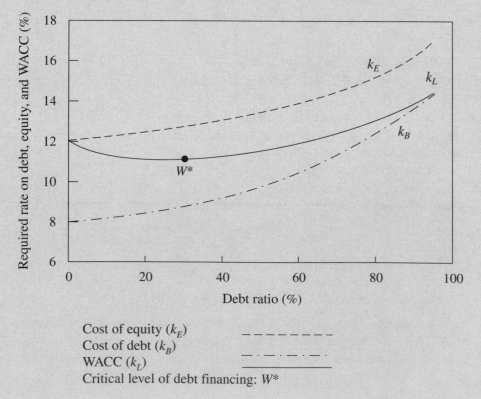

iii) All financing costs rise with greater financial leverage under the traditional view of capital structure so the optimal capital structure of a firm contains no debt.

iv) The weighted average cost of capital falls when debt financing is first added to the capital structure but then rises when financial risk becomes very high.

6. Which of the following statements *best* describes the significance of the degree of operating leverage (DOL) of a firm?

   i) DOL measures the sensitivity of a firm's profits to changes in selling prices.

   ii) DOL is smallest when the firm is at its break-even point and earning no profits.

   iii) DOL is positive at all sales levels below the break-even point.

   iv) DOL measures the sensitivity of a firm's earnings before interest and taxes (EBIT) to changes in sales.

7. Which of the following statements about bankruptcy costs is true?

   i) Indirect bankruptcy costs are incurred by third parties and are then billed to the bankrupt firm.

   ii) Legal fees are an example of indirect bankruptcy costs.

   iii) Indirect bankruptcy costs are incurred when a firm is under threat of bankruptcy, whereas direct bankruptcy costs are the result of actual bankruptcy.

   iv) The loss from the forced sale of assets below market prices is an example of indirect bankruptcy costs.

8. In a world with bankruptcy costs, which type of firms are the most likely to borrow more?

   i) Firms with higher business risk

   ii) Firms with predominantly intangible assets

   iii) Firms with predominantly tangible assets

   iv) Firms in lower tax brackets

Quantitative Multiple Choice Questions

1. A manufacturing firm has a production capacity of 25,000 units, and the units have a selling price of $100 each. The variable cost per unit is $30 and fixed operating costs are $333,000 per year. What is the degree of operating leverage?

   i) 0.8097

   ii) 1.0000

   iii) 1.2350

   iv) 2.456

2. A company has 10,000,000 outstanding shares and no debt. It has a choice between financing a new project by issuing 2,000,000 common shares that will sell for $15 each, or by issuing 2,000,000 preferred shares valued at $15 each that pay a dividend of $1.5 per share annually. The company's tax rate is 35%. At what level of earnings before interest and taxes (EBIT) is the company indifferent between the two financing choices?

   i) $ 2,000,000

   ii) $ 9,090,091

   iii) $27,692,308

   iv) $51,428,571

3. Winnonto Inc. (WI) is an unlevered firm. It is expecting cash flows to be as indicated below, forever. The firm's shareholders expect 16% return per year and the firm pays out all of its after-tax earnings as dividends. If WI has a corporate tax rate of 40%, what is the value of the firm to its shareholders?

State of the economy	Bad	Fair	Good	Very good
Probability	0.20	0.30	0.40	0.10
EBIT ($ Millions)	1.5	3.5	6.5	10.5

   i) $10.50 million
   ii) $12.50 million
   iii) $16.45 million
   iv) $18.75 million

4. A company has sales of $220 million and operating income (EBIT) of $145 million. The degree of operating leverage (DOL) is 1.67 at this level of sales. If sales were to increase to $228 million, what would the new level of operating earnings be, approximately?
   i) $158 million
   ii) $154 million
   iii) $147 million
   iv) $144 million

5. Charloteville Corp.(CC) expects its EBIT to be $120,000 every year indefinitely. The firm can borrow at 12%; however, it currently has no debt and its cost of equity is 18%. If the tax rate is 40%, what will CC's value be if it borrows $80,000 and uses the proceeds to repurchase shares?
   i) $698,667
   ii) $680,000
   iii) $432,000
   iv) $400,000

6. When a firm's degree of operating leverage is 8, what percentage change in sales would lead to a 3% increase in operating profit?
   i) 3.75%
   ii) 2.67%
   iii) 0.375%
   iv) 0.267%

7. VCS Corp. is considering a recapitalization plan. It has 7 million common shares outstanding but no preferred shares or debt. It plans to issue $18 million debt with an interest rate of 9% and repurchase shares at $32 a share. VCS has a tax rate of 35%. What is the EBIT level that would make VCS indifferent to the recapitalization plan?
   i) $25.94 million
   ii) $20.16 million
   iii) $12.10 million
   iv) $11.34 million

8. Saskton Corp. is an all-equity-financed firm with a value of $22 million. The cost of equity is 15%. It plans to issue $8 million debt at an interest rate of 8% to repurchase some

shares. Saskton is in the 45% tax bracket. What will be Saskton's weighted average cost of capital after the debt has been issued?

   i) 15.00%
   ii) 14.02%
   iii) 13.88%
   iv) 12.89%

9. VMT Corp. has a degree of operating leverage (DOL) of 2.23. Its current year's EBIT is $6.8 million. If it plans to increase EBIT to $7.8 million in the next year, by how much must VMT increase its sales in the coming year?

   i) 5.75%
   ii) 6.60%
   iii) 8.00%
   iv) 14.71%

Quantitative Problems

Problem 1

Eastern Inc. manufactures playground equipment. It has two production facilities, one in Levis, Quebec and the other in Fredericton, New Brunswick, and an assembly plant in Truro, Nova Scotia. The Levis facility produces plastic components, including swing seats, climbing apparatuses, and connections. The Fredericton facility produces structural steel components. The Truro assembly plant creates custom-designed equipment for clients from these components and used vehicle tires.

The exhibit below includes forecast income statements for the Levis and Fredericton facilities for the coming year. Both sell 100% of their output to the Truro assembly plant at a 50% mark-up over their production costs, and each has its own debt financing and related interest costs. The 50% mark-up is believed to properly reflect market prices for these components. The Truro assembly plant has been extremely profitable for several years, due to its unique designs that have resulted in long-term contracts with a number of school boards and real-estate developers.

Eastern Inc. Levis and Fredericton Facilities Forecast Income Statements		
	Levis	**Fredericton**
Sales	2,050,000 units	60,000 units
	$10.00 per unit	$100.00 per unit
Sales	$20,500,000	$6,000,000
Variable production costs	8,200,000	950,000
Fixed production costs	5,800,000	3,550,000
Earnings before interest expense and income taxes	6,500,000	1,500,000
Interest expense	800,000	1,650,000
Earnings before income taxes	5,700,000	(150,000)
Income taxes at 40%	2,280,000	(60,000)
Net income (loss)	$ 3,420,000	$ (90,000)

Required

a) Explain the meaning of degree of operating leverage. Is it the same at all sales levels? When would DOL be negative?

b) Calculate the break-even levels of sales volume for the Levis and Fredericton facilities. Are they currently above or below their break-even sales levels?

c) Calculate DOL for the Levis and Fredericton facilities. Interpret and compare your results.

Problem 2

You have been hired by a family-founded Canadian manufacturing firm that continues to have all key management positions held by members of the founding family. The family is very conservative in managing the company and has never used debt financing. In fact, they follow the philosophy "never a borrower be." Your training in corporate finance suggests that there are both potential costs and potential benefits of borrowing, particularly in an environment in which there are market imperfections such as corporate and personal taxes and bankruptcy costs. The company's corporate tax rate is 40%, the personal tax rate on interest income is 44%, and the personal tax rate on income from the shares is 6.7%.

Required

Explain the costs and benefits of borrowing in a setting in which these market imperfections exist. First explain whether there would be any advantage to debt financing based on the existence of taxes alone, and then consider whether bankruptcy costs would favour the use of debt financing.

Problem 3

Three years ago, Sasha Khan and Kerri Song, graduates of a university software engineering program, founded Keri Kan Co. (KKC) to commercialize their software products developed for any organization to archive its corporate information more effectively than ever before. KKC is an all-equity company financed with Sasha and Kerri's own savings and savings from their families and friends. The business has been very successful. Now Sasha and Kerri are exploring financing initiatives to expand their operation. The amount of working capital required is $2.7 million. The following banks have offered to lend money to KKC:

- Bank West offers a term loan at an interest rate of 7.5%, compounded daily.
- Bank Central offers a simple interest term loan at an interest rate of 7%, with a compensating balance of 10% and interest payments made quarterly.
- Bank East offers a discount interest term loan at a 7.5% interest rate, compounded monthly.
- Island Bank offers a discount interest term loan with a 7% annual interest rate and a compensating balance of 5%.

Required

Write a memo to Sasha and Kerri to address the following:
- One advantage and one disadvantage of issuing new common shares
- One advantage and one disadvantage of introducing debt into KKC's capital structure
- The effective annual interest rate for each loan proposal
- Your recommendation of which offer Sasha and Kerri should accept and why

Cases

Case 1: ReginON Corporation (ROC)

The capital structure of ROC is depicted in Case Exhibit 4-1. Other companies in the firm's industry rely less heavily on debt than ROC, and the industry norm is a debt-to-firm-value ratio of 45%. ROC is assessing the implications of altering its capital structure to match the norm in its industry. ROC could alter its capital structure by issuing shares and using the proceeds to pay down debt, which costs 9% per annum. The corporate tax rate is 40%.

Case Exhibit 4-1
Capital Structure of ROC

Market value of equity (300,000 outstanding shares)	$5,750,000
Market value of current liabilities	1,500,000
Market value of long-term debt	4,750,000

Required

a) Calculate the total debt-to-value ratio for ROC at the current time.

b) How much long-term debt would ROC have to pay down to achieve the industry average debt-to-value ratio? In your solution, consider how firm value will be affected by the tax shields associated with debt financing. Prove that your answer does indeed result in the desired debt-to-value ratio. Show your calculations.

c) Determine the value of outstanding equity after the capital structure has been altered. Will the value per share go up or down, as a result of the restructuring? Explain briefly.

Case 2: HamilOak Corporation (HOC)

HOC has 4 million shares outstanding and no debt. Earnings before interest and tax (EBIT) are projected for three scenarios:

1. $30 million under normal economic conditions
2. $10 million for an economic downturn
3. $40 million for an economic expansion

The probability for the normal scenario is 40% and the probability is 30% each for the other scenarios.

HOC is considering a recapitalization plan. Debt would be issued for $100 million with a 9% interest rate. The proceeds would be used to buy back 2 million shares at their book value of $50 a share. The corporate tax rate is 35%.

Required

Write a brief report to discuss HOC's recapitalization plan. In particular, for each of the three scenarios, calculate HOC's EPS and return on investment (ROI = EPS divided by book value share price) in two situations—first before any new debt is issued and then after the recapitalization. Calculate the leverage-indifference EBIT level and discuss the risk associated with recapitalization. Briefly explain why you would or would not recommend HOC to proceed with the recapitalization plan.

Case 3: Edmontuk Inc. (EI)

EI is currently an all-equity firm. It needs to raise $5 million in additional funds. After raising the funds, it expects earnings before interest and taxes (EBIT) to be $1,200,000. The firm's unlevered cost of equity, k_U, is 14%, and its before-tax cost of debt, k_B, is 9%.

Required

a) If there are no corporate taxes, in a perfect Modigliani and Miller (M&M) world, what is the value of EI if it issues common shares to raise the needed funds? Alternatively, what is the firm's new cost of equity and the value of the firm if it issues debt to raise the needed funds? What is its opportunity cost of capital? What is the fundamental determinant of the value of the firm in the M&M no-tax case?

b) Now assume that the corporate tax rate is 40%.
   i) What is the all-equity value of EI?
   ii) What is EI's value if $5 million in debt is issued? What is the new k_E? What is the new opportunity cost of capital?
   iii) Assume the debt is now $6 million. What is EI's value? What is the new k_E? What is the new opportunity cost of capital?

c) Based on your answers to parts a) and b), what role do debt financing and corporate tax play in a firm's capital structure decision? What other factors does a firm need to consider?

Chapter 5
Dividend Policy

CHAPTER OVERVIEW

This chapter focuses on the question of whether shareholder wealth is affected by dividend policy. Changes in dividend policy have both favourable and unfavourable effects on a firm's share price. Higher dividends mean higher immediate cash flows to investors. Although this is good news, it also implies reduced expected growth for the firm because less money is available for reinvestment. The optimal dividend policy balances these opposing forces and maximizes share price.

In Section 5.1, you learn the basic theory proposed to explain dividend policies that may be observed in practice. The question is whether one policy is more effective than another in increasing shareholder wealth. It is shown that under perfect market conditions, dividend policy has no effect on the value of the firm. However, in accounting for transaction costs, tax differentials, information asymmetries, and other real market imperfections, dividend policy is indeed found to affect share price.

Section 5.2 reviews the general features of dividend policies. You learn that there are dividend policy features that the market finds desirable and the reasons for their desirability. You also review the characteristics of the three basic dividend policies: the constant payout ratio policy, the residual policy, and the constant dividend policy.

In Section 5.3, you learn the details of the payment procedures for distributing cash dividends to shareholders. Knowing the record date is particularly important for financial managers as well as for investors.

Finally, Sections 5.4 and 5.5 review the characteristics of stock dividends, stock splits, and share repurchases as alternatives to cash dividends.

In explaining the effects of dividend policy, this chapter assumes that the capital budget, investment policy, and capital structure are all fixed. In order to isolate the impact of dividend policy from the effects of investment strategy and capital structure, we require this assumption. Thus, dividend policy involves the decision of *whether or not* to pay cash dividends, not *how* the cash is obtained. In cases where the cash is not available and the firm's policy is to pay dividends, it is assumed that the firm will sell shares to raise the required cash.

Learning Objectives

After completing this chapter, you will be able to:

- Explain how dividend policy affects share value under perfect market conditions.

- Explain the effect of shareholders' risk and the preference for current income.

- Explain tax differential effects, signalling, and transaction costs as factors that make dividend policy relevant.

- Identify and explain the characteristics of dividend policies in publicly traded firms.

- Demonstrate how dividends are declared and paid.

- Demonstrate the effect of cash and stock dividends on shareholder wealth. Explain the effect of various dividend policies on a firm's financial statement accounts.

- Demonstrate how share repurchases can serve as substitutes to cash dividends under perfect market conditions.

This knowledge will provide you with the professional skills to:

- Advise on the capital structure of the organization to maximize the organization's value.

- Advise on business decisions in the context of larger economic and geo-political conditions.

- Recognize market factors and adapt business decisions to the context of the organization's sector and industry.

- Evaluate and advise on growth strategies of an organization or individual, in particular on the impact of dividend distributions.

- Advise on business decisions, in this case dividend payments, in the context of the legal framework.

- Consider alternative solutions and shape recommendations.

- Manage cash flow and working capital.

- Apply professional ethical standards to a specific situation.

- Develop financial forecasts and plans.

HOW THIS CHAPTER RELATES TO OTHER CHAPTERS IN THIS BOOK

The relationship between a firm's dividend policy and share price has been the subject of many theoretical explanations and propositions. Different views have been proposed to explain why firms adopt one policy or another. Regardless of the hypothesis, the dividend decision is usually regarded as an output of the investment decision, the financing decision, or both.

Investment and financing decisions and policies form the content of this book. Chapters 1, 2, and 6 provide practical applications of theory towards making the investment decision. Chapters 3, 7, 8, and 9 explore different financing products and their adoption in the real world. Chapters 2 and 4 consider the theory behind financing choices. Thus, understanding both investment and financing decisions is integral to gaining insight into dividend policy.

Once again the content of this chapter is implicit in all others. The knowledge here may be carried both forward and back; we have considered investments and financing choices before and continue to do so throughout the remainder of this book.

5.1 THEORETICAL FOUNDATION

Dividends are distributions of earnings to shareholders paid primarily in cash or shares. After a company has distributed preferred dividends, the residual net earnings may be distributed as common-share dividends or kept by the company as retained earnings to be reinvested in the business, or some combination may be determined between the two. The term **dividend policy** refers to a firm's long-term policy toward the distribution of earnings. In this section we consider arguments leading to different theoretical viewpoints and the practical implications arising from them with regard to different dividend policies.

In practice, companies vary widely in their **payout ratios**, the percentages of earnings they pay as dividends. Payout ratios also vary greatly from one industry to another. Mature companies, such as banks, may pay out a substantial percentage of their earnings as dividends to their shareholders. In contrast, growing companies, such as those in high technology industries, may need to keep a high proportion of earnings within the company to finance new projects.

The board of directors determines a company's dividend policy in accordance with the goals set for the company. Dividends are usually paid quarterly. However, unlike interest on debt, dividends are discretionary. The board determines the payout ratio and may defer the declaration of dividends indefinitely. In practice, however, dividends are paid if justified by earnings. Failure to declare an anticipated dividend weakens investor confidence and may jeopardize the future borrowing power of the firm.

There are several views on the effect of dividend policy on share price. The rest of this section deals with these views.

Traditional "Bird-in-Hand" View

The basis of one of the initial views on why dividend policy affects share price is the adage, "a bird in the hand is worth two in the bush." The **"bird-in-hand" view** suggests that shareholders prefer to have cash dividends paid to them now rather than wait for potential payments in the future, given the uncertainty associated with future earnings.

The "bird-in-hand" view is criticized for an important reason. It is true that investors perceive future capital gains as riskier than more predictable current dividends. However, paying dividends will not necessarily increase shareholder wealth by more than the increase that might result from a policy of retaining earnings to finance new projects. Investors demand a higher rate of return on equity if the future expected cash flows are riskier. Investors also demand a higher rate of return when the dividend payout is reduced. The firm will be able to pay the higher rate if the retained cash can be invested in new projects with high rates of return. Otherwise, the firm will pay out the cash in higher dividends.

Investors choose whether to invest in a high- or a low-dividend-paying alternative depending on their risk/return trade-off preference. The magnitude of the dividend payment is irrelevant to the decision. For example, suppose a shareholder desires a large cash income from an investment. Yet this investor prefers investing in a low-dividend-paying firm because it offers a higher expected rate of return on investment. This investor's goal can be achieved by investing in a low-dividend-paying firm and periodically selling part of the investment to obtain the desired income. Theoretically, retaining cash for future investment increases the share price and the total value of the investment for the shareholder. The investor can keep the size of the investment constant by selling a portion of holdings equal to the amount of the appreciation. This strategy is equivalent to investing in a similar firm with a 100% dividend payout ratio, as the size of the shareholder's investment will be constant.

Homemade dividend is a term used to indicate the ability of shareholders to sell portions of their investments to generate the desirable pattern of cash flows. When investors can generate homemade dividends, the "bird-in-hand" view does not hold. Minicase 5-1 demonstrates how an investor can create homemade dividends. Note that the information in Minicase 5-1 will also be used in the three subsequent minicases.

MINICASE 5-1 HOMEMADE DIVIDENDS

Kelly owns 2,000 shares in Thrifty Retail Stores (TRS). Currently, the share price is $32, and there are 2.5 million outstanding shares. The firm's expected earnings are $12 million per year in perpetuity. The firm can invest in a new project with initial outlays of $12 million. It can provide cash flows of $2.85 million per year in perpetuity. Alternatively, the firm can pay the earnings in dividends and sell shares to finance the new project. The firm is financed with 100% equity and pays no taxes. Kelly pays no personal taxes.

Question 1: Should TRS invest in the new project?

The firm's total market value without the new project is $80 million ($32 × 2.5). This value is a consequence of the $12 million of perpetual earnings. The required rate of return to equity k_E is:

$$k_E = \frac{\text{perpetual cash flows}}{\text{total value}} = \frac{\$12}{\$80} = 15\%$$

Therefore, the net present value of the new project is:

$$\text{NPV} = \frac{\text{perpetual cash flows}}{\text{discount rate}} - \text{initial costs} = \frac{\$2.85}{0.15} - \$12 = \$7 \text{ million}$$

As the net present value is positive, TRS should invest in the new project.

Question 2: How much cash would Kelly receive from owning 2,000 shares if the firm distributes 100% of the earnings as dividends to existing shareholders and finances the project with a new equity issue?

The firm has $12 million to distribute on 2.5 million shares. Thus, the dividend per share is $4.80 ($12 ÷ 2.5). Kelly would receive $9,600 in total dividends ($4.80 × 2,000).

Question 3: What is Kelly's total wealth if the firm pays no dividends and uses the earnings to finance the new project?

The firm's expected earnings after undertaking the project are $14.85 million ($12 + $2.85) in perpetuity. Capitalizing these earnings at the required rate of return of 15% yields $99 million.

If the firm retains all earnings to finance the new project, the share price after announcing the new project will be $39.60 ($99 ÷ 2.5). Thus, Kelly's total wealth would be $79,200 ($39.60 × 2,000).

Case Continued >

Question 4: Explain how Kelly can create her own dividends if the firm chooses to finance the project with internal funds rather than pay dividends.

Kelly can sell enough shares to receive the $9,600 that she would have received as dividends. Given the new share price of $39.60, Kelly will have to sell 242 shares ($9,600 ÷ 39.60) to create her homemade dividends. The proceeds from the sale will be $9,583.20 because of rounding.

Perfect-Market View

In 1961, Miller and Modigliani (M&M) argued that under perfect market conditions, dividend policy has no effect on either the price of a firm's shares or the firm's cost of capital. Dividend policy is irrelevant.[1] M&M argued that the value of a firm is determined by its basic earning power and its risk class. Value depends on the firm's asset investment policy rather than on how earnings are split between dividends and retained earnings.

M&M proved their proposition under a set of restrictive assumptions:

1. There are no personal and corporate income taxes.

2. The flotation and transaction costs are zero.

3. Dividend policy has no effect on a firm's cost of equity.

4. A firm's capital investment policy is independent of its dividend policy.

5. There is no asymmetric information because investors and managers have the same information regarding the future investment opportunities of the firm.

Demonstrate the irrelevancy of dividends by attempting the You Apply It below.

YOU APPLY IT DEMONSTRATING THE IRRELEVANCE OF DIVIDEND POLICY ON FIRM VALUE WHEN M&M ASSUMPTIONS 1 TO 5 ARE SATISFIED

Thrifty Retail Stores from Minicase 5-1 decides to pay the earnings of $12 million in dividends and issue new shares to finance the $12 million project.

Questions

Question 1: What is the price per share after announcing the project and selling the new share issue?

Question 2: What is Kelly's total wealth from her 2,000 shares if the firm pays $4.80 of dividends per share and sells shares to finance the project?

Question 3: Is the dividend policy relevant?

You Apply It Continued >

[1] Merton H. Miller and Franco Modigliani, "Dividend Policy, Growth and the Valuation of Shares," *Journal of Business*, Volume 34, October 1961, pp. 411–433.

Answers

Question 1: What is the price per share after announcing the project and selling the new share issue?

With the new project, TRS will have total cash flows of $14.85 million ($12 + $2.85), regardless of whether the initial outlays come from retained earnings or external financing. In Minicase 5-1, it was determined that these cash flows are worth a total value of $99 million. It was also determined that if the project were financed internally, the price per share would be $39.60 ($99 ÷ 2.5).

If new shares are sold so that TRS can pay for the project and for the dividends, TRS will have to raise $12 million in cash. The new shareholders, who will contribute $12 million, will then own 12.12% ($12 ÷ $99) of the firm. The original shareholders will retain 87.88% (100% − 12.12%) of the shares.

Let N denote the total number of shares after the new share issue. Because the original shareholders own 2.5 million shares, N should satisfy:

$$0.8788 \times N = 2,500,000$$

Solving for N yields 2,844,788 shares.

Therefore, the price per share after announcing the project and selling the new share issue is:

$$\$99,000,000 \div 2,844,788 = \$34.80$$

Question 2: What is Kelly's total wealth from her 2,000 shares if the firm pays $4.80 of dividends per share and sells shares to finance the project?

Kelly's wealth when the firm pays dividends and sells shares to finance the project is:

$$
\begin{aligned}
& \text{her share of the cash dividends} + \text{market value of her shares} \\
& = (2,000 \times \$4.80) + (2,000 \times \$34.80) \\
& = \$79,200
\end{aligned}
$$

Question 3: Is the dividend policy relevant?

Kelly's wealth is the same whether the firm finances the new project with internal funds or pays the cash in dividends and sells new shares to finance the new project ($79,200 in either case). Similarly, the firm's value is $99 million regardless of how the firm chooses to finance the project. Under conditions of perfect markets, there are no taxes and transaction costs, information is readily available, and a firm's dividend policy is irrelevant.

Dividend Relevance View

M&M assumed that dividend policy does not affect the required rate of return on equity. They suggested that under conditions of perfect and efficient markets, increasing a firm's dividends per share does not reduce the basic degree of risk of common equity. If a dividend payment would require management to issue new shares, it only transfers the risk and ownership from current owners to new owners. The current investors who trade the uncertain capital gain for a cash dividend ultimately reinvest their dividends in the same or similar firms. Thus, there is no reduction in risk.

In practice, however, taxes and transaction costs can make dividend policy important in determining the cost of equity. Thus, the assumptions of the M&M irrelevance view do not hold. This section explains the following factors that make dividend policy relevant: transaction and flotation costs, tax differential effects, the signalling hypothesis, and the clientele effect. While these factors are interrelated, they are presented separately to emphasize their effects.

Transaction and Flotation Costs When investors pay transaction costs to trade securities and firms pay flotation costs to sell new securities, dividend policy *does* matter. Investors who desire current income but have shares in a firm that does not pay dividends will have to sell part of their holdings to create homemade dividends. However, transaction costs make homemade dividends expensive and deter investors who want current income from buying securities that do not pay high dividends. They will invest in high-dividend-paying firms to avoid transaction costs.

Similarly, the existence of flotation costs when firms raise new funds through sales of securities tends to make firms reluctant to pay dividends. According to the irrelevance view, a firm can pay high cash dividends and at the same time sell shares to raise cash for internal investments and to finance growth. Under conditions of perfect markets, these actions affect ownership structure but do not increase or decrease value. However, the existence of flotation costs makes funds from the market more expensive than retained earnings. Because of flotation costs, it is optimal for a firm to retain as much cash as may be needed to finance new projects with net present values that are greater than or equal to zero.

Demonstrate the relevancy of dividends by attempting the You Apply It minicase below.

YOU APPLY IT EFFECT OF TRANSACTION AND FLOTATION COSTS

Thrifty Retail Stores from Minicase 5-1 and the You Apply It minicase above pays 2% of the face value of any new share issue in flotation costs. Also, share purchases and sales are subject to transaction costs. These costs are calculated as $45 per trade plus $0.02 per share.

Questions

Question 1: The firm pays no dividends and uses earnings to finance the new project. What are the net proceeds that Kelly can receive from selling 242 shares at $39.60? What will her total wealth be after the sale?

Question 2: The firm pays $12 million in dividends and sells shares to finance the new project. Including flotation costs, how much does TRS have to raise to net $12 million?

Question 3: What is the price at which shares can be sold?

Question 4: How many shares does the firm have to sell to raise the required amount after flotation costs?

You Apply It Continued >

Question 5: After the sale, what will the total value of the firm and the value per share be?

Question 6: What will Kelly's total wealth be after the firm pays dividends and sells shares?

Question 7: Is the dividend policy relevant?

Answer

Question 1: The firm pays no dividends and uses earnings to finance the new project. What are the net proceeds that Kelly can receive from selling 242 shares at $39.60? What will her total wealth be after the sale?

The share price after announcing the new project is $39.60. Selling 242 shares at $39.60 per share will produce $9,583.20. However, Kelly has to pay transaction costs on the sale:

$$\text{Transaction costs} = \$45 + (0.02 \times 242) = \$49.84$$

The net proceeds for Kelly will be $9,533.36. Transaction costs reduce the value of the homemade dividends.

Under this internal financing option, Kelly's total wealth after the sale is:

$$[(2,000 - 242) \times \$39.60] + (242 \times \$39.60) - \$49.84 = \$79,150.16$$

Question 2: The firm pays $12 million in dividends and sells shares to finance the new project. Including flotation costs, how much does TRS have to raise to net $12 million?

The firm has to raise $12 million in cash plus the flotation costs of 2% on the share issue, or a total of $12,244,898 ($12 million/0.98) to net $12 million. Total flotation costs are $244,898.

Question 3: What is the price at which shares can be sold?

The price at which the shares can be sold is:

$$\begin{array}{c} \text{share value before} \\ \text{the dividend} \end{array} - \begin{array}{c} \text{dividend} \\ \text{per share} \end{array}$$
$$= \$39.60 - \$4.80 = \$34.80$$

Question 4: How many shares does the firm have to sell to raise the required amount after flotation costs?

The firm has to sell:

$$\begin{array}{c} \text{total cash including} \\ \text{flotation costs} \end{array} \div \begin{array}{c} \text{share price} \\ \text{of new issue} \end{array}$$
$$= \$12,244,898 \div \$34.80$$
$$= 351,865 \text{ shares}$$

Question 5: After the sale, what will the total value of the firm and the value per share be?

The total value of the firm after the sale is:

$$(\text{"old" shares} + \text{"new" shares}) \times \$34.80 - \text{flotation costs}$$
$$= [(2,500,000 + 351,865) \times \$34.80] - \$244,898$$
$$= \$99 \text{ million}$$

You Apply It Continued >

To calculate the value per share, first determine the total number of shares:

$$\text{Total shares} = 2,500,000 + 351,865 = 2,851,865$$

$$\text{Value per share} = \frac{\text{Total value}}{\text{Total shares}}$$

$$\text{Value per share} = \frac{\$99,000,000}{2,851,865} = \$34.71$$

Question 6: What will Kelly's total wealth be after the firm pays dividends and sells shares?

Kelly's wealth after the firm pays dividends and sells shares to finance the project will be equal to the sum of her share of the cash dividends plus the market value of her share holdings.

$$\text{Dividends} = 2,000 \times \$4.80 = \$9,600$$

$$\text{Value of her shareholdings} = 2,000 \times \$34.71 = \$69,420$$

$$\text{Total wealth} = \$79,020$$

Question 7: Is the dividend policy relevant?

Transaction and flotation costs decrease Kelly's wealth whether the firm finances the new project with internal funds or pays the cash in dividends and sells new shares to finance the new project.

In the first You Apply It minicase above, where dividends, transaction costs, and flotation costs were zero, Kelly's wealth after the announcement of the project was $79,200, regardless of whether the firm pays dividends. However, Kelly's wealth is adversely affected by transaction costs when the firm chooses to finance the project with internal funds because she is forced to sell shares to produce homemade dividends (Question 1). Her wealth after considering transaction costs is $79,150.16, which is $49.84 less than when transaction costs are zero.

Kelly's wealth is also adversely affected by flotation costs when the firm sells shares in the market to pay the cash dividends and, at the same time, finance the project (Question 6). Her wealth after considering flotation costs is $79,020, which is $180 less than when transaction costs are zero. So the dividend policy is relevant in that Kelly's wealth is greater under the second alternative.

The fact that transaction costs are less than flotation costs determines the preferable investment alternative for an investor like Kelly. Shareholders who need current income are better off selling shares to create income and having the firm retain all cash to finance the new project. These arguments should not, however, imply that the optimal alternative for one group of shareholders is optimal for all. Consider next the effects of differing tax treatments.

Tax Differential Effects According to the **tax-differential view of dividend policy,** the difference in the tax treatment of dividend income and capital gains should make dividend policy important in determining the value of a firm. When the effective personal tax rate on capital gains is higher than the effective personal tax rate on dividends, investors will require higher rates of return on low-dividend shares than they require on high-dividend shares. Consequently, shares with high dividends will sell at a premium compared to low-dividend shares.

In Canada, recent changes in the *Income Tax Act* have complicated the tax differential effects. Up to a federal marginal tax rate of 22%, capital gains are taxed at a higher rate than dividends. Above 22%, capital gains are taxed at a lower rate than dividends. However, it is important to remember that taxes on capital gains are deferred until the gains are realized, while dividends are taxed in the year during which they are received. Consequently, under certain circumstances, the effective tax rate on capital gains may be lower than the effective tax rate on dividends even at marginal rates below 22%. (Minicase 5-2, which follows, deals with this issue.) The ability of investors to defer capital gains without paying taxes complicates the relationship between dividend policy and firm value.

The effect of the tax differential between capital gains and dividends is further complicated by the tax status of institutional investors. Tax-exempt institutions, such as pension plans, are not affected by the differences in tax treatment between capital gains and dividends. More importantly, in Canada dividends received by corporate shareholders from taxable Canadian corporations are deductible in computing Part I tax. As a result, corporate investors are willing to pay a premium for shares that pay high dividends.

The existence of a group that favours high dividends, another group that is indifferent, and a third group that favours retention of earnings with no distribution of dividends makes it difficult to predict the overall effect of the tax differential on dividend policies. However, the existence of different tax clienteles can be predicted and investors will invest in securities that suit their needs. As long as there are enough investors in each group, the preferences resulting from tax biases will not affect share prices. Empirical evidence supports the tax-differential view of dividend policy and suggests that for every dollar increase in dividends, investors require an additional 23 cents in before-tax return.

Minicase 5-2 illustrates the tax differential effects.

MINICASE 5-2 CHOICE OF DIVIDENDS OR CAPITAL GAINS UNDER THE CONDITION OF A CONSTANT EFFECTIVE PERSONAL TAX RATE

Suppose there are no transaction or flotation costs for Thrifty Retail Stores (TRS). However, Kelly pays 42% personal taxes on dividends and on capital gains. Kelly bought her 2,000 shares at $32 per share shortly before the firm announced the new project.

Additional information:

Dividends per share	$ 4.80
Share price after announcing the new project	39.60
Share price after cash dividend and sale of shares to finance project	34.80

Note: In Canada, the effective personal tax rate on dividends can be lower or higher than the effective personal tax rate on capital gains, depending on the tax bracket. This minicase assumes that the two rates are equal in order to derive a general conclusion.

Case Continued >

How would personal taxes affect Kelly's preference between the firm's alternatives of paying a cash dividend and selling shares to finance the new project or using the cash to finance the new project?

If TRS pays dividends:

If the firm pays the dividends in cash and sells shares to finance the new project, Kelly will receive $9,600 (2,000 × $4.80) in dividends before taxes. As she pays 42% tax on the dividends, her net cash inflows from the firm will be $5,568 ($9,600 × 0.58).

Kelly's wealth is:

$$\begin{array}{c} \text{value of dividends} \\ \text{after tax} \end{array} + \begin{array}{c} \text{market value} \\ \text{of her shares} \end{array}$$

$$= \$5,568 + (2,000 \times \$34.80)$$

$$= \$75,168$$

If TRS uses earnings alone to finance the new project:

Kelly's total wealth is $79,200 ($39.60 × 2,000). However, she needs approximately $5,568 in cash to substitute for the loss of dividends. Kelly can sell enough shares to receive the $5,568 after taxes. She will have to pay capital gains taxes of 42% on the difference between the selling price and her purchase price ($32.00). Let N be the number of shares required to be sold to receive the desired $5,568 plus taxes. Then:

$$N \times \text{new share price} = \text{desired amount} + (\text{capital gains per share} \times N \times T_{PC})$$

where

T_{PC} = effective personal tax rate on capital gains

The second term on the right-hand side calculates the amount of personal tax on the capital gains realized from the sale of N shares. For the case at hand, this relationship is:

$$N \times 39.60 = \$5,568 + [(\$39.60 - \$32.00) \times N \times 0.42]$$
$$N \times 39.60 = \$5,568 + (3.192 \times N)$$
$$36.408N = \$5,568$$
$$N = 153 \text{ shares}$$

Kelly's total wealth is:

$$\begin{array}{c} \text{after-tax cash from} \\ \text{the sale of 153 shares} \end{array} + \begin{array}{c} \text{market value of her} \\ \text{remaining shares} \end{array}$$

$$= (153 \times \$39.60) - [(\$39.60 - \$32.00) \times 153 \times 0.42] + [(2,000 - 153) \times \$39.60]$$

$$= \$5,570.42 + \$73,141.20$$

$$= \$78,711.62$$

Comparing the resulting total wealth, it could be concluded that the retention of earnings will maximize Kelly's total wealth. However, the total wealth calculated in each *Case Continued >*

case is not completely after-tax wealth, as there are unpaid tax liabilities on the capital gains. If the firm pays the cash in dividends and sells shares to finance the new project, the unpaid tax liabilities will be:

$$2{,}000 \times (\$34.80 - \$32.00) \times 0.42 = \$2{,}352$$

Thus, Kelly's total after-tax wealth if she chooses to liquidate her total investment now will be $72,816 ($75,168 − $2,352).

If the firm retains all cash to finance the new project, Kelly's unpaid tax liabilities will be:

$$(2{,}000 - 153) \times (\$39.60 - \$32.00) \times 0.42 = \$5{,}895.62$$

Thus, Kelly's total after-tax wealth if she chooses to liquidate her total investment now will also be $72,816 ($78,711.62 − $5,895.62).

In conclusion, if the effective personal tax rate on dividend income is equal to the effective personal tax rate on capital gains, and Kelly liquidates her investment immediately after the firm announces the new project and pays the dividend, Kelly's wealth is the same whether the firm pays all earnings as dividends or retains the cash to finance the new project.

This conclusion can be extended to a more general one. If the effective personal tax rate on dividends is higher than the effective rate on capital gains, investors who liquidate their investments immediately after the dividend will prefer earnings retention because they will receive the income as capital gains. If the effective personal tax rate on dividends is lower than the rate on capital gains, they will prefer the dividend payment.

In Canada, the effective personal tax rates on capital gains and dividend income vary according to the marginal federal tax rate and whether or not the dividends are eligible. Exhibit 5-1 shows the differences in taxes paid for the next $1.00 of the three types of investment income, assuming that the provincial tax rate is 50% of the calculated federal

---

Exhibit 5-1
Tax Paid for the Next $1 of Investment Income in Year 2007

Marginal federal tax rate	Interest income[1]	Capital gains[2]	Dividend income—eligible[3]	Dividend income—other than eligible[4]
16%	0.2400	0.1200	0	0.0500
22%	0.3300	0.1650	0.066	0.1625
26%	0.3900	0.1950	0.1530	0.2375
29%	0.4350	0.2175	0.2183	0.2938

[1] Tax (interest) $= (1 + Tp)T_F$

[2] Tax (capital gains) $= (1 + T_p)(\frac{1}{2})(T_F)$

[3] Tax (dividends) $= (1 + T_p)(1.45)(T_F - 0.189655)$ when the eligible dividend rate of 45% gross up and 18.9655% tax credit is used

[4] Tax (dividends) $= (1 + T_p)(1.25)(T_F - 0.133333)$ when the other-than-eligible dividend rate of 25% gross up and 13.3333% tax credit is used

tax. Note, the first federal rate used was 16% whereas the actual rate is 15.5%. For more information on federal tax brackets and rates, see the Web Links section at the end of this chapter.

These results hold when investors liquidate their investments immediately after the decision to pay dividends. However, most investors keep their investments for much longer periods. These investors prefer earnings retention to dividends because the tax liability on capital gains is deferred. The present value of tax liabilities on capital gains may indeed end up being less than the taxes on dividends, even when the rate on capital gains is moderately higher than the rate on dividends. Thus, the ability to defer taxes often makes the effective tax rate on capital gains lower than the rate on dividends, favouring the choice of retaining earnings rather than paying dividends.

Test your knowledge. Try the You Apply It minicase below.

YOU APPLY IT DIVIDEND POLICY AND TAXES

Adi Dabeault is looking for a long-term investment for $50,000. His broker suggests two alternatives. Adi can invest in Provincial Utilities (PU), which is known for its stable but other-than-eligible dividends. Currently, the price per share of PU is $4. PU has recently increased the dividend per share to $0.48. No changes are expected in the near future. Dividends are paid regularly on December 31.

Another investment alternative for Adi is Secure International Growth (SIG) mutual fund, which invests in a highly diversified international portfolio. SIG makes no distribution to its unit holders, as it invests exclusively in growth common stocks that do not pay dividends. Over the past 10 years, the unit price has been increasing at an annual rate of 12% and the pattern is expected to continue long-term. The current unit price is $20.

Assume that Adi is in the highest federal tax bracket of 29% (ignoring surtaxes). He lives in Saskatchewan, where provincial tax is 50% of the federal tax (ignoring surtaxes).

Questions

Question 1: If Adi buys PU shares on January 1, 20X1, what is the after-tax cash flow from his investment after one year?

Question 2: What is Adi's effective tax rate on dividend income?

Question 3: What is Adi's after-tax and before-tax rate of return if he invests in PU shares?

Question 4: The share price, dividend per share, and tax rates will not change over the next 10 years. What will Adi's investment in PU be worth after 10 years if it is compounded at an after-tax rate of return of 8.4742%?

Question 5: Adi buys SIG units on January 1, 20X1 for $20 per unit and liquidates his investment on December 31, 20X1 for $22.40 per unit. What is the after-tax cash flow from his investment?

Question 6: What is Adi's effective tax rate on capital gains income?

Question 7: What is Adi's after-tax and before-tax rate of return if he invests in SIG units and liquidates his investment after one year?

You Apply It Continued >

Question 8: Adi invests in SIG units. Assuming that the unit price appreciates at the rate of 12% and that tax rates do not change over the next 10 years, how much will Adi receive after tax if he liquidates his entire investment in exactly 10 years' time?

Question 9: If Adi's plan is to invest the money for 10 years, which investment alternative (PU or SIG) will produce the highest after-tax future value?

Question 10: If Adi plans to invest the money for 2 years, which investment (PU or SIG) will produce the highest after-tax future value?

Answers

Question 1: If Adi buys PU shares on January 1, 20X1, what is the after-tax cash flow from his investment after one year?

With $50,000 and a share price of $4, Adi will be able to buy 12,500 shares. Each share will pay $0.48 in dividends. Thus, Adi will receive $6,000 before taxes.

Keep in mind that other-than-eligible dividends in Canada are taxed using the gross-up method. The taxpayer grosses up dividends by 25% and subtracts 13.33% from the federal tax rate that will be applied to the grossed-up amount. Therefore, Adi's federal and provincial tax bill on the dividends is:

$$\$6,000 \times 1.25(0.29 - 0.1333) \times 1.50 = \$1,762.88$$

Adi's after-tax cash flows from his investment after one year will be $4,237.12.

Question 2: What is Adi's effective tax rate on dividend income?

Adi's effective tax rate on dividend income is:

$$T_{DE} = \$1,762.88 \div \$6,000 = 29.38\%$$

Question 3: What is Adi's after-tax and before-tax rate of return if he invests in PU shares?

As a result of investing $50,000, Adi will receive $4,237.12 per year after tax. Therefore, his after-tax rate of return is:

$$\$4,237.12 \div \$50,000 = 8.4742\%$$

Adi's before-tax rate of return is:

$$8.4742 \div (1 - 0.2938) = 12\%$$

which is the same as

$$\$6,000 \div \$50,000 = 12\%$$

Question 4: The share price, dividend per share, and tax rates will not change over the next 10 years. What will Adi's investment in PU be worth after 10 years if it is compounded at an after-tax rate of return of 8.4742%?

Compounded at the after-tax rate of return of 8.4742%, Adi's investment after 10 years will be:

$$\$50,000 \times (1 + 0.084742)^{10} = \$112,780.64$$

Question 5: Adi buys SIG units on January 1, 20X1 for $20 per unit and liquidates his investment on December 31, 20X1 for $22.40 per unit. What is the after-tax cash flow from his investment?

You Apply It Continued >

With the $50,000 investment and a price of $20 per share, Adi can buy 2,500 units. At the sale price of $22.40, Adi's investment will be worth $56,000. His before-tax profit will be $6,000.

Adi's profit is capital gain. In Canada, only 50% of capital gains are taxed. The taxable portion of the capital gains is taxed at a federal tax rate of 29% and a provincial tax rate of 50% of federal taxes. Therefore, Adi's taxes on the $6,000 of capital gains are:

$$\$6,000 \times 0.50 \times 0.29 \times 1.50 = \$1,305.00$$

The after-tax capital gain is $4,695.00 ($6,000.00 − $1,305.00).

Question 6: What is Adi's effective tax rate on capital gains income?

Adi's effective tax rate on capital gains income is:

$$T_{GE} = \$1,305.00 \div \$6,000 = 21.75\%$$

Question 7: What is Adi's after-tax and before-tax rate of return if he invests in SIG units and liquidates his investment after one year?

As a result of investing $50,000 for one year, Adi will receive $4,695.00 after tax. Therefore, his after-tax rate of return is:

$$\$4,695.00 \div \$50,000 = 9.39\%$$

Adi's before-tax return is:

$$9.39 \div (1 - 0.2175) = 12\%$$

which is the same as

$$\$6,000 \div \$50,000 = 12\%$$

Question 8: Adi invests in SIG units. Assuming that the unit price appreciates at the rate of 12% and that tax rates do not change over the next 10 years, how much will Adi receive after tax if he liquidates his entire investment in exactly 10 years' time?

At the growth rate of 12% per year, Adi's investment will compound to:

$$\$50,000 \times (1.00 + 0.12)^{10} = \$155,292.41$$

He will have to pay capital gains tax on the amount above $50,000. This amount is $105,292.41. His tax bill will be:

$$\$105,292.41 \times 0.50 \times 0.29 \times 1.50 = \$22,901.10$$

After 10 years, Adi's after-tax cash flows from the investment in SIG units will be:

$$\$155,292.41 - \$22,901.10 = \$132,391.31$$

Question 9: If Adi's plan is to invest the money for 10 years, which investment alternative (PU or SIG) will produce the highest after-tax future value?

Adi should choose the alternative of investing in SIG units because they will provide an after-tax future value that is $19,610.67 ($132,391.31 − $112,780.64) higher.

Question 10: If Adi plans to invest the money for 2 years, which investment (PU or SIG) will produce the highest after-tax future value?

The future value of the PU investment after 2 years is obtained by compounding the $50,000 by the after-tax return for 2 years. The process yields:

$$\$50,000 \times (1 + 0.084742)^2 = \$58,833.26$$

You Apply It Continued >

The future value of the SIG investment after 2 years is obtained by compounding $50,000 by the before-tax return for 2 years and subtracting the capital gains taxes due after liquidation. Capital gains taxes are determined by multiplying the capital gains by the effective capital gains tax rate of 21.75%. The process yields:

$$\text{Future value before-tax} = \$50,000 \times (1 + 0.12)^2 = \$62,720$$
$$\text{Capital gains} = \$62,720 - \$50,000 = \$12,720$$
$$\text{Taxes on capital gains} = \$12,720 \times 0.2175 = \$2,766.60$$
$$\text{After-tax future value} = \$62,720.00 - \$2,766.60 = \$59,953.40$$

Investing in SIG shares is preferable if Adi is planning to invest for only 2 years.

Signalling Hypothesis Most firms that pay dividends exhibit stable patterns of a constant dividend payment made on a regular basis. Dividends are increased only when management is relatively certain that the higher dividend payout can be maintained indefinitely. Dividends are decreased when the firm is no longer able to sustain the current level of dividends. Given this type of behaviour, the **signalling hypothesis** states that changes in dividends are considered to be useful information to investors concerning a company's future prospects.

For example, consider the Toronto Dominion Bank (TD). TD has changed its dividends in the past, but changes have been in the same direction as the changes in earnings. If TD increases its dividends now, the market will interpret the increase as a signal indicating that earnings will also increase to support the new dividend. Consequently, the market will react by bidding the shares up until the market price equals the present value of the future expected earnings.

Similarly, if TD decreases its dividends, the market will expect a similar long-term change in the firm's earnings. Consequently, the share price will be discounted to reflect the market's perception of its new value.

It must be emphasized that the quality of information contained in dividend changes depends on the firm's established pattern of dividends. In the absence of a regular pattern, it is hard to interpret changes. Moreover, interpretations differ from one firm to another depending on the established pattern.

For example, if a firm has established a pattern of annual dividend increases, the market will expect the dividend to grow by the rate of the increases. If by the expected date of the usual increase, the firm does not announce the expected increase, the market will lower its expectations regarding the growth rate of the dividend. Consequently, the market price of the shares will be discounted to reflect the market's new expectation. For such a firm, the *magnitude* of the change is as important as the direction of the change. The firm might increase its dividend and yet suffer a drop in share price because the increase is less than expected.

In contrast, if a firm has an established pattern of constant dividend payments with occasional changes, the market will not react if a regular announcement date passes without changes in the dividend. Moreover, the price reaction to an increase will be positive regardless of the magnitude of the increase.

Despite the existence of various patterns, it is widely believed that investors interpret an increase in the current dividend payout as a message that management anticipates a permanently higher level of cash flows from investment. Ross argued in 1977 that an increase in dividends is often accompanied by an increase in share price, while a dividend cut generally leads to a share price decline.[2] Price changes indicate that dividend announcements contain important information or "signalling" content. An increase in dividend payout is a clear message because:

- it cannot be duplicated by firms that do not anticipate higher earnings, and
- management has an incentive to "tell the truth."

Thus, investors are more likely to believe the firm's financial reports if the firm announces earnings increases that are accompanied by a dividend increase.

M&M (1961) suggested that the increase in share price in response to a dividend announcement does not necessarily mean that investors prefer cash dividends to retained earnings.

Consider the following article, which shows that the conclusions from the above paragraphs do not always hold and that an increase in dividends is therefore not necessarily accompanied by an increase in share price.

According to the article, IBM expected the increase in dividend discussed in the article to cause an increase in share price. However, comments made by IBM's CEO, along with sputtering growth in earnings and revenue, counteracted any positive signalling effects of the dividend increase.

Speaking of Dividends

Sandra Ward

Big Blue Rides a Roller Coaster
Hefty dividend hike can't calm the tide

All seemed right with the world Wednesday morning. At least, the world according to International Business Machines. Big Blue's first-quarter earnings beat expectations. Its stock price changed hands at levels more than double the low period of three years ago. For the first time since it hacked its quarterly payout to the bone in 1993, the giant computer maker boosted its dividend by 40%, to 35 cents a share. The new dividend will be payable June 10 to holders of record May 10. IBM was back—briefly.

Before the day was out, investors turned on the same shares they had driven up nearly five points earlier in the session, sending them a punishing 9% lower. More than 16 million shares traded, nearly four times IBM's average daily volume. Big Blue's swoon led to a 70-point drop in the Dow Jones Industrial Average. As weighted in the Dow, IBM's share of the damage: about 29 points. The stock finished the day down 10¼, at 105¼.

If the dividend hike was designed to stem the tide, it wasn't enough. Nor was Chairman and Chief Executive Louis V. Gerstner's statement that management will continue to "carefully consider other uses of cash, including share repurchases, acquisitions and debt reductions."

---

[2] Stephen A. Ross, "The Determination of Financial Structure: The Incentive Signalling Approach," *Bell Journal of Economics*, Volume 8, Spring 1977, pp. 23–40.

Investors grew distracted by signs of sputtering earnings growth and skimpy revenue growth. More troubling was IBM's admission that personal computer sales to the corporate market had gone soft, something widely suspected and greatly feared. Also, the computer giant confessed that its formerly bustling computer-chip business is under pressure from falling prices. Ditto for the computer-storage operation.

Adding to the company's frustrations is the rising dollar: foreign-currency translations pinched profits. Indeed, IBM execs painted the current quarter as the one with the most potential to disappoint in comparison with year-ago results. Currency translations are expected to knock 25 cents a share off profits.

For the first quarter, IBM saw operating earnings grow by a modest 4.2% before a one-time charge of $435 million reduced net income to $774 million, or $1.41 a share, down from $1.29 billion, or $2.12, in the year-earlier period. The company logged revenues of $16.56 billion in the quarter, compared with $15.74 billion in the same period last year. Still, hardware sales and margins weakened as the company worked at making a transition to new mainframes, a shift that could take up to four years.

With the market gyrating wildly these days and investors increasingly nervous about the outlook for corporate earnings, it wasn't just what IBM executives said, it was how they said it, apparently, that provoked such a stampede. "Bearish times" were detected.

Also testimony to the jittery nature of Wall Street was the fretting that accompanied a discussion of actions Big Blue is considering, such as possible divestitures and continued cost cutting. Typically such moves would be greeted enthusiastically on the Street, yet here they seemed a source of anxiety as securities analysts sensed a shift in direction.

The **clientele effect** implies that different groups of shareholders prefer different dividend payout policies. Some shareholders prefer current income and higher payout ratios to the retention of earnings for future growth. Examples include seniors, who rely on their investments for spending, and pension plans, which may need regular cash flow to pay pensioners. Other shareholders may prefer low dividend payouts so that the firm can reinvest the proceeds in new investments. They hope that their returns will be realized as capital gains in the future as they have no need for current income.

In a perfect market where there are no taxes or transaction costs, investors should be indifferent between high and low dividend payments. Investors who do not need current income but receive current dividends would simply reinvest them in the same firm's stock or in other similar investments. However, when investors must first pay taxes on dividend income and then pay transaction costs to reinvest, these investors would prefer the firm to retain most of its earnings. These arguments suggest the existence of clientele groups separated on the basis of their preference for dividend payments or capital gains.

The clientele effect, which emphasizes that the existence of taxes leads to different clientele groups, is necessarily related to flotation and transaction cost effects as well as to tax differential effects, as explained earlier. (The tax differential view suggests that differences in tax rates on capital gains and dividends lead to various dividend policies.)

The existence of clientele groups implies that a firm will attract a specific clientele group depending on its dividend policy. Yet it seems unlikely that firm value will be affected by the clientele argument. As long as the supply of high-dividend-paying securities balances the demand by investors for high dividends, the market should not discriminate among firms based on the proportion of their earnings paid in dividends.

The clientele effect, however, may provide a possible explanation for management's reluctance to alter established payout ratios. Although changes to established payout ratios might attract other shareholders, such changes may cause current shareholders to exchange their shares for ones that match their preferred dividend policy. The exchange will result in transaction costs and capital gains taxes for the current shareholders. Although empirical studies indicate the existence of a clientele effect, this does not imply that one dividend policy is better than any other dividend policy.

Expectations View

According to the **expectations view of dividend policy**, the share-price reaction to a dividend announcement is not entirely governed by dividend policy. It is also affected by investors' expectations about the dividend payments. Expectations are based on internal factors, such as past dividend decisions and investment strategies, and external factors, such as the general economy, industry conditions, and level of interest rates. A movement in share price is seen only if there is a difference between actual and expected dividends. Following are three different scenarios for a dividend announcement:

■ If the dividend announcement is as expected, there is no change in share price.

■ If the dividend announcement is better than expected, an increase in share price occurs.

■ If the dividend announcement is worse than expected, a decrease in share price occurs.

Other Considerations

A firm's dividend decision is influenced by many other factors, such as the following.

Legal and Mandated Restrictions Dividend policies are affected by restrictions imposed by legislative agencies. For example, the *Canada Business Corporations Act* prohibits dividend payments unless the firm meets the solvency test. **Solvency** is a firm's ability to pay its liabilities after the dividend payment. The test is intended to ensure that the payment of dividends does not reduce the realizable value of a firm's assets below the aggregate of its liabilities and equity capital.

Firms may also be subject to specific constraints. Lenders impose restrictions in the form of protective covenants attached to debt and preferred-share contracts. The objective of restrictions is to ensure that the firm will live up to its promises to debtholders. Such restrictions limit the firm's ability to decrease the size of working capital, issue new debt, and pay dividends. For example, a common restriction requires that working capital be maintained at a certain level before dividends can be paid on common shares. Any violation of these requirements makes loans immediately due and gives the lender the right to foreclose on a loan.

Finally, constraints may be imposed indirectly by certain investors. For example, laws prohibit some institutions from investing in common shares that do not have established records of dividend payments. Similarly, the policy of some investors will prohibit them from spending the principal of their investments. Such investors will invest in securities that pay dividends. Companies may purposely pay high dividends to satisfy the needs of this investment group. For example, utility companies such as Bell Canada, Aliant Inc., and TELUS Corporation are known to pay high dividends.

Firm Liquidity The ability of a firm to pay cash dividends is sometimes restricted by lack of liquidity. A firm may show a large amount of retained earnings on the balance sheet, but this does not mean it is in a position to pay dividends. Dividends are typically paid with cash. Thus, the cash flows of the firm, not the amount of retained earnings, determine its ability to pay dividends.

Earnings Volatility Earnings volatility constrains a firm from increasing dividends. When a firm's earnings fluctuate widely, it will have a low payout ratio. The firm will be conservative in paying dividends to ensure its ability to pay the same dividends when earnings are low. In contrast, when a firm has relatively stable earnings, it can pay a larger percentage of its earnings as dividends.

Control Many firms, particularly medium and small ones, try to keep control of ownership in the hands of some existing shareholders. Such firms will try to finance their projects first with internal financing and consequently have low payout ratios to retain earnings to meet their cash needs.

Consider the next article, which describes a managerial perspective on the relevance of dividend policy in practice. The article considers dividend policy as an integrated financial strategy that affects the company's target capital structure and expected funding needs. It explains the impact of factors such as financial flexibility, signalling, and the clientele effect on FPL Group's dividend decision. As the financial environment becomes more competitive, a company's financial strategy and dividend policy must change accordingly.

Of Dividends and Financial Flexibility

Dennis Soter

On May 9, 1994, Juno Beach, Fla.-based FPL Group, the parent company of Florida Power & Light, announced a 32 percent reduction in its quarterly dividend payout. This cut, the first-ever by a healthy utility, ended FPL's 47-year string of annual dividend increases, the longest of any electric utility and third longest of any company listed on the New York Stock Exchange.

In addition to the dividend cut, FPL's board authorized management to repurchase up to 10 million shares of common stock over three years, with 4 million shares earmarked for repurchase over the next 12 months. (In fact, the company repurchased exactly 4 million shares during the last eight months of 1994.) Although much of the cash saved from the dividend cut would be returned to investors in the form of stock repurchases, the rest would be used to repay debt, thereby reducing leverage.

Ever since Nobel Prize–winners Franco Modigliani and Merton Miller postulated in 1961 that a company's dividend policy is irrelevant to its stock price, money managers, Wall Street analysts, and corporate practitioners have debated the issue. This view—that investors care only about total returns and not whether they are realized as cash dividends or price appreciation—assumes that a company's value is determined by its future free cash flows. Dividends represent merely a financial policy decision: How much cash should be distributed to stockholders—and what form should such distributions take?

FPL decided to cut its dividend for a number of reasons. With competition looming in both power generation and distribution, the utility expected its increased business risk to be reflected in more volatile cash flows and less predictable earnings. It concluded that its quarterly dividend payout of 62 cents per share and payout ratio—which had averaged 90 percent over the prior four years—were too high, and engaged Stern Stewart & Co. to assist in developing a new dividend policy that would enhance financial flexibility. The result was to cut the dividend to 42 cents per share and target a future payout ratio of between 60 percent and 65 percent of the prior year's earnings.

To understand the relationship between dividends and financial flexibility, consider the following: For every $1 paid in dividends, a company must earn $1.60 before taxes, since dividends are paid out of after-tax earnings. (This assumes a combined marginal federal and state income tax rate of 37.5 percent.) If the company's cost of borrowed funds is 8 percent, each dollar in dividends could service interest expense on $20 of debt principal. Dividends, therefore, represent a significant fixed cost that destroys financial flexibility by reducing debt capacity—fully 20 times the amount of dividends paid. With 190 million shares of common stock outstanding, FPL expected to save about $150 million in dividends in the first year alone. If this entire amount were used to service interest expense on new borrowings, FPL's debt capacity would, in theory, increase by more than $3 billion. (At year-end 1993, total interest-bearing debt was $4.4 billion.)

In addition, changes in the U.S. tax code since 1990 had made capital gains more attractive to stockholders than dividends, since dividends are taxed at ordinary income rates of up to 39.6 percent; stock sales, however, are taxed at the capital gains rate of 28 percent. Moreover, capital gains taxes are due only on the difference between the repurchase price and the stockholder's tax basis in the stock. And, those stockholders who choose not to sell their shares can defer taxes indefinitely.

The stock market's initial reaction to FPL's announcement was negative: On the day of the announcement, FPL's stock price fell from $31.88 to $27.50. But as Wall Street realized that the dividend cut was not a negative signal about the company's prospects, the stock rebounded. Three weeks later, FPL's stock closed at $32.17 (adjusted for the quarterly dividend of 42 cents); one year later, FPL's stock price closed at $37.75, giving stockholders a one-year post-announcement return (including dividends) of 23.8 percent, well above the 14.2 percent of the S&P 500 Index and more than double the 11.2 percent of the S&P Utilities Index over the same period. In the meantime, while FPL lost some stockholders unhappy with the lower payout, its new financial strategy has attracted additional institutional ownership—up from 34 percent at the end of 1993 to 47 percent at year-end 1995.

Dividend policy must be viewed as part of an integrated financial strategy that includes a company's target capital structure and its expected funding needs. Integral to the financial strategy are the company's business strategy and the associated risks. When the competitive environment is expected to change, a company's financial strategy and policies—including dividends—must change accordingly. The stock market's response to FPL's bold dividend action vindicated management's decision.

Dennis Soter is a partner of Stern Stewart & Co., a New York–based financial advisory firm. He is responsible for the firm's Corporate Finance Advisory Services and Middle Market EVA Advisory Services.

Source: *Corporate Finance,* September 1996.

5.2 DIVIDEND POLICY IN PRACTICE

The first section of this chapter described the theory proposed to explain the behaviour of firms in setting their dividend policies. This theory does not predict a consistent relationship between dividend policy and firm value. Yet it provides insights that can be used by managers to set dividend policies.

Similarly, dividend policies of publicly traded firms fail to provide evidence of a consistent relationship. However, a study of dividend policies in practice shows several important features. Furthermore, it appears that, in practice, firms choose from several feasible alternatives.

Important Features of Dividend Policies

Dividend policies appear to be influenced by two dominant features: stability and industry norms.

Stability Observing the pattern of corporate dividends over time reveals preference for stability. Generally, corporations' earnings fluctuate more widely than their dividend payments. It seems that corporations often set their dividend payments lower than expected earnings to ensure the same dividend level during years of high and low earnings. Firms resist cutting dividends to avoid conveying negative signals about their prospects. Section 5.1 indicated that this conclusion is consistent with the signalling hypothesis and expectations view of dividend policy.

Corporations also try to convey stability of earnings through the payment pattern. The majority of dividend payments are made quarterly, although some firms pay dividends semi-annually or annually. There is a tendency to keep the frequency and the timing of dividend payments consistent over time. In their annual reports, companies often emphasize the consistency of their dividend payments.

The proportion of earnings paid in dividends is generally a function of the firm's maturity. Young and growing firms need cash to invest in new projects. During this stage, the firm is better off keeping earnings rather than paying dividends and selling new equity to finance expansion and growth. Sometimes a small, growing firm is not able to raise funding at all. Consequently, the firm will face hard rationing—a concept detailed in Chapter 2.

The pattern of not paying dividends during the early stages of a firm's life cycle may also be a sign of preference for stability. During these early stages, earnings are highly uncertain and fluctuate widely from one year to the next. Thus, concerns about stability prohibit the firm from paying dividends for fear that these dividends will have to be temporarily cut in the future because of lack of earnings to support them.

Dividend stability and uninterrupted increases in the payout ratio are good signs of stability and high quality. Also, dividend increases can have an immediate impact on share prices, as they signal improved operations and a strengthened balance sheet.

Management's preoccupation with dividend stability may lead it to occasionally pay **extra** or **special dividends**, over and above the regular dividend. The term "extra" cautions investors that the payment may not be repeated the following year unless the firm's earnings are high enough to warrant payment.

A special dividend is often paid when a firm finds itself with a substantial amount of cash, for example after the sale of property or division. It may also occur when a firm that has accumulated cash for takeovers and acquisitions decides to abandon its plans. Finally, firms with huge sums of idle cash may become targets for takeovers. They declare special dividends as an anti-takeover measure.

Normally, extra and special dividends are declared at the end of the fiscal year. This practice allows a firm to declare payment after reviewing results from operations and ensuring its ability to pay the dividend. As a result, extra or special dividends should not convey any signals concerning the long-term prospects of the firm.

Exhibit 5-2 shows a sample special dividend announcement:

Exhibit 5-2
A Special Dividend Announcement

June 21, 2007—SPECIAL DIVIDEND: The ABC company has declared a special dividend of $0.05 per common share payable on July 30, 2007 to shareholders of record June 10; ex-dividend May 31, 2007.

To maintain the perception of a stable dividend policy, management may distribute dividend payments known as "dividends-in-kind." For example, a firm may sometimes pay dividends in the form of shares in another corporation or in a subsidiary. Exhibit 5-3 shows that Some Company paid dividends in the form of shares in their subsidiary, the Other Company:

Exhibit 5-3
A Dividend-in-Kind Announcement

Nov. 15, 2007—DIVIDEND-IN-KIND: Some Company has declared a dividend-in-kind of 0.48 of a common share of subsidiary The Other Company for each Some Company common share held. The dividend will be paid on or after Dec. 15, 2007 to shareholders of record Dec. 1, 2007; ex-dividend Nov. 28, 2007. Based on a value of $25.50 per Other Company share as of Nov. 14, 2007, the dividend is equivalent to $12.24 for every Some Company share held.

In conclusion, there is strong evidence suggesting the existence of an optimal dividend policy. There is also agreement among practitioners and financial economists that changes in dividends convey useful information. This information and the resulting signals depend on shareholder and market expectations of what the dividend payments should be. This fact suggests that dividend policies should be set conservatively to maintain stability and avoid disappointing market expectations.

Industry Norms Financial managers often consult industry norms when setting their dividend policies. Empirical studies generally show that dividend payout ratios vary across industries. This evidence suggests that the investment opportunities and business risk facing a particular industry are important factors in determining dividend payout ratios. For example, a growing industry, such as the software sector, is likely to be associated with low-payout dividend policies. Such an industry needs huge funds for investment and faces substantial business risk, both of which are reasons for low dividend payout ratios. Indeed, it is difficult to find software companies paying any dividends.

In contrast, companies in a mature industry, such as telephone and other utility companies, or banks, can afford higher payout ratios because of either relatively limited investment opportunities or lower business risk. As a proxy for the level of dividend distribution among industries, Exhibit 5-4 shows the dividend yields for a sample of Canadian companies in various industries: telephone, financial, and software and other technologies.

Exhibit 5-4
Dividend Yields for a Sample of Canadian Companies at June 1, 2007

Telecommunications companies		Financial firms		Software and other technology companies	
Company	Dividend yield	Company	Dividend yield	Company	Dividend yield
BCE	3.40%	Bank of Montreal	3.70%	Nortel Networks	0.0%
Rogers Communications Inc.	0%	Royal Bank	3.00%	Absolute Software	0.0%
TELUS Corporation	2.10%	Toronto Dominion	2.70%	Epic Data International	0.0%

Source: Reproduced with permission of Yahoo! Inc. ® 2007 by Yahoo! Inc. YAHOO! and the YAHOO! logo are trademarks of Yahoo! Inc.

Alternative Dividend Policies

Generally, firms choose one of three different dividend policies:

- the constant dividend payout ratio policy
- the residual dividend policy
- the constant dollar dividend policy

Constant Dividend Payout Ratio Policy The **constant dividend payout ratio policy** is used by firms that wish to pay out a constant percentage of earnings in dividends on a regular and predictable basis. For example, a firm may pay 30% of earnings as dividends and retain the remaining 70% for internal uses.

Strictly following a constant dividend payout ratio policy implies that the firm's dividend payments vary considerably from one year to the next. As earnings fluctuate, the dollar value of dividend payments also fluctuates. However, because high uncertainty of dividends is not desirable for shareholders, some firms use a long-term target for a dividend payout ratio. The actual payout ratios tend to increase during periods of depressed earnings and decrease during periods of good earnings to make the long-term dividends as stable as possible. We display this concept in Minicase 5-3. Note that the information in this minicase also forms the basis of Minicases 5-4 through 5-6.

MINICASE 5-3 CONSTANT DIVIDEND PAYOUT RATIO POLICY

Fast Shipping and Transportation (FST) has projected net earnings for the next five years as shown in Exhibit 5-5. The firm has 12.5 million outstanding shares.

Exhibit 5-5
FST's Projected Net Earnings after Interest and Taxes for the Next Five Years ($ Millions)

	Year 1	Year 2	Year 3	Year 4	Year 5
Net earnings	$45.00	$25.00	$60.00	$75.00	$21.00

Question 1: The firm's dividend policy is to pay 40% of earnings in dividends. What are the projected dividends per share over the next five years?

Exhibit 5-6 shows FST's projected dividends per share.

Exhibit 5-6
FST's Projected Dividends per Share ($ Millions except Per-Share Figures)

	Year 1	Year 2	Year 3	Year 4	Year 5
Net earnings	$45.00	$25.00	$60.00	$75.00	$21.00
Earnings per share	3.60	2.00	4.80	6.00	1.68
Dividend per share	1.44	0.80	1.92	2.40	0.672

Question 2: What are the expected earnings per share, expected dividends per share, standard deviation of expected earnings per share, and standard deviation of dividends per share?

Expected earnings per share = $3.616

Expected dividends per share = $1.4464

Standard deviation of expected earnings per share = $1.64

Standard deviation of the dividends per share = $0.656

$$\text{Expected dividends per share} = \text{expected earnings per share} \times \text{dividend payout ratio}$$

$$\text{Standard deviation of dividends per share} = \text{standard deviation of earnings per share} \times \text{dividend payout ratio}$$

Therefore, under a strict policy of a constant dividend payout ratio, dividend instability is a direct function of the instability of earnings. The higher the uncertainty of earnings, the higher the uncertainty of dividends will be.

Case Continued >

Question 3: Chen is a major shareholder. As he is not a well-diversified investor, he considers the coefficient of variation (from Chapter 2) to be the measure of risk relevant to his situation. What is the coefficient of variation (CV) of FST's expected dividends per share?

$$CV = \$0.656 \div \$1.4464 = 0.4535$$

In this case, the CV indicates that one unit of percent return increases risk by 0.4535%.

Residual Dividend Policy

Residual Dividend Policy A **residual dividend policy** is used by firms that wish to pay dividends only if earnings and cash flows exceed the amount of funds needed to finance all investment projects that have zero or positive net present values. This policy is considered optimal when the rate of return that the firm can earn on the reinvested earnings exceeds the rate of return investors can obtain on their own. If funds can be invested internally more profitably than outside the firm, payment of dividends would require the firm either to forgo profitable investment opportunities or to raise funds from the market.

A firm using the residual dividend policy would determine the dividend payment as follows:

1. Determine the amount of funds needed to finance the accepted investment projects.

2. Use the optimum debt ratio to determine the amount of equity required for the new investments.

3. Finance the required equity with retained earnings to the greatest extent possible.

4. Pay dividends only if the residual amount is positive.

Strictly following a residual dividend policy implies that the firm's dividend payments vary considerably from one year to the next. The variations depend on the fluctuations in earnings and the availability of profitable investment projects. As high uncertainty of dividends is not desirable for shareholders, some firms use a modified version of the basic residual policy to decrease dividend uncertainty. During periods of high earnings and low investment needs, these firms pay out less than they can afford. They use the difference to pay dividends during years of tight earnings or high need for investment funds.

MINICASE 5-4 RESIDUAL DIVIDEND POLICY

Revisiting Minicase 5-3, Fast Shipping and Transportation's dividend policy is to pay any cash after financing all profitable investment projects. The firm's capital structure includes 40% debt and the firm would like to maintain this structure. Exhibit 5-7 provides relevant information on FST's dividend policy over the next five years.

Question 1: What is the expected value of dividends per share over the next five years?
The expected value of dividends per share over the next five years is $1.84.

Case Continued >

Exhibit 5-7
FST's Dividends over the Next Five Years ($ Millions except Per-Share Figures)

	Year 1	Year 2	Year 3	Year 4	Year 5
Net earnings	$45.00	$25.00	$60.00	$75.00	$21.00
Investments	35.00	40.00	40.00	35.00	35.00
Equity required for investments[1]	21.00	24.00	24.00	21.00	21.00
Dividends[2]	24.00	1.00	36.00	54.00	0.00
Dividends per share[3]	1.92	0.08	2.88	4.32	0.00

---

[1] Equity required for investments = 60% of investments

[2] Dividends = net earnings − equity required for investments

[3] Dividends per share = dividends ÷ 12.5 million shares

Question 2: What are the expected investments, standard deviation of investments, and standard deviation of dividends per share?

$$\text{Expected investments} = \$37.00 \text{ million}$$
$$\text{Standard deviation of investments} = \$2.45 \text{ million}$$
$$\text{Standard deviation of dividends per share} = \$1.66$$

The expected dividends per share and standard deviation of dividends per share under the residual dividend policy are respectively higher than the expected dividends and standard deviation using the fixed payout ratio (from Question 2 of Minicase 5-3).

Question 3: Given that the CV under the constant dividend payout policy is 0.4535, should Chen prefer the residual or the constant dividend payout ratio policy? Why?

The CV of FST's expected dividends per share under the residual dividend policy is:

$$CV = \$1.66 \div \$1.84 = 0.9022$$

Given that Chen is primarily concerned with the CV, he should prefer the dividend policy that reduces the CV. Chen would prefer the constant dividend payout ratio policy because it provides the lowest risk per dollar of expected dividends.

Question 4: Would the residual dividend policy always increase the CV?

Question 2 of Minicase 5-3 demonstrated that the degree of risk of the dividends of a firm following a policy of constant dividend payout is directly related to earnings volatility. In contrast, the residual dividend policy has a higher or lower risk per dollar of dividends depending on the correlation between the firm's earnings and the cash required for investment purposes.

For example, the correlation is negative when the firm's earnings and its investment needs exhibit the following pattern. In periods with a high level of earnings, the level of cash required for investments is low, while in periods with low earnings, the level of cash needed for investments is high. In this case, a residual dividend policy leads to higher

Case Continued >

dividend variability because the variability of earnings is further magnified by the variability of investment needs. This is precisely what happens with FST.

In contrast, the correlation is positive when the level of earnings and level of cash required for investment demonstrate similar changes. That is, in periods in which the level of earnings is high, the level of cash needed for investment is also high. In periods in which the level of earnings is low, the level of cash is also low. In this case, a residual dividend policy will lead to lower dividend variability, as the variability of earnings is reduced by the variability of the investment needs. Minicase 5-5 reveals this possibility.

MINICASE 5-5 EFFECT OF INVESTMENT NEEDS ON THE RESIDUAL DIVIDEND POLICY

Fast Shipping and Transportation from Minicase 5-3 continues with its dividend policy of paying out any cash after financing all profitable investment projects. The firm wishes to maintain its capital structure, which includes 40% debt. Exhibit 5-8 provides relevant information on FST's dividend policy and investment needs.

Exhibit 5-8
FST's Dividends per Share over the Next Five Years
($ Millions except Per-Share Figures)

	Year 1	Year 2	Year 3	Year 4	Year 5
Net earnings	$45.00	$25.00	$60.00	$75.00	$21.00
Investments	37.00	17.00	52.00	67.00	12.00
Equity required for investments[1]	22.20	10.20	31.20	40.20	7.20
Dividends[2]	22.80	14.80	28.80	34.80	13.80
Dividends per share[3]	1.824	1.184	2.304	2.784	1.104

———

[1] Equity required for investments = 60% of investments

[2] Dividends = net earnings − equity available for investments

[3] Dividends per share = dividends ÷ 12.5 million shares

Question 1: What is the expected value of dividends per share over the next five years?
The expected value of FST's dividends per share over the next five years is $1.84.

Question 2: What are the expected investments, expected dividends per share, standard deviation of investments, and standard deviation of dividends per share?

Expected investments = $37.00 million
Standard deviation of investments = $20.74 million
Standard deviation of dividends per share = $0.6448

Case Continued >

Question 3: Calculate the CV of FST's expected dividends per share and compare the results with those obtained in the previous minicase:

$$CV = \$0.6448 \div \$1.84 = 0.3504$$

The expected dividends per share increased while the standard deviation of dividends per share dropped. As a result, the coefficient of variation dropped from 0.4535 in Minicase 5-3 to 0.3504 in this minicase. The new pattern of investments makes the residual dividend policy preferable over the constant dividend payout ratio policy because it reduces the variations of the firm's expected dividends.

Constant Dollar Dividend Policy The **constant dollar dividend policy** is used by firms that wish to pay out a fixed-dollar amount on a regular and predictable basis. The policy acknowledges shareholders' desire for stability in dividend payments. Proponents of this strategy argue that it is optimal because it minimizes uncertainty about dividend payments. Reducing uncertainty increases the satisfaction of shareholders who desire current income and reduces the cost of equity financing.

A firm that follows a constant dollar dividend policy will change its dividend payout only after careful consideration to avoid the effects of signalling. An increase in dividends will be considered only when earnings have increased and seem stable enough to maintain the new dividend level. Similarly, dividend payments are rarely cut, even if earnings fall below the level that can support the dividends in any particular year. In this case, the firm will borrow or issue new equity to make the dividend payments. Generally, borrowing is preferable because it signifies a temporary shortage of cash rather than a permanent one. The firm permanently decreases dividends only when earnings are not likely to recover to their original level.

Setting the periodic dividend payment is most difficult when a firm follows the constant dollar dividend policy. The process starts by estimating over a predetermined planning horizon, usually five years, the residual funds after financing profitable projects. At a maximum, the firm will pay the cash flows that are not used internally for investment purposes. Of course, the actual need for funds will not be known with certainty until the projects are finished. General economic and industry conditions change from one period to the next, which significantly changes the cash needs of the firm. Nevertheless, the estimates provide a range of possible expenditures and a corresponding range of feasible dividend payout ratios. Once the ranges are established, the firm must decide on the target payout ratio. The decision depends on industry averages and practices and the mix of the firm's shareholders.

Given the target payout ratio and the projected earnings over the planning horizon, the firm should set its periodic dividend payment at a level that can be maintained over the entire planning horizon. The significance placed by the market on dividend changes makes it important to minimize decreases. The firm should set dividend payments below the expected sustainable level to compensate for the uncertainty of earnings forecasts.

Minicase 5-6 extends Minicase 5-3 once again to illustrate the constant dollar dividend policy.

MINICASE 5-6 CONSTANT DOLLAR DIVIDEND POLICY

Fast Shipping and Transportation prefers a constant dollar dividend policy. Management wishes to set the dividend payment so that it does not have to raise long-term funds to pay dividends or to finance profitable investment projects. The firm's capital structure includes 40% debt, and the firm would like to maintain this structure. The firm will spend respectively $35, $40, $40, $35, and $35 million on new investments over the next five years. The firm has 12.5 million shares outstanding.

Question 1: What is the maximum yearly dividend per share over the next five years?

Question 1 of Minicase 5-5 showed that the average value of dividends per share over the next five years is $1.84 per share. This is the maximum amount of dividends per share that can be paid per year over the next five years without forcing the firm to raise long-term funds to pay dividends or finance new investments. However, this dividend payment will require the firm to lend and borrow in the short-term market to smooth out the fluctuations.

Question 2: What is the annual distribution of earnings between dividends and retained earnings and what are the firm's annual borrowing or lending needs?

The firm has 12.5 million shares outstanding and the expected value of dividends per share is $1.84. Therefore, the firm will pay an average of $23 million (12.5 million × $1.84) in dividends annually. Exhibit 5-9 shows the distribution of earnings between

---

Exhibit 5-9
Distribution of Earnings between Dividends and Retained Earnings and the Firm's Annual Borrowing or Lending Needs ($ Millions)

	Year 1	Year 2	Year 3	Year 4	Year 5
Net earnings	$45.00	$25.00	$60.00	$75.00	$21.00
Investments	35.00	40.00	40.00	35.00	35.00
Equity required for investment[1]	21.00	24.00	24.00	21.00	21.00
Earnings available for dividends[2]	24.00	1.00	36.00	54.00	0.00
Dividends[3]	23.00	23.00	23.00	23.00	23.00
Cumulative surplus (deficit)[4]	1.00	(21.00)	(8.00)	23.00	0.00

[1] Equity required for investment = 60% of investments

[2] Earnings available for dividends = net earnings − equity required for investment

[3] Dividends = 12.5 million shares × expected dividend per share

[4] For simplicity, interest to be paid on the borrowed money is ignored.

Case Continued >

dividends and retained earnings and the firm's yearly borrowing or lending needs. The exhibit shows that the firm will have a cumulative surplus after the first year, but then a cumulative deficit until the fourth year. The firm uses its ability to borrow and lend in the financial markets to smooth the stream of dividend payments to shareholders.

5.3 PAYMENT PROCEDURES

Recall that unlike interest on debt, dividends on common shares are not contractual obligations. The board of directors decides whether to pay a dividend, the amount to be paid, and the payment date. Firms with established dividend records often pay dividends quarterly, semi-annually, or annually.

Important Dates

Five important dates relate to the payment of dividends:

- The **announcement date** is the date on which the amount of dividends per share, the record date, and the payment date are announced, after approval of a dividend by the company's board of directors.

- The **dividend-on date** is the last day that an investor can buy shares in time to be entitled to the dividend declared on those shares.

- The **ex-dividend date** is the day after the dividend-on date.

- The **record date** is the cut-off point that determines who is entitled to receive the declared dividend. All shareholders who are registered as owners of shares at the close of business on the record date are entitled to receive payment.

- The **payment date** is the date on which the dividend is paid to all shareholders who are entitled to receive the dividend.

These dates and their sequence are shown in Exhibit 5-10.

Exhibit 5-11 shows a sample dividend announcement from a Canadian corporation, demonstrating dividend payment procedures and the related dates.

Announcement Date Many publicly traded corporations announce their board of directors' decision to declare a dividend by posting a press release on their Web site and placing ads in financial newspapers. In our example, the date that Allbanc announces these dividends is August 2, 2007. Notice the press release announcement includes the type and class of shares affected and the amount of dividend per share, as well as timing information.

Payment Date Allbanc's payment date in this announcement is August 31, 2007.

Exhibit 5-10 Dates Related to the Process of Dividend Payments

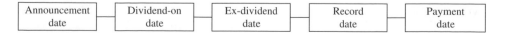

| Announcement date | Dividend-on date | Ex-dividend date | Record date | Payment date |

Exhibit 5-11
Press Release for a Dividend Payment

PRESS RELEASE

TORONTO, Aug. 2, 2007 /CNW/ —The Board of Directors of Allbanc Split Corp. II (the "Company") has declared today dividends of $0.26563 per Preferred Share and $0.07 per Capital Share, payable on August 31, 2007 to holders of record at the close of business on August 15, 2007.

Holders of Preferred Shares are entitled to receive quarterly fixed cumulative distributions equal to $0.26563 per Preferred Share. The Company's Capital Share distribution policy is to pay holders of Capital Shares quarterly distributions in an amount equal to the distributions received by the Company on the underlying portfolio shares in excess of the fixed Preferred Share distributions and forecasted administrative and operating expenses of the Company.

Allbanc Split Corp. II is a mutual fund corporation created to hold a portfolio of publicly listed common shares of selected Canadian chartered banks. Capital Shares and Preferred Shares of Allbanc Split Corp. II are listed for trading on The Toronto Stock Exchange under the symbols ALB and ALB.PR.A respectively.

Source: Reproduced with permission of Yahoo! Inc. ® 2007 by Yahoo! Inc. YAHOO! and the YAHOO! logo are trademarks of Yahoo! Inc.

Record Date The record date is important for shares that are actively traded because share ownership is continually changing. The record date is typically set two to four weeks in advance of the payment date to allow time for processing. Allbanc's record date for these dividends is August 15, 2007.

Dividend-On Date and Ex-Dividend Date The dividend-on date and ex-dividend date are important for investors who are buying or selling shares close to the record date, because they specify whether it is the buyer or the seller that is entitled to the dividend when it gets paid. In Canada and the U.S., share purchases settle three business days after a trade is executed (you may have heard this referred to as "T+3," which represents the trade date plus three days). Therefore, if an investor wants to receive the dividend, the investor has to buy the shares at least three days before the record date, and that way they will be the registered owner of the shares on the record date. The last day that an investor can buy shares in time to be entitled to the dividend declared on those shares is the dividend-on date. Because of the settlement rules, the dividend-on date is always three business days before the dividend record date. In our example, for an investor who wants to receive the dividend declared on Allbanc's shares, the dividend-on date is Friday, August 10, 2007. Any shares traded after the dividend-on date will not have settled by the record date. This means that on the record date, the seller would still be listed as the registered shareholder, and would therefore be the one entitled to the dividend, even though they had already sold the shares. Because of this, the business day after the dividend-on date is known as the ex-dividend date, and shares are said to be trading ex-dividend as of this date. For Allbanc, the ex-dividend date for this announcement is Monday, August 13, 2003.

Payment Processing

The paying firm will process the payments differently depending on the types of registration:

- *Direct registration:* Direct registration occurs when the shares are registered in the name of the actual owner. In this case, cheques in the amount of the dividend are mailed directly to the owner.

- *Registration in street names:* Street registration refers to arrangements by which a security firm holds shares in trust for the actual owners. The share certificates carry the name of the trustee. Thus, the issuing company's files indicate that the trustee owns the securities.

Dividend payments are made to the security firm whose name appears on the share certificate. However, the trustee keeps records of the actual owners and acts as a liaison between the issuer and the owners, crediting the dividends to the shareholders' accounts.

Valuation Issues

In theory, the opening price on the ex-dividend date should be less than the settlement price of the day prior (dividend-on date) by the exact amount of the dividend. The change in price should reflect the status of the share, which is no longer entitled to the dividend payment. However, the dynamic nature of share prices and the many factors that influence share price on a particular day make it impossible to observe this phenomenon in practice. For example, on a day of a rising stock market, the momentum may drive up the price of a share that just went ex-dividend.

Dividend Reinvestment Plans

Some major firms give their common shareholders the option of participating in an automatic **dividend reinvestment plan**, an arrangement whereby the firm directs dividends of participating shareholders to the purchase of additional shares. Only shareholders who agree to participate in the plan receive additional shares in place of cash dividends. For tax purposes, the shares received are treated as ordinary cash dividends, even though the dividends are not received as cash. Therefore, participating shareholders have to pay taxes on the reinvested dividends.

Share purchases in most dividend reinvestment plans are made in the open market under the direction of a trustee. Participating shareholders are periodically sent a statement showing the number of shares, including fractional shares in some cases, bought under the plan and at what price. Since under a reinvestment plan the firm uses authorized dividends to purchase additional shares in bulk, the investor saves commissions in the process. To buy the same number of shares, an individual investor would normally pay higher commissions, particularly if odd lots are involved. Generally, an **odd lot** is a stock transaction that is not an exact multiple of 100 shares. However, participants who eventually sell odd lots of shares from the reinvested dividends may face higher transaction costs. **Odd-lot order costs** are additional costs that may be incurred when selling securities in odd lots.

Another advantage of a dividend reinvestment plan is that it functions like an automatic savings plan that solves the problem of reinvesting small amounts of cash. Participating shareholders gradually increase their portion in the firm's ownership.

5.4 STOCK DIVIDENDS AND STOCK SPLITS

Stock Dividends

Stock dividends are additional shares distributed to existing shareholders. No cash is involved in the distribution. Instead, there is an accounting transfer from the retained earnings account to the common shares account. Normally, stock dividends increase the number of shares outstanding without increasing the total value to shareholders. The dividend is usually expressed as a percentage of the shares held by a shareholder. For instance, a shareholder with 100 shares would receive five shares as the result of a 5% stock dividend.

Stock dividends are often paid by a rapidly growing company that needs to retain a large amount of earnings to finance future growth. The stock dividend conserves the cash needed to operate the business.

Stock dividends are generally more expensive to administer than cash dividends. Moreover, when a firm replaces cash dividends with stock dividends because of financial difficulties, investors view this information as a negative signal.

Often, firms maintain the cash dividend per share following the issuance of a stock dividend. Such action causes an overall increase in the cash dividends. When stock dividends are accompanied by an increase in overall cash dividends, they are interpreted as a signal that management has raised its expectation of future earnings.

Stock Splits

A **stock split** is an action taken by a firm to increase the number of shares outstanding without issuing new shares and selling them in the market. In effect, the firm issues new shares and distributes them to current shareholders in proportion to their ownership in the original shares. The book value per share is also split to reflect the new number of shares. Total shareholder wealth and total firm value are the same as before the split.

For example, consider a firm with a current market value of $90 per share and a book value per share of $20. The company may wish to split the shares two for one. The resulting book value per share will be $10. Similarly, in principle, the market value per new share will be $45. The total number of shares has doubled while the total firm's value is unchanged. A shareholder who has 500 shares has a pre-split value of $45,000. After the split, the shareholder will have 1,000 shares, each worth $45, for a total wealth of $45,000.

Despite the seeming uselessness of this exercise, companies often split their shares. Practitioners argue that investors tend to purchase shares that are priced within the preferred range of $10 to $100. Thus, whenever a firm's share price reaches the high end of the range, management may execute a stock split to lower the price per share to a more desirable trading level. A split makes ownership more affordable to a broader base of investors. It increases marketability and facilitates equity financing if required in the future.

Often, stock splits are accompanied by an increase in total dividends. For example, the pre-split dividend of a stock may be $2.50 per share. After a two-for-one split, each stock will receive $1.25 in dividends unless overall dividends are increased. The dividend per share may be increased by paying $1.50 in dividends for the post-split shares, which is equal to a $3.00 dividend per share on a pre-split basis. Increasing dividends after splitting stocks is generally considered to be a sign of good financial health.

Reverse Stock Splits

Reverse stock splits are actions by a firm that decrease the number of shares outstanding. In effect, the firm replaces the old shares with a new issue distributed to current shareholders. The number of shares received by a shareholder will be proportionate to ownership in the original shares. Again, total firm value and individual shareholder wealth are unchanged.

For example, consider a firm with a current market value of $5 per share. The company may wish to reverse-split the share one-for-five. In principle, the resulting market value per new share will be $25, as the total number of shares decreases to one-fifth of the original number. However, the total firm value is unchanged. A shareholder who had 500 shares worth $2,500 before the reverse split will have 100 shares each worth $25, for a total wealth of $2,500 after the reverse split.

Companies reverse-split their shares when management feels that the share price is below the desirable trading level. Stock exchanges also typically have minimum share price requirements for listed companies. If a company's share price falls and remains below the minimum level for a period of time, the stock may be delisted from the exchange. This has serious implications for raising financing. Low-priced shares are perceived to be low performers. Thus, when a firm's share price falls below a desired level, management may execute a reverse stock split to return share price to a more desirable trading level. Investors generally interpret reverse stock splits as a sign of financial weakness.

Exhibit 5-12 depicts a press release announcing a reverse split stock for the Terra Nova Financial Group. The reverse split is 1-for-10 shares, effective to all holders of record June 14, 2007, whereby shareholders receive one share for each ten shares held.

Exhibit 5-12
Reverse Split Announcement

Press Release   **Source:** Terra Nova Financial Group, Inc.

Terra Nova Financial Group, Inc. Announces 1-for-10 Reverse Stock Split

Friday May 25, 10:26 am ET

CHICAGO, May 24 /PRNewswire-FirstCall/ —Terra Nova Financial Group, Inc. (OTC Bulletin Board: TNVF—News), a leading financial services company specializing in trading and brokerage services, announced that its Board of Directors unanimously approved yesterday a 1-for-10 reverse stock split of the company's outstanding common stock and an amendment to the Company's amended and restated articles of incorporation to reduce the number of authorized shares to 150 million, subject to obtaining shareholder approval. To become effective, the reverse stock split must be approved by at least two-thirds of the shares of common stock outstanding, which will be sought by means of a written consent from shareholders of record on June 15, 2007.

Continued >

"The Board approved the measure with the intent that it will encourage investor interest and improve the marketability of the Company's common stock to a broader range of investors," said Bernay Box, Chairman of the Board. The Company's common stock would continue to trade on the OTC Bulletin Board on a split-adjusted basis.

Under the terms of the reverse stock split, each 10 shares of issued and outstanding common stock will be combined into and become one share of common stock. No fractional shares will be issued. Subject to approval of the reverse stock split, the number of the company's authorized shares of common stock will also be reduced from 800 million to 150 million, without any change in the par value of $0.01 per share. The shares issuable to holders of any outstanding series of convertible preferred stock or convertible notes upon conversion, or to holders of outstanding options or warrants upon exercise, will be adjusted proportionately to reflect the reverse stock split. In addition, the number of shares authorized for issuance under the Company's equity compensation plans will be proportionately reduced if the reverse stock split is approved by shareholders.

If approved by shareholders, the reverse stock split and reduction to the number of authorized shares would become effective upon final approval by the Board of Directors and filing of an amendment to the Company's Amended and Restated Articles of Incorporation.

Instead, any fractional shares remaining as a result of the reverse stock split will be rounded upwards to the nearest whole share.

Source: Reproduced with permission of Yahoo! Inc. ® 2007 by Yahoo! Inc. YAHOO! and the YAHOO! logo are trademarks of Yahoo! Inc.

Differences between Stock Dividends and Stock Splits

The only difference between stock dividends and stock splits lies in their accounting treatment. A stock dividend requires an accounting entry transfer from the retained earnings account to the common shares account and an accompanying pro rata distribution of new shares to the existing shareholders. The dollar amount that must be transferred from the retained earnings account is equal to the number of shares outstanding times the percentage of the stock dividend times the market price of the share at the payment date.

In the case of a stock split, there is no change on the balance sheet. The number of outstanding shares increases, but the dollar amount of common shares remains unchanged. In both cases, however, total common shareholders' equity remains unchanged.

5.5 SHARE REPURCHASES AND THE DIVIDEND DECISION

A company may reacquire its shares by paying cash to shareholders in return for their share rights. Such **share repurchases** decrease the number of shares outstanding. The repurchased shares that are held in the company treasury as opposed to being immediately resold are called **treasury shares**. They are issued shares, but they are not counted as outstanding. In Canada, the practice is to retire treasury shares because companies registered under the *Canada Business Corporations Act* are discouraged from using treasury shares. Furthermore, treasury shares do not have voting privileges and they receive no dividends. They are not included in any of the ratios that measure values per common share, such as earnings per share.

Share Repurchases as Alternatives to Cash Dividends

When a firm has cash accumulated from earnings and it wishes to distribute the cash to shareholders, it can purchase its own shares in the open market instead of paying cash dividends. As the firm purchases shares, the number of outstanding shares decreases and the per-share value increases in book as well as market value. The following minicase proves this point.

In a perfect market, repurchasing shares is the ideal alternative to a cash dividend. As you learned in Section 5.1, in the absence of all taxes and transaction costs shareholder wealth is unaffected when a firm either makes a dividend payment and issues new shares to replace the cash or retains the cash for internal use. Similarly, when a firm wishes to distribute cash, shareholder wealth is not affected, whether the distribution is in direct cash dividends or in share repurchases. Shareholders benefit from share repurchases because the remaining shares appreciate in value by an amount equal to

MINICASE 5-7 SHARE REPURCHASE AND THE DIVIDEND DECISION

Precision Calculation Instruments (PCI) has expected annual earnings of $45 in perpetuity. It has 100 shares outstanding and no debt in its capital structure. The required return on equity is 10%.

Question 1: What is the market price per share of PCI?

The total value of the firm should be equal to the present value of the expected earnings capitalized at the 10% discount rate. Therefore, PCI's total value should be:

$$V = \$45 \div 0.10 = \$450$$

Given that the firm has 100 shares outstanding, the market price per share is $4.50.

Question 2: PCI announces that it is using $50 in cash to keep its transaction accounts with the banks above a critical level to avoid fees. However, after the introduction of a synchronized payment system that will become operational in one month's time, the $50 will no longer be needed. The new system will be cost-free to PCI. The firm is planning to keep the $50 surplus cash idle for emergency needs. What will the market price per share be after the announcement?

The announcement does not change the earnings forecast for PCI. The firm continues to earn $45. Assuming the discount rate does not change (although it might, as the

Case Continued >

existence of cash to satisfy emergency needs may lower risk), the earnings have a value of $450. Thus, the market price per share after the announcement continues to be $4.50.

Question 3: After careful analysis, PCI realizes that keeping the cash serves little purpose, as the firm has had only minor emergencies in the past. The firm announces plans to use the $50 surplus cash to pay dividends. What will the market price per share be after the announcement and prior to the payment of the dividend?

The announcement implies that the firm's earnings will not be affected. The firm continues to earn $45 despite the payment of $50 in dividends, as this cash will not be used in operations. Capitalizing the earnings at the 10% discount rate produces $450 ($45 ÷ 0.10).

The $450 is the present value of PCI's earnings. Because the number of outstanding shares remains 100, each share should have at least $4.50 of value because of its entitlement to earnings. In addition, PCI has $50 in cash that will soon be paid in dividends. Each share will receive $0.50. Therefore, after the announcement and prior to the payment of the dividend, the total market value per share will be $5.

Question 4: Instead of announcing the payment of cash dividends, the firm announces that it will use the $50 in surplus cash to repurchase shares. What will the market price per share be after the announcement?

The announcement implies that the firm's earnings will not be affected by the repurchase plan. The firm continues to earn $45 despite using $50 in cash to repurchase shares. Capitalizing the earnings at the 10% discount rate produces $450 ($45 ÷ 0.10).

The $450 is the present value of PCI's earnings. Following the announcement and prior to repurchasing any shares from the market, the number of outstanding shares remains 100. Thus, each share should have at least $4.50 of value because of its entitlement to earnings. In addition, PCI has $50 in cash that will be used to repurchase shares. The present value of this cash per share is $0.50. Therefore, after the announcement and prior to repurchasing shares from the market, the total market value per share will be $5.

Using the $50, PCI can purchase 10 shares. The firm will have 90 shares outstanding, and these shares will be entitled to $45 of earnings. Capitalizing these earnings at 10% yields $450 or $5 per share.

Question 5: PCI can invest the cash in Treasury bills to yield 6% interest. What is the firm's value in this case?

PCI's earnings increase because of this decision. The $50 produces:

$$\$50 \times 0.06 = \$3$$

Therefore, PCI's total earnings are $48 ($45 + $3), and the total value of PCI is:

$$\$48 \div 0.10 = \$480$$

The price per share will be:

$$\$480 \div 100 = \$4.80$$

Question 6: PCI can invest the cash in government bonds to yield 10% interest. What is the firm's value in this case?

PCI's earnings increase. The $50 produces:

$$\$50 \times 0.10 = \$5$$

Case Continued >

Therefore, PCI's total earnings are $50 ($45 + $5), and the firm's value is:

$$\$50 \div 0.10 = \$500$$

The price per share is:

$$\$500 \div 100 = \$5$$

Question 7: What advice would you offer PCI?

In the context of perfect capital markets, both methods of distribution have an identical effect on shareholder wealth. In the case in which taxes and transaction costs exist, PCI should distribute excess cash as a dividend. This option increases shareholder wealth because the firm cannot reinvest the cash to earn a return equal to or higher than the required rate of return on equity.

the cash used in the repurchase. Shareholders who wish to receive cash instead of higher value in their shareholdings can sell a portion of their holdings to substitute for the cash dividend.

In practice, however, markets are characterized by the existence of asymmetric taxes and transaction costs. In Canada, share repurchases made through open-market purchases cause shareholders to incur a capital gain. Consequently, shareholders lose the potentially more favourable tax treatment of dividends as compared to capital gains (depending on their tax bracket and the eligibility of dividends). However, share repurchases made by tender offer or negotiated purchases are deemed by the Canada Revenue Agency to be dividends and they benefit from the potentially more favourable tax treatment as compared to capital gains, again depending on the tax bracket of the shareholder and eligibility of the issuer. Thus, although the argument for the existence of asymmetric taxes is somewhat limited, the existence of transaction costs in the form of issuing cost remains significant.

Advantages and Disadvantages of Share Repurchases

There are at least three advantages to share repurchases as an alternative to cash dividends.

- Repurchase announcements are viewed as a strong management signal that the shares are undervalued. In a world where asymmetric information exists, repurchase announcements can lead to substantial appreciation in share price.

- Shareholders have a choice with share repurchases. They can tender the shares, receive the cash, and pay taxes on the dividend. Alternatively, they can refuse to tender. With a cash dividend, a shareholder has no choice other than to receive the payment and pay the taxes.

- If a firm distributes surplus cash in the form of dividends to shareholders, the market may view the payment as a signal that the firm is increasing dividends permanently. In this situation, the firm must maintain the new level of dividends or the market will penalize the firm by lowering share price. Therefore, when there is risk that a dividend payment may be perceived as permanent, it is better for the firm to repurchase shares with the surplus cash than to pay dividends. Share repurchases will not alter the market's expectations regarding dividends.

Similarly, there are disadvantages to share repurchases as alternatives to cash dividends.

- Share repurchases may give investors the impression that the firm has limited investment opportunities.
- The firm may bid up the share price, hence paying too much for the shares. In this situation, the selling shareholders would gain at the expense of the remaining shareholders.
- If the Canada Revenue Agency establishes that the repurchase was primarily to avoid taxes, penalties may be imposed on the firm.

Other Reasons Why Firms Repurchase Their Shares

Other than as an alternative to cash dividends, share repurchases have been triggered by many motives.

Shares Trading Below Intrinsic Value Management may consider that the company's share price is undervalued in the market. The share provides an attractive investment opportunity that can be exploited by the firm. This strategy is effective if management can identify when the share is undervalued. If management possesses information not available to the market, it is easy to identify such instances.

Success depends on the stock market's recognition that the share is indeed undervalued. In such a case, the announcement of a share repurchase program will lead market participants to bid the share price up until it reaches its true value. The repurchase plan will lead to profits for the remaining shareholders who do not sell their shares to the firm.

Altering the Existing Capital Structure Shares may be repurchased to alter the capital structure of a firm. For example, a firm may have had an optimal capital structure five years ago, but in the meantime, profits from operations have increased equity substantially. Thus, the firm may sell bonds to raise funds and repurchase shares. The result would be a decrease in the equity-to-total-asset ratio and financial leverage would be closer to its optimal level.

Eliminating Small Shareholdings A firm may want to eliminate small shareholdings. In such a repurchase plan, the firm will offer to buy the shares of existing shareholders at a premium. The benefit to the firm is in minimizing the costs of servicing shareholders. These costs include printing and mailing annual and quarterly reports, proxy materials, and dividend cheques. Most of these costs are fixed per shareholder, which means that servicing an account holding 100 shares or 1,000 shares is almost equal. Eliminating small shareholdings lowers overall servicing costs. Shareholders sell their shares to obtain the premium price and avoid the potentially higher commissions on odd-lot sales.

Consolidating Ownership Some firms repurchase shares to consolidate ownership in the hands of management or large blocks of shareholders. One way of consolidating ownership is to buy shares in large blocks directly from minority shareholders. The purchase price in this case is set at a substantial premium above the market price. Another way to consolidate ownership is to repurchase shares from investors who are not affiliated with the insider group. Finally, a majority shareholder or the firm's management may buy enough shares to give them the power to take the firm private. These motives, however, are not necessarily consistent with the maximization of shareholder wealth.

Protecting against Takeovers Shares may be repurchased as protection against takeovers. Companies frequently become targets for takeovers when they have large amounts of unused cash. A cash-rich firm will be targeted by a firm that is facing liquidity constraints at a time when it has many profitable projects that need to be financed. The acquirer will try to buy the target firm by offering its own shares in exchange for the shares of the target company. If successful, the acquirer will obtain the cash and invest it in the profitable investment projects. Share repurchases eliminate the surplus-cash incentive for potential bidders.

Given that the cash is surplus, it is likely to be invested in money market securities that normally pay lower yields than the required rate of return on equity. Therefore, using surplus cash to repurchase shares increases the price of the remaining shares and reduces the potential return to bidders.

Methods of Repurchase

There are several popular methods by which firms repurchase their shares. Each method is appropriate under certain circumstances and has advantages and disadvantages.

Open-Market Purchases In an **open-market purchase**, also known as a **normal-course issuer bid**, the firm acquires the shares from stockbrokers at the going market price. Such repurchase programs are convenient when the firm's motive is to buy shares to be used for employee benefit programs such as stock options or for the exercise of warrants and convertible securities.

Open-market purchases have several advantages:

- They are less expensive than other purchases because no premium is involved.
- They can be extended over a long period of time to ensure market support.
- They increase the liquidity of the share.
- They attract less attention than other methods and produce minimal impact on the market.

There are disadvantages to open-market share repurchases:

- If the shares are thinly traded and no blocks are traded during the purchase program, it may take a long time to purchase the target number of shares.
- The price may appreciate before purchases are concluded. The firm would then pay a premium for its purchases.

Exhibit 5-13 shows an announcement by Burger King Holdings Inc. for an open-market purchase, referred to as a normal-course issuer bid.

Tender Offers Firms call on shareholders to tender their shares within a particular time period in exchange for a specified price per share. An **offer to purchase** is a method of share repurchase whereby the firm states a price at which it will repurchase shares and offers that price to existing shareholders. On the other hand, a **Dutch auction tender offer** is a method of share repurchase whereby the firm specifies the maximum and minimum purchase prices it is willing to accept and the maximum and minimum number of shares that it is willing to buy. Interested shareholders then communicate to the firm the price at which they are willing to tender their shares.

The most important decision in a tender offer is determining the size of the premium. The premium must be large enough to attract enough shareholders to tender their shares. The premium varies depending on the structure of the shareholders. For example, if shareholders are institutional investors who have indicated willingness to tender, the premium can be as low as 5%. On the other hand, if shareholders are predominantly individual investors or the trading volume is very low, the premium should be set high enough to attract these shareholders. The premium can be as high as 25%.

Tender offers have several advantages:

- They are convenient when the firm wishes to purchase a large number of shares in a short period of time.

- They provide the opportunity for all shareholders to tender their shares. If the number of shares tendered is greater than the number that the firm wishes to purchase, purchases are made on a pro rata basis.

- They are generally considered by the market to convey a more positive signal than open-market purchases.

- They are more effective than open-market purchases in eliminating small share-holdings.

The disadvantages of tender offers are:

- They are more expensive to the firm than other repurchase methods, as the purchase premium is often high.

- Transaction costs are higher than with open-market purchases.

Negotiated Purchases A **negotiated purchase** is a share repurchase that takes the form of acquiring a large block of shares from one or more holders, negotiating the price in the process. Large block purchases are often made to complement open-market or tender-offer purchases. Sometimes the seller initiates them. In this case, the purchase price is at a discount from the market price rather than at a premium. In other cases, management may buy large blocks of shares from belligerent shareholders to eliminate their ability to challenge management. In this case, the purchase price will be at a substantial premium over the prevailing market price.

The main advantage of negotiated purchases is that they may be concluded at a lower cost than other purchases. This occurs because:

- Transaction costs may be lower due to the large volume per block.

- They may be negotiated at a discount from the market price rather than at a premium.

The disadvantages of negotiated purchases include:

- They are not reliable, as it can be difficult to locate block holders willing to sell their shares.

- They provide little support to the market over the long term.

CHAPTER SUMMARY

This chapter focuses on the basic theories of dividend policies. You learned the general features of these policies and how they are influenced by market imperfections such as transaction costs, taxes, and information asymmetries. This chapter considered the payment procedures for distributing cash dividends to shareholders, in addition to analyzing the characteristics of stock dividends and stock splits. It concluded by determining whether or not share repurchases are viable alternatives to distributions of cash dividends.

Key Terms

announcement date,   page 311

"bird-in-hand" view,   page 283

clientele effect,   page 298

constant dividend payout ratio policy,   page 304

constant dollar dividend policy,   page 309

dividend,   page 283

dividend policy,   page 283

dividend reinvestment plan,   page 313

dividend-on date,   page 311

Dutch auction tender offer,   page 322

ex-dividend date,   page 311

expectations view of dividend policy,   page 299

extra or special dividends,   page 302

homemade dividend,   page 284

negotiated purchase,   page 323

offer to purchase,   page 322

odd lot,   page 313

odd-lot order costs,   page 314

open-market purchase or normal-course issuer bid,   page 321

payment date,   page 311

payout ratios,   page 283

record date,   page 311

residual dividend policy,   page 306

reverse stock splits,   page 315

share repurchases,   page 317

signalling hypothesis,   page 296

solvency,   page 299

stock dividends,   page 314

stock split,   page 314

tax-differential view of dividend policy,   page 289

treasury shares,   page 317

Web Links

Dividend Calendar

■ http://www.sp500.us/ An online calendar that can be sorted by stock symbol, company name, market cap, yield, rate, dividend date, or payment date, allowing the user to see the latest date by which they must own the specific U.S. company's stock in order to collect a dividend.

Dividend Facts You May Not Know

■ http://www.investopedia.com/articles/stocks/07/dividend_implications.asp Although geared toward the casual investor, this February 2007 article by the staff of Investopedia.com provides an overview of some of the implications of paying dividends that may not be known to the average investor.

InvestorWords.com

■ http://www.investorwords.com/1509/dividends.html An online glossary of investment terms. The entry for "dividends" yields a definition of the term with hyperlinked terms, links to related terms, and a link to articles and other tools related to the term searched.

RefDesk

■ http://www.refdesk.com/index.html A one-stop reference desk for links to breaking news around the world, search engines, statistics, and online tools, including online calculators, calendars, dictionaries, and lists of links to authoritative Web sites on subjects ranging from Biographies to Zip Codes.

SEDAR

■ http://www.sedar.com/ The System for Electronic Document Analysis and Retrieval (SEDAR) is the Canadian Securities Administration's online filing system for Canadian company public documents.

Study Finance: Dividend Policy Self-Paced Overview

■ http://www.studyfinance.com/lessons/dividends/ Developed by a professor at the University of Arizona, this is a self-paced overview of dividend policy. Click on "Exit" in the upper right hand corner of the main page to access overviews of other finance topics such as the valuation of corporate securities and capital budgeting.

Unclaimed Dividends Search System

■ https://strategis.ic.gc.ca/sc_mrksv/bankruptcy/ud/engdoc/intro.html From the Office of the Superintendent of Bankruptcy Canada, this online searchable database allows creditors to easily search for unclaimed dividends. The most current statistics state that there are almost 60,000 records in the database with over $10 million in unclaimed dividends.

U.S. Securities and Exchange Commission

■ http://www.sec.gov/ The body that oversees the securities market and helps to protect investors. The SEC Web site contains a link to EDGAR filings as well as a tutorial on how to access the EDGAR database, the Electronic Data Gathering, Analysis, and Retrieval system which houses all the forms that companies are legally required to file with the SEC.

Self-Test Questions

Qualitative Questions

Answer each of the following questions in point form:

1. What is the traditional view regarding the relationship between dividend policy and firm value?

2. Why is dividend policy irrelevant under perfect market conditions?

3. What is the impact of transaction and flotation costs on dividend policy?

4. How do taxes affect dividend policy?

5. According to the signalling hypothesis, how do dividends relate to share value?

6. What are the clientele and expectation arguments of dividend policy?

7. What are some of the other factors that affect dividend policies?

8. What forms of dividends are distributed?

9. What characteristics are often observed in real-life dividend policies?

10. What are some key strategies to paying cash dividends?

11. What are the five important dates for the distribution of dividends?

12. What is the relationship between stock dividends, stock splits, and dividend policy?

13. How can share repurchases serve as substitutes for cash dividends?

14. What methods are used by firms to repurchase shares?

Qualitative Multiple Choice Questions

1. Which of the following dividend policies is likely to provide common shareholders with the *most* stable dividend income?
    i) Constant dividend payout ratio policy
   ii) Residual dividend policy
  iii) Constant dollar dividend policy
  iv) Constant dollar dividend policy plus extras

2. If a company engages in a share repurchase via a normal-course issuer bid, which of the following is true?
    i) The firm acquires the shares from stockbrokers at the going market price.
   ii) The firm calls upon shareholders to tender their shares within a particular time period in exchange for a specified price per share.
  iii) The firm acquires a large block of shares from one or more shareholders, negotiating the price in the process.
  iv) The firm states a maximum price it is willing to pay and offers that price directly to all of its shareholders at the firm's annual shareholders' meeting.

3. Which of the following statements *best* describes an advantage of share repurchases as an alternative to cash dividends?

 i) The firm may bid up the share price, paying too much for the shares to the selling shareholders.

 ii) Shareholders have a choice with a share repurchase—they can tender their shares or they can refuse to tender.

 iii) The firm can use a share repurchase program to signal to investors that shares are currently overvalued.

 iv) An unexpected share repurchase will alter the market's expectations regarding future dividends.

4. On January 5, 2003, ABC Corp. declared a quarterly dividend of $0.25 per share, payable on March 1, 2003 to shareholders of record on February 1, 2003. The ex-dividend date is January 30, 2003. In order to receive the dividend, an investor must buy the share on or before which of the following dates?

 i) January 29, 2003

 ii) January 30, 2003

 iii) January 31, 2003

 iv) February 1, 2003

5. Which of the following statements regarding the relevance of dividend policy to firm value is true in an imperfect world where there are taxes, transaction costs, and flotation costs?

 i) When the effective personal tax rate on capital gains is higher than the effective personal tax rate on dividends, shares with high dividends will sell at a discount compared to low-dividend shares.

 ii) Tax-exempt institutions are willing to pay a premium for shares that pay high dividends, but this will not affect share prices, as long as the existence of tax clienteles can be predicted and as long as there are enough investors in each tax situation.

 iii) If flotation costs for new securities are reduced, firms will be more reluctant to pay dividends.

 iv) If transaction costs to sell shares are increased, firms should be more reluctant to pay dividends.

6. When the rate of return that the firm can earn on reinvested earnings exceeds the rate of return that investors can obtain on their own, what is the optimal dividend policy according to the residual dividend policy approach?

 i) 100% earnings retention and zero dividends

 ii) 0% earnings retention and pay out all earnings as dividends

 iii) Pay out dividends as a constant percentage of earnings

 iv) Pay out dividends as a residual, after financing all positive NPV investment projects

7. Which of the following statements *best* describes the clientele effect explanation of dividend payout policies?

 i) Seniors who rely on their investments for spending and whose post retirement income is low may prefer low-dividend payouts.

 ii) The existence of tax clienteles implies that each firm will attract a specific group of investors, depending on their dividend policy.

iii) The clientele explanation of dividends provides a reason why firms may want to alter their established dividend policies in order to attract a different investor group.

iv) Investors are in different tax clienteles, depending on their income levels, with high-income individuals paying higher taxes on capital gains income, so that they prefer growth stocks with low-dividend payouts.

8. Which of the following *cannot* explain why cutting dividends often leads to a share price drop?
  i) Traditional "bird-in-hand" view
  ii) Perfect market view
  iii) Signalling hypothesis
  iv) Clientele effect

9. Which of the following statements is true about dividend reinvestment plans (DRIPs)?
  i) Shareholders don't pay taxes on the reinvested dividends.
  ii) DRIPs affect a company's balance sheet in the same way as stock dividends do.
  iii) Shareholders have no choice but to participate in DRIPs.
  iv) Shareholders solve the problem of reinvesting small amounts of cash.

10. Which of the following statements about a residual dividend policy is true?
  i) The dividend payout ratio is constant.
  ii) The dollar dividend payment grows at a constant rate.
  iii) Share dividends are paid regularly only if earnings are growing.
  iv) The dividend paid each period is a function of current earnings and current investment opportunities.

11. Which of the following will *not* be affected by a stock dividend?
  i) The common shares account
  ii) The retained earnings account
  iii) The number of shares outstanding
  iv) The cash account

12. Which of the following statements applies to a share repurchase?
  i) There is no cash-flows effect to the company.
  ii) Shareholders have a choice with share repurchases.
  iii) Shareholders' ownership in the company will decrease.
  iv) The number of shares outstanding remains unchanged.

Quantitative Multiple Choice Questions

1. A company has expected earnings of $4,250,000 and 350,000 outstanding common shares. It regularly pays out 35% of its earnings as dividends. An analyst has reviewed historical financial statements for the firm and determined that the standard deviation of the company's earnings per share is $5.60. What is the standard deviation of the firm's dividends per share?
  i) $1.68
  ii) $1.96
  iii) $2.76
  iv) $4.25

2. An investor has $250,000 to invest. He has a federal income tax rate of 29% and lives in Saskatchewan, where his provincial tax rate is 50% of the federal tax. Ignore surtaxes. He buys shares on January 1, 2007 at a share price of $25 each and these shares have an expected annual eligible dividend of $2.25 to be paid on December 31. What is the expected after-tax dividend income (to the nearest dollar) from his investment after 1 year?

  i) $15,975

  ii) $17,589

  iii) $19,226

  iv) $22,500

3. St. André Corp. has a target capital structure that consists of 40% debt and 60% equity. The company expects that its capital budget for the upcoming year will be $5 million. If St. André reports net income of $3.75 million and it follows a residual dividend policy, what will its dividend payout ratio be?

  i) 0%

  ii) 20%

  iii) 30%

  iv) 45%

4. Vicouver Corp. believes that its common shares are undervalued at a market price of $26.46 each. It plans to repurchase 5 million of its 50 million shares outstanding. The firm's managers expect that the share repurchase will have no effect on either net income or the company's price/earnings (P/E) ratio. The firm's net income is $126 million. What will the share price be following the share repurchase?

  i) $7.06

  ii) $26.46

  iii) $29.40

  iv) $32.45

Quantitative Problems

Problem 1

Calgina Company has a policy of maintaining a debt-to-equity ratio of 55%. Management has approved 4 new investment projects that will require a total investment outlay of $3,500,000. The firm's weighted average cost of capital is 12%, and it has net earnings of $2,500,000. Calgina follows a residual dividend policy. It is considering whether to maintain this policy, or to conserve cash and substitute a stock dividend or a stock split for the cash dividend this year.

Required

a) Under current Calgina Company policies, what amounts of debt and equity should be used to finance the 4 projects, and how are these amounts to be financed?

b) Calculate the firm's cash dividend payment for this year.

c) **i)** What is the most that Calgina can invest if it pays no cash dividend this year?

   ii) How much new debt must Calgina issue in order to maintain the 55% debt-to-equity ratio?

d) Explain what a stock dividend is and how it is recognized in the company's books.

e) Explain what a stock split is and how it is recognized in the company's books.

Problem 2

In 2007, WhiteHouse Corp. (WHC) paid dividends totalling $7.2 million on net income of $18 million. The year 2007 was a typical year, and for the past 5 years earnings have grown at a constant annual rate of 7%. However, in 2008, earnings are expected to increase to

$28.8 million because of an exceptionally profitable new product line being introduced, and the firm expects to have profitable investment opportunities of $16.8 million. After 2008, the company will likely return to its previous 7% growth rate. WHC's target capital structure is 30% debt and 70% equity.

Required

a) Calculate WHC's total dividends for 2008 if it follows each of the following policies:
- **i)** Its 2008 dividend payment is set to force dividends to grow at the long-run growth rate in earnings.
- **ii)** It continues the 2007 dividend payout ratio.
- **iii)** It uses a pure residual dividend policy (30% of the $16.8 million investment is financed with debt and 70% with common equity).
- **iv)** It employs a regular-dividend-plus-extra policy, with the regular dividend being based on the long-run growth rate and the extra dividend being set according to the residual policy. Also calculate the extra dividend for 2008.

b) Which of the preceding four policies would you recommend? Explain briefly.

c) Suppose that investors expect WHC to pay total dividends of $18 million in 2008 and to have the dividend grow at 7% after 2008. The share's total market value is $360 million. Calculate the firm's cost of equity.

d) In addition to cash dividends, identify other possible forms of shareholder remuneration that can be used.

Cases

Case 1: Antibury Inc.

Antibury Inc. (AI) had 1,500,000 outstanding common shares, and paid $1.45 per share in dividends last year. The current share price is $15. For the past 8 years, the company has maintained a policy of paying out 70% of earnings as cash dividends. Case Exhibit 5-1 contains the projected balance sheet for AI for the upcoming year end, assuming no dividends. Earnings after tax are projected at $3,257,143.

Case Exhibit 5-1
Projected Balance Sheet (Assuming No Dividends)
Antibury Inc. Projected Balance Sheet December 31, 200X

Assets
Current assets

Cash	$12,000,000
Accounts receivable	2,400,000
Inventories	3,500,000
	17,900,000
Equipment	5,140,000
Land	3,160,000
	$26,200,000

Continued >

Liabilities and shareholders' equity

Current liabilities

Accounts payable		$3,400,000
Notes payable		1,300,000
	CL	4,700,000
		~~4,700,000~~
Long-term debt	LTL	5,000,000
Common shares		1,500,000
Retained earnings		15,000,000
		$26,200,000

Required

a) If AI maintains its steady 70% cash dividend payout policy, what will be the total cash dividend payout and the total-debt-to-total-equity ratio following the payout? What dividend payment will a holder of 200 common shares receive? Show your calculations.

b) Suppose that AI retains all of its cash in order to finance a purchase of a large piece of real estate that will be used for future development of a new distribution centre. Instead of a cash dividend, a 30% stock dividend will be paid. Assess the impact of a stock dividend as follows:

  i) What will the holder of 200 common shares receive?

  ii) How will the balance sheet change, given the stock dividend, and what will the total-debt-to-total-equity ratio be if earnings are projected to be unchanged after the real estate purchase?

  iii) What can this same shareholder expect to receive in cash dividends next year if AI returns to its steady 70% cash dividend payout policy?

c) Suppose that AI has no investment plans and would like to pay out 70% of its earnings to shareholders in the form of a share repurchase this year, and then will return to its policy of paying cash dividends in future years. Earnings are projected to be unchanged. Assess the impact of a share repurchase as follows:

  i) Calculate the number of shares AI can repurchase if the share price remains at $15.

  ii) Calculate the number of shares that will remain outstanding.

  iii) In the next year, when cash dividends are resumed, calculate the per-share dividend and the amount of dividends to be received by the original or former holder of 200 shares.

d) Referring to your analysis in parts a) to c), briefly explain which of the three policies would be most attractive to shareholders.

Case 2: JoliBrand Corp.

JoliBrand Corp. (JBC) currently has the capital structure described in Case Exhibit 5-2. It has significantly less debt than others in the industry. The industry norm has a total debt to market value ratio of 60%.

JoliBrand Corp. can alter its capital structure by issuing debt at 10% yield to repurchase shares at the market price. The corporate tax rate is 34%.

Case Exhibit 5-2
JoliBrand Corp. Capital Structure

Market value of equity	$81,000,000
Number of outstanding shares	10,000,000
Market value of current liabilities	$22,000,000
Market value of debentures	$48,000,000

Required

a) Assuming a perfect Modigliani and Miller (M&M) world except for corporate taxes, explain how much additional debt JBC must issue to achieve a capital structure comparable to the industry norm.

b) Assuming that the additional debt to be issued is $18,000,000, how many shares must JBC repurchase when adopting its new capital structure? How many shares will remain outstanding and what will the value of each share be in view of the new structure?

c) JBC currently pays annual dividends of $2 per share. Assuming that the additional debt to be issued is $20,000,000 and it is used to repurchase the maximum number of shares (Hint: compute the new share price), describe the cash flow impact of the change in capital structure. That is, how much will interest costs rise and how much will dividend payments to common shareholders fall? What is the net effect?

d) Identify *two* alternative dividend payout policies, other than constant dollar dividend policy, that JBC could use for its common shares, and explain how they differ from the constant dollar dividend policy that was assumed in part c).

Chapter 6

Special Financing and Investment Decisions

CHAPTER OVERVIEW

Chapters 1, 2, and 4 suggested that under perfect market conditions, the value of a project is independent of its financing. As demonstrated in Chapter 4, the existence of transaction costs, flotation fees, bankruptcy costs, asymmetric taxes, and other market imperfections means that the financing and investment decisions for some projects cannot be separated. In this chapter, you learn how to incorporate the impact of financing decisions into the investment analysis of a project. The adjusted present value approach is introduced as a new way to account for the finance-related cash flows from a project, lease, or merger target.

Section 6.1 provides an introduction to project financing. You review the details and purposes of the various project financing arrangements that may be observed in practice. You also consider the advantages and disadvantages of these arrangements compared to direct financing.

Section 6.2 demonstrates how to incorporate the impact of financing decisions into investment analysis. The focus is on incorporating the impact of incremental bankruptcy costs and various types of government assistance such as subsidies and investment tax credits. This type of analysis requires that finance-related cash flows be identified and discounted at an appropriate level of risk. In Chapters 1 and 2, you discounted the firm's cash flows at the weighted average cost of capital. Cash flows for new projects are discounted at a rate that adjusts for project risk that is either higher or lower than the weighted average cost of capital. Finance-related cash flows are not any riskier than debt and are discounted at the after-tax cost of debt. The adjusted present value (APV) method and the equity residual method are two major ways that finance-related cash flows can be added to a project's net present value. Minicases are used to demonstrate the two methods.

Section 6.3 introduces leasing as an alternative to financing the purchase of an asset by borrowing. It begins by describing the different kinds of leases. You study the characteristics of lease contracts that make leasing similar to the purchase of an asset by borrowing. You then learn how the equivalent loan approach can be used to determine whether to lease or to buy with borrowing. The amount of the equivalent loan can then be used to calculate the net value to leasing (NVL). A computer illustration is used to demonstrate the equivalent loan approach so as to evaluate the decision to lease. Finally, you study the various advantages and disadvantages of leasing as a substitute to borrowing.

Section 6.4 reviews the types of mergers and the various motives for mergers. Operating and financial synergies, strategic considerations, market power, the desire to obtain management expertise, and tax considerations may be motives for mergers. In the section, you study the strategies of mergers and acquisitions. You also learn how to tailor the techniques of capital budgeting to the analysis of merger targets and to use data from previous merger cases to estimate an offer price for the shares of the target.

Section 6.5 considers the leveraged buyout (LBO) as a special way to acquire a target firm. The section covers the special circumstances under which a leveraged buyout is executed. It also describes the characteristics that make a company a good LBO target. The financing arrangements often associated with LBOs are also covered.

Learning Objectives

After completing this chapter, you will be able to:

- Identify and explain the various project financing arrangements.

- Calculate the adjusted present value of a project.

- Compare and contrast the adjusted present value, weighted-average cost of capital, and equity residual methods of incorporating finance-related effects into investment analysis.

- Explain the merits and limitations of leasing as an alternative to debt financing.

- Analyze decisions to lease assets using the equivalent loan approach.

- Identify and analyze the advantages and disadvantages of lease financing.

- Identify the motives for and explain the strategies of mergers and acquisitions.

- Calculate the value of a proposed merger or acquisition using the basic methods.

- Describe how acquisition occurs through leveraged buyouts and explain the financing arrangements associated with them.

This knowledge will provide you with the professional skills to:

- Identify and analyze risk factors with respect to special projects.

- Implement and advise on measures to mitigate risk around the special concerns of large projects.

- Evaluate and advise on capital investments, mergers and acquisitions, and the sale of a business.

- Analyze leases versus loans with respect to advising on financing to meet the organization's goals.

- Evaluate and advise on growth strategies of an organization.

- Analyze and advise on tax planning issues.

- Advise on business decisions in the context of the legal framework.

- Advise on issues of corporate governance.

- Assess the value of a business.

HOW THIS CHAPTER RELATES TO OTHER CHAPTERS IN THIS BOOK

This chapter is a natural extension of Chapters 1, 2, and 4. It shows that investment decisions always have side effects on financing and these consequences cannot be ignored in practice. Also, you will see that there is more than one way to take these consequences into account. You can either calculate NPV by discounting at an adjusted discount rate (usually the WACC), or you can discount at the opportunity cost of capital and then add or subtract the present value of financing side effects. The second method is called the adjusted present value or APV method.

Furthermore, in Chapter 2 we discussed the use of common stock and various types of debt. In this chapter, we examine some other types of long-term financing arrangements used by financial managers. In addition, this chapter provides a basic understanding of these alternative sources of financing and the variety of means by which a firm can raise funds.

6.1 INTRODUCTION TO PROJECT FINANCING

When a firm finances a large project on a stand-alone basis, the process is known as **project financing**. Generally, project financing is an alternative when a project is large and consists of assets that can be maintained as independent economic units. That is, the project is expected to generate reasonably steady cash flows from operations. These cash flows must service the debt used to finance the project and provide the required rate of return on the equity invested in the project. Often, a project will have one or more sponsors who provide the required equity capital for the project. Additional financing is obtained through lenders and lessors. Projects are usually operated as separate legal entities.

Project sponsors benefit from the profits of a project in proportion to their equity investment. Projects have their own debt obligations, which are separate from the debts of the sponsoring companies. Examples of projects that may be financed on a stand-alone basis include oil refineries, chemical plants, paper mills, pipelines, power-generating facilities, mines, dock facilities, and vacation resorts.

Project Financing Arrangements

Project financing may take place under several types of contractual arrangements depending on the particular circumstances and activities of a project. The terms are designed to spread the risk among the sponsors and minimize agency problems and costs such as monitoring. The reduction of a project's business risk decreases the variability of earnings and therefore reduces the cost of debt and the cost of capital.

Completion and Quality Assurance Arrangements Completion and quality assurance arrangements require the sponsor to guarantee that the project will be completed on time and will meet certain specifications or quality tests, such as satisfactory production for a specified period of time. Otherwise, the sponsor will have to repay the debt immediately and in full to creditors.

Completion and quality assurance arrangements are desirable when the sponsor provides technology and expertise to finalize the project. If the sponsor abandons the project before completion, it will be difficult and expensive to find a substitute. More importantly, such arrangements may require the sponsor to be responsible for the quality of the output long after completion. For example, a mining company that sponsors a project to open a new mine may be required to guarantee the successful development of the mine and the quality of the ore extracted.

Completion risk relates to the possibility of technical failure, cost overruns, or the inability to raise additional funds. Often, sponsors reduce completion risk by contracting with a construction company to deliver the project ready for operations. Creditors prefer having completion and quality assurance arrangements in place to guarantee that sponsors will not abandon a project before its completion.

Technological risk relates to the possibility that a project does not meet performance requirements because of technology type, scale, or premature obsolescence. The terms of a quality assurance arrangement may include a guarantee by the sponsor to the creditors against technological risk.

Raw Material Supply Arrangements

Raw material supply risk entails the risk that raw materials become depleted or unavailable during the life of a project and that other sources of raw materials are expensive. Raw material supply arrangements require one or more of the sponsors to guarantee the supply of raw materials to the project during or after completion. Such arrangements are desirable when one or more of the sponsors have control over the supply of raw materials. If the guarantor fails to ensure the supply as needed, it will be required to pay the debt and compensate other sponsors. For example, a uranium mining company that sponsors an electric power-generating project may guarantee the supply of uranium for the project.

Output or Service Purchase Arrangements

A **purchase arrangement** is a method of project financing by which one or more sponsors guarantee to purchase part or all of the output or services produced by a project. Failure to purchase as agreed obligates the guarantor to pay the debt and compensate other sponsors.

Output or service purchase arrangements are made when the sponsors are the primary customers of the project. They participate in the project to satisfy their needs for a product or a service or just a component for their final products. Examples of projects for which purchase arrangements are beneficial include pipeline projects, oil refining projects, and the building of general processing facilities. Failure on the part of the sponsor to purchase the production deprives the project of the cash flows needed to pay expenses and service debt.

Purchase arrangements are made as guarantees against the risks that a product or service may not be saleable in the future at a price that ensures demand. This scenario may occur if the price is affected by a rise in operating or raw materials costs. Also, the price of a product can rise above expected levels due to changes in tax laws, import or export duties, and other political risks. These factors are particularly important when the project is undertaken in a foreign jurisdiction. Alternatively, the demand for a product may be lower than expected because of substitute products in the market.

Completion, Quality Assurance, and Purchase Arrangements The terms of a pure purchase arrangement specify that the sponsors guarantee to purchase any output ready for delivery. However, some purchase arrangements require the sponsor to purchase whether the product is available for delivery or not. In this case, the sponsor guarantees the completion of the project on time, the efficiency of the operating procedures, the quality of the output, and the market for the product or service. Essentially, the sponsor is guaranteeing the entire project against default.

Completion, quality assurance, and purchase arrangements provide guarantees against all risks associated with a project and, in addition, may include terms covering types of risk beyond the control of the sponsors, such as the risk of flood, fire, storm, theft, and other factors that may interrupt operations.

Cash Flow Guarantee Arrangements Another type of arrangement in which the sponsors effectively guarantee a project against default is the **cash flow guarantee arrangement**. In this method of project financing, one or more of the sponsors are required to make up any deficiency in cash flows required to service the debt, thus reducing the risk of the project. Cash supplements may be provided in the form of equity contributions or repayment of cash dividends previously received. This type of arrangement covers all risks.

Advantages of Project Financing

Following are examples of how project financing provides sponsors with significant advantages compared to direct financing:

- Sponsors can *share the benefits* from the same project. For example, it may not be economically feasible or justifiable to build a facility for a product or service if only one end user is willing to commit to purchasing the product. A purchase agreement ensures that sponsors can pool their interests and share in the benefits of the project.

- Sponsors can *share the risks* of a new project. For example, the costs of a project may be too large for one sponsor and there may be high probability that the project will not be as successful as expected. Instead of bearing the entire risk of failure, a sponsor may secure participation and risk-sharing by other partners. Alternatively, the sponsor may be able to pass some of the risk on to suppliers, customers, and sometimes, creditors.

- Sponsors can *expand their debt capacity* beyond what might be possible with direct financing. For example, a firm's bond indenture may restrict its ability to issue new debt. Project arrangements can be structured so that the company's debt provisions will not affect any debt financing. Moreover, project arrangements can transfer operating risk to others, allowing the sponsor to finance the project.

- Sponsors can share the business and financial risk in some project financing arrangements to *reduce the risk caused by high or bad debt*. The result is a lower cost of debt and a lower cost of capital. The sponsor will realize a higher net present value for the project through a lower cost of financing. For example, output or service purchase arrangements guarantee the demand for the project's products. Consequently, the risk of bankruptcy is lower than for a similar firm that has no ready customers. Given the lower business risk, lenders should be willing to finance the project at a relatively low rate. It must be emphasized, however, that this advantage may not be obtained on all projects.

Disadvantages of Project Financing

The disadvantages of project financing are higher costs. For example:

- The arrangements are *often complex* and result in *substantial fees* to lawyers and investment bankers.

- Although some project financing arrangements lower risk and the cost of capital, other project financing arrangements *may require lenders to take more risk* than they normally do when lending directly to the sponsor. In these cases, they will demand a premium and the cost of financing the project will be higher.

  To illustrate, consider firm AAA, which has an excellent credit rating. A group of three potential customers, BB_1, BB_2, and BB_3, approach this firm to satisfy their demand for a product. These customers have marginal credit ratings because they face tough competition from foreign competitors. Firm AAA can meet this demand using one of the following alternatives:

  - AAA can build the plant and supply the three customers as long as they demand the product. The entire cost of the plant will constitute about 10% of AAA's assets.

  - BB_1, BB_2, and BB_3 can participate in an output purchase project financing arrangement in which they share equally in the risks and rewards of the project. The costs of the plant will be approximately 50% of the assets of each partner. AAA will guarantee to build the plant and ensure the quality of the product. The debt, however, will be guaranteed equally by all three partners.

  - One of the three firms, for example, BB_3, can seek financing and build the plant. This firm will agree to supply the other two companies. Again, AAA will guarantee to build the plant and ensure the quality of the product. The debt will be guaranteed by BB_3.

  The first alternative is preferable from a lender's point of view. AAA is of high credit quality and the planned plant is small compared to its total assets. The third alternative is the least desirable, as the risk of default is substantial.

  If, however, the first alternative is not available, the choice is between the second and third alternatives. Project financing will reduce the risk.

  In the second alternative, in which all three partners guarantee the debt equally, project financing decreases risk to the lender more than in the third alternative, where debt is guaranteed by one firm.

- Project financing sometimes *requires guarantees from a financial institution*. In this case, fees are paid to the institution.

6.2 INTERACTIONS OF INVESTMENT AND FINANCING DECISIONS

Setting the Stage

Before considering the interactions of investment and financing decisions, it is useful to review some important conclusions from previous chapters.

- Chapter 1 suggested that the value of a project is independent of its financing under perfect market conditions. For the purposes of financial decision making, investment and financing decisions can be separated. Therefore, a firm should not worry about how it finances a project before it determines whether it should accept or reject the project. This conclusion was important to your study of the pricing of real assets.

■ Chapter 2 considered the investment decision from an expected return-risk point of view. Because investment and financing decisions can be separated, risk can be incorporated into the pricing analysis of real assets.

■ Chapter 4 addressed capital structure issues, touching on the extent to which the choice of financing sources influences the value of the firm. Under assumptions of perfect markets, investment and financing decisions are indeed independent.

■ Chapter 4 also demonstrated that the existence of transaction and bankruptcy costs, flotation fees, taxes, and other market imperfections causes the firm's capital structure to change its value. If a firm is considered as a portfolio of projects, the capital structure decision also influences the value of any project that the firm undertakes. The financing and investment decisions cannot be separated for some projects when market imperfections exist.

In this section, you learn how to incorporate the impact of financing decisions into investment analysis. Essentially, you need a way to determine how a project's value is affected by the choice of financing. The value of any project depends on two main factors—the cash flows expected from the project and the discount rate that will be used to discount the cash flows. Therefore, it should not be surprising that the methods used will adjust the cash flows or the discount rate, or both, to account for financing effects.

Adjusted Present Value Method

The **adjusted present value (APV) method** separates the cash flows of a project into two sets. The first set contains the cash flows that will be obtained from the project, assuming it will be financed with all equity (unlevered). The second set contains the incremental cash flows that will be obtained if the firm uses a source other than equity to finance the project. The value of each cash flow is discounted at a rate that reflects its inherent risk. The value of the project is then:

$$\text{Value of project} = \text{NPV of unlevered project} + \text{NPV of cash flows associated with financing}$$

Essentially, the APV method adjusts the unlevered NPV to account for the effects of the financing decision. Formally, the APV method can be stated as:

$$\text{APV} = \text{base-case NPV} + \text{present value of the cash flows associated with project financing}$$

$$= \text{NPV}_B + \text{ITS} - \text{FCNS} + \text{TSFC} + \text{ITCS} - \text{IBC} + \text{OFRE}$$

(Equation 6-1)

where

$\quad$ APV $=$ adjusted present value

$\quad$ NPV$_B$ $=$ base-case NPV

$\quad$ ITS $=$ present value of interest tax shield

$\quad$ FCNS $=$ present value of flotation costs of new securities

TSFC = present value of tax shield on flotation cost amortization

ITCS = present value of financing-related investment tax credits and subsidies

IBC = present value of the incremental bankruptcy costs

OFRE = present value of other financing-related effects

The following notes highlight the calculation procedures.

Base-Case NPV To calculate the base-case NPV of a project, it is necessary to estimate both the cash flows expected from the project and the appropriate required rate of return to discount these cash flows. In Chapter 1, you learned how to identify and estimate the cash flows expected from a project. This knowledge can be applied to estimate the cash flows for calculating the base-case NPV. The required rate of return used to discount these cash flows should be the unlevered firm's discount rate. This required rate of return reflects the risk of a firm without any debt.

In Chapter 2, you learned how to estimate an appropriate risk-adjusted discount rate for a project. The capital asset pricing model (Equation 2-13, p. 107) specifies that the required return on a project should be equal to the risk-free rate plus a risk premium. The premium is determined as a multiple of the premium over the risk-free rate that the average investor expects from the market. The multiple is determined by the project's beta.

Chapter 2 emphasized that financial leverage increases a firm's beta. Equation 2-16 indicates that the levered firm's beta is higher than the unlevered firm's beta. In other words, if a firm has no leverage, its required rate of return on projects should be less than the rate required by a levered firm with similar business and operating risks.

Equations 2-15 and 2-16 (pp. 110, 116) estimate the required rate of return used to calculate the base-case NPV. In practice, the beta of a firm can be estimated by determining the equation of the characteristic line, as suggested in the You Apply It minicase on page 104. The data used in the calculations will likely be historical, reflecting the firm's situation during and immediately after the period over which the data is collected. If the firm was not levered during this period, the unlevered firm's beta is used in Equation 2-15 to estimate the unlevered firm's discount rate. This rate is used to calculate the base-case NPV.

For most corporations, however, the beta reflects the financial leverage during the period over which the data was collected. In this case, Equation 2-16 is used to calculate the unlevered beta, which is then used in Equation 2-15 to determine the unlevered firm's discount rate. The cash flows are then discounted by this rate to determine the base-case NPV.

Present Value of the Interest Tax Shield As explained in Chapters 3 and 4, the main advantage of using debt is that interest payments are deducted from income before calculating taxes. Dividends, however, are paid from after-tax income. Therefore, a firm with a positive tax rate T will find that its tax bill is reduced as more debt is used to replace equity in its capital structure. Interest payments shield the firm's income from taxes and tax savings increase cash flows. The present value of these incremental cash flows is added to the base-case NPV.

The interest tax shield is the product of the firm's tax rate and the interest payment. Each dollar of interest payments reduces before-tax income by one dollar and saves the firm tax dollars. The rate used to discount the cash flows from the interest tax shield should be equal to the after-tax cost of the firm's debt, because they have the same risk level.

Formally, the present value of the interest tax shield may be calculated as:

$$\text{ITS} = \frac{T \times \text{IP}_1}{1 + k_D} + \cdots + \frac{T \times \text{IP}_i}{(1 + k_D)^i} + \frac{T \times \text{IP}_{i+1}}{(1 + k_D)^{i+1}}$$

$$+ \cdots + \frac{T \times \text{IP}_n}{(1 + k_D)^n} \qquad \text{(Equation 6-2)}$$

where

ITS = present value of the interest tax shield

IP_i = interest payment in period i, where $i = 1, \ldots, n$

T = corporate tax rate

k_D = after-tax required rate of return on the firm's debt

n = number of periods over which the interest payments are made, which may be less than the useful life of the project

Flotation Costs of New Securities   Flotation costs are costs incurred by a firm when issuing new securities. These costs include lawyers' fees, underwriting and selling fees, offering memorandum printing expenses, and distribution costs. The present value of flotation costs is considered a cost of project financing.

It must be emphasized that incremental flotation cash flows need to be considered. In the base-case NPV calculation, the cost of equity includes the flotation costs of issuing equity. The assumption that the firm finances with debt instead of equity implies that equity flotation costs are replaced by debt flotation costs. Therefore, the financial manager needs to consider only the debt flotation costs incurred and the proportion of equity flotation costs that was not replaced by debt.

No flotation costs are incurred if a project is entirely financed by retained earnings. Consequently, the flotation costs of issuing debt are the only relevant flotation costs.

If a new share issue is used to finance a project entirely, the flotation costs of equity should be subtracted from the flotation costs of debt to obtain the incremental flotation costs related to financing. In this case, the incremental flotation costs may be negative, as issuing equity may be more expensive than issuing debt.

If the new equity is a combination of retained earnings and a new equity issue, only the costs of issuing the new equity will be subtracted from the flotation costs of the new debt.

Tax Shield on Flotation Cost Amortization   Under Canadian tax laws, flotation costs can be divided equally over the years to maturity of securities or over five years, whichever is less, and deducted from income as expenses. Thus, the after-tax flotation costs are equal to the cash flotation costs minus the present value of the tax shield resulting from the deduction of flotation costs as expenses over the allowable years.

Calculating the present value of the tax shield from deduction of flotation costs as expenses is similar to calculating the present value of the tax shield from interest payments. Each dollar of flotation costs will shield one dollar of income and save tax dollars. The tax savings are cash flows that will be realized over a maximum of five years. The present value of these cash flows can be obtained by discounting them at the firm's after-tax cost of debt. Formally, the present value of the tax shield on flotation costs may be calculated as:

$$\text{TSFC} = \frac{T \times \text{FCA}_1}{1 + k_D} + \cdots + \frac{T \times \text{FCA}_i}{(1 + k_D)^i} + \frac{T \times \text{FCA}_{i+1}}{(1 + k_D)^{i+1}}$$
$$+ \cdots + \frac{T \times \text{FCA}_n}{(1 + k_D)^n} \qquad \text{(Equation 6-3)}$$

where

TSFC = present value of the tax shield on flotation cost amortization
FCA_i = flotation cost amortization in period i, where $i = 1, \ldots, n$
T = corporate tax rate
k_D = after-tax required rate of return on the firm's debt
n = number of periods over which the flotation costs are amortized (five years or the maturity of the securities, whichever is less)

Financing-Related Investment Tax Credits and Subsidies If a firm receives investment tax credits or subsidies because it uses debt rather than equity, the cash flows obtained from these incentives must be included in the present value calculations. Accounting rules in Canada require that investment tax credits and subsidies provided by any level of government be accounted for using the income approach. This approach requires that government assistance received be credited to income either by an increase in revenues or a decrease in expenses during the period to which it relates. Government assistance that relates to current expenses, such as research and development, transportation, and interest expenses, would be included in the determination of net income for the period. When government assistance relates to expenses of future accounting periods, the appropriate amounts should be deferred and amortized to income as related expenses are incurred. These rules also apply to investment tax credits.

Therefore, if a firm receives assistance related to a specific asset, the initial cash flows required to purchase the asset must be reduced by the amount of the assistance. Such assistance affects the base-case NPV and should not be included as part of the present value of the financing-related investment tax credits and subsidies (ITCS). A subsidy is considered non-finance related if there is no stipulation in the agreement for the firm to use debt. In this case, the subsidy is discounted at the after-tax cost of debt.

Only subsidies, credits, and investment tax credits that relate to the mode of financing must be included in calculating ITCS. For example, lump sum amounts that are provided to assist in paying interest on a loan are cash flows related to financing and need to be considered in calculating ITCS.

Similarly, if a firm receives assistance related to operating costs, such as to lower fixed or variable costs or to increase revenues, the cash flows from this assistance are credited to income as appropriate. These cash flows affect the base-case NPV, but they are not related to financing. They should not be included as part of the present value of the financing-related investment tax credits and subsidies.

Again, investment tax credits and subsidies should be discounted at the after-tax cost of debt. This practice recognizes that these cash inflows are not riskier than debt. The firm will receive them as long as it remains viable.

Incremental Bankruptcy Costs The use of debt to finance a project may increase the possibility of bankruptcy and the costs associated with liquidation. Subtracting the present value of the after-tax bankruptcy-related costs from the base-case NPV would capture this effect.

$$PV(BC) = \text{probability of financial distress} \times (1 - T) \times BC \quad \textbf{(Equation 6-4)}$$

where
  BC = bankruptcy costs

The incremental present value of bankruptcy costs must be considered. This incremental present value may be calculated as:

$$IBC = PV(BC)_D - PV(BC)_E \qquad \textbf{(Equation 6-5)}$$

where

  IBC = incremental present value of bankruptcy
  $PV(BC)_D$ = present value of bankruptcy costs under debt financing
  $PV(BC)_E$ = present value of bankruptcy costs under equity financing
  $PV(BC)$ = probability of financial distress $\times (1 - T) \times$ bankruptcy costs

Applying the APV Method You have already used the APV method to calculate the value of a levered firm in the presence of corporate taxes. Equation 4-7 in Chapter 4 (reproduced here as Equation 6-6 for convenience) shows that the value of a levered firm is equal to the unlevered firm's value plus the value of the tax savings. Formally, this relationship is:

$$V_L = V_U + T_C D \qquad \textbf{(Equation 6-6)}$$

where

  V_L = levered firm's value
  V_U = unlevered firm's value
  T_C = corporate tax rate
  D = amount of debt

The unlevered firm's value is the base-case NPV. The term $T_C D$ is the present value of the interest tax shield. As explained in Chapter 4, the equation is derived by assuming the firm is operating in an environment of perfect and efficient markets. In this case, flotation costs, government assistance or subsidies, and bankruptcy costs do not exist.

Equation 6-6 assumes cash flows are constant and occur as an infinite series. Such a distribution of cash flows is known as a perpetuity. Both interest payments and tax breaks on these payments are considered perpetuities. Consequently, the calculation of the present value of the interest tax shield yields:

$$ITS = \frac{k_D \times D \times T_C}{k_D} = T_C \times D \qquad \textbf{(Equation 6-7)}$$

In practice, however, when a firm borrows money, the loan is tied up with an asset through a mortgage or lease. In the case of a mortgage, the payments, including principal and interest, are made over a period of time less than or equal to the useful life of the asset. Over the payment period, the value of the tax shield decreases as the interest payments on the outstanding debt balance decrease.

Minicase 6-1 demonstrates the APV method. Note that the information in this minicase is also the basis for Minicases 6-2 and 6-3.

MINICASE 6-1 ADJUSTED PRESENT VALUE (APV) METHOD

A newly formed company, Squeezed Fruit Juices (SFJ), is evaluating an investment in a new processing plant to produce a new product. Relevant financial data are as follows.

Initial investment	$20,000,000
Annual revenues from project	6,000,000
Annual variable costs if financed with retained earnings	2,350,000
Project financing:	
Common-share issue	6,000,000
New debt	14,000,000
Debt-to-asset ratio	70%
Debt repayment terms:	
Interest rate at end of every year	11%
Repayment of principal due at end of every year	$1,000,000
Flotation costs (new shares and new debt)	500,000
Investment tax credits and subsidies:	
Federal government investment tax credit	
(three annual instalments of $300,000)	900,000
Provincial government subsidy (of operating costs)	2,000/year
SFJ's tax rate	32%
Required return on equity to shareholders	14%
Useful life of plant	20 years
Salvage value	$2,000,000
CCA rate of plant and equipment	10%

The new debt is consistent with SFJ's optimal debt ratio of 70%. The East West Bank (EWB) has agreed to help the firm in issuing mortgage bonds with the plant as collateral. EWB insists that SFJ should pay back the principal in level payments of $1 million at the end of every year until the securities are all paid off. Also, interest on the outstanding balance is due at the end of every year.

If it makes the investment, the firm will receive $900,000 in investment tax credits from the federal government. They are intended to help SFJ establish itself in a market dominated by well-established competitors. Moreover, the provincial government has promised to subsidize the operating costs of the plant by $2,000 per year over the life of the project.

The CCA class will remain open after the 20-year period.

Question 1: What is the present value of the operating cash flows of the project if SFJ finances the project with equity?

Case Continued >

The cash flows for a year are:

$$
\begin{aligned}
\text{After-tax cash flows} &= (\text{revenues} - \text{variable costs}) - \text{taxes} \\
&= (\text{revenues} - \text{variable costs}) \times (1 - \text{tax rate}) \\
&= (6{,}000{,}000 - 2{,}350{,}000) \times (1 - 0.32) \\
&= \$2{,}482{,}000
\end{aligned}
$$

These cash flows should be discounted at the required return on equity in order to find the value of the unlevered project:

$$
\begin{aligned}
\text{Present value of operating cash flows} &= \$2{,}482{,}000 \times \text{PVIFA}_{(14\%,\ 20\ \text{years})} \\
&= \$16{,}438{,}610
\end{aligned}
$$

Question 2: Calculate the present value of the CCA tax shields over the 20-year period.

The present value of the perpetual CCA tax shields for the $20 million capital cost can be obtained from Equation 1-17 (p. 42) as follows:

$$
\begin{aligned}
\text{PVTS} &= \left[\frac{C \times d \times T}{2(d + k)}\right]\left[\frac{2 + k}{1 + k}\right] \\
&= \left[\frac{\$20{,}000{,}000 \times 0.10 \times 0.32}{2(0.10 + 0.14)}\right]\left[\frac{2 + 0.14}{1 + 0.14}\right] \\
&= \$2{,}502{,}924
\end{aligned}
$$

The present value of lost CCA tax shields due to the salvage of $2 million can be calculated using Equation 1-18 as follows:

$$
\begin{aligned}
\text{PVTSL}_n &= \left[\frac{S_n}{(1 + k)^n}\right]\left[\frac{d \times T}{d + k}\right] \\
&= \left[\frac{\$2{,}000{,}000}{(1 + 0.14)^{20}}\right]\left[\frac{(0.10 \times 0.32)}{(0.10 + 0.14)}\right] \\
&= \$19{,}403
\end{aligned}
$$

The present value of the CCA tax shields is:

Perpetual tax shield	$2,502,924
Less: Lost tax shield due to salvage	19,403
	$2,483,521

Question 3: The salvage price is expected to be $2 million, to be obtained after 20 years. What is the present value of the expected salvage price?

The present value of the expected salvage price discounted at 14% is $145,523.

Question 4: What is the present value of the investment tax credits provided by the federal government?

Government assistance in the form of investment tax credits has been provided in three annual instalments over the first three years of the project. Their present value can be calculated as an annuity at the after-tax cost of debt. The after-tax cost of debt is:

$$
11\% \times (1 - 0.32) = 7.48\%
$$

$$
\begin{aligned}
\text{Present value of investment tax credit} &= \$300{,}000 \times \text{PVIFA}_{(7.48\%,\ 3\ \text{years})} \\
&= \$780{,}441
\end{aligned}
$$

Case Continued >

Question 5: What is the present value of the operating cost subsidies?

The $2,000 of operating cost subsidies will reduce costs by $2,000 per year for the next 20 years. This means the after-tax income will increase by:

$$\$2,000 \times (1 - 0.32) = \$1,360 \text{ per year}$$

for the next 20 years. These cash flows should be discounted at the after-tax cost of debt, which is equal to 7.48%. Thus:

$$\text{Present value of the operating cost subsidy} = \$1,360 \times \text{PVIFA}_{(7.48\%, \ 20 \text{ years})}$$
$$= \$13,886$$

Question 6: Should the project be accepted if the firm finances with all equity?

The net present value of the project if it is financed with all equity is:

BASE CASE NPV

$$\$16,438,610 + \$2,483,521 + \$145,523$$
$$+ \ \$780,441 + \$13,886 - \$20,000,000$$
$$= -\$138,019$$

The project should *not* be accepted if the firm finances with all equity since its base-case net present value is negative.

Question 7: Prepare a schedule to show SFJ's annual interest payments until the entire debt is paid off.

The firm's beginning balance is $14 million, as the initial cost of the project is $20 million and the firm is using $6 million of its cash to finance the plant. As principal payments are $1 million per year, the loan will be paid back in 14 years. Exhibit 6-1 shows the annual interest payments over the 14-year period.

Exhibit 6-1
Schedule of Interest Payments for SFJ ($ Millions)

Year	Beginning balance	Interest	Principal payment	Remaining balance
1	$14.00	$1.54	$1.00	$13.00
2	13.00	1.43	1.00	12.00
3	12.00	1.32	1.00	11.00
4	11.00	1.21	1.00	10.00
5	10.00	1.10	1.00	9.00
6	9.00	0.99	1.00	8.00
7	8.00	0.88	1.00	7.00
8	7.00	0.77	1.00	6.00
9	6.00	0.66	1.00	5.00
10	5.00	0.55	1.00	4.00
11	4.00	0.44	1.00	3.00
12	3.00	0.33	1.00	2.00
13	2.00	0.22	1.00	1.00
14	1.00	0.11	1.00	0.00

Case Continued >

Question 8: Calculate the present value of the tax shields.

SFJ will receive an annual tax shield equal to the interest payment times the tax rate of 32%. These tax shields should be discounted back at the after-tax cost of debt (7.48%).

Exhibit 6-2 shows the calculations required to obtain the present value of the tax shields.

Exhibit 6-2
Present Value of Tax Shields on Interest Payments

Year	Interest	Tax shields	$PVIF_{7.48\%}$	PV of tax shields
1	$1,540,000	$492,800	0.9304	$458,501
2	1,430,000	457,600	0.8657	396,144
3	1,320,000	422,400	0.8054	340,201
4	1,210,000	387,200	0.7494	290,168
5	1,100,000	352,000	0.6972	245,414
6	990,000	316,800	0.6487	205,508
7	880,000	281,600	0.6035	169,946
8	770,000	246,400	0.5615	138,354
9	660,000	211,200	0.5225	110,352
10	550,000	176,000	0.4861	85,554
11	440,000	140,800	0.4523	63,684
12	330,000	105,600	0.4208	44,436
13	220,000	70,400	0.3915	27,562
14	110,000	35,200	0.3643	12,823
			PV of tax shields =	$2,588,647

Question 9: What is the after-tax present value of the flotation costs?

Flotation costs can be deducted from income as expenses over a five-year period. Thus, for five years, the firm can reduce taxable income per year by $100,000. The tax reduction from these deductions is $32,000 per year for five years. Thus, the present value of tax savings is discounted at the after-tax cost of debt as follows:

$$\text{Present value of tax shields} = \$32,000 \times \text{PVIFA}_{(7.48\%,\ 5\ \text{years})}$$
$$= \$129,537$$

The after-tax present value of the flotation costs is:

$$\$500,000 - \$129,537 = \$370,463$$

Question 10: After considering the financing effects, is the project acceptable for investment?

The adjusted present value of the project is:

$$\text{APV} = -\$138,019 + \$2,588,647 - \$370,463 = \$2,080,165$$

As the APV is positive, the project should be accepted.

The positive APV in Minicase 6-1 emphasizes that the financing-related benefits of a project must be considered to make the final decisions to accept or reject the project. According to the base-case net present value, the project should clearly be rejected. However, as all the financing-related benefits are added, the project becomes desirable with a positive adjusted present value.

Moreover, the result indicates that debt financing lowers the cost of capital and provides valuable tax savings. These benefits cannot be ignored in practice, as they increase the adjusted present value of the project and can make the difference between acceptance and rejection.

Weighted Average Cost of Capital Method

The traditional approach by which the finance-related effects can be incorporated into investment analysis, the **weighted average cost of capital (WACC) method** is to adjust the weighted average cost of capital, which is used to discount the cash flows. The process can be summarized in a few steps:

1. Calculate the cash flows from the project, assuming all equity financing.

2. Calculate the WACC for the firm.

3. Discount the cash flows at the WACC.

4. Estimate the cash flows that were not considered in the first step and discount them at the appropriate rate to derive their present values.

5. Add all the present values and subtract the initial outlays.

Formally, the net present value of a project may be calculated as:

NPV = present value of the after-tax cash flows from operations
+ present value of the salvage price
+ present value of the investment tax credits and subsidies
− present value of the after-tax flotation costs
− initial outlays   **(Equation 6-8)**

While the procedure seems simple, the following notes clarify several areas where difficulties are often encountered.

Cash Flows For the purposes of the WACC method, the after-tax cash flows are estimated as if the project is financed with all equity. The cash flows are the same as those calculated for the base-case NPV using the adjusted present value method.

Weighted Average Cost of Capital In Chapter 4, you used Equation 4-9 to calculate WACC. For convenience, that equation is reproduced here as Equation 6-9.

$$k_L = \left(\frac{D}{V}\right)k_B(1 - T_C) + \left(\frac{E}{V}\right)k_E \qquad \textbf{(Equation 6-9)}$$

where
k_L = weighted average cost of capital
E = market value of the firm's common equity
D = market value of the firm's debt
V = total market value of the firm, which equals debt plus equity

T_C = corporate tax rate

k_B = before-tax cost of debt

k_E = cost of common equity

Equation 6-9 calculates the proper rate to discount the cash flows from a project that has the same risk as the existing projects of the firm, meaning that the project's cash flows and the firm's existing cash flows have the same probabilities of occurrence. In addition, the use of the firm's weighted average cost of capital to calculate the NPV of a new project assumes that the new project has the same capital structure as that of the firm and that the capital structure of the project is the same over the project's useful life.

In practice, these assumptions do not necessarily hold. How can the WACC method be adjusted to overcome the limitations? There are several methods for making the adjustment. Each method estimates a beta for the project and uses this beta in the capital asset pricing model to estimate a cost of equity for the project. The estimated cost of equity is then used in Equation 6-9 to estimate the WACC for the project.

Analyzing Subjective Data The beta of a project can be estimated directly. The You Apply It minicase on page 111 of Chapter 2 demonstrated how to calculate beta by analyzing subjective data about a project's future cash flows. The section entitled "Practical Difficulties in Estimating Project Betas" on page 112 described the difficulties of this process. It explained that a project beta should be adjusted for the project's financial leverage.

Using the Betas of Similar Firms as Proxies to Project Betas A widely used method of estimating project betas is to use the beta of a competitor whose main business has risks similar to those of the new project. The financial manager should adjust the beta of the proxy firm to reflect the financial leverage of the new project.

Estimating Betas for Classes of Risky Projects Many firms estimate project betas by classifying projects according to risk classes. Projects that have the same risks as the firm's existing projects are classified as average-risk projects and are assigned the same beta as the company's shares. The cash flows of these projects are discounted by the firm's weighted average cost of capital to determine the project's NPV.

Other projects are classified in terms of their specific risk characteristics. If the degree of risk of a class is considered higher than average, the beta of this class will be higher than that of the firm's own shares. Thus, the rate used to discount the cash flows from projects in this class should be higher than the firm's WACC, which is charged to the average class. If the degree of risk of a class is less than that of the average group, the betas of the class will be lower and their discount rate should be lower as well.

Adjusting the Discount Rate for a Project's Financial Leverage Project betas must be adjusted for financial risk when the capital structure of a project differs from that of the firm. In Chapter 2, you used Equation 2-16 to determine the levered firm's beta. For convenience, that equation is reproduced here as Equation 6-10.

$$\beta_L = \beta_U + (1 - T)(D/E)\beta_U \qquad \textbf{(Equation 6-10)}$$

where

β_L = levered firm's beta

β_U = unlevered firm's beta

T = corporate tax rate

D = market value of the firm's debt

E = market value of the firm's equity

The debt-to-equity ratio (D/E) measures the firm's degree of financial leverage. Equation 6-10 indicates that the levered firm's beta is always higher than the unlevered firm's beta, and the higher the financial leverage, the higher the levered firm's beta will be.

The equation can be used to adjust project betas for financial leverage. There are three steps to this process:

1. Determine the beta of the firm (e.g., from the market using regression analysis, as in the You Apply It minicase on p. 116 of Chapter 2). This beta is known as the beta of the levered firm (β_L).

2. Use Equation 6-10 to calculate β_U using the firm's overall debt-to-equity ratio.

3   Apply Equation 6-10 again to calculate β_L of the project. β_U will be the beta obtained in Step 2, and D/E will be the debt to equity ratio of the project under consideration.

Equation 6-10 can be used whether you are calculating the project beta by analyzing subjective data, obtaining betas of proxy firms, or classifying the project in a particular risk class.

Other Cash Flows   It may be preferable to isolate some of the cash flows related to a project from the cash flows generated from operations. For example, you may not want to include a one-time cash flow expected in the second year of a project's life in a series of cash flows because it would prohibit using the annuity function as a financial calculation.

From a theoretical point of view, each cash flow can be discounted at a different rate. For example:

■   Salvage price discounted at the levered cost of equity

■   Tax shields on flotation costs discounted at after-tax cost of debt

■   After-tax investment tax credits discounted at after-tax cost of debt

■   After-tax subsidies discounted at after-tax cost of debt

Differences between the WACC and APV Methods

The differences between the WACC method and the APV method can be summarized as follows:

■   With the APV method, the cash flows are discounted at the unlevered firm's cost of equity. In contrast, with the WACC method, the same cash flows are discounted at the WACC.

■   With the APV method, the present value of the interest tax shield is added to the base-case NPV. This addition accounts for the deductibility of interest as an expense before calculating taxes. With the WACC method, this deductibility is accounted for by averaging the cost of equity and the after-tax cost of debt to obtain the WACC. This produces a WACC lower than the cost of equity. Because the cash flows from operations are discounted at a lower rate, the WACC produces a present value for these cash flows that is higher than the present value produced by the APV approach for the base-case.

Minicase 6-2 extends Minicase 6-1 to demonstrate the WACC method.

MINICASE 6-2 WEIGHTED AVERAGE COST OF CAPITAL (WACC) METHOD

Squeezed Fruit Juices' (SFJ) current debt-to-total-value ratio is consistent with borrowing $14 million and issuing $6 million in common shares for the project. (The debt-to-total-value ratio remains constant for the entire useful life of the project.) Currently, the risk-free rate is estimated at 7% and the expected rate of return on the market is 12%. The required rate of return on the unlevered firm's equity is 14%. The firm's tax rate is 32%.

Question 1: What is the weighted average cost of capital for SFJ if it decides to issue $14 million in debt at 11% and $6 million in common shares to finance the project?

The required rate of return on the levered firm's equity is calculated using Equation 6-10.

First, calculate the unlevered firm's beta using the capital asset pricing formula (Equation 2-13):

$$E(R_U) = R_f + [E(R_M) - R_f]\beta_U$$

This equation yields:

$$0.14 = 0.07 + \beta_U(0.12 - 0.07)$$

Solving for β_U yields $\beta_U = 1.4$.

Now use Equation 6-10 to calculate the beta for the levered firm:

$$\beta_L = \beta_U + (1 - T)(D/E)\beta_U$$
$$= 1.4 + (1 - 0.32)(14/6)(1.4) = 3.621$$

The required rate of return on the levered firm's equity should be:

$$E(R_L) = k_E = 0.07 + 3.621(0.12 - 0.07) = 25.11\%$$

$$k_L = \left(\frac{14}{20}\right) \times 0.11 \times 0.68 + \left(\frac{6}{20}\right) \times 0.2511 = 12.77\%$$

Question 2: Use the weighted average cost of capital to determine whether or not the firm should accept the project.

Additional information:

Initial investment	$20,000,000
Annual revenues from project	6,000,000
Annual variable costs	2,350,000
Useful life of plant	20 years
Salvage value	$2,000,000
CCA rate of plant and equipment	10%
PV (after-tax subsidies)	$13,886
PV (investment tax credits)	780,441
PV (after-tax flotation costs)	370,463

Case Continued >

The cash flows from operations were calculated earlier for the APV method. (Note that the CCA asset class remains open after the 20-year period.) Now calculate their present value by discounting them at the WACC rate.

The present value of the after-tax operating cash flows discounted at the WACC rate is:

$$PV(\text{operating cash flows}) = \$2,482,000 \times PVIFA_{(12.77\%, \, 20 \text{ years})}$$
$$= \$17,679,310$$

The CCA tax shields in perpetuity using the WACC rate are:

$$PVTS = \left[\frac{\$20,000,000 \times 0.10 \times 0.32}{2(0.10 + 0.1277)} \right]\left[\frac{2 + 0.1277}{1 + 0.1277} \right]$$

$$= \$2,651,574$$

The PV of the lost tax shields is also discounted at the WACC rate as follows:

$$PVTSL_n = \left[\frac{\$2,000,000}{(1 + 0.1277)^{20}} \right]\left[\frac{(0.10 \times 0.32)}{(0.10 + 0.1277)} \right]$$

$$= \$25,406$$

The present value of the CCA tax shields is:

Perpetual tax shields	$ 2,651,574
Less: Lost tax shields due to salvage	25,406
	$ 2,626,168

Theoretically, the WACC method indicates that the salvage price of $2 million should also be discounted at the WACC rate. The present value of the salvage value is:

$$PV(\text{salvage value}) = \left[\frac{\$2,000,000}{(1 + 0.1277)^{20}} \right] = \$180,783$$

Given the uncertainty of estimating this cash flow at the end of the 20-year life of the project, it may be more appropriate to discount at a higher rate to reflect a greater level of risk, such as the cost of equity. The present value of the salvage value discounted at the cost of equity (25.11%) is:

$$PV(\text{salvage value}) = \left[\frac{\$2,000,000}{(1 + 0.2511)^{20}} \right] = \$22,656$$

The present value of the after-tax subsidies ($13,886), investment tax credits ($780,441), and after-tax flotation costs ($370,463) are the same as calculated earlier for the APV approach. Using these values in Equation 6-7 yields:

$$NPV \text{ of project} = \$17,679,310 + \$2,626,168 + \$22,656 + \$13,886$$
$$+ \$780,441 - \$370,463 - \$20,000,000$$
$$= \$751,998$$

As the net present value is positive, SFJ should undertake the project. Notice that the NPV using the WACC is different from that calculated by the APV method (in the previous demonstration case). At the end of this section, you will learn the reason for this difference.

Equity Residual Method

The **equity residual method** is a valuation method that first determines the cash flows that can be distributed to shareholders after paying operating costs, financing costs, and debt repayments, and then calculates the present value of these cash flows. Formally, the NPV of a project is given by:

$$\text{NPV}_{\text{ER}} = \sum_{i=1}^{n} \frac{[(\text{RNV}_i - \text{CCA}_i - \text{IP}_i) \times (1 - T) + \text{CCA}_i] - \text{DP}_i}{(1 + k_E)^i} - C_0 + D$$

     + present value of the salvage price

     + present value of the investment tax credits and subsidies

     − present value of the flotation costs   **(Equation 6-11)**

where

    NPV_{ER} = net present value of the project (equity residual method)

     RNV_i = revenues minus variable costs during period i

     CCA_i = amount of capital cost allowance in period i

       IP_i = interest payment in period i

     DP_i = debt principal payments in period i

        D = initial proceeds from the debt issue

       C_0 = initial investment outlays

       k_E = cost of equity

The following notes clarify several areas where difficulties are often encountered.

Cash Flows   For the purposes of the equity residual method, the after-tax cash flows per year are estimated after deducting interest payments to debtholders. These cash flows are equal to earnings after interest and taxes plus the CCA. Then the principal payments on the debt are deducted. All other cash flows can be distributed to shareholders.

Cost of Equity Capital   Because the cash flows considered in this method can be distributed to shareholders, they must be discounted at the cost of equity capital. Sometimes it is appropriate to use the firm's overall cost of equity capital as the discount rate. This is appropriate when a project has the same risk as the firm's overall assets, the firm is expected to use debt for the project consistent with the firm's overall capital structure, and the capital structure is expected to stay stable throughout the project. When these assumptions do not hold, the cost of equity capital for the project must be adjusted to reflect the project's business risk and financial leverage. As suggested earlier for the WACC method, Equation 6-9 may be used to adjust the cost of equity capital for financial leverage.

An interesting question arises when the capital structure changes annually over the life of the project. For example, the Squeezed Fruit Juices project starts with high leverage, but the leverage gradually decreases as the firm pays back the debt. After year 14, the project is financed with all equity. Should Equation 6-9 be used to calculate the cost of equity capital for every year and a different discount rate used for each year? This practice may be desirable, but the rates obtained would likely be rough estimates.

Although it may be easy to estimate the debt-to-equity ratio, it is likely to be difficult to reasonably forecast the other parameters. For example, β_U may change over time. Also, the risk-free rate and the expected return on the market are likely to change from one period to the next. All these changes will make it difficult and impractical to adjust the discount rate on an annual basis.

Nevertheless, if a project's capital structure is expected to change considerably over time, it is appropriate to make some adjustment. For example, the cost of capital can be estimated when leverage is expected to be the highest and when leverage is expected to be the lowest. Then judgment can be used to choose a discount rate between the two extremes.

Equation 6-10 can be used any time a firm needs to adjust a project beta for financial leverage. Thus, it can be used whether you are calculating the project beta by analyzing subjective data, obtaining betas of proxy firms, or classifying the project in a particular risk class.

Other Cash Flows As with the WACC method, in the equity residual method it may be preferable to consider some project cash flows in isolation from the cash flows generated from operations. Again, it can be argued that the cost of equity capital should be used to discount all the cash flows from a project, regardless of their source. However, for the sake of consistency, this section takes the view that some cash flows may be discounted at different rates than the cost of equity capital. Cash flows such as the tax shields on flotation costs, investment tax credits, and subsidies are examples of cash flows that you would treat separately both for convenience and to apply a different discount rate than the equity cost of capital. The tax shields on flotation costs, investment tax credits and subsidies are discounted at the after-tax cost of debt. The salvage price should always be discounted at the cost of equity.

Minicase 6-3 demonstrates the equity residual method using the Squeezed Fruit Juices example once again.

MINICASE 6-3 EQUITY RESIDUAL METHOD

SFJ's management realizes that the firm's capital structure is expected to change considerably over time. At the start of the project, leverage will be highest, with the debt-to-equity ratio equal to 14/6. After year 14, the project will be financed entirely with equity. Thus, in the first year, the cost of equity capital for the firm is 25.11% (calculated in Minicase 6-2), while after year 14, it will be 14% (again, see Minicase 6-2). Consequently, SFJ's management estimates the cost of equity capital over the life of the project to be 19.25%. This rate is considered to be appropriate because it is less than the average of 25.11% and 14%. The first rate is the cost of capital assuming the leverage of the first year will be preserved throughout the life of the project. The 14% rate is the cost of capital assuming no leverage. As the debt will be completely paid off in year 14, the average cost of capital over the life of the project will be less than the average of 14% and 25.11%.

Question 1: Calculate the net present value of the cash flows from SFJ's project using the equity residual method and including the salvage value, but excluding investment tax credits, subsidies, and flotation costs. The following information is relevant to the calculation of cash flows.

Case Continued >

Initial investment	$ 20,000,000
Annual revenues from project	6,000,000
Annual variable costs	2,350,000
Project financing:	
Common share issue	6,000,000
New debt	14,000,000
SFJ's tax rate	32%
CCA rate of plant and equipment	10%

For the purposes of the equity residual method, the cash flows from operations are those that can be distributed to shareholders after paying interest, taxes, and principal payments on the debt. The operating incomes and the tax shields on CCA can both be treated in the same way as in the previous two methods.

$$\text{Present value operating cash flows} = \$2,482,000 \times \text{PVIFA}_{(19.25\%, \ 20 \ \text{years})}$$
$$= \$12,512,262$$

The PV of the CCA tax shields in perpetuity using the levered equity rate is:

$$\text{PVTS} = \left[\frac{\$20,000,000 \times 0.10 \times 0.32}{2(0.10 + 0.1925)}\right]\left[\frac{2 + 0.1925}{1 + 0.1925}\right]$$
$$= \$2,011,432$$

The lost CCA tax shield due to salvage is:

$$\text{PVTSL}_n = \left[\frac{\$2,000,000}{(1 + 0.1925)^{20}}\right]\left[\frac{(0.10 \times 0.32)}{(0.10 + 0.1925)}\right]$$
$$= \$6,470$$

The CCA tax shields are:

Perpetual tax shields	$2,011,432
Less: Lost tax shields due to salvage	6,470
	$2,004,962

The major difference with the equity residual method is the inclusion of both principal and interest payments on the loan as cash flows to be discounted. Exhibit 6-1 under the APV method has the details of the loan, and Exhibit 6-3 shows the applicable cash flows discounted at the levered equity rate of 19.25%.

The salvage value using the levered equity rate is calculated as before:

$$\text{PV(salvage value)} = \left[\frac{\$2,000,000}{(1 + 0.1925)^{20}}\right] = \$59,137$$

Therefore the net present value of the cash flows from the project (excluding the investment tax credits, subsidies, and flotation costs) is:

$$\text{NPV of project} = \$12,512,262 + \$2,004,962 - \$8,346,224 + \$59,137$$
$$- (\$20,000,000 - \$14,000,000) \qquad \text{NEXT PAGE}$$
$$= \$230,137$$

Case Continued >

Exhibit 6-3
Present Value Calculations for Loan Cash Flows Using the Equity Residual Method

Year (1)	Interest (2)	Tax (3)	Net interest (4) = (2) − (3)	Principal (5)	Cash flow (6) = (4) + (5)	PV factor (7)	PV cash flow (8)
1	$1,540,000	$492,800	$1,047,200	$1,000,000	$2,047,200	0.8386	$1,716,782
2	1,430,000	457,600	972,400	1,000,000	1,972,400	0.7032	1,386,992
3	1,320,000	422,400	897,600	1,000,000	1,897,600	0.5897	1,119,015
4	1,210,000	387,200	822,800	1,000,000	1,822,800	0.4945	901,375
5	1,100,000	352,000	748,000	1,000,000	1,748,000	0.4147	724,896
6	990,000	316,800	673,200	1,000,000	1,673,200	0.3477	581,772
7	880,000	281,600	598,400	1,000,000	1,598,400	0.2916	466,093
8	770,000	246,400	523,600	1,000,000	1,523,600	0.2445	372,520
9	660,000	211,200	448,800	1,000,000	1,448,800	0.2051	297,149
10	550,000	176,000	374,000	1,000,000	1,374,000	0.1720	236,328
11	440,000	140,800	299,200	1,000,000	1,299,200	0.1442	187,345
12	330,000	105,600	224,400	1,000,000	1,224,400	0.1209	148,030
13	220,000	70,400	149,600	1,000,000	1,149,600	0.1014	116,569
14	110,000	35,200	74,800	1,000,000	1,074,800	0.0850	91,358

PV of loan cash flows (payments and interest) $ 8,346,224

Question 2: What is the net present value of the project after considering all effects?

The present values of the after-tax subsidies ($13,886), investment tax credits ($780,441), and after-tax flotation costs ($370,463) are the same as calculated earlier for the APV approach. Therefore, the final NPV is:

$$NPV = \$230,137 + \$13,886 + \$780,441 - \$370,463$$
$$= \$654,001$$

Comparing the Three Methods

The adjusted present value method, weighted average cost of capital method, and equity residual method are comparable but do not produce the same results. Following are advantages and disadvantages of each method.

Adjusted Present Value (APV) Method

Advantages

■ The APV method adjusts for interest tax shields that are generated by debt securities for the financing of a project. This advantage is particularly desirable when the debt used to finance a project is significantly different from the firm's other debt-financing arrangements. The special nature of the debt may include provisions, such as a sinking fund, that need to be specifically considered in the analysis and that cannot be captured by the traditional WACC approach.

■ The APV method adjusts for the differences in capital structure between the various projects undertaken by the firm. In practice, some projects may be financed with a debt-to-equity ratio significantly different from the one the firm normally uses.

■ The APV method enables the evaluation of projects with capital structures that will change over time. In practice, this feature is important because firms are normally required to pay off the debt gradually over time and do not rebalance their capital structures. For example, in Minicase 6-1, the debt-to-equity ratio for the new plant project starts at 2.33 ($14 million ÷ $6 million) times and drops gradually to zero in year 15. Using the WACC method in this case would overestimate the value of the project.

Disadvantage The main disadvantage of the APV method is that it discounts the cash flows that will be used to pay debtholders at the rate required on the unlevered firm's equity. Keep in mind that these payments are considered in calculating the base-case NPV. Only the tax subsidy of debt is discounted at the after-tax cost of debt. Therefore, in comparison with the other two methods, the APV discounts the cash flows needed to repay debtholders at the high discount rate. On the other hand, the APV method enables the financial manager to discount the cash flows at the required rate of return for the unlevered firm's equity. The use of leverage in the firm's capital structure requires that cash flows be discounted at a higher rate. For example, the required rate of return on a levered firm's equity is 25.11% using the WACC method (see Minicase 6-2) compared with the required rate of return on an unlevered firm's equity of 14% using the APV method (see Minicase 6-1). Payments to debtholders should not be discounted at a higher rate than the cost of debt because this will underestimate the project's value. In contrast, cash flows to shareholders should not be discounted at a lower rate than the required rate of return on the firm's equity since this will overestimate the project's value. The overall result depends on the relative magnitude of the two. Therefore, the APV method may over- or underestimate the project's value.

Weighted Average Cost of Capital (WACC) Method

Advantage This method is the easiest to implement. It is particularly useful when project risk is equal to the firm's overall risk and the overall capital structure of the firm is applied uniformly for all projects of the firm.

Disadvantages

■ The WACC method is not effective in evaluating projects for which the capital structure is significantly different from the firm's overall structure. The WACC must be adjusted for the project's capital structure.

■ The method is not effective in evaluating projects with special financing arrangements, the features of which change the overall value of the project under consideration. It is easier to evaluate such projects using the APV approach.

■ The method assumes that the debt-to-equity ratio will be constant over time. In practice, this assumption may not hold, particularly when the firm is required to pay off the debt gradually over time and does not intend to rebalance the capital structure immediately, as for example in Minicase 6-1. Using the WACC method in this case would overestimate the value of the project.

Equity Residual Method

Advantages

- The equity residual method corrects for the changes in the required rate of return on equity over time. This is particularly useful when the discount rate is expected to change over time and when a project's life extends for longer than ten years.

- The method is useful when the debt ratio is expected to change over time.

- The method avoids the need to estimate WACC. It is necessary to estimate interest payments to debtholders and dividends to preferred shareholders to be deducted from the cash flows. Only the required rate of return on equity needs to be estimated for the period over which the project is considered.

- It is easier to use when cash flows are not even over time. On a period-by-period basis, it estimates the operating cash flows, deducts both the interest and principal payments from the cash flows, and discounts the result by the rate of return required on the unlevered firm's equity.

- When compared with the APV method, it is more accurate because it discounts at the high rate only those cash flows intended for distribution to shareholders.

Disadvantages

- The method is cumbersome because the cash flows of the project per period must be estimated.

- It assumes that the project stands alone, which may lead to the temptation of considering a separate rate of return on equity for each project. Although the method may be desirable for some projects, it may ignore the diversification effects that the firm enjoys when it operates a portfolio of several projects simultaneously.

It is clear from these advantages and disadvantages that no single method is superior to the other two under all circumstances. Consequently, financial managers need to be familiar with all three methods and decide which method to use to evaluate a given project, depending on the circumstances.

Summary

Exhibit 6-4 summarizes the important aspects of the three methods.

6.3 EVALUATING LEASE FINANCING

A **lease** is an arrangement in which the **lessor**, the entity or individual who owns the asset, makes the asset available to the **lessee**, the individual who will have the full use of the asset, in return for periodic lease payments. Leasing allows the lessee to obtain the right to use an asset without having to own it. It is an alternative to borrowing and owning an asset.

Types of Leases

Operating Lease An **operating lease** is a contract that entitles a lessee to the right to use an asset for a specified period in exchange for specified payments on a regular basis. The term of the agreement may be much shorter than the useful life of the asset. Also, the payments

---

Exhibit 6-4
Factors to Consider in Investment Analysis

APV method	WACC method	Equity residual method
• Debt used to finance project is significantly different from firm's other debt arrangements.	• Project risk = firm's risk.	• Debt used to finance project is significantly different from firm's other debt arrangements.
• Significant differences in capital structure of firm's projects.	• Financial structure of firm is applied to all projects.	• Significant differences in capital structure of firm's projects.
• Capital structure changes over time.	• Capital structure is not likely to change over time.	• Capital structure changes over time.
• Some cash flows are stable over time (considered constant). Makes calculations easier without compromising accuracy.	• Project is small compared to firm's assets.	• Required rate of return on equity is expected to change over time.
• Debt has special provisions that need to be considered in the analysis.		• Cash flows are not even and should be estimated on a period-by-period basis.
		• Discounts at the high rate only cash flows to shareholders.

---

received from one lessee are normally less than the cash flows needed to recover the full cost of the equipment. As a result, a lessor may lease the asset several times before recovering the full costs. Common examples of assets financed with operating leases are office copiers, computers, and vehicles.

Some operating leases require the lessor to handle all maintenance and servicing. This type of lease is called a **service lease**. Moreover, operating leases often require the lessor to pay any taxes due on the asset and to provide adequate insurance coverage. The costs are generally included in the rental rate or paid directly by the lessee.

Capital Lease A **capital lease** is a lease contract that generally encompasses the entire life of the asset. In this way, all of the risks and rewards of ownership in the leased asset are transferred from the lessor to the lessee for the term of the lease. In return, the lessee agrees to make periodic payments throughout the lease term. A capital lease is usually non-cancellable, except at a significant cost to the lessee.

The service provided by the lessor to the lessee is generally limited to financing the asset. All other responsibilities related to the possession of the asset, such as maintenance, are borne by the lessee. The lessee normally also pays insurance and taxes.

In contrast to operating leases, capital leases, also known as **financial leases**, are designed so that the cash that will be received from one lessee will cover the entire costs associated with purchasing, owning, and leasing the asset. Thus, from the lessor's point of view, the present value of the cash flows should be at least equal to the purchase price of the asset. For the lessee, financial leasing is essentially similar to borrowing from a financial institution and buying the asset. A loan requires periodic payments of interest and principal, while a financial lease requires periodic lease payments.

Sale and Leaseback Arrangement A **sale and leaseback arrangement** is a form of lease in which a company sells an asset that it owns to another party for cash and then contracts to lease the asset back for a specified term. Typically, the asset is sold for its market value and is leased using a capital lease. In essence, the lessee sells the asset to reacquire capital that is tied up in a long-term asset. The lessor in a sale and leaseback arrangement is often an insurance company, finance company, leasing company, limited partnership, or institutional investor.

Direct Lease A **direct lease** entails acquiring the right to use a new asset through a lease. In this case, the lessor may be the manufacturer of the asset or a financial institution. Direct leases are often capital leases in which the lessor provides 100% financing of the equipment.

The distinguishing feature of a direct lease as opposed to a regular capital lease is the role of the lessee. In a direct lease, the lessee decides on the type and options of the equipment to be leased. The lessee is responsible for finding the equipment from the manufacturer and negotiating the warranties, terms of delivery, installation, and maintenance agreements, as well as the price.

If the manufacturer is willing to finance the lease, the lessee also negotiates the terms of the lease, either separately or as part of the purchase deal. If a financial institution finances the purchase, the lessee negotiates the terms of the lease directly with the institution. After agreement, the financial institution buys the asset for cash and leases it to the lessee, who will start making the lease payments.

Leveraged Leasing A **leveraged lease** is a form of capital lease in which the lessor finances the cost of the asset with debt secured by the same asset. In a leveraged lease, the lessor's equity is combined with debt from third-party investors to acquire the property. Leveraged leases are designed to provide financing for expensive items involving $500,000 or more in capital outlays. Generally, the economic life of the asset exceeds five years.

There are three parties in a leveraged lease: the lessee, the lessor, and a lender. The lender normally provides up to 80% of the capital in debt. The loan is secured by the asset through a mortgage and the lease is assigned to the lender. As such, the lender has first claim on the lease payments and will be able to foreclose on the asset if the lessee defaults on the lease payments.

Leasing as a Substitute for Debt Financing

When a firm is deciding whether to lease an asset, it has already decided to make an investment in the asset. The decision to lease does not involve justifying the use of the asset, as the firm has already decided that the project that requires investing in the asset will contribute a positive net present value. Therefore, the decision is about financing: whether the firm should lease the asset or borrow in order to buy it.

Lease payments have similar characteristics to debt payments in that they are contractual obligations to the lessor. Both lease and debt payments are considered when estimating cash flows that can be used to service debt. Therefore, lease payments use up the firm's debt capacity in the same way as debt payments. Moreover, if lease payments are not made fully and on time, the lessor can demand the asset back and sue the lessee for the missed lease payments. The lessor becomes a general creditor and can force the firm into bankruptcy. Thus, the firm's default risk is the same whether its contractual payments are lease or debt service payments.

Lease payments have the same effect as debt payments on the variability of a firm's cash flows. They have to be made whether the cash flows from operations are above or below the expected level. Both lease and debt payments magnify the variability of the net cash flows to shareholders. Therefore, both types of payments are a source of financial risk.

Leasing and borrowing to buy also have similar patterns of cash flows. Both alternatives enable the firm to make use of the asset immediately. Leasing ensures that the lessee does not have to borrow the initial capital outlays that would be required to purchase. Also, with both alternatives, periodic cash outflows are required to service the debt or to make the lease payments.

There are differences between leasing and borrowing to buy. In the case of operating leases, the entire periodic lease payment can be claimed as a tax-deductible expense. (A notable exception is the monthly limit placed on the leasing expense of an automobile.) In contrast, only the interest part of debt service payments is tax-deductible. On the other hand, a lessee cannot claim any capital cost allowance when leasing equipment using an operating lease. Also, the lessee will not benefit from the asset's residual value at the end of an operating lease period.

Analysis of the Lease Financing Decision

It is assumed that the decision to invest in the particular asset has already been made based on a capital budgeting analysis as described in Chapter 1. What remains to be established is whether the lease is an attractive source of financing.

Proper Evaluation of the Lease-versus-Buy Decision

Relevant Cash Flows When a firm leases an asset rather than purchasing it, it avoids paying the purchase price up front. This is a benefit of leasing and can be treated as a cash inflow. However, if purchase of the asset would have entitled the firm to an investment tax credit from the federal or provincial government, this cash flow would be lost to the firm if it leased the asset instead.

Investment tax credits and subsidies are treated in one of two ways. If the credits or subsidies are related to capital expenditures, such as the purchase of a machine, their value should be deducted from the cost of the equipment. CCA calculations should be based on the capital costs of the equipment less the investment tax credit.

Normally, credits for the purpose of asset purchases are provided at the time of purchase and are subtracted from the capital cost of the asset. If payment of the investment tax credit is to be made in future years, the present value of the credit should be used to reduce the capital cost of the asset. The discount rate should be the after-tax cost of borrowing.

Alternatively, investment tax credits may be provided to decrease costs or to increase revenues. In this case, any immediate investment tax credits should reduce the initial costs or increase revenues by an equivalent amount. The investment tax credits received in the future will increase future cash inflows. They may be accounted for by adding them to future revenues or subtracting them from future costs. Alternatively, the after-tax present value of these credits can be added to the present value of the project.

As the tax credit provided by the provincial government is intended for the purchase of the asset, the credit should be deducted from the capital cost of the equipment. CCA calculations should be based on the capital costs of the equipment less the investment tax credit. The discount rate should be the after-tax cost of borrowing.

Hence, the initial investment outlay saved by leasing would be:

$$\text{Initial investment outlay} = \text{purchase price} - \text{investment tax credit}$$

The cash flows to be considered when evaluating whether to lease are the firm's after-tax lease payments, the CCA tax shields, and the salvage value of the purchased asset when it is eventually sold. The firm must also consider the incremental difference in after-tax operating costs or other expenses that result from borrowing and leasing. Operating costs (including costs associated with servicing and maintaining the equipment, property taxes, and insurance) would be saved under the lease option. However, the firm would lose any investment tax credits from the federal or provincial government on the purchase of the asset.

In summary, the cash flows associated with the leasing decision are the initial investment outlay, the after-tax leasing payments, the incremental difference in after-tax operating costs between borrowing and leasing, the CCA tax shields, the salvage value, and the investment tax credits.

Equivalent Loan For all practical purposes, lease financing may be viewed as a substitute for debt financing. When a firm leases an asset through a capital lease, the fixed payments that it is obliged to make increase and its debt ratio also increases, which means that it uses up some of its ability to use debt financing. The proper analysis of the leasing decision is, therefore, a comparison of leasing and borrowing to purchase. If the firm leases, it saves having to make the initial cash outlay, but it commits to cash outflows. To compare leasing with borrowing to purchase, you will need to identify an **equivalent loan** that would commit the firm to exactly the same cash outflows as the lease. If the amount that could be borrowed under the equivalent loan is more than the initial investment outlay saved under the lease, then borrowing to purchase is preferable. If the amount that could be borrowed is less than the initial investment outlay saved under the lease, then leasing is preferable. If the amount that could be borrowed is equal to the initial investment outlay saved under the lease, then the firm will be indifferent in its choice to lease or borrow to purchase.

If you borrow $50,000 at a before-tax interest rate of 10% and promise to pay off the loan with equal annual payments over five years, the annual payment can be determined by equating the amount of the loan to the present value of the annual payments (calculated by discounting the annual payments at the before-tax interest rate). Thus, the amount of the loan would equal the present value of the annual payments on a before-tax basis using the before-tax interest rate as the discount rate. Similarly, the amount of the loan also equals the present value of the after-tax cash flows associated with the loan, discounted using the after-tax interest rate, which is the before-tax interest rate × (1 − corporate tax rate).

The amount of the equivalent loan, which requires the same cash outflows as under the lease, can be determined by finding the present value of the after-tax cash outflows under the lease by using the after-tax interest rate on debt for the firm.

Therefore, the equivalent loan would be given by

Equivalent loan $=$ PV(after-tax lease payments)
$-$ PV(incremental difference in after-tax operating costs or other costs between the borrowing and leasing alternatives)
$+$ PV(CCA tax shields)
$+$ PV(salvage value)
$+$ PV(investment tax credits under purchase option)   **(Equation 6-12)**

where, in general, all the present values would be calculated by discounting the relevant after-tax cash flows at the firm's after-tax cost of borrowing.

The salvage value of the asset is deemed to be riskier than the other cash flows, and it should be discounted at a higher discount rate to reflect its greater level of risk. Because of the uncertainty associated with estimating the salvage value at the end of the project's life, this cash flow may be discounted at the project's weighted average cost of capital to reflect its greater level of risk.

Recall from Chapter 1 that the present value of the CCA tax shields from the purchase of an asset is the present value of the CCA tax shields assuming that the asset will be kept forever, less the present value of the CCA tax shields lost assuming that the asset is sold for its salvage value at year n. Equation 6-13 shows the present value of the CCA tax shields.

$$
\text{PV(CCA tax shields)} = \left[\frac{CdT}{2(d + r)} \right]\left[\frac{2 + r}{1 + r} \right]
$$
$$
- \left[\frac{S_n}{(1 + k_L)^n} \right]\left[\frac{dT}{(d + r)} \right] \quad \text{(Equation 6-13)}
$$

where
C = initial undepreciated capital cost of the asset
d = CCA rate of the class to which the asset belongs
T = corporate tax rate
S_n = salvage value of the asset at the end of year n
r = after-tax interest rate on debt
k_L = weighted average cost of capital

Since the salvage value is deemed to be risky, the present value of the CCA tax shields lost is discounted back to the present at the weighted average cost of capital k_L. As a result, the third term on the right-hand side of Equation 6-13 is determined by discounting the salvage value by the weighted average cost of capital k_L.

Net Value to Leasing The **net value to leasing (NVL)** is the difference between the initial investment outlay saved under the lease and the value of the equivalent loan. Thus, the NVL is:

NVL $=$ initial investment outlay $-$ equivalent loan   **(Equation 6-14)**

The NVL measures the cost savings realized by the firm if it leases rather than borrows to buy. The decision criterion for the **net value to leasing** or **NVL method** is simple. If the NVL is positive, the firm has positive cost savings and leasing is preferable over borrowing to buy. If the NVL is negative and the firm leases, it incurs costs greater than the amount required for borrowing to buy.

The application of the NVL method is well suited to a case in which the firm, as a lessee, must make a decision on whether to finance by leasing or to purchase by borrowing. In such a case, the lessee benefits from the cost savings incurred because of lease payments.

The following You Apply It minicase demonstrates the lease-versus-buy analysis for Royal Builders Corp. (RBC).

YOU APPLY IT LEASE-VERSUS-BUY ANALYSIS FOR ROYAL BUILDERS CORP.

Royal Builders Corp. (RBC) has decided that a cement mixer, which has a purchase price of $50,000, is worth acquiring. RBC is considering two choices: purchase of the cement mixer or lease of the cement mixer.

Purchase Option

If RBC purchases the mixer, it will be entitled to an investment tax credit from the federal government of 10% of the purchase price. RBC will be able to deduct CCA at the rate of 30%. It can fund the purchase with a bank term loan of $50,000 with an interest rate of 9% over a period of five years. The cement mixer can be sold at the end of five years for $6,000. RBC will incur pre-tax costs associated with maintenance of the equipment, property taxes, and insurance of $2,000 per year. These operating costs are incurred at the end of the year. The provincial government will provide an investment tax credit of $1,000 per year. (Note: The provincial government tax credit is a before tax benefit.)

Lease Option

The lease will require payments of $12,855 per year for five years, to be paid at the beginning of each year, while operating cash flows and the tax shield due to the lease payment will occur at the end of each year.

RBC has a corporate tax rate of 40%. The weighted average cost of capital for the asset purchase is 15%. Should RBC lease the cement mixer?

Answers

Part 1: Calculate the initial investment outlay of the equipment.

$$\text{Initial investment outlay} = \text{purchase price} - \text{investment tax credit}$$
$$= \$50,000 - (0.10 \times \$50,000) = \$45,000$$

Part 2: Calculate the leasing costs.

If RBC purchased the cement mixer through a bank loan, the interest rate would be 9%. Therefore, the after-tax cost of debt is:

$$9\% \times (1 - 0.40) = 5.40\%$$

You Apply It Continued >

Because the series of lease payments occur at the beginning of the year, the present value of the annuity due is calculated as follows:

$$\$12,855 \times \text{PVIFA}_{(5.4\%, \ 5 \ \text{years})} \times (1 + r) = \$58,017.82$$

The lease payments are deductible for tax purposes. The tax shield due to the lease payment each year is:

$$\$12,855 \times 0.40 = \$5,142$$

Because the tax shield is received at the end of each year, the present value of the tax shield due to lease payments at the after-tax cost of debt is:

$$\$5,142 \times \text{PVIFA}_{(5.4\%, \ 5 \ \text{years})} = \$22,018.15$$

The present value of the lease payments on an after-tax basis is:

$$\$58,017.82 - \$22,018.15 = \$35,999.67$$

It is now necessary to calculate the present value of the incremental difference of the after-tax operating costs between the borrowing and leasing alternatives. In this case, there are no operating costs associated with leasing, and only the after-tax operating costs incurred under the borrowing alternative are considered. As a result, after-tax operating costs for the borrowing alternative would be:

$$\$2,000 \times (1 - 0.4) \times \text{PVIFA}_{(5.4\%, \ 5 \ \text{years})} = \$5,138.42$$

The present value of the CCA tax shield lost by leasing rather than buying can be calculated by using Equation 6-13. The capital cost of the asset is $45,000, the CCA rate is 30%, the after-tax interest rate is 5.40%, the weighted average cost of capital is 15%, the tax rate is 40%, and the salvage value of the cement mixer at the end of five years is $6,000.

The first term in Equation 6-13 represents the CCA tax shield available on purchase of the asset, if the asset were held indefinitely. This value is:

$$\left[\frac{\$45,000 \times 0.30 \times 0.40}{2(0.30 + 0.054)} \right] \left[\frac{2 + 0.054}{1 + 0.054} \right] = \$14,863.47$$

The second term in Equation 6-13 represents the CCA tax shield lost to the purchaser of the asset due to sale of the asset for its salvage value. This is:

$$\left[\frac{\$6,000}{(1 + 0.15)^5} \right] \left[\frac{0.30 \times 0.40}{(0.30 + 0.054)} \right] = \$1,011.21$$

Notice that the salvage value of this part of the equation is discounted at the weighted cost of capital to reflect the uncertainty associated with estimating this cash flow at the end of the project's life.

The present value of the CCA tax shields lost by RBC if it leases the asset is:

$$\$14,863.47 - \$1,011.21 = \$13,852.26$$

The present value of the salvage value lost by leasing would be:

$$\$6,000 \div (1 + 0.15)^5 = \$2,983.06$$

The present value of the investment tax credits lost under the lease option is:

$$\$1,000 \times (1 - 0.4) \times \text{PVIFA}_{(5.4\%, \ 5 \ \text{years})} = \$2,569.21$$

You Apply It Continued >

Part 3: Calculate the equivalent loan.

   Using Equation 6-12, the equivalent loan is:

$$\$35,999.67 - \$5,138.42 + \$13,852.26 + \$2,983.06 + \$2,569.21$$
$$= \$50,265.78$$

Because the amount that could be borrowed under the equivalent loan ($50,265.78) is more than the initial investment outlay ($45,000) saved under the lease, borrowing to purchase is preferable to leasing. The equivalent-loan approach has the added advantage of indicating the amount of conventional debt that lease financing can displace. In this case, leasing displaces $50,265.78 in conventional debt.

Part 4: Calculate the net value to leasing.

   The net value to leasing using Equation 6-13 would be:

$$\$45,000 - \$50,265.78 = -\$5,265.78$$

Since the net value to leasing is negative, RBC should not lease the asset.

A more complicated scenario of the leasing decision is now demonstrated using a spreadsheet analysis.

Computer Activity: Equivalent-Loan Approach to Leasing

This computer illustration analyzes the decision on whether to lease or to purchase by borrowing. Specifically, the illustration demonstrates the equivalent-loan approach to leasing and calculates the NVL. This approach identifies an equivalent loan that commits the firm to the same cash flows as the lease would. The analysis assumes that the equipment is a worthwhile investment.

LEARNING OBJECTIVE

■ Design and use a worksheet to calculate the amount of the equivalent loan and the NVL.

Description

Cold Cutts Incorporated (CCI) has decided to acquire refrigeration equipment for its new store in downtown Calgary. An NPV analysis indicates that the acquisition creates shareholder wealth. In order to minimize the firm's costs, Mr. Cutts, owner and manager, wants to evaluate whether to purchase by borrowing or to lease the new refrigeration equipment.

   If CCI decides to borrow to buy, Mr. Cutts expects that the CCA class will be kept open after the refrigeration equipment is sold. Annual operating costs for the buying alternative are paid at the end of each year. Under the leasing alternative, the lessor maintains the machine and pays any costs related to insurance, delivery, and installation.

   For the leasing alternative under consideration, annual payments are made at the beginning of each year, with the first payment due on delivery and installation of the refrigeration equipment.

Cost	$126,000
Delivery and installation	6,000
Investment tax credit to purchase equipment	20,000
CCA rate (Class 8)	20%
Useful life	10 years
Salvage value	$25,000
Annual operating costs	12,000
Weighted cost of capital	15%
CCI's tax rate	30%
Borrowing alternative:	
10-year term loan	9%
Leasing alternative:	
10-year financial lease	$13,500/year

Mr. Cutts has asked you to determine whether he should lease or borrow to buy the new refrigeration equipment.

Required

a) Calculate the initial investment outlay of the refrigeration equipment.

b) Calculate the present value of the after-tax lease payments.

c) Calculate the present value of the after-tax operating costs that will be incurred under the borrowing option.

d) Calculate the present value of the CCA tax shields.

e) Calculate the present value of the salvage value.

f) Calculate the amount of the equivalent loan.

g) Calculate the NVL.

Procedure

Excel FN2L6P1.xls

Starting up:

1. Open the file FN2L6P1.xls. The file is organized into three worksheets as follows:

L6P1DATA	A worksheet that contains information required to calculate NVL
L6P1A	A partially completed worksheet set up to calculate the amount of the equivalent loan and the NVL
L6P1AS	A solution worksheet that reports the amount of the equivalent loan and the NVL for the decision to lease the refrigeration equipment

2. Click the L6P1DATA sheet tab and study the layout of the worksheet. Rows 5 to 16 contain the data required to calculate the amount of the equivalent loan and the NVL.

To complete Question a):

1. Click the L6P1A sheet tab. Rows 4 to 34 are set up for you to calculate the amount of the equivalent loan and the NVL.

2. Enter in cells E7 to E9 the appropriate amounts for the purchase cost, the delivery and installation cost, and the investment tax credit.

3. Enter in cell F10 the formula to calculate the initial investment outlay.

To complete Question b):

1. Enter in cell E14 the formula to calculate the annual after-tax lease payment.

2. Enter in cell F15 the formula to calculate the PV of the after-tax lease payments for years 1 to 10.

To complete Question c):

1. Enter in cell E19 the formula to calculate the annual after-tax operating costs from borrowing.

2. Enter in cell F20 the formula to calculate the PV of the after-tax operating costs for years 1 to 10.

To complete Question d):

1. Enter in cells E23 and E24 the appropriate formulas to calculate the perpetual CCA tax shields on the purchased asset and the lost tax shield on the salvage value.

2. Enter in cell F25 the formula to sum the perpetual tax shield on the purchased asset and the lost tax shield on the salvage value in order to calculate the CCA tax shields.

To complete Question e):
Enter in cell F28 the formula to calculate the present value of the salvage value.

To complete Question f):
Enter in cell F31 the formula to calculate the amount of the equivalent loan.

To complete Question g):
Enter in cell F34 the formula to calculate the NVL.

Commentary

a) The first part of the equivalent-loan approach is to calculate the initial investment outlay. Cell F10 of the solution sheet L6P1AS shows:

$$\text{Initial investment outlay} = \text{Purchase price} + \text{delivery and installation cost} - \text{investment tax credit}$$
$$= \$126{,}000 + \$6{,}000 - \$20{,}000$$
$$= \$112{,}000$$

In terms of leasing, the initial investment outlay of owning the asset represents a savings to the lessee. The lessee does not have to buy the asset for cash. Delivery and installation costs should be included in the purchase cost if the lessor agrees to deliver and install the equipment.

b) The second part of the equivalent-loan approach comprises four steps. The first step in determining the costs of leasing is to determine the present value of the after-tax lease payments. The lease payments are deducted from income as expenses. Thus, they lead to tax savings, and the after-tax costs are used to calculate the present value.

The discount rate required to calculate the present value of lease payments is equal to the after-tax cost of borrowing on a secured basis. Because the underlying asset secures lease payments, the rate on the firm's secured loans is more appropriate to discount lease payments. The discount rate is the after-tax cost of borrowing. As the bank is willing to lend to CCI at 9% to acquire the machine, the after-tax cost of borrowing is equal to:

$$9\% \times (1 - 0.3) = 6.3\%$$

Most lease contracts require the lessee to make the first lease payment up front. In these cases, the present value of the after-tax lease payments can be calculated as the present value of an annuity due.

The after-tax lease payment per period is:

$$\$13,500 \times (1 - 0.30) = \$9,450$$

Cell F15 of the solution sheet L6P1AS shows that the present value of these payments is $72,895.06.

c) The second step is to calculate the present value of the after-tax operating costs under the borrowing option. Sometimes, the lessor may agree to service and maintain the equipment without direct charges associated with these services. In this case, the costs of operating the equipment are less than the costs of operating under ownership and represent savings under the leasing option. Other costs that may be incurred with owning but not with leasing include property taxes and insurance.

As the operating cost savings are relatively certain and occur at the end of the year, the rate at which they should be discounted should reflect this fact. The after-tax cost of borrowing should be the relevant rate for this purpose. The present value can be calculated as:

$$PV(\Delta OC) = \frac{(1 - T)\Delta OC_i}{1 + r} + \frac{(1 - T)\Delta OC_{i + 1}}{(1 + r)^{i + 1}}$$
$$+ \cdots + \frac{(1 - T)\Delta OC_n}{(1 + r)^n} \qquad \textbf{(Equation 6-15)}$$

where

ΔOC_i = savings in operating costs in period i because of leasing, where $i = 1, \ldots, n$

Cell F20 of the solution sheet L6P1AS shows that the present value of the after-tax operating costs under the borrowing option is $60,955.41.

d) The third step is to determine the present value of the CCA tax shields. The CCA tax shields can be calculated using Equations 1-17 and 1-18 from Chapter 1. These equations are adapted as Equations 6-16 and 6-17 for your convenience. Equation 6-16 calculates the present value of the perpetual tax shield. The sum of purchase cost and delivery and installation cost must be adjusted by subtracting the investment tax credit. Equation 6-17 calculates the present value of the CCA tax shields from selling the asset in year n.

$$\text{PVTS} = \left[\frac{C \times d \times T}{2(d + r)} \right]\left[\frac{2 + r}{1 + r} \right] \qquad \textbf{(Equation 6-16)}$$

$$\text{PVTSL}_n = \frac{S_n}{(1 + k_L)^n} \times \frac{dT}{(d + r)} \qquad \textbf{(Equation 6-17)}$$

where

PVTS = present value of the perpetual tax shield
PVTSL_n = present value of the tax shield loss
C = capital cost paid to acquire the asset less the investment tax credit
d = CCA rate
S_n = salvage value in year n
r = after-tax interest rate on debt
k_L = weighted average cost of capital

The present value of the perpetual tax shields of the purchased asset and the present value of the tax shield lost because of the sale of the asset are discounted at the after-tax cost of borrowing. Because of the uncertainty concerning the salvage value, this cash flow is discounted at the firm's weighted average cost of capital.

$$\text{PVTS} = \frac{(\$132{,}000 - \$20{,}000) \times 0.20 \times 0.30}{2(0.20 + 0.063)}$$

$$\times \frac{2 + 0.063}{1 + 0.063} = \$24{,}794.17$$

$$\text{PVTSL}_n = \frac{\$25{,}000}{(1 + 0.15)^{10}} \times \frac{0.20 \times 0.30}{(0.20 + 0.063)} = \$1{,}409.80$$

Cell F25 of the solution sheet L6P1AS shows that the present value of the tax shield lost is $23,384.37 if the firm leases the refrigeration equipment.

e) The fourth step is to calculate the present value of the salvage value. The cash flows from the sale of the refrigeration equipment are, however, highly uncertain. Therefore, the discount rate for these cash flows should be the firm's weighted average cost of capital.

The salvage price is $25,000, and it should be discounted at the weighted average cost of capital, which is equal to 15%.

$$\text{PV}(S_n) = \frac{\$25{,}000}{(1 + 0.15)^{10}} = \$6{,}179.62$$

Cell F28 of the solution sheet L6P1AS shows that the present value of the salvage value is $6,179.62.

f) The third part of the equivalent-loan approach determines the amount of the equivalent loan. The equivalent loan represents the maximum amount that the lessee can borrow if the firm dedicates its future incremental cash flows to service a conventional loan. The amount of the equivalent loan includes cash flows resulting from leasing payments, less any incremental difference in operating or other expenses between the borrowing and leasing alternatives. In other words, it represents the incremental after-tax operating savings because of the leasing alternative. The equivalent loan amount also includes the present value of the CCA tax shields and the present value of the salvage value because these cash flows would normally be used to service a conventional loan.

Equivalent loan = PV(after-tax leasing payments)
 − PV(incremental difference in after-tax operating costs
   or other costs between borrowing and leasing options
 + PV(CCA tax shields)
 + PV(salvage value)

Cell F31 of the solution sheet L6P1AS shows that the amount of the equivalent loan is $41,503.63.

g) Using the equivalent-loan approach, the NVL can now be determined. This step requires subtracting the equivalent loan from the initial investment outlay.

NVL = Initial investment outlay − equivalent loan

Because the amount that could be borrowed under the equivalent loan ($41,503.63) is less than the initial investment outlay ($112,000) saved under the lease, leasing is preferable to purchase by borrowing. Cell F34 of the solution sheet L6P1AS shows that the NVL is $70,496.37.

Conclusion

This computer illustration demonstrates how the equivalent-loan approach can be used to make the decision whether to borrow to buy or to lease. The decision focuses on identifying an equivalent loan that commits the firm to exactly the same cash flows as would be incurred in the leasing alternative. A cost/benefit analysis should be performed beforehand to establish that the acquisition creates shareholder wealth. If the amount that could be borrowed under the equivalent loan is more than the initial investment outlay saved under the lease, then borrowing to purchase is preferable to leasing. If the amount that could be borrowed is less than the initial investment outlay saved under the lease, then leasing is preferable. If the amount that could be borrowed is equal to the initial investment outlay saved under the lease, then the firm will be indifferent in its choice between leasing and borrowing to purchase. Notice that the difference between the initial investment outlay and the equivalent loan is equal to net value to leasing (NVL). The equivalent-loan approach, however, has the added advantage of indicating the amount of conventional debt that lease financing can displace. In this illustration, leasing displaces $41,503.63 in conventional debt.

Benefits of Leasing

Leasing can provide several benefits. These benefits differ depending on whether the lease is classified as operating or capital. Also, the benefits vary depending on the particular situation of the lessee.

General Benefits of Leasing

- Leasing provides different patterns of tax breaks to the lessor and the lessee. In the case of an operating lease, the *lessor* obtains tax credits associated with equipment ownership and is entitled to claim capital cost allowances for the equipment. The *lessee* can claim the lease payments as expenses in the year they are incurred. Therefore, leasing may be beneficial if the lessor can utilize the tax credits and tax deductions associated with ownership more efficiently than the lessee.

- The leased equipment remains the property of the leasing company. This provides more security than a mortgage, enabling risky customers who may be turned down for a loan to still qualify for leasing.

- Lower risk means lower costs. In practice, a lessee will lease equipment if the net value to leasing is positive. To calculate the present value of the lease payments, the lessor discounts lease payments from the lessee. If the discount rate is high, the lease payments have to be higher to make the same net present value. Thus, lower risk means a lower discount rate and lower lease payments by the lessee.

- Leasing may allow a company to finance the acquisition of equipment in spite of restrictive covenants in its loan agreements or bond indentures that would limit its ability to raise new debt to purchase the equipment. Unless similar constraints are placed on the ability of the firm to lease, leasing can be an effective substitute for debt financing. However, lenders are often careful to include restrictions against leasing as well as borrowing.

- The lessee can save the transaction costs associated with borrowing to buy the equipment. When the leased item has a ready secondary market, the credit-checking process can be simplified and the lessor is likely to use standardized procedures. Access to active secondary markets allows the lessor to sell the equipment if returned earlier than expected, which makes default risk less of a concern. In contrast, lenders will perform the same level of credit analysis regardless of how the firm intends to use the proceeds, and the resulting transaction costs may be passed on to the borrower. By leasing, the firm avoids these costs.

Special Benefits of Capital Leases

- Capital leases can be made for terms longer than the terms of bank loans. Thus, the cash flows needed to cover the lease payments are less than those needed to amortize a loan. This preserves cash for other purposes.

- Leasing companies have more expertise than their customers in the assets they lease. This factor is particularly important when the lessee is a small or medium-sized business. In this case, leasing may save the firm the costs and time needed to search for a suitable asset.

- The lessor may agree to service and maintain the equipment and to insure it against the risk of obsolescence. This occurs when the lessor is the manufacturer or a finance company affiliated with the manufacturer. The costs of these services are factored into the lease payments. However, the lessee may benefit because the lessor can be more efficient in performing these functions.

Special Benefits of Operating Leases In contrast to capital leases, operating leases are usually made on a short-term basis and are renewable by mutual agreement. This feature provides additional benefits to the lessee.

- The lessee can obtain the asset for as long as desired and can return it to the lessor. This is particularly convenient when the asset is intended for temporary use. The lessee can avoid the risk of selling or disposing of the asset when it is no longer needed.

- The lessee can avoid the risk of obsolescence. The typically short-term nature of operating leases enables the lessee to exchange an obsolete asset for a newer one with little or no penalty.

Disadvantages of Leasing There are some disadvantages to leasing.

- For some firms, leasing can be more expensive than borrowing and buying. A firm that enjoys a high credit rating, ready access to the capital market, and has the ability to take advantage of the tax benefits of ownership is likely to incur lower costs and more tax savings by borrowing to purchase than by leasing an asset.

- In the case of an operating lease, the lessee loses the tax savings associated with the tax depreciation of the asset.

- Operating leases are not available on all assets. Moreover, the options available on assets intended for leasing are generally standard, and the need for options varies from one lessee to another.

6.4 MERGERS AND ACQUISITIONS
Similarities and Differences

Firms grow either by generating new investments internally or by acquiring other businesses. Mergers and acquisitions have played an important role in the growth of firms over the past two centuries, increasing rapidly during the late 1970s and throughout the 1990s. In 2000, the total value of global mergers and acquisitions activity peaked at U.S.$3.5 trillion. About 50% of these activities involved U.S. companies. The financial press reports daily activities related to mergers and takeovers. Exhibit 6-5 contains excerpts from such an announcement.

In Canada, a **merger**, or more precisely, a **statutory amalgamation** is a combination of two or more companies in which ownership interests are joined. For a merger to occur, a buyer must acquire all the target company's assets and liabilities. A merger is normally accomplished by an exchange of shares, cash, or other securities for the target company's shares. In a merger, the target company loses its corporate identity.

An alternative approach to a merger is an **acquisition** either of a target company's shares or of its assets. In the case of an acquisition of shares, a buyer acquires control of a target company by paying cash or another type of consideration for shares so as to gain voting control of the target company. However, the target company continues to exist under its original name. A disadvantage of an acquisition of shares is the possibility of a holdout of minority interests that refuse to sell their shares. As a result, the two companies cannot be completely integrated until a formal amalgamation occurs.

In the case of an acquisition of assets, a buyer acquires a target company's assets. The buyer can acquire individual, specific assets by paying cash, shares, or other securities issued by the buyer. Usually, the target company ceases to exist after the acquisition of the assets. A disadvantage of an acquisition of assets is the high level of associated legal and administrative costs.

In this course, the terms "merger" and "acquisition" are used interchangeably.

Tax Consequences Under the Generally Accepted Accounting Principles (GAAP), mergers must be accounted for using the purchase method, in accordance with the *CICA Handbook* section 1581. The *Income Tax Act*, however, provides its own specific rules and criteria for corporate mergers. In some situations, for example, the *Act* provides for a tax-deferred rollover for corporations that have amalgamated. The details of these provisions are relatively complex and beyond the scope of this textbook.

Types of Mergers

Mergers can be classified in terms of their impact on the industry or industries to which the merged companies belong.

- A **horizontal merger** combines two or more firms that are direct competitors in the same product lines and markets. This type of merger leads to a larger market share by the resulting company. Horizontal mergers are often encouraged when the target company is financially weak or under threat of failure. Well-capitalized and profitable financial institutions, in particular, are encouraged to acquire smaller and financially weak ones to save them from bankruptcy. In recent cases, the Canada Deposit Insurance Corporation provided incentives to acquiring banks to allow them to take over financially weak trust companies.

- A **vertical merger** combines a company and its direct customer or a company and its direct supplier. The resulting company carries out more phases of product design, development, production, marketing, or sales internally.

- A **congeneric merger**, also known as a **product-extension merger**, combines companies selling different but related products in the same market. For example, a consumer goods company that produces dental care products may acquire a company that produces cosmetic products.

- A **conglomerate merger** is a combination of two (or more) firms that operate in entirely unrelated markets and/or industries and have none of the previous relationships or similarities. A steel company that acquires a clothing manufacturer is an example of a conglomerate merger.

Governments in Canada, the United States, and other developed countries are concerned with large horizontal mergers. Antitrust legislation is in place to prevent mergers that may lead to monopolistic powers by the resulting company. Exhibit 6-6 contains excerpts from an article that shows how regulators can delay and sometimes stop a merger or takeover attempt when they perceive a potential for monopolistic markets.

Exhibit 6-6
Example of a Merger Delay

Potash hits obstacle in bid for German firm

Potash Corporation of Saskatchewan Inc. hit another obstacle Friday in its quest to acquire control of Europe's largest potash company.

The German Federal Cartel Office issued an order prohibiting Potash Corporation's $211-million purchase of 51% of **Kali & Salz Beteiligungs AG**, a subsidiary of German conglomerate **BASF AG**.

Potash said it intends to fight the antitrust body's ruling that the acquisition would give Potash a lock on the market that would decrease competition.

"We and BASF will be filing a joint appeal with the German minister of economics in the next couple of weeks," said Potash Corp. senior vice-president Betty-Ann Heggie. "The minister then has four months, theoretically, to rule on it."

Potash Corp. stock (POT/TSE) closed Friday at $107.65, down 70 cents. Heggie said Potash Corp. chief executive Charles Childers has met with the unions and political leaders in the regions where Kali & Salz has mines.

"He has had a favorable response from the constituents." Heggie discounted the cartel office's ruling that the Potash acquisition would decrease competition.

Source: Material reprinted with the express permission of "National Post Company," a CanWest Partnership.

Motives for Mergers

One of the main reasons for mergers is synergy. Synergy exists when the value of the new firm exceeds the sum of the values of the individual entities. The additional value may come from various benefits provided by the merger. Generally, shareholders cannot obtain these benefits on their own. Synergy can arise from the following six sources.

Operating Economies of Scale and/or Scope Operating economies of scale and/or scope are claimed to be major motives of horizontal mergers. The main result of a horizontal merger is larger market share. Firms claim that increased market share allows them to produce more and gain economies of scale. As a result, the production cost per unit decreases, allowing firms to lower their prices.

Also, firms trying to expand horizontally have argued that they need to merge so that they can compete effectively in world markets. Financial institutions in their drive to acquire trust and insurance companies have advanced this argument.

Firms also claim that vertical mergers produce cost savings. For example, technological developments are costly, which may prohibit a small supplier from investing in product development. A firm may acquire component manufacturers that are critical suppliers but cannot afford to invest in technological improvements.

Finally, firms claim that congeneric mergers reduce the costs of advertising, promotion, and distribution because promoting and selling two related products by two separate firms costs more than promoting and selling the two products by one company. Therefore, congeneric mergers result in savings that may be passed on to customers in the form of lower prices.

Strategic Motives A major motivation behind vertical mergers is the firm's concern about its supply of raw materials. A firm concerned that it may lose access to valuable components may acquire a firm that supplies the component. In this case, the firm would prefer to produce the strategic components itself at higher cost rather than run the risk that a key strategic asset will be controlled by an outside firm.

Similarly, a company may vertically integrate when it is concerned about its product market. However, studies suggest that firms integrate more when demand is highly certain than when it is uncertain.

Market Power and Control Firms with inherently weak market power integrate more than those that have the market position to spread risks and maintain strategic flexibility. A vertically integrated firm with multiple operations in production and distribution can use its market strength at one level of competition to further its interests at another. For example, a firm that achieves most of its value added at the final assembly stage can use its market strength to acquire subassembly operations in order to control product quality directly.

Financial Economies of Scale Financial managers argue that mergers allow a company to become large enough to achieve economies of scale in raising funds from the financial market. They suggest that creditors are more willing to lend to large companies than to medium or small ones. More importantly, new debt or equity issues are associated with substantial fixed costs. Thus, the cost per dollar of new funds decreases with the size of the issue. Managers also argue that larger companies often attract better coverage from security analysts, leading to higher demand for the firm's securities and higher prices. Ultimately, the firm's cost of capital drops.

Increase in Management Capabilities Some firms merge to acquire managerial expertise and skills that are not otherwise available. For example, a firm may not be able to attract good quality managers and employees because the required skills can be achieved only through practical experience. A merger gives the firm direct access to skilled workers and managers without having to train its own. The increase in managerial capabilities and work force efficiency increases the value of the firm's assets.

Fast Growth A firm that wishes to move quickly into a new geographic or product area may search for a target company that already has an established market, sales personnel, management capabilities, and physical facilities. A merger saves the time and effort to develop the firm's own facilities and operations.

The CP acquisition described in Exhibit 6-5 seems to be part of a growth strategy. CP is increasing its access to the U.S. market by expanding its current rail network.

Important Considerations for Undertaking a Merger

When evaluating the benefits of undertaking a merger, managers should consider the following factors.

Diversification Diversification is considered to be the primary motivation behind conglomerate expansion. Managers often state that diversification helps stabilize the firm's earnings stream. Stability of earnings reduces the total risk of equity and benefits shareholders. However, under assumptions of perfect markets, an investor who is concerned about earnings variability can diversify more easily than the firm. Moreover, well-diversified shareholders are more concerned with a share's market risk than its total risk. Higher variability of earnings does not necessarily mean higher market risk.

Good Investment The purchase of assets at below replacement cost is one of the reasons behind mergers. It is argued that combining two companies may enable the bidder to acquire desirable assets at prices below what it has to pay to purchase them directly. This is possible when the market value of the target company is less than the book value or below the replacement cost of the firm's assets. In an efficient market, however, the prices of assets will always equal their intrinsic values. Thus, it is not likely that a bidder will be able to find a company that has a market value substantially below the replacement cost of its assets.

Advantages and Disadvantages of Vertical Mergers

Vertical integration occurs if a company manufactures its own components or provides its own services to produce the final product. Consider the following article.

Pros and Cons of Vertical Integration

Vertical integration is when a company manufactures its own components or provides its own services. But, says Kimya Kamshad, whether this is an economically justifiable option can depend on many factors.

The decision whether to make or buy—or in the language of economists, whether to vertically integrate or contract out—any link in the value chain leading to the final sale of a good will depend on a number of factors that affect the efficient functioning of markets.

Generally speaking, vertical integration is most attractive when different types of market failures exist that threaten profitability. Bringing production in-house allows a company to internalize and thereby overcome market failures. But the strategy is not without its own costs in terms of efficiency and price.

Vertical integration is often the best solution where the activity in question is complex and hard to define under conventional legal contracts. Thus there is a moral hazard problem involved with contracting out if the contracting company cannot be legally covered for all possible contingencies.

One reason many pharmaceutical companies do not contract out activities such as the development of a cure for a particular disease, say AIDS, is that it is difficult to tell whether lack of success in finding a cure arises from insufficient effort on the part of the contractor or an unfruitful line of research.

And with complex transactions, it may be hard to specify quality standards in legal terms—so that to the extent that higher quality is associated with higher costs, suppliers will have an incentive to produce lower-quality goods. This is one often cited reason why many automobile companies manufacture many of their parts in-house. Also, since the information uncovered through R&D is a public good, if it leaks out its value is greatly diminished. Leakages may be harder to control through legal contracts with an independent supplier than if the research is done in-house.

Similarly, vertical integration will be attractive where outside suppliers of the activity are few and are likely to behave opportunistically, i.e. if there are not many suppliers then those that do exist may be able to exercise market power and extract economic rents in supplying the service in question. Such rent extraction by suppliers can be avoided if a company produces the activity in-house.

For example, in California's electricity market in the early 1980s, the state-regulated public utility companies were charging a premium to industrial users for their electricity use that, for politically motivated reasons, was used to subsidize the residential market. As the divergence between the price charged and the actual cost of the electricity became increasingly large, it became cost-effective for many of California's big industrial users of electricity to look to harness the energy produced in their manufacturing processes and generate their own electricity, bypassing the public utilities altogether.

More generally, vertical integration into activities where market power exists among suppliers allows the user to avoid the problem of double margins, i.e. of paying a mark-up to the supplier and basing one's own production levels and price on the marked-up price of the input rather than its true marginal cost. In such cases vertical integration has the added advantages of: creating entry barriers if the integrated company benefits from lower costs than non-integrated rivals, and of providing security against being locked out from a key input in case a rival vertically integrates with the main supplier.

In most countries it is illegal to use vertical integration to monopolize a market. In one recent example, a U.S. federal court ruled against Eastman-Kodak for attempting to monopolize the service and parts market for its photocopiers and business machines by refusing to sell parts to independent service operators that were competing against Kodak's own network of service operators. In doing so, Kodak was raising entry barriers in the market for the supply of parts and servicing by vertically integrating into the provision of this service.

Vertical integration is also particularly attractive where the intermediate activity has large economies of integration with another stage of the value chain. Economies of integration, also known as economies of scope or synergies, occur when the cost of one company performing two distinct activities is less than the cost of two companies performing them separately.

Such economies may arise for a number of reasons such as shared overheads, similar expertise, shared learning, better scheduling and co-ordination of tasks, better market information, reduced information requirements, and lower transactions costs.

For example, many British tour operators have vertically integrated into the airline business, allowing them to co-ordinate the number of air travel seats available to them with the number of spaces they have reserved in resorts, and to share the fixed overheads of their sales and marketing systems. They have also vertically integrated into travel agencies, which provides them with early market information on popular holiday destinations and other passenger trends.

Similarly, pharmaceutical companies developing new drugs often find that by doing the research in-house they can also find ways to lower the final production cost of the finished drug. Or, when automobile manufacturers produce certain key parts in-house, they are able to respond to breakdowns in the final assembly much more quickly.

In-house production will be less attractive where scale economies in the intermediate activity are large and the volume of the intermediate input required by the company is small, leading to a cost disadvantage associated with in-house production.

This is especially true for activities requiring large investments in capital equipment that will not be used at full capacity by a company only producing for its own use. For example, the volume of tires required by an automobile manufacturer may not be sufficiently large to allow for least-cost production of those tires in house.

The automobile company has the option of producing more than its own requirements in order to reach the minimum efficient scale of operations and then selling the excess production on the open market. However, this strategy may be unattractive in that it exposes the company to the risks of the tire market where it may also face the prospects of trying to sell tires to its own rivals in the automotive sector who, for reasons of their own, may prefer independent suppliers.

Other disadvantages of vertical integration include the costs associated with entering a new and possibly unfamiliar business. The corporate press is filled with failed examples of established companies in one sector trying to enter another—one recent example is provided by the case of AT&T's purchase of NCR, aimed at gaining a successful foothold in the computing market and combining the provision of information systems with computing hardware. The combination was so unsuccessful that AT&T has since announced plans to split itself up into three separate companies, one of which will be made up of the computing division.

Another disadvantage of vertical integration is that higher overheads are needed for the vertically integrated operation, which may lead to larger losses in economic downturns than would be incurred if the company was purchasing its supplies on the spot market. The case of the European automotive industry in the recent recession provides a clear example of this where the worst affected companies were often those who did the least contracting-out.

The vertically integrated company must also lock into a particular in-house supplier's technology, which may be inferior to existing or emerging alternatives. Similarly, the incentives of the vertically integrated supplier to provide the best service at the least cost may be less than that of an independent supplier competing for the organization's business.

Mercedes-Benz, among other companies, has been in the financial news in recent years as it has announced moves to increase outsourcing of components formerly produced in-house to save on costs. Indeed, in recent years many European companies have followed the Japanese method of outsourcing many inputs but at the same time reducing the number of suppliers being dealt with, allowing them to build much closer relationships with the remaining suppliers.

The British retail group Marks and Spencer has been extremely successful in developing its own network of independent suppliers with whom it has special long-term relationships. Some large supermarket retailers now share automated check-out information with suppliers and provide them with their own sales forecasts to ensure a steady inflow of new supplies.

Like pure vertical integration decisions, these long-term relationships are not without their own risks and costs. The cost-savings from locking into a single supplier in terms of better information and a higher level of service and/or quality must be balanced against the loss of freedom to deal with other suppliers that may offer more competitive prices and the risk that the supplier may switch to supply a rival and take all the company's confidential market data with it.

Summary

Bringing production in house allows a company to overcome market failures—it avoids the problems of double margins and being locked out from a key input, as well as providing synergies. In-house production will be less attractive, though, where scale economies in the intermediate activity are large and volumes required by the company are small. Other disadvantages include the costs associated with entering a new and possibly unfamiliar business, higher overheads, dependence on a single technology, and lack of incentive. Locking into a long-term relationship with a supplier is another option, but this has its risks.

Source: Courtesy of Dr. Kimya Kamshad.

The article provides several reasons that make vertical integration an economically justifiable option.

- Vertical integration is most attractive when different types of market failures threaten profitability. Bringing production in-house allows a company to internalize and thereby overcome the threat of market failures.

- It is attractive if the activity is complex and difficult to define under conventional legal contracts.

- It is attractive if outside suppliers of an activity are few and apt to behave in an opportunistic manner.

- It is attractive if economies of integration can be achieved. Economies of integration or synergies occur if the cost of one company performing two distinct activities is less than the cost of two companies performing them separately.

  The article also provides several reasons that may make vertical integration undesirable.

- Vertical integration is less attractive if scale economies in the intermediate activity are large and the volume of the intermediate input required by the company is small. This situation creates a cost disadvantage associated with in-house production.

- It is less attractive if there are costs associated with entering a new and possibly unfamiliar business.

- It is less attractive when overhead costs are higher. This situation may lead to larger losses in economic downturns than would be incurred if the company were purchasing its supplies in the spot market.

- It is less attractive if a company must lock into a long-term relationship with a particular in-house supplier's technology, which may be inferior to existing or emerging alternatives.

Strategies of Mergers

Merger strategies differ depending on whether or not the management of the target company approves the merger.

- A **friendly takeover** is a business combination of two (or more) firms through cordial and structured negotiations, supported by the board of directors and management of the firm being acquired. The board recommends to shareholders that they approve the takeover offer because it represents fair value for the company's shares. In many cases, the acquiring company retains many of the acquired company's existing managers to continue to run the business.

- A **hostile takeover** is a combination of two (or more) firms in which the firm being acquired opposes the bid. Such a takeover involves acquiring voting control and ownership of the company by purchasing shares in the open market. A hostile takeover may be attempted by another company or by a well-financed investor who announces that it will pay a certain price for the shares of the target company. Often, the tender price is higher than the prevailing market price of the shares at the time of the tender announcement. If the offer price is high enough, shareholders may vote to accept the offer even if management resists and claims that the company is actually worth more. If the acquirer raises the price high enough, management may change its attitude, converting the hostile takeover into a friendly one.

Anti-Takeover Measures

An **anti-takeover measure** is an action taken by management to fend off a hostile takeover. A firm may take such a measure for two main reasons. First, a hostile takeover almost always means that the successful company will change the managers of the acquired company. Even if they are not dismissed, the existing management will not have the same powers as prior to the takeover. Second, many companies are controlled by a group of shareholders who will resist any changes in ownership structure that may diminish their control. They will urge management to fight a hostile takeover bid.

Over the years, many strategies have been developed by managements and shareholders to repel hostile takeovers. Some of these strategies are designed to inhibit any potential attempts, while others are designed to fight declared takeover attempts.

Strategies Designed to Inhibit Potential Attempts   A firm can use several strategies to inhibit a potential hostile takeover. The first strategy attempts to keep voting power in the hands of a select group. The following measures can be used to achieve this strategy.

- Some firms issue dual-class common shares, where one class has superior voting powers, such as ten votes per share. Superior voting shares cannot be sold but can be exchanged into regular voting shares, which can then be sold in the market.

- Firms may sponsor employee stock option plans and regularly allocate shares to the plans to cover the future exercise of the options. Most of the time, the provisions of a stock option plan allow management to vote the shares of the plan until they are distributed to employees. Thus, the firm can use this voting power as an anti-takeover measure. For example, if a firm is under threat of a hostile takeover bid, management can transfer a block of shares to the plan to increase the number of shares over which it has voting powers.

- The company's charter may be changed to require a significant majority vote, such as 80% of the common shares, to approve a merger that has not been approved by management and the board of directors.

- The terms of the company's directors may be structured so that only a small number of directors are elected per year. In this case, a company bidding to take over will have difficulty quickly electing its own directors to gain control.

Another strategy is to design executive compensation so that key executives will receive large benefits when their contracts are terminated after a takeover without proper cause. Such measures are known as "golden parachutes."

A third strategy is to issue securities that become valuable when an unfriendly bidder obtains control of a certain percentage of shares. These mechanisms are often called "poison pills" or "shareholders' rights plans." One such poison pill is to issue warrants to existing shareholders with very low exercise prices. The warrants cannot be exercised unless an unfriendly bidder has acquired a large block of shares.

Measures Designed to Fight Declared Takeover Attempts   Some actions are designed to make the best of hostile takeover bids. For example, a firm may search for a friendlier bidder, often called a "white knight." If one is found, a bidding war ensues and the shares are bid to higher levels.

Exhibit 6-7 shows that firms look for white knights whenever possible. The exhibit contains excerpts from a newspaper article reporting that Wascana Energy was opening its books so that potential white knights could evaluate the company's assets. Occidental Petroleum Ltd. eventually became the white knight and acquired Wascana.

Husky to look at Wascana:
Regina oil company seeks white knight to ward off Talisman bid

When Regina-based **Wascana Energy Inc.** opens its books to attract potential white knights, **Husky Oil Ltd.** of Calgary will definitely have a look.

Sources say Wascana chief executive Frank Proto has already spoken to a number of potential suitors to ward off a hostile bid from **Talisman Energy Inc.**, although he refuses to comment even on whether a data room would be opened.

On February 12, Talisman made a $1.7-billion bid for Wascana.

"The list of potential Canadian white knights is short, because of the fit that Talisman has with Wascana, and also just because of the size of the transaction," said Peters & Co. Ltd. analyst Craig Langpap.

Husky and the Saskatchewan government share ownership of the Husky heavy oil upgrader in Lloydminster. Also, like Wascana, Husky has a lot of heavy oil in Saskatchewan. "They might have an advantage on some other suitors because whoever takes over Wascana must be acceptable to the Saskatchewan government, and Husky is a well-established Saskatchewan producer," said Langpap.

Other possible suitors are **Canadian Occidental Petroleum Ltd.**, and **Alberta Energy Co. Ltd.** Sources at **Canadian Natural Resources Ltd.** say it is not interested in mounting a bid.

Source: Material reprinted with the express permission of "National Post Company," a CanWest Partnership.

Alternatively, management may negotiate with the bidder to stop the acquisition process for an agreed period of time. During this period, management and the bidder will negotiate a friendly merger.

Other measures are designed to ensure that the shares controlled by the bidder do not exceed those controlled by management or by friendly parties. Management may:

- buy back the shares purchased by the bidder at the purchase price or at a premium;
- use cash or borrow to repurchase a large number of the shares that may be sold to the bidder;
- sell shares to friendly third parties.

Finally, management may take measures to make the acquisition process more difficult or less desirable for the bidder. The target firm may:

- file a suit against the bidder alleging violation of antitrust laws, securities regulations or other laws;
- buy assets that may create an antitrust problem or that the bidder will not want;
- sell an asset that is the main attraction to the bidder;

- borrow a large sum of money and distribute the proceeds as dividends to shareholders (making the acquisition more difficult, as the ability of the bidder to use debt is diminished);
- make a takeover bid for the shares of the bidder.

Agency Problems of Anti-Takeover Measures Several arguments suggest that anti-takeover measures create agency costs for shareholders.

- Generally, tender offers are made at a price higher than the market price of the shares at the time of the announcement. Following the announcement, the share price rises to match the takeover bid. If the takeover bid is unsuccessful and withdrawn, the share price may return to its original level. In this case, shareholders have lost the premium that they would have received from the successful bidder. The loss of premium is a form of agency cost.

- Agency costs are also incurred when potential bidders are deterred from initiating a takeover bid because of anti-takeover measures. In this case, shareholders lose the premium that would be obtained if the potential bidder made an offer. Essentially, anti-takeover measures allow management to continue its control of the firm and prevent shareholders from realizing the full potential of their assets.

In recognition of the potential agency costs associated with anti-takeover measures, institutional investors have been actively fighting anti-takeover measures. Refusal to accept good offers may lead investors to sell their investments in the firm, which puts pressure on share price.

Exhibit 6-8 contains excerpts from a report on a study published by Scottish Amicable Investment Managers showing that the share prices of the majority of U.K. companies that succeeded in fending off hostile takeover bids underperformed the market in the following

---

Exhibit 6-8
Effects of Anti-Takeover Measures

Bruised but not beaten

There can be after-effects for a takeover prey that gets away. When a hostile takeover bid has been successfully repelled, how do the bruised incumbents shape up? Not very well, according to recent research. Back in the summer of 1986, when Standard Chartered Bank escaped a hostile bid by Lloyds, its share price went on to underperform the market by 33%, 47%, and 50% over the next three years. This is an extreme example from a study published by Scottish Amicable Investment Managers earlier this year. But the figures illustrate the underlying conclusion of the report: that the vast majority of U.K. companies which have succeeded in fending off hostile takeover bids in the last decade have underperformed by a considerable margin in the following years. "History suggests that shareholders are better to accept the offer on the table," concludes the report.

Of course, many companies become takeover targets precisely because they are underperforming in the hands of the current management. A failed contested bid can

Continued >

years. Yet the exhibit also shows that many failed contested bids produced beneficial effects. Some target companies restructured their operations and their shares outperformed the market within five years of the abandoned bids.

Evaluating Merger Targets

Theoretically, the evaluation of a merger target is similar to a capital budgeting problem. The techniques described in Chapters 1 and 2 apply if the merger target is considered as an asset or project to be undertaken. The purchase price is compared to the present value of the cash flows generated from the asset. If the present value is greater than the purchase price, the merger project will increase the wealth of the acquirer's shareholders. Thus, the merger should be pursued.

Despite the similarity between the evaluation of projects and the evaluation of merger targets, the latter is complicated by the existence of many factors that do not affect the evaluation of regular projects. Moreover, acquirers have to be careful in estimating the values of target companies because the amounts of money involved are substantial. Overestimating the value of the target company can lead to substantial losses to the acquirer.

When shares of the acquisition target company are actively traded on exchanges, the market price per share may not accurately reflect the value of the share to the acquirer. In practice, the acquirer offers the target company's shareholders a premium above market price to persuade them to sell their shares. Normally, premiums range between 20% and 50% above market value immediately prior to the merger announcement. In many situations, shareholders may hold on for much better offers either from the initial bidder or from a new one.

The acquiring company can avoid paying excessively high premiums by undertaking a valuation of the merger target. Regardless of whether the target firm's shares are traded publicly, a valuation of the target firm provides an appropriate estimate to begin the bidding process.

Essentially, the valuation of a merger target is a present value exercise. The acquirer estimates the present value per share of the target assuming the acquisition will take place. The maximum price that the acquiring firm should be willing to offer per share of the target is equal to the present value per share. As long as the acquiring firm can buy the target at a price less than or equal to the present value, the value of the acquiring firm will increase because of the value of the target firm.

In practice, the price per share at which the acquiring company may be able to buy the shares of the target does not necessarily equal the maximum price that the acquiring company may be willing to pay. The NPV per share is the maximum price per share minus the purchase price per share. If the NPV per share is negative, the target should not be purchased. If the NPV per share is positive, the target should be acquired, as the acquisition will increase the acquiring firm's value. If the NPV per share is zero, the acquiring firm should be indifferent.

If the target has shares outstanding and trading in the market, the NPV per share may be calculated in terms of the current market price per share of the target. In this case, the NPV may be called the maximum premium because it will be the maximum amount above the current share price that the acquirer should be willing to pay to acquire the target.

Evaluation Techniques

There are three main techniques used in the evaluation of merger targets.

Weighted Average Cost of Capital (WACC) Method

This method is an adaptation of the familiar discounted cash flow analysis for capital budgeting. It has several steps:

1. Estimate the initial merger costs. These costs include the purchase price of the target company's shares and the transaction fees. In some cases, the acquirer may sell some of the assets of the target company that it considers undesirable. The resulting net acquisition costs are equal to the costs of acquisition minus the liquidation value of these assets.

    When the target firm has shares trading in the market, the purchase price may be estimated by the current market price immediately prior to the announcement of the merger. If the target firm does not have outstanding shares trading in the market, estimating the initial merger costs requires an assumption regarding the price per share at which the target will be acquired.

2. Estimate the incremental cash flows generated by the new firm because of the acquisition. For this purpose, the financial manager should estimate the useful life of the acquired assets. Then, two sets of pro forma cash flow statements must be prepared for the entire life of the acquired assets. One should be prepared assuming that the firm continues on without the acquisition, while the other assumes that the merger will take place. The difference between the two cash streams constitutes the incremental cash flows from the merger. The incremental cash flows should reflect the increase in revenues and the synergistic benefits from the merger. Also, they should include any capital investments required to maintain the acquired assets in full operating condition.

3. Calculate the terminal value of the acquired assets. This value may be estimated as if the assets will be liquidated by the end of their useful life. In this case, the financial manager must include in the terminal value of the acquired assets an estimation of the firm's going-concern value. For example, the firm may have developed customer goodwill in a new market that makes it easier to sell other products in this market. In this case, it may be better to estimate the terminal value on the basis of a going-concern sale. If the assets are held as a subsidiary, the evaluation should estimate the price at which the subsidiary's shares can be sold.

4. Estimate a discount rate for the cash flows. The discount rate must reflect the risk caused by the additional financing of the acquisition. Equation 6-9 can be used for this process.

5. Calculate the total net present value of the acquisition. The NPV per share is equal to the total NPV of the acquisition divided by the number of shares. If the NPV is positive, the merger at the assumed price will increase the wealth of the acquiring firm's shareholders. Thus, it should be pursued.

Adjusted Present Value (APV) Method The APV method may be used to evaluate mergers and acquisitions. As indicated by Equation 6-1, the base-case NPV must be calculated and then adjusted by the present values of the cash flows arising from merger-related effects.

The base-case NPV is equal to the value of the merger target before the merger. In the case of a target firm that has outstanding shares trading in the market, this NPV is equal to the current market price per share (before the merger announcement) times the number of shares outstanding. For a privately held firm, the base-case NPV must be estimated using the standard valuation techniques for a project.

Merger-related effects include changes in many factors such as financial structure, operating structure, risk, competitive position, economies of scale, and synergies. For example, the merger may bring the debt of the acquirer closer to the optimal capital structure. This change may reduce the cost of capital to the entire firm and increase the value. This increase should be credited to the merger transaction.

Similarly, the merger may increase the acquirer's revenues. For example, if one product of the target complements an existing product of the acquiring firm, the acquisition may increase sales of both products. Again, the incremental amount of sales of the original product should be credited to the merger transaction.

The total net present value of the target firm is the sum of the present value of the merger-related effects and the base-case NPV. Dividing the total value by the number of shares produces the maximum price per share that the acquiring firm should be willing to offer the target. If this maximum offer price per share is greater than the price at which the firm can purchase the target, the purchase will increase the acquirer's value and the merger should be attempted.

The APV alternative is preferable when the merger produces merger-related cash flows that are difficult to capture in the WACC. Moreover, the WACC assumes that the firm will rebalance its capital structure to keep it constant over the evaluation period. When this assumption is not valid, the APV method should be used, because it provides a better approximation of the merger's value.

Comparison with Previous Acquisition Cases This method analyzes past mergers for guidance to determine a reasonable offer price for the target company's shares. Generally, the acquirer's financial managers study past mergers to find cases in which the acquired companies are in the same industry and have the same assets as the target. Once similar cases are identified, the managers use these cases to calculate some ratios based on the offer price. Popular ratios include:

$$\frac{\text{Times earnings}}{\text{per share paid}} = \frac{\text{purchase price per share}}{\substack{\text{fully diluted earnings per share,} \\ \text{excluding non-recurring items}}} \qquad \textbf{(Equation 6-18)}$$

$$\frac{\text{Times cash}}{\text{flow paid}} = \frac{\text{purchase price per share}}{\substack{\text{fully diluted cash flows per share,} \\ \text{excluding non-recurring items}}} \qquad \textbf{(Equation 6-19)}$$

$$\frac{\text{Times book}}{\text{value paid}} = \frac{\text{purchase price per share}}{\text{book value per share}} \qquad \textbf{(Equation 6-20)}$$

$$\frac{\text{Premium}}{\text{paid}} = \frac{\text{purchase price} - \text{market price before merger}}{\text{market price before merger}} \qquad \textbf{(Equation 6-21)}$$

$$\frac{\text{Times replacement}}{\text{cost paid}} = \frac{\text{purchase price of all shares}}{\text{net replacement cost of assets}} \qquad \textbf{(Equation 6-22)}$$

where

net replacement cost of assets = replacement cost of assets less value of liabilities

These ratios are calculated for all previous cases that are similar to the case under analysis. Financial management then determines for each ratio the lowest and highest value it took during past mergers. The range obtained for the ratio is considered a normal range within which the ratio resulting from the current merger should fall. Comparing all the ranges obtained for the ratios, a common range can be established for the target company's share price. A share price offer that falls within the common range is considered to be a reasonable offer.

In practice, a firm may be acquired when its earnings are negative. In this case, the ratio "times earnings per share paid" is negative. A negative ratio should be ignored. For example, consider a situation where times earnings per share paid for the past five mergers were 12, 15, –10, 8, and 16. The target's earnings per share are $2. An offer price range based on the times earnings per share paid will have $16 as the lowest price and $32 as the highest price. The negative ratio is ignored.

The managers will also analyze various financial performance measures for the group of companies acquired in previous mergers and compare them to the same measures of the target company. The purpose is to determine whether the target company is more or less desirable than the previous targets. If it is more desirable, the estimated target price is adjusted upward. If the target is considered to be less desirable, the price is adjusted downward.

Minicase 6-4 demonstrates merger analysis using ratios.

MINICASE 6-4 MERGER ANALYSIS USING RATIOS

Inter Industries Incorporated (III), a diversified conglomerate, is considering the acquisition of Montréal Fashion House (MFH), a medium-sized company that specializes in designing and producing high fashion clothing. III financial staff have identified seven previous mergers in which the target companies are in the same industry and have similar types of assets to MFH. Moreover, the circumstances of the merger in the identified cases were similar to the current circumstances surrounding III's intentions to acquire MFH. The staff have prepared Exhibits 6-9 and 6-10 to assist in estimating an offer price for MFH's shares.

Question 1: Consider the times earnings paid ratios from previous mergers. How can these ratios be used to estimate a range of possible offer prices for MFH?

The ratios suggest that previous similar mergers have been accomplished at ratios that range from a low of 9.6 times to a maximum of 15 times. If past experience is indicative of

Case Continued >

Exhibit 6-9
Key Ratios from Previous Mergers

Merger case	Times earnings paid	Times cash flow paid	Times book value paid	Premium paid	Times replacement cost paid
M_1	9.6	8.2	2.25	25%	1.45
M_2	12.5	10.4	1.75	35	1.75
M_3	13.0	12.0	2.75	50	1.85
M_4	15.0	10.0	2.15	30	2.00
M_5	12.0	9.5	3.00	40	2.15
M_6	10.0	7.0	1.95	38	1.45
M_7	11.0	7.5	2.35	20	1.90

Exhibit 6-10
MFH Selected Income Statement and Balance Sheet Items
(Merger Intentions Are Not Public)

Expected fully diluted earnings per share, excluding non-recurring items	$ 4.75
Expected fully diluted cash flows per share, excluding non-recurring items	$ 6.25
Book value per share	$28.00
Current share price	$38.00
Replacement cost of assets per share	$32.00

the present, a successful offer price for MFH would lead to a times earnings paid ratio within the range 9.6 to 15. Given that the earnings per share for MFH are $4.75, the offer price can range from a minimum of $45.60 (9.6 × $4.75) to a maximum of $71.25 (15 × $4.75).

Question 2: Using the key ratios from previous mergers, calculate a minimum price and a maximum price that may be offered to MFH shareholders.

Using calculations similar to those in Question 1, Exhibit 6-11 reports the offer price ranges obtained using the various ratios.

Question 3: Determine a range for the offer price that excludes all offer prices that would be considered extreme based on past merger cases.

An offer price is considered extreme based on past merger cases if it falls outside the range of prices established by past mergers. For example, a price of $74 is considered to be extreme if compared to the prices paid in the past for earnings per share. These prices range from $45.60 to $71.25. However, the same price of $74 is not extreme if compared to prices paid in the past for cash flows or book value per share. These prices range from $43.75 to $84.00 per share. Therefore, a range that excludes all offer prices that would be considered extreme based on past merger cases would be $49.00 to $57.00 inclusive, based on the maximum of the minimum values and the minimum of the maximum values.   *Case Continued >*

Exhibit 6-11
Ranges of Possible Offer Prices for MFH Shares

Item considered	Level of MFH item	Minimum Prior ratio	Minimum Offer price	Maximum Prior ratio	Maximum Offer price
Expected fully diluted earnings per share, excluding non-recurring items	$ 4.75	9.60	$45.60	15.00	$71.25
Expected fully diluted cash flows per share, excluding non-recurring items	$ 6.25	7.00	$43.75	12.00	$75.00
Book value per share	$28.00	1.75	$49.00	3.00	$84.00
Current share price	$38.00	20%	$45.60	50%	$57.00
Replacement cost of assets per share	$32.00	1.45	$46.40	2.15	$68.80

6.5 LEVERAGED BUYOUTS

A **leveraged buyout (LBO)** is the acquisition of a company by using little capital and large amounts of debt. The debt is secured by pledging the acquired company's assets as collateral. An LBO is performed by a firm or a group of investors that buys a subsidiary or an entire company. Most often, the target company's assets serve as security for the loans taken out by the acquiring firm. The buyers hope to repay the loans out of the cash flow of the acquired company. In addition, buyers are usually part of the management team of the target company. They use a leveraged buyout to retain control by converting a company from public to private.

LBO targets are generally companies or subsidiaries with undervalued assets. The purpose of purchasing these assets is to achieve a quick improvement in operations and higher residual cash flows to the owners. LBOs taking place over the past two decades that returned profits to the owners often resulted in a major turnaround in the profitability of the firm. Buyers seem to have been successful in turning the businesses around quickly and increasing the values of the purchased assets.

In some cases, success in increasing value is primarily credited to the highly qualified managers who were employed by the firm before the LBO. These managers find themselves with greater power to use their knowledge and the flexibility to make decisions promptly. They are able to respond quickly to market conditions and customer demand. In other cases, success is attributed to new managers hired immediately after the purchase. They improve the firm's efficiency, reduce waste, or increase sales, any of which lead to better profits and cash flows to the owners. Consequently, the firm's value under new ownership is expected to increase significantly.

While LBOs generally start with high leverage, those that succeed in turning their fortunes around have lowered their leverage ratios gradually after the purchase.

Investors typically sell part of the assets after purchase to pay off the debt. Often, the leverage ratio of a successful LBO decreases within a few years to a level comparable to the industry leverage.

The high leverage that characterizes LBOs enables key personnel to obtain significant ownership in the newly formed firm. If the LBO is successful, the owners gain substantial wealth from improving the operating performance of their firms. The leverage ratios decrease because the value of the firm increases while debt remains constant. Most successful LBOs go public again within three to five years from the date of the purchase. However, if the owners of the new firm cannot turn the business around and make profits, they end up in bankruptcy and they and their creditors suffer huge losses.

The evolution of the market for LBOs provides interesting insights into how the financial market operates. Many of the early LBOs in the mid-1970s produced returns as high as 50% to their owners. The financial market responded quickly by providing funds for such activities. Consequently, corporate raiders were armed with huge amounts of money and a willingness to buy.

By the early 1980s, takeover activities were common. As more LBO hunters entered the market, prices of takeover targets increased and the rate of failure immediately after purchase increased substantially. With the bidding wars, many buyers discovered after purchasing the assets that they paid prices too high to be recovered by improvements in operations. As the rate of bankruptcies increased in the mid- and late 1980s, leveraged buyout financing became restricted to the soundest of deals. In almost all recent leveraged buyouts, public shareholders received a premium over the current market value for their shares.

Good Targets for Leveraged Buyouts

An ideal candidate for a leveraged buyout has some or all of the following characteristics:

- The industry in which the firm operates is relatively stable or mature, with well-known production technology. The industry's assets tend to preserve their value over time, as the rate of economic deterioration is slow. This factor is important because the buyers will likely need some time to pay off some of the debt before they can renew or upgrade equipment.

- The target company is itself well established, with well-known and diversified product lines. This characteristic provides for stable cash flows and the ability to service high levels of debt.

- The firm's assets have good collateral values. For example, accounts receivable are not overdue and inventories are mostly finished goods and non-perishables. This makes the current assets suitable for collateral and lenders will be willing to lend a high proportion of the value of these assets.

- The firm's current capital is mostly equity, giving the buyer the opportunity to use a large amount of debt to buy out other shareholders.

- The purchase is likely to be finalized without overloading the firm with debt that has service requirements beyond the firm's ability to generate cash flows.

These characteristics imply that an ideal candidate for a leveraged buyout is a firm with low business risk. Firms with low business risk are able to take on high financial risk.

Financing a Leveraged Buyout

The financing structure of a leveraged buyout depends on a firm's assets, their suitability for collateral, and the magnitude of the firm's business risk. Generally, an investment banker acts as an intermediary for the deal and brings together the various contributors. The banker determines the proportion of funds that must be raised through debt.

Senior debt is usually provided by financial institutions, such as banks or finance companies, for terms of five to ten years. Often, the rate is floating and set at a premium above the prime rate. The premium varies depending on the degree of risk of the LBO but ranges from 100 to 400 basis points.

Subordinated debt is provided by life insurance companies or by special funds accumulated from pension plans. The terms of this debt range from 10 to 20 years and the rate is usually fixed. Generally, the capital structure will contain several tiers of subordinated debt with declining degrees of security. The highest-rated subordinated debt will normally have a BBB rating or lower.

Preferred shares are used when a firm exhausts its ability to use interest tax shields. Often, subordinated debtholders also buy some preferred shares.

Common equity is often provided by the acquirer, leveraged buyout funds, management, and subordinated lenders.

Using Leasing to Finance a Leveraged Buyout

The article that follows considers the advantages and difficulties of leasing as an alternative to LBO financing. It indicates that many LBO companies are ideal lessees because they want to reduce cash expenditures and frequently are unable to take full advantage of depreciation benefits. In addition, the article suggests that under certain circumstances a lease is better suited than traditional sources of LBO financing (senior and subordinated debt) to finance fixed assets—particularly when the lives of the assets will support longer financing terms and the LBO company cannot use tax benefits efficiently. An example is provided to explain the cash flow savings from lease financing and the impact it has on the capital structure of the LBO.

FUNDING AN LBO WITH EQUIPMENT LEASE FINANCING

DIANE S. BRANDT AND DEAN THOMAS RISKAS

Leveraged buyout transactions (LBOs) have become an appealing form of finance to accomplish a variety of corporate objectives, as evidenced by the tremendous increase in LBO activity in recent years. Many LBO companies are ideal candidates for equipment lease financing because they want to reduce cash expenditures and frequently are unable to take full advantage of depreciation benefits. Yet, for a variety of reasons, LBOs have made limited use of equipment lease financing—generally applying it after the buyout closes, and rarely as part of the initial financing of the LBO.

While a lease to a recent LBO may offer a premium yield, lessors can earn even greater risk-adjusted returns by providing lease financing as part of the initial capital structure of the

LBO. This is because, under certain circumstances, a lease is better suited than traditional sources of LBO financing (senior and subordinated debt) to finance fixed assets—particularly when the lives of the assets will support longer financing terms and when the LBO company cannot use tax benefits efficiently. Compared to debt, a lease can offer both a lower financing cost and lower payments. Because an LBO company's projected cash flows usually dictate its initial capital structure, the cash flow savings created when a lease is used in lieu of debt can be very valuable.

However, the nature of LBO transactions and the manner in which they are typically completed present major challenges to incorporating lease financing at the formation of the LBO. These challenges place special organizational and operating demands on lessors. This article will: illustrate the value to an LBO of using a lease as a source of initial funding; examine the obstacles to leasing in the LBO environment; and outline ways in which a lessor can organize its efforts for success.

Value of a Lease in Funding an LBO

When structuring a buyout, an LBO sponsor frequently measures the attractiveness of a financing alternative by both its interest cost and cash flow attributes. The value of a lease can be illustrated for a hypothetical LBO by comparing the lease financing rates and payments to those of the LBO debt which the sponsor would otherwise employ.

The hypothetical LBO company is the paper division of a forest products company, which will be purchased for $100 million. The LBO sponsor and management of the new company will provide equity of $15 million. The balance of the financing, $85 million, will be comprised of $60 million of senior debt and $25 million of subordinated debt. The senior debt, which will be secured by the company's fixed assets, has a 12.5 percent interest rate and a seven-year term with fully amortizing level payments. The subordinated debt has a 15 percent interest rate and a ten-year term, with seven years of interest-only payments. In addition, the subordinated lender receives stock warrants that are expected to add 1000 basis points to the cost of the loan. The LBO sponsor is considering using a sale-leaseback of $20 million of the company's processing equipment in lieu of a portion of the debt. The lease is priced at an effective interest rate of 12.5 percent (comparable to senior debt) with level payments over a ten-year term.

When lease financing is substituted for debt, the most cost-effective strategy is to replace the more expensive subordinated debt or equity dollar for dollar. However, it generally is not possible to reduce only subordinated debt or equity because the lease removes some of the collateral and cash flows upon which the senior lender bases its loan. Consequently, a lease is likely to replace a combination of senior and subordinated debt and equity. In this example, the $20 million lease is assumed to replace $14 million of senior debt and $6 million of subordinated debt; i.e., a 70 percent/30 percent blend. The actual mix of debt replaced by a lease will vary depending upon the debt terms and whether the senior lender looks primarily to the company's assets or to its cash flows for purposes of determining the loan amount.

Financing Cost Savings

As can be seen in Table 1, the lease provides meaningful financing rate savings when measured against the weighted average cost of the LBO debt. The effective interest

Table 1 Comparison of Pre-Tax Financing Costs

	Effective interest cost	
	Excluding warrants	Including warrants
Lease financing	12.50%	12.50%
Mix of debt replaced:		
• 70% senior debt	12.50%	12.50%
• 30% subordinated debt	15.00%	25.00%
Weighted average	13.25%	16.25%
Financing cost savings	.75%	3.75%

rate for the lease is 12.5 percent, which is 75 basis points to 375 basis points lower than the interest rate for the blended LBO debt, depending on whether the cost of the warrants is included.

The actual cost of the lease, and yield to the lessor, is several percentage points higher than that shown in Table 1 because the lessor, rather than the LBO company, receives the tax benefits and residual value from ownership of the equipment. However, if the LBO company cannot efficiently use tax benefits, the cost of the lease generally will still be lower when measured on an after-tax discounted cash flow basis. And, if the LBO sponsor expects to sell or refinance the LBO company before the end of the lease, as it often does, the loss of residual value may be less important than the cash flow savings created by the lease.

In some cases, it may be appropriate for a lessor to charge a higher price than assumed in Table 1. In these cases, it may be preferable to obtain the additional return in the form of warrants or other equity participation, rather than a higher lease rate, in order to ensure that the lease offers a cash flow advantage over competing LBO debt.

Cash Flow Savings

When the lower effective cost of the lease is combined with a lease term that is longer than the debt term, the LBO company's cash outflows can be reduced. Table 2 compares the annual cash payments for the lease and the blended LBO debt during the critical early years following the buyout. Annual debt service is $3.9 million compared to annual lease payments of $3.5 million, a savings of $400,000 per year.

Impact on the LBO Capital Structure

The combination of the lower financing cost and reduced cash flow obligations of an equipment lease can greatly impact one of the LBO sponsor's key structuring concerns: the annual cash flow available to satisfy the debt coverage requirements of the senior and subordinated lenders. In our example, the LBO company is able to reduce expensive subordinated debt by $6 million, and, at the same time, the $400,000 of annual cash flow savings improves its debt coverage ratios. By increasing debt coverage, the LBO company has a cash cushion, and may be able to negotiate more favourable interest rates or other terms with its lenders.

Alternatively, the $400,000 of cash savings created by the lease could be used to support additional debt of approximately $2 million, thus allowing the LBO company to

Table 2 Comparison of Cash Flows ($ in Thousands)

	Financing amount	Annual payments
Debt financing:		
• Senior debt	$14,000	$3,030
• Subordinated debt	6,000	900
	$20,000	$3,930
Lease financing	$20,000	$3,530
Cash flow savings	—	$ 400

be purchased at a higher price ($102 million) without diminishing the debt coverage ratios or other financial standards. Or, if the LBO sponsor intends to leave the purchase price at the same level, the amount of equity can be reduced by $2 million, a considerable reduction considering the proposed equity infusion of $15 million.

Commitments at the close of the buyout to lease-finance future capital expenditures can provide an LBO company with additional cash flow savings. In the absence of forward financing, the total cost of the new equipment generally is deducted from the projected cash flow available to service the company's debt. Lease financing can thus free up cash to support a higher level of acquisition debt or to improve the company's projected debt coverage ratios.

Impediments to LBO Leasing

In spite of its obvious advantages, equipment leases are rarely used as a source of LBO funding. There are a number of legitimate, though surmountable, reasons for this.

Undeveloped LBO Market

Because the leasing industry has not actively pursued the LBO market, LBO sponsors generally are unaware of the magnitude of benefits that may be attained by using a lease to finance an LBO. Historically, many big-ticket lessors, the natural candidates to undertake such an effort, have focused on investment grade credits even though, often, affiliates of these leasing companies provide senior and/or subordinated debt to LBOs. Only recently have a few lessors ventured into the LBO market; many lessors continue to view LBO credit risks as inconsistent with their investment objectives.

Improper Timing

In most cases where equipment leasing has been considered by an LBO sponsor, the LBO company's capital structure has already been in place. This timing creates two impediments. First, restrictive debt covenants may limit or prohibit the sale and leaseback of the restructured company's assets. Second, the advantages of an equipment lease are less compelling after the buyout than when it is part of the LBO's initial capital structure; only then can the cash flow savings created by the lease be used to negotiate better debt financing terms (due to improved debt coverage ratios) or to reduce the levels of equity and warrants.

Difficulties in Completing an LBO Lease

The time available to arrange firm financing commitments for an LBO transaction is often very limited—sometimes a matter of a few days. As a result, LBO sponsors frequently deal with only a few funding sources with which they have experience and can rely upon for timely commitments. Most leasing companies have not organized their credit review and approval processes to provide firm commitments in such short time periods, particularly given the greater due diligence demands of LBO financing.

An LBO transaction is complex and must balance the requirements of a variety of financial participants: senior and subordinated lenders and preferred and common stock-holders. The participant most likely to be affected by the lease is the senior lender, which may object to a lease because it is accustomed to controlling all of the LBO company's collateral. The additional layer of financing imposed by a lease can further complicate the LBO transaction, particularly the negotiation of intercreditor rights. Because most LBO sponsors are not as knowledgeable about structuring and documenting a lease as they are about debt and equity, it is more difficult and time-consuming for them to incorporate the lease into the LBO.

Organizing for Success in the LBO Market

To be successful in the LBO market, a lessor must offer its financing in a manner that is workable in the LBO environment. This is best accomplished when the lessor makes a major commitment of capital and resources to a dedicated LBO leasing activity; staffs it with senior leasing and LBO personnel; and establishes investment criteria and operating policies that are responsive to LBO sponsors' needs for flexibility, confidentiality, and timely decisions.

Understanding LBO Credit Risks

Lessors will find that the credit risk characteristics of the financial participants in an LBO can vary significantly. There is obviously a high degree of risk for the equity holders and, to a lesser extent, subordinated lenders. However, senior lenders are relatively safe, as evidenced by the fact that they typically lend to LBO companies at only a small premium above their prime rate. An LBO equipment lease can have similar credit characteristics to those of the LBO senior debt. Consequently, a favourable relationship can exist between the credit risk and the attractive returns that can be achieved.

It is essential that the lessor thoroughly understand the structure and dynamics of the various LBO financing components in order to be able to: (1) distinguish between good and bad LBOs; (2) measure the risk associated with its lease to the LBO; (3) price the lease commensurate with its risk; and (4) structure and document the lease in such a way as to control the lessor's risk as much as possible.

Evaluation of an LBO credit is different than for a less leveraged business. Financial statement analysis can be more complicated; e.g., purchase accounting can distort the numbers and requires a shift from a balance sheet to a cash flow orientation. Due diligence is more extensive and demands in-depth sensitivity analyses to assess the appropriateness of the capital structure and the impact of variances in operating assumptions on the company's ability to service its financing. The intercreditor relationships and roles of the other financial participants also must be carefully examined: What incentives and capabilities do they have to support the company in the event of financial trouble? Finally, intangibles must be considered: What impact will higher leverage, increased financial incentives, and the watchful eye of the LBO sponsor have on management performance?

Major Commitment of Resources and Capital

Participation in the LBO leasing market requires a major commitment of capital and other resources over an extended period. The LBO leasing market is new [as of 1989] and needs to be developed. Because most leasing companies do not currently have established relationships with LBO sponsors, breaking into the sponsor's financing "inner circle" will take a significant investment of senior personnel, time, and effort. Therefore, a lessor must be willing to view the LBO leasing activity as a long-term venture.

LBOs are well known for the considerable sizes they can take: While the vast majority of buyouts occur in the $50 million to $500 million range, billion dollar transactions are not uncommon. The lease usually will range from 10 percent to 50 percent of the overall financing. The amount of capital directed to LBOs should be appropriate to this task and sufficient to underscore to LBO sponsors that the lessor is committed to this market. Also, given the relatively higher level of credit risk, the lessor's capital allocation should be sufficient to allow it to achieve diversification.

Targeting a Market Segment

The LBO market is huge—over $100 billion in 1988. In addition to a wide range of transaction sizes, industries vary considerably, including manufacturing, retail, communications, transportation, wholesale, and service businesses. And there is no particular geographic concentration.

As with any type of leasing, the LBO lessor will want to target one or more market segments that match its investment objectives and the risk-reward characteristics it is willing to assume. It can then tailor its marketing efforts, credit policies, and operating procedures to the specific needs of that niche. For example, if a lessor has particular expertise in a type of equipment (such as high-tech) or a type of financing (such as facilities), it may want to emphasize these capabilities in its discussions with LBO sponsors. Conversely, the lessor should identify the types of LBOs in which it does not wish to participate, such as turnarounds or those involving hostile takeovers.

Whatever the target market, a lessor will be more successful if it can provide both sale-leasebacks and lease-lines of credit. Generally, it will be important to accommodate a variety of equipment types and lease terms under a single master lease agreement.

Appropriate Staffing

LBO lease financing requires the marriage of two complex disciplines—LBO finance and tax-oriented leasing—in order to properly evaluate credit risk, structure and negotiate the lease, and overcome potential intercreditor issues and lender objections. Initially, the LBO leasing activity should include both people who are highly experienced in LBO finance (ideally as lenders) as well as people who have strong big-ticket leasing backgrounds (ideally in leveraged leases), with the goal of developing a staff of individuals each of whom are skilled in both disciplines.

LBO sponsors are accustomed to negotiating with lenders who almost always are key decisionmakers within their organizations. Therefore, it is essential that the leasing company's representatives are senior and able to act with authority. Also, the heavy financial analysis and due diligence demands of an LBO and the ongoing need to closely monitor the LBO requires the support of senior analysts. Ideally, the staff should be dedicated solely to the LBO leasing activity in order to provide the flexibility and response time required in an LBO.

Operating Policies and Investment Guidelines

While LBO financing requires more due diligence than traditional lease financing, the time available to approve a transaction is often very short. Unless the lessor is responsive on a timely basis, many attractive investment opportunities will be lost and the success of the LBO leasing activity itself may be jeopardized. Therefore, streamlined structuring, pricing, due diligence, and approval processes should be developed. In particular, the lessor should examine the approval limits and authorities vested in its officers with a view toward providing the officers with as much flexibility as possible.

Well-thought-out investment guidelines can facilitate the approval process. However, guidelines should not be overly restrictive, due to the diversity of LBOs and the propensity of LBO sponsors to restrict the number of financing sources to an inner circle. The lessor will likely need to strike a balance between the desirability of targeting a specific market and the need to accommodate a wider diversity of transactions than is typical of traditional lease markets.

Conclusion

Under certain circumstances, a lease is better suited than traditional sources of LBO financing to finance fixed assets. As a result, lessors can earn attractive returns with favourable risk-reward characteristics. Lessors that want to tap this market's potential must be willing to make a major commitment of capital and senior personnel to the market and to organize their efforts to be responsive to the unique characteristics of LBO financing.

Source: Reprinted with permission of Equipment Leasing & Finance Foundation, www.leasefoundation.org

The article explains the difficulties that limit the use of leasing in LBO financing:

- Leasing companies often attempt to lease to LBO companies after the capital structure has been finalized. By that time, leasing is no longer attractive to LBO companies.

- LBOs are arranged quickly. It can be difficult to complete lease agreements quickly, as most leasing companies have not organized their credit review and approval processes to provide firm commitments in such short time periods.

- Leasing companies are not responsive to the LBO sponsors' needs for flexibility, confidentiality, and timely decisions.

- Leasing executives are not properly trained to evaluate the various risks associated with LBO financing.

- The financial needs of LBOs are often large and well beyond the ability of most leasing companies.

- Leasing companies need intensive and focused marketing efforts to attract potential LBOs. The LBO lessor will want to target one or more market segments that match its investment objectives and the risk-reward characteristics it is willing to assume.

CHAPTER SUMMARY

This chapter explains project financing and leasing as special financing arrangements. You learned how to incorporate the impact of financing decisions into investment analysis using the adjusted present value, weighted cost of capital, and equity residual methods. The chapter covers corporate expansion through mergers, acquisitions, and leveraged buyouts. You learned that advantages such as operating and financial synergies, strategic and tax considerations, market power, and the desire to obtain management expertise may be motives for mergers. The basic analytical tools and decision rules of capital budgeting are modified and applied to evaluate these investment decisions.

Key Terms

acquisition,   page 373

adjusted present value (APV) method,   page 339

anti-takeover measure,   page 381

capital (or financial) lease,   page 359

cash flow guarantee arrangement,   page 337

congeneric (or product-extension) merger,   page 375

conglomerate merger,   page 375

direct lease,   page 360

equity residual method,   page 353

equivalent loan,   page 362

flotation costs,   page 341

friendly takeover,   page 381

horizontal merger,   page 374

hostile takeover,   page 381

lease,   page 358

lessee,   page 358

lessor,   page 358

leveraged buyout (LBO),   page 390

leveraged lease,   page 360

merger or statutory amalgamation,   page 373

net value to leasing (NVL) method,   page 363

operating lease,   page 358

project financing,   page 335

purchase arrangement,   page 336

sale and leaseback arrangement,   page 360

service lease,   page 359

vertical merger,   page 375

weighted average cost of capital (WACC) method,   page 348

Important Equations

Adjusted present value

$$\text{APV} = \begin{array}{c}\text{base-case}\\ \text{NPV}\end{array} + \begin{array}{c}\text{present value of the cash flows}\\ \text{associated with project financing}\end{array}$$

$$= \text{NPV}_B + \text{ITS} - \text{FCNS} + \text{TSFC} + \text{ITCS} - \text{IBC} + \text{OFRE}$$

(Equation 6-1)

where

APV = adjusted present value
NPV_B = base-case NPV
ITS = present value of interest tax shield
FCNS = present value of flotation costs of new securities
TSFC = present value of tax shield on flotation cost amortization
ITCS = present value of financing-related investment tax credits and subsidies
IBC = present value of the incremental bankruptcy costs
OFRE = present value of other financing-related effects

Present value of interest tax shields

$$\text{ITS} = \frac{T \times \text{IP}_1}{1 + k_D} + \cdots + \frac{T \times \text{IP}_i}{(1 + k_D)^i} + \frac{T \times \text{IP}_{i+1}}{(1 + k_D)^{i+1}}$$

$$+ \cdots + \frac{T \times \text{IP}_n}{(1 + k_D)^n}$$

(Equation 6-2)

where

ITS = present value of the interest tax shield
IP_i = interest payment in period i, where $i = 1, \ldots, n$
T = corporate tax rate
k_D = after-tax required rate of return on the firm's debt
n = number of periods over which the interest payments are made, which may be less than the useful life of the project

Present value of the tax shields on flotation costs

$$\text{TSFC} = \frac{T \times \text{FCA}_1}{1 + k_D} + \cdots + \frac{T \times \text{FCA}_i}{(1 + k_D)^i} + \frac{T \times \text{FCA}_{i+1}}{(1 + k_D)^{i+1}}$$

$$+ \cdots + \frac{T \times \text{FCA}_n}{(1 + k_D)^n}$$

(Equation 6-3)

where

TSFC = present value of the tax shield on flotation cost amortization
FCA_i = flotation cost amortization in period i, where $i = 1, \ldots, n$
T = corporate tax rate
k_D = after-tax required rate of return on the firm's debt
n = number of periods over which the flotation costs are amortized (five years or the maturity of the securities, whichever is less)

Present value of the after-tax bankruptcy costs

$$\text{PV(BC)} = \text{probability of financial distress} \times (1 - T) \times \text{BC} \quad \textbf{(Equation 6-4)}$$

where
    BC = bankruptcy costs

Incremental present value of bankruptcy costs

$$\text{IBC} = \text{PV(BC)}_D - \text{PV(BC)}_E \qquad \textbf{(Equation 6-5)}$$

where
        IBC = incremental present value of bankruptcy
   PV(BC)_D = present value of bankruptcy costs under debt financing
   PV(BC)_E = present value of bankruptcy costs under equity financing
    PV(BC) = probability of financial distress $\times$ $(1 - T)$ $\times$ bankruptcy costs

Value of the levered firm

$$V_L = V_U + T_C D \qquad \textbf{(Equation 6-6)}$$

where
   V_L = levered firm's value
   V_U = unlevered firm's value
   T_C = corporate tax rate
   D = amount of debt

Present value of interest tax shields

$$\text{ITS} = \frac{k_D \times D \times T_C}{k_D} = T_C \times D \qquad \textbf{(Equation 6-7)}$$

Net present value of a project

    NPV = present value of the after-tax cash flows from operations
            + present value of the salvage price
            + present value of the investment tax credits and subsidies
            − present value of the after-tax flotation costs
            − initial outlays   **(Equation 6-8)**

Weighted average cost of capital

$$k_L = \left(\frac{D}{V}\right) k_B (1 - T_C) + \left(\frac{E}{V}\right) k_E \qquad \textbf{(Equation 6-9)}$$

where
   k_L = weighted average cost of capital
   E = market value of the firm's common equity
   D = market value of the firm's debt
   V = total market value of the firm, which equals debt plus equity
   T_C = corporate tax rate
   k_B = before-tax cost of debt
   k_E = cost of common equity

Beta of a levered firm

$$\beta_L = \beta_U + (1 - T)(D/E)\beta_U \qquad \textbf{(Equation 6-10)}$$

where
   β_L = levered firm's beta

β_U = unlevered firm's beta

T = corporate tax rate

D = market value of the firm's debt

E = market value of the firm's equity

Net present value of a project using the equity residual method

$$NPV_{ER} = \sum_{i=1}^{n} \frac{[(RNV_i - CCA_i - IP_i) \times (1 - T) + CCA_i] - DP_i}{(1 + k_E)^i} - C_0 + D$$

+ present value of the salvage price

+ present value of the investment tax credits and subsidies

− present value of the flotation costs **(Equation 6-11)**

where

NPV_{ER} = net present value of the project (equity residual method)

RNV_i = revenues minus variable costs during period i

CCA_i = amount of capital cost allowance in period i

IP_i = interest payment in period i

DP_i = debt principal payments in period i

D = initial proceeds from the debt issue

C_0 = initial investment outlays

k_E = cost of equity

Equivalent loan amount

Equivalent loan = PV(after-tax lease payments)

− PV(incremental difference in after-tax operating costs or other costs between the borrowing and leasing alternatives)

+ PV(CCA tax shields)

+ PV(salvage value)

+ PV(investment tax credits under purchase option) **(Equation 6-12)**

Present value of CCA tax shields

$$PV(\text{CCA tax shields}) = \left[\frac{CdT}{2(d + r)} \right]\left[\frac{2 + r}{1 + r} \right]$$

$$- \left[\frac{S_n}{(1 + k_L)^n} \right]\left[\frac{dT}{(d + r)} \right] \quad \textbf{(Equation 6-13)}$$

where

C = initial undepreciated capital cost of the asset

d = CCA rate of the class to which the asset belongs

T = corporate tax rate

S_n = salvage value of the asset at the end of year n

r = after-tax interest rate on debt

k_L = weighted average cost of capital

Net value to leasing

NVL = initial investment outlay − equivalent loan **(Equation 6-14)**

Present value of savings in operating costs because of leasing

$$PV(\Delta OC) = \frac{(1 - T)\Delta OC_i}{1 + r} + \frac{(1 - T)\Delta OC_{i+1}}{(1 + r)^{i+1}} + \dots + \frac{(1 - T)\Delta OC_n}{(1 + r)^n}$$

(Equation 6-15)

where

ΔOC_i = savings in operating costs in period i because of leasing,
where $i = 1,\dots,n$

Present value of perpetual tax shields

$$PVTS = \left[\frac{C \times d \times T}{2(d + r)}\right]\left[\frac{2 + r}{1 + r}\right]$$ **(Equation 6-16)**

Present value of tax shield loss on salvage value

$$PVTSL_n = \frac{S_n}{(1 + k_L)^n} \times \frac{dT}{(d + r)}$$ **(Equation 6-17)**

where

$PVTS$ = present value of the perpetual tax shield
$PVTSL_n$ = present value of the tax shield loss
C = capital cost paid to acquire the asset less the investment tax credit
d = CCA rate
S_n = salvage value in year n
r = after-tax interest rate on debt
k_L = weighted average cost of capital

Times earnings per share paid

$$\text{Times earnings per share paid} = \frac{\text{purchase price per share}}{\text{fully diluted earnings per share, excluding non-recurring items}}$$ **(Equation 6-18)**

Times cash flow paid

$$\text{Times cash flow paid} = \frac{\text{purchase price per share}}{\text{fully diluted cash flows per share, excluding non-recurring items}}$$ **(Equation 6-19)**

Times book value paid

$$\text{Times book value paid} = \frac{\text{purchase price per share}}{\text{book value per share}}$$ **(Equation 6-20)**

Premium paid for a merger

$$\text{Premium paid} = \frac{\text{purchase price} - \text{market price before merger}}{\text{market price before merger}}$$ **(Equation 6-21)**

Times replacement cost paid

$$\text{Times replacement cost paid} = \frac{\text{purchase price of all shares}}{\text{net replacement cost of assets}}$$ **(Equation 6-22)**

where

net replacement cost of assets = replacement cost of assets less value of liabilities

Web Links

AllBusiness.com Types of Leases

- http://www.allbusiness.com/3103-1.html Provides a brief overview of the different types of leases, tax implications, and other tips and information on finding leasing providers and negotiating or ending a lease. Allbusiness.com also offers articles, forms, directories, and other information for small business professionals.

Harvard Business Online Teaching Resources

- http://www.hbsp.harvard.edu Although this is a commercial site with much of the information requiring a password to access, there are many articles, videocasts, and other commentary freely available to the public.

Investopedia

- http://www.investopedia.com/ Investopedia contains free links to definitions, articles, and tutorials on the three finance methods as well as many of the other subjects covered in this chapter.

Institute of Mergers, Acquisitions, and Alliances (MANDA)

- http://www.manda-institute.org MANDA is an educational and research body that promotes the use and benefits of mergers and acquisitions (M&A). Their Web site offers links to articles, publications, research, and topical discussions in the M&A field.

Strategis Lease or Buy Calculator

- http://strategis.ic.gc.ca/epic/site/oca-bc.nsf/en/ca01851e.html Produced by Industry Canada, Strategis is a consumer and business website that provides tools, statistics, and information for Canadians to build a strong economy. This link is for a Lease or Buy Calculator specifically for financing vehicles.

Self-Test Questions

Qualitative Questions

Answer each of the following questions in point form:

1. What are the various project financing arrangements?
2. How is the base-case NPV calculated for a project?
3. How are the finance-related benefits and costs calculated for the adjusted present value approach to project evaluation?
4. What are the similarities between leasing and debt financing?
5. What are the differences between leasing and borrowing to buy?
6. How are decisions to lease assets analyzed?
7. What are the advantages common to operating and capital leases?
8. In what way are financial and operating economies of scale valid motives for mergers and acquisitions?
9. How is an offer price for the shares of a merger target estimated through comparison with previous merger cases?

10. How does acquisition occur through leveraged buyouts and what are the likely results?

11. What are the financing arrangements associated with LBOs?

Qualitative Multiple Choice Questions

1. Which of the following firms would be a good target for a leveraged buyout (LBO)?
    i) A firm that uses well-known, mature production technology
    ii) A firm that is heavily in debt and has difficulty meeting payment obligations
    iii) A firm that is in a new and specialized business
    iv) A firm whose assets are mostly intangible

2. Which of the following statements about different methods of analyzing investment projects is true?
    i) The main disadvantage of the APV method is that it discounts the cash flows that will be used to pay debt holders at the rate required on the unlevered firm's equity.
    ii) The WACC method is effective in evaluating projects for which the capital structure is significantly different from the firm's overall structure.
    iii) The equity residual method is effective when debt has special provisions that need to be considered in the analysis.
    iv) The APV method requires that the capital structure be constant over time.

3. Which of the following statements *best* describes an advantage or disadvantage of a vertical merger?
    i) Vertical mergers are attractive if the activity is complex and difficult to define under conventional legal contracts.
    ii) Vertical mergers are more attractive if economies of scale in the intermediate activity are large and the volume of the intermediate output required by the company is small.
    iii) Vertical mergers are more attractive when overhead costs are higher.
    iv) Vertical mergers are more attractive if there are costs associated with entering a new and possibly unfamiliar business.

4. Which of the following statements is true about the weighted average cost of capital method (WACC) of capital budgeting?
    i) The WACC method is the most difficult to implement.
    ii) The WACC method is effective in evaluating projects for which the capital structure is significantly different from the firm's overall capital structure.
    iii) The WACC method assumes that the debt-to-equity ratio will be constant over time.
    iv) The WACC method is particularly useful when project risk differs from the firm's overall risk.

5. What can the merger between two beer companies, Adolph Coors Co. and Molson Inc., be classified as?
    i) A horizontal merger
    ii) A vertical merger
    iii) A congeneric merger
    iv) A conglomerate merger

6. Which of the following is *least* likely to produce a synergy effect?
    i) Operating economies of scale and/or scope
    ii) Market power and control

iii) Increase in management capabilities

iv) Diversification

7. Which of the following statements correctly describes the main features of an operating lease?

    i) The lessee pays property taxes and insurance on the asset.

    ii) The term of the agreement is the useful life of the asset.

    iii) Some leases require the lessor to handle all maintenance and servicing.

    iv) The lessee has no recourse in returning the equipment to the lessor if it becomes obsolete or is no longer needed.

8. Which of the following statements correctly describes the general benefits of leasing?

    i) Operating leases enable the lessor to claim the investment tax credits and tax deductions associated with ownership.

    ii) Leasing is always cheaper than borrowing and buying because the lessee can claim the entire lease payments as expenses.

    iii) Lessees can provide certain types of leased equipment as security for mortgages.

    iv) Leasing provides similar benefits regardless of whether the lease is classified as operating or capital.

9. Anti-takeover measures are designed to deter potential bidders from attempting a hostile takeover. Which of the following is a valid anti-takeover measure?

    i) Creating a class of shares with superior voting powers, such as ten votes per share

    ii) Selling a block of shares to the employer-sponsored employee benefit plan, which gives bondholders the power to vote the shares of the plan

    iii) Changing the company's charter to require equal voting rights per share for all shareholders, regardless of the number of shares they hold

    iv) Structuring the terms of the company's directors so that the terms of all directors will expire once a bidder owns a controlling block of shares

Quantitative Multiple Choice Questions

Use the following information to answer Questions 1 and 2:

A company is assessing the NPV of a potential leasing arrangement, to determine whether to lease or purchase an asset. If the company proceeds with a lease arrangement, the lease requires payments of $70,000 per year for 5 years to be paid at the beginning of each year. The tax shield due to the lease payment would occur at the end of each year. The weighted average cost of capital for the asset purchase is 15%. If purchased, the asset would be financed with a 6% bank loan. The corporate tax rate is 35%.

1. What is the appropriate discount rate to use when calculating the present value of the lease costs?

    i) 3.9%

    ii) 6.0%

    iii) 9.75%

    iv) 15%

2. Assuming a discount rate of 15%, what is the equation for calculating the present value of the lease costs?

    i) $PV = \$70,000 \times (1 - 0.35) \times PVIFA_{(15\%,\ 5\ years)}$

    ii) $PV = \$70,000 \times [PVIFA_{(15\%,\ 5\ years)} - 1] - \$70,000(0.35) \times PVIFA_{(15\%,\ 5\ years)}$

    iii) $PV = \$70,000 \times [1 + PVIFA_{(15\%,\ 5\ years)}] - \$70,000(0.35) \times PVIFA_{(15\%,\ 5\ years)}$

    iv) $PV = \$70,000 \times [1 + PVIFA_{(15\%,\ 4\ years)}] - \$70,000(0.35) \times PVIFA_{(15\%,\ 5\ years)}$

3. A company is considering investing in a new project in its existing line of business, which it will finance with 33% debt and 67% equity. The usual financing mix for this firm is 50% debt and 50% equity, and the firm has an equity beta of 1.35 and a debt beta of zero. The risk-free rate of interest is 4% and the expected return on the market portfolio is 11%. What rate of return should the firm require on this new project if the tax rate of the firm is 40%?

   i) 7.7%

   ii) 9.3%

   iii) 11.7%

   iv) 17%

Quantitative Problems

Problem 1

Delta Company is evaluating an investment project that has several financing side effects. The project involves establishing a facility to assemble children's toys in a sparsely populated area of northern Ontario, in response to a mandate of the federal government to support employment in the region. The facility has an expected useful life of 15 years. It would require an initial investment of $10,000,000. Of this amount, $8,500,000 would be for equipment with a 20% CCA rate and the remainder of the purchase price would be for the land and building. Assume no CCA is allowed for the land or for this building. There is no salvage value for the equipment, but the land and building can be sold to the federal government for a guaranteed price of $1,500,000 in 15 years. The CCA class would remain open after the 15-year period.

Annual revenues are expected to be $4,000,000 and annual variable costs, if the facility is financed with retained earnings, are estimated at $2,500,000. In order to provide incentives to firms, the federal government is offering a subsidy for operating costs, to a maximum of $250,000 per year for 15 years. The $250,000 represents before-tax savings and these are taxable. The company has a tax rate of 40% and is currently financed with all equity. The required return on shareholders' equity is now 15%.

Suppose that Delta would finance this investment with $5,000,000 of new debt with an interest cost of 6% per annum and $5,000,000 of newly issued shares. Flotation costs for both would total $350,000. These costs can be amortized over a 5-year period on a straight-line basis. The debt would be issued for a 15-year term and would pay annual interest only, with all principal to be repaid at maturity.

Required

a) Calculate the adjusted present value (APV) of this investment proposal. Determine whether the proposal should be accepted, and briefly explain why or why not.

b) Explain how the tax deductibility of interest is accounted for under each of the APV method and the WACC method of capital budgeting.

Problem 2

SIGMA Inc. manufactures small household appliances and employs many disabled workers in its assembly operation. A proposal to expand plant capacity will cost $600,000 for new equipment, including specialized facilities to accommodate special needs of the workforce. If the expansion is undertaken, operating income will increase by $120,000 per year for the 7-year life of the new equipment.

The provincial government will provide a low-interest loan for the expansion costs. The loan will be at a reduced rate of 5%, which is below the regular 7.5% borrowing rate for firms with the characteristics of SIGMA. The loan will be for a 7-year term, with annual interest payments at end of year and the principal amount due on maturity. SIGMA has a corporate tax rate of 35%. SIGMA is now entirely equity financed. If the expansion proposal is undertaken, SIGMA will then be financed 25% with debt and 75% with equity. The new equipment has a 20% CCA rate and no expected salvage value.

Required

a) Calculate the cost of equity financing for SIGMA, with and without the expansion of the plant. Assume that the unlevered beta of SIGMA is 1.1, the expected return on the market is 10%, and the risk-free rate of interest is 6%.

b) Calculate the weighted average cost of capital for SIGMA, both with and without the effects of the expansion proposal. Identify which of the weighted average costs of capital is lower, and explain why.

c) State three reasons to explain why the adjusted present value (APV) method would be more appropriate for evaluation of this project than the net present value (NPV) method would be.

d) Calculate the base-case NPV for the expansion proposal.

e) Should SIGMA undertake the expansion proposal? Support your answer using the adjusted present value method. Show all calculations.

Problem 3

EXAM

Halifax Corp. is evaluating an investment proposal with the characteristics outlined below. The project will be financed initially with 75% debt, but as cash flows are received, debt will be reduced and ultimately eliminated. The average levered cost of equity over the entire 4-year project life is estimated at 16%. The weighted average cost of capital for Halifax projects financed in the regular pattern is 11%, and debt can be obtained at a per annum rate of 6%. The debt principal will be repaid in 4 equal annual payments, with interest charged each year on the outstanding balance. The equity investment will be made from retained earnings, so no new shares need to be issued.

Halifax Corp. Investment Proposal	
Initial investment	$15,000,000
Annual revenues from project	7,000,000
Annual variable costs	1,220,000
Salvage value	2,500,000
CCA rate of plant and equipment	30%
Tax rate	50%

Required

Evaluate this investment proposal using the equity residual method, and advise Halifax Corp. on whether to undertake the project.

Problem 4

NOT EXAM

LaSalle Corp. wants to acquire a $200,000 machine. LaSalle has a 40% marginal tax rate. If purchased, the machine would be a Class 10 asset with a CCA rate of 30%. The salvage value is expected to be $20,000 at the end of 10 years. To finance the purchase, LaSalle could borrow at an annual pre-tax interest rate of 10% over a period of 10 years. LaSalle would also incur annual maintenance expenses of $1,000. These expenses will not be incurred if the machine is leased. The lease rate would be $28,000 per year for 10 years, payable at the beginning of each year. LaSalle's weighted-average cost of capital is 12%.

Required

a) What alternative, leasing or buying, should be chosen, according to the equivalent loan amount approach? Explain.

b) Determine the pre-tax lease payment that will make LaSalle indifferent between leasing and buying.

Problem 5 HW

Sudbury Corp.'s existing project portfolio, which is worth $700,000, has an expected IRR of 10% and a standard deviation of 2%. The company is considering adding a new project that has an expected IRR of 11% and a standard deviation of 3%. The new project costs $200,000. The correlation coefficient between returns from the portfolio and the new project is 0.9. A comparable firm, which is in the same business line as the new project, has a firm beta of 1.2 and a 50%–50% debt–equity ratio. This firm is taxed at a 40% corporate tax rate. Sudbury is going to finance the new project with 30% debt and 70% equity. It has a 30% corporate tax rate. The expected return on Canadian Treasury bills is 5%. The TSX stock market index is expected to increase by 10% in the coming year.

Required

Prepare a brief report to recommend whether to accept the new project. Be sure to discuss how to use a risk-adjusted discount rate to evaluate a project on its own merits and whether to consider the relationship between a portfolio and an individual project when evaluating a new project.

Cases

Case 1: Victoria Corp.

Victoria Corp. requires new equipment for its food processing division, to cut vegetables prior to canning. Two alternative brands of equipment are being considered. Brand X equipment is highly specialized and can only perform the cutting process that Victoria Corp. currently requires. It is in a CCA class with a 20% CCA rate. Brand Y equipment can be used for a variety of processes and is primarily used by firms for a process that Victoria Corp. does not perform in its manufacturing plant. The Brand Y equipment is in a different CCA class with a 25% CCA rate. Victoria Corp. has a tax rate of 45%.

Victoria Corp. has many assets in the class that the Brand X equipment belongs in. The pool balance is always positive, and assets remain in the pool after the Brand X equipment is salvaged. However, Victoria Corp. has no other assets in the class that the Brand Y equipment belongs in and none will be acquired in the coming 4 years.

Output from Brands X and Y equipment is of the same quality and quantity, so the differences between the two choices relate to their costs. These are described in Case Exhibit 6-1.

Case Exhibit 6-1
Equipment Costs for Brands X And Y
(All Figures in Thousands)

	Brand X	Brand Y
Original investment cost	$700	$550
Expected useful life	4 years	4 years
Annual operating costs	$20	$40
Annual maintenance costs	$15	$12
Salvage value	$100	$80

Required

a) Using a discount rate of 12%, calculate and compare the present value of after-tax costs for Brand X and Brand Y equipment. Which brand of equipment should Victoria select?

b) Suppose that the manufacturer of the Brand Y equipment offers its customers a leasing alternative. Instead of purchasing the equipment, Victoria Corp. can lease it for 4 years, paying $347,000 at the start of each year. This amount includes annual maintenance costs, but not annual operating costs. Note when calculating present values that the tax shields on both the lease payments and the operating costs occur at the end of each year and that the operating costs occur at the end of each year, but the lease payments are made at the start of each year. Assume no leasing alternative exists for the Brand X equipment. Assess this opportunity to lease the Brand Y equipment, continuing to use a 12% discount rate. Does it change your decision about which brand to acquire?

Case 2: Saskatoon Industries

Saskatoon Industries has decided to replace a major piece of industrial equipment and must now decide how to finance the acquisition. The equipment costs $690,000 to purchase and install and is expected to have a useful life of 5 years, after which it will be sold on the open market and is expected to have a salvage value of $200,000. Saskatoon has a required return on equity of 14% and a large number of outstanding common shares held by many small investors. Saskatoon is financed 50% with debt and 50% with equity.

The new equipment will be one of a large group of assets with a CCA rate of 20%. As this equipment is involved in the firm's main line of business, the asset class is expected to always contain assets and to have a positive balance.

One financing alternative is a bank loan at the rate of 7% per annum, which is consistent with current debt. Another alternative is to lease the equipment for $200,000 per year for 5 years with the payments at the start of each year. The payments are tax deductible and it is assumed that the tax shields on the lease payments will occur at the end of each year rather than at the start. The corporate tax rate is 40%. If the company leases the asset, it will not be responsible for maintenance and insurance costs of $40,000 per annum due at year end, but it will have the same basic operating costs as if it had purchased the equipment. If Saskatoon purchases the equipment, it will be entitled to an investment tax credit of 5% of the purchase price.

Required

a) Calculate the weighted-average cost of capital of Saskatoon. Assume that the capital structure weights are always 50/50, as stated above, regardless of how this new asset is financed.

b) Identify which discount rate is appropriate in a lease-versus-purchase decision. If more than one discount rate will be used in the analysis, identify when each is appropriate and explain why.

c) Calculate the net value to leasing this piece of equipment; specifically, calculate and identify the initial investment outlay and the equivalent loan in your analysis.

d) Summarize your analysis and make a recommendation on how this firm should finance its equipment acquisition.

Case 3: East Travel Ltd.

East Travel Ltd. (ET), based in Canada, is one of the world's largest integrated tourism companies. ET specializes in the organization, marketing, and distribution of holiday travel packages. With the return of the tourism market to its former levels from the industry downturn after September 11, 2001, ET's revenues increased by 10% while its net income jumped by 15%. As a result, cash is accumulating. The public company is considering how to spend this large amount of cash. One alternative is to pay cash dividends to the shareholders. Another is to grow the business by setting up new affiliates or by purchasing an existing company. ET has identified a company to purchase: West Travel Ltd. (WT). While ET serves customers in eastern Canada and organizes tours within Canada and to Europe, WT serves clients in western Canada and focuses on tours to east Asia. ET's financial staff identified several previous mergers which took place within this industry in the past five years and prepared Case Exhibits 6-2 and 6-3 to assist in estimating an offer price for WT shares.

Case Exhibit 6-2
Key Ratios from Previous Mergers

Merger Case	C1	C2	C3	C4
Premium paid	20.00%	30.00%	35.00%	45.00%
Times earnings paid	9.50	20.00	15.00	12.00
Times cash flow paid	10.50	7.50	12.50	11.00
Times book value paid	3.00	1.95	2.50	2.75
Times replacement cost paid	1.35	1.55	2.00	1.85

Case Exhibit 6-3
Key Income Statement and Balance Sheet Items of WT

Item Considered	Level of WT Item
Share price	$35
Earnings per share	$ 5
Cash flow per share	$ 6
Book value per share	$25
Replacement cost per share	$30

Required

a) ET declares that a cash dividend of $1.00 per share will be paid on January 31, 2007 to shareholders of record at the close of business on January 19, 2007. Which date is the last day for Jane, a potential buyer, to purchase ET shares in order to receive the declared cash dividend payment?

b) State three factors that ET should consider when establishing its dividend policy.

c) To distribute cash to shareholders, which alternative to cash dividends is the most appropriate? Explain briefly from the perspectives of both the company and its shareholders.

d) What type of merger would the ET-WT merger be an example of?

e) State two reasons for ET wanting to merge its business operations with WT.

f) Calculate a minimum and a maximum share price for each ratio and determine a range of share prices that may be paid by ET for WT, excluding all other prices that would be considered extreme based on previous mergers.

Case 4: Asian Auto Co.

Asian Auto Co. (AA) is an Asia-based auto maker. It has been exporting its vehicles to North America for several years. With a significant gain in the market share at the expense of its competitors, it has now decided to establish an assembly plant in North America. The new plant will produce and sell 100,000 vehicles per year at an average selling price of $30,000 per vehicle in the North American market.

There are two alternative locations available: one in the United States and another in southern Ontario. The required equipment costs $800 million and has a useful life of 10 years and no salvage value for both locations. Assume that AA will adopt the same Canadian CCA system for both locations and that the CCA rate for the equipment is 20%. AA could use a building that it already owns for the new plant in the U.S. location, but would have to invest an additional $200 million to build the new plant in the southern Ontario location. The CCA rate for the building is 4%.

The after-tax operating profit margin (not including tax savings from CCA) is 6% for the U.S. location, and 6.6% for the Ontario location because the Canadian public health-care system would eliminate AA's health-care costs for its employees.

AA will be in the 40% tax bracket. The risk-free interest rate is 4% and the market risk premium is 5%. Currently, AA has a debt ratio of 40% and a before-tax interest rate of 6%. AA plans to finance the project with equity capital that has the same risk as the firm as a whole. The average debt ratio, tax rate, and beta for the auto industry are 50%, 50%, and 1.2857, respectively.

To attract AA to choose the Ontario location, both the Canadian federal and Ontario provincial governments have promised to provide some financial aid. The federal government offers a 10-year, 4% loan in the amount of $100 million, while the Ontario government will subsidize before-tax operating costs at $25 million per year for 5 years to help cover research and employee training costs.

Required

Evaluate the investment opportunity in the two locations and present your recommendation on which location to build the new plant.

a) Briefly explain the adjusted present value (APV) method, the weighted average cost of capital method, and the equity residual method. Which method is the most appropriate to use in this case?

b) **i)** What is the discount rate used to calculate the base-case NPV?

  ii) What is the initial investment for the U.S. location and for the Ontario location?

  iii) What is the present value of the after-tax operating cash flows for the U.S. location and for the Ontario location?

  iv) What is the present value of the CCA tax shields over the 10 years of the new plant's life for the U.S. location and for the Ontario location?

  v) What is the net present value of the plant for the U.S. location and for the Ontario location, before the governments provide any financial incentive?

  vi) Without government financial aid, which location should AA choose, based on the project's NPV?

c) **i)** What is the present value of the federal government's low-interest loan subsidy?

  ii) What is the present value of the operating cost subsidies provided by the Ontario government?

  iii) With government financial aid, which location should AA choose?

Chapter 7
Treasury-Risk Management

CHAPTER OVERVIEW

This chapter deals with a number of interrelated aspects of treasury risk. Treasury risk includes interest-rate risk, foreign-exchange risk, and commodity-price risk.

Section 7.1 focuses on the task of identifying the type of risk, an important task for the treasury-risk manager because the type of risk largely determines the appropriate risk management strategy. The fundamental concerns are whether the risk concerns interest rates, foreign exchange, or commodity prices. However, you also must determine whether an increase or a decrease in the given risk factor is of concern.

In Section 7.2, you study the different ways that risk exposure can be measured. Measuring risk is a difficult but necessary task for the treasury-risk manager. The magnitude of the risk a firm faces determines whether or not management should invest resources to manage the risk.

In Section 7.3, you extend the concepts from Section 7.2. This section uses the measurement techniques as a foundation for some basic risk management techniques. More complicated techniques that involve financial derivatives will be explored in Chapters 8 and 9. The essential element of risk management at this level is matching assets and liabilities.

A summary of the general risk management approaches that firms may take is covered in Section 7.4. Arguments are presented to support the view that shareholders as well as other stakeholders benefit from a well-planned risk management strategy.

Section 7.5 extends the study of risk to the arena of international trade, which involves risks other than foreign-exchange risk. This section provides an analysis of these other risks and the various international trade financing arrangements that can be used in their management. The financing instruments reviewed are letters of credit, bankers' acceptances, factoring, and forfeiting. A brief explanation of the risk management services provided by the Export Development Corporation is included.

An understanding of risk and risk management will give you a good basis for understanding derivative securities, which will be covered in Chapters 8 and 9.

Learning Objectives

After completing this chapter, you will be able to:

- Define and distinguish between examples of interest-rate risk: single-transaction risk, income risk, and capital risk.

- Define and explain foreign-exchange risk and commodity-price risk.

- Illustrate the concepts of duration and volatility to measure risk exposure.

- Explain the micro approach to measuring risk exposure.

- Explain the macro approach (gap analysis and sensitivity analysis) to measuring risk exposure.

- Identify and explain the basics of managing risk using risk measurement methods.

- Define and distinguish among the four approaches to risk management.

- Identify and explain the various risks of international trade and the financing instruments that may be used to manage these risks.

This knowledge will provide you with the professional skills to:

- Identify and analyze risk factors with respect to the treasury management function.

- Identify financial-risk strategy and challenges in the organization's environment.

- Assess or define a financial-risk management strategy.

- Implement and advise on measures to mitigate risk as part of the treasury management function.

- Advise on financing to meet the organization's goals.

- Advise on business decisions in the context of larger economic and geopolitical conditions, specifically analyzing international opportunities and their attendant risks.

HOW THIS CHAPTER RELATES TO OTHER CHAPTERS IN THIS BOOK

In this chapter, we take an in-depth look at how treasury risk should be measured and how it affects the market value of a firm's assets, liabilities, and shares. Recall that in Chapter 1, we concluded that management's primary concern should be maximizing the price of the firm's common shares. Risk, indeed, has a profound impact on stabilizing profits or share value.

Treasury risk is one of the toughest and potentially most damaging forms of risk that all businesses face. Thus, financial managers today focus heavily on the *management of risk*—attempting to control their exposure to loss caused by changes in interest rates, foreign exchange rates, and commodity prices. Successful risk management requires effective tools that provide financial managers with the weapons they need to achieve their corporation's goals. In this chapter, several of the most important risk management tools are highlighted and discussed. Suffice it to say, a good understanding of risk and risk management provides a solid basis for understanding derivative securities, another interesting and highly sophisticated financial topic, which will be introduced in Chapters 8 and 9.

7.1 TYPES OF TREASURY RISK

Risk is the fluctuation in a firm's profits or in the market value of its assets, liabilities, or shares. **Treasury risk** includes risks that arise from changes in interest rates, foreign exchange rates, or commodity prices. These risks are normally managed by the treasury department of an organization. Although other types of financial risk may impact treasury, the minicases in this section illustrate the three major types of treasury risk and their possible effects on a firm.

Interest-Rate Risk

Interest-rate risk is the fluctuation in a firm's income or expenses or in the market value of its assets, liabilities, or shares that results from changes in interest rates. Interest-rate risk can affect a single transaction or the firm's entire portfolio of assets and liabilities.

Interest-rate risk also arises from changes in the shape of the yield curve. The **yield curve** is the graphical relationship among interest rates for different maturities. Changes in the relationship between short- and long-term interest rates, or between different medium-term rates, for example, can result in unexpected gains or losses.

Note that the information used in Minicase 7-1 is also used as the basis of Minicases 8-7 and 8-8.

MINICASE 7-1 INVESTOR'S RISK FROM A DROP IN RATES—SINGLE-TRANSACTION RISK

Today is March 1. Lora is reviewing her cash forecast for the next few months. Her records show that a customer is expected to pay $5 million on March 29. She is planning to use this money to pay for recently purchased equipment to be delivered in May and paid for by May 29. She is planning to invest the $5 million in the money market. Usually, she buys Treasury bills to avoid default risk. Currently, 61-day Treasury bills are yielding 5.50%. At this rate, interest plus principal will exactly match the price and delivery charges of the equipment.

However, Lora's transaction is still subject to risk. Her expectation is that the rate will drop by 0.50% (or 50 basis points, because each basis point is 1/100th of a percent) to 5.00% by the time she receives the money. If it occurs, this drop will result in a cost of forgone interest income of approximately:

$$(0.005 \times \$5,000,000) \times 61 \div 365 = \$4,178.08$$

Interest plus principal will be short $4,178.08 of covering the cost of the equipment, and Lora will have to look for other sources to make up the shortfall. In addition, if rates drop, the firm will report lower income at the end of the quarter.

As Lora does not have the $5 million in hand, she is not in a position to take advantage of the higher interest rate now available (5.50%). Thus, if rates drop to 5.00%, the $4,178.08 in forgone interest will represent an opportunity loss.

Lora's risk is the probability of a decline in interest rates. However, whenever there is a possibility of loss, there is also a possibility of gain. Lora's income from the investment could be higher than the 5.50% current rate. For example, if by the time she receives the cash, the Treasury bill rate is 6.00%, Lora will have an opportunity gain of $4,178.08 instead of an opportunity loss. Although this upside risk is not a concern to investors, it cannot be isolated from downside risk and, therefore, any actions Lora takes to reduce risk may ultimately reduce potential gains as well as losses.

The rest of this chapter approaches risk from the position of a treasury manager who is concerned about managing risk of loss. This approach is taken to stress the practical applications of hedging.

Lora's case is a simple demonstration of potential interest-rate risk. Although the potential loss is minor for the given scenario, the majority of transactions in large corporations involve amounts greater than $5 million. Moreover, most market participants, such as large corporations, have many transactions per year, so that repeated losses can accumulate and adversely affect net income. Indeed, changes in interest rates can affect the entire portfolio of the firm's assets and liabilities and have a substantial impact on net income. Minicase 7-2 illustrates income risk.

MINICASE 7-2 INCOME RISK FROM CHANGES IN INTEREST RATES

PKG Inc. is a large food processing and packaging company with assets and liabilities as shown in Exhibit 7-1. Income from operations has been relatively stable, averaging $53 million per year. Given this stability, management has relied heavily on debt. Currently, PKG's debt to total assets ratio is about 60%. The firm's policy is to pay all earnings in dividends. Today is January 2, 20X2, and the company is considering alternatives for refinancing its long-term debt, which matures soon.

Exhibit 7-1
PKG Inc. Balance Sheet
December 31, 20X1 ($ Millions)

Assets		Liabilities	
Current assets		**Current liabilities**	
Cash and securities	$ 15.00	Accounts payable	$ 32.75
Accounts receivable	63.00	Accruals	4.25
Inventory	172.00	Short-term loans	52.00
	250.00		89.00
Capital assets		**Long-term liabilities**	
Equipment	135.00	Bonds	207.00
Plant	103.00		
Other assets	6.00	**Shareholders' equity**	$198.00
Total assets	$494.00	Total liabilities and shareholders' equity	$494.00

The company is relying on the recent drop in interest rates to boost return on equity. Savings will come in part from lower interest on short-term loans, where the rate is currently around 7.50%. Also, large savings are expected on the company's long-term debt.

Case Continued >

This portion of the debt currently pays 10.50% annual interest but will mature soon and will be refinanced at a lower rate. Management is predicting either stable or slightly rising rates over the next five years.

For this reason, management is inclined to raise the money by selling one-year securities and refunding yearly for the next five years. The company can raise one-year funds at 7.50%. Alternatively, selling five-year bonds at 9.50% can raise the same amount.

Exhibit 7-2 calculates return on equity over five years following a decision by PKG to sell five-year, fixed-rate bonds. This exhibit is prepared under the assumption that short-term rates will rise sharply after one year, contrary to management's forecast (interest rates are chosen arbitrarily to demonstrate income risk).

Exhibits 7-3 and 7-4 are prepared under the assumption that PKG will sell one-year securities and refund them yearly. Similarly to Exhibit 7-2, Exhibit 7-3 is prepared under the assumption that short-term rates will rise sharply after one year, contrary to management's forecast. Exhibit 7-4 is based on the assumption that interest rates will not rise as steeply. These exhibits show the impact on return on equity if rates rise after the first year following the decision.

A comparison of Exhibits 7-2 and 7-3 shows the risk PKG is taking if it chooses the one-year alternative over the five-year, fixed-rate bonds. Exhibit 7-2 shows that the five-year, fixed-rate alternative would enable the company to guarantee a relatively stable return on equity with an expected average over the next five years of 9.574%. This return is still slightly unstable because of the changes in the rates on the short-term portion of the debt.

Exhibit 7-2
PKG Inc. Proforma Income Statements
under a Five-Year, Fixed-Rate Loan ($ Millions)

Year ending December 31	20X1	20X2	20X3	20X4	20X5	20X6
Net operating profits	$53.0000	$53.0000	$53.0000	$53.0000	$53.0000	$53.0000
Interest expenses:						
Short-term rate	7.50%	7.50%	9.75%	10.75%	11.75%	12.75%
Short-term interest	3.9000	3.9000	5.0700	5.5900	6.1100	6.6300
Long-term rate	10.50%	9.50%	9.50%	9.50%	9.50%	9.50%
Long-term interest	21.7350	19.6650	19.6650	19.6650	19.6650	19.6650
Earnings before taxes	27.3650	29.4350	28.2650	27.7450	27.2250	26.7050
Taxes at 32%	8.7568	9.4192	9.0448	8.8784	8.7120	8.5456
Net income	$18.6082	$20.0158	$19.2202	$18.8666	$18.5130	$18.1594
Return on equity	9.40%	10.11%	9.71%	9.53%	9.35%	9.17%

Exhibit 7-3 demonstrates the impact of a steep rise in interest rates when the firm chooses to roll the debt yearly. The exhibit shows how return on equity fluctuates as the rate changes. In 20X2, shareholders would be rewarded by an 11.71% return, a rate substantially higher than the rate in 20X1. However, if interest rates rise sharply, the return on equity drops quickly to 7.04% in 20X6, when the short-term rate is 12.75%. The expected average return on equity is now 9.042% over the next five years.

Case Continued >

Exhibit 7-3
PKG Inc. Proforma Income Statements
under Steep Interest Rate Increases ($ Millions)

Year ending December 31	20X1	20X2	20X3	20X4	20X5	20X6
Net operating profits	$53.0000	$53.0000	$53.0000	$53.0000	$53.0000	$53.0000
Interest expenses:						
Short-term rate	7.50%	7.50%	9.75%	10.75%	11.75%	12.75%
Short-term interest	3.9000	3.9000	5.0700	5.5900	6.1100	6.6300
Long-term rate	10.50%	7.25%	9.50%	10.50%	11.50%	12.50%
Long-term interest	21.7350	15.0075	19.6650	21.7350	23.8050	25.8750
Earnings before taxes	27.3650	34.0925	28.2650	25.6750	23.0850	20.4950
Taxes at 32%	8.7568	10.9096	9.0448	8.2160	7.3872	6.5584
Net income	$18.6082	$23.1829	$19.2202	$17.4590	$15.6978	$13.9366
Return on equity	9.40%	11.71%	9.71%	8.82%	7.93%	7.04%

Exhibit 7-4
PKG Inc. Proforma Income Statements
under Moderate Interest Rate Increases ($ Millions)

Year ending December 31	20X1	20X2	20X3	20X4	20X5	20X6
Net operating profits	$53.0000	$53.0000	$53.0000	$53.0000	$53.0000	$53.0000
Interest expenses:						
Short-term rate	7.50%	7.50%	7.75%	8.00%	8.25%	8.50%
Short-term interest	3.9000	3.9000	4.0300	4.1600	4.2900	4.4200
Long-term rate	10.50%	7.25%	7.50%	7.75%	8.00%	8.25%
Long-term interest	21.7350	15.0075	15.5250	16.0425	16.5600	17.0775
Earnings before taxes	27.3650	34.0925	33.4450	32.7975	32.1500	31.5025
Taxes at 32%	8.7568	10.9096	10.7024	10.4952	10.2880	10.0808
Net income	$18.6082	$23.1829	$22.7426	$22.3023	$21.8620	$21.4217
Return on equity	9.40%	11.71%	11.49%	11.26%	11.04%	10.82%

Finally, Exhibit 7-4 shows the impact of a moderate increase in the one-year interest rate on the return on equity. In this scenario, the return on equity decreases from 11.71% in 20X2 to 10.82% in 20X6, with an expected average over the next five years of 11.264%. Notice that the short-term interest rates are much lower than the coupon interest rate of 9.50% required to sell five-year bonds. Clearly, choosing the short-term option exposes the firm to substantial risk. Yet, the company may be rewarded with higher return on equity. As suggested by Exhibit 7-3, however, the risk may be too great to accept. Changes in interest rates can lead to variations in net income beyond what may be tolerated by shareholders.

Changes in market factors, such as interest rates, impact both income (profitability) and the value of assets and liabilities. Some treasury managers may choose to focus primarily on **income risk**, the fluctuation in net income resulting from changes in interest rates. Others may prefer to focus on **capital risk**, the fluctuation in the market values of financial or other assets resulting from changes in interest rates. As the value of an asset is a direct function of the income expected from the asset, income risk and capital risk are related; reducing one reduces the other. For example, a borrower may focus on income risk because an increase in interest rates raises the cost of borrowing, whereas an investor might focus on capital risk. Minicase 7-3 demonstrates capital risk. Note that the information in this minicase also forms the basis of Minicases 7-6, 7-7, and 7-9.

MINICASE 7-3 CAPITAL RISK FROM CHANGES IN INTEREST RATES

Louise is an account manager at PNSN Inc., a Canadian investment company specializing in managing pension plans for small businesses. Louise has a large number of claims due in three years' time. The funds allocated to cover these liabilities have been invested in Government of Canada bonds, which are due to mature tomorrow. How should Louise manage the accumulated funds over the next three years to ensure that the claims can be paid?

One strategy is to invest the funds in three-month securities. As the securities mature, funds will be reinvested at the new prevailing rate at the time of reinvestment. Louise obtains the current market quotations shown in Exhibit 7-5 and realizes that the yield on three-month securities is the lowest in comparison with the yields on other maturities.

Exhibit 7-5
Current Annual Yields on Three-Month Treasury Bills and Government Bonds That Pay 9% Coupon Rates Semi-Annually

Maturity	3 months	1 year	2 years	3 years	4 years	5 years
Yield to maturity	4.50%	5.50%	6.50%	7.40%	8.20%	9.00%

A second strategy is for Louise to invest the coming proceeds in three-year Government of Canada bonds. By doing this, she will earn 7.40% to maturity, and the maturity date will match her requirement for funds. At 7.40%, she will earn more than the 4.50% rate for three-month securities. Economists are forecasting that the yield curve (Exhibit 7-5) will remain unchanged for some time.

A third strategy is to buy five-year bonds that are currently yielding 9.00% and selling at par value. The bonds can be sold in three years, and at that time they will have two years left to maturity. Assuming that the yield curve does not change, Exhibit 7-5 indicates that the yield on similar two-year bonds will then be around 6.50%. Given their *Case Continued >*

9.00% coupon yield, the bonds would be sold at a premium from purchase price, providing an overall return much higher than 9.00%.

The risk with the first strategy is that if interest rates remain stable or drop further, the return may be inadequate. On the other hand, if interest rates rise substantially, this strategy will have a high payoff, as higher reinvestment rates will make up for the early low yield.

The second strategy matches the maturity of the three-year bonds with Louise's cash flow requirement, meaning that she knows her return with certainty. Unless she has some unexpected reason to sell the three-year bonds early, she will earn 7.40% by holding them to maturity.

The third strategy of buying the five-year bonds in the hope of selling them after three years at higher prices is subject to capital risk. This risk arises from the possibility that rates may increase over the three-year period so that the required return on the two-year bonds in three years from today becomes higher than the coupon rate of 9.00%. In this case, Louise will have to sell the bonds at a discount from face value, resulting in a lower return.

Despite the risk, Louise decides to take the third alternative.

In practice, it is not possible to know beforehand which alternative is optimal. The choice depends on the decision maker's expectations and tolerance for risk. In this section, it is assumed that Louise took the third alternative so that her situation can be revisited in the next section (in Minicase 7-6) for illustrative purposes.

Louise's problem is a typical one faced by bond investors. The alternatives suggested are representative of a larger array of choices, with each strategy representing a different mix of risk and potential return. The investment strategy is defined by the risk created by possible changes in interest rates.

Foreign-Exchange Risk

Foreign-exchange risk occurs because fluctuations in the profit or share value of a firm may be caused by changes in the foreign exchange rate. International businesses face foreign-exchange risk because the values of transactions in different currencies vary with exchange rate fluctuations. Risk arises from uncertainty about the future exchange rate of a particular currency. Even firms that produce exclusively for the domestic market may face exchange-rate risk. For example, some of the firm's raw materials may be imported. In this case, if the foreign exchange rate of the Canadian dollar drops, the costs of the raw materials will be higher in Canadian dollars. Minicase 7-4 illustrates how profitability can be affected by foreign-exchange risk.

In general, a decline in the value of the domestic currency benefits exporters, whose products and services become relatively cheaper to international buyers, while an increase in the domestic currency's value makes exported goods and services relatively more expensive to foreign buyers. Similarly, a decline in the value of the domestic currency hurts importers, who have to pay for imported goods in other, more expensive currencies, while an increase in the value of the domestic currency benefits importers. In reality, a firm might be both an importer and an exporter, and relationships between economies and competitors can change independently of exchange rates.

MINICASE 7-4 TRANSACTION RISK FROM CHANGES IN THE FOREIGN EXCHANGE RATE

Roy has just signed a contract by which he agrees to deliver equipment worth US$5 million to a customer in the United States in one month. Three months after delivery, payment will be made in U.S. dollars. Roy is happy with this order because the timing of the cash inflow from the sale will match the date on which a large loan (in Canadian dollars) will be due. In fact, the amount of the expected U.S. dollar cash inflow will exactly match the amount needed to retire the loan if the exchange rate stays at its current level. At the time of writing, the U.S. dollar is trading at $1.0055 Canadian.

Question 1: What is the risk that Roy faces if the value of the Canadian dollar increases (U.S. dollar decreases) from US$1 = C $1.4600 to US$1 = C$1.4400?

Roy's risk is a rise in the value of the Canadian dollar. If the Canadian dollar rises to US$1 = C$1.44, the cash inflows will be C$7.2 million (US$5 million × 1.4400), leaving a shortfall of $100,000 ($5 million × 0.0200) to retire the loan. Roy will then have to look for other sources to obtain the $100,000 difference. Moreover, net income earned by the firm will be reduced by $100,000.

Question 2: What will happen if the value of the Canadian dollar drops (U.S. dollar increases) to US$1 = C$1.4800?

For this transaction, a drop in the value of the Canadian dollar will be advantageous because it will increase the value of the U.S. dollars receivable when converted to Canadian dollars. If the Canadian dollar drops to US$1 = C$1.4800, Roy will receive C$7.4 million (US$5 million × 1.4800). He will have an additional C$100,000 (US$5 million × 0.0200) cash inflow.

Question 3: How is Roy's risk different from the risk of an importer?

Because an importer buys products denominated in other currencies, an importer's risk is that the value of the Canadian dollar will drop. For example, consider an importer who is buying merchandise worth US$5 million. At the current exchange rate of 1.4600, this importer will have to pay C$7.3 million. If the value of the U.S. dollar rises to US$1 = C$1.4800, the cash required to pay for the merchandise will be C$7.4 million (US$5 million × 1.4800). The importer will have to pay an additional C$100,000 ($5 million × 0.0200) for the merchandise.

Commodity-Price Risk

Commodity-price risk is the fluctuation in the profit or market value of a firm's shares that results from changes in commodity prices. Firms face commodity-price risk because the values of transactions are sensitive to changes in the price of commodities needed in the production operations of the firm.

Firms that require a commodity in their production process face the risk of loss if commodity prices rise and those price increases cannot be passed along to the final consumer. Similarly, firms that produce a commodity or commodity-based product face the risk of loss if commodity prices fall and those price declines are not compensated (by increased profits from production, for example).

Even firms that do not directly need a commodity may face commodity risk because a rise in the general level of prices, known as inflation, may affect other factors of production. For example, a retailer may not directly use diesel in its operations. Yet a rise in the price of diesel may increase the costs of the company if suppliers charge higher rates for delivery. Minicase 7-5 illustrates commodity price risk.

MINICASE 7-5 COMMODITY-PRICE RISK

Today is January 4, and James, the purchasing manager of LSTR Inc., is looking at last year's results. LSTR designs, manufactures, and distributes jewellery to retailers across Canada. After the introduction of several new designs, sales have been growing at the rate of 8%. Assuming a similar growth rate, James estimates the coming year's demand for gold by his company will reach 46,500 troy ounces (a troy ounce, abbreviated oz., is the standard unit of measure for gold, where one pound is equal to 12 troy ounces and each ounce is 31.103 grams).

Nevertheless, James is concerned. Demand for the new popular line seems to be price sensitive, and the price of gold is rising. Yesterday, it reached US$390.50 per oz., and market experts believe that the price could go much higher. If this happens, it could mean disaster for LSTR. If the prices of LSTR's products are held constant at their current levels while the price of the raw material (gold) rises, the profit margin will be lower than the current margin and operating profits will decline. Alternatively, if the higher price of gold is passed on to customers, overall demand may drop and lead to lower profits. Moreover, LSTR may lose some customers permanently if they switch to less expensive products produced by competitors. James believes that LSTR will start to experience these effects if the price per oz. exceeds US$400.

In the next three months, LSTR is planning to make two major purchases, one in late February, involving 13,600 oz., and the other in late March, involving 12,200 oz. LSTR faces the risk that a significant increase in the price of gold in the meantime could result in reduced profits or potential losses to the firm. James will have to make some decisions about how to manage this risk.

James is not worried about foreign-exchange risk, as the company has been hedging this risk for a long time.

The minicases in this section have demonstrated interest-rate, foreign-exchange, and commodity-price risks. Often firms are exposed to several of these risks at the same time. For example, an international firm that relies on debt to finance its operations and a particular commodity for its production activities may be subject to risk from all three sources. Section 7.2 demonstrates how these risks interact.

7.2 MEASURING RISK EXPOSURE

In Section 7.1, treasury risk was defined as the probability of loss or reduction of profit, or a change in the market value of its assets or liabilities, as a result of changes in three major factors: interest rates, foreign exchange rates, or commodity prices.

Measuring risk exposure means determining the potential magnitude of the loss that may occur because of given changes in a particular market factor or combination of factors.

Measuring risk exposure is an important step in managing risk because the effort invested in managing risk depends on the magnitude of potential loss.

The conclusions from Chapter 1 indicate that management's primary concern should be maximizing the price of the firm's common shares. Risk, indeed, has an impact on share value. Although some risks identified in the minicases in Section 7.1 may not directly affect share prices, they will affect the firm's profits or the fluctuations of profits over time, which in turn will affect the value of the firm. Corporations are not the only organizations that manage treasury risk. Some governments, for example, manage interest-rate risk, foreign-exchange risk, and commodity-price risk on behalf of a variety of stakeholders. Managers often concentrate on managing profits or cash flows. Given that profits and their stability are directly related to share values, risk management that focuses on increasing profits or stabilizing profits should lead to maximizing shareholder or stakeholder value.

Two different approaches to measuring risk exposure are known as the micro and the macro approaches.

Micro Approach to Measuring Risk Exposure

The **micro approach** measures risk exposure by examining risks on a transaction-by-transaction basis. The risks described in Section 7.1 are generally associated with particular transactions, assets, or liabilities. The source of risk in each situation can be attributed to interest-rate, foreign-exchange rate, or commodity-price changes. Exposure is measured in terms of how a particular transaction can affect income. A manager can then deal with these particular risks individually.

Risk exposure from single transactions is measured by estimating the magnitude of losses or profits that may occur from changes to the source of risk. Generally, there is a direct relationship between the two that can be easily estimated.

Measuring Interest-Rate Risk Exposure of a Single Fixed Income Security—Duration In Minicase 7-3, Louise decided to invest in five-year bonds, despite the fact that she will require the funds in three years' time. She is concerned about the risk of this strategy and would like to measure the sensitivity of the investment's market value to changes in interest rates. In particular, she would like to know what increase in interest rates would result in a loss of 2% of the value of the five-year bond when she sells it in three years.

One way to answer this question is to use the concept of duration. Duration measures interest rate risk by calculating the sensitivity of a bond's price to changes in interest rates. Duration, which is stated in years, depends on time to maturity of the bond as well as its cash flows (coupon interest, if any). Duration is a useful concept because once interest rate sensitivity is known, you can estimate the potential loss (or gain) resulting from a change in interest rates. In other words, duration tells the manager how sensitive to interest rate changes a particular set of cash flows (e.g, a bond) will be.

Duration is a measure of the average maturity of a stream of payments generated by a financial security. It is the weighted average of the time until expected cash flows from a security will be received. The weight of each cash flow's time to receipt is the present value of the cash flow divided by the current market value of the security. The formula for calculating duration is as follows:

$$D = \frac{\sum_{t=1}^{n}\left[\frac{CF_t}{(1+i)^t} \times t\right]}{\sum_{t=1}^{n}\left[\frac{CF_t}{(1+i)^t}\right]}$$ (Equation 7-1)

where

D = duration

CF_t = dollar value of the cash flow expected at time t

t = number of units of time (normally years or semi-annual periods) until cash flow payment

i = yield to maturity on the security under consideration

n = number of anticipated cash flows

A couple of observations are in order. First, notice that the denominator is the current market value of the security. Second, a zero coupon bond (strip bond), which pays no coupon interest, promises only one future cash flow at maturity. This means all the cash flows are zero except the cash flow at maturity CF_n, which is also the face value of the strip. Thus, Equation 7-1 shows that the duration of a zero coupon security is always equal to the term to maturity of the security.

In Minicase 7-6, Equation 7-1 is used to calculate the duration of Louise's five-year bond (from Minicase 7-3), that is, how sensitive it will be to changes in interest rates.

MINICASE 7-6 EXAMPLE OF DURATION CALCULATION

The following data are used to calculate the duration of Louise's five-year bond:

Bond's coupon rate, paid semi-annually	9%
Maturity	5 years
Yield to maturity	9%
Market value	$1,000

Most North American bonds have interest that is stated per year, compounded and paid semi-annually. Thus, there are 10 six-month periods (5 years × 2), and the discount rate is 4.5% per period (bond yield divided by 2). Exhibit 7-6 summarizes the required calculations.

Case Continued >

Exhibit 7-6
Duration Calculation

Time t	CF_t	PV (factor)	PV(CF_t) at a discount rate of 4.5%	$t \times PV(CF_t)$
(1)	(2)	(3)	(4)	(5) = (1) × (4)
1	$ 45	0.9569	$ 43.0622	43.0622
2	45	0.9157	41.2078	82.4157
3	45	0.8763	39.4333	118.3000
4	45	0.8386	37.7353	150.9410
5	45	0.8025	36.1103	180.5515
6	45	0.7679	34.5553	207.3318
7	45	0.7348	33.0673	231.4710
8	45	0.7032	31.6433	253.1466
9	45	0.6729	30.2807	272.5263
10	1,045	0.6439	672.9044	6,729.0443
		Sum	$1,000.0000	8,268.7905

Price of the bond = the sum of column (4)
= $1,000.0000

Duration of the bond = sum of column 5 ÷ price
= 8,268.7905 ÷ 1,000.0000
= 8.2688 semi-annual periods

Duration of the bond in years = 8.2688 ÷ 2 = 4.1344 years

Notice that the sum of the entries in column (4) is the market value of the bond.

A security's duration provides information about the change in the security's market value as a result of interest rate changes. The longer the duration of a security, the higher the security's volatility to changes in interest rates will be. As interest rates rise, prices of fixed income securities will fall. For example, if Security A has a longer duration than Security B, a 1% increase in the yield on A and on B will decrease the values of both A and B. However, the decrease in the value of A will be greater than the decrease in the value of B.

Using Equation 7-1, it can be shown mathematically that:

$$\frac{\left(\dfrac{\Delta V}{V}\right)}{\Delta r} \approx \frac{-D}{1 + \dfrac{i}{m}} \qquad \text{(Equation 7-2)}$$

where
D = duration measured in years
V = market value of the security
ΔV = change in market value of the security
Δr = change in interest rates
i = yield to maturity
m = number of compounding periods per year

The ≈ sign implies that the relationship approximately holds, as the difference between the left- and right-hand expressions is small.

Equation 7-2 is also used to define the concept of volatility. **Volatility (v)** is another measure of the sensitivity of a security's market value to changes in interest rates. It is represented by the left-hand side of Equation 7-2. Volatility is directly proportional to duration: the higher the duration, the higher the volatility. However, whereas duration is expressed in years, volatility can be expressed as a percentage change in the price of the security. The volatility or sensitivity of Louise's bond to changes in the six-month required yield can be approximated by:

$$v = \frac{-D}{1 + \dfrac{i}{m}}$$

$$= \frac{-4.1344}{1 + \dfrac{0.09}{2}} = -3.9564$$

Similarly, Equation 7-2 can be recast as:

$$\Delta V = \frac{-D \times V}{1 + \dfrac{i}{m}} \times \Delta r \quad \text{or} \quad \frac{-D \times V \times \Delta r}{1 + \dfrac{i}{m}} \qquad \textbf{(Equation 7-3)}$$

This form of the equation is useful because it shows the approximate change in the market value of the bond for a given change in the interest rate. For example, if the interest rate rises by 1%, the market value of the bond drops by:

$$\Delta V = \frac{-4.1344 \times \$1,000}{1 + \dfrac{0.09}{2}} \times 0.01 = -\$39.56 \text{ or } -3.96\%$$

To confirm that this is so, calculate the value of the $1,000 bond with a coupon rate of 9% compounded semi-annually for five years with a yield to maturity of 10%. The calculation is shown in Exhibit 7-7.

Exhibit 7-7
Calculation of Present Value at 10%

Time t (1)	CF_t (2)	PV (factor) (3)	PV(CF_t) at a discount rate of 5% (2) × (3) = (4)
1	$45	0.9524	$42.8571
2	45	0.9070	40.8163
3	45	0.8638	38.8727
4	45	0.8227	37.0216
5	45	0.7835	35.2587
6	45	0.7462	33.5797
7	45	0.7107	31.9807

Continued >

8	45	0.6768	30.4578
9	45	0.6446	29.0074
10	1,045	0.6139	641.5393
		Sum	$961.3913

Remember that the volatility equation is a relationship that is approximate rather than equal. The volatility equation calculated a drop of $39.56 in the market price for a 1% rise in interest rates, resulting in a price of $1,000 − $39.56 = $960.44. Thus, the volatility equation is a good approximation of market value.

Using Equation 7-3, you can also predict the approximate change in interest rates that would cause a specified change in market value to occur. Minicase 7-7 continues on from Minicase 7-6 and illustrates this process.

MINICASE 7-7 RELATIONSHIP BETWEEN CHANGES IN INTEREST RATES AND CHANGES IN A BOND'S MARKET VALUE

Louise decided that she would sell the five-year bonds if they lose 2% of their market value at the time she purchased them ($1,000). Louise's bond has a yield to maturity of 9% compounded semi-annually and a duration of 4.1344 years. What increase in interest rates will be needed to produce this loss?

The answer can be obtained using Equation 7-3 and solving for Δr. The 2% change in market value of the security, ΔV, is equal to $1,000 \times 0.02 = $20. This yields:

$$-\$20 = \frac{-4.1344 \times \$1,000}{1 + \dfrac{0.09}{2}} \times \Delta r$$

$$\Delta r = \frac{-\$20}{-3,956.36} = 0.0051$$

Therefore, Δr must be 0.0051. Louise will suffer a 2% loss ($20 per $1,000 bond) and sell the bonds if the annual non-compounded rate rises by 51 basis points above the rate of the bonds.

Macro Approach to Measuring Risk Exposure

The **macro approach** measures risk exposure by examining an entire set of transactions that the firm may undertake over a given period of time. The logic behind the macro approach is that, in practice, risks are often interrelated. Changes in one source of risk may change the economic environment, which in turn may lead to changes in other sources of risk. For example, a higher rate of inflation may lead to higher interest rates and commodity prices. These changes may in turn lead to changes in the value of the dollar. The firm is thus exposed to interest-rate, foreign-exchange, and commodity-price risks.

Depending on the firm's circumstances, these risks may completely or partially offset each other. For example, a rise in interest rates may adversely affect a firm's income because it leads to higher interest payments on debt. Yet, this risk may be partially offset because of a rise in inflation and the impact it will have on cash flows. Depending on the competitive environment, the firm may be able to pass on some or all of the cost increases to customers through higher prices for the product.

In other situations, the different risks that affect the firm may all influence income or share value in the same way, thereby increasing overall risk. For example, a rise in interest rates may lead to higher costs of funds and lower income. At the same time, a rise in interest rates may lead to a higher value of the dollar. If some of the firm's income is denominated in foreign currency, because of export sales for example, the value of these sales in Canadian dollars will decline, leading to a further reduction in income.

Given the interrelationships among interest rates, foreign exchange rates, commodity prices, and other sources of risk, the firm's overall risk involves a complex combination of transactions. The various assets and liabilities of the firm may be treated as a portfolio in which changes in the value of one asset or liability may be partially offset by changes in the value of another. Combinations of factors may increase or decrease risk to the organization. Thus, measuring the risk exposure of the entire firm is more complex than measuring that of a single transaction.

Regression Analysis Regression analysis is an analytical technique used to estimate linear relationships between the value of a firm and various sources of risk. Historical values are regressed against historical changes in the factors under consideration to obtain the coefficients of the linear regression equation.

You used regression analysis in Chapter 2. Indeed, the familiar beta of returns on a security determines the sensitivity of the security's return to the market's return. As explained in Chapter 2, beta is calculated by regressing the historical return on the security against the historical return on the market. Then, the resulting beta is used to estimate the characteristic line by which the future return on the security can be estimated for a given market return.

In a similar approach, the sensitivity of a firm's income to changes in oil prices could be measured by regressing the historical income of the firm against historical oil prices. The resulting "beta" could be used to estimate a linear relationship between the firm's income and oil prices and, consequently, to estimate future expected income of the firm for given levels of oil prices.

However, because linear relationships rarely exist, the relationship identified by the regression line is a *rough estimate* of the true relationship. Moreover, given that regression analysis relies on historical data to obtain the coefficients, extending the relationship to the future may not be appropriate, because changes may impact the effectiveness of the regression model. Nevertheless, a linear relationship helps the treasury manager to better understand the relationship between a market factor (such as oil prices) and the overall impact on the firm (such as income). As a result, it may help the manager to decide whether or not to hedge. Hedging is discussed in more detail in later chapters.

Gap Analysis The gap analysis approach was initially developed for measuring the interest-rate risk of financial institutions, such as banks. It is explained here as a tool to measure and manage interest-rate risk. Gap analysis attempts to identify gaps between assets and liabilities that expose the institution to interest-rate risk.

Gap analysis is a measure of interest rate-risk, derived from the difference between the values of interest-rate-sensitive assets and interest-rate-sensitive liabilities. That is:

$$\text{Gap} = \text{rate-sensitive assets} - \text{rate-sensitive liabilities} \quad \textbf{(Equation 7-4)}$$

A financial institution's traditional business involves taking money from depositors (liabilities to the bank) and lending money to borrowers (assets to the bank). Most depositors choose relatively liquid terms for their deposits, which means that the interest rate they receive changes as market interest rates change. However, most borrowers choose fixed-rate terms, such as five-year mortgages. On these assets, the bank's return is fixed. Gap analysis is a way to measure the interest-rate risk that arises from the fact that the interest-rate sensitivity of assets is not the same as the interest-rate sensitivity of liabilities. In other words, they are mismatched, and gap analysis gives some idea of the resultant risk.

An asset or liability is said to be **rate sensitive** if it is repriced when the interest rate changes. As a result, it will be assigned a new rate. For example, a floating-rate loan in which the loan rate is reset daily at prime plus 2% is a rate-sensitive loan. As the prime rises or falls, the loan rate will be changed to reflect the change in the prime. In contrast, a **rate-insensitive** asset will not be assigned a new rate if interest rates change. For example, a five-year closed mortgage is interest-rate insensitive for five years. Whether interest rates rise or fall, the mortgage rate will not change.

The characterization of an asset as rate sensitive or insensitive depends on the time period under consideration. For example, a six-month fixed-rate term deposit is rate insensitive if the gap is being measured over a six-month period. However, if the gap is calculated over a *one-year period*, the six-month term deposit is rate sensitive, as it will be assigned a new rate within six months. Gap analysis may segregate assets and liabilities by maturity or repricing date in time "buckets." For example, the first time bucket might contain assets with six-month maturities, the next bucket assets with one-year maturities, and the subsequent time bucket assets with two-year maturities. The same is done for liabilities, and then the time buckets of assets and liabilities are compared for gaps. The gap analysis example that follows will focus simply on rate-sensitive and non-rate-sensitive assets and liabilities as a group.

A **positive gap** means a firm has more rate-sensitive assets than liabilities. A **negative gap** means that the firm has more rate-sensitive liabilities than assets. A financial institution that has a negative gap faces risk from rising interest rates. If rates rise, more of the liabilities are assigned higher rates, while only a small portion of assets are assigned higher rates. This situation increases the average cost of funds as well as the average return on assets. However, the increase in the average cost of funds is higher than the increase in the average return on assets. This leads to a lower average net interest margin and lower income for the institution. Minicase 7-8 illustrates the use of gap analysis.

MINICASE 7-8 GAP ANALYSIS

Exhibit 7-8 shows a schedule of assets, liabilities, and expected net interest income for WRTRST Inc. This trust company has $1.45 billion in assets, of which $900 million represent rate-sensitive assets. It also has $1.1 billion in rate-sensitive liabilities. Therefore, $200 million of fixed-rate assets are financed by rate-sensitive liabilities, which is the size of the gap for WRTRST. Simply, the gap can be calculated using Equation 7-4:

$$\text{Gap} = \$900 - \$1,100$$
$$= -\$200$$

Given the average rates of return on assets and the average costs of liabilities, the expected net income of WRTRST for next year will be $23.55 million. As Exhibit 7-8 indicates, return on assets is expected to be slightly higher than 1.62%.

Case Continued >

Exhibit 7-8
Schedule of Assets, Liabilities, and Expected Net Interest Income of WRTRST Inc.

Assets	Amount ($ millions)	Average yield (%)	Liabilities	Amount ($ millions)	Average cost (%)
Cash	$ 50	0.00%	Non-earning	$ 10	0.00%
Rate-sensitive	900	7.70	Rate-sensitive	1,100	6.70
Fixed-rate	500	9.00	Fixed-rate	220	7.75
			Equity	120	N/A
Total	$1,450		Total	$1,450	

Expected interest income = $(0.00 \times 50) + (0.077 \times 900) + (0.09 \times 500) = \$114.30$

Expected interest cost = $(0.00 \times 10) + (0.067 \times 1,100) + (0.0775 \times 220) = \$90.75$

Net interest income = $\$114.30 - \$90.75 = \$23.55$

Net return on assets = $\$23.55 \div \$1,450 = 1.62\%$, gap = $-\$200$

If interest rates over the coming year exceed expected levels by 1%, and the increase affects all securities equally, what will happen to WRTRST's net interest income and net return on assets?

Exhibit 7-9 shows the effect of a one-percentage-point interest rate increase on WRTRST's net interest income and return on assets. First, notice that only the rates on the rate-sensitive assets and rate-sensitive liabilities change. Second, the increase in rates leads to increases in both the interest income and the interest cost of liabilities. However, because there are $200 million more of rate-sensitive liabilities than of rate-sensitive assets, the interest costs of liabilities increase by more than the increase in the interest income on assets. Consequently, net interest income decreases by exactly $2 million (from $23.55 million to $21.55 million) or by approximately 8.49%. Similarly, return on assets drops from 1.62% to 1.49%, a drop of 8.02%.

Exhibit 7-9
Schedule of Assets, Liabilities, and Realized Net Interest Income of WRTRST Inc.

Assets	Amount ($ millions)	Average yield (%)	Liabilities	Amount ($ millions)	Average cost (%)
Cash	$ 50	0.00%	Non-earning	$ 10	0.00%
Rate-sensitive	900	8.70	Rate-sensitive	1,100	7.70
Fixed-rate	500	9.00	Fixed-rate	220	7.75
			Equity	120	N/A
Total	$1,450		Total	$1,450	

Expected interest income = $(0.00 \times 50) + (0.087 \times 900) + (0.09 \times 500) = \$123.30$

Expected interest cost = $(0.00 \times 10) + (0.077 \times 1,100) + (0.0775 \times 220) = \$101.75$

Net interest income = $\$123.30 - \$101.75 = \$21.55$

Net return on assets = $\$21.55 \div \$1,450 = 1.49\%$, gap = $-\$200$

The decrease in the net interest income (NII) could have been predicted by calculating the product of the gap and the expected change in interest rates as follows:

$$\Delta \text{NII} = \Delta r \times \text{gap} \qquad \textbf{(Equation 7-5)}$$

where

ΔNII = change in net interest income

Δr = expected change in interest rates

Using the data in Minicase 7-8, the change in net interest income if interest rates rise by 1% will be:

$$\Delta \text{NII} = 0.01 \times -200 \text{ million} = -\$2 \text{ million}$$

Thus, gap analysis can be considered as a measure for assessing interest rate risk exposure in situations where the rate sensitivity of assets does not match the rate sensitivity of liabilities. Indeed, Equation 7-5 can be used to produce general conclusions regarding the gap. These conclusions are summarized in Exhibit 7-10. For example, Equation 7-5 shows that if the gap is negative and rates are expected to decrease (Δr negative), the change in the net interest income is positive. The first row of Exhibit 7-10 illustrates this scenario. It shows that if the gap is negative and interest rates decrease, both interest income and interest costs decrease as the rate-sensitive assets and liabilities are repriced at lower rates. However, as the gap is negative, there are fewer rate-sensitive assets than rate-sensitive liabilities. Thus, the decrease in interest income is less than the decrease in interest costs, and the change in net interest income is positive.

Exhibit 7-10
Gap as a Measure of Interest-Rate Risk

Sign of gap	Rate change	Interest income	Interest cost	Δ in income compared with Δ in cost	Net interest income
Negative	−	Decrease	Decrease	Less than	Increase
Negative	+	Increase	Increase	Less than	Decrease
Positive	−	Decrease	Decrease	Greater than	Decrease
Positive	+	Increase	Increase	Greater than	Increase
Zero	−	Decrease	Decrease	Equal to	No change
Zero	+	Increase	Increase	Equal to	No change

Using a Spreadsheet to Measure Risk Exposure

Additional ways to measure risk exposure for the entire firm are sensitivity analysis and scenario analysis. Sensitivity analysis is not the same as scenario analysis. With **sensitivity analysis**, an individual variable, such as a change in interest rates, is altered to show the sensitivity of the forecasted results to the value of the variable. **Scenario analysis** entails changing sets of variables to create alternative scenarios and provide a better understanding of the overall most likely, best, and worst scenarios. Simulation may be used for both scenario and sensitivity analysis. Simulation provides a probabilistic overview as long as the correlations among input variables are correctly built into the model.

Scenario analysis is the process by which a financial manager studies the sensitivity of changes in one or more risk sources and observes the outcomes. The manager can assess the sensitivity of asset or liability values to changes in risk sources, such as interest-rate, foreign-exchange, or commodity-price risk. Using mathematical models and a computer program, the manager can simulate complex, real-life situations. The program can be used to create random changes in selected variables and to measure the impact of these changes on the income statement or the balance sheet. Although complex software programs are available to do scenario analysis with many variables, it can also be done using a simple spreadsheet program.

The financial manager will need to forecast the expected values of the variables and their probability distributions. These relationships can then be modelled so that the computer can automatically draw values for the random variables to create scenarios and prepare a balance sheet or income statement under each scenario. After a large number of runs, the manager generates N estimates for a selected set of key variables and ratios. These values can be used to estimate the expected value of the variables and their standard deviations. From these estimates, it should be possible to obtain an idea about the risk sources and how they affect asset or liability values.

There are two major benefits to using sensitivity and scenario analysis with computers and simulation models. First, simulation models can represent situations in which many different variables can interact and change. Second, the process of building the simulation model leads the analyst to a better understanding of the problem.

There are, however, difficulties with simulation. Generally, it is difficult to specify the functional relationships among the parameters and variables. Thus, in attempting to create a realistic model, the treasury manager may end up with a very complex model from which little can be learned.

Computer Activity: Measuring Interest-Rate, Foreign-Exchange, and Commodity-Price Risks

This computer illustration shows how to perform a scenario analysis of a firm's risk exposure. Specifically, it demonstrates how a firm's net income and return on equity are affected by changes in interest rates, foreign exchange rates, and commodity prices.

LEARNING OBJECTIVE

■ design and use a spreadsheet to perform a scenario analysis of a firm's risk exposure.

Description

FSTRK Inc. is a medium-sized trucking company based in Winnipeg, Manitoba. The company ships products between Canada and the United States. Business is fairly stable, as FSTRK has secured long-term contracts with many customers on both sides of the border. With few exceptions, trucks leave Canada loaded, unload at their destinations, reload, and drive to new destinations. Scheduling is arranged to maximize the loading factor. This makes FSTRK a profitable firm while the rest of the industry is struggling.

FSTRK's income statement for the year ended December 31, 20X1 (Exhibit 7-11) shows some risk exposure. Last year, FSTRK generated $18 million in revenues from American customers. Converted to Canadian dollars at C$1.36 per U.S. dollar, these revenues represented about 42.59% of total revenues. FSTRK's dividend policy is to distribute all net income as dividends, and the company is planning no share issues during 20X2. The income statement indicates that FSTRK's revenues are sensitive to exchange rate fluctuations.

Exhibit 7-11
FSTRK Inc. Income Statement
Year Ended December 31, 20X1

Sales	20X1
Canadian revenues	$33,000,000
U.S. revenues in C$	24,480,000
Total revenues	57,480,000
Expenses	
Fuel (diesel)	15,435,000
Wages and salaries	9,000,000
Interest expenses:	
Short-term debt	2,100,000
Long-term debt	8,075,000
Advertising	1,200,000
Rent and insurance	8,000,000
Total expenses	43,810,000
Net operating income	13,670,000
Taxes	5,468,000
Net income	$ 8,202,000
Return on equity	10.52%

In addition, FSTRK's revenues are sensitive to oil prices. As the company's fleet of trucks consumes a large amount of diesel, any rise in the price of diesel adversely affects revenues.

Finally, FSTRK is subject to interest-rate risk. FSTRK's balance sheet at December 31, 20X1 is presented in Exhibit 7-12. It shows that FSTRK is exposed to interest-rate risk, as more than 60% of its assets are financed with debt. The $85 million from long-term debt is due for refinancing in the year 20X6. Management is concerned that the rates may be higher when it comes to debt refinancing. Management, however, is more concerned about the short-term portion of the debt. In particular, FSTRK has $28 million in short-term notes that are repriced frequently. If rates rise, interest payments on this debt will rise and net income will decrease. Alternatively, the firm can fix the cost of this debt by issuing long-term bonds. The problem is that current long-term rates are higher than short-term rates, a situation that will lead to an immediate drop in income.

Exhibit 7-12
FSTRK Inc. Balance Sheet
December 31, 20X1

Assets		**Liabilities**	
Current assets		**Current liabilities**	
Cash	$ 12,000,000	Accounts payable	$ 4,000,000
Accounts receivable, C$	6,000,000	Accruals	1,500,000
Accounts receivable, US$	5,440,000	Short-term notes	28,000,000
Inventory	15,000,000	**Long-term liabilities**	
Capital assets		Bonds	85,000,000
Equipment	126,000,000	**Shareholders'**	
Other	32,000,000	**equity**	77,940,000
Total assets	$196,440,000	Total liabilities and shareholder's equity	$196,440,000

Required

Use a spreadsheet to show the effect of changes in diesel prices, foreign exchange rates, and interest rates on FSTRK's net income and return on equity.

Procedure

1. Open the file FN2L7P1.xls. The file is organized into the following worksheets:

L7P1DATA	A worksheet that contains the data for the scenario analyses
L7P1	A partially completed worksheet set up to construct pro forma income statements for the five scenarios
L7P1S	A solution worksheet for the pro forma income statements

2. Click the L7P1DATA sheet tab and study the layout of the worksheet. Rows 5 to 14 contain information required to construct the pro forma income statements. Rows 17 to 19 contain the changes in each of the variables associated with scenarios 1 to 5. Rows 27 to 45 contain the FSTRK's 20X1 income statement.
3. Click the L7P1 sheet tab and study the layout. Enter in row 11 the appropriate formulas to convert the US$ revenue earned by FSTRK into Canadian dollars. Be sure to reference the data table values from the L7P1DATA worksheet when constructing your formulas.
4. Enter the appropriate formulas in rows 15, 18, 19, and 25 to complete the scenario analysis.
5. Enter in row 28 the formula to calculate the return on equity (ROE) and in row 29 the percentage change in ROE from the base case for each of the five scenarios.
6. Save your completed worksheet and print a copy.
7. Click the sheet tab L7P1S and compare your results. Resolve any differences.

Commentary

Exhibit 7-13 shows the effects of a 1% or −1% change in diesel prices, exchange rates per U.S. dollar, and short-term interest rates.

Exhibit 7-13
Effect of One-Percent Changes in Interest Rate, Commodity, and Foreign Exchange Rates

Year ending December 31	20X1	20X2 Scenario 1	20X2 Scenario 2	20X2 Scenario 3	20X2 Scenario 4	20X2 Scenario 5
Change in diesel prices		1%	1%	1%	1%	1.3961%
Price/barrel of diesel	$49.00	$49.49	$49.49	$49.49	$49.49	$49.68
Change in US$ rate		−1%	1%	0%	1%	1%
Exchange rate per US$	1.3600	1.3464	1.3736	1.3600	1.3736	1.3736
Change in short-term rates		1%	0%	−1%	1%	1.3961%
Short-term interest	7.50%	7.5750%	7.500%	7.4250%	7.5750%	7.6047%
Change in long-term rates		0%	0%	0%	0%	0%
Long-term interest	9.50%	9.50%	9.50%	9.50%	9.50%	9.50%
Change in return on equity		−3.07%	0.66%	−0.98%	0.51%	0%
Return on equity		10.20%	10.59%	10.42%	10.58%	10.52%

Column C of the solution worksheet L7P1S shows the effect of a 1% adverse change per variable over the next year. Cell C29 shows that this scenario causes the return on equity to decrease by 3.07%.

Column D shows the effect of a 1% adverse change in diesel prices in combination with a 1% favourable change in the foreign exchange rate and no change in interest rates. Cell D29 shows that the return on equity will increase by 0.66%. Thus, Scenario 2 shows that FSTRK's net income is more sensitive to foreign exchange rate changes than to changes in diesel prices.

Column E shows the effect of a 1% adverse change in diesel prices against a 1% favourable change in short-term interest rates and no change in the exchange rate. Cell E29 shows that return on equity will decrease by 0.98%. Thus, the sensitivity of FSTRK's net income to changes in the price of diesel is more important to the firm than the sensitivity to changes in short-term interest rates. In contrast, cell F29 shows that return on equity is affected favourably by changes in the foreign exchange rate compared with changes in both diesel prices and short-term interest rates.

Column G shows that a 1% favourable change in the exchange rate can neutralize 1.3961% simultaneous increases in each of diesel prices and short-term interest rates.

Conclusion

Scenario analysis has been used to show the sensitivity of FSTRK's net income and return on equity under various scenarios of changes in diesel prices, foreign exchange rates, and interest rates. These five scenarios are just a selection of those that can be analyzed. Such methods provide valuable information for measuring exposure and for-mulating a hedging strategy.

Using Volatility Analysis to Measure Portfolio Risk

The concept of duration is also used to assess the volatility of a portfolio of assets or liabilities. The duration of a portfolio is the weighted average of the durations of the assets or liabilities that make up the portfolio. The weight of each asset or liability is the proportion of the portfolio's value contributed by that asset or liability. The duration of a portfolio can be calculated as:

$$D_P = \frac{D_1 V_1 + D_i V_i + \ldots + D_n V_n}{V_1 + V_i + \ldots + V_n} \qquad \text{(Equation 7-6)}$$

where

D_P = duration of a portfolio
D_i = durations of i securities (where $i = 1, \ldots, n$)
V_i = market values of i securities (where $i = 1, \ldots, n$)

As an example, consider a portfolio that has the bonds described in Exhibit 7-14. The portfolio's duration is 3.78 years.

MINICASE 7-9 VOLATILITY ANALYSIS

In Minicases 7-6 and 7-7, you looked at the effect of a change in interest rates on the value of a single bond. Louise has now invested in a portfolio of four bonds, all with a face value of $1,000 and with varying interest rates and terms to maturity. Exhibit 7-14 outlines her portfolio.

Exhibit 7-14
Louise's Portfolio

Bond	Rate	Compounded	Term	Market value (V)	Yield to maturity
B_1	6%	Semi-annually	3 years	$1,000.00	6%
B_2	7%	Annually	4 years	943.31	8.74%
B_3	8%	Quarterly	6 years	861.55	11.20%
B_4	10.75%	Annually	5 years	1,028.43	10%

The calculation of the duration for bond B_1 is shown in Exhibit 7-15.

Exhibit 7-15
Duration Calculation for Bond B_1

Time t	CF_t	PV (factor)	PV(CF_t) at a discount rate of 3%	$t \times$ PV(CF_t)
(1)	(2)	(3)	(4)	(5) = (1) × (4)
1	$30	0.9708	$29.1262	29.1262
2	30	0.9426	28.2779	56.5557
3	30	0.9151	27.4542	82.3626

Case Continued >

4	30	0.8885	26.6546	106.6184
5	30	0.8626	25.8783	129.3915
6	1,030	0.8375	862.6088	5,175.6528
	Sum		$1,000.000	5,579.707

The duration of bond B_1 will be $5,579.707 \div 1,000.000 = 5.5797$ semi-annual periods. The duration of bond B_1 in years will be $5.5797 \div 2 = 2.7898$ years. The duration of the other bonds in the portfolio are listed in Exhibit 7-16.

Exhibit 7-16
Portfolio Duration Calculations

Bond	Duration (D)	Market value (V)	$D \times V$
B_1	2.790	$1,000.00	2,790.000
B_2	3.612	943.31	3,407.236
B_3	4.713	861.55	4,060.485
B_4	4.132	1,028.43	4,249.473
Sum		3,833.29	14,507.194

Duration of the portfolio = $14,507.194 \div \$3,833.29 = 3.78$ years

The duration of Louise's portfolio is 3.78 years, which is the average of the four individual durations, weighted by their market value. Despite the fact that the portfolio contains bonds maturing in three, four, five, and six years, it will respond to interest rates as though it were a zero coupon bond with maturity in 3.78 years (recall that the duration of a zero coupon bond is equal to its maturity, because there is only one cash flow at maturity). The duration of a portfolio can be used to estimate the sensitivity of the portfolio's value to changes in the discount rates. Keep in mind that Equation 7-3 approximates the relationship between the duration of an asset and the sensitivity of the asset's value to changes in the discount rate.

Two issues need to be settled before applying Equation 7-3 directly to a portfolio:

1. *Determine the appropriate discount rate by which to discount the numerator.* You know that, for a single asset, the rate is the annual yield on the asset divided by the number of compounding periods per year. A portfolio has several assets, each of which may have a different yield. Also, different assets may have a different number of compounding periods. A general rule for dealing with this situation is:
   - determine i/m (ratio of annual yield to number of compounding periods per year) for each asset;
   - calculate the weighted average of these yields, where the weight of an asset is the percentage of the portfolio's value contributed by the asset;
   - use (1 + weighted average) to discount the numerator.

2. *Estimate the impact of an expected change in interest rates on each of the yields of a portfolio's assets.* For a single asset, a change in yield may be easy to predict. A portfolio has several assets; each may have a different yield, and each yield may change differently from the others. To overcome the difficulty of estimating each yield, the financial manager will often forecast the expected change in interest rates and then assume that the change will affect the yields of the portfolio's assets equally. *Case Continued >*

Therefore, for a portfolio, Equation 7-3 should be modified as:

$$\Delta V_P = \frac{-D_P \times V_P}{1 + d_W} \times \Delta r \quad \text{or} \quad \frac{-D_P \times V_P \times \Delta r}{1 + d_W} \qquad \textbf{(Equation 7-7)}$$

where

V_P = portfolio's value

D_P = portfolio's duration

Δr = change in interest rates

d_W = weighted average discount rate, where the component rate for an asset is the yield to maturity per compounding period

For the portfolio of bonds in Exhibit 7-14, the values for V_P and D_P have been calculated. The next step is to determine d_W, the weighted average discount rate. The yields to be used in the weighted average yield calculations should be, respectively, 3%, 8.74%, 2.8%, and 10%. Note that this is calculated as the yield-to-maturity rates divided by the number of compounding periods per year. The weighted average discount rate should be:

$$d_W = \frac{0.03 \times \$1,000}{3,833.29} + \frac{0.0874 \times \$943.31}{3,833.29} + \frac{0.028 \times \$861.55}{3,833.29} + \frac{0.10 \times 1,028.43}{3,833.29}$$

$$= 6.25\%$$

This discount rate can then be used to calculate the impact of an expected change in rates of 1% on the overall portfolio. Therefore, if rates rise by 1%, it can be estimated that the value of the portfolio will decrease by:

$$\Delta V = \frac{-3.78 \times \$3,833.29}{1.0625} \times 0.01 = -\$136.37$$

To verify that this is a good approximation of the change in the portfolio, recalculate the market value of the four bonds based on a yield to maturity that is 1% per annum higher than the original data. The calculation produces the values shown in Exhibit 7-17.

Exhibit 7-17
New Portfolio Value

Bond	Original market values	Market values at 1% higher yield to maturity	Difference
B_1	1,000.00	$ 973.36	$ 26.64
B_2	943.31	912.65	30.66
B_3	861.55	823.13	38.42
B_4	1,028.43	990.76	37.67
Total	$3,833.29	$3,699.90	$133.39

Therefore, the change in market value as predicted by the volatility equation is a reasonable approximation of the change in market value of the portfolio.

7.3 BASIC RISK MANAGEMENT

The purpose of measuring risk is to understand and manage it. As shown in the minicases in Section 7.1, unmanaged risk can have a severe effect on a firm's future. Many factors have increased the need for risk management. They include the increased volatility of financial markets, the increased globalization of business, and the increase in competition for most businesses. Like risk measurement, risk management can be accomplished on a micro or a macro level.

Risk management is intended to reduce or eliminate risk arising from market factors, such as interest rates, foreign exchange rates, or commodity prices. The treasury manager needs to determine whether the risks that an organization faces are worth managing. This decision is based on the expected potential loss to the organization and the costs of mitigating those risks.

Clearly, there is a need for a mechanism to transfer risk from organizations that wish to reduce or eliminate it to organizations that are willing to accept it. This is the subject of hedging, which will be discussed in more detail in the remainder of this chapter and in Chapters 8 and 9. It is possible to manage risk by finding offsetting transactions that will reduce, if not eliminate, potential losses. For example, an importer that buys raw materials from Japan (and is therefore exposed to the value of the Japanese yen) might try to find an outlet for some of its products or services in Japan. By developing sales in Japan, the firm ensures it will earn Japanese yen income to help offset its purchase requirements. In practice, for many organizations such a strategy may not be possible, and if it is, it would take time to implement and would require long-term planning.

Gap Analysis and Risk Reduction

In Section 7.2, you learned that one way to measure risk exposure is to use gap analysis. By identifying the gap between rate-sensitive assets and liabilities, the firm can measure the level of exposure it faces. Once the level of exposure is known, management can take steps to manage the risk.

One intuitively simple method of managing risk is to narrow the gap by matching rate-sensitive assets and liabilities. Remember that the sensitivity of assets and liabilities to changes in interest rates is largely a factor of their length of time to maturity. By classifying rate-sensitive assets and liabilities by their maturities, it is possible to assess the gap between the two on a term-by-term basis.

By carefully managing the gap between rate-sensitive assets and liabilities, it is possible to control both the extent and the direction of exposure that a firm will experience if interest rates change. In practice, it is unlikely that you will be able to completely eliminate the gap by matching both the term and the rate of financial assets to financial liabilities. In addition, the portfolios of many firms include major non-financial assets, such as plant, equipment, or intellectual property.

Duration and Risk Management

Duration is a method of measuring risk based on the volatility of assets or liabilities with fixed cash flows. Duration may be used to measure risk on a transaction-by-transaction basis. You were shown how managers calculate duration as a measure of risk. These techniques isolate a risk from a single transaction (such as ownership of a bond) and therefore do not encompass other risks that the firm may face.

Duration enables an organization to measure the sensitivity of an asset or a liability, or a portfolio of assets or liabilities, to changes in interest rates. A useful way of thinking of duration is to use the economic concept of price elasticity. Duration can be interpreted as the price elasticity of a given financial asset or liability. This makes duration a useful tool in managing risk.

In Section 7.2 we discussed matching maturities of assets and liabilities. A more sophisticated form of matching involves duration, rather than maturity. Basically, if you balance the duration of a firm's assets with the duration of its liabilities, you will have hedged against changes in the values of these securities caused by changes in interest rates. Hedging in this way is known as **portfolio immunization**.

In practice, this technique is not as simple as it sounds. As the term to maturity and interest rates change, the duration of a given security changes. Therefore, the firm's portfolio of assets and liabilities will need to be readjusted constantly to ensure that the duration of assets and liabilities continues to balance.

Also, short- and long-term rates may change in different directions over time, resulting in changes to the term structure of interest rates. Such changes to the yield curve will also require a "rebalancing" of the durations of the firm's portfolio of assets and liabilities.

As Chapter 3 pointed out, there are many different kinds of fixed-cash-flow securities. Bonds can come with a variety of provisions that may change the maturity of the security. For example, bonds with an extension or a retraction provision allow the bondholder to either extend or retract the term of the bond. Inability to precisely determine the term of a bond issue will make the duration calculation difficult and complex.

In addition, as we have seen with gap analysis, one of the biggest challenges many firms face is the fact that their portfolios of assets and liabilities often include non-financial assets. Because of the technical difficulties related to the use of these techniques, financial derivatives have evolved to meet the needs of hedgers. The use of financial derivatives to hedge against risk will be covered in Chapters 8 and 9.

7.4 RISK MANAGEMENT CONSIDERATIONS

Hedging fulfils an essential risk transfer mechanism: to transfer risk from organizations that do not desire it to organizations willing to accept it. Hedging means taking an offsetting market position that will reduce or eliminate some of the market risk that an organization faces. In many cases, though not all, it is an active strategy involving derivatives.

Hedgers are mostly governments, corporations, or financial institutions that produce, process, manage, or rely on the actual underlying physical commodity, asset, or financial instrument to generate revenues. They hedge against adverse movements in interest rates, foreign exchange rates, or commodity prices by taking positions in the financial derivatives markets. They hope that changes in these markets will offset changes in the cash markets.

In a study conducted for the Commodity Futures Trading Commission in the United States, Wiesemeyer and Bernard found that no more than 7% of American farmers hedge with futures.[1] The farmers cited several reasons for not hedging:

■ Hedging before crops are harvested increases risk because the final size of the crop is highly uncertain.

■ Lack of knowledge of the hedging process is a major factor.

---

[1] J. Wiesemeyer and R. Bernard, "Futures/Options Pilot Farm Program Not on Autopilot," *Future*, Volume 17, Number 6, 1988, pp. 48–49.

- The size of the futures contract does not match the level of their production. They claim that taking a mismatched position, such as selling barley futures in 20 metric tons (one contract on the Winnipeg Commodity Exchange) when they expect a crop of 15 metric tons may increase rather than decrease their risk.

- They believe that margin calls make hedging with futures risky. (Margin calls will be covered in Chapter 8.)

On the other hand, hedgers often cite several benefits from risk management:

- A company can secure a positive profit margin on sales because it can guarantee the cost of working capital loans.

- It can lock in a suitable price for physical inventories or financial assets.

- It can guarantee predictable production costs by fixing raw material prices, such as for oil, gold, and various other commodities.

- A firm can reduce the need to transact in the cash market. This reduces the costs of carrying inventory because the firm can substitute futures positions for cash positions.

Chapters 8 and 9 will provide further information on the technical details of using financial derivatives for hedging purposes.

General Risk Management Approaches

Almost all business entities are interested in risk management. The most common businesses actively engaged in the practice of treasury- or financial-risk management include financial institutions, exporters, importers, farmers, mining companies, oil producers, manufacturers, and institutional investors. Given this diversity of potential beneficiaries, policies and approaches are not the same for all those who practise risk management.

There are four different approaches to managing risk:

- **Opportunistic approach:** Management has superior ability to forecast financial or commodity prices. Decisions are made based on the forecast to benefit from changes in these prices.

- **Passive approach:** Ignores risk and relies on the ability of the company to ride the fluctuations. The manager assumes that over the long run any gains or losses will balance out.

- **Defensive approach:** Taken when adverse changes in the interest rate, foreign exchange rate, or commodity prices threaten substantial losses that may lead to bankruptcy. The manager takes action in the financial market to insure against major risks.

- **Compromise approach:** A firm develops a complete hedging strategy to minimize its risk exposure and follows it with some exceptions. The exceptions occur when management strongly believes it can benefit by taking an opportunistic position in the market or when the risks are not so high. This strategy takes more management time but may create positive returns from hedging.

Exhibit 7-18 summarizes for each approach the conditions under which it may be appropriate and the magnitude of administrative costs needed for implementation.

Exhibit 7-18
Risk Management Approaches

Approach	Appropriate when:	Administrative costs
Opportunistic	Management has superior forecasting ability	Very high
Passive	Risks are moderate	None
Defensive	Risks are high	Low
Compromise	Risks are not so high	High

The choice of one approach to managing risk over the others depends on the risk management policy, the organization's tolerance for risk, the costs of hedging, the competitive environment, and other factors.

Employees, managers, customers, and creditors are stakeholders of the firm, as are shareholders. In other organizations, such as governments, stakeholders also include taxpayers and recipients of tax-funded services. Treasury-risk management leads to stability in income and asset values, long-term continuity, and more loyalty on the part of stakeholders.

Although shareholders can engage in their own hedging, it is preferable for management to engage in treasury-risk management on behalf of shareholders. If the risk-return trade-off can be optimized through treasury management, the long-term value of the firm's shares should be maximized. In addition, when management engages in risk management, it ideally communicates explicitly to investors what strategies are pursued. This disclosure is desirable because it permits shareholders to understand the risks the company faces. Such disclosure is often made in the notes to the financial statements.

Once a firm decides to adopt a treasury-risk management strategy, it may be optimal to centralize the hedging functions. Centralization is generally most effective in larger organizations where decisions are made individually by divisions or subsidiaries. A centralized system for managing risk minimizes the hedging actions that must be undertaken, as some transactions may offset the risks of others (portfolio diversification effects). Without centralization, these transactions may be hedged separately, increasing costs. Also, centralization provides for adequate performance evaluation of risk management operations. It is often desirable for a firm that has many divisions and/or multinational operations and for which the treasury-risk management function can be separated from other functions. In very large multinational organizations, a separate division may be created to undertake all financial-risk management activities.

Corporations need to actively manage their risks in today's competitive environment. It is essential to establish risk and reward objectives to optimize risk-adjusted cash flows. A guaranteed cash flow is, of course, usually more valuable than one that is contingent on a future foreign exchange rate or other market changes.

In the following article, Wally Hassenrueck accounts for what went on when Husky Oil decided to take advantage of declining U.S. interest rates.

Interest-Rate Risk Management:
A Corporate Case Study

Wally Hassenrueck

This article is intended to demystify the entire process of creating an interest-rate risk management strategy and provides a useful guide to preparing your own strategy. It is based on the interest rate strategy originally developed for 1994 and 1995 by Husky Oil Ltd.

Husky Oil Ltd. is an integrated oil and gas company privately owned by the Li family group of Hong Kong and CIBC. Like most oil and gas companies, a substantial portion of Husky's debt is normally US$-denominated, in part because of the perceived natural hedge between the liability and oil and gas assets that are US$-driven.

To take advantage of declining U.S. rates, the company had decided to convert a major portion of its long-term debt to U.S. dollars and to place that debt on the short end of the curve. By the end of the first quarter of 1993, 100% of the long-term debt was U.S-dollar denominated and 77% of this debt was being rolled at 30-day LIBOR. Long-term debt was at historically high levels as Husky was nearing completion of 2 sizable capital projects, and there was some desire to protect against increasing interest rates to ensure that cash flow would be available for debt repayment. In April 1993 Husky decided to develop a strategy to hedge its interest-rate exposure.

The key steps in the process are:

- To assess current and future market development;
- To develop a personal risk profile;
- To evaluate and select the hedging instruments;
- To implement the strategy;
- To assess and refine the strategy.

Let's start by reviewing the market conditions and Husky's situation in the spring of 1993, when the strategy was first developed.

The market conditions: Both the U.S. and Canada had experienced a severe economic downturn. The Canadian economy was still suffering, but the U.S. economy had started to turn the corner. Economic stats were mixed and, although the market wasn't entirely certain whether this recovery was real, there was a sense that the party was too good to last. U.S. floating rates were heading up, but how far and how fast was still debatable. 90-day LIBOR rates had averaged 3.25% for both February and March and, although financial institutions were starting to forecast rate increases, the timing of the increases ranged from mid-year 1993 to early 1994, with a fairly gentle rate of increase. One financial institution was calling for Fed funds to increase from 3% to 4.5% within the 18-month period. Another was calling for Fed funds to increase by 125 basis points starting at the end of 1993. FRA rates were implying an increase in 90-day LIBOR to a "dizzying" 4% by the end of 1993.

A corporate looking to hedge at this time was faced with both the uncertainty of rate movements and a yield curve that produced a fairly healthy step up over current short rates. For example, the spread between a 5-year swap and 6-month LIBOR was 235 basis points. The swap rates themselves had increased by about 25 basis points over the levels seen 6 months earlier. Even a 2- or 3-year swap required a step up of 110 and 155 basis points, respectively, an increase that was a little difficult to swallow for corporates that had seen 90-day LIBOR hover around the 3.25% level for an extended period.

Before we could finalize a strategy, we had to form an opinion about what the future would bring. Since reliable crystal balls are in notoriously short supply, we use a three-step process:

1. Canvass the market to collect the current forecast;

2. Identify and evaluate underlying assumptions;

3. Integrate forecasts, develop a personal view.

The first step is checking to see what other people think, otherwise known as "checking with the gurus." We tend to canvass institutions that in our opinion have the ability to interpret market events and have a reasonable track record in forecasting. To ensure that we have a range of opinions we also include forecasts from institutions that are outrageous, controversial, or off the wall. If nothing else they make this process a little more entertaining. We typically include the views of 3 to 4 institutions in our summary of the views of the market.

The second step is to look at the underlying assumptions. If forecasts vary significantly, the underlying assumptions should give a clue about the view of the world reflected in the forecast.

We typically collect the assumptions made about U.S. and international economic growth, international interest-rate and currency movement expectations, inflation projections, forecast Fed intervention and so on, and we evaluate them to decide whether the forecast is consistent with the assumptions and whether we agree with the assumptions and the forecast.

Finally, you have to develop your own view. It is highly unlikely that all the forecasts and all the assumptions will line up neatly and reach exactly the same conclusion. In fact, it's highly likely that the forecasts may be all over the map in terms of magnitude and direction. The challenge is to reconcile the views and determine which you believe is most correct.

Developing this personal view is absolutely fundamental to developing a successful strategy. In our experience, taking the time to determine what we believe the world looks like today and what it is likely to look like tomorrow helps us to focus on and to articulate the nature, magnitude, and probability of the risk. So, for example, we would use this process to decide if rates were heading up or down, how quickly and how far rates would move and how likely it was that the universe would unfold as we'd predicted.

Not only does this process help you to focus, it also increases the comfort level with the program, something that is obviously important if you are committing significant dollars to a hedge program. In our experience picking apart the forecasts of others and developing our own view significantly raises the comfort level.

This process also increases the commitment to the program. We found that participation in the development of the corporate view reduces the risk of repudiation if the actual results turn out to be something less than expected.

Every company must look at what works for it. We like to use a process that involves the treasury team, from senior management to the senior analyst level. It is critical that senior management be involved at this stage. Since the hedging program is supposed to protect the company against the risks that it sees, senior management should be involved in the assessment of that risk. I would recommend hands-on involvement, not just a review of the finished risk assessment.

At Husky, we tend to use a process in which every member of the treasury team individually develops his or her forecast and rationale. Each person presents and defends or abandons her forecast. The corporate forecast is then developed as a consensus view. For an interest-rate hedging program, the corporate forecast would include a view on the direction of interest-rate movements, the timing and magnitude of the movements, and quarterly rate forecasts for a 12- to 24-month period.

As a result of this process, we developed the following interest rate outlook:

1. U.S. rates were close to the bottom and may have already bottomed out;

2. Although economic statistics were still giving mixed signals, U.S. rates could start to move up by mid-year if the stats started to show a clearer evidence of the recovery;

3. The timing and magnitude of future movements of U.S. rates would depend on the strength of the economic recovery;

4. This would not be a 1-year cycle. Rates would continue to increase or at best trade sideways in 1995;

5. U.S. rates would continue to be lower than Canadian rates and should continue to provide Husky with the most attractive rate of financing, provided interest-rate savings were not eroded by a weakening Canadian dollar.

Our view led us to the following conclusions:

1. If we wanted to avoid the anticipated increase in rates, there was a need to act fairly quickly;

2. Our strategy had to include a short-term component and a longer-term component, because this would not be a 1-year cycle;

3. Because we were less certain of rate increases more than 1 year out, we wanted the flexibility to make up our mind at a later date.

The second major step in the development of the strategy was a corporate risk profile. Developing a corporate risk profile means identifying the risk you face; the risks you want to accept; and the risks you want to hedge. This profile is unique for every company and should be developed before you construct a hedging program. For an interest-rate hedging program it might consist of an analysis of the floating-rate exposure by currency; a sensitivity analysis of the P&L impact of interest-rate increases; an identification of the constraints that determine the scope and cost of the hedge program; construction of the price protection matrix and identification of the company's optimum position on this matrix; and the features, if any, for which the company is willing to pay some money.

In developing this profile, you should ask questions such as:

■ What risk do I face?

■ How sensitive are these risks to pricing changes?

■ Can I handle some uncertainty or do I prefer absolute certainty?

■ Have I done this before?

■ Am I comfortable with new products?

- To what extent am I prepared to commit?
- Is there a level at which I must have protection?
- Am I willing to pay for that level? If not how much am I willing to pay?
- Am I willing to pay for anything else?
- Can I afford to do nothing?

There are two steps in the development of the risk profile:

1. to identify the risks you face, and
2. to identify your appetite for risk.

You could also label these two steps as:

1. What keeps you awake at night; and
2. How much risk can you take and still sleep at night?

Let's look briefly at Husky's risk profile. As well as the commodity and currency risk that comes with the oil and gas business, Husky faced a substantial exposure to increased rates. Because of the remaining capital requirements and the upcoming requirement to reduce debt, cash flow had to be protected from the effect of rate increases to ensure that these commitments could be met. In addition, given that the majority of debt was placed at the short end of the yield curve, Husky arguably faced the risk of greater volatility in rates if it remained at the short end.

As far as Husky's appetite for risk was concerned, Husky had always managed its debt aggressively. Under the right circumstances, we were quite prepared to hedge a significant portion of our debt. Since we wanted some certainty about our interest expense, we were prepared to lock in and extend term, if the price was right.

Regardless of how strongly we feel that our view of the market is reasonable and correct, we invariably leave room in any strategy for the possibility that we may not be right. Thus, although we were prepared to hedge a significant portion, we were not prepared to hedge 100%, and we preferred a phased implementation, linked either to the passage of time or actual changes in rates.

The level of protection that can be achieved and the price–protection trade-off really come down to whether the company is prepared to pay for protection at a particular level. If the company is not prepared to consider anything other than zero-cost strategies, protection will be limited to zero-cost ranges. In Husky's case, although we were not prepared to pay an arm and a leg, we were willing to pay a reasonable amount for protection at a given level.

Note that determining how much you are willing to pay and the level at which you want to be protected is a somewhat iterative process. Although rough guidelines may be set upfront, the prices and levels should be finalized as you analyze the products available.

(From conversations with various banks, I gather that many corporates have a certain reluctance to pay for protection. While it might be easier to sell a strategy that doesn't require any payment, I think you have to examine very carefully whether the protection you get really fits your assessment of the market and whether it's really adequate. At the same time you have to remain realistic or you'll pay enormous sums of money to protect against an event that in your view has a slim to nil chance of occurring.)

In addition to being willing to pay for protection at the right level, Husky will consider paying for flexibility. Flexibility may include the right to choose to act rather than be forced to act, such as in an option versus a swap, or may include the right to choose to act at more than one time, such as in an option with multiple exercise dates. Whether flexibility is something you want to pay for depends on how strongly you hold to your view and whether you're restricted to a zero-cost hedging program.

In summary, the Husky risk profile looked something like this:

- We had a significant exposure to rate increases.
- We were willing to extend term and move up the yield curve.
- We were willing to hedge a significant portion of debt.
- We were willing to pay something for the right level of protection.
- We had a preference for flexibility.

A third step in developing a strategy is the evaluation and selection of the hedging instruments. Like most corporates we tend to see a steady stream of banks and products. Unfortunately, too often we have the impression that we are seeing the flavour of the month and not the products that are really applicable to our situation and profile.

Although we recognize the difficulties in developing and marketing products geared to individual situations, the tendency to market what's hot means that the corporate spends a fair amount of time sifting through the available products and invariably goes back to the financial institution to request a special twist or spin on the generic product. We have also found that institutions tend to market individual products and not strategies. In our experience, it's pretty rare to get a truly useful answer when we say, "Here's our view of the world. Here's what we're trying to protect ourselves against. Here are the ideas we have for protection. What other ideas do you have?"

Although the banks are good at pricing specific products and levels, the corporate may have to spend more time than it would like on developing alternatives. We have found a few people who are excellent at "the idea game," and we tend to go back to them even to the extent of following them from one bank to another. Finding these individuals involves a certain amount of trial and error, since they don't come with business cards that read "Financial Wizard." As a corporate, you have to identify the individual you can trust, who consistently has workable ideas that match your requirements and who is familiar with the range of product that may meet your needs.

Product assessment: Rather than reviewing all the products available, let's examine the assessment and analysis that should be done to select the products that work best for you. If in the assessment process you can't answer the following questions, you need to think very seriously about using the product.

1. *Do I understand it?* Do I understand how the product works? How it performs under various market conditions, including those that I think might be likely and unlikely? What variables most affect the pricing? Can I explain it to others? If you don't understand it, don't use it.

2. *What will the product do for me and what will it do to me?* What conditions are required to increase or decrease my risk if I select this product? How does the

product interact with other hedging instruments that I'm using or planning to use? How does this product interact with the other risks, for example financial or operational risks, that I face? Does the use of this product put me over the top in terms of total risk?

We have all read about the high-profile problems in the derivatives area. The claims and counter-claims seem to centre around trying to identify who had responsibility to determine what a product would do to the client under market conditions that were not foreseen at the time the hedges were placed. In my opinion, the client has the responsibility to determine the "what-ifs," to assess what happens to the product as well as what happens to the company under various scenarios.

3. *Is there a cheaper and more effective alternative?* Although this question may seem self-evident, this is often the most difficult item to assess. Part of the problem is the lack of creativity in the financial community. Often an attempt to canvass the institutions for alternatives may not be very fruitful. In my experience, unless a client is creative and suggests other alternatives that the institution can then go away and price, the list of suggested alternatives may not be very extensive and may be very conventional. We find that a good portion of the time that we spend on developing a hedging program involves trying to determine what else is out there, how it performs and how it compares in terms of cost and coverage to conventional alternatives.

4. *How does the product perform if I'm wrong?* Prior to committing to any product or strategy you must consider what happens if you haven't guessed right. For example, if you think rates are going to trend sideways or come off, what are your cash requirements and what is the impact on your P&L if rates increase? Can you live with the position? Do you need to limit your downside? Can you commit right now or do you need the flexibility of choosing your course of action at a later date when you have a better idea of what will happen to rates? Do you need to provide an emergency exit?

Your financial analysis should be designed to answer these questions. Husky typically takes a quick look at the performance of the product or strategy under various market scenarios, including, for example, constant rates, moderately increasing/decreasing rates, and sharply increasing/decreasing rate scenarios. If the product is somewhat unconventional or if, in our opinion, the bank is somewhat unfamiliar with the product, we will request a copy of the pricing and the cash flow analysis to satisfy ourselves that the product has been correctly constructed and priced.

So where did we end up? What did we consider and what did we select?
Our short list, which perhaps wasn't all that short, included FRAs; conventional floating-fixed swaps; forward start swaps; accreting or step-up swaps; at-the-money swaptions; zero-cost tunnel swaptions; and at-the-money tunnel swaptions.

The best way to narrow down the list and to check out possible combinations is to test each alternative against your view of the market, your objectives and your risk profile. For example, if I believe that there is some uncertainty as to the future movement of rates, does the product lock me in immediately or does it allow me to act at a later date? If my objective is to avoid immediate rate increases, does the product require me to step up the yield curve immediately? If I want to pay little or nothing for protection, is the product beyond my budget? What you are really trying to do is achieve the best possible fit between your company, its objectives, and the products available.

An integral part of selecting the products for your hedging strategy is to determine the size of the hedge: What percentage of your debt do you want to hedge in total? How do you want to allocate it between your alternative products? Again this decision should be driven by your view and objectives, but the most important item here is your risk profile. If as a company you are not comfortable with hedging a significant portion of your debt, your total hedge should obviously not be equal to the majority of your debt. If you are trying out a new product for the first time, even if you feel comfortable with your analysis of the product, a modest portion of your hedge should be allocated to the new product until you develop a track record of how the hedge actually performs.

So what did we decide to use?

1. We decided to use FRAs to create a short-term hedge for 1 year. Our rationale here was:

   ■ We could achieve short-term rate protection by extending LIBOR maturities or by using FRAs. If we locked in with a 1-year LIBOR, we would immediately increase our interest rates. If we chose maturities greater than one month but less than one year, we were still exposed to rate increases on the rollover dates.

   ■ The FRA curve at the time called for a relatively modest increase in LIBOR rates of 62.5 basis points over the year. We thought that rate increases would exceed that level.

   ■ We found that the 6- and 12-month FRA strips were trading very close to cash rates. Both the 6-month strip and the 12-month strip were only 1 basis point over LIBOR.

   ■ FRA strips would also not require an immediate step up the yield curve and would allow us to achieve the same effective rate as the 6- or 12-month LIBOR.

   ■ Assuming that we chose to match our LIBOR terms to the FRA term, the FRA would give us the same degree of certainty on our financing cost as the 1-year LIBOR.

2. We decided to purchase an American-style swaption with a 1-year option period and a 1-year fixed period and sell the European-style swaptions, creating a tunnel swaption. The upper tunnel limit would be set at 5.5%, the lower tunnel limit would be set at less than or equal to 12-month LIBOR plus 75 basis points, resulting in a premium payable of 18–20 basis points.

Our rationale for selecting this was as follows:

■ If we entered into a conventional swap, this would require an immediate step up on the yield curve of 110 to 155 basis points.

■ If we chose an accreting swap or a step-up swap, it would allow us to buy down the rate in earlier years while agreeing to pay higher rates in the later years. Since the rate structure was locked in up front, the later years could be at above-market rates if rates did not increase to the levels in the swap.

■ The longer-term hedge should kick in after the short-term hedge. We didn't want to double up on our hedge positions, so some form of forward start swap or option was preferable.

■ Although the step up would be delayed, a forward start swap would reflect the current yield curve and would result in approximately the same average cost as a conventional swap.

- We found that a straight swaption was fairly expensive. The option premium would produce a breakeven rate that was about 55 basis points over the strike price.

- When we tried to create a zero-cost tunnel swaption with the upper limit at the money, we created one that we felt was too narrow. Since the bank had the right to receive the lower limit from Husky if rates were less than the lower limit, the higher the bank's strike price, the higher the probability that we'd end up with an above-market rate. To give you an idea of this risk, the bank's strike price on a one-year option period was about 75 basis points over the 9×12 FRA and 110 basis points over 12-month LIBOR.

- We found that if we were prepared to pay some premium, we could widen the tunnel by adjusting either the bank's strike price or the Husky strike price. We found that we could widen the tunnel by almost 60 basis points in exchange for paying a premium of 18 basis points. The placement of the tunnel was based on our forecast increase in LIBOR rates and our view on the rates at which we would like to be fixed.

- We planned to match our hedges to our underlying LIBOR rolls. If the bank could exercise at any time, we could end up with a mismatch between our LIBOR maturities and the exercise date. In addition we liked the idea of limiting the bank's right to exercise to just one date. For the lower end of the tunnel, we thus preferred a European-style option.

- As far as our ability to exercise was concerned, we liked the idea of being able to exercise on any date if it suited our operational requirements. We thus preferred an American-style option on the upper end.

- We weren't entirely comfortable with the cost of fixing a 2-year period, although in hindsight those rates looked awfully good. Adding another year to the term resulted in break-even rates of close to 6% in years 2 and 3.

3. Lastly we decided that the short-term hedge should cover 50% of our floating-rate debt and the long-term hedge should cover approximately 25% of our floating-rate debt. Our rationale here was:

   - The size of the hedging program had to allow for the anticipated debt repayments in the next two years.

   - The size of the hedging program had to consider that one of our facilities totalling about 20% of our debt at that time had some rate hedging built in in the form of an average 6-month LIBOR arrears setting mechanism.

   - The size of the hedging program, particularly further out, had to reflect our view of the probability of future rate increases.

Implementation: Having senior management involved in the development of the strategy simplifies the process of approval and implementation. At our company, we tend to involve management in the development of Husky's view of the market. The evaluation and selection of the products and the development of the strategy is then carried out by the treasurer's staff, and the recommendations are presented for approval to senior management. Obviously, management style and familiarity with the products will determine the extent of management involvement in the approval process. But the earlier they are involved, the better.

If the strategy is being developed for the first time, management will likely want some time to review the proposal and assess the consequences. Our approval process was quite streamlined, but there was still a lag of 3 months between the presentation of the strategy and the placement of the first hedge. Part of the delay occurred, though, because we were waiting for the right market opportunity.

As far as timing was concerned, given our view of the market we felt some urgency to get the FRAs in place. But we were prepared to wait to pull the trigger on the longer-term hedges. As is often the case, we thought that we would wait to see if our view of the world was actually going to happen.

To simplify our lives we decided to match the FRAs to the rollover dates of our floating-rate debt. Given the liquidity in the U.S. FRA market, we didn't anticipate any problems in the market's ability to accommodate our tranches, which ranged in size from US$25 million to US$260 million.

Our main concern was to identify target levels and market opportunities to determine whether all or only a portion of the FRA strip should be put in place at one time.

Husky has always been more comfortable actively managing its position and choosing its levels rather than passing on the responsibility for execution to one or a few banks on a best price basis. As a result we watched the market daily for about four months. We would watch the FRA rates for different points on the yield curve and regularly monitor the cash market to determine which market presented the best opportunity.

Approximately 85% of the total FRAs placed were done on this basis. For the remainder, target levels were set and orders placed with the banks with whom we felt comfortable. We would typically not shop the FRA. Instead we would determine which banks were consistently aggressive in their pricing or had a particular appetite for a specific term. For example, we found that one bank had a view on the year-end turn that was quite different from the other banks'. As a result, any of the FRAs that crossed this period were much more aggressively priced than what we saw from the other banks. We would monitor pricing by either obtaining indicative pricing prior to trading or by monitoring live quotes received over time.

So what did we actually implement?

Since we don't live in a perfect world, it's not surprising that things didn't work out exactly as we had planned. The short-term hedge—the FRA program—was expanded to 65% of our floating-rate debt and was extended to a total of 17 months, with the last FRA maturing in March 1995. The option strategy was never implemented, in part because of our desire to wait and see what happened and because of the timing and magnitude of the rate increases in early 1994.

We achieved an average rate of just under 3.85% on our FRAs. As a result, our cash interest expense for 1994 was about $3.5 million less than it would have been if we had funded ourselves in the 90-day LIBOR market and about $1 million less than if we had limited the short-term hedge to the original 50%. For 1995, we estimate that our interest expense will be about 20 basis points higher than if the long-term hedge had been implemented. Over the two years I estimate that we are still significantly ahead on our interest expense.

So what did we learn from all this?

1. We learned that while it's easy in hindsight to look at any hedging program and say that what we learned is that we should have locked in the maximum amount for a longer term at the bottom of the market, I don't think that such a conclusion

is useful in improving future performance. What is useful is to recognize the difficulty in selecting the top and bottom of the market and to recognize the importance of developing a market view and a strategy with which you are comfortable. This is perhaps the difference between a good price and the best price.

2. We learned that even though a strategy has been approved it is still difficult to commit. It's a very human reaction to want some additional confirmation that a rate increase is imminent before placing the first hedge. I would recommend that implementation be discussed in specific detail, including such things as size of order, timing, level, etc., as part of the development of the strategy and fine-tuned as necessary during the actual implementation.

3. We learned that there's no easy answer to the question of what is the appropriate trade-off between flexibility and the courage of your convictions. Accepting and implementing a strategy may mean that you lose the ability to take advantage of market opportunities. Retaining too much flexibility defeats the purpose of a strategy, since you run the risk that the opportunity to hedge may disappear while you're waiting for a clearer indication of how and when rates will change.

    We tried to strike a balance by placing the FRAs in pieces around the time of the underlying maturity or by not placing the entire strip for any given tranche at one time. How you handle this problem will depend on your need for certainty and your comfort level with managing the timing of the placing of the hedge.

    Our main concern was to identify target levels and market opportunities to determine whether all or only a portion of the FRA strip should be put in place at one time.

4. We were a little surprised at how frequently the futures market differed from the cash market and how frequently combining a LIBOR with an FRA strip produced a more attractive rate than the cash rate. We now regularly check to see which alternative will give us the best rate if we are rolling a LIBOR tranche in excess of 90 days.

5. Even though a strategy may not be fully implemented, it may produce spin-off benefits. Although the tunnel option was not implemented, the analysis and evaluation of the various option configurations greatly increased our comfort level with this hedging product and was a factor in the development of our 1995 option program.

6. Early involvement by senior management ensured a consensus in our view of the market, products and execution levels. Not only did this simplify the approval process and streamline implementation, it allowed us to fine-tune the implementation by allowing us to move quickly to take advantage of market opportunities.

Wally Hassenrueck is Manager, Financial Assets Management, for Husky Oil in Calgary. Her responsibilities include financial exposure management, cash management, and foreign exchange. This article is based on her presentation at the 12th Annual Cash and Treasury Management Conference in Toronto in 1995.

Source: *Canadian Treasurer*, June/July 1995, pp. 15–17, 20–23.

As indicated in the article, Husky Oil had decided to convert a major portion of its long-term debt to U.S. dollars and to place that debt on the short-term end of the yield curve. By the end of the first quarter of 1993, 100% of the long-term debt was U.S.-dollar-denominated and 77% of this debt was being rolled at 30-day LIBOR. (The London InterBank Offered Rate is, roughly speaking, the prime rate in the

Eurodollar market.) Long-term debt was at historically high levels, Husky was nearing completion of two sizable capital projects, and there was some desire to protect against rising interest rates to ensure that cash flow would be available for debt repayment. In April 1993, Husky decided to develop a strategy to hedge its interest rate exposure.

The article provides a good explanation of the steps that must be followed by a firm when it decides to hedge. These steps are:

- assess the current and future market development (forecasting);
- develop a risk profile for the company;
- evaluate and select the hedging instruments;
- implement the strategy;
- assess and refine the strategy on an ongoing basis.

It is important to understand these steps and the reasons why they are recommended.

7.5 FINANCING INTERNATIONAL TRADE

International trade finance is similar to domestic trade finance. Credit is provided by the supplier (exporter), the buyer (importer), one or more financial institutions, or any combination of these. When the buyer finances the transaction, either internally or externally with its bank, the credit is known as **buyer credit**. If the supplier funds the entire trade, the credit is known as **supplier credit**. In some cases, the exporter or importer may require bank financing to support the cash flows.

One of the major risks of international trade is foreign-exchange risk. Previous sections covered ways of managing this risk. This section addresses additional risks and complications and how they can be managed. The treasury-risk manager plays a role in managing the risks of international trade.

In addition to foreign-exchange risk, international trade has special commercial and political risks that may be managed by the proper choice of financing instrument. Some of these additional risks include:

- The exporter may question the importer's ability to make payment. This credit question exists in domestic trade relations, but in international trade the information available to resolve this problem is often scarce.
- The government may impose exchange and other controls that prevent payment to the exporter.
- The importer may not trust that the exporter will ship the goods ordered.
- Trade barriers or time lags in international transportation may delay delivery time.

Terms of Payment in International Trade

Many basic methods of payment can be used to settle foreign trade, each with varying degrees of risk to the exporter and importer. These include the open account, consignment, draft or bill of exchange, letters of credit, and prepayment arrangements. This section focuses on drafts and letters of credit.

Drafts A **draft arrangement** or **bill of exchange** is an agreement in which an importer promises to pay the exporter the amount of the draft either at a specified future date (**time draft**) or on presentation (**sight draft**). A typical situation requires the intermediation of two banks, one representing the exporter and the other representing the importer.

Generally, the exporter ships the product and, at the same time, forwards the shipping documents to its bank. In turn, the exporter's bank forwards the documents to the buyer's bank. Under a *time draft*, the exporter instructs the buyer's bank to release the documents once the importer accepts the draft. On acceptance and receipt of the shipping documents, the importer can obtain the merchandise before paying. From this point, the exporter is relying on the buyer's honour and financial integrity to pay the draft at maturity. Thus, the exporter is still facing a high risk. The draft provides increased comfort, because the buyer's bank and the exporter's bank will participate in the collection process. Moreover, the draft is a binding financial contract recognized by law should the exporter be forced to sue the importer for collection.

Under a *sight draft*, the buyer is required to pay once shipment has been made and the exporter presents the draft to the buyer for payment. The buyer's bank will release the shipping documents only after the buyer makes the payment. This arrangement is more secure than a time-draft arrangement.

Letters of Credit A **letter of credit** is a document that effectively commits a bank to the creditworthiness of its client in order to substantiate the client's future business dealings with a third party. Letters of credit are issued as time or sight drafts and guaranteed by the importer or exporter's bank (the issuing bank) on behalf of the importer. The bank is lending its creditworthiness to the buyer. International trade letters of credit are also known as commercial or import/export letters of credit. In addition to the draft, the letter of credit includes the commercial invoice, the bill of lading, and other documents that may be required.

A **bill of lading** is a formal document that substantiates the nature of, ownership of, and responsibility for goods from point of loading to destination. It is prepared by the shipper or carrier of the goods on the carrier's form and is signed by the carrier or the carrier's agent. Bills of lading are issued normally by ship lines throughout the world and by railways and licensed truckers in Canada and the United States. In the bill of lading, the carrier acknowledges having received at a designated point a specified number of packages containing the goods. The packages are described by numbers or marks. The carrier undertakes to transport these packages to a named destination and deliver them to the order of a named consignee.

Letters of credit may be revocable and irrevocable. A **revocable letter of credit** may be modified or cancelled at any time without informing the beneficiary. It provides little protection to the exporter; consequently, it is used only on rare occasions. In contrast, an **irrevocable letter of credit** cannot be altered or terminated without the approval of the beneficiary.

Irrevocable letters of credit provide protection to both the exporter and the importer. The exporter receives more protection with a letter of credit than with a simple sight draft. As long as the documents conform to the letter-of-credit agreement, the issuing bank is obligated to make payment to the exporter, regardless of the buyer's ability or willingness to pay.

Similarly, the importer is protected, as payment is not required until the exporter presents the shipping documents to the issuing bank and the bank is satisfied that they are in good order. The letter of credit does not, however, guarantee that the goods invoiced and shipped are those purchased.

International Trade Financing Using Letters of Credit

Letters of credit are widely used instruments for financing foreign trade. The issuing bank guarantees payment to the exporter if the conditions of the agreement are met. Normally, the importer will have an existing relationship with the bank. If the importer has enough cash to pay the transaction, the importer pays the issuing fees plus the price of the merchandise. Otherwise, the importer may use its line of credit with the issuing bank or take a working capital loan. The important aspect of the letter of credit is that the exporter will receive payment as long as the issuing bank is solvent and creditworthy.

In cases where the exporter doubts the ability of the importer's bank to pay, it may demand a *confirmed* letter of credit. As a result, a bank, normally the exporter's bank, guarantees payment to the exporter and assumes the risk of failure of the issuing bank. When political risks are high, the use of a confirmed letter of credit may be desirable, even if the issuing bank is well known and financially sound.

Bankers' Acceptances Bankers' acceptances (BAs) are written demands, accepted and approved by a bank, stipulating a commitment to pay a certain amount at a given point in time. They are often created in conjunction with an export/import letter of credit. For example, the bank issuing the letter of credit may draw a time draft covering the amount of the payment for the benefit of the exporter. The exporter then presents the time draft along with the shipping documents to its local bank. The exporter's bank in turn sends the draft plus the other documents to the importer's bank. The importer's bank examines the documents, and if they are in order, it stamps the draft "ACCEPTED," thereby creating a bankers' acceptance. The accepting bank will charge an "Accepting Fee" for lending its creditworthiness to the acceptance. The exporter receives the face value of the draft, now the acceptance, at maturity. In this case, the exporter is providing financing for the importer.

Sometimes the exporter may need immediate cash. Because the bank has accepted the draft, the exporter may be able to sell the acceptance to a bank in the money market. As this would be a loan to the exporter, the market price will be less than the face value of the draft to compensate the investor (lender) for the interest cost.

Bankers' acceptances that are traded in the market are generally issued in denominations of $100,000. Once issued, they are often sold by the accepting bank and traded in the secondary market. They are discount securities in that no contractual periodic interest payment is made. Rather, the bankers' acceptance is issued at a discount and matures at face value, the difference being interest to the lender. Normally, maturities range from one month to a year, but the majority are issued with three-month maturities. They enjoy high credit ratings because of the fact that although they are corporate debt, the acceptance gives them the bank's creditworthiness. They are also relatively liquid.

Accounts-Receivable Financing Exporters extend credit when customers cannot purchase without credit. When an exporter supplies credit without guarantees from a bank, for example, through open account or a draft, the accounts receivable of the exporter increase. The exporter can reduce credit, foreign-exchange, and political risks by conducting its own credit analysis and checking.

In many situations, an exporter needs cash immediately. In this case, the exporter can use accounts-receivable financing. This can be done either through pledging of accounts receivable or by factoring. Banks, finance companies, or independent factors may provide the loan.

Pledging Pledging is a financing agreement in which accounts receivable are used as security for a credit extended by a lender. The security is paper assets, the quality of which depends on the borrower's integrity in reporting actual sales. The lender reviews the invoices and rejects those that do not meet the acceptable credit standards for pledging. The final loan is usually less than 100% of the pledged receivables. Banks normally lend 50% to 80% of a borrower's receivables that have not aged more than 60 days. Pledging gives the lender recourse to the borrower. If the importer does not pay, the export firm, not the lender, will take the loss. The risk of default on the accounts receivable remains with the borrower.

Factoring Factoring is a financing agreement in which a firm sells its accounts receivable, usually at a discount to the lender, without recourse. In contrast to pledging, the factoring company (lender) assumes the risk of default on bad accounts. Thus, it must do the credit checks. Accordingly, factors provide not only money but also a credit department for the borrower.

Generally, an agreement is made between the seller and the lender to specify legal obligations and procedural arrangements. When the seller receives an order from a buyer, a credit approval slip is written and forwarded to the factoring company for a credit check. If the factoring firm does not approve the credit, the seller refuses to fill the order. If the credit is approved, the sale will be made and the invoice is stamped to notify the buyer to make payment directly to the factoring firm.

Factoring provides several benefits to the exporter:

- The exporter receives funds immediately to be used for other purposes.

- The exporter is relieved of the administrative costs of collecting the receivable.

- The exporter does not have to maintain an international credit-checking department. Normally the factor performs credit checking.

- The factor assumes all credit, foreign-exchange, and political risks.

- Some arrangements allow the exporter to choose any combination of the previous services by changing the provisions of the factoring agreement. Usually, credit-checking commissions range between 1% and 3% of the amount of invoices accepted by the factor. Interest on the money borrowed is usually one to three percentage points above prime.

Forfeiting Forfeiting is similar to factoring except that the receivables are longer term and have higher values. Generally, the importer issues a promissory note to the benefit of the exporter, who in turn sells the note, without recourse, to the forfeiting bank. The bank does the credit checking, lending, collecting, and risk bearing.

Forfeiting is different from factoring in a few aspects:

- Forfeiting involves the purchase of receivables from which payments are expected over several years rather than several months, as in factoring. For example, the receivables may occur because of the construction of an airport facility or warehouse, or the purchase of equipment. In these cases, financing is required over several years and the exporter may not be capable of providing ongoing funds.

- Given the nature of the purchases in forfeiting transactions, the amounts covered are usually large. Sometimes, the agreements involve several financial institutions, known as a syndicate. Each participant assumes a portion of the underlying risk and profit.

- Given the long-term nature of forfeiting agreements and the large amounts involved, the risks are usually higher than in factoring. For this reason, a bank in the importer's country may be required to guarantee the payment by a letter of credit.

Forfeiting is desirable when cash flows are expected over several years and the exporter is either not capable of waiting or not willing to wait until they are paid. Forfeiting is particularly attractive when the amounts involved are large and constitute a significant portion of the exporter's cash flows. In such cases, the exporter needs the cash to pay wages, raw material, taxes, interest on the debt, and other recurring cash outflows. The forfeiting bank can use the promissory note as collateral to supply these cash needs and wait until the ultimate payment is made. Similar to factoring, forfeiting should be pursued by an exporter when credit, political, and commercial risks are high. Under these conditions, the exporter is better off having the forfeiting bank handle the risk assessment and bear the risk.

The Export Development Corporation

A study of managing the risks of international trade by Canadian exporters is not complete without considering the services of Export Development Canada (EDC). The EDC is a Crown corporation that was established in 1969 to assist exporters in financing their sales with loans, loan guarantees, and credit insurance.

The most important service of the EDC is credit insurance, which is provided to cover commercial and political risks. Commercial risks include buyer's default caused by insolvency, unlawful termination of agreement, and unlawful rejection of product. Political risks include loss caused by war, revolution, cancellation of import or export permits, and inability to exchange foreign currency on account of political unrest or unusual circumstances. Up to 90% of losses can be insured.

The EDC also insures direct investments made by Canadians in foreign countries. Canadians who make direct investments in plant, equipment, mines, and other projects can insure their interests against political risks. The provision of credit to foreign purchasers of Canadian goods and services is also an important part of the EDC's services. The EDC provides qualified foreigners with up to 85% financing for the purchase of Canadian goods, services, or equipment. The product to be financed must meet a Canadian content test to qualify for financing. Normally, the EDC sets up an arrangement with a foreign institution, such as a bank, where it approves a line of credit to the foreign bank, and the bank lends the money to the foreign purchasers of Canadian goods and services. When foreign buyers obtain financing from the EDC's line of credit and a foreign bank guarantees the loan, the credit is known as buyer credit.

Alternatively, the exporter may obtain supplier credit from the EDC. In this case, the importer issues promissory notes to the benefit of the exporter. Then the exporter obtains a guarantee on the promissory notes from a financial institution located in the importer's country. The guarantee enables the exporter to sell the notes to the EDC for cash. In this case, the EDC operates like a factor to the exporter.

For additional information, visit the EDC Web site (see the Web Links section of this chapter).

CHAPTER SUMMARY

This chapter addresses the practical details of identifying and measuring interest-rate, foreign-exchange, and commodity-price risks from transactions. You learn the fundamental concepts and approaches to risk management. You also learn the basics of financing international trade, including letters of credit, bankers' acceptances, factoring, and forfeiting.

Key Terms

Important Equations

Duration of a security

$$D = \frac{\sum_{t=1}^{n}\left[\dfrac{CF_t}{(1+i)^t} \times t\right]}{\sum_{t=1}^{n}\left[\dfrac{CF_t}{(1+i)^t}\right]}$$

(Equation 7-1)

where

D = duration

CF_t = dollar value of the cash flow expected at time t

t = number of units of time (normally years or semi-annual periods) until cash flow payment

i = yield to maturity on the security under consideration

n = number of anticipated cash flows

Volatility of a security's value to changes in the required yield per discounting period

$$\frac{\left(\dfrac{\Delta V}{V}\right)}{\Delta r} \approx \frac{-D}{1 + \dfrac{i}{m}}$$

(Equation 7-2)

where

D = duration measured in years

V = market value of the security

ΔV = change in market value of the security

Δr = change in interest rates

i = yield to maturity

m = number of compounding periods per year

Change in market value of a security for a given change in interest rate

$$\Delta V = \frac{-D \times V}{1 + \dfrac{i}{m}} \times \Delta r \text{ or } \frac{-D \times V \times \Delta r}{1 + \dfrac{i}{m}}$$

(Equation 7-3)

Gap analysis of a firm

$$\text{Gap} = \text{rate-sensitive assets} - \text{rate-sensitive liabilities}$$

(Equation 7-4)

Change in net interest income

$$\Delta NII = \Delta r \times \text{gap}$$

(Equation 7-5)

where

ΔNII = change in net interest income

Δr = expected change in interest rates

Duration of a portfolio

$$D_P = \frac{D_1 V_1 + D_i V_i + \ldots + D_n V_n}{V_1 + V_i + \ldots + V_n}$$ (Equation 7-6)

where

D_P = duration of a portfolio

D_i = durations of i securities (where $i = 1, \ldots, n$)

V_i = market values of i securities (where $i = 1, \ldots, n$)

Change in a portfolio's value as a function of a weighted average expected change in individual yields

$$\Delta V_P = \frac{-D_P \times V_P}{1 + d_W} \times \Delta r \quad \text{or} \quad \frac{-D_P \times V_P \times \Delta r}{1 + d_W}$$ (Equation 7-7)

where

V_P = portfolio's value

D_P = portfolio's duration

Δr = change in interest rates

d_W = weighted average discount rate, where the component rate for an asset is the yield to maturity per compounding period

Web Links

Bank for International Settlements

- http://www.bis.org/index.htm Research, working papers, publications, statistics, and committee proceedings from the bank for central banks.

Glossary of International Trade Terms

- http://www.exportsource.ca/gol/exportsource/site.nsf/en/es02712.html From Team Canada Inc., a network of federal departments and agencies, this glossary lists some of the key terms and definitions in international trade financing.

Government of Canada Treasury Risk Management Framework

- http://www.fin.gc.ca/treas/frame/gctrmf06_e.html From the Department of Finance Canada and the Bank of Canada, this reference document describes the management of government funds in Canada.

MoU between the Department of Finance and Bank of Canada

- http://www.fin.gc.ca/treas/Goveev/mou-trm-e.html The Memorandum of Understanding (MoU) regarding the treasury management policy framework and roles and responsibilities between the Government of Canada's Department of Finance and the Bank of Canada. See also http://www.fin.gc.ca/treas/frame/gctrmf06_e.html for HTML or PDF versions of the framework.

Export Development Canada

■ http://www.edc-see.ca Export Development Canada provides financing, insurance, and bonding services to Canadian exporters, as well as foreign market expertise. Its Web site includes a Weekly Commentary, Latest News Releases, and an Exporting 101 section.

Risk Center

■ http://www.riskcenter.com/ An online news service providing up-to-the-minute stories and data for financial risk professionals.

Risk Glossary

■ http://www.riskglossary.com/link/interest_rate_risk.htm This is a risk consultant's commercial Web site that contains a glossary of terms related to risk management with links to related books and forum discussions.

Treasury & Risk

■ http://www.treasuryandrisk.com/ This Web site offers access to selected current and archived magazine articles and financial white papers on a variety of treasury and risk topics.

Self-Test Questions

Qualitative Questions

Answer each of the following questions in point form:

1. What types of interest-rate risk may a treasury-risk manager face?

2. What other types of risk can a treasury-risk manager face?

3. How is duration used to measure risk?

4. How is gap analysis used to measure interest-rate risk in financial institutions?

5. How are gap analysis and duration calculations used to create basic hedges?

6. What are the general approaches to risk management?

7. International trade may expose a firm to risks other than foreign-exchange risk. What are these other risks?

8. What financing arrangements can be used to manage risks in international trade?

Qualitative Multiple Choice Questions

1. Which of the following is a formal document that substantiates the nature of, ownership of, and responsibility for goods from the point of loading to the destination?
   i) Bankers' acceptance
   ii) Letter of credit
   iii) Factoring agreement
   iv) Bill of lading

2. Which of the following statements *best* describes the pledging of accounts receivable?
   i) A financing agreement in which a firm sells its accounts receivable, usually at a discount to the lender, without recourse
   ii) A financing agreement in which the risk of customer default on the accounts receivable remains with the borrower

iii) A financing agreement used primarily for very large receivables that are long term in nature

iv) A financing agreement in which the borrowing firm does not receive any amounts collected on the receivables above the loan amount provided by the lender

3. Which of the following statements about factoring accounts receivable is true?

   i) Factoring involves the purchases of receivables from which payments are expected over several years, rather than several months.

   ii) The amounts covered are generally large and the agreements are long term in nature.

   iii) The exporter incurs the administrative costs of collecting the accounts receivable.

   iv) The exporter receives funds immediately to be used for other purposes.

4. In international trade financing, which of the following statements about factoring and forfeiting arrangements is correct?

   i) Forfeiting arrangements tend to be used for very short term receivables.

   ii) Factoring arrangements tend to be used for very large receivables.

   iii) In factoring arrangements, receivables are used as security for credit extended by a lender, whereas in forfeiting arrangements, the exporting firm sells its receivables to the lender.

   iv) Forfeiting is similar to factoring, except that the receivables are longer term and have higher values.

5. Which of the following statements *best* describes a document used in international trade?

   i) A letter of credit effectively commits a bank to the creditworthiness of its client in order to substantiate the client's future business dealings with a third party.

   ii) A banker's acceptance substantiates the nature of, ownership of, and responsibility for goods from point of loading to destination.

   iii) Under a sight draft, the exporter instructs the buyer's bank to release the documents once the importer accepts the draft.

   iv) A bill of lading is a written demand, accepted and approved by a bank, stipulating a commitment to pay a certain amount at a given point in time.

Quantitative Multiple Choice Questions

1. An investor has a 4-year, $1,000 Government of Manitoba bond. The bond has a coupon rate of 8%, payable annually. The current yield to maturity on Government of Manitoba bonds is 4%. What is the duration of the bond?

   i) 3 years

   ii) 3.28 years

   iii) 3.61 years

   iv) 4 years

2. A portfolio is worth $10 million with equal weight for 3 bonds. The durations for the bonds are 2, 3, and 5 years, and the weighted average discount rate is 2.5%. What will be the change in the portfolio's value if all interest rates go up by 1%?

   i) −$100,000

   ii) −$250,000

   iii) −$325,170

   iv) −$333,333

3. A North American bond has 2 years to maturity. It has a $1,000 face value and a 10% coupon rate with interest paid semi-annually. The required rate of return on bonds of similar risk and maturity, with semi-annual interest payments, is currently 8%. What is the duration of this bond?

  i) 1.86 years

  ii) 1.93 years

  iii) 2.07 years

  iv) 3.73 years

4. Frank has just signed a contract by which he agrees to deliver equipment worth US$10 million to a customer in the United States in 2 months. One month after delivery, payment will be made in U.S. dollars. Currently, the U.S. dollar is trading at C$1.40. What will happen to the Canadian dollar value of the receivable if the U.S. dollar drops in value to C$1.35 in 3 months?

  i) The value will decrease by C$264,455.

  ii) The value will increase by C$264,455.

  iii) The value will decrease by C$500,000.

  iv) The value will increase by C$500,000.

Quantitative Problems

Problem 1

Susan is planning to invest about $100,000 in Government of Canada bonds for at least 4 years. The bonds compound annually and pay out the interest at maturity. On consulting her broker, she obtains the information below.

Cash Rates on Government of Canada Bonds					
Maturity	1 year	2 year	3 year	4 year	5 year
Cash rate	4%	4.35%	4.65%	4.90%	5.20%

a) How many alternatives are available to Susan, given that she is limited to investing in only the maturities specified in the table?

b) What will Susan's returns be for each of these alternatives, assuming the yield curve does not change?

c) Susan needs $123,000 in 4 years' time. Given this information, what is Susan's best option? Show your calculations.

Problem 2

An investor has both shares and bonds in his investment portfolio. The bond holdings include two issues, each with a $1,000 face value. Issue A is for a natural gas pipeline firm with very stable earnings. The bonds pay an interest rate of 3% each half-year, and the bonds have 2 years until they mature. The current market yield on comparable bonds if newly issued would be 2% each half-year. The investor owns 200 of these bonds.

The investor also owns 150 Issue B bonds, issued by a high-tech robotics firm. These bonds pay an interest rate of 8% per annum and mature in 4 years. The current market yield on comparable bonds if newly issued would be 10% per annum.

a) Calculate the value of each bond issue holding and of the bond portfolio as a whole.

b) Calculate the duration of each bond issue and the duration of the bond portfolio.

c) Calculate the volatility of each bond issue.

d) Explain which of the bond holdings, Issue *A* or Issue *B*, is riskier. Consider both business risk and interest-rate risk in your explanation.

Problem 3

Kim has one $1,000,000 bond that was part of an inheritance. The bond has a three-year term to maturity and compounds quarterly with a coupon rate of 8%.

a) Calculate the duration of the bond.

b) What is the volatility of the bond?

c) If Kim decides that a 1% change in market value will indicate that it is time to sell the bonds, what increase in interest rates will trigger the sale?

Problem 4

According to the article by Wally Hassenrueck,

a) What are the steps that a company planning to hedge should follow to assess current and future market developments?

b) What are the benefits of formulating an internal view regarding the current and future state of the market?

Problem 5

Adam has a portfolio of three different types of bonds in his RRSP, *A*, *B*, and *C*. Each of these bonds has $1,000 par value. Adam's bond portfolio is shown below.

			Adam's Bond Portfolio		
Bond	**Quantity**	**Interest rate**	**Payment frequency**	**Maturity (years)**	**Yield to maturity**
A	10		Zero coupon	5	6%
B	5	8%	Semi-annually	3	6.6% compounded semi-annually
C	8	7%	Annually	4	6.2%

a) What is the current market value for each type of bond?

b) What is the duration of each of bonds *A*, *B*, and *C*?

c) What is the duration of Adam's bond portfolio?

d) For purposes of using Equation 7-7 to calculate the volatility of Adam's bond portfolio, what is the current weighted average discount rate on the portfolio?

e) What is the volatility of the portfolio?

f) If rates drop by one percentage point, what happens to the value of the portfolio, and what is the magnitude of the expected change?

Cases

Case 1: Baywater Soup Company

The Baywater Soup Company is concerned about the current state of the economy. The company is highly leveraged with both long- and short-term debt. The peak soup-sales season has just passed and the company has invested excess funds in short-term securities. Case Exhibit 7-1 shows the company's balance sheet as at April 30, 20X1.

Case Exhibit 7-1
Baywater Soup Company Balance Sheet
As at April 30, 20X1

Assets		Liabilities	
Current assets		**Current liabilities**	
Cash	$ 13,450,000	Accounts payable	$ 4,360,000
Short-term investments	5,125,000	Accruals	1,235,000
Accounts receivable	6,720,000	Short-term notes	23,000,000
Inventory	16,645,000		
Long-term investments	50,000,000	**Long-term liabilities**	
		Mortgage on plant	31,500,000
		Bonds	90,000,000
Capital assets			
Plant	42,000,000	**Shareholders'**	
Equipment	120,875,000	**equity**	104,720,000
Total assets	$254,815,000	Total liabilities and shareholders' equity	$254,815,000

The current rates on Baywater's various investments and liabilities are as shown in Case Exhibit 7-2.

Case Exhibit 7-2
Average Yields and Costs of Investments and Liabilities

Assets	Amount in $ millions	Average yield %	Liabilities	Amount in $ millions	Average cost %
Non-earning	$199.690	0.00%	Non-earning	$5.595	0.00%
Rate-sensitive	5.125	3.25	Rate-sensitive	23.000	3.00
Fixed-rate	50.000	5.00	Fixed-rate	121.500	4.75
Total	254.815		Equity	104.720	N/A
			Total	254.815	

Required

a) Calculate the expected interest income.
b) Calculate the expected interest cost.
c) Calculate the expected net interest income or loss.
d) Calculate the net return on assets.
e) Calculate the gap.
f) If interest rates rise 1%, what will the change be in net interest income or loss?

Chapter 8
Futures and Forwards

CHAPTER OVERVIEW

In Chapters 1 to 7, you studied the valuation techniques of financial and real assets under the assumption that the transactions will be completed imminently. In other words, the asset that has been purchased is delivered to the buyer immediately or in the near future, and the money for payment is delivered immediately. Transactions such as these are said to take place in the cash or spot market.

In this chapter, the focus shifts to situations in which the agreement to purchase or sell an asset is reached in the present but delivery takes place at some future date, on terms set out in the agreement. Specifically, in this and the next chapter, you study futures, forwards, options, and swaps. These securities are known as derivative securities because their value depends on (or is derived from) the value of an underlying asset.

Section 8.1 covers the characteristics and features of futures and forward contracts and the environment in which they are traded. Generally, futures and forward contracts are agreements to sell or buy a specified asset for future delivery. The buyer has the obligation to buy the underlying asset at the specified price regardless of whether it is profitable to do so or not. Similarly, the seller has the obligation to sell at the specified price. Other than nominal transaction costs, the buyer and seller do not have to exchange any money at the time of the agreement. Futures contracts and forward agreements may result in substantial losses or profits to the trader, which is why they are most often used by hedgers or professional speculators.

The basic valuation concepts of futures and forwards are explained in Section 8.2. You learn that their prices are primarily a function of cash prices plus the costs of holding the cash asset until delivery. Cash prices normally reflect the market's expectation of future asset prices. Holding costs are affected by interest rates, inventory holding costs, dividend payments, and other factors that depend on the traded asset.

Section 8.3 highlights the important concepts involved in hedging with futures and forwards. The issues involved in this section are important and require considerable attention in order to follow the detailed treatment of managing risk using futures and forward contracts.

Learning Objectives

After completing this chapter, you will be able to:

- Describe futures contracts, margin requirements, and the role of the clearing house in futures trading.

- Explain the basics of futures valuation and calculate the price of a futures contract.

- Demonstrate the process of hedging using futures and calculate its cost under different interest rate changes.

- Explain hedging using forward contracts.

This knowledge will provide you with the professional skills to:

- Identify, analyze, and advise on financial instruments to minimize risk and their impact on the organization.

- Identify, analyze, and advise on financial instruments to minimize the financial risk of the issuer, investor, or lender.

- Research, evaluate, and advise on the appropriate accounting treatment for complex transactions with respect to valuation of financial instruments.

- Assess or design a financial-risk management strategy.

HOW THIS CHAPTER RELATES TO OTHER CHAPTERS IN THIS BOOK

Business enterprises are subject to numerous risks related to commodity-price, interest-rate, equity-price, and exchange rate fluctuations in the financial markets. Back in Chapter 2, the trade-off between risk and return was discussed. If an action can reduce risk without reducing any returns in excess, then the action can enhance value. For an investor, one of the most obvious ways to reduce financial risk is to possess a broad diversified portfolio of stocks and debt securities, including international securities and debt of varying maturities. However, derivative securities (usually simply called *derivatives*) can also be used to reduce the risk associated with financial and commodity markets.

Derivatives are securities. Their prices are determined or driven by the price of other securities. Futures and forward contracts are both derivative securities. It will be seen that their payoffs are dependent on the value of the other securities. Options and swaps, which are discussed in Chapter 9, also are derivatives. As the value of derivatives depends on the value of other securities, these can be powerful tools for both hedging and speculation. These applications will be investigated in the next two chapters, starting in this chapter with futures and forwards.

8.1 FUTURES AND FORWARDS

Characteristics of Futures and Forward Contracts

Futures and forwards, as well as options and swaps, are derivative contracts. They are called **derivatives** because their value is derived from the value of an underlying asset. The underlying asset could be a bond, currency, commodity, or interest rate. In place of an underlying asset, the derivative can even be based on the more or less probable outcome of an event, such as weather conditions. You will look first at futures and forward contracts and later broaden your scope to include options and swaps.

A **futures** or **forward contract** is an agreement to trade an asset on a specified future date at a specified price. The seller promises to sell the underlying asset at the agreed price and deliver on the delivery date. The buyer promises to buy at the agreed price and accept delivery on the agreed delivery date. In contrast, the **spot market** is a market for trading assets where there is an immediate exchange of the asset for cash.

The major difference between futures and forwards is the way they are traded. **Futures contracts** are transacted on an organized exchange, and all aspects of the contract and trading in it are governed by the exchange and its clearing house. **Forward contracts** are traded directly between buyer and seller in the over-the-counter market. All aspects of a forward contract are governed by the parties to the contract, one of which is usually a bank or financial institution.

The price at which an asset is to be delivered at a specified future date is called the **futures** or **forward price**. The **cash price**, also called the **spot price**, is the price at which the asset can be purchased today. The difference between the futures or forward price and the spot price is called the **basis** of the specific future or forward. No exchange of assets or money takes place at the time the contract is signed. The exchange of cash for assets takes place, if at all, on the delivery date.

At the time of an agreement to sell, the seller does not necessarily own the underlying asset. By agreeing to sell an asset he does not own, the seller assumes a **short position** in the futures or forward market. In contrast, the purchase of a futures or forward contract on a security or commodity is referred to as a **long position**.

Exhibit 8-1 contains an example of an outstanding futures contract for coffee. According to the contract details, this contract was traded through the New York Coffee and Sugar Exchange Inc. (now part of the New York Board of Trade). The original contract is a standardized form and the underlined areas (date of the contract, name of the buyer, name of the seller, purchase price, and delivery dates) are filled in by the two parties when the contract is signed. Standardized futures contracts relieve traders of dealing with the specifics of each contract. They also increase liquidity and marketability.

**Exhibit 8-1
An Outstanding Coffee Futures Contract
Contract "C" (new) (Colombian Coffee Contract)**

Montréal _September 15, 20X7_

(We/I) _Coffee Roasters International (CRI)_ have this day (~~sold~~/bought) and agreed to (~~deliver to~~/receive from) _South Columbia Coffee Beans (SCCB) Inc._ 32,500 lbs. (in about 650 bags) of Columbian coffee, grading from No. 2 to No. 6 inclusive, provided the average grade shall not be better than No. 3, nor worse than No. 5. Delivery of better than No. 3 is allowed provided that the premium for No. 3 grade is paid. No premium shall be paid for Softish Coffee grading worse than No. 4.

At the price of _120.00_ U.S. cents per pound for Columbian No. 4, Strictly Soft, Fair to Good Roast, Solid Bean with additions or deductions for grades, ports of shipment and description (quality) according to the differentials established or to be established by the Committee on Coffee of the New York Coffee and Sugar Exchange for the delivery month specified below in accordance with Section 88(9) (a) of the By-Laws of said Exchange. The delivery must consist of Coffee from one port only.

The Coffee to be Fair to Good Roast, Solid Bean, and the description (quality) to be Strictly Soft, Soft, or Softish. No delivery permitted of Hard Coffee.

Continued >

Deliverable from licensed warehouse in the Port of New York between the first and last days of _January 20X8_ inclusive, the delivery within such time to be at the seller's option upon either five, six or seven days' notice to the buyer as prescribed by the Trade Rules.

Either party may call for margin as the variations of the market for like deliveries may warrant, which margin shall be kept good.

This contract is made in view of, and is in all respects subject to, the By-Laws, Rules and Regulations of the New York Coffee and Sugar Exchange, Inc.

Signatures:

Buyer(s): _Coffee Roasters International (CRI)_
Seller(s): _South Columbia Coffee Beans (SCCB) Inc._

Source: Reprinted with permission of Eric Kirzner.

Note that the contract ensures the buyer of a specified quality of coffee, given that many different grades of coffee exist.

The signed contracts of the buyer and the seller both become financial instruments that can be traded in the market. The contract price is US$1.20 per pound. The buyer's side of the contract will have positive value (profits) when the market price of the underlying asset is higher than the contract price. For example, if on October 10, 20X7, the market price of coffee for delivery in January is US$1.35, the buyer's side of the contract has a positive value equal to:

$$\text{Buyer's contract value} = (\$1.35 - \$1.20) \times 32{,}500 = \$4{,}875$$

In this case, the contract gives the buyer the right to purchase from the seller at a price $0.15 per pound lower than the market price of $1.35 per pound. The buyer will not be willing to trade the contract for less than $4,875 because that is his profit if he keeps the contract. Any other party in the market to buy the same kind of coffee for delivery in January 20X8 should be willing to pay up to $4,875 to purchase the contract from the buyer.

In contrast, the seller's side of the contract will have a negative value (loss) if the market price of the underlying asset is greater than the contract price. For example, on October 10, 20X7, the seller's side of the contract has a negative value equal to:

$$\text{Seller's contract value} = (\$1.20 - \$1.35) \times 32{,}500 = -\$4{,}875$$

The mechanism of a forward contract is quite similar to this example of a futures contract, except that the two participants trade directly with each other, negotiating the desired amount, quality, quantity, and delivery date.

Futures and forward trading is a zero-sum game if transaction costs are ignored. In other words, excluding any initial transaction costs to buy or sell, the amount that will be lost by the seller will be gained by the buyer, or vice versa. Exhibit 8-2 summarizes the profits and losses in futures or forward trading.

Futures and Forward Traders

The major participants in futures and forward trading are hedgers and speculators. A **hedger** is a person or firm that has a direct interest in the actual commodity or asset underlying the

Exhibit 8-2
Profits and Losses in Futures and Forward Trading

	Market price	Result	With the contract:
Buyer: guaranteed and obligated to purchase at the contract price	Decreases	Loss	The buyer is obligated to buy at a price higher than the market price.
	Increases	Profit	The buyer is secured to buy at the contract (lower) price.
Seller: guaranteed and obligated to sell at the contract price	Decreases	Profit	The seller is secured to sell at a price higher than the market price.
	Increases	Loss	The seller is obligated to sell at the contract (lower) price.

futures contract. Hedgers have a specific requirement to buy or sell, and their participation is an effort to minimize the risk of price fluctuation that results from their core business. For example, hedgers who use agricultural commodity futures and forwards include farmers, grain companies, and flour mills. The term "hedging" relates to protecting oneself (in this case, from financial losses), since a hedge can be seen as a form of protective barrier. Hedgers who use financial futures and forwards include banks, trust companies, and investment companies.

Hedgers use forwards or futures to secure a sale price or a purchase price for the underlying asset. Buyers expect to use the underlying asset some time in the future, and they want to guarantee the purchase price now. Sellers expect to have the underlying asset sometime in the future, and they want to guarantee a sale price. Hedgers attempt to avoid price risk by passing the risk to a speculator who is willing to accept it or by transacting with another hedger who is trying to cover a diametrically opposed risk position.

Turn now to the following article and see what Paul G. Barr has to say about large-volume traders of derivative securities in general and of futures in particular.

INSTITUTIONS CUT DERIVATIVES USE

PAUL G. BARR

Greenwich, Conn.—Fixed-income derivatives trading volume plummeted among pension funds, investment managers and mutual funds, a Greenwich Associates report shows.

In addition, the share of trading in exchange-traded futures and derivatives among investment managers and mutual fund managers fell, although pension funds' share held steady, the survey shows.

But the results don't surprise institutional investors.

In a survey of many types of institutional derivatives users, pension fund use of interest rate and cross-currency swaps fell to $100 million on average from $6.2 billion; investment manager use fell to $100 million on average from $1 billion; and mutual fund use fell to $100 million on average from $6.1 billion.

Pension fund use of interest rate options, caps, collars, floors, or swaptions among survey respondents rose to $500 million on average from $100 million, while investment manager use fell to $800 million on average from $2.2 billion, and mutual fund use fell to $300 million on average from $600 million.

Pension funds' share of futures and exchange-traded fixed-income derivatives volume held steady at 13%, while investment managers' share fell to 15% from 21%, and mutual funds' share fell to 12% from 34%.

Frank Feenstra, principal with Greenwich, said the big derivatives-linked losses taken in the past few years woke up a lot of senior people at institutional investment firms to the realization that they didn't know how derivatives were being used. Because the firms didn't want to get burned, they curtailed the use of all derivatives, he said.

The number of users also declined, with smaller investors possibly getting out for good, Mr. Feenstra said. The cost of managing positions and understanding what they're doing might be too great for smaller investors, he said.

The Greenwich survey results confirmed what some institutional investors have seen in the derivatives markets.

"I'm not at all surprised by the survey," said John Isaacson, chief investment officer for Payden & Rygel Investment Counsel, Los Angeles. The results are consistent with his experience in 1994 and 1995.

"We just got a steady stream of calls" from pension sponsors looking at how to define derivatives in order to limit their use, he said. A problem with that, though, is that new structures are constantly being created, and using a definitional method of limiting their use will not work, he said.

In addition, many investors were at least rewriting investment guidelines, if not banning derivatives' use, he said.

For clients who requested it, Payden & Rygel has increased its reporting to clients on derivatives usage.

But he had a message for clients: "Don't get rid of derivatives if it can truly reduce volatility."

At Payden & Rygel, portfolio managers have not altered their use of derivatives in response to losses, Mr. Isaacson said. Derivatives are used primarily for hedging currency positions.

Robert Arnott, chief investment officer and chief executive of First Quadrant Corp., Pasadena, Calif., said he isn't surprised by the drop in volume among pension funds and money managers in using over-the-counter derivatives.

He said the decline "is probably, in fact almost certainly, happening in the OTC swap market, where some of the exotic custom-designed fixed-income swaps and other over-the-counter derivatives have turned out to be so costly—indeed, devastatingly costly to some institutional investors who did not have the sophistication to fully understand what they were buying.

"But we have seen no evidence at all of a decline in interest in using exchange-traded bond futures—plain-vanilla derivatives—where the daily settlement of gains and losses makes it much more difficult to get into serious trouble unexpectedly building up losses over months."

William Miller, chairman of the End Users of Derivatives Association, a Washington education and resource group for derivatives users, noted other factors—like a less volatile interest rate environment—might have contributed to decreased use of derivatives.

If interest rates don't move as much, there's less of a need to use derivatives to try to limit volatility, Mr. Miller said.

He also said if derivatives use by pension funds and investment managers has fallen as overall use increases, maybe those investors should question whether they are managing risk properly.

Some institutional investors, who asked to not be identified, wondered if the Greenwich study was a good reflection of how pension funds and money managers use fixed-income derivatives, particularly given the continued growth of the overall use of OTC derivatives.

The Greenwich survey included 1,110 institutions overall, including 96 pension funds with internal management, 449 investment managers, and 97 mutual funds.

Source: Reprinted with permission, *Pensions & Investments* (July 12, 1996). Copyright Crain Communications Inc.

The term **derivative securities** refers to futures, options, swaps, and other securities that derive their values from other assets. The article suggests that most of the traders in derivatives are institutions, such as investment firms and pension plans, that are trying to avoid interest rate volatility. Small investors also trade derivatives, but the volume traded by these investors is declining. An important conclusion of the article is that traders should be well educated about derivatives; otherwise, they may expose themselves to unwanted risks. The article also indicates that for small investors, the costs of managing positions and understanding the risks and details of derivatives and their trading are high.

A **speculator** is a person or firm that purchases and sells futures or forward contracts with the sole intention of making a profit by closing out the position at a price that is higher than the initial price. Speculators buy contracts on underlying assets for which they have no intention of taking actual delivery, or sell contracts on assets they do not own. Until they close out their positions (by passing the contract on to another party before the delivery date), they accept the risk of price fluctuations in the underlying assets. Despite the negative publicity that speculators often receive, they are essential participants in every market because they add liquidity by buying when no one else wants to and by selling when everyone else is buying. Without speculators, there could not be an active market.

In the case of futures, hedgers and speculators may or may not be members of the exchange on which they trade. If they are not members, they execute their buy and sell orders through a member broker. A **broker** is a financial intermediary who facilitates the buying and selling of securities for investors. In the case of futures, brokers facilitate the exchange of futures contracts for a commission. **Floor traders** buy and sell futures for their own accounts or on behalf of others. They are professional speculators. Their positions are short term, rarely exceeding four or five hours. They have the advantage of being on the floor of the exchange to seek profits from short-term price differentials.

In the case of forwards, most speculators are large institutions, such as banks, trading houses, or investment dealers. Hedge funds may also be speculators in the forward market. These institutions employ professional traders who make forward contracts to other parties, such as corporations and governments. They also trade actively in the forward market with one another. The interbank forward market is large and liquid. In some markets, such as foreign exchange, the volume traded in the futures markets is only a tiny fraction of the volumes traded between banks in the forward market.

A hedger who wishes to buy or sell a forward contract would contact a financial institution, such as a bank or trading house. The amount, delivery date, and price would be determined based on the hedger's requirements. Unlike trading prices in the futures markets, which are reported to all market participants, prices in the forward market represent a private agreement to purchase or sell between the bank and the bank's customer.

Futures Price Quotations

Information on financial and commodity futures trading is reported in financial newspapers on a daily basis. This information is also available online.

To find out more about the basics of the futures contract, go to the Montréal Exchange Web site (see the Web Links section later in this chapter). From the *Publications* drop-down menu on the top of the Web page, select *Guides and strategies*. Then select the *BAX descriptive brochure*. This document contains general information about BAX^{TM} futures.

From the MX *Products* drop-down menu, select *Interest rate derivatives → BAX*. This Web page outlines the details of the contract for three-month Canadian bankers' acceptance (BA) futures. The underlying interest of this contract is a notional three-month bankers' acceptance, which means that this contract can be used to hedge or speculate on three-month BA interest rates. The contract specifications include trading unit, contract size, contract type, and other information.

To review BAX^{TM} quotes, go to *Stock Options and Futures Quotes* (located under *Quick Links* on the left from the Montréal Exchange home page). From the *Interest Rate Derivatives* drop-down menu, select *BAX* and click *OK*. This Web page contains a table of selected information for each quote. (A snapshot of this quote table is shown in Exhibit 8-3.) Click on a listing in the first column (Month / Strike) to review the detailed information for that quote.

Exhibit 8-3 Bourse de Montréal BAX Quote Table

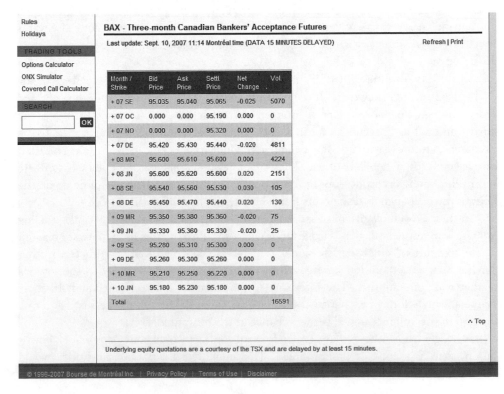

Month / Strike	Bid Price	Ask Price	Settl. Price	Net Change	Vol.
+ 07 SE	95.035	95.040	95.065	-0.025	5070
+ 07 OC	0.000	0.000	95.190	0.000	0
+ 07 NO	0.000	0.000	95.320	0.000	0
+ 07 DE	95.420	95.430	95.440	-0.020	4811
+ 08 MR	95.600	95.610	95.600	0.000	4224
+ 08 JN	95.600	95.620	95.600	0.020	2151
+ 08 SE	95.540	95.560	95.530	0.030	105
+ 08 DE	95.450	95.470	95.440	0.020	130
+ 09 MR	95.350	95.380	95.360	-0.020	75
+ 09 JN	95.330	95.360	95.330	-0.020	25
+ 09 SE	95.280	95.310	95.300	0.000	0
+ 09 DE	95.260	95.300	95.260	0.000	0
+ 10 MR	95.210	95.250	95.220	0.000	0
+ 10 JN	95.180	95.230	95.180	0.000	0
Total					16591

BAX - Three-month Canadian Bankers' Acceptance Futures

Last update: Sept. 10, 2007 11:14 Montréal time (DATA 15 MINUTES DELAYED)   Refresh | Print

Rules
Holidays

TRADING TOOLS

Options Calculator
ONX Simulator
Covered Call Calculator

SEARCH

OK

⌃ Top

Underlying equity quotations are a courtesy of the TSX and are delayed by at least 15 minutes.

© 1996-2007 Bourse de Montréal Inc. | Privacy Policy | Terms of Use | Disclaimer

The information in the three-month Canadian bankers' acceptance futures quote table is organized as follows:

- Column 1 indicates both the delivery month and year.
- Columns 2 and 3 are the bid and ask price.
- Column 4 shows the last price index of the day. The price index is defined as:

$$\text{Price index} = 100 - i_d \hspace{2cm} \textbf{(Equation 8-1)}$$

where

i_d = annual discount rate in percent

- Column 5 shows the change for the day.
- Column 6 shows the volume for the day.

Check the current quotes. On August 1, 2007, the table indicated that the three-month bankers' acceptance futures contract for June 2009 delivery was settled at 94.950. This information implies that a buyer of this contract would be promised delivery in June 2009 of three-month Canadian bankers' acceptances to yield an annual rate of 5.05% (100 − 94.950). Note that these contracts have been standardized so that the difference between the futures price and 100 is the relevant interest rate. It is very likely that the information that you see today if you visit this Web site will be different, as the market will change.

Note that a hedger trying to protect against rising three-month BA rates would be hedging against a declining three-month BA price, and therefore would be selling a futures contract. Similarly, a hedger trying to protect against a decline in three-month BA rates would be hedging against an increase in three-month BA prices, and therefore would be buying a futures contract.

For settling the futures contracts, it is not necessary to calculate the prices. Go to the Montréal Exchange menu tab: MX Products and choose BAX. Under Price Fluctuation, it states that "0.005 = C\$12.50 per contract for the nearest three listed contract months, including serials" and "0.01 = C\$25 per contract for all other contract months" for easy calculation. These contracts have been standardized so that an increase of one basis point in the index implies a \$25 profit to the buyer of a contract and a \$25 loss to the seller.

The Clearing House

Every futures exchange has a clearing house that plays an essential role in the trading of futures contracts. The clearing house for three-month BA futures contracts is the Canadian Derivatives Clearing Corporation (CDCC). The **clearing house** acts as seller to the buyer and as buyer to the seller. It undertakes these roles simultaneously but never acts as the primary seller or the primary buyer. Exhibit 8-4 illustrates the role of the clearing house in a futures market.

In doing so, the clearing house guarantees every futures contract. For example, if the seller defaults, the clearing house will honour the seller's obligation while trying to collect from the defaulting seller. This process eliminates credit checking of market participants and increases the liquidity of contracts. If and when delivery takes place, the clearing house arranges the delivery from the seller to the buyer.

The major risk facing the clearing house is default risk. For example, when a buyer defaults, the clearing house covers the losses and pays the seller as required. The clearing

Exhibit 8-4 Role of the Clearing House in a Futures Market

house reduces its risk by requiring traders to post collateral for their trade, known as margin. The clearing house controls and manages margin requirements for traders. Brokers may charge additional margin.

For forward contracts, no clearing house is necessary. The major participants in the forward markets are international banks, whose credit rating is relatively high and whose business activities are subject to significant regulation. Participants deal only with other participants if they are of acceptable credit quality. A hedger who wishes to use forward contracts for hedging treasury risk will need to set up an appropriate credit facility with a bank in order to use forwards. Unlike futures contracts, there is no transaction cost, such as brokerage commission, to transact a forward. The dealer's profit is built into the overall forward price.

Margin Requirements

The **margin requirement** represents cash or securities provided by a futures exchange trader as collateral, essentially to ensure that the trader is capable of honouring payment and covering losses. Margin requirements are set by both the clearing house and the exchanges to help limit their risk exposure and maintain the integrity of futures contracts and traders. Margin requirements will often be different for speculators and hedgers.

There are two critical levels for the margin.

- The **initial margin** is the collateral required when the contract is signed. For a $1 million, three-month bankers' acceptance contract, this initial margin, as quoted from the Bourse de Montréal, is $850 for a speculator holding a simple position. The hedger's margin would be $800 for the same position. These amounts are the minimum margin requirements of the exchange. Both the seller and the buyer deposit the required margin in an account controlled by the clearing house. If, for example, the price of the underlying asset falls $500 below the agreed price over the three months, the buyer's account will be debited $500 and the seller's account will be credited $500.

- The **maintenance margin** or **maintenance performance bond** is the minimum balance that a brokerage firm will permit commodity futures traders to keep in their margin accounts. If the balance falls below the maintenance margin, the brokerage firm will call a trader to put additional cash in the margin account to bring it back to the initial margin requirement. In the example cited in the previous paragraph, if the buyer's initial margin was $850, out of which he lost $500, the buyer's net margin is reduced to $350. If the maintenance margin is $400, the buyer will receive a request, known as a **margin call** or **performance-bond call**, to add cash to the margin account to bring the total back to $850. Of course, the seller is allowed to withdraw from his balance as long as it remains above the initial margin.

Marking to market is the process of updating margin accounts on a daily basis to reflect the market value of the trader's position. If a trader receives a margin call but fails to replenish the margin, the broker liquidates the trader's position to avoid losses and commences action to recover the position.

In the following article, Louis-Philippe Hémond gives practical examples of some of the concepts introduced so far. The article describes the role of the clearing house and the margin requirements associated with futures trading. It also illustrates how margin requirements work.

Back to Basics: Interest-Rate Futures

Louis-Philippe Hémond

In the following article Louis-Philippe Hémond explores the fundamentals of futures markets. He describes their operations and discusses the roles of the clearing house and margin requirements, using practical examples to illustrate his explanation.

Until recently, futures trading was an activity limited to contracts on agricultural products and other commodities. A futures contract is a standardized and transferable agreement to buy or sell a given commodity, on a specified future date, at a predetermined price. In a typical transaction, the buyer of a future (sometimes referred to as "the long") agrees to purchase, and the seller ("the short") agrees to deliver, a specific item according to the standardized terms of the contract. In contrast, a cash—or "spot"—market transaction involves the simultaneous pricing and transfer of the physical ownership of the item being sold.

Trading in futures contracts on financial instruments began in the early 1970s, after almost a decade of accelerating inflation that exposed market participants to unprecedented levels of exchange- and interest-rate risk. Today, financial futures represent more than half of all traded futures.

The terms of futures contracts are standardized. All the specifications of the contracts traded on a futures exchange are determined by that exchange. Specifications include the item to be delivered, the time and location of delivery, the currency to be used for payment, and the deliverable grade of the commodity. The only item negotiated when trading futures contracts is price.

Futures market participants typically fall into two categories: hedgers and speculators. A hedge is a futures market transaction that serves as a temporary substitute for a spot-market transaction. Hedges are used to take advantage of current prices to "lock in" the price of a future spot transaction. Hedgers use futures to offset *now* the risks associated with a spot transaction to take place *later*. In most cases, hedgers have a commercial interest in the futures' deliverable item as well.

Speculators, on the other hand, assume a long or short position solely to profit from price changes. They have no interest in the underlying item or commodity of the futures contracts. Speculators assume, for their own profit or loss, the risks that the hedgers want to offset. They are welcomed by futures exchanges because they provide the market with liquidity, in exchange for potentially unlimited profits.

Futures market speculation involves assuming either a short or long futures position solely to profit from price changes, and not in connection with ordinary commercial pursuits. A person who buys wheat futures after hearing of a nuclear disaster in the Soviet Union is speculating that wheat prices will rise as a result. However, a grain dealer with a contract to buy grain from the Soviet Union who purchases wheat futures in this case would be hedging his position.

Futures exchanges perform many important functions within the futures market. One of their principal functions is to organize and support the physical trading area. In general, trading can only take place in this location, often called "the pit," during specified

---

Contract Standardization

When trading in futures contracts, buyers and sellers will negotiate the price they are ready to pay or accept for the item. All other items are standardized.

For example, when dealing in 10-year Government of Canada Bond Futures, the following characteristics form the contract:

Trading unit: C$100,000 nominal value of Government of Canada bonds, with a coupon of nine per cent.

Delivery grade: Any Government of Canada bond with 6.5 to 10 year maturity remaining (other rules apply).

Delivery day: Any business day in delivery month (at the seller's choice). Made and settled through Central Depository Service (CDS) on the 5th business day following tender of a delivery notice.

Last trading day: On the seventh business day preceding the last business day of the delivery month.

Quotation: Per C$100 nominal value.

Daily price limit: Three points per contract above or below the previous day's settlement price.

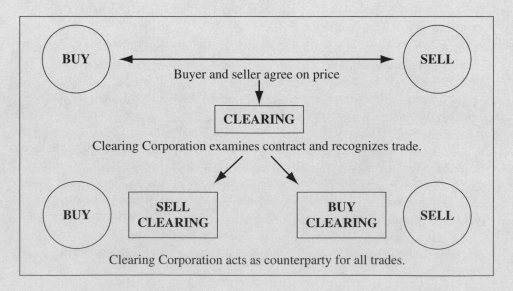

business hours. Access to the pit is limited to members and their representatives, or to trading permit holders.

In order to ensure a high-quality market for futures users, exchanges must establish and enforce strict rules, and have the power to discipline members and permit holders. Rules and regulations of a futures exchange often specify such things as the necessary qualifications to trade in the pit or to sell futures to customers, the priority of order execution (i.e., clients' orders must be filled before professionals' orders), and so on.

Futures exchanges also serve a very important function in price finding. Since all trading occurs within a given physical space during specified hours, and because the transactions are disseminated to all the brokers and futures trades outside the pit, it becomes the reference for the best available bid or ask.

The financial stability of futures trading is protected by an independent body called the clearing corporation. Once a trade has occurred in "the pit" the information is communicated to the clearing corporation. It then either recognizes or disallows the trade. Recognition is granted if, among other things, both the buyer and the seller meet the minimum capitalization and margin requirements. If the trade is recognized, the clearing corporation breaks the contractual bond between the buyer and the seller, and assumes the role of counterparty to each part of the contract.

The original buyer and seller do not need to deal with one another again. Their contractual obligations now rest with the clearing corporation. It, in turn, guarantees the performance of the contract for both parties. Should one party to the original contract fail, the other party will not be affected. The intervention of the clearing corporation and contract standardization result in simplified trading. Transaction costs are reduced, there is little or no counterparty credit risk and it is easy to liquidate the futures obligation before the delivery period. Changes in futures pricing will increase the value of the contract for one party at the expense of the other party. In the early days of trading futures contracts, traders adversely affected by price movements often disappeared as the settlement date drew near. In response, futures exchanges adopted the practice of requiring a performance bond, called a "margin requirement," from buyers and sellers of futures contracts. In addition, traders are required to report any gains or losses on their outstanding futures positions at the end of each trading session. This practice is called "marking to market."

All futures exchanges now require member firms to maintain margin accounts. Brokers who execute orders on behalf of customers must collect margin deposits from them before undertaking any trade. Minimum margin requirements are set by the exchanges. Most brokers require that their customers maintain margins higher than the minimum levels set by the exchanges. Any gains or losses realized when the contracts are "marked to market" at the end of a trading session are added to or subtracted from the trader's margin account. If margin account balances fall below a specified minimum, called the maintenance margin, traders face a margin call and must deposit the additional margin (variation margin) to their accounts.

There are several differences between futures markets and forward markets such as the market for Forward Rate Agreements. A forward contract, like a futures contract, is a formal commitment between two parties that specifies the terms of a transaction to take place at a future date. Unlike futures contracts, however, forward contracts are custom-tailored agreements that in most cases cannot be transferred to a third party, but they can

How Do Margins Work?

A buyer purchasing 100 Canadian Bankers' Acceptance Futures (BAX) valued at $1,000,000 each is required to deposit initial and maintenance margins of $1,500 per contract. Each basis point variation is worth $25.

Day 1

The buyer purchases 100 BAX at 86.32 and must deposit the initial margin of $1,500 per contract.
Margin: 100 × $1,500 = $150,000

Day 2

The BAX contract closes at 86.50, an increase of 18 basis points. The day's profit will be credited to the maintenance margin account.
Margin: 18 × $25 × 100 = $45,000

Day 3

The BAX contract closes at 86.45, down five basis points over the previous day. The resulting loss will be subtracted from the maintenance margin account.
Margin: 5 × $25 × 100 = $12,500

Day 4

The BAX contract price falls another three basis points to 86.42 and the buyer decides to sell the futures.
Margin: 3 × $25 × 100 = $7,500

The margin funds are then liberated.

Day 1 (initial margin)	$150,000
Day 2 (gain)	+ $45,000
Day 3 (loss)	− $12,500
Day 4 (loss)	− $7,500
Margin returned	**= $175,000**

be easily reversed. Forward markets are not regulated but are subject to rules established by the private parties directly involved in the forward transaction. Each trade is made according to an agreement governing that transaction. The price is determined by private negotiation. Margin deposits may not be required. The integrity of the agreement is only as strong as the integrity of the buyer and the seller associated with the transaction. Expiration dates and offset rules can be negotiated. Daily trading volume is usually not available.

Forwards involve day-to-day loss supervision and can be tailored to suit the needs of the buyer or seller. However, futures are generally less expensive, and can be transferred more easily.

Louis-Philippe Hémond is a Chicago-based consultant who was recently assistant director of The Montréal Exchange's Derivative Products Department. Prior to that, he gained extensive experience in the securities industry as a registered representative, first with Tasse & Associates, and then with Wood Gundy.

Source: *Canadian Treasury Management Review*, Vol. 7, Number 5, May/June 1991, pp. 1–3, 7.

The following minicase will work through the calculations of maintaining a margin account for a futures contract.

MINICASE 8-1 MARGIN REQUIREMENTS FOR FUTURES CONTRACTS

Today is December 3, 20X1. Clark has decided to enter the futures market. He has $2,000,000 to speculate with. He decides to purchase 200 three-month Canadian bankers' acceptance futures (BAX). The market quotes 97.95 as the price for a March 20X2 settlement. Clark enters the contract and sets up his margin account with his stockbroker on December 3.

Question 1: Assuming that his stockbroker uses the Bourse de Montréal margin requirements, how much must Clark deposit for his initial margin?

Clark is a speculator so his margin rate would be $850 per contract. Therefore, his initial margin requirement is:

$$200 \times \$850 = \$170,000$$

Question 2: At the end of December 4, the BAX closes at 98.23. What adjustment is made to Clark's margin account?

The price has changed by 28 basis points. Each basis point change is worth $25. Therefore the change in each contract is:

$$\$25 \times 28 = \$700$$

Clark has 200 contracts; therefore, his maintenance margin account is credited with

$$200 \times \$700 = \$140,000$$

Question 3: On December 5, the BAX falls to 98.15, a total of 8 basis points for the day. What is the effect on Clark's margin account?

$$8 \times \$25 \times 200 = \$40,000 \text{ is debited to his account}$$

Question 4: At the close of trading on December 6, the BAX has dropped to 97.65. What effect does this have on Clark's account?

At 97.65, the BAX is down 50 basis points from 98.15. The change in Clark's margin account would be:

$$50 \times \$25 \times 200 = \$250,000$$

The balance in Clark's margin account is now: $170,000 + 140,000 − $40,000 − $250,000 = $20,000. Clark will get a margin call to ask him to replenish his margin account to the $170,000 minimum margin requirement.

Daily Price Limits

The daily process of marking individual accounts to market limits the risk to the clearing house of price fluctuations that occur during one day. In addition, **daily price limits** specify a range of prices around the opening price within which trading can take place. No trading can take place at prices over the upper limit or under the lower limit. If the contract price hits the upper limit, the contract is said to be *limit up*. If the price hits the lower limit, the contract is said to be *limit down*.

Daily price limits are frequently imposed on commodity futures. For example, the Winnipeg Commodity Exchange normally imposes a $10 per metric tonne ($200 per contract) daily price limit, up or down, on the 20 metric tons canola contract. If the opening price on a particular trading day is $330 per metric ton, the lower price limit will be $320 per ton and the upper price limit $340 per metric ton. Limits may be raised or lowered as is appropriate.

The imposition of daily price limits on some futures contracts does not limit a futures trader's risk in any way. Limits are there to protect the clearing house and permit traders to replenish margin accounts. Daily price limits may temporarily delay the realization of losses, for example, for one day. During this delay, the reasons for the extreme price changes may disappear and the futures price may return to a normal level.

While price limits may affect futures trading, trading in forwards in the over-the-counter markets is subject to no such limits. Forward prices can and do move spectacularly when major news or events surprise the markets. As a result, it is almost always possible to transact a forward, regardless of the volatility of the market, provided that an international financial centre is open for business and a counterparty can be found.

Covering a Futures or Forward Position before the Delivery Date

A futures or forward contract can be covered or closed out with an offsetting position. For example, a trader who sells Swiss francs forward for March delivery can offset this transaction by buying the same amount of Swiss francs for March delivery. If this were a Swiss franc futures contract, the sold contract and the purchased contract would have the same delivery period (March) and likely be traded on the same exchange. The resulting profit or loss would be credited to or debited from the trader's margin account. The broker closing out the transaction would note that it was a closing transaction.

If the sale of Swiss francs had been executed using a forward contract, and the seller no longer had a need to sell Swiss francs for delivery in March, the bank with which the original forward was negotiated would be contacted to arrange an offsetting purchase of Swiss francs. The resulting profit or loss would belong to the hedger.

Approximately 95% of futures transactions do not result in actual delivery of the underlying assets, whereas a majority of forward contracts do involve delivery.

Difference between Futures and Forward Contracts

The major difference between futures and forwards is that futures trade on an organized exchange, while forwards trade in the over-the-counter market between large institutions.

Exchanges govern the specifications and trading of futures contracts, including when and how they may be traded. Forward markets, such as the one for foreign exchange, trade around the clock in major financial centres, provided that a bank willing to do the transaction can be located. Forward trading is facilitated by interbank brokers, who act as intermediaries between banks for various forward maturities. Constant arbitrage (the purchase and sale of identical or nearly identical assets to earn a risk-free profit) between forward and futures markets reduces any discrepancies between futures and forward price differences other than transaction costs and provides liquidity to both markets.

Forward contracts can be advantageous to traders. The buyer and the seller can tailor the delivery dates, underlying asset, quantity to be delivered, and other features to fit their particular needs. In addition, because forward contracts are transacted between creditworthy counterparties, there are no margin requirements. Unlike futures, forwards are not usually marked to market daily, though many users of forwards perform a regular mark to market for their own risk management purposes.

Futures have an advantage over forwards in that they are often available in small contract sizes. For example, currency futures contracts are available for amounts under $100,000, whereas forwards usually trade in multiples of US$5 million (though smaller amounts can be transacted). Unlike forwards, futures contracts are available to organizations with poor credit quality or even to individuals, provided that margin requirements are met.

Prices in the futures markets are determined through a bidding process on an organized exchange and are publicly available. Forward contract prices are negotiated between counterparties and are not publicly available.

One disadvantage of forwards is the absence of a clearing house. This means that the seller and buyer are responsible for ensuring adequate creditworthiness of the other party. In practice, most banks and large investment dealers trade in the forward market. As a result, only moderate- to high-credit-quality organizations are able to transact forwards.

8.2 BASIC VALUATION CONCEPTS OF FINANCIAL FUTURES AND FORWARDS

The valuation of futures and forwards focuses on factors that influence the relationship between the future price and the spot (cash) price. In this section, you learn how to determine the futures or forward price if you know the spot or cash price. As defined in Section 8.1, the difference between the futures price and the spot price is called the basis.

For simplicity, it is assumed in this section that there are no margin or marking-to-market requirements. Thus, the pricing formulas derived under this assumption are primarily applicable to forward contracts. As a result, the prices obtained by the derived formulas represent estimates of real futures prices. Adjusting for the costs of margin and marking to market are possible, but the explanations are lengthy and the analysis complicated. The following material captures the basic principles underlying the pricing of futures or forwards.

Law of One Price

The **law of one price** states that the futures price of an asset is determined from the spot price of the same asset or the cash price of any product related to the asset. Cash prices of related products (which can be obtained from processing the basic product) should reflect the processing costs. The futures price, when the product is the same as the basic product but delivery occurs on a future date, should include storage or carrying costs.

Minicase 8-2 illustrates the law of one price.

MINICASE 8-2 USING THE LAW OF ONE PRICE TO CALCULATE A FUTURES PRICE

Today is September 1, 20X1. Lisa realizes she will need 1,000 bushels of grain on March 20, 20X2. Currently, a bushel of grain is selling for $3.50 for immediate (spot) delivery. However, if Lisa buys now she will have to pay storage costs. She estimates that these costs will be $450. Alternatively, she can buy a grain futures contract for delivery March 20, 20X2. If she does this, she does not have to pay any money when she signs the contract on September 1, 20X1. Therefore, she will be able to invest her money in the meantime. The annual rate of return on a three-month Treasury bill (risk-free asset) is 4%.

What should the price of grain for delivery on March 20, 20X2 be?

According to the law of one price, the futures or forward price should equal the cash price plus the storage costs plus the loss of interest income that would have been earned on the purchase price.

Spot price per bushel	$ 3.50
Storage costs per bushel ($450.00 ÷ 1,000)	0.45
Loss of interest [$3.50 × $(1 + 0.04 × 1/4)^{200 \div 91}$ − $3.50]	0.08
Futures or forward price	$ 4.03

For the loss of interest calculations, begin by approximating the interest rate to calculate the Treasury bill rate over a fraction of a year. The annual rate of 4% is multiplied by the fraction of the year over which the Treasury bill will be outstanding. The interest approximation in this situation is consistent with industry practice. (For example, when your broker quotes a 6% annual rate on a three-month Treasury bill, you will receive 1.5% interest over the three-month period.) Finally, calculate the effective rate over the 200 days (6 months = 181 days, plus 19 days for March) by assuming that Lisa can reinvest the proceeds every three months (91 days). The result is 200/91 compounding periods.

A General Model for Futures and Forward Prices

According to the law of one price, spot prices are the primary influence on futures prices. In a perfect and efficient market in which the transfer of an asset from one period to the other is frictionless and net supply is constant, the spot price and the futures price would be the same. Arbitrage activities would force futures prices to be near spot prices to keep trading profits near zero.

As suggested in Minicase 8-2, there are costs involved in moving assets through time. For non-financial assets, there are significant holding costs associated with carrying the assets. Costs are incurred to use and maintain storage facilities, insurance costs are incurred to cover damage to the stored assets and spoilage costs may be incurred because of the deterioration of the product's quality.

For financial assets, the holding costs are negligible. However, there are interest costs associated with holding some financial assets, such as non-dividend-paying stocks. Buying such an asset now for cash results in loss of interest on the cash paid to acquire the asset.

Assuming that net product supplies are fixed over time, the futures price and the cash price for financial futures are, in general, related by:

$$F_{0,T} = S_0(1 + Rf_{0,T} - Rh_{0,T})$$ **(Equation 8-2)**

where

$F_{0,T}$ = futures price at time 0 for delivery at time T
S_0 = spot price at time 0
$Rf_{0,T}$ = rate at time 0 on the risk-free asset maturing at time T
$Rh_{0,T}$ = rate of cash payments expected to be paid by the underlying asset between time 0 and time T

For futures on non-financial assets, Equation 8-2 should be modified to account for holding costs. The equation becomes:

$$F_{0,T} = S_0(1 + Rf_{0,T} - Rh_{0,T}) + H_{0,T}$$ **(Equation 8-3)**

where

$H_{0,T}$ = holding costs from time 0 to time T

Pricing Interest-Rate Futures Some of the most heavily traded financial futures contracts are based on debt securities, the prices of which are primarily dependent on interest rates. Such products include Eurodollar deposits, bankers' acceptances, Government of Canada bonds, and U.S. Treasury bonds. The markets for cash securities are considered to be efficient, and their supply and demand conditions are continually changing over time.

The basic valuation model for financial futures (Equation 8-2) must be adjusted to price interest-rate futures.

- The holding cost in Equation 8-3 can be dropped because financial futures are considered to be intangible, requiring virtually no handling of the physical product.

- Assuming that the rate at time 0 on the risk-free asset maturing at time T (the rate forgone for not holding the asset) equals the rate of cash payments expected to be paid by the underlying asset between time 0 and time T, the difference $(Rf_{0,T} - Rh_{0,T})$ would be zero.

- When dealing with interest-rate futures, the spot price of a security already reflects expectations about future prices. The relationship depends on the term structure of interest rates.

Pricing Stock-Index Futures In Canada, stock-index futures contracts are available based on the S&P/TSX 60 Index. The price of the index is a capitalization-weighted average of the prices of the 60 largest and most liquid stocks in Canada. The value of an index futures contract, and therefore the underlying asset, is the price of the index times the index multiplier of 200, because a contract consists of 200 units.

Futures on stock indexes are **cash settled**, meaning that when the futures contract expires, the seller delivers to the buyer the current cash value of the index rather than the assets that make up the index. An index buyer who holds an index futures contract to expiration will receive (or pay) the difference between the value of the underlying asset when the purchase occurred and the value of the underlying asset at contract expiration. Minicase 8-3 illustrates these points. Note that the information used in this minicase also forms the basis of Minicase 8-4.

MINICASE 8-3 CASH SETTLEMENT OF A STOCK-INDEX FUTURES CONTRACT

On March 16, 20X0, Jim bought a futures contract on the S&P/TSX 60 Index for delivery on June 15, 20X0. The futures price is $600.20, and the index closed at $599.33. Thus, Jim agreed to buy the futures contract at:

$$200 \times \$600.20 = \$120,040$$

However, on expiration, the index closed at $625. Therefore, the value of the index at expiration is $125,000. The seller delivers to Jim the difference of $4,960.

Although index futures are settled in cash, their values are affected by the same factors that affect the prices of the stocks in the index:

- *Dividends*: Shareholders are entitled to dividends, while holders of index futures are not. When a stock goes ex-dividend, the share price tends to decrease by the amount of the dividend. Thus, the index level drops and the value of the index contract is affected.
- *Interest rates*: They affect all financial securities, including stocks.
- *Expected capital gains*: Expectations of future capital gains affect the spot price, regardless of the interest-rate and dividend effects.

Combining all these factors leads to a general pricing formula for index futures:

$$F_{0,T} = S_0[1 + Rf_{0,T} - E(D_{0,T})] \qquad \textbf{(Equation 8-4)}$$

where

$E(D_{0,T})$ = expected rate of dividends over the contract period, which represents an opportunity loss for the holder of the futures contract as the holder is not entitled to the dividends

Capital gains effects are captured in the term S_0, as the current price is expected to reflect the present value of the capital gains expected in the future.

MINICASE 8-4 PRICING A STOCK-INDEX FUTURES CONTRACT

Continuing with Minicase 8-3, the annual rate on three-month Treasury bills on March 16, 20X0, is 5.21% and the annual rate of dividends paid on the S&P/TSX 60 stocks is 4.63%. If the S&P/TSX 60 Index closed at $599.33, what would the value of the S&P/TSX 60 Index futures contract for delivery on June 15, 20X0 be?

$$\begin{aligned}
\text{Value} &= 200 \times \$599.33(1 + 0.0521 \div 4 - 0.0463 \div 4) \\
&= 200 \times \$600.20 \\
&= \$120,040
\end{aligned}$$

Thus, the futures contract was fairly priced.

Case Continued >

Once again, interest approximations are used to estimate the interest over a three-month period on a Treasury bill. In this case, the approximation reflects the market practice of pricing Treasury bills.

Pricing Currency Futures The foreign-exchange market is the largest in the world, as well as being one of the most efficient markets since currencies are generic assets that can be bought and sold easily by large financial institutions. The price of a foreign currency in the market reflects all available information. Consequently, the current futures price reflects the current spot price after adjusting for interest rate differentials between the two currencies.

The adjustment for interest costs has both opportunity costs and benefits. Buying a foreign currency leads the buyer to sacrifice interest income on the domestic currency. However, the buyer can use the foreign currency to earn the foreign rate of return. Therefore, the net interest costs depend on the relative levels of interest rates on the two currencies.

As a result, the forward or futures price for a currency may be higher or lower than its spot price, depending on the currency being bought or sold and on interest rates. Minicase 8-5 illustrates this concept. Note that the information used in this minicase also forms the basis of Minicase 8-6.

MINICASE 8-5 PRICING CURRENCY FUTURES

Grace has $100,000 to invest for six months. Currently, the annual rate on the six-month term deposit denominated in Canadian dollars is 3.5%.

Instead of investing in Canadian term deposits, Grace can buy U.S. dollars (US$) at C$1.43 per dollar and invest the proceeds in a U.S.-dollar-denominated term deposit. The current annual interest rate on six-month U.S. dollar term deposits is 4.5%. However, Grace is concerned about the exchange rate after six months when her term deposit will mature and she will need the money. She can guarantee the exchange rate in the forward market. The six-month forward exchange rate is C$1.4275 per US$. Given this information, should Grace invest the money in a Canadian dollar or U.S. dollar term deposit?

The value at maturity from investing in the Canadian dollar term deposit is:

$$\$100,000 \times (1 + 0.035 \div 2) = \$101,750$$

For a meaningful comparison between this alternative and the alternative of investing in a U.S. dollar term deposit, the two investments should be exposed to the same risk. Grace must arrange to exchange the proceeds from the U.S. dollar term deposit in the forward exchange market. Calculating the value at maturity from investing in U.S. dollars takes several steps.

First, she has to exchange the Canadian dollars for U.S. dollars. She will obtain:

$$C\$100,000 \div 1.43 = US\$69,930$$

Then she will calculate the future value of a U.S.-dollar-denominated six-month term deposit at 4.5%. This will be:

$$US\$69,930 \times (1 + 0.045 \div 2) = US\$71,503$$

Case Continued >

The exchange of the proceeds from the U.S. dollar term deposit at the current forward rate will yield:

$$US\$71,503 \times C\$1.4275 = C\$102,071$$

Therefore, Grace should invest in the U.S. dollar term deposit.

Note: Although this simple example is used to illustrate relative interest rates and their impact on forward exchange rates, in reality, such a calculation would be based on the exact number of days in the proposed term (rather than half a year). In addition, U.S. deposit interest is based on a 360-day year, while Canadian deposit interest is based on a 365-day year, and this would also need to be taken into account.

Comparing the two alternatives in Minicase 8-5 shows that the U.S. dollar alternative is slightly better. However, in an efficient market, this investment opportunity would rarely occur because arbitrage activities would quickly correct the differential between the two alternatives. Banks and financial institutions constantly look for such opportunities to earn a risk-free profit through arbitrage. The market pressure on interest rates and the spot and forward exchange rates would force the market to correct until the two alternatives were equal.

When the two alternatives are equal, markets are said to be in *equilibrium*. The relationship between spot and forward exchange rates and the interest rates in the domestic and foreign currencies at equilibrium is represented in the equation:

$$F_{0,T} = S_0 \frac{\left(1 + \dfrac{R_D}{N_D}\right)^{M \times N_D}}{\left(1 + \dfrac{R_F}{N_F}\right)^{M \times N_F}} \qquad \textbf{(Equation 8-5)}$$

where
$F_{0,T}$ = forward rate at time 0 quoted in domestic currency at which the foreign currency can be purchased for delivery at time T
S_0 = spot rate at time 0 quoted in domestic currency at which the foreign currency can be purchased for immediate delivery
R_D = annual interest rate on the domestic currency
R_F = annual interest rate on the foreign currency
N_D = number of times per year the domestic interest rate will be compounded
N_F = number of times per year the foreign interest rate will be compounded
M = number of years until the maturity of the forward contract

This relationship is known as interest-rate parity.

The interest-rate parity relationship can be used to determine the forward exchange rate in relation to the cash exchange rate. The relationship shows that for a given spot rate, interest rates on domestic and foreign currencies play an important role in determining the forward exchange rate. The domestic rate contributes positively to the forward exchange rate, while the foreign rate contributes negatively. Minicase 8-6 illustrates interest-rate parity.

MINICASE 8-6 INTEREST-RATE PARITY

Given the following information, what should the forward exchange rate of the U.S. dollar be in order to make Grace (from Minicase 8-5) indifferent in her choice between the two alternatives?

Annual rate on a 6-month term deposit denominated in Canadian dollars	3.5%
Annual rate on a 6-month term deposit denominated in U.S. dollars	4.5%
Spot rate to buy U.S. dollars	C$1.4300

$$F_{0,T} = \$1.4300 \frac{\left(1 + \dfrac{0.035}{2}\right)^{1/2 \times 2}}{\left(1 + \dfrac{0.045}{2}\right)^{1/2 \times 2}} = \$1.4230 \text{ Canadian dollars per U.S. dollar}$$

8.3 HEDGING WITH FUTURES AND FORWARD CONTRACTS

Hedging describes the use of futures, options, or other means to manage an existing risk. It involves the initiation of a position in the futures or options market that is intended as a temporary substitute for the purchase or sale of the actual commodity or asset at a later date. In other words, hedging is the creation of a position in the derivatives market to offset an existing risk in the cash market.

A wide variety of derivative securities are available for hedging purposes. The most popular ones are futures, forward contracts, options, and swaps. Also, combinations of these securities are increasingly used to custom design the hedging instrument to fit particular needs. This section demonstrates the principle of hedging using futures and forward contracts.

Basics of Hedging with Futures and Forwards There are two kinds of hedges. A **long hedge** gives the hedger the obligation to *buy* an asset at a future date at an agreed price, effectively locking in a purchase price. A **short hedge** gives the hedger the obligation to *sell* an asset at a future date at an agreed price, effectively locking in a selling price. For both kinds of hedges, futures or forwards may be used.

Trading futures or forwards for hedging or speculation results in cash profits or losses. Every dollar change in the value of the underlying asset will be reflected in a gain or loss on the futures or forward contract. However, in the case of hedging when the futures position (such as the sale of a forward contract) is offset by a cash position (such as owning the underlying asset), the profits or losses from futures trading should offset the losses and profits from the underlying asset positions and minimize risk. These cash profits and losses are summarized in Exhibit 8-5.

Exhibit 8-5
Cash Profits and Losses in Futures or Forward Trading

	Market value of asset	Result	Explanation
Long position: locked in purchase price	Decrease	Cash loss	Obligated to buy at the high price
	Increase	Cash profit	Secured to buy at the low price
Short position: locked in sale price	Decrease	Cash profit	Secured to sell at the high price
	Increase	Cash loss	Obligated to sell at the low price

Futures or forwards can be used to hedge interest-rate, foreign-exchange, and commodity-price risks in fairly similar ways. The process can be generalized to more complicated situations with several transactions.

Two more definitions are important to know at this point. A **direct hedge** is an arrangement in which the asset underlying a futures or forward contract is the same as the asset being hedged. A **cross hedge** is an arrangement in which the asset underlying a futures or forward contract is different from the asset being hedged. As long as the two assets are similarly sensitive to changes in the factor leading to fluctuations in value, the hedge will reduce risk.

Presuming that a decision to use futures, rather than forwards, has been made, the process of hedging with futures requires three decisions:

- *Decision 1:* Whether to buy or sell futures contracts.

- *Decision 2:* Which delivery date to choose. As suggested in Section 8.1, buying a futures contract for hedging does not necessarily involve delivery. The contract can be sold later in the market once the need for the hedge disappears. The delivery date must be chosen so that it is longer than the period over which hedging is desirable. The question of which delivery date is most appropriate does not have a widely accepted answer. However, it is safe to choose a contract with a delivery date that extends at least one month beyond the date on which the hedge is to be concluded. Such a contract is likely to be the most liquid contract at the time of conclusion.

- *Decision 3:* How many contracts to buy. Also in Section 8.1, you learned that futures contracts are standard contracts in which only multiples of the underlying asset can be traded. This decision is determined using the hedge ratio.

Calculating the Hedge Ratio The **hedge ratio** is the number of futures contracts that need to be purchased or sold in order to hedge and cover all risk safely. Because futures contracts are only available in standardized amounts, there are several ways to determine the hedge ratio. The simplest model provides what is known as the **naive hedge** or **1:1 hedge**, in which the position in the futures market is equivalent to the position in the spot market. For example, if your exposure in the spot market is 500 troy ounces of gold and the gold futures contract traded on the Commodity Exchange in the United States has a size of 100 troy ounces, then you should have a position in 5 (500 ÷ 100) gold futures contracts to hedge your risk. Although the naive hedge is simple to use, it is unlikely that a perfect 1:1 hedge will be available in most situations.

One model that is used in practice is known as the **duration-based hedge ratio** or the **price sensitivity hedge ratio**. Other more complicated models may be used. The principle is that the number of futures contracts used should be set in such a way that the change in value of the futures position will offset the change in value of the spot position, given a small change in interest rates.

The hedge ratio can be estimated by comparing the changes in volatility of the hedging instrument to the changes in the volatility of the underlying instrument. In this type of model, the Greek symbol ρ (rho) reflects the correlation of the changes in volatility of the rate to be hedged to the changes in volatility of the rate on the security underlying the futures contract.

In the case of simple, one-transaction hedging decisions, the following equation can be used to determine the hedge ratio for futures contracts on assets or liabilities that are sensitive to interest-rate risk.

$$ HR = \rho \times \frac{V}{F_F} \times \frac{M_C}{M_F} \qquad\qquad \textbf{(Equation 8-6)} $$

where

HR = hedge ratio, total number of contracts needed
V = market value of the assets or liabilities to be hedged
F_F = face value of the security underlying the futures contract
M_C = maturity of the assets/liabilities to be hedged
M_F = maturity of the security underlying the futures contract
ρ = correlation of the change in volatility of the rate to be hedged in relation to the change in volatility of the rate on the security underlying the futures contract

The ratio V/F_F calculates how many futures contracts are needed to hedge the assets or liabilities that are at risk, assuming M_F and M_C are equal and ρ is 1. It implies that twice as many contracts are needed if the amount to be hedged is two times as much as the face value of the security underlying the futures contract. For example, a three-month, $2 million bankers' acceptance could be hedged with two futures contracts on a three-month bankers' acceptance with $1 million face value per contract. The intuition is that the risk is proportionate to the face value; for example, the risk doubles if the face value doubles.

Similarly, the ratio M_C/M_F calculates how many futures contracts are needed to hedge the assets or liabilities that are at risk, assuming V and F_F are equal and ρ is 1. It implies that three times as many contracts are needed if the maturity of the asset to be hedged is three times as long as the maturity of the security underlying the futures contract. For example, a nine-month, $1 million bankers' acceptance could be hedged with three three-month bankers' acceptance futures contracts with a face value of $1 million per contract. The intuition is that the risk is proportionate to the length of time to maturity; for example, the risk triples if the maturity triples.

Recall that with futures contracts, you are not free to choose M_F and F_F. As explained in Section 8.1, futures contracts are standardized by the exchanges. For example, the asset underlying the three-month bankers' acceptance futures contract always has a $1 million face value and three months to maturity. If forward agreements are used, M_F and F_F can be designed as desired.

The Greek symbol ρ reflects the correlation of the changes in the volatility of the rate on Treasury bills and the changes in volatility of the rate on bankers' acceptance futures. This relationship implies that the Treasury bill rates decrease by ΔTB, while bankers' acceptance (BA) futures rates decrease by ΔBA. These two changes are related by the following equation:

$$\Delta TB = \rho \times \Delta BA \qquad \text{(Equation 8-7)}$$

An estimate of ρ can be obtained by calculating the correlation between a series of rates on the asset to be hedged and a series of rates on the security underlying the futures contract. However, practitioners often use subjective judgment to estimate ρ.

Although Equation 8-7 is expected to hold on average for a large number of observations, the actual change may be more or less than calculated. **Basis risk** is the inherent risk that the rates on both sides of a hedge do not move in such a way as to satisfy the original purposes of the hedge. To simplify the minicases, this chapter assumes there is no basis risk. In reality, basis risk often exists and increases with cross hedging.

Minicase 8-7 demonstrates the process of hedging the interest-rate risk of a single transaction.

MINICASE 8-7 HEDGING THE RISK OF A SINGLE TRANSACTION

Returning to Minicase 7-1, Lora's risk is a drop in interest rates. If rates drop, the prices of Treasury bills will rise and Lora will have to pay more to purchase the same bills. She can avoid this risk by buying a futures contract on a security that has the same sensitivity to interest rate changes as Treasury bills. This minicase shows how Lora can use a cross hedge to reduce her risk if there is a decrease in interest rates. The more similar the characteristics of the Treasury bills and the futures contract underlying asset are, the better the hedge will be.

The ideal situation would be for Lora to purchase futures on Treasury bills now in the futures market to hedge the later purchase of Treasury bills in the cash market. However, as indicated in Section 8.1, there are no futures on Canadian Treasury bills. Thus, Lora has to find an asset that is as sensitive to changes in interest rates as a Treasury bill and on which futures contracts are traded. For example, Lora could use futures on bankers' acceptances, which are similar to Treasury bills. When the rates on Treasury bills change, the rates on bankers' acceptances change in the same direction. Credit quality is the major difference between the two instruments. Using bankers' acceptance futures to hedge Treasury bill prices is an example of a cross hedge.

Having decided to hedge using bankers' acceptances, Lora has three more decisions to make:

- *Decision 1:* Lora must decide whether to buy or sell futures. Given that her risk is from a rise in the price of Treasury bills, she must buy bankers' acceptance futures to lock in the purchase price.

- *Decision 2:* What delivery date should Lora choose? To keep the hedge liquid beyond the time she requires it, Lora wants a delivery date that extends at least one month beyond the date on which the hedge is to be concluded. In her case, June delivery is appropriate.

Case Continued >

Note: The simplifying assumption is that Lora will purchase a three-month Canadian bankers' acceptance futures contract, which is available with quarterly maturities of March, June, September, and December. Serials are available that consist of the two nearest non-quarterly months.

■ *Decision 3:* How many contracts must Lora buy? In the case of three-month bankers' acceptance futures contracts, the underlying asset is a three-month bankers' acceptance with $1,000,000 face value.

So far, you know that the assets to be hedged are the Treasury bills that will be purchased on March 29 to mature on May 29 (61 days). The security underlying the futures contract is a $1,000,000 face value three-month bankers' acceptance to be delivered in June. Almost all information is in place to use Equation 8-6 to determine how many futures contracts Lora needs. However, ρ is still needed.

To estimate ρ, calculate the correlation between a series of Treasury bill rates and a series of bankers' acceptance rates. For Lora's case, assume that ρ is 0.95. This means, roughly speaking, that the Treasury bill rates are 95% as volatile as the bankers' acceptance rates.

Using Equation 8-6 and $\rho = 0.95$, the hedge ratio for Lora's case can be estimated as:

$$HR = 0.95 \times (\$5,000,000 \div \$1,000,000) \times (61 \div 91) = 3.18 \text{ contracts}[1]$$

As only multiples of a whole contract can be purchased, Lora can buy either three or four contracts. Generally, the number is rounded off to the nearest integer. In this case, the decision would be to purchase three contracts.

Once the decision on how many contracts are to be traded is made, the steps needed to execute the investment plan in conjunction with the hedging process can be summarized as shown in Exhibit 8-6.

Exhibit 8-6
Executing the Investment Plan

March 1:	Buy 3 three-month bankers' acceptance futures contracts for June delivery.
March 29:	Close position in the futures market by selling the futures contracts that were purchased March 1.
	Buy $5 million at face value of Treasury bills after receiving the cash from the customer.
May 29:	Redeem the Treasury bills for their face value and use the cash as desired.

---

[1] It is important to note that the calculation of the hedge ratio for Lora's case should technically use the discounted value (market value) of the asset to be hedged. This would result in the following calculations:

$$\text{Price} = \$4,926,308$$

This price would then be used in the hedge ratio formula:

$$HR = 0.95 \times (\$4,926,308/\$1,000,000) \times (61/91) = 3.137 \text{ contracts}$$

Notice that the risk from a drop in interest rates no longer exists after March 29, when the cash is received and the funds are used to purchase Treasury bills as desired. Because the risk no longer exists, the futures contract is no longer required and must be sold in the market.

Pricing Bankers' Acceptances Using Futures Contracts Suppose that on March 1, the futures rate on bankers' acceptances for June delivery is 6.0%. That is, the futures contract promises the buyer the delivery of bankers' acceptances at a price that will guarantee the buyer a yield of 6.0%. The price of a bankers' acceptance that has a $100 face value can be calculated as:

$$ \text{Price} = \frac{\$100}{1 + \left(\text{yield} \times \dfrac{\text{days to maturity}}{365} \right)} \qquad \textbf{(Equation 8-8)} $$

This formula is used to determine the price of a short-term, pure discount security that has a $100 face value. Essentially, it calculates the present value of the $100, which is the only future cash inflow expected at maturity from a discount security. As the period over which the security will be outstanding is a fraction of one year, the discount rate is equal to the same fraction of the yield.

The practice of using the simple interest convention to calculate the price of a bankers' acceptance is consistent with market practice. Moreover, the practice implies that the effective yield from investing in three-month bankers' acceptances will be the annual quoted rate compounded quarterly. This result is obtained because the proceeds from the bankers' acceptance can be reinvested at the end of every three-month period when the bankers' acceptance matures.

Using Equation 8-8 to price three-month bankers' acceptances that have a $100 face value at 6.0% yields a price of $98.5262:

$$ \text{Price} = \frac{\$100}{1 + \left(0.06 \times \dfrac{91}{365} \right)} = \$98.5262 $$

The outcome of the hedge will be known on March 29, and it will depend on the changes in interest rates. Suppose the change were a drop of 0.01% or 1 basis point. This means that on March 29, traders are willing to buy bankers' acceptances for June delivery to yield 5.99%. The delivery price would be:

$$ \text{Price} = \frac{\$100}{1 + \left(0.0599 \times \dfrac{91}{365} \right)} = \$98.5286 $$

Thus, for each one-basis-point drop in the futures rate, the price of bankers' acceptances with a $100 face value for June delivery will increase by:

$$ \$98.5286 - \$98.5262 = \$0.0024 $$

Accordingly, the futures contract, which promises to deliver $1,000,000 of face value, will increase in value by:

$$ 0.0024 \times \$1,000,000 \div 100 = \$24 $$

It is important to understand that the maturity of the security underlying the futures contract does not change with the passage of time. In this example, the bankers' acceptance futures contract was purchased on March 1. At that time, the seller is obliged to sell to you, and you are obliged to purchase, a three-month bankers' acceptance for June delivery. On March 29, you and the seller still have the same obligations. The maturity of the futures contract is independent and has no bearing on the maturity of the underlying security. Only the rate on the security underlying the futures contract will change as the delivery date of the futures contract approaches.

In Section 8.1, you were introduced to the Bourse de Montréal Web site (see also the Web Links on page 502) on which the quotes for three-month Canadian bankers' acceptance futures contracts are available. Remember that the indicated prices are points of 100, which means that a quoted price is not the price at which the bankers' acceptances will be delivered. Rather, it is a *price index* from which the rate and the delivery price can be calculated. The rate is equal to 100 minus the index.

Recall that a one-basis-point change in the index implies a $25 profit or loss to the futures trader. It must be emphasized that $25 per basis point is a rough approximation used by the Bourse de Montréal to settle three-month bankers' acceptance contracts, although using Equation 8-7 to calculate the price change in a futures contract will generally produce a different per-contract loss or profit. However, for the rest of this chapter, the convention of $25 per basis point will be used in dealing with a futures contract for which the underlying asset has three months to maturity and a face value of $1 million. (Exchanges around the world use the same convention for contracts with similar specifications.) The Equation 8-7 calculations are provided to help you achieve a better understanding of the concepts and to show the reason for using the $25 convention.

Hedging Strategy for Interest Rate Changes The following minicase illustrates the results from hedging under two scenarios of interest rate changes.

MINICASE 8-8 HEDGING STRATEGY FOR INTEREST RATE CHANGES

Returning again to Lora's case, two scenarios are possible for interest rate changes between March 1 and March 29. In one scenario, rates drop, as Lora expects. In the other scenario, rates rise, contrary to Lora's expectations. Both scenarios show that the realized rate on the hedged investment is almost equal to the original 5.5% interest rate of the Treasury bills.

Scenario 1: Rates drop as expected.

On March 29, the cash rate for Treasury bills due to mature on May 29 happens to be 5%, a drop of 50 basis points from the rate on March 1. Given this drop in the Treasury bill rate, the rate on 91-day bankers' acceptances for June delivery will also drop. Given the relationship in Equation 8-7 and the value of ρ as 0.95, the change in the Treasury bill rate will trigger the following change in the bankers' acceptance:

$$\Delta BA = 50 \div 0.95$$
$$= 52.63 \text{ or } 53 \text{ basis points}$$

Therefore, the rate on 91-day bankers' acceptances for June delivery is 5.47% based on the March 1 futures rate of 6%. Suppose also that there is no basis risk.

Case Continued >

Lora's opportunity costs from the drop in rates can be interpreted as follows. Had Lora been able to buy the Treasury bills on March 1, she would have had to pay:

$$Price = \frac{\$100}{1 + \left(0.055 \times \frac{61}{365}\right)} = \$99.0892$$

Now, on March 29, the rate on Treasury bills is 5.0%. Lora must now pay:

$$Price = \frac{\$100}{1 + \left(0.05 \times \frac{61}{365}\right)} = \$99.1713$$

This means an opportunity loss of $0.0821 per $100 of face value. In total, Lora's opportunity loss is:

$$(\$5,000,000 \div 100) \times 0.0821 = \$4,105$$

Similarly to the maturity of the asset underlying the futures contract, the maturity of the asset that will be hedged will not change over time. Lora wants to invest in Treasury bills for a period of 61 days. She will look in the market for the desirable maturity. (It is assumed that such maturity can be found.) Therefore, her analysis will be for 61-day Treasury bills, regardless of whether the calculations are done on March 1 or on March 29. The maturity of the asset to be hedged is independent from the delivery date of the futures contract (June 1) and from the date on which the cash transaction will be undertaken and the futures transaction will be settled (March 29).

Lora's opportunity loss in the cash market will be offset by a profit in the futures market. Now that the rates have dropped, the bankers' acceptance price index has risen by 53 basis points. Lora sells the three futures contracts and earns on the sale:

$$\$25 \times 53 \times 3 = \$3,975$$

This cash profit partially offsets the opportunity losses in the cash market. However, the result can be interpreted a little differently. On March 1, Lora wanted to pay:

$$(\$99.0892 \times \$5,000,000) \div \$100 = \$4,954,460$$

to purchase the Treasury bills. On March 29, their prices have increased, and now Lora has to pay:

$$\$99.1713 \times \$5,000,000 \div \$100 = \$4,958,565$$

However, her futures position netted her $3,975. Thus, her net cost of purchasing the Treasury bills, given the hedge, is:

$$\$4,958,565 - \$3,975 = \$4,954,590$$

This price is very close to the original price (a difference of $130). Her implicit rate on the hedged investment is:

$$\left(\frac{\$5,000,000 - \$4,954,590}{\$4,954,590} \times \frac{365}{61}\right) = 5.48\%$$

which is almost equal to the original 5.5% rate.

Case Continued >

Notice that the hedge is not perfect in that it did not completely offset the risk. Even with the hedge, Lora's return has dropped by 2 basis points. One of the reasons for the discrepancy is the rounding off of the hedge ratio to three contracts. In practice, there are other factors that may also lead to a discrepancy.

Scenario 2: Rates rise contrary to expectations.

On March 29, the cash rate for Treasury bills due to mature on May 29 rises to 6%, an increase of 50 basis points from the rate on March 1. Given this rise in the Treasury-bill rate, the rate on 91-day bankers' acceptances for June delivery also rises, suppose by 53 basis points. That is, the rate on 91-day bankers' acceptances for June delivery is 6.53%. Suppose also that there is no basis risk.

As calculated in Scenario 1, had Lora been able to buy the Treasury bills on March 1, she would have had to pay $99.0892 per $100 of face value. Now, on March 29, the rate on Treasury bills is 6.0%, and Lora must pay $99.0072.

$$\text{Price} = \frac{\$100}{1 + \left(0.06 \times \dfrac{61}{365} \right)} = \$99.0072$$

This means an opportunity gain of $0.082 ($99.0892 − $99.0072) per $100 of face value. In total, Lora's opportunity gain is:

$$(\$5,000,000 \div \$100) \times 0.082 = \$4,100$$

Lora's opportunity gain in the cash market is offset by a loss in the futures market. Now that the rates have risen by 53 basis points, the bankers' acceptance price index will drop by 53 basis points, subjecting Lora to a cash loss of:

$$\$25 \times 53 \times 3 \text{ contracts} = \$3,975$$

This cash loss partially offsets the opportunity gains in the cash market. However, the result can be interpreted in a different way. On March 1, Lora wanted to pay:

$$(\$99.0892 \times \$5,000,000) \div \$100 = \$4,954,460$$

to purchase the Treasury bills. On March 29, the prices of Treasury bills have decreased, and now Lora can purchase them by paying:

$$(\$99.0072 \times \$5,000,000) \div \$100 = \$4,950,360$$

However, her costs from the futures position are $3,975. Thus, her net cost of purchasing the Treasury bills, given the hedge, is:

$$\$4,950,360 + \$3,975 = \$4,954,335$$

This price is very close to the original price. Her implicit rate on the hedged investment is 5.52%, that is:

$$\left(\frac{\$5,000,000 - \$4,954,335}{\$4,954,335} \times \frac{365}{61} \right) = 5.52\%$$

which is almost equal to the original 5.5% rate.

Case Continued >

As in Scenario 1, the hedge is not perfect. In this case, however, the difference worked to Lora's benefit. Despite the hedge, Lora's return has increased by 2 basis points. The rounding off of the hedge ratio to three contracts is one of the reasons for the discrepancy. In practice, other factors may also create a discrepancy.

Hedging with Forward Contracts

The problems of rounding off and basis risk from cross hedging can be partially eliminated by using forward contracts in place of futures contracts. As explained in Section 8.1, a forward contract is transacted directly between participants, or through an interbank broker, which is an advantage to the traders. Most trade sizes are relatively large and most participants are financial institutions, such as banks, corporations, and governments.

For example, Lora could have made a deal with a bank to purchase a forward contract to cover her risk exposure perfectly. She could have purchased forward $5 million face value of 61-day Treasury bills at the forward rate. The rate would then be determined by negotiations between the seller and the buyer based on the market price for Treasury bills in 61 days.

Forwards that are widely used for hedging include foreign-exchange forwards, which are used to lock in an exchange rate for some future delivery date. Forward-rate agreements (FRAs) are interest rate forwards that are used to protect against a decline or increase in interest rates for a specific period of time commencing in the future.

For example, suppose a company normally requires $1 million funding during its busy quarter, which begins six months from today. If management is concerned about rising rates, it may decide to lock in a borrowing rate today by purchasing an FRA through its bank. If the FRA rate is 5%, the company would effectively have locked in its borrowing costs on $1 million for a three-month period. At the beginning of the period covered by the FRA, if interest rates are higher than 5%, the bank will reimburse the company for the three-month difference. On the other hand, if rates are lower than 5%, the company will reimburse the bank for the three-month difference.

CHAPTER SUMMARY

Chapter 8 explains the features of futures and forwards, the environment in which they are traded, and the techniques used in their evaluation. You study the basic techniques of hedging risk with the aid of derivative securities, such as futures and forward contracts.

Key Terms

basis risk,   page 492

basis,   page 469

broker,   page 473

cash or spot price,   page 469

cash settled,   page 485

clearing house,   page 475

cross hedge,   page 490

daily price limits,   page 481

derivative securities,   page 473

derivative,   page 468

direct hedge,   page 490

duration-based or price sensitivity hedge ratio,   page 491

floor trader,   page 473

forward contract,   page 469

futures contract,   page 469

futures or forward contract,   page 468

futures or forward price,   page 469

hedge ratio,   page 490

hedger,   page 470

hedging,   page 489

initial margin,   page 476

law of one price,   page 483

long hedge,   page 489

long position,   page 469

maintenance margin or maintenance performance bond,   page 476

margin call or performance-bond call,   page 477

margin requirement,   page 476

marking to market,   page 477

naive or 1:1 hedge,   page 490

short hedge,   page 489

short position,   page 469

speculator,   page 473

spot market,   page 469

Important Equations

Price index

$$\text{Price index} = 100 - i_d \qquad \text{(Equation 8-1)}$$

where
i_d = annual discount rate in percent

Futures price for financial futures

$$F_{0,T} = S_0(1 + Rf_{0,T} - Rh_{0,T}) \qquad \text{(Equation 8-2)}$$

where
$F_{0,T}$ = futures price at time 0 for delivery at time T
S_0 = spot price at time 0
$Rf_{0,T}$ = rate at time 0 on the risk-free asset maturing at time T
$Rh_{0,T}$ = rate of cash payments expected to be paid by the underlying asset between time 0 and time T

Futures price for non-financial assets

$$F_{0,T} = S_0(1 + Rf_{0,T} - Rh_{0,T}) + H_{0,T} \qquad \text{(Equation 8-3)}$$

where
$H_{0,T}$ = holding costs from time 0 to time T

General pricing formula for index futures prices

$$F_{0,T} = S_0[1 + Rf_{0,T} - E(D_{0,T})] \qquad \text{(Equation 8-4)}$$

where
$E(D_{0,T})$ = expected rate of dividends over the contract period, which represents an opportunity loss for the holder of the futures contract as the holder is not entitled to the dividends

Forward exchange rate using the interest rate parity relationship

$$F_{0,T} = S_0 \frac{\left(1 + \dfrac{R_D}{N_D}\right)^{M \times N_D}}{\left(1 + \dfrac{R_F^{\bullet}}{N_F}\right)^{M \times N_F}} \qquad \text{(Equation 8-5)}$$

where
$F_{0,T}$ = forward rate at time 0 quoted in domestic currency at which the foreign currency can be purchased for delivery at time T
S_0 = spot rate at time 0 quoted in domestic currency at which the foreign currency can be purchased for immediate delivery
R_D = annual interest rate on the domestic currency
R_F = annual interest rate on the foreign currency
N_D = number of times per year the domestic interest rate will be compounded
N_F = number of times per year the foreign interest rate will be compounded
M = number of years until the maturity of the forward contract

Hedge ratio

$$HR = \rho \times \frac{V}{F_F} \times \frac{M_C}{M_F} \qquad \text{(Equation 8-6)}$$

where

HR = hedge ratio, total number of contracts needed
V = market value of the assets or liabilities to be hedged
F_F = face value of the security underlying the futures contract
M_C = maturity of the assets/liabilities to be hedged
M_F = maturity of the security underlying the futures contract
ρ = correlation of the change in volatility of the rate to be hedged in relation to the change in volatility of the rate on the security underlying the futures contract

Change in value of Treasury-bill rates as a function of the bankers' acceptance futures rates

$$\Delta TB = \rho \times \Delta BA \qquad \text{(Equation 8-7)}$$

Price of a short-term, pure discount security

$$Price = \frac{\$100}{1 + \left(yield \times \dfrac{days\ to\ maturity}{365} \right)} \qquad \text{(Equation 8-8)}$$

Web Links

Canadian Derivative Clearing Corporation (CDCC)

■ http://www.cdcc.ca/accueil_en.php According to its Web site, the CDCC "is the issuer, clearinghouse, and guarantor of equity, index and interest rate financial derivative contracts traded on the Montréal Exchange."

Financial Web

■ http://www.finweb.com/investing/ Contains articles grouped together by broad topic. See this link for the section listing articles on futures and forwards contracts.

FXStreet—Forwards and Futures

■ http://www.fxstreet.com/education/related-markets/forwards-and-futures/2007-05-16.html A portal for the foreign-exchange market, this article provides an overview of futures and forwards from advantages and pricing to futures trading.

Institute for Financial Markets

■ http://www.theifm.org/tutorial/contracts6.htm A non-profit foundation that offers training, sales, and the development of educational materials for the futures industry. The Web site offers quizzes, exercises, and a glossary of terms.

Investopedia Futures Tutorial

■ http://www.investopedia.com/university/futures/ An eight-part tutorial that reviews the fundamentals of futures, including a brief history, strategies, the players, and options for trading in futures.

Montréal Exchange/Bourse de Montréal

■ http://www.m-x.ca/accueil_en.php The Montréal Exchange/Bourse de Montréal is Canada's oldest exchange. Its Web site includes current news, stock market quotes, derivatives, and a variety of current and historical data.

National Futures Association for Financial Markets

■ http://www.nfa.futures.org/ From the self-regulating body of the U.S. futures industry, this Web site features access to the Background Affiliation Status Information Center (BASIC), a searchable database of information about individuals and firms working in the futures industry.

Self-Test Questions

Qualitative Questions

Answer each of the following questions in point form:

1. What is a financial futures contract?
2. How do forwards differ from futures?
3. What is the role of the clearing house in futures trading?
4. What are margin requirements?
5. How are futures prices generally determined?
6. How are futures on stock indexes priced?
7. What are the advantages of using a futures or forward contract to hedge?

Qualitative Multiple Choice Questions

1. According to the law of one price, which of the following formulas is the correct calculation of the futures price of an asset?
   i) Futures price = cash price + storage costs + forgone interest income that can be earned on the purchase price
   ii) Futures price = cash price − storage costs + forgone interest income that can be earned on the purchase price
   iii) Futures price = cash price + storage costs − interest income that can be earned on the purchase price
   iv) Futures price = cash price − storage costs + interest income that can be earned on the purchase price

2. What can a producer do to hedge the risk of a drop in the price of its product?
   i) Buy a futures contract
   ii) Sell a futures contract
   iii) Sell a put option
   iv) Buy a call option

3. Which of the following statements *best* describes the duration of a fixed income security?
   i) The maturity date of the final payment, when the principal is repaid to the lender
   ii) The time between interest payments (annual versus semi-annual versus quarterly)

iii) The average maturity of the stream of payments the security generates for the lender

iv) A measure of the sensitivity of the value of the security to changes in the time to maturity

4. A company is hedging with futures contracts using a duration-based hedge ratio. The company is determining the number of futures contracts that need to be purchased in order to hedge and cover all risk safely. For what level of changes in interest rates will the company set the number of contracts purchased, so that the change in value of the futures position will offset the change in value of the spot position?

   i) Small changes in interest rates

   ii) Any change in interest rates

   iii) Large changes in interest rates

   iv) Changes in interest rates that do not exceed a predetermined level

5. Which of the following statements is correct with respect to futures and forward contracts?

   i) Futures contracts can be tailored to fit the particular needs of the buyer and seller.

   ii) Forward contracts involve a clearing house that covers and guarantees the contract so that if the buyer defaults, the seller does not have to sue the buyer or take the loss.

   iii) Cancellation of a futures contract requires negotiations between the buyer and the seller.

   iv) Forward contracts lack the liquidity associated with futures contracts as there are no secondary markets for forward contracts.

6. Which of the following statements about futures contracts is true?

   i) The seller promises to sell the underlying asset at the agreed price and to deliver on the transaction date.

   ii) At the time the contract is signed, the buyer promises to buy, pays the price of the asset, and expects delivery on the exercise date.

   iii) The seller is said to be in a short position because he does not necessarily own the underlying asset.

   iv) A futures contract is essentially two contracts; each on its own is a financial liability.

7. Which of the following statements correctly identifies one of the major participants in futures trading?

   i) A person or firm that has an interest in the actual commodity and would like to buy it sometime in the future

   ii) A person who expects to have the underlying asset sometime in the future and wants to guarantee an open interest

   iii) A firm that has no intention of using the underlying asset now or in the future but wishes to make profits without risk

   iv) Speculators who are in the market for quick, riskless profit

8. Which of the following statements *best* describes futures contracts?

   i) The cash price of a futures contract is the price at which an asset promised for future delivery can be purchased today.

   ii) Futures contracts are agreements to trade an asset on the current date at a specified price.

   iii) At the time of signing a futures contract, the seller owns the underlying asset.

   iv) Futures contracts, like option contracts, need not be exercised at maturity.

9. If a company is to profit from the falling prices of a given asset, what should it do?

   i) Buy futures contracts

   ii) Buy call options

   iii) Buy put options

   iv) Buy forward contracts

Quantitative Multiple Choice Questions

1. Diane needs 10,000 bushels of grain in 3 months. Currently, 1 bushel of grain is selling for $2.73 for immediate delivery, but if Diane buys the grain now, she will have to pay storage costs of $5,500. She is considering purchasing a futures contract for delivery 3 months from now, so that instead of purchasing the grain today, she will invest her money in Treasury bills. Three-month Treasury bills offer an annual rate of return of 6%. According to the law of one price, what should the futures price of grain for delivery in 3 months be?

   i) $2.73

   ii) $2.77

   iii) $3.24

   iv) $3.32

2. Which of the following statements about the pricing of bankers' acceptances is true?

   i) The simple interest convention is used to price bankers' acceptances, though this is inconsistent with market practice.

   ii) The use of the simple interest convention implies that the effective yield from investing in 3-month bankers' acceptances will be the annual quoted rate, compounded quarterly.

   iii) The discount interest convention is used even though the proceeds from the bankers' acceptance cannot be reinvested at the end of every 3-month period when the bankers' acceptance matures.

   iv) The discount interest convention is consistent with market practice and is therefore used to price bankers' acceptances.

3. Today is January 15, 200X. Peter has decided to enter the futures market. He has $3,000,000 to speculate with, so he decides to purchase 300 three-month Canadian Bankers' Acceptance Futures (BAX). The market quotes 98.45 as the price for the March 200X settlement. Peter enters the contract and sets up his margin account with his stockbroker. His margin is $850 per contract and the contract size is $10,000. At the end of January 16, 200X, suppose that the BAX closes at 98.75. What adjustment must be made to Peter's margin account on January 16, 200X?

   i) $9,000

   ii) $90,000

   iii) $225,000

   iv) $255,000

4. A speculator, Mary, enters the futures market in three-month bankers' acceptance futures (BAX). The market quotes 80.90 as the price for settlement in three months' time. Mary enters the market by purchasing 50 contracts and must set up her margin account with $850 per contract. The next day, the BAX closes at 81.05. What adjustment must be made to Mary's margin account?

   i) The margin account will be credited with $750.

   ii) The margin account will be credited with $18,750.

iii) The margin account will be credited with $42,500.

iv) The margin account will be credited with $61,250.

5. The futures rate on bankers' acceptances for contracts maturing in three months is 5%. If the bankers' acceptance has a $100 face value, what will its delivery price be?

   i) $95.23

   ii) $98.77

   iii) $100.00

   iv) $101.25

Quantitative Problems

Problem 1

Alexandra has $1,000,000 to invest for six months. The annual interest rate is currently 4% on six-month term deposits denominated in Canadian dollars. One alternative would be to invest in a six-month U.S. dollar term deposit, which has an annual interest rate of 4.5% for a six-month term. The spot exchange rate is US$1 = C$1.65. Another alternative would be to invest in a three-month term deposit denominated in Canadian dollars, with an annual interest rate of 5%.

Required

a) Calculate the forward exchange rate at which Alexandra would be indifferent between the Canadian- and U.S.-dollar-denominated six-month term deposits.

b) For a three-month term beginning three months from now, calculate the forward interest rate that would make Alexandra indifferent between a six-month Canadian term deposit and a series of two three-month Canadian term deposits.

c) Suppose that Alexandra does not have the funds today, but that she will receive the funds in one month's time. She then has to invest the funds for a five-month period and requires sufficient investment proceeds to pay a large invoice six months from now. If she is concerned that interest rates will fall over the next month, how could she use futures to hedge against this risk of having sufficient funds to fund the payments? Explain briefly.

d) Identify *three* differences between forward and futures contracts.

Problem 2

Joel has $100,000 to invest for one year. Currently, the annual rate on a one-year term deposit denominated in Canadian dollars is 3%. However, Joel can invest in a U.S.-dollar-based term deposit at 2.5%. The current exchange rate is US$1 = C$1.60. The one-year forward exchange rate is $1.64.

Required

a) Using the rates quoted, determine whether Joel would be better off investing in the Canadian term deposit or in the U.S. term deposit. Explain the steps Joel would need to follow to hedge the U.S. term deposit with a forward contract that would eliminate all exchange rate uncertainty.

b) Calculate the forward exchange rate that would make an investor indifferent between the two investments.

Problem 3

Danny has £50,000 to invest for one year. He needs this amount in British pounds sterling as he plans to visit England exactly one year from today. However, he is tempted to invest in U.S. dollars because the current rate on one-year pound sterling–denominated deposits is only 4.25%.

   Danny can buy U.S. dollars at the rate of US$1.5656 per pound. He can invest the proceeds in a term deposit denominated in U.S. dollars. The current interest rate on one-year term deposits denominated in U.S. dollars is 4.5%. He can guarantee the exchange rate at which he can change the dollars back to pounds in the forward market. The one-year forward exchange rate is US$1.5725 per pound.

a) What is the value at maturity of Danny's investment in pounds if he takes the alternative of a one-year term deposit in U.S. dollars?

b) What rate of return will Danny receive on his investment? Should he invest in the dollar-denominated deposit?

c) What should the forward exchange rate be to make Danny indifferent between the two alternatives?

Problem 4

Amy is planning to invest about $100,000 in Treasury bills for at least one year. On consulting her broker, she obtains the information contained in the following table.

Cash Rates on Treasury Bills				
Maturity	3 months	6 months	9 months	12 months
Cash rate	4%	4.35%	4.65%	4.90%

a) How many alternatives are available to Amy given that she is limited to investing in only the maturities specified in the table?

b) Amy believes it is better to invest in a three-month Treasury bill followed by a nine-month Treasury bill, as she may need the cash after three months. According to the expectations theory of forward exchange rates, what is the forward rate on nine-month Treasury bills for delivery three months from today?

c) What is the forward rate on six-month Treasury bills for delivery three months from today?

Problem 5

How and why are futures cash settled?

Problem 6

A Canadian equipment manufacturer, XYZ Inc., has just received its first order from a foreign customer. The customer is a U.S. firm that requires its invoice to be denominated in U.S. dollars. The customer has agreed to pay US$15,000 three months from now if the equipment is shipped and installed one month from now. If XYZ Inc. cannot tolerate uncertainty about the exchange rate, it can borrow U.S. dollars today and convert the funds to Canadian dollars at the current spot exchange rate of C$1 = US$0.63. Then the U.S. sale proceeds can be used to repay the loan, including interest. The interest rate for the three-month loan will be 2%. Alternatively, XYZ Inc. can sell the U.S. dollars forward.

a) What would be the Canadian dollar proceeds from the sale if XYZ Inc. borrowed against the sale and converted the loan proceeds to Canadian dollars on the spot market? Show your calculation.

b) If the Canadian interest rate on a three-month loan is currently 2.75%, use interest rate parity to determine what the three-month forward exchange rate should be. What would be the Canadian dollar proceeds from the sale in three months' time at this rate? Show your calculations.

c) Explain how XYZ Inc. should compare the two choices described in parts a) and b).

Cases

Case 1: Farmer's Friend Inc.

Farmer's Friend Inc. (FFI) is a manufacturing firm in Michigan that produces farm equipment for the U.S. market. FFI buys most of its raw material from Canadian Steel Corp. (CSC) in Ontario, Canada. The terms of sale usually allow FFI until late spring to make payments to CSC because of the seasonal nature of FFI sales revenues, which peak in the spring. It is now mid-November and FFI has a payment of C$10 million due at the beginning of next June. The exchange rate is currently US$0.72 = C$1.

Currency options on the Canadian dollar, which trade on the Philadelphia Exchange, have a size of C$50,000. Options are available with expiration dates in March, June, September, and December. Two series of options are available, the first with a strike price of $0.71 and the second with a strike price of $0.75. Option premiums are shown in Case Exhibit 8-1:

Case Exhibit 8-1
Price Quotations for Currency Options on the Canadian Dollar

	Calls				Puts			
Series	December	March	June	September	December	March	June	September
US$0.71/C$	0.02	0.03	0.04	0.05	0.55	0.71	1.07	1.43
US$0.75/C$	0.01	0.02	0.03	0.04	0.90	1.27	1.45	1.62

Currency futures contracts of C$100,000 are also available to FFI. They are available with delivery dates in March, June, September, and December on the Chicago Mercantile Exchange. Price quotations for these futures contracts are shown in Case Exhibit 8-2:

Case Exhibit 8-2
Price Quotations for Futures Contracts on the Canadian Dollar

Expiration	Open	High	Low	Settlement
December	0.730	0.735	0.725	0.731
March	0.718	0.728	0.705	0.724
June	0.712	0.720	0.695	0.715
September	0.710	0.715	0.690	0.712

In order to achieve its budget cost level, FFI cannot pay more than US$0.74.

Required

Assume the role of assistant to the treasurer of FFI and prepare a draft report for her to present to the president of the company. The president has little familiarity with financial matters so you must be very clear and comprehensive in your report. Your report should include the following:

a) Explain the foreign-exchange risk FFI faces. What would the cost of the payable be if paid today at the spot exchange rate? What impact would a change in exchange rate have on this cost?

b) Identify the main differences between a futures contract and an options contract.

c) Assess the opportunity FFI has to hedge with futures contracts and what the outcome would be if the value of the Canadian dollar were to either rise to US$0.78 by June or fall to US$0.69. In your analysis, describe all of the transactions FFI must undertake in order to complete the futures hedge and to pay the amount due to CSC. Express the outcomes both in terms of the U.S. dollar cost of the Canadian dollars required and in terms of the resulting effective exchange rate. Assume each futures contract involves a transaction cost of US$40.

d) Assess the opportunity FFI has to hedge with options contracts and what the outcome would be if the value of the Canadian dollar were either to rise to US$0.78 by June or to fall to US$0.69. In your analysis, describe all of the transactions FFI must undertake in order to complete the options hedge and to pay the amount due to CSC. Express the outcomes both in terms of the U.S. dollar cost of the Canadian dollars required and in terms of the resulting effective exchange rate. Assume each options contract involves a transaction cost of US$50.

e) Summarize your report with a recommended course of action for FFI. Take the view that the two possible outcomes for the Canadian dollar, US$0.78 or US$0.69, are equally likely.

Case 2: Northeast Industries

You have just been hired as an assistant to the treasury manager of a large manufacturing firm, Northeast Industries. The company produces and exports industrial equipment and manufactures its own packing crates from raw lumber. The firm has several types of treasury risk, including exposure to variations in product prices, exchange rates, and interest rates. To date, futures contracts have not been used to hedge exposures, but they are under consideration. Several questions have been raised by the members of the board, and you have been asked to present information about futures at the upcoming board meeting.

Required

a) Explain the features of futures contracts, including daily mark-to-market and margin requirements.

b) Explain the difference between a hedger and a speculator in terms of trading in futures contracts.

c) Explain the role of the futures clearing house. What functions does the clearing house perform, how is it compensated, and what are the risks associated with the clearing house function?

d) Identify *three* disadvantages of forward contracts as compared with futures contracts.

e) Commodity futures prices are determined according to the law of one price. Use the following futures contract information to determine an appropriate futures contract price:
- Spot price per 1,000 board feet (or "mbf") of lumber = $260
- Current three-month Treasury bill rate = 4%
- Storage cost for 50,000,000 mbf of lumber = $300,000
- Current date is 182 days prior to contract maturity and a quarter is assumed to include a period of 91 days

f) Illustrate how currency futures prices are determined according to interest-rate parity. Use the following scenario as your example:
- Canadian interest rate on a one-year term deposit = 3%
- U.S. interest rate on a one-year term deposit = 4%
- Current spot exchange rate: US$1 = C$1.60

Case 3: Dorval Inc.

Dorval Inc., a Canadian producer of rollerblades, has developed an extensive market in the U.S. northeast. In a recent sale, a major U.S. customer went bankrupt after paying only half of its invoice. The invoice was denominated in U.S. dollars and the receipts Dorval did collect were received 90 days late and were converted to Canadian funds at a less favourable exchange rate than expected. This experience has sparked an intense debate among Dorval management on the benefits of export sales, the credit risks involved, and the exchange-rate uncertainty associated with invoicing in foreign currency.

It is now May 1, 20X1, and Mark Bigley, marketing manager at Dorval, has just announced a sale of 2,000 units of premium rollerblades to another U.S. customer. The sales agreement involves a unit price of US$50, with shipment to occur on June 1, 20X1, and payment to be due on August 1, 20X1. Dorval has been actively pursuing this new customer for several months and will honour this commitment. The task now is to effectively manage the risks associated with the sale.

The bank Dorval normally deals with offers two alternatives. Under Alternative 1, Dorval can sell the U.S. dollar proceeds forward now at a rate of US$1 = C$1.75. The current spot rate is US$1 = C$1.70. The borrowing rate Dorval currently pays on its line of credit to the bank is 0.5% per month on outstanding balances. Dorval has drawn down on its line of credit significantly in recent years and has a sizeable balance.

Alternative 2 involves Dorval selling its U.S. dollar receivable to a factor affiliated with the bank. The face value of the receivable is discounted by 5% as a factoring fee. Dorval would receive the funds immediately upon shipping the product and invoicing its customer. The bank has already contacted the factor and approval has been obtained for this invoice.

Dorval management believes that the exchange rate will be stable for the next three months, remaining at US$1 = C$1.70 with 80% probability. They believe there is a 10% chance of the rate moving to US$1 = C$1.60 and a 10% chance it will move to C$1.80.

Required

a) Explain the foreign-exchange risk and credit risk associated with the new sales commitment at Dorval. Describe the amounts involved, relevant dates, and the proceeds to Dorval if no hedge is undertaken. Calculate expected proceeds from the sale, in Canadian dollars, based on the opinions of Dorval management.

b) Evaluate the forward hedging opportunity. Calculate the proceeds Dorval would earn from the sale under this strategy. Include an explanation of what will happen under this strategy if the customer does not pay Dorval on schedule.

c) Evaluate the factoring opportunity. Calculate the proceeds Dorval would earn from the sale under this strategy. Identify *two* advantages to Dorval of selling its future export receivable to the factor.

d) Prepare a memo to the president of Dorval recommending the course of action Dorval should follow. Refer to your analyses in parts a), b), and c) and to the facts presented in the question. Include your recommendations with respect to both foreign-exchange risk and credit risk.

Chapter 9
Options and Swaps

CHAPTER OVERVIEW

This chapter deals with options and swaps. A major part of the chapter is devoted to the subject of hedging using options and swaps.

Section 9.1 focuses on the features and characteristics of options and the environment in which they are traded. Option holders have the right but not the obligation to buy or sell at the agreed price. In contrast, option writers have no rights but have the obligation to sell or buy at the specified price. Consequently, option holders have to make an upfront investment, called the option premium, to obtain these rights without undertaking any obligations. Option writers receive the premium for undertaking obligations without obtaining any rights. Because the maximum loss to the buyer of an option is the premium paid for it, buying options is considered to be less risky than trading futures.

The concepts and principles underlying the valuation of options on common shares are analyzed in Section 9.2. You learn that the value of an option depends on several factors, including the exercise price of the option, the time to expiration, the volatility of the return on the underlying asset, and the level of interest rates. You use the basic Black-Scholes option-pricing model to estimate the values of European options.

Section 9.3 illustrates how many securities issued by a firm contain embedded options. The values of these options increase the prices of the securities holding them. The financial manager should be able to identify these options to ensure that any securities containing options are priced to include the values of the options.

Section 9.5 explains the features and characteristics of currency and interest-rate swaps, the circumstances under which swaps may be created, and the advantages of swaps. Three minicases are used to illustrate the cash flow movements between the two parties of a swap.

Sections 9.4 and 9.6 will take you through the use of options and swaps in hedging against treasury risk. Through extended minicases, you study the use of options to hedge interest-rate risk from a single transaction and swaps to hedge currency risk over several years and many transactions.

These sections present much new material and detailed illustration. You will need to allocate your study time judiciously in order to develop a sound grasp of the ideas and to achieve the learning objectives. This subject matter cannot be effectively absorbed in one long session.

Learning Objectives

After completing this chapter, you will be able to:

- Explain the basics of option valuation and the factors that influence option values.

- Calculate the value of an option using the Black-Scholes model.

- Explain why option-like features are used with some issues of corporate securities.

- Demonstrate the process of hedging using options on futures and calculate the cost under different interest rate changes.

- Explain the general rules for hedgers under both rising and falling interest rates.

- Explain the use of currency swaps and interest-rate swaps and identify the circumstances under which they may be created.

- Demonstrate the process of hedging using currency and interest-rate swaps.

- Describe the four primary costs of hedging.

This knowledge will provide you with the professional skills to:

- Identify, analyze, and advise on financial instruments to minimize the financial risk of the issuer, investor, or lender.

- Research, evaluate, and advise on the appropriate accounting treatment for complex transactions, in this case, options and swaps.

- Manage cash flow and working capital using financial instruments.

- Assess or design a financial-risk management strategy.

HOW THIS CHAPTER RELATES TO OTHER CHAPTERS IN THIS BOOK

In a dynamic and competitive global business environment, risk management is becoming increasingly important and sophisticated, which is why finance students should understand it. In Chapter 7, the different approaches to managing risk exposure were examined. In Chapter 8, some of the characteristics of futures and forward contracts were highlighted, with a particular emphasis on how these derivatives can be used to hedge financial risks.

Along with forwards and futures (outlined in Chapter 8), options and swaps (as seen in this chapter) represent another important class of derivative contracting. The main purpose of this chapter is to explain how the concepts and techniques developed in valuing options and swaps may be applied to issues in corporate finance. This sets the stage for a more detailed advanced study of derivatives in corporate finance later as well as for future practice in the field.

9.1 OPTIONS

Characteristics of Options

An **option** is the right (but not the obligation) to buy or sell an asset at a specified exercise price within a specified period or on a specified date. The **writer** is the party who sells the option. The **holder** is the party who buys the option.

The **exercise price** or **strike price** of an option is the price specified in the contract at which the underlying asset will be traded on exercise of the option.

A **call option** gives the holder the right but not the obligation to *buy* an asset at a fixed exercise (strike) price within a specified period or on a specified date. In turn, the writer of the call option is obligated to *deliver* the asset to the holder at the specified price if the holder exercises the option.

A **put option** gives the holder the right but not the obligation to *sell* an asset at a fixed exercise (strike) price within a specified period or on a specified date. The writer of a put option is obligated to *buy* the underlying asset if the put option holder exercises the option.

The **underlying asset** of an option is the asset specified in the contract to be traded on exercise of the option.

The **expiry date** or **exercise date** is the last day on which an option holder can demand delivery. If the expiry date passes and the holder of the option does not exercise this right, the option becomes worthless. There are two kinds of options, American and European. **European options** can be exercised *only* on the expiry date. **American options** can be exercised *on or before* the expiry date. The names are not related to the places where these options are currently traded.

The **option premium** is the price that the holder pays to acquire the option.

In both calls and puts, the holder (buyer) of the option determines whether to exercise the option and the timing of exercise.

Financial options are options written on financial assets, such as bankers' acceptances, currencies, or Treasury bills. **Commodity options** are written on commodities. **Futures options** are options written on futures contacts.

The following two minicases are designed to assist you in understanding important concepts related to call and put options.

MINICASE 9-1 EXAMPLES OF CALL OPTIONS

Julie is the owner of Northern Flour Mills (NFM). She just signed a call option that gives her the right (but not the obligation) to buy 1,000 bushels of wheat at $3.40 per bushel on or before March 1, 20X2. Julie pays $200 for the option.

In this example, Julie is the option holder. The option writer (or option seller) is a commodities trading house with whom she has dealt in the past. The underlying asset is 1,000 bushels of grain, the exercise price is $3.40 per bushel, and March 1, 20X2 is the expiry date. The option premium is $200, the amount Julie paid to obtain the option. The option is an American option, as it can be exercised on or before the expiry date of March 1, 20X2.

Julie also buys a call option on a three-month wheat futures contract. The call contract gives Julie the right but not the obligation to buy the three-month futures contract on March 1, 20X2. (This is a European call.) The asset underlying the futures call is a futures contract for 1,000 bushels of grain at $3.50 per bushel to be delivered June 1, 20X2. Therefore, if Julie exercises the call, she will hold a futures contract that gives her the right and the obligation to buy the underlying asset of the futures contract, namely 1,000 bushels of wheat, at $3.50 per bushel three months from March 1, 20X2 (June 1).

Some of the technical details on the trading of options were simplified in Minicase 9-1 in order to clarify important concepts related to options. In the industry, the following conventions and practices are observed:

- All option contracts on a futures contract are sold through exchanges or registered brokers.

- Wheat futures contracts are sold on the Chicago, Kansas, and Minneapolis exchanges in denominations of 5,000 bushels, and on the Winnipeg exchange in denominations of 20 metric tons.

- The expiry dates for a wheat futures contract are March, May, July, September, and December. There is no June contract.

- A real option contract on a wheat futures contract would be American style (not European as in Minicase 9.1).

- An option contract normally expires the last Friday preceding the first notice day, that is, the third Friday of the month preceding the contract month.

- A futures contract does not have an underlying value, only a quantity. The call option has an exercise price that enables the option holder to buy this underlying quantity at a given price (in Julie's case, $3.50/bushel).

- A wheat futures contract has a specified expiry date.

MINICASE 9-2 EXAMPLE OF A PUT OPTION

Jeannine is the manager of Delicious Bakeries Inc. (DBI). Jeannine signs a contract whereby she will have the right (but not the obligation) to sell, for delivery on March 1, 20X2, 10,000 kilograms of flour at $0.50/kg. Jeannine paid $150 to obtain this put option.

In this example, Jeannine is the option holder. The option writer (or option seller) is a commodity trading house. The underlying asset is 10,000 kg of flour, the exercise price is $0.50/kg and March 1, 20X2, is the exercise date. The option premium is $150 (the amount paid for the option). The option is a European put option, as it can be exercised only on the expiry date of March 1, 20X2.

The preceding options are written on real assets—grain and flour. In practice, the underlying assets are diverse and may include agricultural commodities, metals, minerals, exploration rights, weather, commercial properties, common shares, currencies, interest rates, and financial futures contracts.

Trading Options

Options trade through an exchange or in the over-the-counter market. An **options exchange** is an organized market in which traders buy or sell options. Options that trade in the over-the-counter market are often of large value. Many transactions involve the use of options. For example, when an airline company buys the right to purchase airplanes from a manufacturer, the airline company is buying a call option in which the underlying asset is the airplane specified in the contract. Our focus will be on options that can be used to manage financial risk through hedging activities.

In over-the-counter markets, writers and holders transact directly or through an institutional broker. Most active participants in the over-the-counter market are financial institutions and large trading houses, as well as corporations. The parties negotiate the terms of the option and the final terms, depending on the requirements of the parties involved. The following terms of a contract are usually negotiated: contract amount, premium, exercise price, exercise privileges, and expiry date.

Calls and puts had been available in a "grey" market for many years prior to the mid-1970s. However, trading in options really began to accelerate following the introduction of an options pricing model by Fischer Black and Myron Scholes in 1973. Listed stock options began on the Chicago Board Options Exchange in 1973. Options on Canadian stocks started on the Bourse de Montréal in 1975 and the Toronto Stock Exchange in 1976. Currently, the only exchange-traded options in Canada are traded on the Bourse de Montréal and the Winnipeg Commodity Exchange. Many options, however, trade actively in the over-the-counter market between banks and their counterparties.

Equity option contracts are traded in standard units of 100 shares, with expiry dates three, six, and nine months after introduction in the market. New equity options are added yearly and options on shares that are no longer being traded are discontinued.

Option contracts are traded until 4 p.m. on the third Friday of the expiry month. They expire on the Saturday at noon, immediately following the last trading date.

Exchange-traded equity options can have as many as ten different expiry dates. The exercise prices are set at approximately the price of the share; one at approximately 20% above the share price, and one at approximately 20% below the share price at the time of listing. In the over-the-counter market, expiry dates typically extend to about one year but may be as long as the parties determine is appropriate.

Information on options trading is reported in financial newspapers. Exhibit 9-1 is used to explain briefly the information reported on financial futures options. Similar interpretations can be made for equity and other options. Publication of information on over-the-counter options is not required but this information is often reported through financial data systems. Over-the-counter trading volumes often exceed those of the exchange-traded market.

Exhibit 9-1 shows how options on three-month Canadian bankers' acceptance (BA) futures are typically reported in a financial newspaper.

The first column of the exhibit reports the strike (exercise) level of the bankers' acceptance futures index. This level determines the discount rate (100 minus the index) to be used for determining the strike (exercise) price of the bankers' acceptances that will be traded if exercise occurs. For example, the strike price of 94.50 means that the discount rate will be 5.50%.

Columns 2, 3, and 4 show, respectively, the premiums (in percentage points) that were used March 21, 20X5, to settle trades in calls with expiry months of March, June, and September. Columns 5, 6, and 7 report the settlement premiums for puts.

The quotes available on the Montréal Exchange Web site (see the Web Links section later in this chapter) are in a different format, but much the same information is available. To review OBXTM quotes, go to Stock Options and Futures Quotes (located under Quick Links on the left). From the Interest Rate Derivatives drop-down menu, select OBX and click OK. This brings up the quotes page for three-month Canadian bankers' acceptance futures options. The first column indicates the series and strike price. Click on one of the listings to review the detailed information for that option. Note that "C" in the code indicates a call and "P" indicates a put. For example, June 08 96.500 (OBX M08C9650) is a call option.

Exhibit 9-1
Sample Quotations on Three-Month Canadian Bankers' Acceptance Futures Options for March 21, 20X5

Strike	Calls—Settle			Puts—Settle		
Strike (1)	Mar (2)	Jun (3)	Sep (4)	Mar (5)	Jun (6)	Sep (7)
94	1.24	s	s	0.35	s	s
94.25	1.07	s	s	0.42	s	s
94.50	0.91	1.75	1.32	0.50	r	0.07
94.75	0.76	1.50	1.10	0.58	r	0.11
95	0.62	1.25	0.90	0.68	r	0.15
95.25	0.50	1.00	0.72	0.80	0.01	0.21
95.50	0.39	0.76	0.55	0.92	0.02	0.28
95.75	0.29	0.54	0.40	1.07	0.04	0.38
96	0.21	0.34	0.28	1.23	0.10	0.50
96.25	s	0.19	0.18	s	0.19	0.65
96.50	s	0.08	0.11	s	0.33	0.82
96.75	s	0.03	0.06	s	0.52	1.02
97.00	s	0.01	0.03	s	0.75	1.23
97.25	s	r	s	s	1.00	s
97.50	s	r	s	s	1.25	s

Prev. open int. 16,167   Prev. open int. 6,934

Note: $1,000,000, points of 100%; 0.01 = $25 per contract
   r = option not traded
   s = no option offered

The premiums are listed in percentage points. As the underlying amount to be traded is $1,000,000 of three-month bankers' acceptances, one percentage point means a premium equal to:

$$\$1,000,000 \times 0.01 \times (3 \text{ months}) \div (12 \text{ months}) = \$2,500$$

Thus, one basis point, which is 0.01 of 1%, means a premium of $25 (0.01 × $2,500). As shown in Exhibit 9-1, the premium per basis point is reported to be $25 per contract. For example, the price of the March call with a 94.50 strike price is:

$$0.91 \times 100 \times \$25 = \$2,275$$

The prices of June and September calls with a strike price of 94.50 are $4,375 and $3,300, respectively. The prices of the puts are calculated similarly.

Role of the Clearing Corporation The Canadian Derivatives Clearing Corporation (CDCC) acts as the issuer, clearing house, and guarantor of all exchange-traded derivative products, such as options on BA futures.

One of the primary functions of CDCC is to act as a guarantor to ensure the integrity and stability of Canadian derivatives markets. In providing a guarantee, CDCC stands ready at all times to transfer, hedge, and fulfil obligations arising from contracts or to liquidate a defaulting member's position in exchange-traded derivatives, such as options.

There is no clearing house for over-the-counter options. Counterparties deal directly with each other and parties to the trade must be confident that the other party is creditworthy.

For additional information on CDCC's services, visit the CDCC Web site.

Call Option Holder The holder of a call option expects an increase in the price of the underlying asset. Firms might use call options as a means to hedge risk caused by fluctuations in commodity prices. For example, a manufacturing firm buys protection against an increase in the price of a commodity, such as oil. If there is a price increase in the underlying commodity, the call option will have value. The holder can either sell the call at a higher premium and use the proceeds to offset the price increase of the underlying commodity, or use the call option to buy the underlying asset at the exercise price.

MINICASE 9-3 A BASIC CALL OPTION TRANSACTION

Juliann holds a call option on Speculating Immensely Inc. Speculating Immensely is currently trading at $54.50 per share. The call option provides Juliann with the right to purchase 100 shares of Speculating Immensely Inc. for $50.00 at any time from today, June 15, 20X3, until expiry on January 30, 20X4. Juliann paid $2.50 per share for the option. She decides to exercise her option and use it to purchase the stock, paying $50 × 100 = $5,000 for 100 shares. Including the option premium, Juliann has paid in total $5,000 + (100 × $2.50) = $5,250.

The seller of the option, on the other hand, is obligated to deliver the 100 shares when Juliann exercises the option. The option seller may already own the shares. Alternatively, if the shares have to be purchased at the current market price to make delivery to Juliann, the option seller will have a loss of ($54.50 × 100) − $5,250 = $200.

The worst-case scenario for a firm that buys a call occurs when the price of the underlying asset drops below the exercise price. In this scenario, there is no value in exercising the option and the holder will lose the entire value of the option premium. However, for a hedger that needs to buy the underlying asset in any case, the losses on the option premium will be offset by savings obtained through its purchase at lower prices. This can be seen in Minicase 9-4.

MINICASE 9-4 BASIC CALL TRANSACTION WITH LOSS TO HOLDER

Juliann, from Minicase 9-3, holds on to her option and the price of Speculating's stock plummets to $45 per share. Juliann has no reason to exercise the option, because she can now buy the shares in the market for less than her option at $50. Remember that she is not obligated to exercise her option; she can let it expire, but she will lose the option premium of $250.

The option seller, on the other hand, is ahead by the option premium less any brokerage fees. If the price of the stock had increased and Juliann had chosen to exercise the option, the seller would have been obligated to deliver the shares. However, because the stock price has declined, the option expires worthless, and the option seller keeps the $250 received as the option premium from the option buyer.

Call Option Writer The writer of a call option receives an option premium in exchange for taking on the obligation to deliver the underlying interest if the option is exercised. The call option writer might expect a decrease in the price of the underlying asset so that the call will expire with no value to the holder. As a result, the writer would earn the option premium less any brokerage fee. Alternatively, the call option writer might already own the underlying asset and be content to sell it at the strike price. If the option is exercised, the call writer will sell the underlying asset at the strike price and the option premium received will increase the effective selling price.

The worst-case scenario for a call option writer occurs when the market price of the underlying asset rises higher than the exercise price and the writer must cover the holder's claim to the shares. This can lead to potentially unlimited risks as the writer is required to purchase the underlying asset at the current market price and deliver it to the holder at the exercise (strike) price. This scenario was illustrated in Minicase 9-3.

Put Option Holder The holder of a put option buys protection against a decrease in the price of the underlying asset. Put options enable firms that are sellers of assets, such as natural resources, to hedge risk caused by fluctuations in asset prices or foreign currency values. The put option can protect the firm from a decrease in the currency value of sales revenue to be remitted at some point in the future. If there is a decrease in the price of the underlying asset, the put option holder can sell a put at a higher premium and use the proceeds to offset the decrease in price. Alternatively, the put holder can use the option to sell the underlying asset at the strike price. A basic put option transaction is described in Minicase 9-5.

MINICASE 9-5 A BASIC PUT OPTION TRANSACTION

Chris holds a put option on Bankers and Trust Company. The put option gives him the right to sell 100 shares of Bankers and Trust Company for $90.00 per share sometime between today, January 15, 20X4, and July 1, 20X4. Chris paid $2.00 per share for the option when Bankers and Trust was trading at $97.50. On March 31, Chris exercises his option when Bankers and Trust Company stock is trading at $80.00 per share. If Chris already owns 100 shares of Bankers and Trust, he can use the option to sell at $90.00 per share or $9,000. He paid $2.00 × 100 = $200 for the put option. Therefore, the effective selling price is $9,000 − $200 = $8,800. Alternatively, he can sell the put option for a higher premium.

The worst-case scenario for a put holder occurs when the price of the underlying asset increases to a higher level than the exercise price. In this scenario, the holder will lose the full option premium paid since the option expires with no value—a situation similar to the one in which the price of the underlying asset falls below the exercise price for a call option holder. This is illustrated in Minicase 9-6.

Suppose the share price of Bankers and Trust from Minicase 9-5 does not fall below the exercise price. At the expiration of the put option, the price per share of Bankers and Trust is $95.50. Chris has no reason to exercise this option and will let it expire, because he can sell at better prices in the market. As a result, he loses the option premium of $2.00 \times 100 = $200.

Put Option Writer The writer of a put option might expect an increase in the price of the underlying asset such that the put will expire with no value to the holder. Alternatively, the writer might wish to acquire the underlying asset by writing a put. Consequently, the writer will earn the premium of the put option (less any transaction costs) as shown in Minicase 9-6. A significant decrease in the price of the underlying asset causes the writer to incur losses, because the put writer will be forced to buy the underlying asset at the strike price. These losses are reduced by the option premium received for writing the option and are limited only by the fact that the price of the underlying asset cannot fall below zero.

Differences between Options and Futures/Forwards

Traders use options to accomplish the same objectives as can be accomplished with futures or forwards. It is important to remember, however, that with options, the decision to exercise is entirely with the holder of the option. If there is no economic benefit to exercising the option, the holder will let the option expire.

Profiting from an Increase in the Price of the Underlying Asset Consider a company that would like to profit if the price of a given asset increases. The company has three alternatives to make a profit:

- buy a futures or forward contract
- sell put options
- buy call options

Each alternative has different risk and return characteristics. For example, the purchase of a futures or forward contract allows for unlimited profit potential if the underlying asset's price increases. There is a potential for substantial loss on the futures or forward contract until the price of the underlying asset reaches zero. As a result, these strategies are used for hedging and speculation. The risk/return analysis for the choice of buying a futures contract is explored in Minicase 9-7.

Selling a put option produces profits once there is an increase in the price of the underlying asset. The put option will be exercised only if the market price is below the strike price. As a result, profits are limited to a maximum equal to the initial put premium received. Potential losses are limited only by the fact that while the put option writer can be forced to buy the underlying asset at the strike price, the asset's value can theoretically fall only to zero. Thus, potential losses to the put writer are equal to the exercise price.

MINICASE 9-7 RISK AND RETURN ON THE PURCHASE OF A FUTURES CONTRACT

David purchases 10 futures contracts. Each contract is for the purchase of 1,000 barrels of oil at $30 a barrel. David must provide a 15% margin requirement. His margin account will contain $10 \times 1,000 \times \$30 \times 0.15 = \$45,000$. He closes the account when oil reaches $45 a barrel. His margin account is at $10 \times 1,000 \times (\$45 - \$30) + \$45,000 = \$150,000 + \$45,000 = \$195,000$. David has profited from the increase in the underlying asset. However, if the price had fallen dramatically to zero, David's losses would equal $10 \times 1,000 \times \$30 = \$300,000$.

MINICASE 9-8 RISK AND RETURN RESULTING FROM THE SALE OF A PUT OPTION

Jessica decides to write a put option on 100 shares of Canadian Winemakers Inc. (CWI), which is currently trading at $23.47 per share. The put option allows the holder to sell 100 shares of CWI for an exercise price of $24.00 on January 30, 20X7. The option premium is $3.50 per share, so Jessica receives $350 from the option holder. On January 30, 20X7, the market price of CWI shares is $25.75. Therefore, the put option expires unexercised and Jessica retains the option premium. However, if CWI's share price had become worthless in the interim, the option holder would have had the right to sell CWI shares to Jessica for $24.00 each on January 30, 20X7. Jessica would have lost ($24.00 × 100) − $350 = $2,050 on the transaction.

Buying a call option produces potentially unlimited profits if there is an increase in the price of the underlying asset above the exercise price by an amount larger than the call premium paid. If prices decrease, the company loses only the call premium; thus, it does not have the same risk exposure as with a long futures or forward position.

MINICASE 9-9 RISK AND RETURN RESULTING FROM THE PURCHASE OF A CALL OPTION

Frank purchases a call option on 100 shares of DreamsComeTrue.com. The option gives him the right to buy 100 shares of DreamsComeTrue.com for $12.50 per share on September 1, 20X5. DreamsComeTrue.com is currently trading for $11.75 per share. Frank paid $1.50 per share for the option. On September 1, 20X5, DreamsComeTrue.com is trading for $15.75 per share. Frank exercises his option and pays 12.50 × 100 or $1,250

Case Continued >

for a total cost for the shares of $1,400. The potential profit on this transaction for Frank is limited only by how high the market for the shares can go. However, if on September 1, 20X5, the shares of DreamsComeTrue.com are worthless, then Frank will not exercise his option. The option will expire and Frank will lose the option premium of $150.

Exhibit 9-2 shows that each alternative will earn a profit if there is an increase in the price of the underlying asset, as was illustrated in Minicases 9-7 through 9-9.

Exhibit 9-2
Profit and Loss Potential on Futures/Forwards and Options If the Price of the Underlying Asset Is Expected to Increase

Transaction	Potential profit	Potential loss
Buy futures or forwards	Unlimited	Unlimited until price reaches zero
Sell a put	Limited to put premium	Limited to exercise price less premium
Buy a call	Unlimited	Limited to call premium

To characterize profits or losses as limited does not mean that they are small on a percentage basis. For example, the potential profit from selling a put is characterized as "limited" because the dollar profit is limited to the premium. However, on a percentage basis, earning the premium represents a 100% profit. Similarly, the potential loss from buying a call option is characterized as "limited to the call premium." On a percentage basis, loss of the premium means 100% loss on the investment.

Therefore, the "limited loss" characterization does not necessarily mean that buying options involves less risk than buying the underlying securities. The term "limited" refers to the fact that the option buyer knows with certainty the maximum loss. In addition, buying an option often involves a smaller investment than buying the underlying asset.

Profiting from a Decrease in the Price of the Underlying Asset
If the concern is that prices of the underlying asset will decrease, a company can benefit from asset price declines. In this case, the company would take a position in the derivatives market to gain from a decrease in the price so as to offset its cash position. Again, the company has three alternatives:

- sell a futures or forward contract
- buy put options
- sell call options

Exhibit 9-3 lists the potential outcomes. Although the futures or forward position may lead to unlimited losses, it may also lead to large gains (limited as the asset price reaches zero). The purchase of a put option also offers the potential for gain (less the premium paid), but the loss is limited to the initial put premium. Another alternative, the sale of a call, limits the gain to the premium received on the call and has unrestricted losses, because the call writer will be forced to deliver the underlying asset, regardless of current market prices, if the call is exercised.

Keep in mind that the purpose of Exhibits 9-2 and 9-3 is to explain that options and futures/forwards can accomplish the same objective for a trader. Yet options have risks that are different from those associated with futures and forwards. A comparison of the alternatives of buying options or futures/forwards as opposed to buying *the underlying security* is an entirely different issue.

9.2 BASIC VALUATION CONCEPTS OF FINANCIAL OPTIONS

In this section, you will learn how option premiums are determined. You will study the relationship between the premium and the exercise price, the time to expiration, the level of current interest rates, and the volatility of the return on the underlying asset. The section concludes by introducing the Black-Scholes option-pricing model, which can be used to price financial and other options.

Relationship between the Premium and the Exercise Price

Option pricing is relatively complex, and it depends on measuring several factors simultaneously. Option premiums or prices depend, among other things, on the value of the underlying asset. If the exercise price of a call option is less than the market price of the underlying asset, the price of the call option is at least equal to the difference. For example, in Minicase 9-1, the exercise price is $3.40 per bushel. If the market price is $4.00 per bushel, the premium of the option is at least $0.60 per bushel (or $600, as the contract is for 1,000 bushels). If the exercise price is higher than the market price, the holder of the option will not exercise because it will be more advantageous to purchase the grain in the open market than to use the option to buy at the contract price.

Similarly, the premium of a put option is a function of the exercise price. If the exercise price is higher than the market price, the put's premium is at least equal to the difference. For example, in Minicase 9-2, if the market price per kilogram of flour is $0.45, the price of the put is at least $0.05/kg (or $500 for the entire contract). In this case, Jeannine will exercise her option. If the market price is greater than the exercise price, she will not exercise her option because it would be more advantageous for her to sell in the open market than to use the option to sell.

At any point, the market price of the underlying asset may be above, below, or equal to the option's exercise price. This price comparison helps to determine the option's value. When the current market price of a call option is above the exercise price, the holder can exercise the option and immediately sell the underlying asset for more than the exercise price. In this case, the option is said to be **in the money**. The greater the price differential, the greater the value of the option will be.

A put option is in the money if the underlying asset's market price is below the exercise price. The holder can acquire the asset at a price below the contracted sale price and sell it to the writer at the contracted price for immediate profit.

When an option holder cannot exercise the option at a favourable price compared with the exercise price, the option is said to be **out of the money**. A call option is out of the money when the market price of the underlying asset is below the exercise price. A put option is out of the money when the market price exceeds the exercise price. An option is **at the money** if the market and exercise prices are equal.

Value of an Option at Expiration You learned from the opening paragraphs of this section that the option premium is directly related to the difference between the exercise price and the current market price of the underlying asset. Now consider an equity call option at or near its expiry date. The option's value is a function of share price. Just before expiration, if the share's market price exceeds the exercise price, the option value is positive. However, if the market price is less than the exercise price, the option value is zero. An option cannot be worth less than zero. Minicase 9-10 illustrates these concepts.

MINICASE 9-10 VALUE OF A CALL OPTION AT EXPIRATION

Tony owns a call option on Middle Crust Resources (MCR). The option has an exercise price of $20 per share and expires in February 20X2 (the third Friday is February 15). Tony bought the option on September 25, 20X1, paying a premium of $1.25 per share.

Today is February 15, 20X2, the expiry date of Tony's call option. If MCR's market price is $20, Tony will be indifferent as to whether or not to exercise his option because he can buy the shares from the option writer or in the market at the same price. As both prices are equal, the option has no value. If MCR's market price is less than $20, Tony will have no incentive to exercise his option because he would lose money. Instead, he can buy the shares in the market at a lower price than the exercise price. Consequently, the market price of the call option is again zero.

Now suppose that on February 15, 20X2, MCR's market price is $21. Tony can exercise the option, which entitles him to buy the shares at $20 each, or for $1 less than the market price. He will not sell the option unless he receives at least $1 per share as a premium.

The value of a call option on the expiry date can be graphed as a function of the market price (the underlying asset). Exhibit 9-4 shows the value of Tony's call option on the day the option matures as a function of MCR's share price on the same day. The

Case Continued >

Exhibit 9-4 Value of Tony's Call Option at Expiration

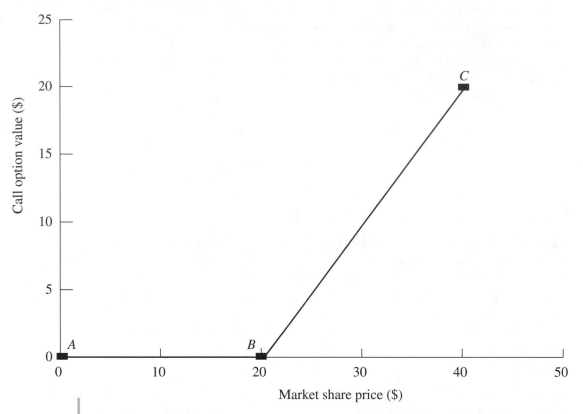

value is zero as long as MCR's market price is less than or equal to the exercise price of $20 per share. If the market price is higher than the exercise price, the value of the call option is positive and exactly equal to the difference between the two prices.

Value of an Option before Expiration

Before expiration, the premium of an option can be divided into two parts: the intrinsic value and the time value.

The *intrinsic value of a call option* is defined as the greater of zero or:

$$\left(\begin{array}{c} \text{Market} \\ \text{price of share} \end{array} - \begin{array}{c} \text{exercise} \\ \text{price} \end{array} \right)$$

That is:

$$\begin{array}{c} \text{Intrinsic} \\ \text{value} \end{array} = \text{maximum} \left(0, \begin{array}{c} \text{market price} \\ \text{of a share} \end{array} - \begin{array}{c} \text{exercise} \\ \text{price} \end{array} \right) \quad \textbf{(Equation 9-1)}$$

The intrinsic value is zero *if the exercise price is greater than or equal to* the market price of the share and positive otherwise. Given that the exercise price is fixed, the intrinsic value is a direct function of the share price. Indeed, the intrinsic value is the price the call writer gives up if the option is exercised and the value the call holder receives by exercising the option. (Generally, it is not wise to exercise early, but if someone does, it is said that the person will receive the intrinsic value.)

Exhibit 9-5 shows the value of a call option before expiration. Line *ABC* represents the lower bound of the option value. This line represents the intrinsic value for the

Exhibit 9-5 Value of a Call Option before Expiration

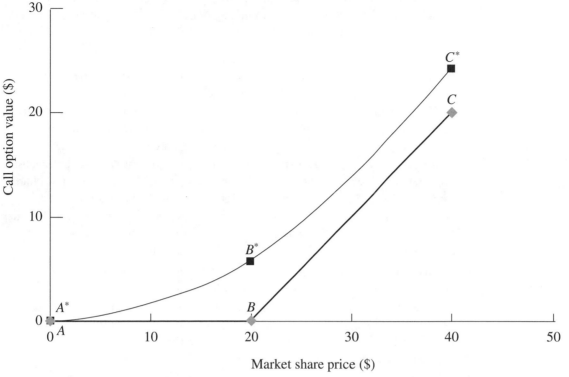

■ Intrinsic value plus time value
◆ Intrinsic value of the call

possible levels of the share price. The intrinsic value is the minimum price at which a trader would be willing to trade the option.

In contrast, the *intrinsic value of a put option* is defined as:

$$\begin{array}{l}\text{Intrinsic} \\ \text{value}\end{array} = \text{maximum} \left(0, \begin{array}{c}\text{exercise} \\ \text{price}\end{array} - \begin{array}{c}\text{market price} \\ \text{of a share}\end{array} \right) \quad \textbf{(Equation 9-2)}$$

The intrinsic value is zero *if the exercise price is less than or equal to* the market price of the share and positive otherwise. Given that the exercise price is fixed, the intrinsic value is a direct function of the share price. The intrinsic value of a put option is the value the put holder receives by exercising the option.

The *time value of a call option or a put option* is defined as:

$$\begin{array}{l}\text{Time} \\ \text{value}\end{array} = \text{premium} - \begin{array}{c}\text{intrinsic} \\ \text{value}\end{array} \quad \textbf{(Equation 9-3)}$$

The time value represents the willingness of holders to pay more than the intrinsic value for an option. *Call holders* hope that the volatility of the share price creates an opportunity in which the share price is higher than the exercise price. *Put holders* hope that the volatility of the share price creates an opportunity in which the share price is lower than the exercise price. As long as there is time to expiration, the time value of the option will be positive, even if the intrinsic value is zero. At expiration, an option is worth the intrinsic value.

At least three factors account for the time value of options. These factors are described for a call option, but the analysis can be easily extended to put options. First, going back to Exhibit 9-5, notice the value of the call option moving along the ABC curve. The difference between the A*B*C* curve and the lower bound option value line is the time value of a call option.

- *In general, the longer the period to the expiry date, the greater the option's time value will be.* This conclusion is based on two facts. First, the longer the period to expiration, the more time is left for the common share to increase in value. Given the opportunity to increase, the share price may rise in the future above its present value and the exercise of the option may be profitable. Second, the exercise price is paid in the future. The longer the period to the expiry date, the lower the present value of the exercise price will be. For example, at a current interest rate of 10%, the present value of an exercise price of $10 to be paid at the end of one year is $9.09. In contrast, the present value of an exercise price of $10 to be paid at the end of two years is $8.26. Other factors being constant, an option with an expiry date that is two years away will have a higher value than an option that has an expiry date only one year away.

- *The present value of the exercise price is a function of the time to maturity of the option and of the prevailing interest rate used in the discounting process.* The delayed payment of the exercise price is particularly valuable if interest rates are high and option maturities are long. Other factors being constant, an increase in interest rates reduces the present value of the exercise price, and investors are willing to pay a higher premium for the option. The opposite is true if interest rates fall.

- *Price volatility of the common share is important in option valuation.* Price volatility increases the chances of favourable outcomes for the option holder (i.e., when share price exceeds exercise price) and hence increases the value of the option. Option holders gain from large positive share returns (upside potential) but do not suffer from large negative share returns (downside protection).

MINICASE 9-11 VALUE OF A PUT OPTION BEFORE EXPIRATION

Margaret owns a put option on Middle Crust Resources (MCR). The option has an exercise price of $20 per share and expires in February 20X2 (the third Friday is February 15). Margaret purchased the option on October 12, 20X1, paying a premium of $0.75 per share.

Exhibit 9-6 shows the value of the put option before expiration. Line *EFG* represents the intrinsic value of the put option. The intrinsic value is zero as long as MCR's share price is greater than or equal to $20. If the share price is less than $20, the intrinsic value of the put option is equal to the difference. The intrinsic value of the put is limited to the exercise price.

Line A*B*C* in Exhibit 9-5 showed the call premiums before the expiry date for various scenarios of market price. The call premium, denoted by line A*B*C*, is always greater than the intrinsic value, which is represented by line *ABC*. Similarly, line E*F*G* shows that the put premiums before the expiry date are greater than the intrinsic value as denoted by line *EFG* for various scenarios of market price. In both cases, the time value of the options is positive because the difference between the premium and the intrinsic value is positive.

Case Continued >

Exhibit 9-6 Value of Margaret's Put Option before Expiration

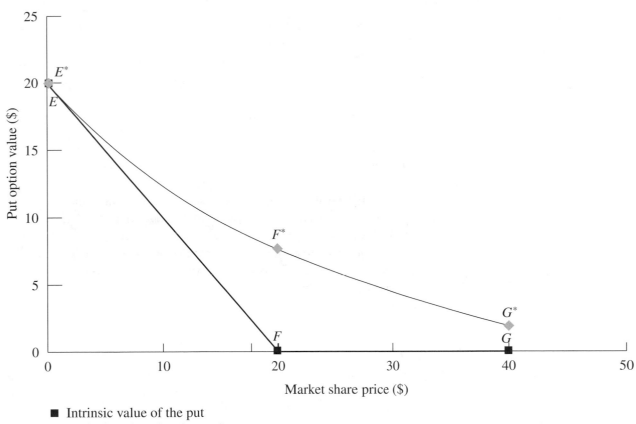

- ■ Intrinsic value of the put
- ◆ Intrinsic value plus time value

Although this discussion and Minicases 9-10 and 9-11 have focused on equity options, the same theory applies to other options, such as options on foreign exchange, interest rates, or commodity prices, for example.

Black-Scholes Option-Pricing Model

The **Black-Scholes option-pricing model** is one of the pioneering models of option valuation. Black and Scholes developed the model in 1973 for pricing common share options. It was later modified for use in pricing options on futures contracts or on physical or real assets.

The Black-Scholes model was developed to value European options. Because the model does not account for the possibility of early exercise, it tends to undervalue in-the-money options slightly. Nevertheless, the Black-Scholes model continues to be the most popular model for estimating option values.

Calculations of option prices are usually done with the aid of option pricing software. Dozens of option pricing formulas have been developed as a result of the Black-Scholes model. Understanding this model is very important for your learning because of its significance as a foundation for options pricing.

> **Value of a Call** The Black-Scholes option-pricing model for a call is given by:

$$C = SN(d_1) - EN(d_2)e^{-rT} \qquad \text{(Equation 9-4)}$$

$$d_1 = \frac{\ln\left(\dfrac{S}{E}\right) + rT}{\sigma T^{1/2}} + \frac{\sigma T^{1/2}}{2} \qquad \text{(Equation 9-5)}$$

where

C = call premium

$d_2 = d_1 - \sigma T^{1/2}$

S = share price

$N(\cdot)$ = cumulative distribution function for a standardized normal random variable that has a mean of zero and standard deviation of 1; $N(d_1)$ is the probability that an outcome will be less than or equal to d_1 (Use a calculator with statistical functions or the cumulative probability table in Appendix B on page 578 to determine the value of $N(\cdot)$ as needed.)

E = exercise price of the asset underlying the option

r = risk-free rate

T = time to expiration measured in years

σ = standard deviation of the continuously compounded rate of return on the underlying asset

$\ln(\cdot)$ = natural (base e) logarithm function

e = natural logarithm base (converts returns to continuously compounded equivalent)

Note: A natural logarithm refers to a logarithm with a base of e where $e = 2.718282$. Mathematically, the expression

$$\left[1 + \frac{1}{n}\right]^n$$

tends toward the value of e as n becomes a very large number. You solve for the natural logarithm function when determining the value of a Call. This procedure is required to determine the natural logarithm function of the ratio of share price to exercise price. On a business calculator, first compute the ratio of share price to exercise price, then compute the natural logarithm by pressing the ln key.

The terms in the Black-Scholes formula may be interpreted as follows. Under risk neutrality, $SN(d_1)$ is the present value of the expected payoff from buying the underlying share at expiration. The expected payoff is calculated at time T, conditional on the call option being in the money. $N(d_2)$ calculates the probability that the call will expire in the money. The present value of the exercise price is discounted at the continuously compounded risk-free rate. Therefore, $EN(d_2)e^{-rT}$ is the present value of the expected cost of exercising the call option at expiration, conditional on the call option being in the money.

Note: To calculate the probability $N(d^*)$ that a call will expire in the money, a technique known as interpolation is used. The cumulative probability table in Appendix B can be consulted to determine the upper

$[N(d_U)]$ and lower $[N(d_L)]$ limits. Both of these limits are used to estimate a more precise value of $N(d^*)$. The formula for interpolation is:

$$N(d^*) = N(d_L) + \left[\frac{d^* - d_L}{d_U - d_L} \times [N(d_U) - N(d_L)]\right] \quad \textbf{(Equation 9-6)}$$

where

$N(d^*)$ = probability that an outcome will be less than or equal to d^*
d_L = value of d in the table that is smaller than and nearest to d^*
d_U = value of d in the table that is greater than and nearest to d^*

MINICASE 9-12 CALCULATING A CALL PREMIUM

Tony from Minicase 9-10 owns a call option on Middle Crust Resources (MCR). The option has an exercise price of $20 per share and expires on February 20, 20X2. Tony bought the option on September 25, 20X1, paying a premium of $1.25 per share.

Today is October 24, 20X1, and MCR's share price is $21. The continuously compounded risk-free rate is 6% per year. The standard deviation of the continuously compounded rate of return on the MCR share is 0.15. What is a fair premium for the option?

The first step is to find the call premium C. According to the data:

S = $21
E = $20
r = 6%
T = 7 days in October, plus 30 days in November, plus 31 days in each of December and January, plus 20 days in February (Total: 119 days or 0.326 years)
σ = 0.15

Use these data to calculate d_1:

$$d_1 = \frac{\ln\left(\frac{\$21}{\$20}\right) + (0.06 \times 0.326)}{0.15 \times 0.326^{1/2}} + \frac{0.15 \times 0.326^{1/2}}{2} = 0.8409$$

Therefore:

$$d_2 = d_1 - \sigma T^{1/2} = 0.8409 - 0.15 \times (0.326)^{1/2} = 0.7552$$

Now calculate $N(d_1)$ and $N(d_2)$. The cumulative probability table in Appendix B shows that no $N(d)$ value is reported for d equal to 0.8409. Instead, 0.8409 falls between 0.84 and 0.85 for which $N(d)$ values are reported. Therefore, it is possible to estimate $N(0.8409)$ using interpolation.

Referring again to the table, for a d_L of 0.84, $N(d)$ is equal to 0.7995, while for a d_U of 0.85, $N(d)$ is equal to 0.8023. Therefore, $N(0.8409)$ can be calculated as:

$$0.7995 + \left[\frac{0.8409 - 0.8400}{0.85 - 0.84} \times (0.8023 - 0.7995)\right]$$
$$= 0.7998$$

Case Continued >

Similarly, notice in the table that d_2 falls between 0.75 and 0.76. Thus, $N(d_2)$ can be estimated as:

$$0.7734 + \left[\frac{0.7552 - 0.7500}{0.76 - 0.75} \times (0.7764 - 0.7734) \right]$$

$$= 0.7750$$

Therefore, the fair premium for this call option can be calculated as:

$$C = (\$21 \times 0.7998) - (\$20 \times 0.7750 \times e^{-0.06 \times 0.326})$$

$$= \$1.60$$

The Black-Scholes option-pricing model confirms the earlier conclusions in this section regarding the relationships between the call premium and the share price, the exercise price, the time of expiration, current interest rates, and the variability in share price.

The values of call options are:

- *positively* related to share price but *negatively* related to the exercise price;
- *positively* related to the time remaining to the expiry date;
- *positively* related to the current interest rate;
- *positively* related to the variability in share price (or the price of the underlying asset).

Put-Call Parity **Put-call parity** is the central relationship between the value of a call option and the value of a put option when the two have the same underlying asset and exercise price. Put-call parity can be explored with option-pricing formulas, but the following is a more practical example for illustration purposes. Minicase 9-13 demonstrates put-call parity.

MINICASE 9-13 ILLUSTRATING PUT-CALL PARITY

Paul owns a call option on stock AB with an exercise price of $30, expiring in three months. Paul also has money invested at the risk-free rate, compounded continuously. The investment's future value on the expiry date is $30. Paul will use the $30 to buy share AB on the expiry date at the exercise price. The share price of AB on the expiry date is given by the distribution in Exhibit 9-7.

Exhibit 9-7
Distribution of AB Share Price at Expiration of the Option

Market price	$15	$20	$25	$30	$35	$40	$45
Probability	0.10	0.12	0.18	0.20	0.18	0.12	0.10

Question 1: What is the distribution of Paul's wealth from holding the call option and the investment and liquidating them on the expiry date?

On the expiry date, Paul is entitled to receive the intrinsic value of the option. The third row of Exhibit 9-8 shows the distribution of the intrinsic value. Also on the expiry date, Paul will receive the value of the investment, which will be $30. The distribution of his total wealth on the expiry date is shown in the last row of Exhibit 9-8.

Case Continued >

Exhibit 9-8
Distribution of Paul's Wealth on the Expiry Date

Share price	$15	$20	$25	$30	$35	$40	$45
Probability	0.10	0.12	0.18	0.20	0.18	0.12	0.10
Intrinsic value	$0	$0	$0	$0	$5	$10	$15
Cash	$30	$30	$30	$30	$30	$30	$30
Wealth	$30	$30	$30	$30	$35	$40	$45

Question 2: Lucille owns one share of AB and a put option on the share with an exercise price of $30. What is the distribution of Lucille's wealth from holding the share plus the put option?

On the expiry date, Lucille is entitled to receive the intrinsic value of the put option plus the share price. Exhibit 9-9 shows the distribution of Lucille's wealth.

Exhibit 9-9
Distribution of Lucille's Wealth

Share price	$15	$20	$25	$30	$35	$40	$45
Probability	0.10	0.12	0.18	0.20	0.18	0.12	0.10
Intrinsic value of put	$15	$10	$5	$0	$0	$0	$0
Value of share	$15	$20	$25	$30	$35	$40	$45
Wealth	$30	$30	$30	$30	$35	$40	$45

Exhibits 9-8 and 9-9 show that on the expiry date, the distribution of outcomes to Lucille and Paul is identical.

Thus, holding a call option plus an investment that will have a future value on the expiry date equal to the exercise price of the option is equivalent to holding the share plus a put option with an exercise price and time to expiration equal to those of the call. Accordingly, the present value that Paul must pay today to acquire his call plus the investment should equal the present value that Lucille should pay to acquire her put plus the share.

If Paul's investment is paying the risk-free rate r continuously compounded, the present value of an investment for which the future value on the expiry date should be equal to the exercise price E can be determined by:

$$\text{Present value} = Ee^{-rT} \qquad \textbf{(Equation 9-7)}$$

Therefore, the relationship among the call premium, the investment for which the future value at expiration will be equal to the exercise price, the put premium, and the share price must satisfy:

$$C + Ee^{-rT} = S + P \qquad \textbf{(Equation 9-8)}$$

where
  P = put premium
  C = call premium

S = share price

E = cash exercise price on option expiration

r = risk-free rate

T = time to expiration of the options

Equation 9-8 defines the put-call parity relationship. This relationship can be used to express the value of a call or put in terms of the value of the other, and the current price, exercise price, time to maturity, and risk-free rate.

Value of a Put

The put-call parity relationship shows that the value of a put can be expressed as a function of the value of a call. The relationship can be written as:

$$P = C + Ee^{-rT} - S \qquad \text{(Equation 9-9)}$$

This equation can be used to derive a formula for a put. Substituting for C its value from Equation 9-4 yields the value of a put P:

$$
\begin{aligned}
P &= SN(d_1) - EN(d_2)e^{-rT} + Ee^{-rT} - S \\
&= Ee^{-rT} - N(d_2)Ee^{-rT} - S + SN(d_1) \\
P &= [1 - N(d_2)]Ee^{-rT} - S[1 - N(d_1)] \qquad \text{(Equation 9-10)}
\end{aligned}
$$

where d_1, d_2, E, r, T, S, and σ are as defined in Equations 9-4 and 9-5.

MINICASE 9-14 CALCULATING THE VALUE OF A PUT

Margaret from Minicase 9-11 owns a put option on Middle Crust Resources (MCR). The option has an exercise price of $20 per share. This option expires on February 20, 20X2. Margaret purchased the option on October 12, 20X1, paying a premium of $0.75 per share. On October 24, 20X1, the call premium was determined to be $1.60, and MCR's share price $21. The continuously compounded risk-free rate is 6% per year. The standard deviation of the continuously compounded rate of return on the MCR share is 0.15. What is a fair premium for the put option?

This question can be answered by working directly with Equation 9-10. However, since the premium for a call with the same exercise price, underlying asset, and expiry date has already been calculated in Minicase 9-12, the put-call parity relationship in Equation 9-9 can be used to calculate the fair premium, P, for the put option.

$$
\begin{aligned}
P &= C + Ee^{-rT} - S \\
&= \$1.60 + (\$20 \times e^{-0.06 \times 0.326}) - \$21 \\
&= \$1.60 + \$19.61 - \$21 \\
&= \$0.21
\end{aligned}
$$

The Black-Scholes option-pricing model confirms the earlier conclusions in this section regarding the relationships between the put premium and the share price, the exercise price, the time to expiration, current interest rates, and the variability in share price. The values of put options are:

- *negatively* related to share price but *positively* related to the exercise price;
- *positively* related to the time remaining to the expiry date;
- *negatively* related to the current interest rate;
- *positively* related to the variability in share price (or the price of the underlying asset).

Notice that only the relationships among the put premium, the share and exercise prices, and the current interest rate are different from those for call options. The following minicase illustrates the various profit/loss scenarios of put options.

MINICASE 9-15 PROFIT/LOSS SCENARIOS FOR PUT OPTIONS

Jackie has 200 shares of General Credit Bank (GCB). The share price is $45. She buys one put (which can be purchased in standard sizes of 100 shares per put) for $300 with an exercise price of $40. She also signs a forward agreement that will expire at the same time as the put to sell 100 shares of GCB at $45 per share.

Question 1: What will Jackie's net profit (loss) be if, on the expiry date, GCB's share price reaches $55?

Given that the share price has increased from $45 to $55, Jackie will realize a profit on the cash position. However, her put will expire worthless because the exercise price is lower than the share price. She will lose the premium she paid on the put. Also, she sold 100 shares in the forward market at $45 per share. Since the share price has increased, she will suffer a loss on this transaction.

Profit on the cash position:	
200 × ($55 − $45)	$2,000
Loss on the put option	(300)
Loss on the forward contract:	
100 × ($55 − $45)	(1,000)
Net profit (loss)	$ 700

Question 2: What will Jackie's net profit (loss) be if, on the expiry date, GCB's share price decreases to $35?

Given that the share price has decreased from $45 to $35, Jackie will realize a loss on the cash position. However, her put will expire in the money because the exercise price is higher than the share price. Also, she sold 100 shares in the forward market at $45 per share. Now that the share price has decreased, she enjoys a gain on this position.

Case Continued >

Loss on the cash position: 200 × ($35 − $45)	$(2,000)
Gain on the put option: 100 × ($40 − $35) – $300	200
Gain on the forward contract: 100 × ($45 − $35)	1,000
Net profit (loss)	$ (800)

Question 3: What will Jackie's profit (loss) be if, on the expiry date, GCB's share price decreases to $25?

Repeating the calculations for Question 2 with the share price replaced by $25 yields:

Loss on the cash position: 200 × ($25 − $45)	$(4,000)
Gain on the put option: 100 × ($40 − $25) – $300	1,200
Gain on the forward contract: 100 × ($45 − $25)	2,000
Net profit (loss)	$ (800)

Question 4: The answers to Questions 2 and 3 are equal. Explain why.

The answers are equal because the loss of $800 will occur as long as the price is $40 or less. A price of $40 at the expiry date leads to the loss of the premium ($300) plus the loss of $5 per share, which was the difference between the share price at the time Jackie purchased the put and the exercise price of the put.

The put option was out of the money by $5 per share, which will be lost partially or fully if the share price at expiration is less than the share price at the purchase date. Indeed, the implicit time value in this case was $8 per share, which was completely lost when the put expired. Therefore, the loss on the put option was $800.

The loss of $800 will not change if the price decreases further, as any decrease below $40 will be gained on the put position. This gain will, however, be offset by a loss on the cash position. Similarly, any gain on the forward position will be offset by a loss on the cash position.

To find out how many practitioners use the Black-Scholes option-pricing formula, consider the following article by Eric S. Hardy. The article points out that inexpensive software is available to determine option prices on a personal computer using the Black-Scholes option-valuation formula. These tools are helpful in making decisions, although they are not likely to provide exact answers. Note that the software information is dated.

OPTION MATH MADE SIMPLE (SORT OF)

ERIC S. HARDY

You've got a hunch a company will pick up a lot of steam and think you should buy a warrant on its shares. But how do you know if the warrant already anticipates the good news?

When financial economists Fischer Black and Myron Scholes published an option valuation formula in 1973, individual investors were scarcely in a position to make use of it. This was eight years before the IBM PC was invented, and Black-Scholes isn't the kind of formula you can easily run on a slide rule.

Today, however, inexpensive software makes it possible to evaluate option prices on a personal computer, using the famous Black-Scholes option valuation formula. If you want to dabble in options—or warrants, which are like long-term options—you should get your hands on one of these programs.

A call option is the right to buy a stock at a certain price before a specified deadline. Options on several hundred public companies trade on the Chicago Board Options Exchange and other places. Warrants are about the same as call options, except that the deadline is usually further away (years, not months). When you buy warrants, you're essentially betting that the underlying company (and its stock price) will do better during the life of the warrant than the market says it will.

Option valuation software can't spit out a list of options that will automatically make money for you. Rather, it's a tool to help you make your own decisions. You can use it, for example, to determine the market's estimation of a stock's volatility. Then you plug in your own assumptions and see if that makes the option a buy.

Example: A three-year warrant on America West Airlines was recently trading at $10. Plug that price—and some other key facts, which we will explain in a moment—into an option program, and it will spit out a 33% volatility estimate.

What does that mean? It means that if 33% is a sound estimate of America West's volatility over the next several years, then $10 is the price at which the America West warrant ought to be trading. But suppose you don't agree with that volatility estimate. You think airline stocks are going to get a lot jumpier over the next several years, and that 50% is a better volatility forecast. If you are right, the warrant is priced too cheaply. So you buy it.

How is an option valued? Six factors are important. The first is the strike, or exercise, price. In the case of the America West warrant, the strike is $12.74—meaning, if you own this warrant you have the right to buy a share of America West at a price of $12.74.

Second is the current price of the stock, 19⅞ in the case of America West. Meaning: Although you probably wouldn't want to cash in the warrant tomorrow, if you did you would pocket a quick $7.14 (and lose what you paid for the warrant). This $7.14 immediate cash-in value sets a floor under the value of the warrant.

Third is the date the warrant expires. This one expires in three years, in August 1999. The further away the expiration, the more the warrant is worth, because the underlying stock will have more time to appreciate.

Factor four is the volatility of the underlying stock. The more a stock moves around, the better chance you have that it will land somewhere well above the strike price and give you a big return on your investment in the warrant. So, the greater the underlying stock's volatility, the more the warrant is worth.

Factor five is the dividend on the stock. The fatter the dividend payout, the less money is left inside the company to make it (and its stock) more valuable, so the less the warrant is worth. To put the same point another way: the fatter the dividend, the more you give up by owning the warrant rather than the stock.

Item number six is a money market interest rate.

As we said, Black-Scholes is a pretty complicated formula. You don't have to understand how it derives an option's value in order to use the software. Most traders don't. What they do know is how to compare warrant prices on the stock exchange with the valuations the software programs spit out. Where the differences are significant, there may be profitable investing and trading opportunities.

Where do you get the software? It's built into some stock quote services. The Bloomberg Financial Markets' $1,640-a-month terminals, for example, deliver delayed option prices and also show the volatility assumptions implied by those prices.

Another source is James Bittman's *Options for the Stock Investor* (Irwin Professional Publishing, $30). The book comes with a diskette containing an option valuation program. You plug in factors like strike price and volatility, and the computer tells you what an option is worth.

What if you don't have any idea what the real volatility is for America West's stock? Here again, the computer is your friend.

You can get a good starting point for your volatility estimate by calculating historical volatility. Start by downloading the daily closing prices for America West for the past year from services such as CompuServe (Go Quotes) and America Online (Personal Finance/Historical Quotes). Feed the numbers into a spreadsheet program. Use the spreadsheet to calculate each day's percentage change.

Using the built-in statistical functions supplied by the spreadsheet, calculate the standard deviation of these numbers. For America West we get 2.66%. Now take this number and multiply it by 15.9 to get an annualized volatility figure. (That 15.9 is the square root of the number of trading days in a year.)

Okay, you now have 42% as a historical annualized volatility for America West common, based on one year's data. From here on, you're working on hunch. If your gut feeling is that the stock is going to be a bit more volatile in coming years—maybe you think jet fuel prices are going to plunge this summer—then you could plug 50% into the program.

With that volatility assumption, the computer says the warrant should trade at $11.11. Assuming you are also a bull on the stock (no use if the volatility is increased

Higher Leverage, Higher Risk						
Company/business	Recent price	Warrant		Value of warrant		
		Strike price	Expiration date	Recent price	At historic volatility	At higher volatility[1]
America West Airlines/airline	19⅞	$12.74	8/25/99	$10.00	$10.55	$10.86
Federated Department Stores/dept. stores	34⅞	29.92	12/19/01	14.13	15.72	16.22
Lone Star Industries/cement	34	18.75	12/31/00	17.00	19.04	19.22
USG/building materials	27⅝	16.14	5/6/98	13.13	13.36	13.43
Viacom/broadcasting	42⅞	60.00	7/7/97	1.13	1.48	1.89

[1] Based on 110% of the annualized volatility over the past 12 months.

Sources: *Options for the Stock Investor* by James Bittman; Telemet America, Alexandria, Va.

because the stock is in a tailspin), the computer's valuation of the America West warrant suggests that the warrant is underpriced.

Bittman's program runs on DOS. If you want a Windows program, order the Chicago Board Options Exchange's Options Toolbox ($30). The CBOE (800-678-4667) also has a lot of free pamphlets that explain options concepts.

The table on page 536 lists five warrants that would be interesting plays for bulls who foresee an increase in volatility in the stocks underpinning the warrants. We used a program called Op-Eval, and dividend forecasts from Value Line.

Source: Reprinted by permission of *Forbes Magazine* © 2007 Forbes LLC.

The article suggests a practical way to estimate the volatility of return for a firm's stock using the following steps:

1. Calculate the historical volatility.
   - Obtain the daily closing prices for the target stock for the past year and enter them in a spreadsheet. You will find that some free Internet finance portals, such as finance.yahoo.com, can provide historical closing data in table format that can be easily imported into a spreadsheet.
   - Use the spreadsheet to calculate each day's percentage change.
   - Use the built-in statistical functions supplied by the spreadsheet to calculate the standard deviation of these numbers.
   - Take this number and multiply it by 15.9 to get an annualized volatility figure. (15.9 is the square root of the number of trading days in a year.)

2. Use your judgment to adjust your estimate of the stock's return volatility. For example, if in your judgment the stock is going to be 25% more volatile in the coming years than it was in the past year, you would add 25% to the stock's standard deviation.

9.3 CORPORATE SECURITIES AND OPTION THEORY

When firms raise funds in the financial market, they issue several types of securities. You studied the nature of these securities in Chapter 3. This section considers options that are used or created when firms issue securities. You will study the nature of these options and the reasons for their use.

Levered Common Shares: An Implicit Call Option

When a firm uses a combination of debt and equity financing, the common shares can be viewed as call options. This view assumes that the firm's debt is zero coupon debt and matures at some time T in the future. If a firm's total value at maturity of the debt is larger than the market value of the debt, debtholders will receive their total claims and shareholders will either issue new debt or new equity to finance payment to debtholders. If a firm's market value is less than the value of the debt, shareholders will choose to default on the debt. The limited liability of shareholders resembles the limited liability of call option holders.

Essentially, a firm that has bondholders and shareholders can be thought of as follows. Bondholders bought the assets of the firm. Then, they sold an ownership call option to shareholders in which the call premium is equal to the initial market value of the shares (total market value of the firm minus the market value of bonds). The option's exercise price is the debt's value at maturity.

At the maturity of the bonds, the firm's value will be less than, equal to, or greater than the market value of the debt. In the first case, shareholders would not exercise their ownership option. Because the market value of the firm is *less than* the value that belongs to bondholders, the value of shareholders' option is zero. The firm's bondholders liquidate the firm and receive the liquidation value. If the market value of the firm were *equal to* or *greater than* the market value of debt, shareholders would exercise their option. They would borrow money equal to the debt value and pay debtholders to keep ownership of the firm.

Exhibit 9-10 illustrates the value of equity as an option on the firm's total value at the maturity date of the debt. The value of the debt at maturity is $40, and the total firm's value is expected to be anywhere between $0 and $100.

Line *KLM* represents the value that can be captured by debtholders at the maturity of their claims, while line *K*L*M** represents the residual value that would belong to shareholders. When the debt matures, if the firm's value ends up to be less than $40, the debtholders would claim the entire value (segment *KL*). Shareholders would receive nothing (segment *K*L**).

If at maturity of the debt, the firm's market value exceeds the $40 debt value, shareholders would exercise the call option associated with common shares. Bondholders would receive exactly the $40 that belongs to them, and shareholders would capture the residual amount. Segment *LM* represents the value that can be captured by bondholders. Given that these claims are limited to $40, the segment is flat. Segment *L*M** represents the value of shareholders' claims. Because the firm's value above $40 accrues to shareholders, segment

Exhibit 9-10 Value of Equity as an Option on the Firm's Value

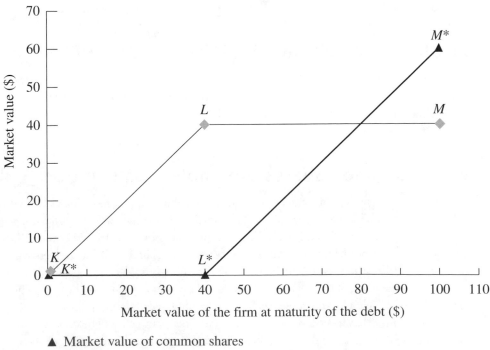

▲ Market value of common shares
◆ Market value of debt

*L*M** rises as fast as the increase in the firm's value (slope equals 45°). Notice that line *K*L*M** is the same as the line representing the value of the call option in Exhibit 9-4.

The assumption of zero coupon bonds simplifies the explanations, but it is not necessary. The situation can be generalized to the scenario in which debt is not entirely zero coupon debt. In this case, multiple call options are needed. Whenever an interest or principal payment is due to bondholders, shareholders have to decide whether or not to exercise their option. If the value of the firm's assets is greater than the required payment, shareholders will exercise their option and buy back the assets from bondholders. Each required payment is, in essence, an exercise price for a call option.

Corporate Securities with Attached Options

Following are examples of options that may be attached to corporate securities to enhance their attractiveness to investors.

Pre-emptive Rights In Chapter 3, you learned that firms often offer common shares directly to their current shareholders through a rights offering. A company distributes certificates to its current shareholders giving them the right to subscribe to additional shares of the company at a given price. Many companies specify in their charters that all share offerings of a particular class should be made exclusively with rights offerings. Pre-emptive rights enable current shareholders to maintain their proportionate holdings of the company.

Rights are essentially call options on newly issued shares. Consequently, each right carries a non-negative market value. This value depends on many factors, such as:

- exercise price
- price of the underlying share
- time to expiration
- variance of the underlying share price
- level of the risk-free rate

In particular, the lower the exercise price in relation to the share price, the more valuable the right will be to the holder. Issuers usually set the exercise price low enough to encourage holders to exercise their rights or to sell them in the market.

In Chapter 3, Equation 3-15 was used to estimate the value of a right during the rights-on period, and Equation 3-16 was used to estimate the right's value during the ex-rights period (see page 194). These equations are derived under the assumption that the time value of a right is usually small and negligible because the time to expiration of rights is normally short. However, as with a call option, the market value of a right consists of time value and intrinsic value. The actual value of a right is equal to the value derived by Equation 3-15 or 3-16 plus the time value. The Black-Scholes formula (Equation 9-4) can be used to estimate the value of a right in the same way it is used to estimate the value of a call option.

Standby Agreements In many rights issues, shareholders may not exercise their rights, as the share price decreases below the exercise price or the subscription price of the rights. Also, in many public issues, when the selling group undertakes to sell the issue on a best efforts basis, the shares may not sell quickly in the market at the expected price. To avoid such situations as well as the possibility that the issuer may end up receiving less than the expected cash from the sale, the issuer may negotiate a standby agreement with an underwriter.

A **standby agreement** requires that the underwriter purchase unsold shares at the subscription price of the offering (in the case of a rights offering) or at an agreed price (in the case of a public issue). The underwriter charges a fee for the standby agreement. In a sense, the underwriter writes a put option that can be exercised by the issuer to sell any remaining shares at the exercise price. The standby fee is the premium for the put.

Warrants   Warrants are long-term claims of holders of bonds, preferred shares, or common shares that confer the right to buy common shares (or other specified corporate securities) at a stated price within a given period of time. Warrants generally have long lives, as long as 10 years, when they are issued. Usually, warrants are used as "sweeteners" to facilitate the sale of bonds, preferred shares, or even common shares. Thus, they are often offered in conjunction with these securities as a package. Once sold in the market, warrants are often detachable and trade on the stock exchanges.

Essentially, warrants are long-term call options on the shares. Unlike standard options, warrants are written by a company on its own shares. On exercise, new equities are created. Therefore, if the warrants are exercised, the issuing firm receives new funds and the number of outstanding shares increases.

Hardy's article (provided in Section 9.2) elaborates on the similarity between call options and warrants:

> *Warrants are about the same as call options, except that the deadline is usually further away (years, not months). When you buy warrants, you're essentially betting that the underlying company (and its stock price) will do better during the life of the warrant than the market says it will.*

Given the similarity of warrants to call options, the prices of warrants are affected by the same factors that affect call options. For example:

- The exercise price negatively affects the values of warrants. The lower the exercise price, the higher the price of the warrant will be.

- The share price positively affects the values of warrants. The higher the share price, the higher the value of the warrant will be.

- The date the warrant expires influences its value. The further away the expiration, the more the warrant is worth because the underlying shares will have more time to appreciate.

- The volatility of the underlying shares is a positive factor for a warrant's value. Hardy's article states: "The more a stock moves around, the better chance you have that it will land somewhere well above the exercise price and give you a big return on your investment in the warrant. So, the greater the underlying stock's volatility, the more the warrant is worth."

- The share dividend has a negative effect on the value of a warrant. Hardy's article states: "The fatter the dividend payout, the less money is left inside the company to make it (and its stock) more valuable, so the less the warrant is worth. To put the same point another way: the fatter the dividend, the more you give up by owning the warrant rather than the stock."

- Money market interest rates affect the value of the warrants. Although Hardy's article does not elaborate on this issue, interest rates have a positive effect on warrant values. The higher interest rates are, the higher the value of a warrant will be. As with call options, the higher rate makes the present value of the exercise price lower and the value of the warrant higher.

Convertibles The conversion privilege is a right attached to bonds or preferred shares that gives the holder the right to exchange the security for common shares. Usually, convertibles are issued as delayed equity financing. They are issued when the stock market or the share price of a firm is considered temporarily depressed and a straight issue of common shares may not be advisable. In this case, the conversion right is given to encourage holders to convert their securities to common shares when the share price exceeds the conversion price.

Convertibles may also be issued as sweeteners when bonds or preferred shares are at higher risk than normal and the required rates of return are high. The conversion option is provided to increase the attractiveness of the securities, as it promises the holders a share in the future growth of the firm.

As with warrants, the shares obtained by an investor after converting a bond or a preferred share are newly issued. However, unlike warrants, the conversion right is attached to the underlying security. It is not detachable and cannot be traded separately on the exchanges. Its value is included in the price of the convertible security. Also, unlike warrants, the conversion of convertibles replaces debt or preferred shares with common shares but does not provide any new cash to the firm. For example, if the conversion is from debt to common shares, the face value of the debt is reduced and the book value of equity is increased by the amount of the debt reduction. The cash account is not affected.

Retractables A retractable bond or preferred share is a security that gives the holder the right to sell the security back to the issuer (in other words, the right to retract the maturity date) for a predetermined price at a specified time in the future. It is a put option with an exercise price equal to the redemption price and an expiry date the same as the redemption date. If the redemption date passes without the put having been exercised, the security to which it is attached remains outstanding until it is redeemed by the issuing firm.

Extendibles An extendible security is a bond or preferred share that gives the holder the right to extend the maturity of the security beyond the existing maturity date. That is, it gives the holder the right to buy a longer-term security for a specified price during a specified period of time. If the option is not exercised, the issuing firm redeems the security held by the investor at the security's maturity date. The extension privilege is a call option.

Pricing Corporate Securities with Built-In Options

When a security has a built-in option, the option adds value to the security and makes it more valuable to the investor than a straight security (one without an option). The value of a security with attached options may be calculated as:

$$\text{Security value} = \text{value of straight security} + \text{option value} \qquad \textbf{(Equation 9-11)}$$

Given the many factors that may affect options attached to corporate securities, it is often difficult to value these options. An option-valuation model, such as the Black-Scholes formula, is useful for estimating the value. Decision-tree analysis, simulation, and other techniques may also be useful.

Despite the difficulty of valuing options attached to corporate securities, they must be recognized as factors that influence the values of the securities. Financial managers should remember the general rules that apply to all options and use them in valuing these options. For example, the greater the uncertainty surrounding the underlying asset, the greater the option's worth will be. Also, the longer the time available before the option expires, the higher the value of the option will be.

9.4 HEDGING WITH OPTIONS

Companies can use options on financial futures to accomplish the same hedging objectives as can be achieved by trading financial futures. This section focuses on the use of options on financial futures for hedging. Options are traded on three-month bankers' acceptance futures, as shown in Exhibit 9-1.

This section uses Lora's situation from Minicases 7-1, 8-7, and 8-8 to demonstrate hedging with options. The mechanics of hedging with options are explained and the general rules for hedging are presented. The same scenarios from Minicase 8-8 (p. 495) are used in this section to emphasize the differences between hedging with futures and hedging with options.

Four Key Decisions

Four key decisions must be made when using options. They are similar to the decisions made when using futures or forwards.

Decision 1: Which type of option to purchase or write. In each case, the price of the underlying asset must be predicted and compared with the exercise price. You must determine what risk the option is intended to mitigate.

Decision 2: The number of options to buy (the hedge ratio) if exchange-traded options are used. A hedge ratio is not normally required for over-the-counter options because an option on the specific underlying asset can be obtained. The appropriate hedge ratio can be estimated in the same way as was used to estimate the hedge ratio for futures (refer to Equation 8-6).

Decision 3: The expiry dates. The expiry date for options is similar to the delivery date for futures. In principle, buying an option or trading a futures contract for hedging does not necessarily involve exercise and delivery of the underlying security. Instead, the contract can be sold later in the market, once the need for the hedge disappears. Therefore, the expiry date is of minor importance but must be chosen so that it is longer than the period over which hedging is desirable. Also, it may be appropriate to use longer expiry options. It is safe to choose options with expiry dates that extend at least one month beyond the date on which the hedge is to be concluded. Such options are likely to be the most liquid contracts at the time when the hedge needs to be lifted.

Decision 4: The suitable exercise prices for the hedge. Again, the answer to the question of what exercise prices to buy is largely unsettled. However, a hedger is better off avoiding the purchase of deep-in-the-money or deep-out-of-the-money options. Perhaps a slightly off-the-money exercise price will provide the best hedging value, as it does not entail a large purchase price and provides good protection.

Over-the-Counter Options

Because many organizations have a need for protection against interest-rate risk, financial institutions offer customized options to protect against higher or lower rates. Whether for exchange rates, commodity prices, or interest rate spreads, for example, there is an active and liquid market for options that these institutions use for their own hedging activities. The types of over-the-counter options available are similar to exchange-traded options, except that a much wider variety of terms, underlying assets, and features are available.

Caps, floors, and collars are specific interest-rate options that are often used. **Caps** protect against rising rates. Essentially, a company buys a series of interest rate options to protect itself over a series of time periods from rising rates. In exchange for an option premium, the company is protected above the strike rate. **Floors** protect against falling rates and constitute a series of interest rate options to protect against declining rates over a series of time periods.

Collars combine caps and floors to form another customized instrument. These involve the purchase of a series of call options on the interest rate (cap), with the sale of a series of options on the same interest rate (floor). They are put together by a bank or financial institution, which will sell the cap and act as the buyer of the interest rate floor from the hedger. In this way, a borrower knows that the cost of funds is limited to the cap rate (due to the purchased option), while the benefit gained from falling interest rates is limited to the floor rate (due to the sold option). When interest rates are between the cap and the floor rate, neither option will be exercised and the hedger will transact at market rates. If rates rise above the cap rate, the cap will be used to limit the cost of funds. If rates fall below the floor rate, the floor will be exercised by the bank and limit the decline in cost of funds.

Importance of Time Value in a Hedged Position

In practice, the time value of an option is observed in the market. As you learned in Section 9.2, time value depends on the volatility of the underlying asset, the time to expiry, and the discount rate, all measured as of the date at which the option is expected to be sold.

You could use an option-pricing formula to obtain a rough estimate of the time value. However, when the time comes to sell the options, you would receive what the market is willing to pay for your option, or the market-determined time value.

The majority of hedgers experience a discrepancy between the realized return on a hedged position and the expected return. When hedging with options, part of the discrepancy is caused by the deterioration in the time value of the option as it approaches the expiry date. Even when the volatility and the discount rate are constant, the time value will deteriorate because of the passage of time.

Now, with this information, it is useful to see how Lora fares when she buys options to hedge her risk. Minicase 9-16 demonstrates the use of call options to hedge interest-rate risk, but the analysis can be extended to the use of options on commodity or currency futures.

Lora is facing the risk that rates may drop. Previous minicases demonstrated how she can hedge her risk using financial futures. Instead of using futures, however, Lora can trade options on futures to hedge her risk.

How would Lora hedge the potential risk using options on bankers' acceptance futures? Remember Lora's risk is from a drop in interest rates on Treasury bills. If this rate drops below the current rate (on March 1) of 5.5%, for example, to 5.0%, the price of the bills will rise and Lora must pay a higher price to buy the same face value. Buying a call will lead to profits if prices rise. Thus, Lora must buy call options.

Ideally, Lora should buy options on Treasury bills but unfortunately, no options are traded on Canadian Treasury bill futures. Thus, Lora must cross-hedge. That is, she must buy call options on a fixed income security that is similar to a Treasury bill in its sensitivity to changes in interest rates.

Now Lora must decide:

- The number of options to buy (the hedge ratio): Using Equation 8-6, she calculates that she needs to buy three call options to cover her risk.

- The expiry dates: A June expiry date is appropriate.

- The exercise prices suitable for the hedge: Lora buys three call options. Exhibit 9-11 describes these options and lists additional information related to the corresponding futures contract. Notice that Lora must pay cash to buy the options. As Exhibit 9-11 shows, this price is 26 basis points per option. Given that the underlying asset is a three-month bankers' acceptance with a $1,000,000 face value, the cash price per basis point is $25 and Lora must pay $1,950 ($25 × 26 × 3) to buy the three options. The options are 10 basis points out of the money [94.10 − (100% − 6%)].

Exhibit 9-11
Call Option Premiums and Futures Rates on Three-Month Bankers' Acceptances

Call options market, three-month BAs			Futures market, three-month BAs	
Expiry date	Exercise price	Premium	Delivery month	Futures rate
June 20X1	94.10	0.26	June 20X1	6.00%

One reason for revisiting Lora's situation in this minicase is to explain the differences between hedging with futures and hedging with options on futures. The same two interest-rate scenarios will now be followed through.

Scenario 1: Rates drop as expected.

On March 29, the spot rate for Treasury bills due to mature on May 28 happens to be 5%, a drop of 50 basis points from the rate on March 1. Given this drop in the Treasury bill rate, the rate on 91-day bankers' acceptances for June delivery also drops. Suppose this rate drops by 53 basis points, which is similar to the assumption made in Minicase 8-8. That is, the rate on 91-day bankers' acceptances for June delivery is 5.47%.

Case Continued >

As calculated, Lora's opportunity cost from the drop in rates is:

$$(\$5,000,000 \div \$100) \times 0.0821 = \$4,105$$

Lora's opportunity loss in the cash market is partially offset by a profit on the options. As the futures rate on bankers' acceptances is now 5.47%, the price index of bankers' acceptance futures for June delivery is:

$$100 - 5.47\% = 94.53$$

This is the current market price of the asset underlying the call options. Thus, the intrinsic value of the call option that has an exercise price of 94.10 is:

$$\text{Intrinsic value} = \text{maximum}(0, 94.53 - 94.10)$$
$$= 0.43\% \text{ or } 43 \text{ basis points}$$

The expiry date of the call option is June 20X1. Thus, the call option still has time value. Assuming that the time value is 28 basis points, the market value of the call is 71 basis points (43 + 28).

In practice, the time value will be observed in the market. On March 29, when the option is expected to be sold, Lora could use an option-pricing formula to get a rough estimate of the time value. However, when the time comes to sell the options, she will receive what the market is willing to pay.

Given that the underlying asset of the option has $1,000,000 of face value, each basis point entails a $25 cash value per option. Thus, Lora will receive:

$$\$25 \times 71 = \$1,775 \text{ per option}$$

Given that Lora purchased three calls, she will receive:

$$\$1,775 \times 3 = \$5,325$$

This amount is not the net profit on the options. Lora had to pay $1,950 to buy the three options. Thus, her net profit from the options is:

$$\$5,325 - \$1,950 = \$3,375$$

This cash profit partially offsets the opportunity losses in the cash market. Subtracting the profit from the cash needed to buy the Treasury bills at the market price shows that Lora's net cost of purchasing the bills is:

$$\$4,958,565 - \$3,375 = \$4,955,190$$

This price is close to the original expected price of $4,954,460, a difference of $730. Lora's implicit yield on the hedged investment is:

$$\left(\frac{\$5,000,000 - \$4,955,190}{\$4,955,190} \times \frac{365}{61} \right) = 5.41\%$$

which is almost equal to the original expected rate of 5.5%.

Notice that the hedge is not perfect in that it did not completely offset the risk. Even with the hedge, Lora's return on investment has dropped by 9 basis points. Moreover, the loss in return is 7 basis points more than the loss of only 2 basis points incurred when hedging with futures. The additional discrepancy is the result of a loss in the time value of the call options.

Case Continued >

Keep in mind that at the time of purchase, the call options were out of the money by 10 basis points and their price was 26 basis points. Thus, their implicit time value was 36 basis points. At the time of sale, the time value was only 28 basis points. Thus, there was a time-value loss of 8 basis points per contract. These losses translate into:

$$\$25 \times 8 \times 3 = \$600 \text{ cash losses}$$

Assuming that these time-value losses did not occur, and subtracting the $600 from the price of $4,955,190, the result is the same price as the one obtained when hedging with financial futures.

Scenario 2: Rates rise contrary to expectations.

On March 29, the spot rate for Treasury bills due to mature on May 28 happens to rise to 6%, an increase of 50 basis points from the rate on March 1. If Lora had been able to buy the Treasury bills on March 1, she would have paid $99.0892 per $100 face value. Now, on March 29, she must pay $99.0072. Given this rise in the Treasury bill rate, the rate on 91-day bankers' acceptances for June delivery also rises. Suppose this rate rises by 53 basis points. That is, the rate on 91-day bankers' acceptances for June delivery is 6.53%.

The rise in the Treasury bill rate means an opportunity gain of $0.082 ($99.0892 − $99.0072) per $100 of face value. In total, Lora's opportunity gain is:

$$(\$5,000,000 \div \$100) \times 0.082 = \$4,100$$

Lora's opportunity gain in the cash market is offset by a loss on the options. Now that the rates have risen by 53 basis points, the bankers' acceptance price index will drop by 53 basis points to 93.47. This is the current market price of the asset underlying the call option. Thus, the intrinsic value of the call option that has an exercise price of 94.10 is:

$$\text{Intrinsic value} = \text{maximum}(0, 93.47 − 94.10)$$
$$= 0 \text{ basis points}$$

As the expiry date of the call option is June 20X1, the time value is not zero. However, since the exercise price is much higher than the current price, the time value is likely to be close to zero. Assuming that the time value is 3 basis points, the loss on the options would be 23 basis points (purchase price of 26 − sale price of 3) per call option or $25 × 23 × 3 = $1,725 total cash losses on the three options.

The same result can be obtained by subtracting the sale price of $225 from $1,950, the purchase price of the options:

$$\begin{aligned}
&\text{Purchase price} - \text{sale price} \\
&= \$1,950 - (3 \text{ basis points} \times \$25 \times 3 \text{ contracts}) \\
&= \$1,950 - \$225 \\
&= \$1,725
\end{aligned}$$

This cash loss partially offsets the opportunity gains in the cash market. Adding this loss to the cash needed to buy the Treasury bills at the market price shows that Lora's net cost of purchasing the bills is:

$$\$4,950,360 + \$1,725 = \$4,952,085$$

Case Continued >

This price is less than the original expected price of $4,954,460, a difference of $2,375. Lora's implicit yield on the hedged investment is:

$$\left(\frac{\$5,000,000 - \$4,952,085}{\$4,952,085} \times \frac{365}{61} \right) = 5.79\%$$

which is higher than the original expected rate of 5.5%.

Notice that the hedge allowed Lora to retain part of the gain in the cash market. Even with the hedge, Lora's return has risen by 29 basis points, the difference between the implicit yield on the hedged investment (5.79%) and the original expected rate (5.5%). The additional return is obtained because Lora's loss in the options market is limited to the premium that she paid to buy the options minus the sale price of the options. She paid $1,950 to buy the options and sold them for $225, for a net loss of $1,725. As the gain in the cash market was $4,100, Lora's net profit is $2,375, which translates to approximately a 29 basis point return.

Conclusions Comparing this result with the one obtained from hedging with futures or forwards under the same scenario shows the major difference between hedging using options and futures or forwards. Generally, futures or forwards hedges lock in the purchase price and hence the yield, regardless of what happens to future interest rates. In contrast, hedging with the purchase of options protects the hedger if rates move adversely, but allows the hedger to participate in the profits should interest rates move favourably. However, as demonstrated in Minicase 9-16, Scenario 1, hedging with purchased options will always involve time-value losses.

General Rules for Hedgers under Falling Interest Rates

From the previous explanations, some general rules for hedging can be derived. As seen in Lora's case, if a company would be adversely affected by a drop in interest rates, it can buy futures or forwards, or it can buy a call option on a financial instrument to hedge this treasury risk. Exhibit 9-12 indicates that each position will earn a profit if future interest rates drop. Each alternative, however, has different risk and return characteristics. While the futures position offers significant gains (limited by the fact that interest rates usually only decline to zero), if interest rates drop as expected, it also leads to unlimited losses if interest rates rise instead. Presuming that the hedger has an underlying need for the

---

Exhibit 9-12
Profit and Loss Potential on Futures/Forwards and Options If Future Interest Rates Drop

Transaction	Potential profit	Potential loss
Buy financial futures/forwards	Unlimited	Unlimited until price reaches zero
Buy call options (on futures or the underlying asset)	Unlimited	Limited to call premium

hedge, profits or losses will be offset by changes in the value of the cash position. Purchasing call options offers lower gains but limits any losses to the initial call premium. It accomplishes the hedging objective while allowing the hedger to participate in the potential gains if rates do not move as expected. Thus, buying options is similar to buying insurance, and the premium is similar to the price of buying insurance protection.

General Rules for Hedgers under Rising Interest Rates

Treasury-risk managers who are facing the risk of rising interest rates can use futures/forwards or options on futures to hedge their risks. They will take positions that produce profits when future interest rates rise, to help offset the higher cost of debt, for example. A hedger has two alternatives: sell futures or forwards, or buy put options on futures or on the underlying financial asset.

Exhibit 9-13 shows the potential outcomes. The short futures position produces unlimited profits if future interest rates rise as expected, but it can generate large losses if rates move adversely. Profits or losses, however, will be almost completely offset by losses or profits in the cash market. Buying a put option produces profits once the future interest rates rise and the futures price falls below the exercise price. However, profits will occur only if the drop in the rate is sufficient to offset the put premium. If rates fall, the company loses only the put premium, or part of it; consequently, it does not have the same rate exposure as a short futures position.

Exhibit 9-13
Profit and Loss Potential on Futures/Forwards and Options If Future Interest Rates Rise

Transaction	Potential profit	Potential loss
Sell financial futures/forwards	Unlimited until price reaches zero	Unlimited
Buy put options (on futures or the underlying asset)	Unlimited until price reaches zero	Limited to put premium

---

9.5 SWAPS

A swap is an agreement between two parties to exchange future cash flows, such as interest payments on debt obligations. Swaps are a recent innovation in financial markets that started trading in the early 1980s but rapidly gained momentum. Several large commercial and investment banking firms have become active dealers in this market. There are several forms of swaps, the most common being currency and interest-rate swaps.

Currency Swaps

A **currency swap** is an arrangement in which two parties agree to exchange currency payments at certain points in the future at agreed prices. Generally, currency swaps are arranged in conjunction with debt issues. Minicase 9-17 illustrates the common features of currency swaps.

International Transport Company (ITC) is a British company operating in Canada. ITC just received £50 million from the sale in England of bonds yielding 7%. Coupon payments are made semi-annually until maturity in 10 years. The company is planning to use the proceeds to expand its operations in North America by acquiring some local Canadian businesses.

Pulp and Paper Canada Inc. (PPC) is looking to expand in the British market. In preparation for building a new plant, PPC sold bonds with a market value of $100 million, yielding 6% paid semi-annually. The bonds will mature in 10 years. The debt obligations of ITC and PPC make good candidates for a currency swap agreement.

ITC has debt denominated in British pounds sterling, which will be used in Canada. First, the company will have to exchange the pounds for Canadian dollars to acquire the local businesses. Second, the revenues will be in Canadian dollars, from which it will service its debt obligations. Therefore, at every coupon payment date, the company needs £1.75 million (£50 × 0.07 ÷ 2) to service the debt. ITC will have to buy the currency in the open market, which exposes it to exchange-rate risk and transaction costs.

PPC is in the opposite situation. The company has debt denominated in Canadian dollars, which will be used in Britain. First, it will have to exchange the dollars for pounds to build its plant. Second, the revenues will be in pounds, from which it will service its dollar-denominated debt obligations. Therefore, at every coupon payment date, the company needs $3 million ($100 × 0.06 ÷ 2) to service the debt. It will have to exchange pounds sterling for Canadian dollars in the open market. This process exposes PPC to exchange-rate risk and transaction costs.

Exhibit 9-14 shows the current situations of PPC and ITC. Each of these companies has to buy currency in the foreign exchange market to pay its debtholders. Indeed, both companies may end up trading with the same foreign exchange dealer. The dealer buys

Exhibit 9-14 Foreign-Exchange Transactions by PPC and ITC in the Absence of a Swap Agreement

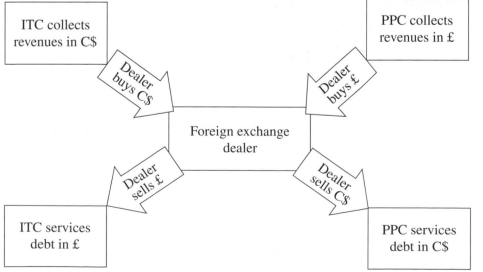

Case Continued >

pounds from PPC at the bid price and sells them to ITC at the ask price. At any point, the ask price is higher than the bid price and the difference is known as the ask-bid spread, which represents the dealer's profits from trading the foreign currency and represents transaction costs to traders.

The current exchange rate is such that each £1 is worth $2. The foreign exchange dealer posts the quotes:

$$\text{Bid price} = \$1.998 \text{ per } \pounds 1$$
$$\text{Ask price} = \$2.002 \text{ per } \pounds 1$$

These quotes indicate that the dealer is willing to buy pounds at $1.998 per pound and sell pounds at $2.002 per pound. The ask-bid spread is $0.004.

If PPC and ITC exchange the money through the dealer, each firm will lose the equivalent of:

$$\frac{\$0.002}{\pounds 1} \times \pounds 50,000,000 = \$100,000$$

The $100,000 represents transaction costs. Instead, PPC and ITC can arrange a currency swap by exchanging the currencies they have now at the cash price. The principal amounts are exchanged immediately between the two at the current price of $2 per pound. PPC, which will have revenues in pounds, can also agree to pay the interest obligations of ITC, also denominated in pounds. In return, ITC, which will have revenues in Canadian dollars, will agree to pay the interest payments due from PPC, denominated in Canadian dollars. Thus, PPC and ITC are able to minimize their risks from foreign exchange fluctuations and at the same time save transaction costs.

Exhibit 9-15 shows the transfer of cash following the swap agreement. Both PPC and ITC service their debt obligations without paying transaction costs to exchange Canadian dollars and British pounds sterling.

Exhibit 9-15 Transfer of Cash between PPC and ITC following the Swap Agreement

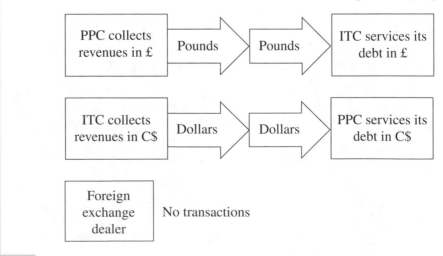

Minicase 9-17 shows that there are two main benefits to currency swaps:

- The partners in a currency swap minimize the risk from foreign exchange. (The role of currency swaps in managing foreign-exchange risk is explained in Section 9.6.)

- The partners in a currency swap eliminate transaction costs, which can be substantial on large sums of money.

Essentially, swap agreements are a combination of forward agreements. For example, in the swap agreement between ITC and PPC, the principal is exchanged in a cash transaction now and currencies to pay the coupon payments in the future are exchanged in several forward agreements. The agreement may also entail exchanging the principals at the maturity of the debt. Variations of this agreement exist when there is a cash transaction and an agreement to reverse the transaction at a later date. This situation occurs when the debt obligations are short term in nature and do not require interim interest payments.

For the sake of simplicity, the preceding example showed a currency swap arranged between two hedgers. However, because they are traded in the over-the-counter market, currency swaps are transacted with financial institutions, so that the counterparty to a currency swap would be a large bank. Large banks are the biggest participants in the currency swaps market, and they not only act as counterparties to hedgers but also actively trade swaps themselves. Although a bank might transact a swap and immediately find another swap to offset it, most banks that trade swaps have no need to find an offsetting swap, as they can offset the risks easily through other markets if necessary.

Interest-Rate Swaps

An **interest-rate swap** is an arrangement in which two parties agree to exchange the payments of a debt obligation. The debt they exchange has different terms but is denominated in the same currency. A popular form of interest-rate swap is an exchange of fixed-rate for floating-rate coupon payments. In this case, the debt obligations of one firm require periodic interest payments based on a floating or adjustable rate, while the coupon payments of the other firm are fixed at a given rate. Minicase 9-18 provides an example of an interest-rate swap.

Interest-rate swaps are the most commonly used swaps. In reality, like currency swaps, they trade in the over-the-counter market between big banks, which are the major participants, and their customers. However, to facilitate understanding of both sides of an interest-rate swap, the following example shows two counterparties transacting directly with each other. Banks that trade swaps deal with many customers and they may or may not offset outstanding swaps. An active financial institution has many ways of managing the risks associated with a swap and may not necessarily offset it with another swap.

MINICASE 9-18 ILLUSTRATING AN INTEREST-RATE SWAP

Firm A has an outstanding bond issue with a $50 million face value and 10% coupon rate paid semi-annually. This debt requires $2.5 million in coupon payments every six months and matures in two years.

Firm B has an outstanding bond issue with a $50 million face value, but the coupon rate is floating. Currently, the rate is 9%, but it is reset at the end of every six months

Case Continued >

equal to the Treasury bill rate at the close of the resetting day plus 2% paid semi-annually. The debt matures in two years.

An agreement to swap these debt obligations would require Firm A to service Firm B's $50 million bonds. Firm A would pay to Firm B at the end of every six months the amount required to pay the coupon payments of Firm B's debt ($50 million times the Treasury bill rate as of six months ago plus 2%). In turn, Firm B would service Firm A's $50 million debt obligations. Debt service payments are $2.5 million every six months. Note that the swap agreement does not require any actions by the bondholders. Each firm remains responsible for its debt and toward its debtholders.

Exhibit 9-16 shows the required debt service payments from Firm A and Firm B to be paid to their bondholders.

Exhibit 9-16
Debt Service Payments Promised to Bondholders

End of:	A's debt payments	T-bill rate	Rate to B: T-bill rate + 2%	B's debt payments
6 months	$2.5	7.0%	9.0%	$2.25
12 months	2.5	8.0	10.0	2.50
18 months	2.5	9.0	11.0	2.75
24 months	2.5	9.4	11.4	2.85

Exhibit 9-17 shows the required debt service payments from Firm A and Firm B when they agree to swap their obligations. The exhibit compares the required debt payments from each firm without the agreement to the debt payments with the agreement. It also shows the exchange of cash that takes place between the two parties.

Exhibit 9-17
Debt Service Payments after the Swap Agreement and the Interchange of Cash to Satisfy the Agreement

Months forward	B's debt payments to bondholders	B's service payments under the swap	Payments (received) by B to (from) A	A's debt payments to bondholders	A's service payments under the swap
6	$2.25	$2.5	$0.25	$2.5	$2.25
12	2.50	2.5	0.00	2.5	2.50
18	2.75	2.5	(0.25)	2.5	2.75
24	2.85	2.5	(0.35)	2.5	2.85

For example, the debt service payments promised by Firm B to its bondholders will be $2.25 million at the end of six months. However, under the swap agreement, Firm B is required to pay $2.5 million no matter what happens to interest rates. Therefore, Firm B will remit the difference of $0.25 million to Firm A, which is obligated to pay $2.5 million to its own bondholders. Yet under the swap agreement, it will only have to pay $2.25 million, the payment of $0.25 million from Firm B to Firm A making up the difference.

Interest-rate swaps are sometimes created to save interest costs for both parties of the transaction. A net quality differential occurs if two firms have different credit ratings. For example, if both Firm X and Firm Y prefer to borrow in the floating-rate market, X, being more creditworthy (having less default risk) than Y, is likely to receive a lower rate than Y.

The same principle applies if they borrow in the fixed-rate market. Again, Firm X, being more creditworthy than Firm Y, is likely to receive a lower rate. However, the quality spread in the fixed-rate market is normally higher than the quality spread in the floating-rate market. Moreover, the quality spread increases as the term to maturity of the fixed-rate loan increases. Therefore, under normal circumstances, the net quality differentials always exist when two firms under consideration have different default risks. The longer the maturity of the fixed-rate loan, the higher the net quality differential will be.

If the borrowers save interest, does it mean that the lenders are not compensated for risks they take? The savings in interest costs realized by the parties to a swap do not mean that the lender receives any less compensation for an equivalent risk. However, because the two transactions decrease the lender's overall risk, the lender's return is also less.

By borrowing in the fixed-rate market instead of the floating-rate market, Firm X changes the degree of risk of its transaction to lenders by:

$$\Delta R_X = R_{FX\,X} - R_{FL\,X} \qquad \text{(Equation 9-12)}$$

where

ΔR_X = difference in risk between the fixed-rate and floating-rate markets
$R_{FX\,X}$ = risk to lenders from lending to X in the fixed-rate market
$R_{FL\,X}$ = risk to lenders from lending to X in the floating-rate market

Lending in the fixed-rate market entails higher risk than lending in the floating-rate market. Thus, ΔR_X is positive, indicating that if Firm X borrows in the fixed-rate market instead of the floating-rate market, lenders face additional risk from the Firm X transaction.

At the same time, by borrowing in the floating-rate market instead of the fixed-rate market, Firm Y changes the degree of risk to lenders for the transaction by:

$$\Delta R_Y = R_{FL\,Y} - R_{FX\,Y} \qquad \text{(Equation 9-13)}$$

where

ΔR_Y = difference in risk between the floating-rate and fixed-rate markets
$R_{FL\,Y}$ = risk to lenders from lending to Y in the floating-rate market
$R_{FX\,Y}$ = risk to lenders from lending to Y in the fixed-rate market

Because lending in the fixed-rate market entails higher risk than lending in the floating-rate market, ΔR_Y is negative. Lenders face less risk from the Firm Y transaction when Firm Y borrows in the floating-rate market instead of the fixed-rate market.

The important result is that the increase in the degree of risk of Firm X's transaction is smaller than the decrease in the degree of risk of Firm Y's transaction. That is, $(\Delta R_Y + \Delta R_X)$ is negative, indicating a net reduction of risk to lenders.

The risk saved by lenders is distributed among Firm Y, Firm X, and the swap dealer, depending on their respective share in the risk and on their relative bargaining powers. For example, in some swap agreements, the dealer fully underwrites the transaction and the swap partners do not share in the savings. Often, the partner with the highest credit rating will have the greatest bargaining power and will receive more of the savings than the other partner. In cases where the dealer does not assume the risk, the swap partner with the highest credit rating is likely to assume more risk and receive more savings than the other partner. Of course, swap agreements entail transaction costs, which also need to be covered from the interest savings.

Minicase 9-19 illustrates how two firms with different credit quality can take advantage of the interest-rate swap market to lower their total borrowing costs.

MINICASE 9-19 USING A SWAP TO SAVE INTEREST COSTS

Northern Saskatchewan Trust (NST) is in the market to borrow $2 million for five years. Because of its small size and lack of diversification in its loan portfolio, NST prefers fixed-rate debt to minimize fluctuations in its interest payments.

Provincial Bank of Canada (PBC) is a large bank with $150 billion in assets. It is in the market to borrow $2 million to finance a loan to a customer. The rate on the loan is floating because of the customer's preferences. Therefore, PBC prefers to borrow on a floating-rate basis.

It happened that NST and PBC talked to the same money market dealer about their needs. The dealer's observations after checking the market are summarized in Exhibit 9-18.

Exhibit 9-18
Quality Spreads and Interest Rates for NST and PBC in the Floating-Rate and Fixed-Rate Markets

	PBC	NST	Quality spread
Fixed-rate market	6.50%	8.50%	2.00%
Floating-rate market	T-bill rate plus 1%	T-bill rate plus 2.25%	1.25%
		Net quality differential	0.75%

Question 1: Under a plan where NST borrows in the fixed-rate market and PBC borrows in the floating-rate market, what is the total interest paid in the first year by both NST and PBC?

Total interest during the first year:

NST's interest cost: $2 million $\times$ 8.50% = $170,000

PBC's interest cost: ($2 million $\times$ 1%) + ($2 million $\times$ T-bill rate)
= $20,000 + ($2 million $\times$ T-bill rate)

Total interest paid by both: $170,000 + $20,000 + ($2 million $\times$ T-bill rate)
= $190,000 + ($2 million $\times$ T-bill rate)

Question 2: If NST borrows in the floating-rate market and PBC borrows in the fixed-rate market, what is the total interest paid in the first year by both NST and PBC?

NST's interest cost: ($2 million $\times$ 2.25%) + ($2 million $\times$ T-bill rate)
= $45,000 + ($2 million $\times$ T-bill rate)

Case Continued >

PBC's interest cost: $2 million $\times$ 6.50% = $130,000

Total interest paid by both: $45,000 + $130,000 + ($2 million $\times$ T-bill rate)
= $175,000 + ($2 million $\times$ T-bill rate)

Question 3: Can NST and PBC make an arrangement by which they can save interest payments and at the same time pay floating- or fixed-interest payments consistent with their preferences?

Yes. NST borrows in the floating-rate market and PBC borrows in the fixed-rate market. Then they arrange an interest-rate swap. The difference in total interest paid by both NST and PBC is $15,000 per year.

With the swap, the interest payments made by NST are fixed, even though it borrowed in the floating-rate market. On the other hand, the interest payments made by PBC are floating, even though it borrowed in the fixed-rate market. The swap allows them to borrow at their preferred terms and save $15,000 per year in interest costs.

Question 4: What is the source of the savings?

The yearly $15,000 savings are obtained by multiplying the $2 million by the net quality differential of 0.75%. Therefore, the savings from the swap are primarily a result of the net quality differential.

Question 5: How often are net quality differentials observed in practice?

Generally, net quality differentials are normal when the two firms have differences in credit quality. For example, if both PBC and NST like to borrow in the floating-rate market, PBC, being more creditworthy (less default risk) than NST, is likely to get a lower rate than NST.

Now suppose that both firms like to borrow in the fixed-rate market. Again, PBC, being more creditworthy than NST, is likely to receive a lower rate than NST. However, the quality spread in the fixed-rate market is normally higher than the quality spread in the floating-rate market. Also, the quality spread increases as the term to maturity of the fixed-rate loan increases. Therefore, under normal circumstances, the net quality differentials always exist when two firms under consideration have different default risks. The longer the maturity of the fixed-rate loan, the higher the net quality differential will be.

Question 6: If the borrowers save interest, does it mean that the lenders will not be compensated for risks they take?

The savings in interest costs realized by the parties to a swap do not mean that lenders receive less compensation for an equivalent risk. Indeed, the overall risk to lenders from the two transactions decreases.

9.6 HEDGING WITH SWAPS

Section 9.5 described swaps as arrangements between two parties in which each party agrees to pay the cash flows on a specified debt obligation of the second party. If the arrangement is an interest-rate swap, one party undertakes a fixed-rate debt payment in return for giving up a floating-rate debt payment. The other party undertakes the floating-rate debt payment and gives up the fixed-rate debt payment.

If the arrangement is a currency swap, one party undertakes a currency-X-denominated debt payment in return for giving up currency-Y-denominated debt payment. The other party undertakes the currency Y payment and gives up the currency X payment.

The objective of an interest-rate swap for a firm is to trade one form of interest-rate risk for another more suitable to its circumstances. For example, consider a bank with a negative gap. As explained in Section 7.2, a negative funding gap means that the bank has more rate-sensitive liabilities than assets. A non-zero gap exposes the bank to risk from interest rate fluctuations. Thus, the bank may be looking to narrow its funding gap to minimize its risk. Having fixed-rate rather than floating-rate service obligations would achieve the bank's objective.

The objective of a currency swap for a firm is to trade one form of currency risk for another more suitable to its circumstances. Minicase 9-20 demonstrates the use of currency swaps.

MINICASE 9-20 HEDGING WITH CURRENCY SWAPS

ALMR is a multinational corporation. The company is planning to build a subsidiary in Sweden to serve the Swedish market. The expansion plan requires $50 million and the company is considering a fixed-rate debt issue to raise the funds. The subsidiary is expected to produce positive cash flows as soon as operations commence. These cash flows will make it possible to make the interest payments. Because cash from the subsidiary will be in Swedish krona (SEK), the company is planning to raise the funds by selling five-year bonds denominated in krona. This move will enable the company to avoid foreign exchange risk and the transaction costs of exchanging krona for dollars. Currently, the Canadian dollar is trading at SEK 3.6463, which means that the face value of the bonds would be SEK 182.315 million.

On contacting the firm's investment banker, ALMR's management finds that a krona-denominated bond issue for $50 million would have to yield almost 11% because ALMR is not well known in the Swedish market. In contrast, the firm is well known in the Canadian market, where it can raise funds at relatively low cost. ALMR's management has guarantees that the Canadian-dollar-denominated bonds would not have to pay more than 8% in coupon payments. ALMR decides to sell five-year dollar-denominated bonds to yield 8%, paid annually, while the principal is to be paid at maturity. The plan is that after five years ALMR will be well known in Sweden, which will allow for a krona-denominated bond issue at a favourable rate.

Question 1: What is the risk that will be taken by ALMR's management if it goes ahead and sells five-year dollar-denominated bonds?

Management will be taking exchange-rate risk. The coupon payments will have to be made in dollars, while the income from which these payments will be made is denominated in krona. Thus, servicing the debt will require exchanging krona for dollars. If the value of the dollar rises against the krona, more income in krona will be needed to make these same coupon payments. For example, annual coupon payments will be $4 million ($50 million at 8%). At the current exchange rate of SEK 3.6463 per dollar, the Swedish subsidiary can cover the coupon payments if operating income exceeds SEK 14,585,200 per year ($4 million at 3.6463). If the exchange rate rises to SEK 4.00 per dollar (9.7% increase), the subsidiary must generate at least SEK 16.00 million in operating income. Of course, if the exchange rate drops, less income will be needed to cover the coupon payments.

In addition to the risks from the coupon payments, the principal also poses some risk. The plan to refund the principal by selling a krona-denominated issue after five years

Case Continued >

exposes the firm to additional currency risk. Currently, SEK 182.315 million is needed for the expansion plan. If the exchange rate rises to SEK 4.00 per dollar, the amount needed to refund the $50 million issue will be SEK 200 million. After reviewing the potential risks, ALMR's management decides that a hedge should be taken.

Question 2: Can ALMR hedge the risk?

In the past, ALMR's management has used forwards and options to hedge foreign exchange risk. Unfortunately in this case, the cash flows span a long period (five years). Forwards and options are not ideally suited to hedge the long-term cash flow obligations or the principal amount to be exchanged in five years. Given the time horizon and the number of cash flows, the investment banker suggests a currency swap. Indeed, the banker has already contacted a dealer in the bank's swap group.

The dealer has identified a Swedish company, FNT Inc., which is in the opposite situation to ALMR. FNT is planning to build a Canadian subsidiary and would like to cover the cash flows from the Canadian dollar-denominated revenues. However, in Sweden, FNT can raise funds at 9.5% whereas in Canada, the rate will be at least 12%. FNT is flexible in its terms and is willing to take risks with the cash flows that cannot be covered by ALMR.

Note: In reality, the swap dealer would not need to identify an offsetting swap, but would transact the swap directly with ALMR. This offsetting swap is shown to facilitate understanding.

Question 3: How does the currency swap work?

Since FNT is flexible, the swap agreement is structured to completely cover the cash flows of ALMR, both before and at maturity. ALMR agrees to remit SEK 14,635,200 annually for five years to the swap dealer. In return, it will receive $4 million to cover the coupon payments. For its part, FNT promises to pay the dealer $4 million annually for five years. In return, it will receive SEK 14,585,200 per year. The dealer retains SEK 50,000 per year for its services to manage the interest payments and SEK 370,000 in the last year to manage the principal amounts. The SEK 14,635,200 paid annually by ALMR is determined by the $4 million annual debt servicing payment of ALMR at the current exchange rate of SEK 3.6463 per dollar plus the SEK 50,000 fee charged by the swap dealer and paid in this case by ALMR.

At maturity (after five years), ALMR agrees to submit SEK 182,685,000 to the dealer in return for $50 million. FNT agrees to submit $50 million to the dealer to receive SEK 182,315,000. Exhibit 9-19 shows the cash flows and hedging results for ALMR and FNT, as well as the cash flows to the swap dealer.

Notice that ALMR experiences cash savings in interest payments in the first and fifth years when the value of the Canadian dollar rises above the current rate of SEK 3.6463. It also experiences cash savings in the fifth year because of the principal payment. On the other hand, FNT experiences cash savings in the second and third years when the exchange rate of the Canadian dollar drops below the current level. ALMR experiences cash losses in the fourth year when the exchange rate happens to be equal to the current exchange rate.

The loss to ALMR is caused by the commission charged by the swap dealer, who retains SEK 50,000 every year and SEK 370,000 in the last year. Generally, this fee depends on the risk assumed by the dealer in the transaction. Usually, the higher the risk assumed by the dealer, the higher the dealer's fees will be. The important result, however, is that ALMR is able to fix its yearly coupon payments at SEK 14,635,200 [Column (e)] and its refunding cost at SEK 182,685,000. Similarly, FNT is able to fix its yearly coupon payments at $4 million per year and its refunding cost at $50 million.

Case Continued >

Exhibit 9-19
Cash Inflows and Outflows of ALMR, FNT, and the Swap Dealer

Interest payment at end of year	Exchange rate* SEK per C$	ALMR without the swap Cash outflows needed in dollars	Cash outflows needed in krona	Cash flows needed with swap	Submitted to FNT	Dealer retains:	Cash inflows (outflows) from swap To ALMR	To FNT
(a)	(b)	(c)	(d) = (b) × (c)	(e)	(f)	(g)	(h) = (d) – (e)	(i) = (f) – (d)
1	SEK 3.6736	$ 4,000,000	SEK 14,694,400	SEK 14,635,200	SEK 14,585,200	SEK 50,000	SEK 59,200	SEK (109,200)
2	3.4523	4,000,000	13,809,200	14,635,200	14,585,200	50,000	(826,000)	776,000
3	3.3874	4,000,000	13,549,600	14,635,200	14,585,200	50,000	(1,085,600)	1,035,600
4	3.6463	4,000,000	14,585,200	14,635,200	14,585,200	50,000	(50,000)	0
5	3.9817	4,000,000	15,926,800	14,635,200	14,585,200	50,000	1,291,600	(1,341,600)
Principal payment	SEK 3.9817	$50,000,000	SEK 199,085,000	SEK 182,685,000	SEK 182,315,000	SEK 370,000	SEK 16,400,000	SEK (16,770,000)
					Overall cash savings		SEK 15,789,200	SEK (16,409,200)

* Exchange rate at time of agreement = SEK 3.6463 per dollar.

The swap dealer transacts directly with the hedger. The dealer determines the amount of cash flows to be swapped and the exchange rate at which they will be exchanged. The agreement may or may not include exchanging the principal amounts at maturity.

As noted earlier, the swap market is active and involves large trades. The market benefits considerably from the participation of large international banks. In the early days of the swap market, the role of banks was limited to intermediating contracts for a fee. As swaps became better known and attracted more participants, banks began to take a more active role.

Banks that trade swaps usually manage a portfolio ("book") of swaps. Alternatively, a bank may hedge the risk inherent in the swap transaction by unbundling the swap and trading forwards or options. Large banks employ dealers, whose job it is to exploit market anomalies in the various markets in which they trade. These activities ensure that pricing is accurate and add breadth and depth to the swap market.

9.7 COSTS OF HEDGING

There are several costs of hedging, including pure transaction costs, the actual cost of hedging, costs related to the maintenance of margin requirements, and costs related to administrative duties.

Pure Transaction Costs Buying futures, options, or other derivative securities for hedging creates pure transaction costs. These costs include the commissions paid to brokers and the bid-ask spread. Generally, pure transaction costs for trading futures are not as high as for options. Currently, the transaction costs of buying a futures contract on three-month bankers' acceptances and later closing the position is about $90. Given that the underlying security has a $1 million face value, this cost is relatively negligible. In contrast, the pure transaction costs of hedging with options are slightly higher.

There is no commission or fee to enter into a forward contract or over-the-counter option. The dealer's profit is built into the price. The bid-ask spread is always a cost, regardless of the hedging instrument used.

Actual Cost of Hedging For option contracts, the cost of hedging can be defined and measured. Essentially, buying an option entails paying a premium to give the buyer insurance against a price decrease (in the case of a put) or a price increase (in the case of a call). The premium to buy an option is the pure cost of hedging in the same way a premium on a life insurance policy is the cost of protection.

In contrast, the cost of hedging with futures cannot be directly defined and measured. Futures that are covered by a cash position reduce risk, but risk reduction cannot occur without cost. Practically, the implicit costs of hedging with futures are the potential cash losses that may be incurred when the price of the underlying asset moves in the direction that causes cash losses to the hedger. Returning to Minicase 8-8 (p. 495), the implicit cost of hedging is the possibility that the rate rises rather than falls. In Scenario 2, a rise of 53 basis points in the futures rate leads to a cash loss of $3,975. This is one of an infinite number of scenarios that may lead to cash losses from the futures contract. The expected present value of all the potential cash losses is an estimate of the cost of hedging with futures. Of course, the cash losses will be offset by opportunity gains in the cash position, which is covered by the futures.

Another way of estimating the costs of hedging with futures is to compare with options. When it is possible to hedge the same situation with either futures or options, the implicit cost of hedging with futures is the same as the cost of hedging with options. For example, buying futures at a hypothetical $10 per unit to hedge against a price increase is equivalent to buying a call option at an exercise price of $10 and selling a put option at the same exercise price. The implicit cost of hedging with futures can be estimated as the premium required to buy the call. As the buyer is trying to reduce the risk of an increase in price, the call premium can be explained as the cost of buying insurance against the increase. However, instead of paying cash for protection, the futures buyer engages in barter. The buyer offers protection to the seller against a price decrease.

Costs Related to Maintaining Margin Requirements As explained in Chapter 8, margin requirements are set by the clearing house and the exchanges to help maintain the integrity of futures' contracts and traders by limiting their risk exposure. They are intended as a good-faith guarantee against default by traders when their positions deteriorate. Marking to market is the process by which futures exchanges adjust margin account balances at the end of every trading day. All losses incurred by a trader must be met by a cash payment, even if the position remains open. Surplus profits may be withdrawn in cash, if desired, or may be used to cover losses on other positions.

There are administrative costs to covering margin requirements. Generally, hedgers will establish a formal line of credit with a bank to absorb the losses. Any fees paid to obtain the line of credit are part of the cost of hedging. Also, there are costs of holding the margin account. Generally, the hedger may be able to earn interest on the margin balance by using Treasury bills or other securities as collateral instead of using cash. Yet, the interest that can be earned is likely to be less than the cost of funds financing the purchase of Treasury bills.

There are no margin requirements when over-the-counter options (or forwards) are used. However, the organization will need to set up credit facilities with a bank in order to buy or sell options with the bank. Outstanding options and forwards will reduce the credit available with the bank, but there is no explicit cost.

Costs Related to Administrative Duties Firms incur costs with the hiring and training of personnel to work in the risk management division or in trading futures, options, or other risk management products. These costs vary depending on the firm's policy and its approach to treasury-risk management.

Consider the following article by David Derwin. It points out that hedging affects not only profits but also growth opportunities, creditworthiness, and competitiveness. Make sure you understand how risk management can increase a firm's value.

THE ECONOMIC VALUE OF RISK MANAGEMENT

DAVID DERWIN

This article emphasizes the importance of developing a currency program to manage foreign-exchange-rate risk and other cash flows affected by market uncertainties and discusses currency-management strategies that use exchange-traded instruments.

Risk management is nothing new. Modern forward agreements were in use as early as the 1600s in England and France. In North America, agriculture futures markets developed in the mid-1800s. What is new is the increasing importance of risk management in corporate policy. It is no longer enough to be the firm with the most effective marketing team, the cheapest source of inputs, or the most efficient production process. Price volatility can force even the best managed firms out of business. If you are not managing risks because of their apparent complexity, you are not being prudent.

When the major assets of a corporation are analyzed, it becomes apparent that its lifeblood—cash flow—is often exposed to market uncertainties. All other assets can be insured, but not all companies insure their cash flows against foreign exchange rate risk (see Figure 1).

Faced with exposure to market risk, a firm has three options:

(1) full exposure;

(2) passive risk management; or

(3) active risk management.

The first option leaves the firm in a speculative position. Since the position is floating freely, the firm has no control over the final value of the cash position. If you do not manage your risk, then it will manage you.

With the second choice, you simply lock in a forward rate. This is an improvement over the first option. However, an organization's management does not passively manage its production process or its advertising strategy, so why should it passively manage its most crucial resource—its cash flow?

In today's competitive environment, corporations need to actively manage their risks. It is essential to establish risk and reward objectives to optimize risk-adjusted cash flows. Cash flows must be discounted to factor in the risk in obtaining them. A guaranteed cash flow is, of course, more valuable than one that's contingent on a future foreign exchange rate. However, it is not enough to simply lock in a forward rate (passive management), because you will forgo any favorable moves that accrue to the net cash position. Figure 2 presents a graphical representation of risk adjusted cash flows under different management scenarios.

Ultimately, risk management increases firm value. Although hedging can result in higher profits, there are deeper ramifications:

(1) Risk management adds value, since it makes internal funds available to invest in new projects and to take advantage of growth opportunities.

(2) Risk management can increase a firm's ability to service debt, since cash flows are more stable. This improves creditworthiness and enables a company to increase its debt capacity and decrease its borrowing rate.

Figure 1 Top Assets of a Corporation

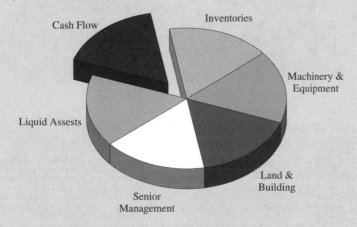

Figure 2 Benefits of Active Risk Management

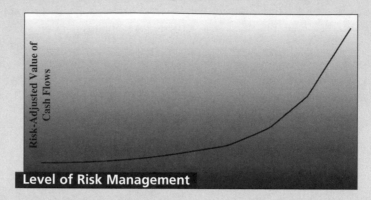

(3) Risk management can improve firm competitiveness, because risk reduces efficiency. Uncertainty about the future makes decisions more difficult. A firm can operate more effectively and increase its market share if it actively manages its risk.

Currencies: The Inherent Risk

Just as the economic growth of a nation fluctuates, so does its currency. To compound the problem, currencies also fall prey to the speculative flow of funds that can exaggerate an upward or downward move. For instance, in Canada, we saw the C$/US$ rate drop almost US$0.03, from US$0.7531 (C$1.3278) to US$0.7251 (C$1.3791) in the weeks before the Quebec referendum. If you had US$1 million outstanding and unmanaged, the fluctuation would have led to a loss or gain of more than C$50,000. Although the referendum was a special event, it is not uncommon to see a two-cent move over the span of 30 days (see Figure 3).

Figure 3 Daily Canadian Dollar

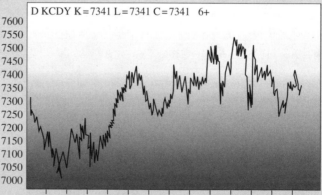

Source: FutureSource.

Let's consider a typical example. On March 16, 1995, the C$ was trading at US$0.7055 (C$1.4174). One month later, on April 13, 1995, the rate was US$0.7287 (C$1.3723) (scenario A). In the same period, under different circumstances, the C$ could have dipped down US$0.02 to US$0.6855 (scenario B). Or it could have remained unchanged at US$0.7055 (scenario C). Table 1 summarizes the effects on the US$1 million outstanding.

Table 1

March 16, 1995
US$1 million = C$1,417,434

April 13, 1995
Scenario A
US$1 million = C$1,372,307

Scenario B
US$1 million = C$1,458,789

Scenario C
US$1 million = C$1,417,434

The variability of the US$1-million cash flow in C$ is approximately C$40,000. This C$40,000 represents the risk you are taking by not managing your exposure. It could pay for someone's salary for the year. In today's competitive environment, every penny counts, and an active currency management program is one way of adding to your bottom line.

Depending on your risk-reward limits and budget constraints, a risk management strategy can be developed to manage a firm's currency exposure. Suppose a Canadian company will receive US$5 million on March 1, 1996. This exporter is therefore long US dollars and short Canadian dollars. The spot rate on Jan. 24, 1995 is 0.7305 C$/US$ or 1.3689 US$/C$. So, the company wants to protect C$6,844,000 (i.e. US$5,000,0000 × 1.3689) against a strengthening C$.

Consider these three simplified strategies:

Strategy A

The company can purchase 68 March 0.7300 strike call options for a premium of 50 basis points (bps). This equals US$34,000 or C$46,540. These options trade on the International Monetary Market on the Chicago Board of Trade. Each option represents C$100,000.

Benefits:

- fully protected if the C$ appreciates above 0.7300 US$/C$ or 1.3700 C$/US$;
- potential to gain on the cash position if the C$ depreciates against the US$;
- a one-time cash outflow of US$34,000/C$46,540 to pay for the option premium; no margin required.

Drawbacks:

- a costly strategy—over C$0.005 per C$1 under management because of the 50-basis-point premium;
- the spot C$ must appreciate to 0.7355 before the strategy breaks even and the protection begins; likewise, the spot C$ must drop to 0.7255 before gains on the strategy occur.

Strategy B

The company can enter into a range forward, if it expects a favorable, yet limited, downward move in the C$ to 0.7200. For instance, the company can lock in a rate between 0.7200 C$/US$ or 1.3889 US$/C$ and 0.7400 C$/US$ or 1.3514 US$/C$. This involves buying

68 March 0.7400 strike call options for 17 basis points and selling 68 March 0.7200 strike put options for 17 basis points. The strategy is put into effect at no cost. However, sometimes it may be possible to do the spread only at a 1 to 5 basis point net cost.

Benefits:

- protected if the C$ moves above 0.7400 C$/US$;

- can participate in a favorable move down to 0.7200, since the company expects the C$ to depreciate;

- the strategy is often put into effect at no cost.

Drawbacks:

- cannot participate in gains if the C$ falls below 0.7200;

- there is a risk of the C$ appreciating to 0.7400;

- requires a performance bond in the form of margin to cover the short puts.

Strategy C

The third strategy allows the company to lock in a floor price while taking advantage of a favorable move in the C$, at a zero net cost. This involves buying 68 March 0.7300 strike call options for 50 basis points. To offset this cost, the company sells 68 March 0.7250 puts for 27 bps, 68 March 0.7200 puts for 15 bps, and 68 March 0.7150 puts for 8 bps. If the C$ appreciates, then the short puts expire worthless, and the cash position is locked in via March 0.7300 calls. If the C$ depreciates, then the underlying US$5 million cash position increases in value. Furthermore, the puts that were sold short will be covered in the futures market at the respective strike prices of 0.7250, 0.7200, and 0.7150.

Benefits:

- full participation in a depreciation of the C$, since you are not locked into a set price that limits a favorable move;

- protection if the C$ appreciates above 0.7300;

- the strategy is put into effect at no cost.

Drawbacks:

- requires a performance bond in the form of margin to cover the short puts.

Strategy C is the most actively managed approach and therefore optimizes risks and rewards. It provides all the benefits of a floor price but with the opportunity to gain on the cash position as well. The main drawback is that it requires margin money; however, this money can be placed in T-Bills to earn interest.

David Derwin is one of four members of Midland Walwyn's Risk Management Group in Winnipeg.

Source: *Canadian Treasurer*, June/July 1995, pp. 22–24.

The article presents three strategies for hedging the foreign-exchange risk of a company that is expecting U.S. dollars to be exchanged for Canadian dollars. The three strategies are used to explain the short-term benefits and costs of hedging. According to the article, depending on risk-reward limits and budget constraints, a risk management strategy can be developed to manage a firm's currency exposure.

The fact that the option holder does not have to exercise the option is a benefit when hedging with options compared with hedging with futures. For example, the same situation could have been hedged by a forward agreement, but the forward agreement does not allow the exporter to benefit from the depreciation of the Canadian dollar. This benefit of options must be compared with the cost of hedging with options. As the article indicates, Strategy A is costly because the cost of protecting one dollar of the Canadian cash at risk is more than C$0.005. This cost is the 50 basis point premium required to buy the calls. A forward agreement does not entail such a high cost.

The article states that Strategy B is put into effect at no cost, or sometimes it may entail a minor cost of only 1 to 5 basis points. This statement ignores the fact that there is a hidden cost to selling the 68 puts. If the Canadian dollar depreciates below US$0.72, the put holder will exercise the option and the writer will suffer losses. Essentially, the present value of these costs is the 17 basis points per contract, which is the premium of selling the puts. Strategy B is similar to buying a forward contract with a delivery price equal to US$0.73. The forward contract protects the hedger if the Canadian dollar moves above US$0.73, but it does not allow the hedger to participate in the profit if the Canadian dollar depreciates to US$0.72. The article properly indicates that the costs of selling puts have margin requirements as a good-faith guarantee.

CHAPTER SUMMARY

In this chapter, you study the basic techniques of hedging risk with the aid of derivative securities, such as options and swaps. You learn that the values of these options increase the prices of the projects or securities holding them.

Key Terms

American option, page 513

at the money, page 523

Black-Scholes option-pricing model, page 527

call option, page 513

cap, page 543

collar, page 543

commodity option, page 513

currency swap, page 548

European option, page 513

exercise price or strike price, page 513

expiry date or exercise date, page 513

financial option, page 513

floor, page 543

futures option, page 513

holder, page 512

in the money, page 523

interest-rate swap, page 551

option premium, page 513

option, page 512

options exchange, page 514

out of the money, page 523

put option, page 513

put-call parity, page 530

standby agreement, page 540

underlying asset, page 513

warrant, page 540

writer, page 512

Important Equations

Intrinsic value of a call option

$$\text{Intrinsic value} = \text{maximum}\left(0, \; \frac{\text{market price}}{\text{of a share}} - \frac{\text{exercise}}{\text{price}}\right) \quad \textbf{(Equation 9-1)}$$

Intrinsic value of a put option

$$\text{Intrinsic value} = \text{maximum}\left(0, \; \frac{\text{exercise}}{\text{price}} - \frac{\text{market price}}{\text{of a share}}\right) \quad \textbf{(Equation 9-2)}$$

Time value of a call option or a put option

$$\text{Time value} = \text{premium} - \text{intrinsic value} \qquad \textbf{(Equation 9-3)}$$

The Black-Scholes option-pricing model for a call

$$C = SN(d_1) - EN(d_2)e^{-rT} \qquad \textbf{(Equation 9-4)}$$

Value of outcome d_1

$$d_1 = \frac{\ln\left(\dfrac{S}{E}\right) + rT}{\sigma T^{1/2}} + \frac{\sigma T^{1/2}}{2} \qquad \textbf{(Equation 9-5)}$$

where

$\quad C = $ call premium

$\quad d_2 = d_1 - \sigma T^{1/2}$

$\quad S = $ share price

$\quad N(\bullet) = $ cumulative distribution function for a standardized normal random variable that has a mean of zero and standard deviation of 1; $N(d_1)$ is the probability that an outcome will be less than or equal to d_1 (Use a calculator with statistical functions or the cumulative probability table in Appendix B, page 578 to determine the value of $N(\bullet)$ as needed.)

$\quad E = $ exercise price of the asset underlying the option

$\quad r = $ risk-free rate

$\quad T = $ time to expiration measured in years

$\quad \sigma = $ standard deviation of the continuously compounded rate of return on the underlying asset

$\quad \ln(\bullet) = $ natural (base e) logarithm function

$\quad e = $ natural logarithm base (converts returns to continuously compounded equivalent)

Interpolation formula to determine $N(d^*)$

$$N(d^*) = N(d_L) + \left[\frac{d^* - d_L}{d_U - d_L} \times [N(d_U) - N(d_L)]\right] \qquad \textbf{(Equation 9-6)}$$

where

$\quad N(d^*) = $ probability that an outcome will be less than or equal to d^*

$\quad d_L = $ value of d in the table that is smaller than and nearest to d^*

$\quad d_U = $ value of d in the table that is greater than and nearest to d^*

Present value of the exercise price at the expiry date

$$\text{Present value} = Ee^{-rT} \qquad \textbf{(Equation 9-7)}$$

Put-call parity relationship

$$C + Ee^{-rT} = S + P \qquad \textbf{(Equation 9-8)}$$

where

$\quad P = $ put premium

$\quad C = $ call premium

$\quad S = $ share price

E = cash exercise price on option expiration

r = risk-free rate

T = time to expiration of the options

Value of a put option in terms of the put-call parity relationship

$$P = C + Ee^{-rT} - S \qquad \text{(Equation 9-9)}$$

Value of a put option using the Black-Scholes formula

$$P = [1 - N(d_2)]Ee^{-rT} - S[1 - N(d_1)] \qquad \text{(Equation 9-10)}$$

where d_1, d_2, E, r, T, S, and σ are as defined in Equations 9-4 and 9-5.

Value of a security with built-in options

$$\frac{\text{Security}}{\text{value}} = \frac{\text{value of}}{\text{straight security}} + \frac{\text{option}}{\text{value}} \qquad \text{(Equation 9-11)}$$

Change in degree of risk from borrowing in the fixed-rate market compared with the floating-rate market

$$\Delta R_X = R_{FX\,X} - R_{FL\,X} \qquad \text{(Equation 9-12)}$$

where

ΔR_X = difference in risk between the fixed-rate and floating-rate markets

$R_{FX\,X}$ = risk to lenders from lending to X in the fixed-rate market

$R_{FL\,X}$ = risk to lenders from lending to X in the floating-rate market

Change in degree of risk from borrowing in the floating-rate market compared with the fixed-rate market

$$\Delta R_Y = R_{FL\,Y} - R_{FX\,Y} \qquad \text{(Equation 9-13)}$$

where

ΔR_Y = difference in risk between the floating-rate and fixed-rate markets

$R_{FL\,Y}$ = risk to lenders from lending to Y in the floating-rate market

$R_{FX\,Y}$ = risk to lenders from lending to Y in the fixed-rate market

Web Links

Canadian Derivative Clearing Corporation (CDCC)

■ http://www.cdcc.ca/accueil_en.php According to its Web site, the CDCC "is the issuer, clearinghouse, and guarantor of equity, index and interest rate financial derivative contracts traded on the Montréal Exchange."

Investopedia's Options Basics

■ http://www.investopedia.com/university/options/ An basic overview of options—what they are, types of options, and how to read an options table.

Montréal Exchange/Bourse de Montréal

- http://www.m-x.ca/accueil_en.php The Montréal Exchange/Bourse de Montréal is Canada's oldest exchange. Its Web site includes current news, stock market quotes, derivatives, and a variety of current and historical data.

Montreal Exchange Options Market

- http://www.m-x.ca/marc_options_en.php A variety of documents about the options market including FAQs, an "Ask an Expert" section, and a monthly newsletter.

Risk Glossary—Option Pricing Theory

- http://www.riskglossary.com/link/option_pricing_theory.htm Summarizes various option-pricing theories including Black-Scholes and derivatives pricing. Includes a list of related internal links, books, and forum discussions.

Smart Money

- http://www.smartmoney.com/ Online version of the magazine with links to articles, tools, and a variety of reports on all aspects of finance.

U.S. Commodities Futures Trading Commission (CFTC)

- http://www.cftc.gov/ The CFTC regulates the futures and options markets. Its Web site includes links to an Education Center, Market Reports, and Newsroom.

Self-Test Questions

Qualitative Questions

Answer each of the following questions in point form:
1. What is the difference between a call option and a put option?
2. What is the difference between a long position in a futures or forward contract and buying a call option?
3. What is the intrinsic value of an option?
4. What determines the time value of an option?
5. Why are common shares of a levered firm regarded as call options?
6. What is a standby agreement?
7. Which corporate securities have call option qualities?
8. Why do firms issue securities with options?
9. What are the advantages of using an option to hedge?
10. What is a swap?
11. How can a currency swap hedge foreign-exchange treasury risk?
12. What are the benefits and costs of hedging?

Qualitative Multiple Choice Questions

1. Which of the following statements about options and their trading is true?
    i) An American call option is a contract specifying that the writer undertakes to buy an asset at the exercise price on the holder's request.

ii) The holder of a put option is obligated to sell the underlying asset if the market price is less than the exercise price.

iii) Options are, without exception, traded on organized exchanges where regulations prevent unlawful use of privileged information.

iv) Similarly to trading in futures, trading in exchange-traded options is managed by a clearing house to reduce traders' risk.

2. Which of the following statements best describes the premiums of put options?

i) They increase if the market price of the underlying asset increases.

ii) They are equal to the time value of the option if the market value of the underlying asset is greater than the exercise price.

iii) They decrease as the volatility of the return on the underlying asset increases.

iv) They increase when interest rates increase.

3. Which of the following statements correctly describes financial options that are attached to corporate securities?

i) They can be implicit call options written by the issuing firm and provided free of charge to security holders.

ii) They can be retraction privileges with which the issuer can call back the security at the face value.

iii) They can be conversion privileges on bonds that are issued when the stock market is considered temporarily depressed.

iv) They can be extension rights on bonds or preferred shares, which give the holders the right to sell the securities back to the issuer.

4. What is the intrinsic value of an option to buy one common share if the exercise price is zero?

i) The market price of the common share

ii) Zero

iii) The market price of the share discounted back at the risk-free rate

iv) The market price of the share discounted back at the market portfolio rate

5. What can a firm do to hedge the risk of an upward movement in raw material prices?

i) Buy a call option

ii) Sell a put option

iii) Buy a put option

iv) Sell a futures contract

6. What could an airline company do to hedge potential oil-price risk?

i) Buy call options

ii) Buy put options

iii) Sell forward contracts

iv) Sell futures contracts

7. Which of the following statements *best* describes an out-of-the-money put option?

i) The market price of the underlying asset is above the exercise price

ii) The market price of the underlying asset is less variable than that of the market portfolio

iii) The market price of the underlying asset is below the exercise price

iv) The market price of the underlying asset is more variable than that of the market portfolio

8. An investor has a bond investment that will mature in one month. She has decided to invest the bond proceeds in the stock market on the maturity date. However, she is

concerned that the stock she has picked to invest in might appreciate significantly from its current level before the bonds mature. Which of the following stock option trading strategies would help her hedge against this price risk?

   i) Buy a put

   ii) Buy a call

   iii) Sell a put

   iv) Sell a call

9. Which of the following courses of action would allow a company to profit if the price of a given asset increases in the future?

   i) Sell futures contracts

   ii) Buy put options

   iii) Sell the asset forward

   iv) Buy call options

Quantitative Multiple Choice Questions

1. A call option on a share of ABC Inc. common stock with a strike price of $40 currently sells for $4.55, and the shares are currently selling for $36 each. The continuously compounded risk-free rate of interest is 5% per year and the call option has 6 months to expiry. What would be a fair price for a put option on a share of ABC stock if it also has 6 months to expiry and a $40 strike price?

   i) $3.01

   ii) $6.60

   iii) $7.56

   iv) $9.56

2. Delta Corp. entered into a currency swap with its bank, providing that Delta borrows $10 million at 10% and swaps for a 12% Euro loan. The spot exchange rate is $1.569 per Euro (€). If interest only is to be repaid on an annual basis, how much would Delta pay annually to the bank?

   i) €188,280

   ii) €637,349

   iii) €764,818

   iv) €1,882,800

3. Tony is planning to purchase a call option on ABX Corp. shares. Currently, ABX is trading at $40 per share. The option's expiry date is 25 days away. During this period, Tony can invest his money at a risk-free rate of 3%, continuously compounded. The call's exercise price is $38 and the option premium is $4.26. What is the time value of the call option?

   i) $2.00

   ii) $2.01

   iii) $2.25

   iv) $2.26

4. An investor exercises a put option with an exercise price of $60 per share. The option costs her $4 per share. Now the share is selling for $46. What is her profit per share?

   i) −$14

   ii) −$10

   iii) +$10

   iv) +$18

5. Consider the following table:

Interest-Rate Swap Opportunity		
	MNO Corp.	**PQR Corp.**
Fixed-rate market	12%	10%
Floating-rate market	Prime + 1%	Prime

PQR borrows long-term at a fixed-rate of 10% and then plans to convert this fixed-rate liability into a floating-rate liability. It enters into a swap deal with MNO. PQR is the floating-payment party, agreeing to pay prime to MNO. In order to share equally the savings in interest costs among them, what rate should MNO pay in the swap as a fixed payment party to PQR in the fixed-rate market?

i) 10.0%

ii) 10.5%

ii) 11.5%

iv) 12.0%

6. A month ago, Susan paid a premium of $0.54 per share to purchase a put option on 100 shares of Brana Corp. with an exercise price of $45 per share. The option expires today, and the current price of Brana stock is $35 per share. Which of the following is the *best* strategy for Susan to follow, and what would be her gain or loss on the transaction, including the premium paid? (Ignore commission in your calculation and assume the only alternatives are to exercise the option or not to exercise the option.)

i) Do not exercise the option and lose $54.

ii) Exercise the option and gain $946.

iii) Exercise the option and gain $1,054.

iv) Exercise the option and gain $4,554.

7. Lisa has to sell her holding of 100 shares of CoCo Inc. now. She bought these shares at a price of $10 per share one year ago, but now the share price is only $6 per share. Fortunately, she purchased a one-year put option when she invested in these shares. Though the option cost $1 per share back then, it entitles Lisa to sell the 100 shares to the option writer or seller at a price of $13 per share. If Lisa exercises the option in selling the 100 shares to the option writer, what would be Lisa's total profit (loss) from the one-year investment?

i) $(500)

ii) $(400)

iii) $200

iv) $300

Quantitative Problems

Problem 1

You have been hired recently as assistant to the treasurer of a small manufacturing firm, Anderson Inc. Anderson requires $15 million to finance the acquisition of equipment for a new plant. Since a fixed asset acquisition is being financed, Anderson prefers to borrow on a long-term basis but the treasurer believes interest rates will fall in the future and recommends a floating-rate loan. The firm can borrow in the fixed-rate market at a 7% rate for a 10-year loan. The available short-term borrowing rate is only 3.5%—the bankers' acceptance (BA) rate (currently 2%) + 1.5%.

In consultation with Anderson's investment banker, you determine that the bank has another client in need of financing that is a riskier firm in every respect. That firm requires $10 million of financing and can obtain it at 10.5% on the fixed-rate market for a 10-year loan, or at 3% above the bankers' acceptance rate on a short-term basis.

Required

Prepare a memo for the treasurer, outlining the possibility of a $10 million interest-rate swap agreement that would be of benefit to your firm. Keep in mind that your audience is unfamiliar with interest-rate swaps, and communicate your explanations simply and clearly. Clearly identify the savings available as a result of the possible swap. Be sure to explain the source of the net savings to the two firms and what factors influence the magnitude of these potential savings.

Problem 2

ABC Corp., a Canadian firm, has an account payable with a British firm coming due in 6 months. The payable requires ABC to pay £200,000 (British pounds sterling). ABC's founder and CEO, Jean Sawyer, has asked you to advise her on the various alternatives for dealing with the exchange risk inherent in this payable. She wishes to know the expected Canadian dollar cost of (1) a forward hedge, (2) borrowing on the money market, (3) an option hedge, and (4) remaining unhedged.

The following information is available. The spot rate today is C$2.48 = £1. The current 6-month forward rate is C$2.47 = £1. The premium for a 6-month option with an exercise price of C$2.45 = £1 is C$0.05 per pound. Interest rates in the two countries are as follows:

	Great Britain	Canada
Six-month deposit rate	4.5%	4%
Six-month borrowing rate	5.5%	5%

Required

Write a brief report to advise Jean on the following:

Which of the four alternatives do you recommend? Be clear on which position to take—buy or sell (with an option hedge, also specify a call, or a put). Support your recommendation with calculations and a discussion of the advantages and also specify disadvantages of each alternative.

Problem 3

Jimmy owns put options on 500 shares of KIM Company. The options have an exercise price of $30 per share and 4 months to expiry. Jimmy paid $1 per option as an option premium. He also just purchased 250 shares of KIM at the current share price of $35. Jimmy is considering signing a forward agreement to buy 100 shares of KIM at $33 per share. The forward agreement will expire at the same time as the put.

a) **i)** Define "put option."

ii) Identify *four* variables that affect put option value, and state whether they affect the value positively or negatively.

b) Explain what a forward agreement to buy/sell a share is.

c) What will be the net profit/loss to Jimmy's portfolio if he does sign the forward agreement and if, on the expiry date of the option and the forward, KIM's share price is:

i) $40?

ii) $25?

Show all of your calculations and explain what is happening in each component of Jimmy's portfolio. Explain whether the variability of returns on his portfolio would increase or decrease if he does not participate in the forward agreement.

Problem 4

Danny owns a call option on Flintstone Mining Company (FMC). The option has an exercise price of $10 per share and expires on March 19, 20X2 (the third Friday is March 19). Danny bought the option on October 25, 20X1, and paid $2.15 per share for the option. The continuously compounded risk-free rate is 5% per year. The standard deviation of the continuously compounded rate of return on the FMC share is 0.12.

a) If today is November 20, 20X1, and the market price of the shares of FMC is $12, what is a fair premium for the option?

b) If today is March 19, 20X2, and the market price of FMC shares is $12, what is the value of the option?

c) If today is March 19, 20X2, and the market price of FMC shares is $9.50, what is the value of the option?

Problem 5

Japan Transport Devices (JTD) is planning to enter the Canadian market through acquisitions. JTD just received ¥2.52 billion from the sale of bonds yielding 3% and sold in Japan. Coupon payments are made annually until maturity in five years. The company is planning to use the proceeds for its expansion purposes. Currently, the Canadian dollar can be purchased in the market at the rate of ¥85 per dollar.

Canada Timber Resources (CTR) is looking to expand in the Japanese market. The expansion plan requires substantial initial investment. In anticipation of this investment, CTR sold bonds with a market value of $30 million, yielding 5% paid annually. The bonds mature in five years. Currently, CTR can exchange the Canadian dollars for yen at the rate of ¥83 per dollar.

a) Why is there a difference in exchange rates for JTD and CTR?

b) What kind of an arrangement could JTD and CTR make between them to avoid transaction costs? Why?

c) CTR and JTD agree to swap the initial investment outlays, the coupon payments over the five-year period, and the final principal payments. If over the five-year period the exchange rate is expected to average ¥84 per dollar and the ask-bid spread is expected to average ¥2 per dollar, what are the savings in transaction costs for each firm?

d) CTR and JTD agree to swap the initial investment outlays, the coupon payments over the five-year period, and the final principal payments. Over the next five years, the exchange rate of the dollar happens to be, respectively, ¥80, ¥84, ¥86, ¥82, and ¥77. Ignoring transaction costs, calculate the cash profits or losses (in dollars) that each party will experience because of the swap. Assume that the exchange rate for the initial investment outlay is ¥84 per dollar.

Problem 6

a) What are the cash flow implications of options trading?

b) Identify *two* differences between forward and options contracts.

Problem 7

With significant increases in the prices of commodities, such as crude oil and gold, inflation is becoming a serious threat to the growth of a healthy Canadian economy. The Bank of Canada, the central bank in Canada, is expected to continue raising its interest rate for overnight loans, which is the benchmark rate for all interest rates on the financial market, in order to keep the inflation under control. The market interest rates are most likely to increase in the future in tandem with the benchmark rate.

General Auto Co. (GA), an Ontario-based auto parts manufacturer, has a $10 million floating-rate loan to mature in 5 years, and a $10 million commercial paper to refinance in 6 months. GA wants to lock in the interest rate on the floating-rate loan at a fixed level. Fortunately, GA has found that Manitoba Mining Co. (MM), a Manitoba-based gold producer, needs to raise $10 million to fund its operations and is willing to take on floating-rate finance. The rates that GA and MM face in the fixed- and floating-rate markets are shown in the table below. All interest rates are compounded annually.

Borrowing Rates for GA and MM		
Company	Fixed-rate market	Floating-rate market
GA	8%	T-bill rate + 1.5%
MM	6%	T-bill rate + 1%

For the commercial paper, GA wants to use futures contracts to lock in the interest rate close to the current 6% level. The futures price quotation for the 3-month bankers' acceptance (BA) futures contract, with a $1 million face value and a delivery date in 6 months, is 98.5. The correlation between changes in the interest rates on commercial paper and BA futures is 0.9.

Required

a) For GA's $10 million floating-rate loan, design an interest-rate swap that would allow GA to fix and lower the rate on its financing by 0.5% and help MM save 1% on its financing. Specifically, answer the following questions:

   i) In order to engage in a swap deal, should MM borrow $10 million in the fixed-rate or the floating-rate market? What is the interest rate?

   ii) In the swap deal, which company, GA or MM, should pay the floating rate, which is assumed to equal the T-bill rate?

   iii) What is the effective interest rate that GA is going to pay on its $10 million financing as a result of the swap deal?

   iv) In the swap deal, which company, GA or MM, should pay the fixed rate? What is the rate?

   v) What is the effective interest rate that MM is going to pay on its $10 million financing as a result of the swap deal?

   vi) Briefly explain why MM would like to take on floating-rate financing even though the market consensus is that interest rates are rising.

b) **i)** How much capital would GA raise if it issued a 9-month commercial paper today?

   ii) To use futures to hedge against an interest-rate increase, should GA buy or sell BA futures? How many futures contracts should GA use?

   iii) Suppose that on the refinancing day 6 months later, the required yield on the 9-month commercial paper is 8.5%. GA issues the commercial paper and closes out its position in futures, which now trade at a price of 96.2. What is the effective annual interest rate obtained by GA, after taking the result of the hedge into account?

Cases
Case 1: Allied Business Corporation (ABC)

Jack has 200 shares of Allied Business Corporation (ABC) in his portfolio with a current share price of $33. Several derivative securities are available relating to the shares of this firm. Jack is interested in buying put options on these shares because he believes that the distribution of possible share prices in 6 months will be as shown in Case Exhibit 9-1:

Case Exhibit 9-1
Jack's Forecast of Future Share Prices for ABC Stock

Scenario	Probability	Share price
i	0.25	$30
ii	0.40	$33
iii	0.35	$35

Call options are also available on ABC shares, with an expiry date in 6 months. Both the call and put options have a strike price of $30, are written on ABC shares, and have 6 months to maturity. The risk-free rate is now 5% per annum and the standard deviation of the ABC share price is estimated to be 12%.

Required

a) Using the Black-Scholes option-pricing model, calculate the premium on the ABC call options. See Appendix B on page 578 for the normal distribution table.

b) Using put-call parity, calculate the premium on the put options.

c) Identify *five* variables that affect put option value and the direction of their effect.

d) Assume that Jack holds 200 shares of ABC, buys puts on 200 shares, and also signs a forward agreement (expiring in 6 months) to sell 100 shares of ABC at $33 each. What is the expected position of Jack in 6 months using his price forecast? For each of three probability scenarios in Case Exhibit 9-1, calculate the total position of this investor, including the value of the shares, puts, and the forward agreement.

Case 2: YYY Corporation

Lucille has just purchased a call option on YYY Corp. Shares of YYY are trading at $40 each, and the exercise price on the call is $38. The option expires in 75 days and during this period, Lucille can invest at the risk-free rate of 3.5%, continuously compounded. Upon careful review of the company's history, Lucille has determined that the variance of returns on YYY shares is 0.14.

Required

a) Using the Black-Scholes option-pricing model, determine the call premium that would be appropriate given the characteristics described above. Appendix B provides the cumulative probabilities of the standard normal distribution function. Round your d_1 and d_2 calculations to the nearest 2 percentage points so that you can directly apply table values and will not need to interpolate.

b) Explain and calculate the time value of the call option. If the time to expiry were 150 days instead of 75 days, calculate the impact this would have on the time value of the call option. Show supporting computations.

c) Determine the appropriate price for a put option on YYY Corp. shares if it also expires in 75 days and has a strike price of $38. When would Lucille be interested in purchasing a put option rather than a call option?

Case 3: JKL Corporation

JKL Corp. is a Toronto-based company specialized in developing and manufacturing dental products. Gold is an essential ingredient of the production process, and therefore JKL needs to have large quantities of gold on hand. It plans to purchase 5,000 ounces of gold in one month. The gold price, quoted in U.S. dollars, has been steadily increasing. Gold futures are traded on the commodity exchange in New York. Each contract is for 100 ounces quoted in U.S. dollars.

JKL sells its products mainly in Canada and invoices its customers in Canadian dollars. Futures contracts on Canadian dollars are traded on the Chicago Mercantile Exchange. Each contract is for C$100,000.

JKL has been using short-term funds to finance its regular operation, and it is now time to refinance its short-term funds. It plans to issue $4 million face value of 9-month commercial paper in 3 months. The current interest rate is 4% on the commercial paper issued by companies with the same credit rating as JKL. Interest rates are expected to rise. The price of the 3-month Canadian bankers' acceptance (BA) futures contract trading on the Montréal Exchange with a $1 million face value and with a delivery date 3 months later has been steadily dropping and is now at 97. It is expected to drop further to 94 another 3 months later. The correlation between changes in yields on commercial paper and BA futures is 0.9.

Required

Prepare a report to address the following issues:

- Identify the risks JKL is exposed to.
- Explain how JKL could hedge each risk with each of the possible vehicles, that is, forward contracts, futures contracts, and options. For each risk, state the appropriate position (buy or sell and the number of contracts to buy or sell) and describe how each vehicle works under two opposite scenarios (assuming that the current gold price is US$450 per ounce, the current exchange rate is C$1.20 = US$1.00, and the 9-month commercial paper trades at a yield of 6% three months later).
- Compare and contrast the three different hedging vehicles.
- Explain how JKL could hedge risk by using means other than derivatives.

APPENDIX B

CUMULATIVE DISTRIBUTION FUNCTION FOR THE STANDARD NORMAL VARIABLE

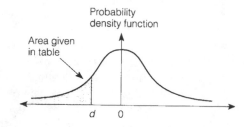

For example, $N(-1.15) = 0.1251$ and $N(1.57) = 0.9418$

d	0.00	0.01	0.02	0.03	0.04	0.05	0.06	0.07	0.08	0.09
−3.0	.0013	.0013	.0013	.0012	.0012	.0011	.0011	.0011	.0010	.0010
−2.9	.0019	.0018	.0018	.0017	.0016	.0016	.0015	.0015	.0014	.0014
−2.8	.0026	.0025	.0024	.0023	.0023	.0022	.0021	.0021	.0020	.0019
−2.7	.0035	.0034	.0033	.0032	.0031	.0030	.0029	.0028	.0027	.0026
−2.6	.0047	.0045	.0044	.0043	.0041	.0040	.0039	.0038	.0037	.0036
−2.5	.0062	.0060	.0059	.0057	.0055	.0054	.0052	.0051	.0049	.0048
−2.4	.0082	.0080	.0078	.0075	.0073	.0071	.0069	.0068	.0066	.0064
−2.3	.0107	.0104	.0102	.0099	.0096	.0094	.0091	.0089	.0087	.0084
−2.2	.0139	.0136	.0132	.0129	.0125	.0122	.0119	.0116	.0113	.0110
−2.1	.0179	.0174	.0170	.0166	.0162	.0158	.0154	.0150	.0146	.0143
−2.0	.0227	.0222	.0217	.0212	.0207	.0202	.0197	.0192	.0188	.0183
−1.9	.0287	.0281	.0274	.0268	.0262	.0256	.0250	.0244	.0239	.0233
−1.8	.0359	.0351	.0344	.0336	.0329	.0322	.0314	.0307	.0301	.0294
−1.7	.0446	.0436	.0427	.0418	.0409	.0401	.0392	.0384	.0375	.0367
−1.6	.0548	.0537	.0526	.0516	.0505	.0495	.0485	.0475	.0465	.0455
−1.5	.0668	.0655	.0643	.0630	.0618	.0606	.0594	.0582	.0571	.0559
−1.4	.0808	.0793	.0778	.0764	.0749	.0735	.0721	.0708	.0694	.0681
−1.3	.0968	.0951	.0934	.0918	.0901	.0885	.0869	.0853	.0838	.0823
−1.2	.1151	.1131	.1112	.1093	.1075	.1056	.1038	.1020	.1003	.0985
−1.1	.1357	.1335	.1314	.1292	.1271	.1251	.1230	.1210	.1190	.1170
−1.0	.1587	.1563	.1539	.1515	.1492	.1469	.1446	.1423	.1401	.1379
−0.9	.1841	.1814	.1788	.1762	.1736	.1711	.1685	.1660	.1635	.1611
−0.8	.2119	.2090	.2061	.2033	.2005	.1977	.1949	.1922	.1894	.1867
−0.7	.2420	.2389	.2358	.2327	.2296	.2266	.2236	.2206	.2177	.2148
−0.6	.2743	.2709	.2676	.2643	.2611	.2578	.2546	.2514	.2483	.2451
−0.5	.3085	.3050	.3015	.2981	.2946	.2912	.2877	.2843	.2810	.2776
−0.4	.3446	.3409	.3372	.3336	.3300	.3264	.3228	.3192	.3156	.3121
−0.3	.3821	.3783	.3745	.3707	.3669	.3632	.3594	.3557	.3520	.3483
−0.2	.4207	.4168	.4129	.4090	.4052	.4013	.3974	.3936	.3897	.3859
−0.1	.4602	.4562	.4522	.4483	.4443	.4404	.4364	.4325	.4286	.4247
−0.0	.5000	.4960	.4920	.4880	.4840	.4801	.4761	.4721	.4681	.4641

d	0.00	0.01	0.02	0.03	0.04	0.05	0.06	0.07	0.08	0.09
0.0	.5000	.5040	.5080	.5120	.5160	.5199	.5239	.5279	.5319	.5359
0.1	.5398	.5438	.5478	.5517	.5557	.5596	.5636	.5675	.5714	.5753
0.2	.5793	.5832	.5871	.5910	.5948	.5987	.6026	.6064	.6103	.6141
0.3	.6179	.6217	.6255	.6293	.6331	.6368	.6406	.6443	.6480	.6517
0.4	.6554	.6591	.6628	.6664	.6700	.6736	.6772	.6808	.6844	.6879
0.5	.6915	.6950	.6985	.7019	.7054	.7088	.7123	.7157	.7190	.7224
0.6	.7257	.7291	.7324	.7357	.7389	.7422	.7454	.7486	.7517	.7549
0.7	.7580	.7611	.7642	.7673	.7704	.7734	.7764	.7794	.7823	.7852
0.8	.7881	.7910	.7939	.7967	.7995	.8023	.8051	.8078	.8106	.8133
0.9	.8159	.8186	.8212	.8238	.8264	.8289	.8315	.8340	.8365	.8389
1.0	.8413	.8439	.8461	.8485	.8508	.8531	.8554	.8577	.8599	.8621
1.1	.8643	.8665	.8686	.8708	.8729	.8749	.8770	.8790	.8810	.8830
1.2	.8849	.8869	.8888	.8907	.8925	.8944	.8962	.8980	.8997	.9015
1.3	.9032	.9049	.9066	.9082	.9099	.9115	.9131	.9147	.9162	.9177
1.4	.9192	.9207	.9222	.9236	.9251	.9265	.9279	.9292	.9306	.9319
1.5	.9332	.9345	.9357	.9370	.9382	.9394	.9406	.9418	.9429	.9441
1.6	.9452	.9463	.9474	.9484	.9495	.9505	.9515	.9525	.9535	.9545
1.7	.9554	.9564	.9573	.9582	.9591	.9599	.9608	.9616	.9625	.9633
1.8	.9641	.9649	.9656	.9664	.9671	.9678	.9686	.9693	.9699	.9706
1.9	.9713	.9719	.9726	.9732	.9738	.9744	.9750	.9756	.9761	.9767
2.0	.9773	.9778	.9783	.9788	.9793	.9798	.9803	.9808	.9812	.9817
2.1	.9821	.9826	.9830	.9834	.9838	.9842	.9846	.9850	.9854	.9857
2.2	.9861	.9864	.9868	.9871	.9875	.9878	.9881	.9884	.9887	.9890
2.3	.9893	.9896	.9898	.9901	.9904	.9906	.9909	.9911	.9913	.9916
2.4	.9918	.9920	.9922	.9925	.9927	.9929	.9931	.9932	.9934	.9936
2.5	.9938	.9940	.9941	.9943	.9945	.9946	.9948	.9949	.9951	.9952
2.6	.9953	.9955	.9956	.9957	.9959	.9960	.9961	.9962	.9963	.9964
2.7	.9965	.9966	.9967	.9968	.9969	.9970	.9971	.9972	.9973	.9974
2.8	.9974	.9975	.9976	.9977	.9977	.9978	.9979	.9979	.9980	.9981
2.9	.9981	.9982	.9982	.9983	.9984	.9984	.9985	.9985	.9986	.9986
3.0	.9987	.9987	.9987	.9988	.9988	.9989	.9989	.9989	.9990	.9990

Chapter 10
Financial Planning

CHAPTER OVERVIEW

Financial planning is the process of analyzing the interactions of a firm's policy decisions, including decisions on capital investment, financing, capital structure, dividends, and liquidity. In Chapters 1 to 9, you learned about the factors that influence these decisions and the tools and techniques that help the financial manager in making them. This chapter extends the knowledge of financial planning acquired in your introductory finance course. It focuses on the financial planning process and emphasizes the role of forecasting, cash budgeting, and strategic planning.

Section 10.1 provides an overview of financial planning, including basic concepts, objectives, and steps of the financial planning process. Financial planning provides an overall picture of the firm's operating, financial, and strategic situations over the short, intermediate, and long terms. An important aim of financial planning is to forecast the firm's future operating and financial situations if the firm's plans are carried out as designed. Financial planning enables the manager to study the feasibility of the plans and the possibility of changing some aspects for better performance and results. More importantly, it allows the manager to test assumptions, study future scenarios, and design contingency plans to ensure the firm's survival.

One of the main steps in the financial planning process is forecasting various macroeconomic and microeconomic factors that affect the firm's performance over the planning horizon. Section 10.2 emphasizes the role of forecasting. Many variables, such as unit sales, product prices, raw material costs, fixed costs, and financing costs, need to be forecasted to develop a financial planning model. The section highlights some of the difficulties in forecasting these variables and ways to deal with them. Multiple regression is applied in the section as a technique to forecast sales.

The main outputs of the financial planning model are the pro forma income statement, balance sheet, and cash flow statement. Section 10.3 explains that these pro forma statements form the basis of financial planning. The income statement shows how a firm's sales, expenses, and net earnings change over the planning horizon. The balance sheet shows how assets and liabilities grow over time. The cash flow statement summarizes the results from operating activities, investment activities, and financing activities, and provides the net cash balances. It provides information for analyzing the interactions of these activities. This analysis is important for financial planning.

Section 10.4 focuses on the short-term planning horizon, which is largely concerned with cash budgeting. Cash budgeting is important in determining when excess cash will be available for short-term investments and when cash shortages will require increased short-term debt. Knowing this in advance allows the finance manager time to ensure efficient use of funds and access to cost-effective sources of funds.

A typical balance sheet divides assets and liabilities into short-term and long-term categories. Section 10.5 addresses the link between these short- and long-term groups. You learn that it is risky to rely on short-term funds for financing long-term assets. However, long-term financing is more expensive. You also learn that the portion of funds obtained from short-term sources depends on factors such as the firm's seasonal working capital needs, its asset liquidity, and shareholders' risk preferences. The section describes the various strategies that firms use to deal with these issues.

Section 10.6 reviews ratio analysis as a tool for studying a firm's past performance. You learn that ratio analysis is effective and powerful in detecting a firm's weaknesses and strengths. Ratio analysis is mainly done by comparing the firm's ratios from the most recent year with those from the past several years. The firm's ratios are also compared with those of similar firms in the same industry. The objective is to detect trends in the ratios and any deviations from industry norms.

Section 10.7 develops a sample financial planning model and uses a computer illustration to demonstrate the use of the model for financial planning and evaluation. The section shows how ratio analysis can be used to determine the feasibility of the firm's plans, the consistency of the plans with the firm's policies, and the risks the firm faces in executing its plans. Scenario analysis should provide managers with the information necessary to prepare for contingencies and to ensure the survival of the firm.

Section 10.8 emphasizes planning as a strategic advantage. It reviews the areas where the firm can have strategic advantages and how financial planning helps to identify these areas. Proper financial planning requires comprehensive databases on various issues of importance to the firm. This information is useful in identifying strategic concerns, such as the firm's weaknesses, strengths, and opportunities, as well as threats to the firm. The financial planning model can then be used to determine the firm's optimal strategies for specific functional areas, such as finance and marketing. Also addressed in Section 10.8 are the ethical concerns and issues that the financial manager may face when considering strategic options. Ethical problems may arise because of agency issues or the existence of asymmetric information. Examples are provided to demonstrate the complexity of dealing with ethical issues. You are reminded that failure to ensure ethical behaviour within an organization can lead to major financial losses to shareholders.

Learning Objectives

After completing this chapter, you will be able to:

- Identify the objectives of corporate financial planning and explain the role of financial forecasting in the process.

- Identify the interactions of the firm's various policies using the cash flow statement.

- Explain the important factors in creating a cash budget.

- Identify and analyze the factors that lead the financial manager to choose between short-term and long-term financing.

- Explain the three strategies of financing the firm's assets with short- or long-term funds.

- Identify a firm's strengths and weaknesses using the results of financial analysis.

- Design and create a financial planning model.

- Analyze a firm's strategic advantage using the financial planning model.

- Identify the ethical issues that may arise from strategic decisions and the approaches to correct them.

This knowledge will provide you with the professional skills to:

- Develop financial forecasts and plans.

- Manage cash flow and working capital.

- Prepare financial statements that are appropriate for users, specifically pro forma statements.

- Develop and administer budgets.

- Advise on financing to meet the organization's goals.

- Assess the value of a business.

- Prepare, analyze, and interpret financial performance measures.

- Assess and advise on performance measurement requirements.

- Develop and assess financial benchmarks.

- Adapt performance measures.

- Evaluate and advise on capital investments, mergers and acquisitions, or the sale of a business.

- Advise on business decisions in the context of larger economic or geopolitical conditions.

- Evaluate and advise on growth strategies of an organization or individual.

- Apply professional ethical standards.

- Protect the public interest, specifically to protect shareholders and the public interested in share activity through ethical application of professional behaviour with respect to financial decision making for an organization.

HOW THIS CHAPTER RELATES TO OTHER CHAPTERS IN THE BOOK

In a business environment characterized by rapid technological changes, globalization, and accelerating competition, strategic financial planning is crucial for growth and survival. Financial planning forces financial managers to think about and forecast the future. It involves building a corporate financial model and identifying the capital requirements needed to carry out the plan. The policy elements of financial planning, such as investment opportunities, dividends, liquidity, and the degree of financial leverage, have been covered and discussed in various chapters in this book. This chapter begins with an overview of the financial planning process. We then examine the key aspects of both long-term (strategic) and short-term (operational) financial planning.

10.1 OVERVIEW OF THE FINANCIAL PLANNING PROCESS

In your introductory finance course, you will have studied financial planning as a useful tool for making strategic decisions that maximize the firm's value. You learned about the elements, objectives, and benefits of the financial planning process. This section provides additional detail on the basic concepts of financial planning. These concepts prepare you for understanding two important aspects of financial planning:

1. the study of the firm's various financial and operating strategies and how their interaction affects the firm's financial performance; and

2. the identification of financial needs and contingency plans required to ensure the survival of the firm under various circumstances.

Basic Concepts of Financial Planning

Corporate financial planning is the process by which a firm formulates a set of consistent business and financial objectives and identifies how they can be achieved. The process begins with the development of a firm's strategic and operating plans over a given planning horizon.

Strategic plans lay out general directions for the firm's future. They identify objectives on which the firm will focus its efforts. For example, a strategic plan may identify the objective of becoming a market leader in one of its products. Other examples of objectives include becoming:

- the supplier of the least expensive product

- the supplier of the highest quality product

- the leader in added features

- highly integrated or highly focused

- highly diversified or highly specialized

- product innovative

Operating plans are detailed schedules of activities used to accomplish the firm's strategic objectives. They include strategies for designing, marketing, producing, and financing new products. As opposed to strategic plans, operating plans are generally more specific, but they must also be consistent with strategic plans. In other words, strategic plans are like the peaks that hikers plan to reach. Operating plans are like maps of the paths that the hikers plan to follow to reach the peaks.

Financial planning is the process by which strategic and operating plans are studied. Through financial planning, the firm projects the financial results from strategic plans and the impact of alternative operating and financial strategies (such as capital structure and dividend policies) on these results. The firm assesses its strategic objectives under different assumptions regarding its future operating environment. Also, financial planning allows the firm to forecast its short-term financial and operating results through weekly, monthly, and quarterly financial statements and cash budgets.

Objectives of Financial Planning Through financial planning, financial managers accomplish several objectives that will vary depending on the firm's strategic objectives. Possible objectives are:

- to forecast the financial results of the firm's strategic and operating plans;

- to predict the impact of various financial policies on the forecasted results;

- to consider how the interactions of capital investment, capital structure, dividends, liquidity, and financing affect various policy decisions;

- to identify short- and long-term financing alternatives that are consistent with the firm's operating and strategic plans;

- to prepare contingency plans for altering the firm's basic financial strategies should future developments deviate from expected outcomes.

There are important differences between the objectives of short-term and long-term financial planning. Generally, managers must consider multiple objectives, such as high returns on investment, high liquidity, and low risk. Sometimes, these objectives conflict with one another. Depending on the planning time frame, one of them will dominate. The shorter the time period, the greater the emphasis on cash management will be and the less focus there will be on obtaining the highest possible return on assets.

The Financial Plan Financial planning is not concerned with specific project-by-project analysis. The **financial plan** consists of both strategic and operating plans, which forecast possible outcomes and results. Therefore, the firm's financial plan requires aggregating the expected results from all of the firm's projects and activities, taking into consideration funds from all sources.

Financial plans are generally prepared for time horizons ranging from three to ten years, depending on the circumstances of the firm. Firms in industries that are not capital intensive, such as software development, engineering design, and retail firms, are likely to have shorter planning horizons that rarely exceed three years. In contrast, companies in capital-intensive industries are likely to have longer planning horizons. For example, utility companies, such as gas distribution, telephone, power generation, and water supply firms, often have planning horizons longer than five years and up to 20 years.

A good corporate financial plan also includes a short-term component, which involves preparing a detailed cash budget for the near term. Similarly to long-term horizons, short-term horizons vary from one firm to another depending on the firm's circumstances. For some companies, a one-year short-term planning horizon is appropriate, while for others, the short-term planning horizon can be one day. Firms with stable cash inflows and disbursements, such as utility companies, are likely to have slightly longer (one-year) short-term planning horizons. Firms with highly uncertain revenues and disbursements, such as service companies, are likely to have planning horizons of one month or less. Firms with large daily cash inflows and outflows and uncertain cash flows are likely to have one-day short-term planning horizons.

The long-term plan reflects the firm's strategic, operating, and financial policy choices over the planning period. In contrast, the short-term plan and the cash budget reflect the firm's operating plan for the coming year. Often, the cash budget is based on the first year of the long-term plan. Most companies update their financial plans annually to incorporate new information.

The emphasis in financial planning is on the analysis of various scenarios rather than on finding the optimal strategy. Financial planning indicates the expected consequences of alternative courses of action. It helps a firm evaluate the returns and risks of alternative plans and determine a reasonable set of strategies and contingencies associated with each plan. Management will still have to decide which plan to implement. Therefore, the real value of financial planning is that it helps the firm prepare for deviations from expected outcomes and formulate contingency plans.

Steps in the Financial Planning Process

Financial planning is a complicated process comprising several steps. These steps are designed to achieve the firm's financial planning objectives. The steps vary from one planning process to another, depending on the firm's objectives. They include:

1. Formulating a statement of the corporation's strategic, operating, and financial objectives over the planning horizon. If a statement already exists, it must be carefully reviewed. This step is required to ensure that the financial planning process is consistent with the overall mission of the firm, its long-term objectives, opportunities, and constraints.

2. Preparing a list of the underlying assumptions of the expected business and economic environment in which the financial plan is prepared. This step is important because general economic conditions will affect alternative actions and the ultimate results.

3. Studying the current projects undertaken by each of the firm's principal divisions as well as any new projects expected to be undertaken during the planning horizon. This step includes preparing period-by-period sales forecasts, estimating costs, and describing the assets needed for each project.

4. Preparing pro forma financial statements, including period-by-period income statements, balance sheets, and cash flow statements for the entire firm, covering the planning horizon. The statements will illustrate the projected operating results and the details of the proposed financing program. This step requires identifying the liabilities required to finance the planned activities.

5. Analyzing the pro forma financial statements to ensure the feasibility of the plan, consistency with the firm's statement of strategic, operating, and financial policies, and the desirability of the outcomes. In this step, the financial manager will study the resulting financial statements using ratio analysis as well as common size and indexed financial statements.

6. Assessing the firm's ability to survive under various scenarios of the future business environment. Scenario analysis is required to determine how the financial situation of the firm would change if the assumptions underlying the planning process differ significantly from the actual results. "What-if" analysis is needed to plan for adverse economic situations, differing responses by competitors, and differing sales and cost figures. The results of this exercise should point out how the managers within each line of business would alter their basic strategies in the event that any of the principal contingencies they foresee should occur.

10.2 ROLE OF FORECASTING

Forecasting is an integral part of financial planning. It is the process of estimating the effects or results of future financial events. Corporations use models to assist them with the forecasting aspect of financial planning. These models vary in detail and degree of sophistication depending on the corporation's situation and the specific needs of the analyst. They are generally constructed around the firm's forecasted cash flows. Models allow the analyst to produce forecasts under various scenarios of operating strategies and financial policies. The objective is to study expected financial performance as well as possible deviations from forecasted performance.

The financial planning model requires forecasts of several key inputs, which determine the ultimate output. The financial analyst uses forecasts of general economic conditions, such as interest rates, stock market activity, household incomes, consumer spending, inflation, and both domestic and foreign government spending. These are the macroeconomic conditions. Similarly, the analyst uses forecasts of many microeconomic variables that influence the cash flows generated from the firm's operations. The analyst must generate forecasts of industry- and company-specific conditions, competitive pressures, sales and variable costs for each line of the firm's business, and many other factors that affect the level and mix of various assets and liabilities.

The output of a financial planning model is a set of pro forma financial statements. The financial manager quantifies the expected financing requirements and identifies the internal and external funding sources to meet the requirements. Thus, the output of a financial planning model is a forecast of the expected sources and uses of funds over the planning horizon. In addition, the pro forma financial statements can be used to study the financial performance of the firm should the plans materialize. The forecast enables management to identify potential risks and take corrective actions to ensure desirable results.

It is important that the forecasts of the various divisions be consistent with the firm's forecast of overall economic conditions. The macroeconomic conditions must be applied logically to each division. Senior management must review and approve the general macroeconomic forecast before it is disseminated to each of the planning units. Then senior management must review and approve the business plans of each unit to ensure consistency with the corporate macroeconomic forecast.

Financial planning should not be done centrally by senior management. Instead, every division should participate in the process by providing its own financial plan. The advantages to a decentralized, bottom-up planning process include:

- better forecasts, as the managers in the organization are closer to the business and have better information to prepare more accurate plans;

- better commitment to the resulting plans, as managers who participate in preparing a plan are more likely to support the plan's execution; and

- better overall participation, because several levels of the organization are involved in the development process.

It is also important that the role of senior management be carefully balanced. Senior management's review should not be designed as a second planning process but as an assurance and control mechanism to ensure consistency between the forecasts of the various divisions and the firm's overall economic forecast. The risk of a second planning process is that if substantial changes are made to the initial forecast, those who participated in the initial planning process may feel that their contribution is not valued and they may not participate seriously in future planning exercises.

The results of any forecast are only as good as the inputs to the forecasting model. Therefore, the firm's economic forecast, which will be used as input in all business plans, must be as realistic as possible. The firm may consult outside experts and economic consulting firms to generate macroeconomic and industry forecasts. Outside opinion can improve forecasting accuracy and eliminate any biases of internal forecasters.

In the final analysis, senior management must keep in mind that forecasting and planning are not to be accepted as 100% accurate. The best management can expect from the exercise is the identification of a set of possible outcomes. Management then hopes that the ultimate results will fall within the preferable range of possibilities. Therefore, financial planning should provide various contingency plans to guide the corporation as events unfold.

Forecasting Sales

The sales forecast is one of the most important inputs to the financial forecasting model. Each department or division in the firm prepares its own sales forecast. These individual forecasts are then aggregated to obtain the firm's overall sales forecast.

Many methods may be used to forecast sales, ranging from simple to sophisticated. One simple method predicts future sales by estimating the sales growth rate over the past several years and assuming that last year's sales figures will increase by the same rate. This forecast would be accurate if the factors influencing the growth rate in the past, such as competitor's reactions, economic conditions, inflation, consumer demand, and the existence of substitute products, remain the same in the future. However, such factors are highly dynamic and likely to change considerably over time, so the growth rate may not be sustainable over the long run.

Extensions of this simple method rely heavily on quantitative and statistical techniques, such as regression and time series analysis. They assume that the growth rate will vary from one period to the next depending on various factors. The analyst uses historical sales figures as inputs to a model from which a sales forecast is derived, based on the historical growth rate of sales and the deviations of sales from the general trend.

MINICASE 10-1 FORECASTING SALES USING MULTIPLE REGRESSION

Bright Colours Dresses (BCD) is a manufacturer of women's fashion dresses. The firm's sales are highly affected by the inflation rate and by the average level of household income. These data are shown in Exhibit 10-1 for the period from 1999 to 2007.

Question 1: Using the data in Exhibit 10-1, what is the multiple regression equation to describe the relationship among household income, the inflation rate, and the level of sales?

For a review of multiple regression analysis, see the computer illustration that follows this minicase.

Case Continued >

Exhibit 10-1
Historical Sales, Inflation, and Household Income Data from 1999 to 2007

Year	Sales ($ millions)	Inflation rate	Household income ($ thousands)
1999	$60.00	3.00%	$45.00
2000	65.00	3.50	44.50
2001	61.00	3.75	45.00
2002	67.00	3.50	45.25
2003	68.00	4.50	45.00
2004	63.00	3.00	45.75
2005	70.00	2.10	46.50
2006	74.00	2.50	47.25
2007	75.00	2.75	48.00

The multiple linear regression from the computer illustration produces:

$$y\text{-intercept} = -152.84$$
$$\text{Inflation coefficient} = 225.04$$
$$\text{Household income coefficient} = 4.64$$

Therefore, the data in Exhibit 10-1 suggest that sales of BCD are related to the inflation rate and to household income by the relationship:

$$\text{Sales} = -152.84 + 225.04(\text{IR}) + 4.64(\text{HI}) + e_i$$

where
- IR = inflation rate measured in decimal form
- HI = household income measured in thousands of dollars
- e_i = a random error, which measures the deviation of the forecast from the actual sales

Question 2: The Bank of Canada just released its annual forecast for 2008. It predicts that inflation is likely to be 5% and average household income is likely to rise to $49,500. Use the multiple regression equation generated in Question 1 to determine the sales that BCD should expect for 2008:

$$\text{Sales} = -152.84 + (225.04 \times 0.05) + (4.64 \times \$49.50) = \$88.092 \text{ million}$$

Question 3: The Bank of Canada's forecast expects that inflation is likely to stay at 5% in 2009 but that the average household income is likely to rise to $51,500. Use the multiple regression equation generated in Question 1 to determine the sales that BCD should expect for 2009:

$$\text{Sales} = -152.84 + (225.04 \times 0.05) + (4.64 \times \$51.50) = \$97.372 \text{ million}$$

Computer Activity: Multiple Regression

LEARNING OBJECTIVE

■ After working through this computer illustration, you should be able to perform a multiple regression analysis using a spreadsheet program.

Description

The data set uses economic information from 1991. It is based on data collected on Canadian cities with greater than 10,000 people. This data set will be used to derive a model in the form of a regression equation that will predict the retail sales based on the independent variables of size of population, number of households, and personal income.

FN2LXR.xls   Excel

Procedure

1. Open the file FN2LXR.xls. Click the Dataset sheet tab.
2. Become familiar with the layout of the Dataset worksheet. Cells A7 to F197 contain the data as described above. The data in your worksheet have been sorted on variable POP1 or size of population.
3. Click the LXR1 sheet tab. This worksheet is set aside for your regression analysis output.

Three Explanatory Variables
Perform a regression analysis using POP1, HSHOLDS, and INCOME1 as independent variables and SALES1 as the dependent variable. Follow the appropriate procedures as described in the following sections.

1. Click the Dataset sheet tab and choose Tools Data Analysis. Then choose Regression from the Analysis Tools box. Click OK.
   (If Data Analysis is not displayed under the Tools menu, click the How To tab on your FN2 Internet CD and follow the "Use Excel" link listed under the "Use software in the course" section. You must ensure that the Analysis Toolpak is installed and activated before proceeding further with this illustration.)
2. Select the range F18:F197 for the Input Y range. (Do not press ENTER.)
3. Select the range C18:E197 for the Input X range. (Do not press ENTER.)
4. Select the Labels checkbox and leave the others unchecked. In the Output section, select the OutputRange radio button. Click the OutputRange text box, type the range LXR1!A5, and click OK. The results will be displayed in sheet LXR1.
5. Save your completed worksheet and print a copy.

Results
You should obtain the following results.
   The regression equation is (rounded to four decimal places):

$$SALES1 = -21.3043 - 3.7798\ POP1 + 14.9178\ HSHOLDS + 0.3634\ INCOME1$$
$$(\text{from cells B21 to B24 of your worksheet or of sheet LXR1S})$$

The *R*-square is 0.9991 (cell B9). This indicates that the regression equation explains 99.91% of the variation in retail sales. This indicates that the model fits the data very well.

The *t*-statistics for HSHOLDS and INCOME1 are quite high. This shows that the coefficients for these variables are statistically significant. Therefore, the variables POP1, HSHOLDS, and INCOME1 are contributing to the explanation of the variation in SALES1.

Conclusion

This computer illustration demonstrated the use of a spreadsheet program to generate a regression equation and statistics that are used to assess the closeness of fit of the equation to the data.

The main advantage of quantitative forecasting methods is that they are easy to use. By integrating them with computers, analysts are able to introduce sophisticated features. Moreover, given their mechanical nature, these methods facilitate scenario analysis.

The main drawback of quantitative forecasting methods is that they use historical data and trends to predict the future. They assume that past experience contains valuable information and that past behaviour will likely be repeated in the future. When these assumptions are valid, quantitative forecasting methods provide fairly accurate estimates of future sales.

In practice, sales can be highly volatile and subject to seasonal and long-term trends. In such situations, using quantitative forecasting models produces unreliable forecasts. Moreover, in some situations historical sales cannot be obtained. For example, a firm wanting to enter a new market in which it has no prior experience, or introduce a new product, will have no input to use in quantitative forecasting models. In such situations, the firm must rely on more subjective forecasting methods. These methods start with a general economic forecast supplied by top management to derive the assumptions relevant to the division. Using these assumptions, the division starts by forecasting industry conditions. Given these conditions, the market demand for the product would then be estimated in units.

Most often, the marketing department of each division produces several estimates of demand based on various scenarios of the economic environment. Each scenario is assigned a probability of occurrence. The expected demand for the product is then estimated as a weighted average of the demands under the various scenarios, with the weights being the probabilities of occurrence. Using its market share as a benchmark, each division estimates its own market demand. Based on the plans of the separate divisions, the financial analyst forms the firm's overall business and financial plan.

Whenever possible, market demand forecasts should be compared with estimates prepared by outside economic or market forecasting agencies. Division personnel should be prepared to explain any significant differences between their forecasts and commercial forecasts.

In practice, the sales forecast produced by a division must be tested for feasibility. A firm's rate of sales growth may not be sustainable or applicable. For example, a sales forecast that requires addition to capacity may not be sustainable if the firm is not willing to expand capacity. In this case, the sales forecast must be limited to the sustainable level.

Estimating the price at which management expects the product to be sold completes the sales forecast. This estimate must take into consideration competitors' reactions to the firm's advertising and promotion strategies. Similarly, the division must factor in its own possible reactions to competitor strategies.

Inputs from various divisions may be needed to complete the financial plan for a particular division. For example, one of the firm's divisions may supply parts to several other divisions. The parts supplier will need the sales forecasts from other divisions to formulate its own production. On the other hand, the capacity of this division may be limited, which may require rationing of the output among the various divisions. This may force the affected divisions to revise their sales forecasts to match the supply of the product. The financial manager must ensure that the financial plans submitted from the various divisions are consistent with each other.

Finally, the sales forecast should take into consideration the effect of the expected inflation rate, as suggested by the forecast of macroeconomic variables. There are two ways to deal with inflation.

■ The **real-terms approach** proposes forecasting all the variables that enter the financial planning model in real terms. This means that the model will assume zero inflation and the results of the final plan will be obtained in real terms. The results can then be adjusted for inflation. For example, if net earnings during the first year are $10 million in real dollars, the earnings in nominal dollars will be $10 million multiplied by one plus the inflation rate. A major assumption of this method is that all variables are equally affected by inflation.

■ The **nominal-terms approach** suggests forecasting all the variables, including sales, operating costs, fixed financial obligations, and capital expenditures, in nominal dollars. As the results of the financial plan are expressed in nominal dollars, no adjustment is needed to the final results. The major advantage of this method is that it allows the financial analyst to apply different inflation rates to different variables. Its major drawback is that it requires the analyst to forecast an inflation rate for each variable of the financial plan.

Forecasting Operating Costs

Operating costs are generally divided between variable costs and fixed costs. Variable costs are those that change directly with unit sales. For example, increasing the sales of a bakery shop will require additional flour proportionate to the increase in unit sales. Similarly, increasing the output of a mining company may require increasing the number of employees to produce the ore.

Based on the expected volume of unit sales, the production department prepares a forecast of labour, materials, and other manufacturing requirements. Financial forecasting models often estimate total variable costs by assuming that costs per unit are fixed. Thus, total variable costs are equal to the unit cost multiplied by the number of units expected to be produced.

In contrast, fixed costs are defined as costs that do not vary directly with unit production. Fixed costs often include overhead expenses, such as

■ operating and maintaining the physical plant

■ economic depreciation (as opposed to accounting amortization) of plant and equipment

■ insurance costs

■ rental expense

■ wages, salaries, and benefits for the managerial and administrative staff

Each business unit is responsible for forecasting its own fixed costs that are required to keep the unit in operation. At the same time, each business unit has to pay a portion of general overhead expenses, such as the costs of the firm's accounting and tax departments, insurance, and executive salaries, which are not directly related to a particular unit. Such charges to the divisions are normally based on a formula to ensure fair allocation.

Most financial forecasting models assume that fixed costs stay unchanged over the planning horizon. It must be emphasized, however, that costs are fixed as long as unit sales do not change substantially. If the firm predicts substantial changes to sales, it may not be appropriate to treat any costs as fixed. For example, if sales are expected to double, the firm may have to build a new plant, buy equipment, or hire executives to run the new facilities. Generally, costs may be fixed over a range of unit sales but become variable as sales fall outside the range.

Estimates of variable and fixed costs are affected by inflation. As inflation rises, the pressure on wages and raw material prices increases variable costs. Moreover, the higher the inflation rate, the higher wage settlements and future prices of raw material will be. Similarly, inflation affects fixed costs, such as executive salaries, insurance, and costs of building a new plant. Thus, uncertainty about inflation makes forecasting operating costs a challenging task.

Forecasting Fixed Financial Obligations

Financial planning models are designed to forecast a firm's project financing requirements and to identify both internal and external funds to meet these financing needs. Debt obligations can be outstanding bonds, bank loans, or short-term securities. Bond indentures specify the timing and amount of interest as well as principal payments on bonds. Loan agreements contain similar information regarding outstanding bank debt. Given the specifications, it is relatively easy to forecast future cash flows required to service and repay long-term debt.

The process becomes more complicated when a firm is planning to raise new debt financing over the planning horizon. The firm must forecast the cost of new funds by estimating the amount of borrowing and the interest rate at the time when the debt will be raised. Indeed, one of the reasons for undertaking financial planning is to identify external financing requirements and determine how interest rates will affect these requirements over the long term.

Similarly, predicting the future costs of short-term borrowing, such as notes payable, corporate paper, and short-term bank loans, is complicated. The interest and principal payments on current short-term debt are known from the available information. Yet additional borrowing is likely to occur as new short-term debt is raised to replace old short-term debt. Forecasting the costs of borrowing in this case requires a forecast of interest rates over the entire planning horizon.

Leases are obligations that require the firm to make fixed cash payments. These payments need to be predicted and included in the financial planning model. Lease agreements specify the cash outflows required by the outstanding leases. Similar to the case of long-term debt, the difficulty is in predicting the costs of new leases that may be needed in the future.

Forecasting Future Capital Expenditures

The financial planning model must include allowances for planned future capital expenditures. Many approved projects require disbursements over several stages rather than one lump-sum payment at the beginning of the project. Most often, the approved capital budgets will contain enough information to help the financial analyst identify the period-by-period capital expenditure requirements. However, the capital expenditures of some projects may not be easy to predict for various reasons, such as inflation and changing industry conditions. The financial planning model must forecast and plan for these expenditures, as they represent future cash outflows.

Forecasting the Cash Flows Needed to Pay Dividends

Financial planning requires estimating the future cash flows needed to service preferred and common shares. Generally, corporations have outstanding common equity, and many of them have preferred-share capital. The financial planning model will indicate whether the firm will need additional outside equity financing over the planning horizon. The amount of money to be raised will be determined by the model, but the financial analyst has to determine whether the financing method should be the sale of common shares or preferred shares.

The financial planning model should plan for the payment of dividends. Forecasting existing preferred-share dividends may be a simple exercise. For most preferred shares, dividends are specified in the prospectus and they are often fixed over a long period of time.

If the preferred shares pay adjustable-rate dividends, estimating the cash flows requires a forecast of the rate that is the basis for the adjustment. For example, if the dividend rate on preferred shares is specified quarterly as the bank rate at the beginning of the quarter plus 2%, then predicting the dividend payments for a particular quarter requires the analyst to predict the bank rate at the beginning of that quarter.

If new preferred shares are planned, predicting the cash flows required to service these shares will be challenging because it will require forecasting the required rate on these shares. The rate on preferred shares often changes with interest rates.

The cash dividends of existing common shares can be forecasted based on the firm's dividend policy. As explained in Chapter 5, although dividends are discretionary, firms prefer to avoid dividend decreases. Therefore, it would be appropriate to assume that common dividends will stay constant over the planning horizon, allowing for changes only if there is an approved plan to change these dividends.

Similarly, if funds are expected to be raised by selling new common shares, the dividends per share will be fixed and equal to the current or expected dividends at the time of the issue. What will be uncertain is the number of shares that will have to be sold to raise the needed funds. For this purpose, the financial analyst must forecast the market price of the common shares at the future date when the share issue will be sold.

10.3 ROLE OF PRO FORMA FINANCIAL STATEMENTS

The firm's published financial statements include an income statement, a balance sheet, a cash flow statement, and accompanying notes to the financial statements. In preparing a financial plan, pro forma statements are required. This section describes the role of the pro forma income statement, balance sheet, and cash flow statement in financial planning.

Income Statement, Statement of Retained Earnings, and Balance Sheet

As explained in your financial accounting courses, the income statement reports the profit (or loss) of a business entity for a specific period of time, usually a year or a quarter. Net income is the difference between total revenues and total costs for the period. In addition, the income statement provides a breakdown of the costs into several categories:

- cost of goods sold, which includes direct costs of producing the goods that are sold (mainly labour and raw materials);

- other expenses incurred in operating the company, such as research and development expenditures, selling and administrative expenses, and income taxes; and

- financing costs, including interest paid to creditors.

A financial analyst can use the pro forma income statement to identify costs that are critical for future performance. The idea is to alert management to the significance of these costs and to indicate ways to control their impact. The income statement also enables the analyst to identify the impact of financing decisions on net income. Specifically, the analyst can determine the sensitivity of the firm's future net income to changes in the capital structure. For example, increasing debt will increase the interest payments to service the debt. Thus, a bigger portion of the firm's revenues will be needed to pay interest. The firm would be subject to higher risk of default should it experience a temporary drop in revenues.

The balance sheet reports the financial position of a business entity at a point in time. It is a critical indicator of the fundamental credit strength of a firm and its capability of financing itself. The balance sheet shows, on a historical cost basis, the assets of the firm, which are the productive resources utilized in its operations, and the liabilities and shareholders' equity of the firm, which are the total claims against the assets.

The pro forma balance sheets derived from the financial planning model show the changes in assets over the planning horizon. The balance sheet equation is:

$$\text{Assets} = \text{liabilities} + \text{shareholders' equity} \qquad \textbf{(Equation 10-1)}$$

Because the equality of the balance sheet equation must be satisfied at all times, the liabilities or equity, or both, have to be increased or decreased following changes in total assets. Forecasting the direction and the magnitude of the required changes in liabilities is one of the major goals of financial planning. Equally important, the financial analyst is interested in knowing whether it is more desirable to raise additional financing through debt or through equity. Analyzing the pro forma balance sheets enables the analyst to answer such questions.

The statement of retained earnings links the income statement with the balance sheet by providing the details of the changes to retained earnings. This would include dividends paid to the holders of the company's preferred and common shares, as well as the change caused by the net income or loss.

Both the pro forma income statement and the balance sheet are used to identify any weaknesses. This analysis gives the firm time to introduce measures to correct the weaknesses before they are reflected in actual results.

Cash Flow Statement

In recognition of the need of external users of accounting statements to have information concerning the investing and financing activities of the firm, the financial statements of profit-oriented enterprises include a cash flow statement along with the income statement and the balance sheet. More importantly, the flow of cash and cash equivalents between a business enterprise and investors, creditors, workers, and customers, serves as a fundamental starting point for analysis of the firm's capital investment projects, corporate acquisitions, and many other key long-term policy choices. Therefore, the cash flow statement plays an important role in the financial planning process.

The pro forma cash flow statement produced by the financial planning model indicates how the cash position of the firm will change during the planning horizon. Changes are caused by

- the portion of net income that is retained in the business
- changes in working capital accounts
- additional borrowing or repayments of debt
- additional issues or retirements of capital stock
- additions or disposals of capital assets

The cash flow statement breaks down the sources and uses of cash into three components:

- cash flows from operating activities, which are further divided between cash and non-cash items from operations
- cash flows from investing activities
- cash flows from financing activities

The cash flow statement is important for several reasons:

- *It identifies the cash generated from the firm's normal operating activities.* Because the cash flow statement takes the net income from the income statement and adds back any non-cash expenses, such as amortization, the cash from operations as measured by the cash flow statement is more indicative of the firm's ability to pay its cash obligations than the net income reported by the income statement.

- *It takes into account that the cash position will change because of changes in net working capital, which occur spontaneously with changes in sales.* For example, if sales increase, inventories, accounts receivable, and accounts payable also increase. However, because the increase in accounts payable is likely to be less than the increase in inventories and accounts receivable, some cash will be needed to finance the increase in net working capital. This information is not immediately available from the balance sheet.

- *It identifies and summarizes the likely changes in capital assets.* It reports any planned acquisitions and the cash needed to finance them. Also, it reports any planned dispositions and the cash generated. This information is not available from the pro forma balance sheet. The information is extremely important for financial planning, as analysts can study the consistency of the information with the projected sales. For example, if the financial plan were predicting a substantial increase in sales, the analyst would be alerted if no major capital expenditures were planned. The obvious question would be, are the new sales estimates justified if no expansions in capacity are planned?

■ *It summarizes the cash deficits or surpluses expected over the planning horizon.* It identifies the cash needed from external sources to support the plans. Indeed, this is one of the most important aspects of financial planning.

The Cash Flow Statement and the Interaction of the Firm's Decisions

Management's decisions on capital budgeting, capital structure, dividend policy, liquidity, financing, and liability management have an impact on the firm's cash position. The cash flow statement is useful in describing some of these interactions.

Interaction of Financing and Operating Decisions The principal net source of funds is the firm's operations. Firms must decide how much debt should be used to finance operations. This decision interacts with the decision to acquire capital assets. Net income is reported after making interest payments. The higher the amount of debt used by the firm, the higher the interest payments will be. Thus, higher operating profits will be needed to cover interest payments. This increases risk, particularly if sales are volatile and uncertain.

The choice of capital assets may contribute to the volatility of operating profits. For example, the choice of a capital-intensive production process may reduce costs over the long run, but will lead to a higher break-even point. This will magnify the volatility of operating profits as sales change.

The financial manager must decide on a proper trade-off between high reliance on capital-intensive processes and high reliance on debt financing. The cash flow statement provides a convenient framework to evaluate these interactions. The cash flows from operating activities should be the focus of the manager when evaluating the trade-offs. Indeed, operating profits alone need not be higher than the interest payments to service the debt. Cash flows from operations, which are operating profits plus amortization, must be greater.

Interaction of Sales Levels and the Volume of External Financing The cash flow statement indicates that a firm's external financing requirement is determined mainly as the difference between the planned capital budget and the amount of financing available from internal sources. Therefore, the higher the size of a firm's capital budget in relation to the amount of cash flows generated internally, the higher the amount of external financing needs will be.

In turn, the projected level of sales directly affects the capital budget. The higher the projected level of sales, the higher the capital budget is likely to be. There are several reasons for this conclusion:

■ Increased sales eventually require expansion in capacity and investment in new plant and equipment.

■ Higher production rates wear out machines more quickly and investment is needed to replace equipment.

■ Higher sales levels also require additional investment in working capital.

Interaction of Dividends and the Size and Mix of External Financing Net income can be distributed to the firm's shareholders or retained for reinvestment in the business. The division of net income between distributions to shareholders and retained earnings depends on several factors, such as the firm's dividend policy, pressing corporate needs for cash, future plans, future cash flows, and outlook and forecast issues. The amount of distribution interacts with both the amount and the mix of external financing requirements.

The higher the proportion of its net earnings that a firm distributes in dividends, the higher the external financing requirements will be. Minicase 10-2 illustrates this relationship. Note that the information used in this minicase is also used as the basis for Minicase 10-3.

MINICASE 10-2 RELATIONSHIP BETWEEN DIVIDEND POLICY AND EXTERNAL FINANCING NEEDS

Banana Moon Inc. (BMI) recorded $10 million in net earnings this year. The firm's dividend policy requires a payout ratio of 60% of earnings in dividends. The firm's expected cash needs for new investments are $6 million.

Question 1: How much should the firm raise in external financing?

$$\text{Retained earnings: } \$10 \times (1 - 0.60) = \$4 \text{ million}$$
$$\text{External financing needed: } \$6 - \$4 = \$2 \text{ million}$$

Question 2: If the firm changes its dividend policy to a 45% payout ratio, what would the external financing needs be?

$$\text{Retained earnings: } \$10 \times (1 - 0.45) = \$5.5 \text{ million}$$
$$\text{External financing needed: } \$6 - \$5.5 = \$0.5 \text{ million}$$

The firm's dividend policy also interacts with the capital structure decision. The higher the dividend payout ratio, the higher the proportion of external funds that must be raised in the form of equity will be. As retained earnings are equity, the larger the retention of earnings, the greater the amount of debt that can be raised without violating the capital structure constraint will be. Minicase 10-3 illustrates this relationship using the case of Banana Moon Inc.

MINICASE 10-3 RELATIONSHIP BETWEEN DIVIDEND POLICY AND CAPITAL STRUCTURE

BMI has a strict policy of financing its assets with 30% debt and 70% equity. Suppose BMI has recorded $10 million in net earnings and expected cash needs for new investments are $6 million.

Question 1: If BMI decides to keep its dividend policy unchanged, whereby 60% of earnings are paid in dividends, how much external equity financing should BMI raise?

BMI needs a total of $6 million for investments. Given the capital structure, 30% of this amount must be obtained from debt and the remainder from equity. Therefore, $1.8 million must be raised in debt and the remainder of $4.2 million must be equity. However, the firm already has $4 million in retained earnings to finance a portion of the required equity. Therefore, the amount of external equity financing must be $0.2 million.

Case Continued >

Question 2: If BMI decides to change its dividend policy to a 45% dividend payout ratio, how much external equity financing should BMI raise?

Again, BMI needs a total of $6 million for investments. Given the capital structure, 30% of this amount must be obtained from debt and the remainder from equity. Therefore, $1.8 million must be raised in debt and the remainder of $4.2 million must be equity. However, the firm already has $5.5 million in retained earnings to finance the required equity. Therefore, no external equity financing is required. Alternatively, the firm can use up to $1.3 million to repurchase some of the outstanding common shares.

Question 3: If the firm decides to keep all the additional equity capital and acquire more debt to finance new investments, how much more debt can it raise?

There is an extra $1.3 million in equity that can be used against any new debt issues to keep the capital structure constant. The proportion of equity in this structure is 70% and debt is 30%. Therefore, the debt-to-equity ratio is:

$$\frac{D}{E} = \frac{0.3}{0.7} = 0.4286$$

This ratio implies that:

$$D = 0.4286E$$

Thus, for every dollar of equity, the firm can raise $0.4286 in debt without affecting the capital structure. The amount of additional debt that can be raised is $0.557 million ($0.4286 \times$ $1.3 million).

In general, the total cash generated by the firm and the total cash used by the firm must be equal for any planning period. Sometimes, the firm will end up with a large cash balance in periods when cash inflows exceed outflows. Other times, the firm will draw down its cash balances or undertake short-term borrowing as cash outflows exceed cash inflows. These undesirable occurrences lead to inefficiencies that can be identified by the pro forma cash flow statement, allowing the financial manager to avoid them with proper financial planning. Moreover, studying the interactions of the various policies of the firm helps the financial manager to decide on a trade-off. The pro forma cash flow statement is very helpful for performing such analysis.

An important subset of planning is **cash management**. Cash management refers to the procedures, tools, and techniques that financial managers use to manage cash. The main objectives of cash management are to reduce the opportunity cost of holding idle cash, to ensure the firm's obligations are paid on time, and to collect payments as soon as they become due.

10.4 SHORT-TERM FINANCIAL PLANNING

Financial managers spend considerable time making short-term financial decisions, including decisions about:

- the amount of cash that should be kept on hand
- the amount of short-term borrowing that the firm should undertake

- the level of inventories that must be carried
- the amount of credit that the firm must extend

In your introductory finance course, you will have studied how to prepare cash budgets to determine future borrowing needs. This section extends the principles of cash budgeting. You study the purposes of cash budgeting, the reasons for the discrepancy between cash inflows and outflows, the methods of forecasting cash disbursements and collections, and other important aspects of cash budgeting. The emphasis is on the role of the financial manager as a decision maker. In this capacity, the manager must have a comprehensive understanding of the issues affecting the cash budgeting and planning process.

The cash budget is a part of the **short-term financial plan**, which is a detailed forecast of the income statement, cash flow statement, and balance sheet over the coming fiscal year. The short-term financial plan reflects the financial decisions that the firm is likely to make in the short run. Generally, plans are prepared for each quarter or month, depending on management preference and the complexity of the firm's situation. Short-term financial planning is designed to reflect seasonal factors that are generally overlooked in long-term planning models.

The short-term financial plan should be fully integrated with long-term financial planning. It is important to keep in mind that the short-term financial plan must be consistent with the projected results of the first year in the long-term financial plan. Essentially, the short-term plan is a detailed description of the coming fiscal year's results, as projected by the long-term financial planning process. For example, the quarterly or monthly income statements and cash flow statements should lead to the full year's statements. The balance sheet in the last sub-period of the short-term financial plan should be the same as the balance sheet of the first year in the long-term financial plan.

Short-term financial planning allows the firm to forecast its cash needs or surpluses over the short-term planning horizon. It identifies the expected cash receipts and estimates disbursements to predict surpluses and deficits.

Another objective of short-term financial planning is financial control. Management can review the performance of the firm at the end of each forecasting interval (month or quarter). If the actual results have deviated considerably from the forecasted results, the firm can adjust its financial or operating strategies to improve performance. For example, if costs are higher than expected, the firm will try to identify reasons for the increase and correct the problem. Fluctuations in sales are another reason that actual results may deviate from forecasted results. In this case, management may try to identify why sales are lower than expected and correct the problem.

Cash Budgeting

A **cash budget** is a planning schedule that summarizes cash receipts and cash disbursements over time. For the purposes of cash management, the cash budget identifies potential financing requirements (lack of cash) or investment opportunities (excess cash). For most firms, the cash budget is an integral part of the short-term financial plan and as such should be consistent with the long-term financial plan.

The frequency with which a cash budget is updated varies from one firm to another, depending on the firm's size and the degree of uncertainty about its cash disbursements and receipts. Generally, large firms update their cash budgets more frequently than smaller firms. Also, firms that experience high uncertainty regarding cash receipts and disbursements tend to update their cash budgets frequently.

The time horizon over which a cash budget is prepared also varies from one firm to another. In practice, firms prepare cash budgets daily, weekly, semi-monthly, or monthly to forecast cash receipts and disbursements two to three months into the future.

For long-term cash budgets of one year or more, annual income statements, balance sheets, and cash flow forecasts are used for the desired horizon. Long-term cash budgets are generated from statements that cover intervals of a year, half-year, quarter, or month.

In contrast, short-term cash budgets, which are updated daily, weekly, or semi-monthly, and span one month to three months or less, rely on subjective estimates of cash receipts and disbursements. Often, a computer program is developed to generate the disbursement schedule and the patterns of small receipts and disbursement clearing. The computer program should incorporate any known large periodic and specific cash inflows and outflows. Daily budgets are often prepared by large firms to forecast short-term financing needs and the availability of cash for overnight deposit or short-term investments.

Purposes of Cash Budgeting Cash budgeting plays a crucial role in financial planning. It enables the firm to predict when and how much cash will be needed. This information helps the firm in planning to pay employees, suppliers, and creditors. Cash budgeting also allows the firm to plan for cash receipts from customers and to prepare for future external financing, if needed. Short-term financing sources include selling commercial paper or bankers' acceptances in the money market and borrowing from banks. Maintaining good working relationships with banks makes it easier for firms to obtain short-term financing.

Essentially, the cash budget enables the firm to monitor closely its sources and uses of cash and to plan the management of these cash inflows and outflows in a timely fashion and at an acceptable cost.

As mentioned in the previous section, the objective of cash management is to minimize the opportunity cost of holding cash balances. In addition, the firm should maintain a reasonable degree of flexibility to obtain funds and meet unexpected needs for cash.

Reasons for the Discrepancy between Cash Receipts and Disbursements
The need for cash budgeting arises primarily from the difference in timing between cash inflows and cash outflows. Exhibit 10-2 illustrates the cash conversion cycle and its components for a typical retailing firm.

The **inventory conversion period** represents the average period of time that elapses between the purchase of raw materials and the sales of finished goods to a customer. Formally, it is calculated as:

$$\text{Inventory conversion period} = \frac{\text{average inventory}}{\left(\dfrac{\text{cost of goods sold}}{365}\right)} \quad \textbf{(Equation 10-2)}$$

The **receivables conversion period** refers to the average period of time elapsing between credit sales to a customer and the receipt of cash from that customer in payment of the customer's account.

$$\text{Receivables conversion period} = \frac{\text{average accounts receivable}}{\left(\dfrac{\text{annual credit sales}}{365}\right)} \quad \textbf{(Equation 10-3)}$$

Exhibit 10-2 Components of the Cash Conversion Cycle

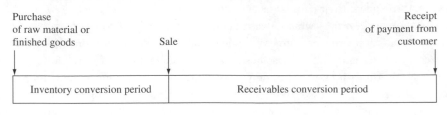

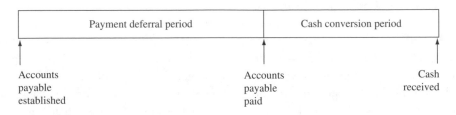

The sum of the inventory conversion period and the receivables conversion period is known as the **operating cycle**.

The purchase of goods gives rise to accounts payable. Payables are typically paid before the firm receives payment from customers. The length of time over which payables are outstanding depends on such factors as payables management policy, supplier's trade credit policies, and the availability of discounts for early payment. Moreover, hourly and salaried employees must be paid as provided by the agreement between the firm and its employees and on a regular basis. The **payables deferral period** refers to the average period of time elapsing between a credit purchase from a supplier and the issuance of the payment for that account.

$$\text{Payables deferral period} = \frac{\text{average accounts payable} + \text{average accruals}}{\left(\dfrac{\text{cost of goods sold}}{365}\right)} \qquad \textbf{(Equation 10-4)}$$

The **cash conversion period** represents the average period of time elapsing between the payment of a supplier and the actual point that payment from sales is received. It shows how long the firm has to wait to receive cash from sales after paying the obligations that produced these sales. During this period, the firm has to use cash from equity or debt to finance the payment of these obligations. Thus:

$$\text{Cash conversion period} = \text{inventory conversion period} + \text{receivables conversion period} - \text{payables deferral period} \qquad \textbf{(Equation 10-5)}$$

Exhibit 10-2 is a simplified illustration of the cash inflow and outflow over time. The inventory conversion period represents the average time it takes the firm to order the inventory and sell it. The receivables conversion period indicates the time it takes the firm to collect on credit sales. In other words, it is the average time it takes customers to pay for purchases. The operating cycle represents the time that elapses between ordering the inventory and collecting cash from selling the inventory.

Net working capital, which is the difference between current assets and current liabilities, can be estimated from the accounts of both the balance sheet and the income statement. The following components are included in the estimation:

- current assets and current liabilities used to finance the cost of goods sold and credit sales (the levels of these assets and liabilities are determined by the inventory conversion [IC], receivables conversion [RC], and payables deferral [PD] periods)
- the average cash level
- current liabilities (e.g., average notes payable and the current portion of long-term debt) that are not used to finance the cost of goods sold

Thus, net working capital is estimated by the following equation:

$$
NWC = \left[(IC - PD) \times \frac{COGS}{365} \right]
$$

$$
+ \left(RC \times \frac{CS}{365} \right) + AC - ANP - CPLD \quad \textbf{(Equation 10-6)}
$$

where

$$
\begin{aligned}
NWC &= \text{net working capital} \\
IC &= \text{inventory conversion period} \\
PD &= \text{payables deferral period} \\
COGS &= \text{cost of goods sold} \\
RC &= \text{receivables conversion period} \\
CS &= \text{yearly credit sales} \\
AC &= \text{average cash level} \\
ANP &= \text{average notes payable} \\
CPLD &= \text{current portion of long-term debt}
\end{aligned}
$$

The effectiveness of the cash manager in shortening the cash conversion period depends on decisions made by other managers in the organization. The cash manager must interact with other functions in the organization, including inventory management, credit management, and payables management. Consequently, internal conflicts may arise in managing the overall cash flow of the organization. The management of the different functions has an impact on the asset accounts of cash, inventories, and accounts receivable. The impact is also reflected in the liability side of the balance sheet. A weak cash flow forces the firm to rely on notes payable, long-term debt, or equity to finance current assets.

The problem with management of the cash conversion period is that the boundaries of authority are disjointed and overlapping. For example, cash managers are concerned with float once the cheque is in the mail but do not generally work with the credit managers in dealing with the credit period and past due accounts, which tends to be the largest part of float. **Float** is the time that elapses between the time the payor forwards a cheque and the time the payee receives the cash.

On the disbursements side, at least two functional departments contribute to the length of time purchases stay unpaid. Essentially, the purchasing manager negotiates the purchase terms and the payables manager decides how long to stretch the payables.

The dilemma for the corporation is that there is no one manager responsible for all the functions that affect the cash flows to and from the firm. One solution may be to have the managers of the various functions cross-trained in the other jobs so that they have a good understanding of how the pieces fit together. This may open lines of communications and, in the long run, facilitate the flow of cash within the organization.

In practice, the level of a firm's cash flows is affected by decisions regarding inventory, payables, credit, and receivables policies. As these policies or practices change, the relative timing of cash inflows and outflows changes. Because the cash conversion cycle may not be sensitive to these policy decisions, the preparation of a cash budget will show the impact of these policies on the pattern of cash inflows and outflows.

In addition, product sales occur randomly throughout the operating cycle. Some sales are made in cash, while others are made on credit. The payment of credit sales also occurs somewhat unpredictably after purchases.

Minicase 10-4 shows how financial statement accounts are used to identify and quantify sources of discrepancy between cash receipts and cash disbursements. The use of the cash conversion cycle provides information on how a firm's decisions regarding inventory, payables, credit, and receivables policies affect cash inflows and outflows.

MINICASE 10-4 ILLUSTRATION OF THE CASH CONVERSION CYCLE

The financial statements of Well Dressers Stores (WDS) are provided in Exhibits 10-3 and 10-4.

Exhibit 10-3
Well Dressers Stores Income Statement
Year Ended December 31, 20X1 ($ Thousands)

Sales	$17,550[1]
Cost of goods sold	12,750
Gross margin	4,800
Selling and administrative costs	
Wages	1,700
Advertising expenses	1,225
Income before interest and taxes	1,875
Interest	865
Income before taxes	1,010
Income taxes (@ 40%)	404
Net income	$ 606

[1] 75% of sales are credit sales.

Case Continued >

Exhibit 10-4
Well Dressers Stores Balance Sheet December 31, 20X1 ($ Thousands)

Assets	20X1	20X0	Liabilities	20X1	20X0
Current assets			**Current liabilities**		
Cash	$ 125	$ 115	Accounts payable	$ 730	$ 650
Accounts receivable	800	700	Accrued expenses	130	120
Inventory	1,000	900	Notes payable	695	645
	1,925	1,715		1,555	1,415
Capital assets	1,740	1,640	**Long-term liabilities**		
			Long-term debt	950	950
Total assets	$3,665	$3,355			
			Shareholders' equity	1,160	990
			Total liabilities and shareholders' equity	$3,665	$3,355

Question 1: What is the inventory conversion period?

Average inventory (thousands): ($900 + $1,000) ÷ 2 = $950

Inventory conversion period:

$$\frac{\$950}{\left(\frac{\$12,750}{365}\right)} = 27.20 \text{ days} = 27 \text{ days (rounded)}$$

Question 2: What is the receivables conversion period?

Average receivables (thousands): ($700 + $800) ÷ 2 = $750
Credit sales (thousands): $17,550 × 0.75 = $13,162.5
Receivables conversion period:

$$\frac{\$750}{\left(\frac{\$13,162.50}{365}\right)} = 20.80 \text{ days} = 21 \text{ days (rounded)}$$

Question 3: What is the operating cycle?

Operating cycle: 27 + 21 = 48 days

Question 4: What is the payables deferral period?

Average payables (thousands): ($650 + $730) ÷ 2 = $690
Average accruals (thousands): ($120 + $130) ÷ 2 = $125
Payables deferral period:

$$\frac{\$690 + \$125}{\left(\frac{\$12,750}{365}\right)} = 23.33 \text{ days} = 23 \text{ days (rounded)}$$

Case Continued >

Question 5: What is the cash conversion period?

$$\text{Cash conversion period: } 27 + 21 - 23 = 25 \text{ days}$$

Question 6: Use Equation 10-6 to estimate the *average* net working capital for WDS over the 20X1 fiscal year.

$$\text{Average cash: } (\$125 + \$115) \div 2 = \$120$$
$$\text{Average notes payable: } (\$645 + \$695) \div 2 = \$670$$

$$\text{NWC: } \left[(27.20 - 23.33) \times \frac{\$12,750}{365}\right] + \left(20.80 \times \frac{\$13,162.50}{365}\right) + \$120 - \$670$$

$$= \$135.18 + \$750.08 + \$120 - \$670 = \$335.26 = \$335 \text{ (rounded)}$$

Thus, WDS's average net working capital over the 20X1 fiscal year is approximately $335,000.

Question 7: What is the *actual* average net working capital for WDS over the 20X1 fiscal year?

Net working capital at year end (thousands): $1,925 − $1,555 = $370

Net working capital at beginning of the year (thousands): $1,715 − $1,415 = $300

Average net working capital (thousands): ($370 + $300) ÷ 2 = $335

Thus, WDS's actual average net working capital over the 20X1 fiscal year is $335,000.

Steps in Cash Budgeting Cash budgeting comprises several activities:

- Estimating the cash outflows needed to meet operating expenses, cover capital expenditures, service outstanding debt payments and preferred-share dividends, pay taxes, and pay common-share dividends. The forecast should take into consideration the size and timing of the cash flows and any seasonal fluctuations in the firm's operational activities.

- Estimating the timing and amounts of cash inflows from cash sales and from collections on accounts receivable. Again, any seasonal fluctuations in the operational activities should be considered in the sales forecast.

- Calculating the difference between the cash inflows and cash outflows to project the amount of daily cash surpluses or deficits. The cash manager determines how to deal with the outcome.

  - In the case of a surplus, the manager must decide whether to make investments in short-term securities, reduce outstanding debt, or take advantage of special purchasing opportunities.

  - In the case of a deficit, the manager will decide the short-term borrowing strategy and whether it is possible to take advantage of any special opportunities.

  - In the case of firms involved in international activities, the cash budget will identify the foreign currency inflows and outflows to allow the manager to plan foreign-exchange hedging transactions.

The first two activities require forecasting the cash inflows and outflows. There are several methods of forecasting.

Direct Forecasting Method The **direct forecasting method** forecasts cash by dividing the forecast period into equal time periods and estimating receipts and disbursements on a category-by-category basis for each period. Major characteristics of this method are as follows:

- It divides the forecast period into equal periods, such as days, weeks, or months, and makes detailed estimates of cash receipts and cash disbursements category by category over the periods.

- It relies on subjective estimates of cash receipts and disbursements. Often, a computer program is developed to generate the disbursement schedule, pattern of small receipts, and pattern of disbursement clearing. The computer program should incorporate knowledge of any large periodic and specific cash inflows and outflows.

- It is used by large firms that prepare cash budgets daily, weekly, or semi-monthly. For frequent forecasts, methods that incorporate management's judgment provide more accurate forecasts than those produced by mechanical or quantitative forecasting methods. The firm's money managers have the time and information to consider all the consequences carefully and to change the forecast based on daily inputs and information.

- It is often used by small businesses. In this case, the cash receipts and disbursements are few in number and the entrepreneur or small business manager can use up-to-date information to change the forecast frequently.

- It is preferable when the firm is small or medium-sized or when sales per order are large and may be accurately forecasted. For example, an airplane manufacturer may use this method, as cash inflows are fairly predictable. The method may also be suitable when cash flows vary considerably from one period to another.

Distribution Method There are many other methods for forecasting cash flows. The following article by James S. Sagner describes the "distribution method." This method is suggested for health care providers in the United States but may also be suitable for service firms.

TREASURY MANAGEMENT: A SIMPLE CASH FORECASTING PROCEDURE

James S. Sagner, PhD

A principal objective of treasury management forecasting is to optimize the sources and uses of a healthcare organization's funds by minimizing bank balances and borrowings. Additional objectives are to help develop financial strategies and to prevent illiquidity, insolvency, or embarrassment.

Treasury management forecasting is accomplished by developing timely information on collected funds positions at an organization's bank and on expected receipts and/or disbursements of large amounts of cash. Too many organizations merely examine present bank balances, determine cash disbursements from check clearing data and expected wire transfers, and invest the balance overnight.

Various statistical procedures to aid in treasury management forecasting are available to treasury managers, including regression, time series, and other sophisticated techniques, as noted in Exhibit 1.

Exhibit 1
Statistical Procedures Used in Treasury Management Forecasting

Time frame	Purpose	Recommended procedures
Long term	To develop financial strategies using debt and equity and to ration capital among alternative projects	Percentage-of-sales or regression, to correlate financial requirements with known independent variables using naïve or sophisticated techniques
Intermediate term	To budget cash as affected by seasonable influences	Cash budgeting to determine monthly status of cash, to arrange for cash sources or postpone expenditures
Short term	To calculate immediate (overnight) position and organization's response	Determine opening position, add/subtract daily activity, and invest/borrow the remainder until the next day

---

The Distribution Method

Treasury managers have had considerable success in forecasting regular cash collection activity using a relatively naive procedure called "the distribution method." Users of this procedure assume that there are repetitive patterns of cash activity by day of the week and day of the month. To develop data for the distribution method, it is necessary to compile actual receipts for two or three months. These data then are analyzed two ways: the percentage of total monthly receipts by business day of the week and the percentage of total monthly receipts collected each business date of the month.

Treasury managers may determine, for example, that an organization experiences its highest level of mailed receipts on Mondays (30 percent, which is typical for many businesses in the United States) and a fairly even distribution the rest of the week.

At the same time, a treasury manager's analysis may show a high collection day on the 1st and 15th business dates of the month, with no particular pattern during the remainder of that month.

Assume that forecast revenues for April 1995, based on the percentage-of-sales or regression methods, are $3.5 million. April 5th, a Wednesday, is the third business day of the month. The factor for that date would be 15 percent (day of the week) times .05 (day of the month), or .0075. That factor then would be multiplied by the expected revenues for the month, or as a surrogate, the revenue experience of the preceding month, so long as no corrective factors must be used for delayed receivables or other changes. The forecast cash inflow for April 5th would be $26,250.

The distribution method of forecasting cash collection activity can be used to look ahead several weeks. A treasury manager would then add anticipated nonregular flows, such as the proceeds of new financing or the sale of equipment. Outflow projections, which are usually based on forecasts of daily check clearings or from the daily controlled disbursements presentment, would be subtracted along with any nonregular payments such as taxes or debt repayment.

The development of a short-term forecasting capability assists in improving the financial performance of healthcare organizations. Bank balances and borrowings are minimized and, in periods of a normal shaped (upward sloping) interest yield curve, investment returns are increased.

James S. Sagner, PhD, is executive vice-president, Sagner/Marks, Inc., a treasury and cash management consulting firm in Chicago, Illinois. Readers' comments and questions are welcome and should be addressed to him at Sagner/Marks, Inc., 117 N. Jefferson Street, Suite 201, Chicago, Illinois, 60661-2306.

Source: Reprinted with permission from *Healthcare Financial Management,* April 1995, copyright Healthcare Financial Management Associaton.

The article describes the steps of the distribution method of forecasting cash receipts as follows:

1. Divide the sources of receipts between regular and non-regular. Regular receipts are those anticipated from normal sales. Non-regular receipts are those anticipated from new financing, sale of assets, or large sales orders.

2. Compile data on actual regular receipts for two to three months.

3. Analyze the data by determining the percentage of receipts paid on each day of the week and each day of the month. The set of percentages is called the distribution of payments. For example, the cash manager may determine that of each month's sales, 5% will be collected on the 14th of the month.

4. Forecast the sales per month for the desirable forecast horizon and use the distribution determined in step 3 to determine the cash receipts anticipated during a particular day of the month. For example, if the sales forecast indicates that next month's sales are expected to be $50,000, the forecast for the 14th of the month will be cash receipts of $2,500.

5. Add the anticipated cash inflows from non-regular items.

In principle, a similar procedure can be developed for cash disbursements. However, the process is most appropriate for transactions that are frequent and uncertain. Also, it assumes that transactions show repetitive patterns over time. The cash disbursements for small item purchases are an example of where such a procedure may be effective in forecasting disbursements. However, firms with good cash control systems may have enough data to predict cash disbursements more accurately than can be done using the distribution method.

Estimating Cash Disbursements When estimating cash disbursements, it is important to separately estimate cash from large transactions and cash from small or high-volume transactions. Large transactions include such items as major capital expenditures, repayment of debt, acquisitions, and common-share dividends and repurchases. Large transactions should be carefully forecasted as they involve large sums of money that cannot be raised on short notice. Small errors in estimating large items can lead to large deviations in the forecast and substantial unexpected needs for cash.

In contrast, small or high-volume transactions include accounts payable in connection with raw materials and supplies, cash purchases, wage and salary expenses, accrued taxes and other liabilities, interest, professional services, health and retirement benefits, and insurance. Generally, these transactions involve small amounts of cash and recur frequently. They can be estimated from past experience because the risk that the actual cash outflows will deviate considerably from the forecast is minor compared with the risk associated with forecasting large transactions.

Forecasting cash disbursements is simplified by the firm's control over the timing of cash payments. For example, the firm determines when to make payment for the purchase of raw materials based on the payment terms the vendor offers. The purchaser may decide to pay promptly if the vendor offers a discount for prompt payment. Firms often maintain computerized payables files that provide a daily record of the firm's payments due on approved invoices.

Similarly, firms set payroll dates and can forecast cash requirements with a high degree of accuracy. Cash required to meet accrued liabilities can also be forecasted with little error. Fluctuations occur as a result of changes in the firm's level of activity.

Estimating Cash Receipts   Similarly to cash outflows, cash receipts should be forecasted separately depending on whether they are from large transactions or smaller and more frequent ones. Relatively large transactions include such items as the sale of capital assets, issuance of securities, and large wholesale transactions. These cash flows should be estimated item by item. Generally, a firm has some control over these items, which can be predicted with a high level of accuracy.

Small or high-volume transactions include cash sales and collections on accounts receivable. The firm can estimate the cash inflows from these items by relying on past experience.

Payment Pattern Method of Forecasting Cash Receipts from Sales   Collections on accounts receivable are normally estimated by assuming that past behaviour will extend into the future. The **payment pattern method** forecasts cash receipts based on an analysis of historical customer payment patterns. The historical pattern is assumed to correctly represent seasonal fluctuations. The following minicase illustrates this approach.

MINICASE 10-5 PATTERN OF RECEIVABLES COLLECTION AND FORECASTED CASH COLLECTION

Northern United Timber (NUT) is a medium-sized manufacturing company. The firm has slightly seasonal demand in that sales peak between November and February. Exhibit 10-5 shows the pattern of receivables collection for NUT over the period January 20X1 to January 20X2.

Question 1: Briefly describe the pattern of collections for NUT.

The firm sells on credit with only a small portion of receivables collected in the same month as sales (current). A maximum of 9.6% of sales (November) will be

Case Continued >

Exhibit 10-5
Pattern of Receivables Collection

Month of sale	Current	+1	+2	+3	+4	Uncollected
		Receivables collected in month				
January 20X1	4.75%	82.25%	7.20%	2.75%	1.40%	1.65%
February	7.65	84.45	3.21	2.10	1.20	1.39
March	3.45	81.65	4.56	6.50	1.80	2.04
April	5.25	86.78	5.08	1.20	0.75	0.94
May	8.35	83.28	4.20	2.14	0.96	1.07
June	6.00	85.18	6.71	1.37	0.55	0.19
July	6.50	80.93	4.48	3.45	3.00	1.64
August	4.70	82.83	3.65	4.06	3.35	1.41
September	5.80	88.15	4.56	0.75	0.25	0.49
October	7.40	87.45	2.95	1.12	0.65	0.43
November	9.60	83.35	3.85	0.55	1.17	1.48
December	6.70	82.15	5.23	3.05	1.42	1.45
January 20X2	4.75	82.25	7.20	2.75	1.40	1.65

collected in the same month. The major portion of NUT's sales (more than 80%) is paid for in the month following the month of sales (+1). Receivables that remain outstanding after the second month are paid in the following three months. Exhibit 10-5 shows that NUT experiences bad debts every month, represented by the percentage of receivables that will never be collected.

Question 2: John is the cash manager of NUT. He is required to produce a cash budget for the 20X2 fiscal year, which starts January 1. He needs to forecast cash receipts from sales. Exhibit 10-6 shows NUT's actual sales levels during 20X1 and forecasted sales levels for each month of the 20X2 year.

What are NUT's monthly forecasted cash collections for 20X2?

Assuming that the historical pattern of collections for NUT will continue in the future, John can use the information in Exhibits 10-5 and 10-6 to estimate the monthly cash collections expected during 20X2. Exhibit 10-7 shows the monthly estimated cash collections for NUT in 20X2 based on the given information.

The cash collections during a particular month are a result of sales during that month and sales from four prior months. For example, the cash collections expected during January 20X2 include:

- 4.75% of January sales (20X2)
- 82.15% of December sales (20X1)
- 3.85% of November sales (20X1)
- 1.12% of October sales (20X1)
- 0.25% of September sales (20X1)

Case Continued >

Exhibit 10-6
Sales over the Past Year and the Upcoming Year's Forecasted Sales ($ Millions)

Month	Actual year's sales in 20X1	Forecasted sales for the coming year
January	$20.00	$21.00
February	19.00	20.00
March	18.00	19.00
April	17.00	19.50
May	17.50	19.50
June	18.50	20.00
July	19.00	20.50
August	19.00	21.00
September	19.10	21.50
October	20.00	22.00
November	21.00	22.00
December	21.50	23.00

Exhibit 10-7
Estimated Cash Collections over the Next 12 Months

Month of sale	Current	−1	−2	−3	−4	Total collections ($ millions)
			Collections from sales of month			
January	1.00	17.66	0.81	0.22	0.05	$19.74
February	1.53	17.27	1.12	0.12	0.13	20.17
March	0.66	16.89	1.51	0.66	0.25	19.97
April	1.02	15.51	0.64	0.58	0.31	18.06
May	1.63	16.92	0.87	0.42	0.29	20.13
June	1.20	16.24	0.99	1.24	0.24	19.91
July	1.33	17.04	0.82	0.23	0.34	19.76
August	0.99	16.59	1.34	0.42	0.15	19.49
September	1.25	17.39	0.92	0.27	0.19	20.02
October	1.63	18.95	0.77	0.71	0.11	22.17
November	2.11	19.24	0.98	0.85	0.62	23.80
December	1.54	18.34	0.65	0.16	0.70	21.39

Combining this information for January yields:

January 20X2 collections

$$= (0.0475 \times \$21.00) + (0.8215 \times \$21.50) + (0.0385 \times \$21.00)$$
$$+ (0.0112 \times \$20.00) + (0.0025 \times \$19.10)$$
$$= \$19.74 \text{ million}$$

The process of forecasting collections as described uses a simple approach. With a spreadsheet or specialized application, the cash manager can increase the sophistication of the process in at least three ways.

- If a firm has different divisions or products, it is necessary to estimate the payment pattern for each to test for variations. Forecasting the payment pattern for each division enables the manager to forecast deviations more accurately.

- Statistical estimation procedures could be used to study the variability of the percentages in Exhibit 10-5. The cash manager can then identify a range of likely values for the collections rather than just a single-point estimate.

- It is important for a firm using the historical pattern approach to continually monitor payment patterns in order to detect significant changes and update the pattern percentages. The set of percentages is determined by economic factors that may change from one period to the next.

The main advantage of the payment pattern method is its simplicity. It starts with an estimate of sales over the planning horizon and uses past experience to estimate cash inflows and outflows. If the payment patterns are predictable and likely to be repeated from one period to another, the method will produce relatively accurate forecasts.

The main disadvantage of the method is its reliance on past experience, which may not be indicative of future behaviour. Moreover, the method uses averages, which makes it inaccurate when the actual cash flows deviate widely around the mean. Without proper adjustments, the method may ignore seasonal changes in payment patterns.

Minimum Operating Cash Balance The **minimum operating cash balance** is the minimum level of cash that a firm holds under normal circumstances. Firms may have more than one motive for holding cash balances:

- The **speculative motive** is the need to take advantage of bargain opportunities, such as discount sales, attractive interest rates, and favourable foreign-exchange rate fluctuations.

- The **precautionary motive** is the need for a financial reserve to meet contingent cash needs as they arise. Cash reserves insure the firm against the risk of failing to pay creditors, suppliers, or employees as payments come due. This risk is often called **liquidity risk**.

- The **transaction motive** is the need to have cash on hand to pay specific bills or is the result of the non-voluntary holding of cash because of the timing of collections. As cash inflows (collections) and outflows (disbursements) are not perfectly synchronized, a firm will often have idle cash. The recent advent of electronic funds transfers and other high-speed, paperless payment mechanisms makes the transaction motive for holding cash substantially weaker than it was a few years ago. Thus, the minimum operating cash balances held by firms for transaction purposes are steadily shrinking in size and approaching zero.

- Another motive is the need for **compliance with loan covenants**, which may require compensating balances. Some lenders require the borrowing firm to keep a specified sum of cash on deposit with the lender as a compensating balance. You learned about the purpose of compensating balances and their impact on the effective rate of borrowing in Section 3.1.

Factors that reduce the need for a large cash balance include:

- The firm's ability to borrow: There can be speculative and precautionary needs for liquidity but not for cash. Firms can arrange open lines of credit or similar facilities to borrow instantly from banks, or they can hold marketable securities to satisfy these motives.

- Firm size: For large firms, **trading costs**, the transaction costs of buying and selling securities, are very small when compared with the opportunity costs of holding cash. Thus, they tend to hold less cash and more marketable securities. In addition, large firms are likely to have more borrowing flexibility than small firms.

- Costs of holding cash: Such opportunity costs include the interest income that could be earned if the cash were invested at least in marketable securities or bank deposits.

The minimum operating cash balance is the optimal and lowest possible cash balance that satisfies short-term cash needs without impeding the firm's ability to make payments and without holding large balances in low- or zero-interest accounts. Determining the minimum operating cash balance entails considering the trade-off between the opportunity costs of holding too much cash (the carrying costs) and the costs of holding too little (the shortage costs). The shortage costs are the expenses associated with arranging a loan or the trading costs associated with selling securities to raise cash.

Annual Cash Budget

The annual cash budget typically includes a monthly breakdown of cash inflows and outflows. The budget summarizes the major activities of the firm and where cash will be generated or used by the activity. This was fully illustrated in your earlier finance course. It is important to remember when constructing a cash budget that management usually sets a minimum balance of cash and securities that must be maintained. Cash surpluses will usually be used to make repayments on short-term financing to improve financial flexibility in the short term.

The annual cash budget will provide a summary of the uses and sources of cash that occur within the firm's three major areas of activity: operating, investing, and financing. It acts as a short-term planning tool, enabling management to forecast cash needs over the coming fiscal year.

Sophisticated budgets may include a monthly breakdown of activities over the entire year and a daily account of cash transactions over at least the first month. A firm needs to be able to monitor its cash position on a daily basis. Large firms will always supplement the annual cash budget with a more detailed one-month moving budget that forecasts cash requirements and cash availability and is updated daily or at least weekly.

In practice, each firm tailors its annual cash budget to suit its particular circumstances. However, cash budgets will contain many of the following features:

- The factors affecting the cash and marketable securities account are divided into operating factors, cash dividends, investment activities, and financing activities.

- Cash and marketable securities are shown at the beginning and at the end of each period. The balance at the beginning of a period is equal to the balance at the end of the prior period unless the firm resets the cash budget periodically to a given level.

- The impact of each set of factors on cash and marketable securities is reported on a monthly basis for the first quarter and on a quarterly basis for the entire year. As indicated earlier, some firms may include a one-month moving budget for the first month, which reports activities on a daily basis.

- A well-constructed cash budget will show the relationship between the cash budget and the firm's operating budget. For example, if the firm's operating results are weaker than forecasted in the operating budget, the cash provided by operations will be less than forecasted. A cash budget based on the pro forma cash flow statement incorporates the long-term financing decisions of the firm, which include the dividend policy and the capital budget. It shows how a change in the firm's operating cash flows affects the funds available for dividends or investment activities. These results may require an increase in financing or a reduction in cash and marketable securities.

The Cash Budget and Financial Control

Financial control is the practice of monitoring the firm's progress in relationship to the overall financial plan and cash budget. One of the objectives of the cash budget and financial planning is to detect variances between forecasted and actual performance. Financial control entails analyzing the variances and prescribing corrective actions.

The cash budget can provide an early warning signal if corporate performance is not going to be as expected. If variances are detected in the cash budget, the reasons are likely to be variances in the operating budget. The firm can initiate corrective actions at all levels to ensure that expected performance will be achieved.

10.5 THE LONG-TERM AND SHORT-TERM FINANCING DECISIONS

This section focuses on the trade-offs that management makes in determining what portion of working capital will be financed with short-term notes payable and what portion will be financed with long-term debt. This will have been covered in detail in your introductory finance course. This section will provide a brief review.

From your introductory finance course, you will know that net working capital refers to the difference between current assets and current liabilities. In other words, net working capital can be viewed as the portion of current assets that is financed with long-term debt. The amount of short-term financing that a firm obtains from accrued liabilities and accounts payable is sometimes called **spontaneous financing**. Increases in spontaneous financing decrease the need to borrow to finance current assets.

Notes payable are the short-term financing arrangements that the firm makes to finance the difference between current assets and spontaneous financing. The amount of notes payable is under the control of management, which may decide its size and mix.

Risk-Return Trade-Off between Short-Term and Long-Term Financing

The decision to finance assets with long- or short-term financing requires a risk-return trade-off. Reliance on short-term financing exposes the firm to the liquidity risk of being unable to pay the firm's maturing debt or other obligations because of a shortage in liquid assets. In principle, this risk is minimized when the firm is financed completely with equity. The firm declares dividends only if it has enough cash to pay them and is not obligated to repay the initial investment to shareholders.

When a firm has only long-term debt financing in its capital structure, the need for liquid assets exists. The firm is obligated to pay periodic interest on the debt. Also, debt contracts may require the firm to pay portions of the principal periodically either to a sinking fund or directly to the lender. These are reported on the balance sheet as the current portion of long-term debt. However, the risk of a cash shortage with small amounts of long-term debt is low compared with the risk when the debt portion of financing is entirely short term. Interest payments are normally made from net cash flows. In situations where the long-term debt is small relative to the assets of the firm, a small portion of current revenues may be sufficient to meet the interest payments.

The current portion of long-term debt is reported in the current liabilities section. It indicates the principal repayments on the firm's long-term debt that will come due during the next reporting period. If the firm accumulates enough cash to pay back the debt as it matures, it will repay the maturing portions without any risk of a cash shortage. However, most firms are likely to raise the cash needed to retire maturing debt by selling new debt or equity securities. In this case, the risk is that the firm may not be able to raise, on reasonable terms, the necessary funds to repay the maturing portion.

As a firm uses short-term debt to finance its assets, the likelihood of incurring liquidity problems increases. The firm's debt payment obligations include the current portion of long-term debt plus the obligation to repay short-term debt. The firm will have additional difficulties in meeting all the obligations from revenues or new borrowing. Essentially, liquidity risk increases as a firm relies increasingly on short-term financing. Ultimately, the firm faces the highest level of liquidity risk when it uses only short-term funds and equity capital to finance its assets.

Given that using short-term funds to finance assets involves higher risk, why are firms tempted to rely on short-term financing? Generally, there are higher costs when a firm borrows long term. The yield curve is most often upward sloping, which means that the interest cost is generally less on short-term borrowing than on long-term borrowing. Therefore, when determining the mix between short-term and long-term liabilities, management must weigh the net costs against the value of reducing liquidity risk.

Approaches to Short-Term and Long-Term Financing Decisions

The two basic approaches to making short-term and long-term financing decisions are the hedging approach and the risk management approach.

When management wishes to completely avoid liquidity risk, it can follow a hedging approach to financing. This approach is based on the principle of matching the maturities of the firm's assets and liabilities. It is similar to the principle of funding gap management, which you studied in Chapter 8.

The risk management approach requires the firm to finance short-term assets by taking on current liabilities of the same maturity and to finance long-term assets by issuing long-term debt and equity securities. Long-term assets include plant, equipment, and other items that generate cash flows to the firm over several periods. During these periods, the firm should, in principle, set aside portions of the cash flow generated by these assets to pay off the debt used to buy them. The maturity of the asset is the time when no more productive services can be generated from the asset. By that time, the firm is supposed to have paid back the debt that generated the funds to purchase the asset. Thus, the matching of maturities requires setting the repayment schedule of the debt to match the cash that can be generated from the asset over its productive life.

Generally, current assets provide benefits to a firm only over a short period. Therefore, under the risk management approach to financing, current assets do not normally qualify to be financed with long-term liabilities or equity. However, current assets fluctuate over time depending on the levels of activity in the firm's operations. When a firm's sales show wide seasonal fluctuations, the levels of current assets show similar wide variations. The minimum level of current assets required to maintain the firm's operations regardless of the level of sales is generally referred to as the **permanent current assets**. **Seasonal temporary current assets** refer to the level of current assets needed above permanent current assets.

Total assets fluctuate considerably over time. Seasonal fluctuations in demand for the firm's services and products will lead to temporary changes in assets. These seasonal changes occur mainly in current assets, such as inventories, accounts receivable, and cash.

Under normal circumstances, capital and other assets increase gradually over time. Long-term assets plus the permanent portion of current assets also rise gradually over time. However, seasonal changes in assets lead to seasonal peaks and troughs in total assets. At the trough, seasonal assets are nil and total assets are equal to long-term assets plus the permanent portion of current assets. At this point, inventories, accounts receivable, and cash are at their minimum levels. As seasonal activities rise, the seasonal portion of current assets rises until it peaks.

Spontaneous current liabilities are current liabilities that result from operations over which management has no influence. As with the level of seasonal current assets, the level of spontaneous current liabilities fluctuates over time depending on the level of activity in the firm's operations. Therefore, spontaneous current liabilities can be classed as permanent or seasonal.

- **Spontaneous permanent current liabilities** refer to the minimum level of accounts payable, accrued liabilities, and accrued taxes payable that arises regardless of the sales level.

- **Spontaneous seasonal current liabilities** refer to the difference between the total spontaneous current liabilities and the spontaneous permanent current liabilities.

Long-term financing rises gradually over time, assuming that the firm keeps a constant capital structure. As long-term assets rise, the amount of long-term financing also rises at the same rate. Similarly, the permanent portion of spontaneous financing rises gradually with the rise in permanent assets. In contrast, the seasonal portion of spontaneous financing fluctuates with the level of activity in the firm's operations.

Net working capital, the difference between current assets and current liabilities, is the amount of additional financing needed by the firm to finance current assets. The previous explanations indicate that the net working capital may be divided between permanent and seasonal portions.

A strict risk-management approach to financing would finance permanent net working capital with long-term liabilities and the seasonal portion with short-term liabilities. This means that, as shown in Exhibit 10-8, the firm would use long-term securities to finance the net working capital represented by the area under the straight line that passes

Exhibit 10-8 Permanent and Seasonal Portions of Net Working Capital

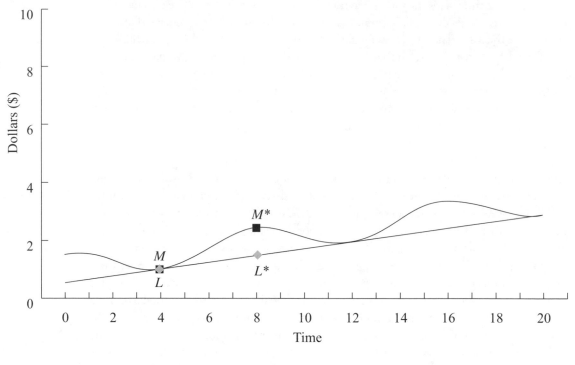

◆ Permanent net working capital (PNWC)
■ Seasonal net working capital (SNWC) + PNWC

through points M and L*. At point M, the long-term liabilities finance all the net working capital needs. However, at point M*, the firm also needs short-term financing to satisfy its full need for net working capital. The amount of financing is represented by the distance between points M* and L*.

The **maturity-matching strategy**—matching the maturities of assets and liabilities—is considered to be a middle ground between the extremely conservative strategy and the aggressive strategy. The **extremely conservative strategy** relies on long-term debt to finance not only all long-term assets but also the permanent and the seasonal portions of net working capital. When the firm faces situations where it has more funds than it needs, the additional funds are invested in short-term securities. Under this strategy, the firm will not have short-term liabilities other than spontaneous financing from accounts payable, accrued taxes payable, and accrued liabilities. This working capital management policy results in a higher level of working capital and a higher current ratio than what strict maturity-matching produces. Moreover, the firm's borrowing costs are higher than the costs under the maturity-matching strategy. At times, the firm will borrow long term only to turn around the funds and invest them at a rate potentially lower than the borrowing rate. The firm prefers to pay additional borrowing costs rather than face liquidity risk.

A less conservative strategy would be to finance a portion of the seasonal net working capital needs with long-term liabilities and the rest with short-term debt. The portion of long-term debt used to finance seasonal assets is called the **liquidity buffer**. Under uncertainty, the assets and liabilities cannot be divided easily between short term and long term. The liquidity buffer gives the firm some protection against liquidity risk from unpredictable circumstances. At times, the firm invests a portion of its funds in short-term securities. At other times, the firm borrows funds for a short term to finance its seasonal net working capital needs.

Many firms, particularly smaller ones, may follow an **aggressive strategy** in which they rely on long-term debt to finance only a portion of the long-term assets and the permanent net working capital. The other portion, as well as the seasonal portion of net working capital, is financed with short-term borrowing, such as bank loans and commercial paper. The firm accepts some liquidity risk to save interest costs. Firms that follow the aggressive strategy will report a small current ratio compared with firms that follow a conservative strategy.

The appropriate current ratio and the size of the liquidity buffer depend to a great degree on the firm's ability to generate cash flows from operations. Liquidity provides protection over a short period, but it cannot serve as a substitute for profitability. Long-term profitability is the best protection against insolvency.

The analyst should expect significant differences in liquidity between industries. Exhibit 10-9 shows two liquidity ratios for selected industries and the differences between industries in terms of these ratios. Moreover, differences exist within a particular industry depending on the size of the assets. Given these differences, it is important that the ratios of any particular company be compared with ratios of firms of similar size in the same industry. The exhibit shows that the ratios for a particular industry or subgroup of the industry are, however, relatively stable over time. You will learn how to use ratio analysis to estimate a firm's liquidity in the next section.

Exhibit 10-9
Current and Quick Ratios for the Median Group of Selected Industries

Industry	Current ratio			Quick ratio		
	2002	2001	2000	2002	2001	2000
Food & beverage	1.1	1.1	1.1	0.6	0.6	0.6
Wholesale & retail	2.2	2.3	1.7	0.9	0.8	0.7
Fabrication & engineering	1.9	1.9	1.6	1.0	1.0	0.9
Biotechnology & pharmaceuticals	7.0	8.7	10.0	6.6	8.1	9.6
Oil & gas	1.7	1.8	1.6	1.5	1.5	1.4
Technology	2.7	2.8	3.5	2.1	2.3	3.1

Source: These data are extracted from Financial Post DataGroup, Industry Reports. Accessed April 9, 2003.

Liquidity and the Cost of Financing

Credit rating services assign ratings to a company's debt securities based on the financial risks investors bear in holding the securities. A firm's short-term securities, such as commercial paper, and long-term securities, such as bonds, are rated.

The rating of commercial paper is essentially an assessment of the fundamental credit quality and relative liquidity of the issuer over a short period of time. Firms that are the most profitable, least leveraged, and most liquid will have the highest rating of their commercial paper. The interest rate required by investors to invest in the commercial paper is inversely related to the credit rating assigned to the paper. Therefore, the lower the liquidity, the lower the credit rating, and the higher the required rate of return will be. The firm's costs of financing increase as the liquidity drops.

Firms in any single industry differ in their choices of current ratios. One reason for the different choices is firms' special circumstances and the conditions of their industries. Another reason is the difference in the risk-return preferences of managers and shareholders. Some firms adopt more conservative working capital management policies than others.

10.6 INTERPRETING FINANCIAL RATIOS

Ratios are diagnostic tools. The accountant studies the ratios of a firm to determine those that indicate problems and then analyzes the accounts used in calculating them. Once a problem account is traced, the accountant studies the individual entries within the account. The objective is to identify the operating or financial problem and to determine the managerial action necessary to correct the problem.

Managers, accountants, financial analysts, investors, and lenders all use ratios to judge a firm's past accomplishments and predict its future performance. The set of ratios used by an investor may be different from the set used by financial managers. Exhibit 10-10 illustrates these differences.

To gain a practitioner's perspective on financial ratios, their uses, and their interpretations, consider the following article by James E. Kristy.

Exhibit 10-10
Ratio Classes Monitored by the Firm, Investors, Lenders, and Creditors

Interested party	Concern	Ratio class
Firm's financial managers	Long-term prospects, ability to pay obligations on time, efficiency, competitiveness, share values, and risk of bankruptcy	All ratios, especially those that stress internal operations: activity, profitability, rate of return, and coverage ratios
Financial analysts and investors	Long-term financial viability, growth, profitability, and ability to generate cash flows after preferred dividends	Profitability and return, financial leverage, market information, and common share ratios
Lenders	Firm's ability to pay contractual obligations as they come due	Liquidity, leverage and coverage, and profitability ratios
Short-term creditors (banks and suppliers)	Firm's ability to pay	Liquidity ratios

---

Conquering Financial Ratios: The Good, the Bad, and the Who Cares?

James E. Kristy

Ratio analysis of financial statements isn't a beanbag. But it needn't be a Rubik's Cube either. Many of the ratios in use today subtract from rather than add to our analysis by obscuring the really important ratios and inviting unwarranted speculation on some of the others.

About 200 ratios are currently used by credit managers, bankers, and financial and investment analysts. A couple of handfuls of these are very useful; about the same number are useless or worse, they may give misleading impressions. The rest are like cold oatmeal . . . they're not apt to do you much harm, but they're no great comfort, either. Here, 14 so-called "key ratios" are examined.

I'm fond of five particular ratios, for which I have adopted or developed standards of excellence and a point scoring system that gives credit managers a quick readout on the financial condition of almost any firm. Those key ratios and their standards are:

Current ratio	2 to 1
Quick ratio	1 to 1
Liquidity ratio	0.40 to 1
Equity/debt ratio	1.65 to 1
Return on equity	14 percent

These five ratios examined together give credit managers about 80 percent of the story of a company's financial strength, as revealed by the standard financial statements. There may still be some data worth exploring, but it's not unlike being a one-month newlywed . . . most of the surprises are behind you.

One reason I rely on so few financial measures is that there is a good deal about the condition of a firm that we simply cannot know, and to construct out of a few bare numbers scenarios that foretell fatal mistakes or great success is an exercise in futility. For example, we might see an unusual increase in accounts receivable and leap to the conclusion that the receivables are badly managed or that they harbour bad debts. But it might be that the company has a new product or a new market from which a rise in accounts receivables is an acceptable consequence. Moreover, the new product might catapult a business into industry leadership, or it might prove to be an expensive dud after a flashy start; who knows? The first thing to learn about ratio analysis is that while some ratios offer fairly solid conclusions, most do not.

Sellers of financial statement data have adopted certain ratios and stuck with them over the years. This article will explore 14 of the most popular ratios.

Ratios have been pigeonholed in various categories. They have been called coverage ratios, solvency ratios, operating ratios, expense ratios, and efficiency ratios to name a few. The classifications I prefer are liquidity, leverage, and profitability, with a minor category called management ratios. This arrangement embraces the fundamental requirements and risks found in nearly every business.

Free enterprise is often made out to be more complicated than it really is. Essentially, a company buys or makes a product or service at a certain cost and tries to sell it at a price higher. When they do, they have profitability. To get started, they must have certain assets and these may be purchased with shareholders' money or creditors' money. The mix of the two we call leverage. And because every business faces daily the payment of debts, expenses, and surprises, they must have some cash on hand and coming. That's why liquidity is crucial.

Almost all companies have these requirements, although the importance of liquidity, leverage, and profitability varies both with the type and age of the business. "Systems of analysis," like the Commercial Credit Matrix, try to synthesize or combine these three elements in a single measure of financial strength which applies to the vast majority of companies regardless of the type of industry they're in.

Each ratio should be tested to see if it addresses these three fundamental requirements. If it does, is it the best ratio for that purpose? If it doesn't, do we really need it?

Current Ratio: Current Assets/Current Liabilities

Function: The granddaddy of financial ratios is a basic measure of liquidity. Because current liabilities have a fixed amount and due date, while the conversion of current assets to cash is less assured, this ratio weighs a certainty against an uncertainty. Companies need more current assets than current liabilities if they are to pay all debts on time.

Standard: 2 to 1 has been accepted by the majority of analysts for nearly a century. Prior to that, it was 3 to 1. This is one of the Commercial Credit Matrix ratios. It's also among five ratios that I call the Long Term Debt Matrix, described in my booklet and software. Whereas in my system, 2 to 1 is the Standard of Excellence for the current ratio, less than 1 to 1 is the Standard of Awful.

Comment: The current ratio is like classic Coke. We tend to take it for granted, but it's hard to beat as a liquidity measure.

Quick Ratio: (Cash Equivalents + Accounts Receivable)/Current Liabilities

Function: A test of liquidity which supplements the current ratio. In this case, inventory and other less liquid current assets are left out, giving us a more immediate indicator of payment ability.

Standard: This is also one of the CCM ratios, and the Standard of Excellence of 1 to 1 was well established long before I came on the scene. A quick ratio of less than .25 to 1 would be worrisome.

Comment: In the CCM system, I combine the current ratio, quick ratio, and—one not in this list—the liquidity ratio (cash equivalents/current liabilities) to get an overall measure of liquidity. Using all three ratios tends to neutralize any "window dressing" . . . boosting the current ratio at year end by using all available cash to reduce payables.

CL to Inventory Ratio: Current Liabilities/Inventory

Function: This ratio purports to tell how much a company must rely on selling its inventory to pay its current obligations. However, it's what's up front that counts; that is, you can't judge this ratio unless you also have the quick ratio, for there may be enough quick assets so that you needn't rely on inventory at all. And if you have the current ratio also you'll learn nothing more from this calculation.

Standard: There is no broad standard because inventory requirements vary so much from industry to industry. That is true of most inventory ratios. An average ratio for industrial companies is about 2.5 to 1.

Comment: Please concentrate with me for a minute: This ratio is approximately the inverse of the current ratio minus the quick ratio. Thus, it gives a rear end view of the current position, which is about as effective a way to analyze the current position as studying equinity by looking at the south end of a north bound horse.

CL/E Ratio: Current Liabilities/Equity

Function: Although called a solvency ratio, this is really a half-baked leverage indicator. Because it ignores long-term liabilities, it is at best a useless and at worst a misleading measure of leverage.

Standard: Some analysts say the ratio should be less than .5 to 1 and that .67 to 1 or higher calls for caution. However, no standard is valid unless the current liabilities equal the total liabilities. In that case, just use the Standard of Excellence for the Equity/Debt ratio in the CCM.

Comment: At one time, this ratio was widely used to measure leverage because few firms had access to long-term financing. Gradually, some companies became established enough to sell bonds and this ratio became an anachronism. Since the advent of high yield (junk) bonds it has become even more outmoded. The ratio has died; we just can't bring ourselves to bury it.

D/E Ratio: Total Debt/Equity

Function: Evaluates leverage in the most direct and uncomplicated way. The equation that gives the balance sheet its name is:

$$\text{Assets} = \text{Debt} + \text{Equity}$$

This ratio reveals the proportion of assets purchased with the investors' money, and the share acquired with creditors' money. Equity acts as a buffer to creditors in the event of liquidation. Also, the higher the leverage (more debt money), the greater the risk that the rigid interest and debt payments cannot be made by fluctuating profit returns. Restrictions on leverage are very common in commercial bank loans.

There are several other names used for this ratio. Total liabilities may be used instead of debt; net worth or just plain "worth" may be substituted for equity, which itself may be called shareholders' equity.

There are also several equivalent ratios which, like Fahrenheit and Celsius, tell exactly the same story using different scales. The list comprises:

- Asset ratio: Total assets/total liabilities;
- Debt to asset ratio;
- Owner's equities to total equities: Equity/(debt + equity);
- Assets and liabilities to total assets;
- Net worth to total liabilities;

- Book value of net worth to total debt;
- Worth to assets;
- Financial leverage ratio: Total assets/net worth; and lastly,
- The leverage ratio in the Commercial Credit Matrix: Equity/debt.

Standard: My Standard of Excellence for the E/D ratio in the CCM is 1.65 to 1, with Awful being anything under .32 to 1. These standards can be converted for use in any of the above ratios by using the basic relationship of Assets = 2.65, Debt = 1, and Equity = 1.65. Thus the standard for Debt/Equity is 1/1.65 = .61 to 1.

Comment: The most popular ratio in this group is Debt to Equity. The one drawback it has is that as the ratio gets higher, the situation is getting riskier, whereas with most other ratios, the higher the number, the better things are. Ratios are abstruse enough without our having to worry about in which direction the safe harbour lies. That's why I use E/D instead of D/E in the Commercial Credit Matrix; for all five of my ratios, higher means better.

FA/E: Fixed Assets/Equity

Function: Advocates of this ratio claim that it

1. indirectly measures liquidity by showing what part of the "permanent" assets are covered by "permanent" capital;
2. acts as a solvency factor showing what portion of the usually heavy losses from a forced sale would be met by stockholders' equity; and
3. indicates the burden of depreciation on current income.

Standard: Advocates say smaller is better and that the yellow light goes on at .75 to 1. The ratio will vary considerably with the industry. The Value Line Industrial Composite had the ratio climb steadily the past five years from 1.07 to 1.24 to 1. Retailers, service companies, and others with few fixed assets will have much lower ratios.

Comment: This ratio constitutes a blunt-axe approach to some delicate problems. There is too much omitted to make it a useful tool. The three functions mentioned above would be better handled by

1. the current ratio;
2. the equity/debt ratio; and
3. return on equity.

Moreover, a low ratio may be due to plenty of equity . . . which is good, or too few fixed assets . . . which is bad when our best gains in productivity come from an increasing use of modern equipment.

Days' Sales Outstanding (DSO) a.k.a. Average Collection Period: Accounts Receivable × 365/Annual Sales

Function: This is a management ratio, probably the single best indicator of the quality of the accounts receivable. It is easy to calculate from information readily available. This ratio can be read as the number of days' sales still not collected or the average number of days it takes to collect a receivable. If the ratio starts creeping up month to month, it may be time to give the collection department a dose of inspiration, or it may be a sign that bad debts are accumulating.

Standard: Some analysts suggest a standard of 1.33 × net terms. I think that's a little stiff and recommend 1.5 × net terms instead. For example, if terms of sale are 2-10, N-30, the Standard of Excellence would be 45 days or less, which happens to be about the national average. It's possible to be too proficient at collecting receivables, so any ratio, say 10 days either side of the standard should get some management attention.

Comment: A company with a pronounced seasonality in its sales may want to use quarterly or bi-monthly instead of annual sales in the calculation. In that case, the multiplier should be changed to correspond with the chosen period. If, for example, quarterly sales are in the divisor, the multiplier should be 91 instead of 365. If month-to-month seasonal changes are extreme, calculate a DSO for each individual month's sales still uncollected and add the DSOs together for the overall figure. So, on June 30 there would be a DSO for June sales, May sales, and April sales still outstanding on June 30, and the sum of these days would be the June 30 DSO.

Some analysts also calculate accounts receivable turnover (annual sales/accounts receivable). No need to do both because they measure the same thing.

Days' Sales in Inventory (DSI): Inventory × 365/Annual Cost of Sales

Function: An excellent management ratio for monitoring the level of inventory. Many companies require an inventory to act as a buffer between production and sales, but the costs associated with inventory (such as the cost of money tied up, handling, warehousing, theft, shrinkage, and obsolescence) can seriously affect profits, so as long as customer demand is satisfied, the less inventory the better.

Standard: There is none, unfortunately, because of a wide variation company-to-company and industry-to-industry, not to mention contrivances like Just-In-Time which make all the past numbers irrelevant. If you're the boss and you need a guideline, figure the DSIs for the past five years and insist on something a little less than the lowest number. In the Value Line Industrial Composite the number never wanders far from 60 days.

Comment: Many analysts prefer inventory turnover (annual sales/inventory) to this ratio, but I don't know why.

Some people calculate this ratio using sales in place of cost of sales. They say it doesn't matter so long as you are comparing the ratio to others calculated the same way. Well, I agree, mostly it's like the difference between a nautical mile and a statute mile; as long as you're a passenger and not the pilot, they are rough substitutes.

From time to time, we see articles in which the author has added the DSO and DSI together to get, say, 100 days for Company A and compares that with 70 days for Company B, and concludes that B has more cash flow. It's a curious error because it is not the number of days in the DSO or DSI that affects cash flow, it is the change in the numbers. If A and B had identical sales for the year and there was no change in their respective DSOs and DSIs, they would have identical cash flows.

S/WC ratio: *Annual net sales/working capital*

Function: working capital, also called "net working capital" = current assets − current liabilities. It is an undependable indicator of liquidity. Every business needs current assets which always comprise cash and usually include accounts receivable and inventory. A rise in sales forces an expansion of these assets. At the same time, a firm will have certain "free" credits, accounts payable and various accruals, which help to finance, or pay for, the current assets. These, too, rise along with sales. Working capital, then, is the part of the current assets not funded by the current liabilities, the part that must be paid with investors' money or long term borrowing. If the WC is too skimpy, it indicates there are too few current assets for the current debt.

Standard: There is no standard of excellence, which is what makes this ratio undependable or even useless. It stands to reason that the more sales a firm has, the more working capital it will need, but actual numbers range all over the lot, even into negatives, so that it is hard to draw conclusions much less make recommendations based on this ratio. For your information, the Industrial Composite ratio has hovered around 8 to 1 for the past five years.

Comment: If a company's S/WC ratio gets much higher than others in the same industry, some analysts accuse them of "overtrading," which means too many sales for the amount of working capital. Overtrading is one of those incongruities like "too much cash," or "too much love," that is difficult to apply in a pragmatic way. Try telling an entrepreneur that he or she has too many sales and they will look at you as if you were speaking Latin or some other bygone language. Never, never treat overtrading by reducing sales; the cure lies in getting more financing.

S/A ratio: *Annual net sales/total assets, a.k.a. asset turnover*

Function: This is a very good management ratio, not so useful in running day-to-day activities, but for understanding the dynamics of your company and sorting out the good ideas from the bad when engaged in strategic planning. S/A tells you how many dollars of sales you have for each dollar of assets, a ratio that may vary somewhat in the short run, but over the long term is fairly steady for each individual firm. Every business requires certain assets to make it go, and if sales are going to rise, the total assets will also go up, and when they do, it will require more investment or borrowing to finance them. S/A provides a guideline for the amount of financing that will be needed.

Standard: The best standard is the company's own historical S/A ratios . . . at least five years' worth. There is considerable variation among companies, some like architectural firms requiring relatively few assets, others like shipbuilders needing plenty. The typical manufacturing company requires one dollar of assets to handle one dollar of annual sales.

Comment: Some analysts talk about "correcting" this ratio if it gets too high or low. In truth, the ratio manages itself. If a company has over capacity, they will stop adding assets until a better balance ensues; if it has too few assets, customer service will suffer and sales will eventually fall without any help. This ratio also appears in its inverse form . . . assets/sales, which tells the same story using a different scale.

AP/S ratio: *Accounts payable/sales*

Function: Supposedly a measure of liquidity, more specifically an indicator of vendor payments. However, the relationship between accounts payable and sales is so slight as to make any use of this ratio a non sequitur. It's sort of like taking a blood test to see if the patient is dead. There are other more direct measures to do the job; for example, the liquidity ratio in my Commercial Credit Matrix (a ratio less than .20 to 1 giving concern for prompt payment), or the more refined days' purchases in accounts payable, or even days' sales in current liabilities.

Standard: I've never seen one published, which doesn't surprise me, the connection between sales and payables being so tenuous. It's rare to see a company with a ratio higher than 9%.

Comment: If you have to lighten the load, this would be a good ratio to toss.

Return on equity (ROE): *Net profit/equity*

Function: This is the fundamental business ratio. If you're ever cast away on a desert island and can take but one ratio with you . . . take this one. It is the ultimate measure of earnings performance. After all the crabbing about taxes, and the excuses for write-offs, and the spin about next year's prospects, this is what you're left with, a measure of performance that's as close to the truth as we can presently come.

Standard: ROE is the earnings ratio in the Commercial Credit Matrix. My Standard of Excellence is currently 14 percent (that's .14 to 1), with a Standard of Awful being less than 3.5 percent. The standard varies, however, with the rate of inflation. If the present low rate of inflation (2 to 3 percent) continues, it would be proper to lower the Standard of Excellence to 12 percent, but I'd suggest waiting a bit.

Comment: This is one of the few financial ratios that can be negative . . . as when a firm has losses instead of profits. Any company, and I mean any company, can have a loss in a given year. On my point-scoring system that would rate a goose egg. But if there are back-to-back losses, I recommend subtracting points from the other ratios because of the serious implications. Losses must be stopped and stopped quickly. Two years' losses running does not necessarily mean bail out, but you should at least make a note of the exits.

Return on assets (ROA): *Net profit/total assets*

Function: This is a very popular profit ratio, especially among larger corporations with numerous divisions and subsidiaries. ROE is a better ratio, but in a large company, equity is a core concept; that is, it is not easily allocated out to divisions or in a meaningful way even to subsidiary corporations. So ROA functions as a good proxy to ROE.

Standard: In a rough way, ROA follows ROE at about half the rate, so that if ROE is 14 percent, ROA is likely to be somewhere near 7 percent. Therefore it's possible to use the ROE standard mentioned above by dividing it by 2 . . . but only as a crude measure.

Comment: Back before the 50s, ROE used to be called ROI, return on investment. But in the recent decades there has been a flowering of special return ratios tailored for specific management reasons, so that ROI is now the generic term for a whole family of profit measures. ROA itself has fathered many others, some of the acronyms which I'll leave with you (explanations will have to wait for another article): RONCE, ROAM, RONA, ROCA, ROBE, ROCANA, ROCE, PROTC, ROO, ROPE, RONABIT, ROANA, ROMI, etc.

Return on sales (ROS): *Net profit/annual sales, a.k.a profit margin*

Function: This is a very popular earnings measure, found in nearly every annual report, often as one of those stairway-to-heaven bar charts. To an outsider looking in, however, the ratio harbours a couple of flaws that render it useless if not misleading. One is that it is possible for the ROS to rise while the ROE is falling, so that you get a mixed signal, or a wrong signal, if you believe as I do that ROE is the better indicator.

Standard: The other drawback is the lack of an overall standard of excellence. The average for all U.S. companies is about 5.5 percent (.055 to 1), but the figures vary from .75 percent for a supermarket to 40 percent for some software firms. Even a company's own historical ratios may be of little use if its marketing strategy has shifted at all from high margin/low volume to high volume/low margin sales.

Comment: One thing I like about this ratio is the perspective it gives on the profit-making process. It shows how slim the margin of profit is for a firm, and how easy it would be to slide into the loss column. I suppose that's why we even get paid for fiddling around with these little numbers. It only takes a modicum of ignorance to turn success into a crushing reverse.

James E. Kristy is a financial management consultant in Bueno Park, Ca. He is author of *Analyzing Financial Statements: Quick and Clean*, available through the NACM Publications Department. His software package, *The Commercial Credit Matrix* (which includes *Analyzing Financial Statements*) is also available through NACM Publications. This article © James E. Kristy 1994. All rights reserved.

Source: James E. Kristy.

The article indicates that about 200 ratios are in use today. However, it suggests that only a few of them are really important. The financial manager should select a group representing the major areas of financial analysis and extract as much information as possible from the selected group. The article claims that as few as five ratios can provide as much as 80% of the information available on a firm. Using too many ratios to analyze a particular aspect of the firm's performance may lead to inconsistent results, as some ratios may obscure the analysis or invite unwarranted speculation. Moreover, once the number of ratios exceeds a range of five to ten, the additional information gained by analyzing more ratios will be minor. Much information about the condition of a firm cannot be known, no matter how many ratios are constructed.

The article adds that the interpretation of ratios cannot be formalized. Each firm will have circumstances that make the interpretation of one or more of its ratios unique and different from the interpretations of other firms' ratios. A ratio that is temporarily out of line with industry ratios because of unusual circumstances should not necessarily indicate that the firm is in a bad situation. The introduction of a new product, the implementation of a new plan, or acquisition of a new business may temporarily distort ratios.

The article describes 14 common ratios and their uses, and suggests standards of excellence for many of them. A firm with good management should have every ratio within a small range of the corresponding standard of excellence. Nevertheless, the article warns that standards of excellence should not be rigidly interpreted, because of the special circumstances of every firm. For example, consider the return on equity. The article suggests 14% as a standard of excellence for this ratio but also suggests that this is a rough benchmark that will be affected by inflation and other factors. The article also states that one or two years of negative return on equity, significantly below the standard, should not be interpreted immediately as a sign of bad performance.

Important Considerations The following considerations are relevant to the interpretation of financial ratios.

Seasonality of Sales During periods of high sales, businesses are likely to experience high levels of current assets and current liabilities. These same businesses experience low levels of current assets and current liabilities during periods of low sales levels. The cyclical pattern of current asset and liability levels leads to a similar cyclical pattern for levels of total assets and total liabilities.

Both asset and liability accounts are influenced by the seasonality of sales. Consequently, the seasonality of sales affects the levels of ratios. For example, the current ratio depends on whether current assets increase or decrease disproportionately to an increase or a decrease in current liabilities. If both current assets and liabilities increase or decrease in the same proportion during a peak sales period, the current ratio is unaffected. In contrast, the current ratio is affected if current assets increase to a greater degree than current liabilities during a peak sales period. For a current ratio that is calculated on the basis of figures estimated during a peak sales period, the reported ratio level will be higher than the normal level that occurs during other periods of the year.

Book Value as Opposed to Market Value When the book value of any class of assets is substantially lower than the market value of these assets, the book value of total assets of the firm is also lower. Using the book value of the asset under consideration or total assets in calculating ratios may lead to meaningless conclusions. For example, the total asset turnover ratio is calculated by dividing sales by average total assets. Using a value for average total assets lower than the economic value of the assets overestimates the total asset turnover ratio. This creates a bias that may lead the analyst to decide that management is doing well in managing assets when the contrary is true.

As another example, the debt ratio is calculated by dividing total liabilities by total assets. If any class of assets is underestimated, total assets are underestimated. Thus, the debt ratio is overestimated, which may lead the analyst to conclude that the firm is overburdened by debt. Yet, the firm may be properly leveraged if the market value of the assets is considered. The biases caused by the use of book value can be minimized by using the market value of assets instead.

Average or Median Ratios for a Peer Group The purpose of a comparison with the industry group is to eliminate biases from particular circumstances of the industry. For example, comparing a firm's leverage ratios with the averages or medians for the industry enables the financial analyst to assess whether or not the firm is using debt properly. Different industry characteristics, however, may lead to situations in which the level of a ratio is appropriate for one industry but unacceptable for another.

Several companies compile and sell ratio information to subscribers and to the public. Robert Morris Associates and Dun & Bradstreet are two main providers in the United States and their coverage extends to Canadian companies. In Canada, *The Globe and Mail*, Financial Post DataGroup, and the Bank of Canada collect extensive information on a large number of industries. Special requests for information may be submitted to be filled instantly or within a couple of days.

Minicase 10-6 illustrates the analysis of a company's financial statement ratios against the median ratios for its peers. Note that the information used in this minicase also forms the basis of Minicase 10-7.

MINICASE 10-6 ANALYSIS OF SELECTED RATIOS FOR OIL INDUSTRIAL LTD.

Oil Industrial Ltd. (OIL), based in High Level, Alberta, is engaged in contract drilling of oil and gas wells in northwestern Canada.

Exhibit 10-11 provides sample medians for a selected set of ratios for the oil and gas industry in Canada. Exhibit 10-12 shows a selected set of financial ratios for OIL.

Exhibit 10-11
Medians for a Selected Set of Ratios for the Extraction Services, Drilling, and Oil and Gas Wells Industry in Canada

Ratio	20X5	20X4	20X3
Quick ratio	0.9	1.2	1.3
Current ratio	0.8	1.2	1.4
Total-asset turnover	1.69	1.46	1.45
Operating profit margin (%)	9.5	6.9	0.3
Return on assets (%)	13.6	6.2	0.5
Return on equity (%)	23.7	18.5	12.5
Debt to equity (%)	81.9	52.3	59.7

Exhibit 10-12
Selected Ratios for OIL over the Years Ending December 31, 20X2 to 20X5

Fiscal year	20X5	20X4	20X3	20X2
Quick ratio	1.14	1.01	1.41	1.53
Current ratio	1.21	1.11	1.69	2.00
Inventory turnover	61.88	32.56	17.48	14.74
Capital-asset turnover	2.67	1.51	1.99	1.63
Total-asset turnover	1.50	0.97	1.15	1.08
Operating profit margin (%)	18.73	15.52	15.32	7.21
Net profit margin (%)	9.45	8.20	8.44	4.17
Operating return on assets (%)	28.10	15.04	17.59	7.80
Return on equity (%)	49.98	30.19	30.75	14.81
Long-term debt to equity (%)	16.00	24.00	10.90	40.80
Total debt to equity (%)	77.82	100.67	74.77	89.67
Interest coverage	22.68	29.35	18.44	4.60
Earnings per share	$ 2.06	$ 1.02	$ 0.63	$ 0.23

Question 1: Compare OIL's ratios with the data in Exhibit 10-11. Is OIL managing its assets efficiently?

In terms of efficiency, OIL has an average total-asset turnover ratio of 1.21 over the period 20X3 to 20X5, which is lower than the industry average of 1.53 over the same

Case Continued >

period. This means that OIL's assets are not generating the sales that are generated by the top half of the peer group. The firm should make efforts to use its assets more efficiently.

Question 2: Compare OIL's ability to generate profits from sales with that of the median firm of the industry.

The operating profit margin shows that OIL has performed substantially better than the median firm in the industry. In 20X5, for every dollar of sales, OIL made 18.73 cents in operating profits. In contrast, the median firm in the industry made 9.5 cents per dollar of revenues. This means that OIL has lower expenses than the median firm in the industry.

Question 3: Explain how both a low asset turnover ratio and a high operating profit margin can occur at the same time.

The product of the asset turnover ratio and operating profit margin determines the return on assets before interest and taxes. Therefore, a low asset turnover ratio may be compensated for by a high operating profit margin. The result may be a return on assets that is equivalent to the return on assets of the average firm in the industry.

It is important to understand that the firm's marketing or operating strategies could lead to such a situation. For example, a firm may adopt a high-profit, low-volume sales strategy. Compared with the average firm in the industry, this firm will experience a high operating profit margin and a low asset turnover ratio. In contrast, a firm that adopts a low-profit, high-volume strategy will experience a low operating profit margin and a high asset turnover ratio. Yet the return (before interest and taxes) on assets may be the same for the two firms.

This question demonstrates that a ratio should be considered jointly with other ratios in order to produce reliable conclusions. Single ratios may be affected by the firm's own policies or by unusual circumstances that lead to ratio values away from the norm. The return-on-equity model is designed to help the financial analyst derive conclusions from combinations of ratios. This model will be considered following the minicase.

Question 4: Describe OIL's debt position.

The total-debt-to-equity ratio for OIL is above the median firm's ratio except for 20X5. This means that prior to 20X5, OIL was highly leveraged compared with the industry. In 20X5, the total-debt-to-equity ratio for OIL improved substantially over the ratio of the median firm in the industry.

Other Techniques Used in Ratio Analysis Ratio analysis can be made more informative by using techniques such as the return on equity model and trend analysis. These techniques highlight important relationships between ratios and their accounts and are helpful in studying a firm's performance over a period of time.

Return-on-Equity Model for Performance Evaluation The return-on-equity (ROE) model, also known as the DuPont model after the group of companies that first developed it, is based on the assumption that return on equity is the most relevant measure that shareholders rely on to judge the performance of management. Thus, the model attempts to divide ROE into as many components as possible. This division allows the financial analyst to detect the primary reasons for high or low ROE. If problems are identified, corrective action can be taken. If evidence of good management is identified from the model, rewards can be given to encourage this behaviour.

The return-on-equity model is based on a simple combination of ratios arranged to reveal the strengths and weaknesses of the firm. It starts with the definition of return on equity:

$$\text{ROE} = \frac{\text{net income}}{\text{average shareholders' equity}} \qquad \textbf{(Equation 10-7)}$$

A simple mathematical transformation yields:

$$\text{ROE} = \frac{\text{net income}}{\text{average total assets}} \times \frac{\text{average total assets}}{\text{average shareholders' equity}} \qquad \textbf{(Equation 10-8)}$$

Therefore,

$$\text{ROE} = \text{ROA} \times \text{EM} \qquad \textbf{(Equation 10-9)}$$

where
    ROA = return on assets
    EM = equity multiplier, which is a measure of financial leverage

At this stage, the analyst can determine the relative contributions of the return on assets and the equity multiplier to the size of the return on equity. The return on assets is a measure of the firm's ability to generate income from its assets. The equity multiplier measures the degree of the firm's financial leverage. Comparing the component ratios with industry ratios enables the analyst to determine the source of weaknesses or strengths. For example, suppose ROE is lower than the industry median. This poor return on equity may be caused by a poor return on assets, low leverage, or both.

If low ROE is caused by a poor return on assets, the analyst needs to decompose ROA into more basic components. Starting with the definition of return on assets, you have:

$$\text{ROA} = \frac{\text{net income}}{\text{average total assets}} \qquad \textbf{(Equation 10-10)}$$

A simple transformation shows that ROA can be determined as the product of two ratios:

$$\text{ROA} = \frac{\text{net income}}{\text{net sales}} \times \frac{\text{net sales}}{\text{average total assets}} \qquad \textbf{(Equation 10-11)}$$

which is the same as

$$\text{ROA} = \text{NPM} \times \text{TAT} \qquad \textbf{(Equation 10-12)}$$

where
    NPM = net profit margin
    TAT = total-asset turnover

Once again, the financial analyst compares these components with industry norms. The low ROA may be caused by low total-asset turnover. Total assets are divided between basic components, such as cash, accounts receivable, inventories, and capital assets. The ratios of these assets to total assets are compared with industry norms. If the low total-asset turnover is caused by higher than usual inventories, it could mean that the firm is using more than the optimal level of inventories to support its sales and should lower inventories.

Alternatively, the low ROA may be caused by a low net profit margin. In this case, additional decomposition of the NPM into basic components is needed. Given that earnings after taxes are obtained after paying direct and fixed operating expenses and taxes, the NPM is equal to:

$$\text{NPM} = 1 - \frac{\text{direct operating expenses}}{\text{net sales}} - \frac{\text{fixed operating expenses}}{\text{net sales}} - \frac{\text{taxes}}{\text{net sales}}$$

(Equation 10-13)

The ratios can be compared with industry norms to determine which component is higher or lower than the corresponding norm. If the fixed operating expenses are determined to be excessive, the analyst can separate them into components, such as occupancy expenses, administrative and advertising expenses, and other fixed expenses. Also, ratios can be developed for comparison with industry norms. Essentially, the financial analyst can continue the process until problems or opportunities can be associated with specific accounts.

Trend Analysis Trend analysis is a financial analysis technique aimed at detecting improvement or deterioration in financial ratios over time. This process compares the firm's performance during the most recent year with prior years. For example, the financial analyst may notice that a ratio is lower (or higher) than desirable. Considered alone, the ratio may be judged as an indication of bad performance. Yet, when the value of the ratio this year is compared with its values over the past several years, a rising (or declining) trend may be detected. In this case, the analyst may conclude that the firm is healthier than might otherwise have been the case.

MINICASE 10-7 ANALYSIS OF THE LIQUIDITY POSITION OF OIL INDUSTRIES LTD.

Consider the ratios of Oil Industries Ltd. (OIL) in Minicase 10-6. OIL undertook an acquisition in 20X4. During the 20X4 fiscal year, total assets increased to $100.629 million from $38.564 million in 20X3.

Question 1: Compare the liquidity position of OIL with the industry and explain the liquidity position of OIL over the period 20X2 to 20X5 using the data in Exhibit 10-12.

Consider the quick and current ratios for 20X5. These ratios are both above 1 in each of the years under consideration. This indicates that current assets are more than current liabilities, even when inventories are excluded from current assets. Compared with the industry's median, OIL has higher quick ratios, except in fiscal year 20X4. The drop in the quick ratio was the result of a drop in OIL's cash balances. However, the main reason for the drop seems to be the acquisition that OIL undertook in 20X4. Similarly to the quick ratio, the current ratio for OIL is higher than the industry's median for the 20X3 and 20X5 fiscal years and lower in the 20X4 fiscal year. Overall, OIL seems to have good liquidity compared with the industry.

However, on its own, a ratio does not mean much. The appropriate level of a ratio depends on many factors that differ from one firm to another and from one industry to the next. A comparison with the firm's ratios of previous years or with industry averages provides a better basis for judgment.

Case Continued >

Question 2: Perform a trend analysis of OIL's performance.

A quick inspection of the quick ratio over time reveals that it decreased from 20X2 to 20X4, after which it recovered. Similarly, several other ratios, such as the current ratio, capital-asset turnover, total-asset turnover, net profit margin, operating return on assets, and return on equity, all deteriorated during 20X4. In contrast, the interest coverage ratio and the earnings per share both increased. A quick judgment is that, excluding the continuous improvement in EPS, OIL's situation worsened considerably in fiscal year 20X4.

However, the analysis so far is subject to a serious bias. During the 20X4 fiscal year, OIL made important acquisitions that significantly changed its operating and financial structures. OIL's assets increased substantially from $38.564 million in 20X3 to $100.629 million in 20X4. It seems that OIL needed some time to bring the new assets to their full potential. The 20X5 results suggest that OIL was able to absorb the impact of the acquisitions entirely in 20X4 and to improve its results in 20X5.

Distorting Factors As indicated in the OIL minicase, special events, such as mergers and acquisitions, leveraged buyouts, major asset sales, large share or debt issues, and changes in accounting practices, can distort ratio analysis and lead to meaningless conclusions. The financial analyst should be alert to these special, nonrecurring events and should try to eliminate their impact on the ratios under consideration.

An important factor that affects ratio analysis for all firms, but some more than others, is accounting practice. Canadian GAAP recommends that firms report capital assets on a historical cost basis. Consequently, the ratios calculated on the basis of such values may not be indicative of a firm's real financial situation. Because the replacement cost of assets may be more relevant to the calculation of ratios, financial analysis should be based on current and expected future conditions and not on historical ones.

The accounting treatment of several balance sheet items causes concern in calculating financial ratios. These items include prepaid expenses, inter-company balances, inventory, marketable securities, goodwill, long-term pension and tax liabilities, minority interests, and reserves arising from asset re-evaluations or foreign currency transactions.

The accounting treatment of several income statement items may cause distortions in the values of ratios. The issues of concern include the calculation of interest expenses, treatment of income from discontinued operations or from nonrecurring transactions, and the capitalization of certain costs.

Another important issue to raise is the treatment of current liabilities in calculating leverage ratios. Many analysts suggest that current liabilities should not be included as debt when measuring the debt ratio because current liabilities are operating rather than financing items. Moreover, current liabilities are considered in studying the company's liquidity and short-term solvency. Despite these arguments, current liabilities are debt that needs to be repaid. Although they are related to operating policies, they constitute an integral part of the financing policy. Indeed, management of current liabilities is one of the areas where financial and operating managers should cooperate to produce optimal results. Furthermore, considering current liabilities in examining liquidity and short-term solvency does not justify excluding them when calculating the debt ratio. The denominator of the debt ratio does not exclude the current assets or those that are covered by current liabilities.

Inflation is one of the factors that may lead to differences between current and historical costs, thus leading to distortions in the income statement. Generally, during periods of high inflation, profits tend to be comparatively overstated. This is the result of inflation-induced gains on inventories and understated amortization expenses. Moreover, as taxes are paid on the overstated profits, the firm will pay more taxes than may be warranted by its actual costs.

The balance sheet is also affected by inflation. Assets are recorded on the balance sheet at their historical cost minus accumulated amortization. Inflation may lead to a situation in which the replacement cost of assets is higher than their book values. Also, debt is recorded at its principal amount net of amortized premiums or discounts. Because shareholders' equity is equal to total assets minus debt obligations, equity will be understated if inflation increases the value of existing assets.

The financial analyst should adjust account balances that are reported in the financial statements to eliminate distortions caused by inflation. There are two areas where adjustments may be needed:

- The accounts of the balance sheet should be adjusted to reflect the current value of capital assets. This adjustment is particularly important when a firm has old properties, such as plant or equipment, that are recorded on a historical cost basis. The impact of inflation should be considered when analyzing proposed capital investment projects. Chapter 2 explained that the analysis should be either entirely in real or entirely in inflation-adjusted terms.

- Changes in the market values of assets and liabilities can make the reported net income and rate of return on equity meaningless. The reported profitability, earnings growth, and payout ratios need adjustment to provide a realistic impression of the firm's performance.

Minicase 10-8 shows the effect that adjustments may have on a firm's financial ratios.

MINICASE 10-8 EFFECT OF ACCOUNTING CHANGES ON RATIO ANALYSIS

Nationwide Warehousing and Storage (NWS) is a thriving medium-sized business with headquarters in Toronto and operations throughout Canada. The firm has warehouses and storage facilities in almost every major city. The company was founded in the early 1900s. During the years of its expansion, the firm's management targeted city limits to acquire land and build the firm's facilities. As a result of urban expansion over the century, city limits of the 1900s are now in the hearts of many Canadian cities.

The firm's capital assets are recorded on a historical cost basis, which reflects the acquisition costs, the capitalized maintenance, and repairs made to keep the facilities in good working conditions. The firm's income statement and balance sheet are shown in Exhibits 10-13 and 10-14.

Question 1: Calculate the operating profit margin, return, and leverage ratios for NWS. **Hint:** Use average values for all balance sheet items.

Exhibit 10-13
Nationwide Warehouse and Storage Income Statement
Year Ended December 31, 20X2 ($ Thousands)

Net sales	$96,897
Employee costs	52,450
Selling and administrative expenses	10,985
Amortization	3,388
Income from operations	30,074
Interest expense	3,817
Income before income taxes	26,257
Income taxes at 34%	8,927
Net income	$17,330

Exhibit 10-14
Nationwide Warehousing and Storage Balance Sheet
December 31, 20X2 ($ Thousands)

Assets	20X2	20X1	Liabilities	20X2	20X1
Current assets			**Current liabilities**		
Cash	$ 1,597	$ 1,397	Accounts payable	$ 645	$ 545
Accounts receivable	13,577	13,177	Accruals	915	835
Inventories	551	471	Bank notes	5,665	5,385
Prepaid expenses	291	191		7,225	6,765
	16,016	15,236	**Long-term liabilities**		
Capital assets	41,269	39,269	Long-term debt	32,500	30,580
Total assets	$57,285	$54,505	**Shareholders' equity**		
			Share capital	825	825
			Retained earnings	16,735	16,335
			Total liabilities and shareholders' equity	$57,285	$54,505

The average value of total assets is $55.895 million, average common equity is $17.360 million, average debt is $38.535 million, and average long-term debt is $31.540 million. Exhibit 10-15 shows the values of the ratios.

Question 2: The firm's capital assets have a current market value that is substantially higher than the net book value. About two months ago, a national real estate development company offered NWS $120 million to purchase all the capital assets. The employees of the firm are considering buying out the shareholders and have requested that you recalculate the ratios using this market value to assess the impact

Case Continued >

Exhibit 10-15
Selected Ratios for NWS

Ratio	Value
Operating profit margin	$30,074 \div $96,897 = 31.04\%
Rate of return ratios	
Operating return on assets	$30,074 \div $55,895 = 53.80\%
Return on assets	$17,330 \div $55,895 = 31.00\%
Return on common equity	$17,330 \div $17,360 = 99.83\%
Leverage ratios	
Debt ratio	$38,535 \div $55,895 = 68.94\%
Long-term debt ratio	$31,540 \div $55,895 = 56.43\%
Debt-to-equity ratio	$38,535 \div $17,360 = 2.22 \text{ times}

---

on the financials of revaluing the assets. (**Note:** In a purchase, there would not be two years of information to average.) What should the values of the ratios displayed in Exhibit 10-15 be?

The market value of capital assets is $120 million. Given this value, the current market value of total assets increases by $78.731 million ($120 million − $41.269 million). Thus, the value of total assets is $136.016 million. On the liability side, retained earnings disappears but common stock changes to $96.291 million. These changes will change the values of the ratios to the values listed in Exhibit 10-16.

Exhibit 10-16
Selected Ratios for NWS Calculated on a Market-Value Basis

Ratio	Value
Operating profit margin	$30,074 \div $96,897 = 31.04\%
Rate of return ratios	
Operating return on assets	$30,074 \div $136,016 = 22.11\%
Return on assets	$17,330 \div $136,016 = 12.74\%
Return on common equity	$17,330 \div ($95,466 + 825) = 18\%
Leverage ratios	
Debt ratio	$38,535 \div $136,016 = 28.33\%
Long-term debt ratio	$31,540 \div $136,016 = 23.19\%
Debt-to-equity ratio	$38,535 \div ($95,466 + 825) = 0.4002 \text{ times}

Except for the operating profit margin, all the ratios will change because of the use of market value.

Question 3: NWS has 82,500 common shares outstanding. The firm's policy is to pay 75% of earnings in dividends. Based on the accounting information, what are the earnings and dividends per share?

Case Continued >

Currently, earnings are $17.330 million. Therefore, the earnings per share are:

$$\$17,330 \div 82.5 = \$210.06$$

The dividends per share are:

$$\$210.06 \times 0.75 = \$157.55$$

Question 4: Based on the market value of assets, what are the earnings and the dividends per share?

The EPS and DPS ratios do not change in this case, as neither the number of shares outstanding nor the earnings changed.

Alternative Methods of Financial Analysis

Financial analysis also includes the preparation of financial statements in order to make comparisons and identify trends more readily. Financial managers use the following techniques to recast financial statements.

Common-Size Financial Statements Common-size financial statements are financial statements expressed on a basis that eliminates the effect of a firm's size on performance evaluation and allows a firm-to-firm comparison. They may be used to compare the performance of a firm to the performance of its competitors. The common-size balance sheet is prepared by expressing the regular items of the balance sheet as a percentage of total assets. The common-size income statement is prepared by expressing the income statement items as a percentage of sales. The purpose of eliminating the effect of size on performance evaluation is to identify performance areas that are out of line with those of competitors.

Indexed Financial Statements An indexed balance sheet is a statement that reports assets and liabilities in terms of the same assets and liabilities measured at the end of a base year. Some financial analysts prepare indexed financial statements to identify trends in financial statements. Similarly, an indexed income statement reports sales, cost of goods sold, and other items in terms of the base year figures. For example, suppose the base year is 20X0 and the inventories of the corporation were $15 million. The inventories during 20X1, 20X2, and 20X3 were $15.75 million, $16.25 million, and 17.25 million dollars, respectively. An indexed financial statement reports inventories in 20X0, 20X1, 20X2, and 20X3 to be, respectively, 1, 1.05, 1.083, and 1.15. This approach shows that the growth of inventories from the base year of 20X0 to 20X3 was 15%.

10.7 LONG-TERM FINANCIAL PLANNING MODEL
Groundwork for the Model

Earlier in this chapter, you learned that financial planning is a process by which a firm formulates a set of business and financial plans and identifies how these plans can be executed. The objectives of financial planning are to study the impact of various financial policies on the firm's operating plans, identify financial plans consistent with the operating strategies, and prepare contingency plans in case future circumstances deviate from expected outcomes. Financial plans can be reflected in the pro forma financial statements. These statements are developed from a full set of financial statements under given economic and corporate assumptions.

This section is primarily concerned with the last three steps of the financial planning process as listed in Section 10.1. You learn how to build a model to construct pro forma financial statements for the purposes of long-term financial planning. Then, you analyze the resulting financial statements using ratio analysis, as explained in Section 10.6. Finally, you learn how to perform a scenario analysis and develop contingency plans to ensure the firm's survival regardless of how the future unfolds.

Preparing Pro Forma Financial Statements

The process of preparing pro forma statements comprises several steps:

1. Prepare a sales forecast.

2. Forecast the direct operating costs based on the sales forecast.

3. Estimate the level of working capital needed to support the forecasted sales level.

4. Forecast the level of capital assets needed to support the sales level.

5. Estimate the operating costs of the firm over the planning horizon.

6. Estimate the amount of financing required to support the forecast of asset growth.

7. Estimate financing costs based on the forecast of financing needs.

8. Determine the split of net income between dividends and retained earnings.

9. Prepare preliminary income statements, balance sheets, and cash flow statements over the planning horizon.

10. Modify the preliminary forecasts to ensure consistency among the various variables and estimates.

It must be emphasized that there are several iterations of these steps. The financial analyst often starts with a preliminary forecast. Once the initial pro forma financial statements are prepared, additional adjustments will be needed to ensure that various costs are consistent with the project's asset levels, financing costs, and operating activities.

Inconsistencies in the preparation of forecasts can occur because of the choice of financing. For example, the amount of external financing depends on the projected cash position, which is resolved after determining the net income and the portion of net income that will be paid in dividends. However, the amount of net income cannot be set before determining the amount of interest expense that will be paid on external financing. Consequently, several iterations are generally needed to make the forecasts consistent.

Also, in the early stages of planning, it is important to review the assumptions underlying the plan, which may involve numerous iterations. For this reason, the base case assumptions should be well known throughout the process. As the assumptions change with each iteration, it is important to study every assumption underlying the plans so that deviations from the base case under scenario or sensitivity analysis can be traced to differences in the assumptions. The base case can then be easily changed if senior management decides to change the assumptions.

Fortunately, the use of spreadsheets facilitates the job of the financial analyst. With the help of a spreadsheet, the financial planning model can be programmed to create an initial estimate, and then used to revise the estimate until all inconsistencies are eliminated.

Analyzing the Pro Forma Financial Statements Using Ratio Analysis

Once financial statements are prepared, the financial analyst can perform ratio analysis. The objective is to analyze the firm's performance with regard to the planned activities and to see whether the projected results are acceptable to management. The principles of ratio analysis and its use in determining the weaknesses and strengths of a firm's past performance were explained in the previous section. The same analysis can be used to identify any weaknesses and strengths in future plans.

Scenario Analysis

The basic financial plan is based on the expected values of many variables. Scenario analysis entails changing these key variables and observing the changes in forecasted results. For example, the firm may be planning to introduce a new product. The financial manager will need to construct pro forma income statements for the project over several years and will need forecasts of many variables. These include general economic conditions, interest rates over several years, the initial costs of the equipment, total market size of the product, the firm's market share, price ranges for the final product, and fixed and variable costs of production. The forecasts are derived from several sources, internal and external to the firm, including outside consultants and customer surveys. Generally, forecasters provide their opinions in terms of most likely, pessimistic, and optimistic scenarios.

Scenario analysis entails preparing financial plans based on the pessimistic, the optimistic, and any other likely forecast. This means that the financial plan will be prepared under different scenarios for any variable that cannot be estimated with certainty. Also, scenario analysis can be employed to determine the variability of the plan to simultaneous changes in several variables. The financial manager prepares the financial plan based on an analysis of all scenarios, choosing the most likely scenario for the plan.

Computer Activity: Scenario Analysis in Financial Planning

This computer illustration demonstrates the use of scenario analysis in long-term financial planning.

LEARNING OBJECTIVES

Design and use a worksheet to:

- perform a ratio analysis of pro forma financial statements that extend over a five-year period;

- study the effect of interest rates on the firm's financial performance over a five-year period;

- study the effect of changes in market demand on the firm's financial performance over a five-year period; and

- study the effect of changes in the costs of materials and labour on the firm's financial performance over a five-year period.

Description

Lynn Goetz is the financial manager responsible for long-term financial planning at Electronic Components Manufacturing (ECM). She is preparing the financial plan for the next five years starting January 1, 20X2, and ending December 31, 20X6. The firm's policy is to prepare a long-term financial plan on an annual basis for a time horizon of five years.

The firm's income statement, statement of retained earnings, and balance sheet for the fiscal year ending December 31, 20X1, are presented in Exhibits 10-17, 10-18, and 10-19. Sales for the next five years are expected to increase by 3.5% annually. Raw material and labour are expected to remain at 40% and 15% of sales, respectively. Advertising and promotion costs will remain stable for next year, but they will increase to $98.871 million by year 20X3 and to $123.589 million in years 20X4 through 20X6.

The firm's capital assets are classified as either equipment or plant. The firm's policy is to use cash equal to the amortization charges to improve or maintain plant and equipment. Consequently, the book values of the current plant and equipment are expected to be stable over the planning horizon. Equipment is amortized at 20%, while plant is amortized at 10%. For planning purposes, the firm assumes that the entire cost of new assets will be subject to amortization during the first year of acquisition.

The firm is planning two major capital investments in 20X3 and 20X4. Further details are shown in Exhibit 10-20. The firm is also expected to pay $25 million in net costs for replacing obsolete machinery during fiscal year 20X2. Additional investments of $25 million and $5 million will be required in 20X5 and 20X6, respectively, to buy equipment for the two new products.

The firm's policy is to keep the debt-to-total-asset ratio at 60%, but it avoids issuing shares to finance small investments. Therefore, it plans to finance the investment expenditures in 20X2, 20X5, and 20X6 with long-term debt. Capital for Products A and B will be financed with 40% equity and 60% long-term debt. Lynn received Exhibit 10-20 from Smart Investment Bankers, the firm's investment banking adviser, which contains a forecast of short-term interest rates (mainly on notes payable to the bank) and long-term interest rates that ECM would likely have to pay to raise funds in the future. The exhibit also contains a forecast of ECM's expected common share prices over the next five years and the cost to the firm if preferred shares are used to raise funds. ECM's management has already approved plans to raise common dividends from $2.00 per share to $2.50. The change will take effect in 20X2, in preparation for an issue of common shares one year later.

In general, the firm's current assets, accounts payable, and accruals are expected to grow at the same rate as sales. However, given the planned capital expenditures over the next five years, these items will actually increase, as indicated in Exhibit 10-22. Notes payable are mainly loans from the firm's line of credit with the bank. The firm is required to repay $16 million of its long-term debt annually over the next five years. The firm's policy is to refund this debt with new issues of long-term debt.

Exhibit 10-17
Electronic Components Manufacturing Income Statement
Year Ended December 31, 20X1 ($ Thousands)

Sales	
Cost of sales:	$435,000
Raw materials	174,000
Labour	65,250
Gross margin	195,750
Selling and administrative expenses	
Advertising and promotion	85,975
Amortization	38,213
Income from operations	71,562
Interest expense	15,531
Income before taxes	56,031
Taxes	23,533
Net income	$ 32,498

Exhibit 10-18
Electronic Components Manufacturing Statement of Retained Earnings December 31, 20X1 ($ Thousands)

Retained earnings, January 1, 20X1	$34,261
Plus: Net income for 20X1	32,498
	66,759
Preferred dividends	$ 2,596
Common dividends	8,000
Retained earnings	$56,163

Required

a) Lynn is planning to conduct an analysis of the strengths and weaknesses of the current financial and operating plans using ratio analysis. For purposes of comparison, she collected key financial ratios for a major competitor, CAM Ltd., and for the industry group (see Exhibit 10-23). Assume the role of financial manager. Write a brief memo (not more than 350 words) to Robert Williams, the controller, summarizing your findings on any possible strengths and weaknesses, and suggest any actions that may improve ECM's performance. Include in your memo a table that summarizes important financial information from your ratio

Exhibit 10-19
Electronic Components Manufacturing Balance Sheet
December 31, 20X1 ($ Thousands)

Assets			Liabilities		
Current assets			**Current liabilities**		
Cash and marketable securities	$	3,985	Accounts payable		$12,472
			Accruals		6,918
			Notes payable		24,115
Accounts receivable		35,624	Current portion of		
Inventories		47,711	long-term debt		16,000
Prepaid expenses		2,338			59,505
Other current assets		1,978			
		91,636			
			Long-term liabilities		
Capital assets			Long-term debt		142,895
Equipment		142,750			
Plant		96,625			
		239,375	**Shareholders' equity**		
Total assets		$331,011	Preferred shares		32,448
			Share capital		40,000
			Retained earnings		56,163
			Total liabilities and shareholders' equity		$331,011

Exhibit 10-20
New Product Launches by ECM

	Product A	Product B
Launch date	20X3	20X4
First year sales	$65.88 million	$119.314 million
Increase in sales	5%/year	5%/year
Cost of materials, year 1	45% of sales	45% of sales
Cost of materials, year 2	45% of sales	45% of sales
Cost of materials, years 3 to 5	40% of sales	38% of sales
Labour costs	20% of sales	18% of sales
Investment in launch year	$75 million	$125 million
Equipment investment	60%	60%
Plant investment	40%	40%

Exhibit 10-21
Forecast of Interest Rates, Share Price, and Preferred Dividend Rates over the Next Five Years

Year	Current	20X2	20X3	20X4	20X5	20X6
Forecasted rates on short-term debt	6.75%	6.20%	6.00%	6.50%	7.00%	8.00%
Forecasted rates on long-term debt	8.75	8.00	7.50	8.25	8.75	9.50
Preferred-dividend rate	8.00	7.25	7.00	7.50	8.50	9.25
Common-share price	$16.00	$16.75	$19.75	$23.35	$23.95	$24.85

Exhibit 10-22
Expected Growth in ECM's Current Assets and Liabilities over the Next Five Years

Year	20X2	20X3	20X4	20X5	20X6
Growth rate	3.5%	20%	30%	1%	1%

analysis of the pro forma financial statements. **Hint:** Use a spreadsheet to generate a financial planning model to produce pro forma income statements, balance sheets, and cash flow statements for ECM over the next five years.

Exhibit 10-23
Selected Ratios for CAM and the Industry Average

	Average over the past five years	
Ratio	CAM	Industry average
Current ratio	1.15	1.20
Inventory turnover ratio	4.87	4.13
Total-asset turnover	1.27	1.15
Gross profit margin	45.00%	45.25%
Return on assets	7.50%	8.00%
Debt ratio	57.00%	60.00%
Long-term debt ratio	46.00%	50.00%
Times interest earned	4.34	4.00
Earnings per share	$ 6.45	$ 6.10

b) Lynn realizes that the forecast of interest rates is highly uncertain. She has revised her forecast as indicated in Exhibit 10-24. Should Lynn be concerned with this faster rise in rates? **Hint:** Remember to start from the initial assumptions.

Year	20X2	20X3	20X4	20X5	20X6
Forecasted rates on short-term debt	7.00%	8.00%	8.50%	9.00%	9.50%
Forecasted rates on long-term debt	8.50%	9.00%	9.50%	10.00%	10.50%

c) After reviewing the marketing strategies for Products A and B with the marketing department, Lynn thinks that the forecasts are highly uncertain. Suppose product A's sales are $35 million for 20X3 (instead of $65.88 million) and product B's sales are $90 million for 20X4 (instead of $119.314 million). How sensitive is ECM's situation to these deviations from the original sales forecasts? **Hint:** Remember to start from the initial assumptions.

d) After reviewing the production plans for Products A and B, it seems that material and labour costs may be substantially higher than projected. One production manager stated that material costs for each product could be as high as 55% of the product's sales for the first two years of production and 50% thereafter. Labour costs for each product could be as high as 30% of the products' sales for the first couple of years of production and 25% afterward. Will ECM face serious losses if such circumstances occur? **Hint:** Remember to start from the initial assumptions.

Procedure

Excel FN2LXP1.xls

Starting up:

1. Open the file FN2LXP1.xls. Notice that it contains worksheets for the four parts of this illustration. Part a) requires seven worksheets; each of the three remaining parts requires five worksheets.

2. Click the LXP1MEMO sheet tab and study the layout of the partially completed worksheet, which you will use to write a summary of your findings.

To complete part a):

1. Three worksheets (PLAN A IS, PLAN A BS, and PLAN A CFS) provide the financial statements needed for the ratio analysis. You may wish to browse these worksheets on-screen or print them.

2. Click the RATIO A worksheet tab. Study the layout of the worksheet. Rows 4 through 14 have been set up for you to enter the appropriate formulas to complete the ratio calculations for 20X2 to 20X6. Ratios have been entered in column B for the major competitor (20X1) and in column H for the industry.

3. Complete the ratio analysis by entering the appropriate formulas in cells C6 to G14. Remember that the calculation of inventory turnover, total-asset turnover, and return on assets requires that the denominator be an average balance.

4. Save and print a copy of the ratios. This file is the base case for subsequent scenario analyses.

5. Click the RATIO AS sheet tab and compare your results. Resolve any differences.

6. Click the LXP1MEMO sheet tab. Click anywhere in the body of the memo template and type your findings.

To complete parts b) and c):

1. Three worksheets (PLAN B IS, PLAN B BS, and PLAN B CFS) provide the financial statements needed for the ratio analysis. You may wish to browse these worksheets on-screen or print them.

2. Click the RATIO B sheet tab. Study the layout of the worksheet. Rows 7 and 9 contain the forecasted rates for both short-term and long-term debt over the period 20X1 to 20X6. Rows 11 through 21 have been set up for you to enter the appropriate formulas to complete the ratio calculations for 20X2 to 20X6. Ratios have been entered in column B for the major competitor and in column H for the industry ratios.

3. Complete the ratio analysis by entering the appropriate formulas in cells C13 to G21.

4. Save and print a copy of the ratios. Click the RATIO BS sheet tab and compare your results. Resolve any differences.

5. Repeat steps 1 to 4 to answer part c).

To complete part d):

1. Three worksheets (PLAN D IS, PLAN D BS, and PLAN D CFS) provide the financial statements needed for the ratio analysis. You may wish to browse these worksheets on-screen or print them.

2. Click the RATIO D sheet tab. Study the layout of the worksheet. Rows 4 to 11 contain the changes in percentages for raw material and the labour component of Product A and Product B over the period 20X1 to 20X6. Rows 13 through 23 have been set up for you to enter the appropriate formulas to complete the ratio calculations for 20X2 to 20X6. Ratios have been entered in column B for the major competitor and in column H for the industry ratios.

3. Complete the ratio analysis by entering the appropriate formulas in cells C15 to G23.

4. Save and print a copy of the ratios. Click the RATIOS DS sheet tab and compare your results. Resolve any differences.

Commentary

a) Worksheet RATIO AS provides the results of the ratio analysis.
Worksheet LXP1MEMO provides an example of a memo that summarizes the results of the ratio analysis. Exhibit A provides the industry ratios, ratios of the major

competitor, the five-year average of the firm, and the ratios over the five-year period for the base case. To make the comparisons, two assumptions are necessary:

- The ratios for the industry are not expected to change in the next five years.
- The new products that will be introduced by ECM will not alter its industry classification.

The memo should summarize the overall strengths and weaknesses of the firm and draw conclusions about each of the ratios. The high inventory turnover ratios that occur throughout the period with especially high ratios in 20X3 and 20X4 and the increasing trend in the cost of raw materials and labour over the five-year period should be mentioned. Also, high long-term debt levels occur in 20X5 because of expenditures on capital assets. Total debt levels are excessive in 20X2 to 20X4. Additional equity issues combined with positive retained earnings brought the total debt ratio down to a manageable level in 20X5. The high level of long-term debt creates an increase in the firm's fixed interest expenses. These observations affect the ratios and should be included in the memo. Finally, recommendations should be given as to how to remedy the observed weaknesses of the firm.

b) Worksheet RATIO BS shows the ratios for ECM over the next five years assuming that interest rates increase faster than the base case. The ratio analysis indicates that higher interest rates make many ratios less attractive to shareholders compared with the performance of the industry and the major competitor over the five-year period. This is especially true of the gross profit margin and the return on assets. However, the firm will not face bankruptcy even if interest rates increase as forecasted because cash flows remain positive, as observed by the pro forma cash flow statements. Moreover, the times interest earned ratio shows that the firm can cover its fixed expenses comfortably.

c) Worksheet RATIO CS shows the ratios for ECM if the first year's demand for Product A is $35 million per year instead of $65.88 million, and for Product B, $90 million instead of $119.314 million. As the scenario analysis indicates, ECM's ratios will be significantly worse than the industry averages for total-asset turnover. The firm faces negative cash flows for 20X4 and 20X5. As indicated by the cash flow statements, cash balances go into the red in 20X5. This could indicate potential insolvency. The firm's return on assets decreases below that of the industry over the five-year period, reflecting a decrease in its financial performance. Moreover, the firm's earnings per share will drop significantly, all of which will cause a significant drop in share price. This could affect the firm's ability to raise funds through equity financing, as it has planned to do in 20X3 and 20X4.

d) Worksheet RATIO DS shows the ratios for ECM if material and labour costs are as high as predicted by the manager. Many of ECM's ratios will be significantly worse than the industry averages. The firm faces negative cash balances in 20X5 and 20X6, which could lead to insolvency. Both the gross profit margin and the return on assets decrease below the industry averages, which indicate the sensitivity of the firm's earnings to these costs. Furthermore, the firm's earnings per share will decrease significantly during the year when Product B is introduced. The decrease will lead to a sharp decline in share price. Again, this will impact the firm's ability to raise funds through an equity issue.

Conclusion

This computer illustration demonstrated the important contribution that scenario analysis can make to improving a firm's long-term financial plan. Scenario analysis shows how changes in key variables affect a firm's forecasted performance. In this illustration, changes to interest rates, market demand, and the cost of raw materials and labour all had an important impact on the financial ratios of the firm. Scenario analysis provides managers with information that can be used to develop action plans to avert serious financial distress.

Limitations of Financial Planning

The financial planning process has certain limitations:

- Perhaps the most serious limitation is that it is *based on forecasts of several key factors*. As the actual future outcome of these factors will inevitably deviate from the forecasted outcomes, the financial planning model will never produce entirely accurate results. Instead, the financial analyst hopes to produce results that are close approximations of the actual ones. The accuracy of the results depends to a great degree on the accuracy of the forecasts.

- The financial planning process is *not designed as a decision-making tool*. The information provided by the process can be used for decision making, but the process itself does not determine the optimal values of the decision variables. In other words, the financial planning process produces qualitative conclusions rather than quantitative values for the decision variables.

- *The assumptions underlying the financial plan become obsolete* as soon as new forecasts of the microeconomic and macroeconomic environment are revealed. Sometimes, changes can be so frequent that by the time the financial plan is finalized, the assumptions are obsolete. In these circumstances, the financial analyst must generate more frequent forecasts. As a result, the firm will incur greater direct costs and opportunity costs in personnel time to collect data and update the plan. Despite this effort, management may perceive the forecasts as unreliable and consequently downplay or ignore their conclusions.

10.8 STRATEGIC DECISIONS AND ETHICAL CONSIDERATIONS

In your introductory finance course, you will have learned that every step in the financial planning process can contribute to the firm's strategic advantage. Understanding the firm's current situation so as to identify the firm's strengths and weaknesses helps in the planning of a valid strategic course. An analysis of the current financial situation will give management an understanding of whether the firm is operating above or below average, which aids in identifying strengths and areas needing improvement. Strategic decision making also requires a good understanding of the firm's customer base and the demographics of the market. The last necessary item for good strategic planning is an understanding of the abilities of the human resources at the firm's disposal.

All of these items contribute to an assessment of the future business environment. A complete analysis of the firm's strengths and weaknesses is necessary for management to properly address them. Also involved in strategic planning is an analysis of the opportunities and threats inherent in the situation. These can include things like identifying a new market or learning of impending changes to the regulatory environment.

Timing is fundamental to strategic efforts and can make or break a business plan, from the timing of the introduction of a new product to the timing of financing needs.

When creating strategic plans it is important to assess the impact of new technology, changing personnel skills, and longer-term social changes. One system of strategic planning works in three stages. The *strategic plan* takes a long-term view of the industry, economic and social changes, developments in technology, competition, and constraints in general. The *operational plan* is more of a financial document—a two-year budget, in effect. It considers fully the economic and market assumptions prior to delving into detailed figures. The final part is the *business plan*. This part ensures the delivery of the financial and business objectives. It involves the departmental and functional action plans on which performance evaluation is based.

Performance evaluation and measurement constitute an integral part of the business plan. Of particular importance and difficulty is measuring non-financial performance. It is important that measures be relevant to the managers of the particular divisions. By using a business plan regularly to measure performance against agreed indicators, managers complement and promote a performance measurement culture within the organization. Benchmarking and inter-company comparative performance reviews can be valuable indicators of how the company is doing against a peer group of companies or the industry as a whole. Planning provides for departmental performance evaluation, which can be used to drive the business.

In other words, strategic plans need to flow into plans for traditional functional areas of business. The proper design and implementation of these strategies allow the firm to build on its strengths or mitigate its weaknesses. Financial planning models are used to study the possible outcomes of the proposed functional strategies in areas including finance and marketing.

The financial planning process allows management to study the implications of corporate strategic options and identify the best financial alternative. The feasibility of options like an anticipated leveraged buyout can be assessed as can the determination of a dividend policy.

Marketing plans provide firms with a strategic advantage. Marketing strategies are broadly classified as market development or product development strategies. Market development refers to plans aimed at capturing a larger share of an existing market for current products. A product development strategy aims at developing new markets for current products or new products for new markets.

Financial planning is used to determine the best approach to follow. New marketing initiatives are studied to assess their contribution to the firm's cash flows. Also, scenario analysis is used to predict the impact of marketing strategies on the firm's future performance.

Ethics and Financial Performance

There appears to be a link between the long-term financial performance of a firm and the ethical behaviour of its decision makers. Evidence of a positive relationship can be found in the newspapers. Each year, numerous articles report on the stock market performance of companies that have consciously made ethical, socially motivated, or environmentally friendly strategic decisions.

An example of such an article, by Shirley Won, follows. It shows that companies that make such decisions are receiving special attention from a growing group of Canadian investors.

WHEN GOODNESS IS ITS OWN REWARD

SHIRLEY WON, INVESTMENT REPORTER

A growing number of Canadians are screening their stocks according to their conscience—and it's reaping dividends.

Rebecca Bateman wants to cash in on the raging bull market but also sleep at night with a clear conscience. "I want to make money—but not at the expense of other people or the environment," says the 41-year-old anthropologist and director of a university outreach program at Vancouver's Simon Fraser University.

That's why she began investing this year in three mutual funds in the Ethical Fund family in her registered retirement savings plan (RRSP). The funds avoid companies that produce tobacco, weapons, and nuclear power. And they also screen for firms that have good environmental records and fair labour practices and do business only in and with countries providing racial equality or equal opportunity.

Ms. Bateman is part of a small but growing number of Canadians who have embraced "ethical investing"—a catch-all phrase for investments screened according to specific social and/or environmental criteria. And these investors are discovering that remaining true to one's social conscience, which usually entails reducing the available universe of stocks or bonds, doesn't necessarily mean sacrificing decent returns.

Consider the performance of funds such as **Ethical Growth Fund** and **Investors Group Inc.'s Summa Fund**, the latter of which avoids firms involved in alcohol, tobacco, pornography, gambling or weapons and those that pollute or support repressive regimes. The 10-year average annual return of these Canadian equity funds beat the 8.8-percent average for their peers as of Sept. 30, 1997 and the 9.3-percent return for the benchmark Toronto Stock Exchange 300 total return index. (See chart.)

Weathered '87 crash

Ethical or socially responsible investing—as some prefer to call it—has had a much higher profile in the United States where a wide array of these guilt-free mutual funds have been part of the investment landscape since the 1970s. It wasn't until 1986 that Canada's first ethical fund—Ethical Growth—was launched by Vancouver City Savings Credit Union. It gained early attention for weathering the October 1987 stock market crash because it had more than 40 percent of its assets in cash, and ended the year with an 8-percent return.

How Ethical Funds Have Fared to Sept. 30

Name	Net assets ($ million)	1-year	3-year	5-year	10-year
			Returns		
Clean Environment Balanced	$ 39.3	38.5%	20.1%	19.7%	—
Clean Environment Equity	110.7	47.6	26.5	23.7	—
Clean Environment Income	3.7	11.1	7.1	—	—
Clean Environment Int'l Equity	10.7	53.3	21.7	—	—
Desjardins Environnement	71.9	44.5	20.0	16.0	—
Ethical Balanced	426.8	33.0	18.7	14.0	—
Ethical Global Bond	12.5	8.6	—	—	—
Ethical Growth	**627.9**	**42.9**	**23.6**	**19.0**	**12.8%**
Ethical Income*	124.4	13.0	13.0	9.7	9.5
Ethical Money Market*	95.0	2.5	4.3	4.3	7.1
Ethical North American Equity*	94.5	49.3	30.2	21.1	10.2
Ethical Pacific Rim	29.9	9.4	—	—	—
Ethical Special Equity	83.2	36.5	—	—	—
Investors Summa	**260.4**	**46.0**	**24.3**	**18.4**	**10.3**
TSE 300 Total Return		**35.4**	**19.9**	**19.1**	**9.3**
Canadian Equity Average		**32.3**	**18.1**	**17.2**	**8.8**

* The track records of Ethical North American Equity, Income and Money Market before Sept., 1992 are not relevant. These funds were acquired by Ethical Funds Inc. at that time and previously did not use social or environmental screens. The North American Equity Fund had previously been a Canadian equity fund.

Source: Globe HySales.

Ethical Growth's assets have mushroomed to $628-million, and the fund is now run by Ethical Funds Inc., which is owned by the Canadian credit union system. And the do-gooder funds have now climbed to 14 with nearly $2 billion in assets—still tiny compared with the more than $270 billion in fund assets being managed in Canada.

But mutual funds don't tell the whole story. Some institutional managers use ethical screens to invest money for foundations, high-net-worth individuals, and religious orders. And more retail investors are demanding portfolios custom tailored to their own social values.

There are financial advisers "who are detecting a growth in this market and want to be part of it," says Eugene Ellmen, author of *The Canadian Ethical Money Guide.* "But most will say it's still a minority of their business."

The Social Investment Organization (SIO)—a Toronto-based non-profit organization that promotes socially responsible investing—says the number of financial planners and brokers who are members has jumped to 81 from a dozen five years ago.

Scott Beech, a 33-year-old graduate university student living in Waterloo, Ont., has units in some U.S. ethical mutual funds that he bought in the early 1990s when he worked in the United States as a software developer. More recently, he has bought stocks through a broker who screens companies according to his values. Mr. Beech will not invest in companies that make tobacco or weapons and is currently avoiding resource stocks. But he holds such environmentally friendly companies as **Ballard Power Systems Inc.** and **Trojan Technologies Inc.** His portfolio also includes high-tech stocks such as **JDS Fitel Inc.**, **Mosaid Technologies Inc.**, and **ATI Technologies Inc.**, because "they are a great investment and aren't doing anything wrong."

Best-of-Sector Approach

In the past couple of years, the performance of ethical funds and individual "ethical" stock portfolios has been given a boost as a result of adopting a "best-of-sector" approach. That involves investing in companies with the best social and environmental records compared with their peers instead of eliminating stocks in "bad" sectors such as mining and forestry because of their negative impact on the environment.

Ethical investing, meanwhile, does have its critics.

Money manager Stephen Jarislowsky, chairman of Montreal-based Jarislowsky Fraser Inc., describes ethical funds as a marketing gimmick and views their constraints as potentially hobbling performance. And he finds holes in their theory.

"Where do you stop?" Mr. Jarislowsky asks. "Tobacco is an easy mark. But then you should never buy Canada Savings Bonds because the government takes enormous taxes out of the tobacco industry and therefore the government isn't ethical."

Mr. Jarislowsky dismisses the best-of-sector approach to ethical investing as "hypocrisy," saying "it's all convenience" to produce more favourable returns.

Michael Jantzi, president of Toronto-based Michael Jantzi Research Associates Inc., concedes the best-of-sector approach is necessary for investment diversification. "In the Canadian market you would eliminate 40 to 45 percent of the market if you took out their resource-base stocks."

But Mr. Jantzi—whose company tracks the social and environmental performance of companies for institutional and retail investment advisers—argues this approach is also a good way of influencing corporate behaviour.

"If you eliminate entire sectors there is no incentive built in," he says. "Our clients don't expect perfection. But what they want to do is have an impact on change and they have decided that one way to do that is through the markets."

Despite careful efforts by funds to screen stocks and bonds, there can be slip-ups. John Linthwaite, president of Ethical Funds Inc., says Vancouver-based Conner Clark Lunn Investment Management Ltd.—which manages Ethical Growth—inadvertently slipped some Ontario Hydro bonds into the fund last June. Those bonds, which violate the fund's anti-nuclear screen because the utility operates nuclear plants, were dumped after being in the portfolio for about two weeks. "It was a mistake," said Mr. Linthwaite, noting that the investment manager had bought the bonds for other clients.

Playing Both Sides

Ethical investing has gained total converts while others hedge their bets. Marian Pitters, 45, who runs her own management consulting business in Toronto, says she has about 50 percent of her fund assets in the **Clean Environment Fund** family, which invests in environmentally friendly companies. The rest is still in what she describes as conventional funds. She does not want to invest in companies that harm the environment or make weapons and cigarettes. But she also doesn't believe in investing in politically correct companies unless they are also "well managed."

Mutual funds make it easier to combine making money with her environmental concerns. "It doesn't have to be a tortuous experience that takes tons of time," she says. "And I have a clearer conscience so I can sleep."

Ms. Pitters also belongs to a women's ethical investment club called The Money Bags, which will not invest in companies making weapons or tobacco. Instead, they have chosen stocks such as **Corel Corp.**, **Intrawest Corp.**, and **Laidlaw Inc**.

There are no Canadian figures, but anecdotal evidence suggests ethical investing has more appeal for women. Alan Harman, a 37-year-old Toronto investment adviser with ScotiaMcLeod Inc., says he has worked with ethical investors for 11 years and 80 percent have been women. "I guess women are warmer and more compassionate," he says. "There is more peer pressure—particularly among men—to make money and maximize their net worth."

Toni Ellis, 42, of Elora, Ont., has been investing "ethically" for about nine years. The mother of two boys, who works part-time in environmental education, says her portfolio includes the Clean Environment Equity Fund and such stocks as **Alcan Aluminum Ltd.** because of its monetary and other contributions to the blue-box recycling program in Ontario. But blue-chips such as **Bank of Nova Scotia**, **Royal Bank**, and **Thomson Corp.** make it into her portfolio because they offer good returns but don't harm the environment. "The concept of making a lot of money on something that is really inherently not good for this planet doesn't sit well with me," she says.

Bottom Line

Ethical investing is not for everyone. But there is evidence that you don't always have to sacrifice competitive returns to appease your social conscience. You may have to accept a practical "best-of-sector" approach when you don't eliminate all the bad actors but reward the best of a "bad" lot.

How to Pick with Your Heart and Mind

Ethical—or socially responsible—investing can be a complex and controversial concept fraught with imperfections.

You can use negative screens and avoid the "bad" guys. Or, you can use positive screens by choosing "good" guys that have strong environmental or social records, or are involved in environmentally friendly technologies.

If you want to invest with your heart as well as your mind, here are some tips as suggested by ethical-industry players in Canada.

♦ **Define your values:** Ethical investing can mean different things to different people. Before you invest your money, figure out your values. Do you just want to avoid the sin stocks like tobacco and alcohol? Are you outraged by weapons makers? Or, are you just concerned about environmental issues?

♦ **Start with mutual funds:** If you are nervous about using social and environmental screens for investing, consider putting a small portion of your portfolio—such as 10 percent—into the so-called ethical funds. Check out their track records. And see if you like their screens because they differ.

Continued >

Source: Reprinted with permission from *The Globe and Mail*

These investors are pursuing what is known as ethical investing. They screen prospective investment targets on the basis of their ethical and environmental records in addition to financial performance. For example, they avoid investing in companies that produce tobacco, alcohol, or weapons, companies engaged in gambling and nuclear power production, and those that pollute or deal with repressive regimes. They favour companies that have good environmental records, have fair labour practices, and conduct their businesses in countries where racial equality and equal opportunities are ensured. The article promotes the "best-of-sector" approach to investing, by which those companies are selected within a sector that have the best score in terms of their ethical, social, and environmental records.

The presence of a large group of investment managers and individuals who favour ethical investing and may be willing to buy the securities of an ethical company at a premium effectively lowers the cost of capital to these favoured companies.

At the same time, there is growing evidence that firms pay a hefty price for making unethical decisions in the form of financial losses resulting from fines, product recalls, environmental cleanups, and lawsuits. However, the most damaging effect of a firm's unethical behaviour is the loss of customer confidence, loyalty, and goodwill. The loss of customer goodwill can lead to the firm's bankruptcy. Because consumer confidence takes time and effort to establish, managers must carefully consider the ethical, social, and environmental issues that arise from their strategic decisions. As agents for shareholders, they are expected to make strategic decisions in the best interests of shareholders.

Ethical Issues in Strategic Planning

One of the reasons why financial managers consider ethical issues when making strategic decisions is the existence of agency relationships and asymmetric information. In Chapter 1, unethical behaviour was shown to occur as a result of the nature of the relationship among the firm's managers, shareholders, and bondholders. Firms issue shares that are purchased by individuals, pension plans, mutual funds, and others. However, these groups of owners are not directly involved in the firm's investment decisions and the allocation of those funds.

Shareholders rely on the firm's managers and on the board of directors to respect their preferences. The relationship between the principals and their agents is called the agency relationship.

Bondholders and creditors also rely on the firm's financial managers to make proper decisions that will enable the firm to fulfil its obligations under debt contracts. Owners and creditors who provide the capital and hold the financial claims on the firm are principals. The financial managers and the board of directors are considered to be agents whose jobs are to represent the best interests of the principals. The agents actually make the decisions.

In the agency relationship, managers breach their responsibility to shareholders if they misuse corporate resources. For example, a manager who uses corporate resources to take a personal trip under the cover of business travel is committing an unethical act. In the agency relationship between finance professional and client, finance professionals or fiduciaries can breach the fiduciary relationship when they counsel clients regarding investments or financial planning. For example, consider a broker who knowingly advises a client to purchase investments unsuitable for the client's personal situation. The broker may promise a naive investor quick gains if the investor makes frequent trades. Yet the real intention of the broker may be to generate commissions.

Asymmetric information can also lead to unethical behaviour. It is unethical for individuals or agents to gain from or misuse private information available to them by virtue of their positions if the information is unavailable to the other party of the transaction. For example, it is unethical for an investment dealer who is involved in negotiating a merger offer to provide information about the offer to private investors or to use the information privately for personal gain.

Similarly, it is unethical to manipulate the financial markets to exploit security price movements for personal gains. An example of this behaviour is the 1997 case of Bre-X Minerals Ltd., in which company executives were accused of falsifying test results to fuel the rise in share price. They were also accused of selling substantial amounts of their shareholdings when Bre-X's share price peaked. The geologist whose report spurred the stock price hysteria was indicted on an insider trading charge. He received a not guilty ruling on that charge. Eventually, the company's real prospects became known and it ceased to exist. Key executives faced lawsuits from shareholders who lost billions of dollars.

CGA-Canada's *Code of Ethical Principles and Rules of Conduct* provides the following guidelines with respect to deceptive information:

> *Members shall not be associated with any information which the member knows, or ought to know, to be false or misleading, whether by statement or omission.*

Rules 401 and 402 indicate that members shall not issue a communication on any financial information that may tend to be misleading. Neither shall members sign or be associated with any letter, report, statement, representation, or financial statement that they know or should know is false or misleading.

Acquisitions Chapter 6 described the process by which a firm acquires another firm. An increase in shareholders' wealth can be accomplished through acquisitions because of synergies and economies of scale in the areas of production, marketing, and financing. There is nothing unethical about such acquisitions. However, there are situations in which acquisitions are driven by unethical motives.

For example, it is well known that executive compensation and power are strongly correlated to the size of the organization. When a company's executives decide to acquire another company, despite a lack of economic reasons to justify the acquisition, the motives may be traced to a quest for power. Shareholders may incur losses because the transactions lead to a drop in the share price over the long run. Such a decision is a violation of the agency relationship between shareholders and managers.

Leveraged Buyouts You learned in Chapter 6 that leveraged buyouts (LBOs) are transactions in which a group of investors buy assets from a firm with a small proportion of the price raised in equity and the remainder in debt. In some cases, the motive of such investors is quick profit. They hope to turn the business around in a short period of time, after which they can sell the assets at a higher price. Some important ethical issues arise in these transactions.

Ethical concerns are raised when the buyers resort to massive layoffs of employees to quickly cut costs and improve profits. The concern is whether the layoffs are necessary. For example, the new owners may lay off employees who are paid high salaries because of their long service with the original firm and replace them with new employees at lower wages.

In addition to the hardships and losses inflicted on employees, layoffs cost society productivity and tax revenues. Moreover, the unemployed will be paid employment insurance benefits. Thus, the owners in some LBOs are subsidized by society for their strategy of cutbacks through social costs, employment insurance costs, and excessive tax shields. The ethical questions are: Should the LBO value increase to offset these costs? Should there be compensation to society for bearing corporate costs?

There are also ethical concerns when the individuals who managed the assets prior to the buyout are the buyers. As you learned in Chapter 6, the managers' motives should be to increase the values of the purchased assets through actions such as improving operations, introducing new products, and improving marketing strategies. The question is why these managers were not able to turn the assets around under the previous ownership. Perhaps the managers knew value-generating information that was not revealed to shareholders prior to the buyout. This would involve a violation of the agency relationship between managers and the original owners. For example, the managers in an oil-drilling firm may conceal the extent of oil reserves in order to acquire the asset in a leveraged buyout and benefit from the reserves.

Financial Restructuring You learned in Chapter 4 that financial structure has implications for risk and expected returns. The higher the leverage, the higher the expected return and the risk will be. **Financial restructuring** refers to managerial actions that are primarily intended to change the capital structure of the firm. Restructuring attempts that are designed to reduce the firm's equity relative to its debt may entail the transfer of wealth from creditors to shareholders. An increase in financial leverage increases financial risk and can severely reduce the value of outstanding bonds.

Although this practice is common, it may have ethical implications. Managers are agents for bondholders as well as for shareholders. In this instance, managers are not acting in the best interest of bondholders, who will lose some of their wealth as a result of restructuring. At the same time, shareholders may not benefit from the restructuring process. In the short run, they may benefit, but the actions could jeopardize the firm's ability to borrow in the future, thereby limiting growth opportunities.

Information Asymmetry and Financial Disclosure Managers and directors of firms are expected to have better information than outsiders. **Information asymmetry** describes a general condition in which an individual or group possesses information that is not known or available to another individual or group. The advantage of having better information has an impact on financial markets and corporate decision making at all levels. A major ethical issue arises from such information asymmetries when managers purposely manipulate the accuracy, breadth, and timeliness of financial statement reports and press releases. This practice is unethical because outsiders, such as investors, analysts, and lenders, expect sound, accurate, and timely information on which to make their capital allocation decisions.

Accountants have ethical and moral obligations to preserve their clients' privileged information. CGA-Canada's *Code of Ethical Principles and Rules of Conduct* provides the following statement to its members on trust and duties toward clients, employers, and interested third parties:

> *Members shall act in the interest of their clients, employers, and interested third parties, and shall be prepared to sacrifice their self-interest to do so. Members shall honour the trust bestowed on them by others, and shall not use their privileged position without their principal's knowledge and consent. Members shall strive to be independent of mind and in appearance.*

Rule 201 indicates that members shall not disclose or use any confidential information concerning the affairs of any client, former client, employer, or former employer. CGA-Canada differentiates between mandatory and discretionary disclosure. *Mandatory disclosure* occurs because the process of law compels a member to disclose a client's affairs. *Discretionary disclosure* of a client's affairs is not forbidden if properly acting in the course of the duties incumbent on a member or where a member becomes aware of an apparent or suspected criminal activity.

For example, privileged information on the discovery of mineral deposits in a new area could be extremely valuable. This type of information would, no doubt, increase the firm's share price. It is unethical to use such insider information for personal gain. There is potential for managers or accountants to be charged with insider trading and fined hefty penalties as a result.

Another abuse of asymmetric information is outright fraud. For example, two parties may exchange information to conclude a trade. One party may mislead the other with false information for personal gain. Accusations of financial fraud usually involve initial public offerings and lending.

Market Manipulation A large firm that has significant market and financial powers may pursue illegal market manipulation. For example, a firm may control the supply of a product to keep the price high, or keep prices artificially low to drive competition out of the market and then raise prices again. Antitrust laws in Canada and the United States prohibit such activities. Moreover, it is unethical for managers to approve of or engage in such practices. Yet such accusations are difficult to prove.

Misuse of Corporate Resources Employees, managers, and directors sometimes use corporate resources for personal benefits. Perks, such as large, costly offices, expensive company cars, and company meetings in expensive resort areas, are examples of agency costs that raise concerns of unethical behaviour.

Shareholders use executive compensation practices to align managers' interests with the firm's objectives. However, these practices also raise ethical concerns if they include:

- unusually large grants of executive stock options;
- a lowering of the exercise price of previously issued executive stock options after the firm's share price has fallen;
- guaranteed bonuses to be paid, regardless of corporate performance;
- long-term employment contracts for managers.

CGA-Canada's *Code of Ethical Principles and Rules of Conduct* provides the following guidance with respect to professional practice:

> *Members shall act openly and fairly towards others in the practice of their profession.*

In dealing with clients or employers, there is a rule that disallows the marketing of goods and services other than their professional services, which would include not accepting a commission or other remuneration from investment dealers for the sale of securities for clients.

CHAPTER SUMMARY

Chapter 10 focuses on the objectives of financial planning and the steps of the financial planning process. Two areas of emphasis are (1) the role of the cash flow statement in summarizing the operating activities, investment activities, and financing activities of the firm, and (2) the role of forecasting. This chapter illustrates cash budgeting as an important tool for short-term financial planning. You learn the nature of the link between short- and long-term financing decisions.

You learn that ratio analysis is effective and powerful in detecting weaknesses and strengths. The chapter explains how financial planning can be used to identify and benefit from a firm's strategic advantages. The ethical concerns and issues that sometimes face the financial manager when making strategic decisions are emphasized.

Key Terms

aggressive strategy,   page 619

cash budget,   page 600

cash conversion period,   page 602

cash management,   page 599

common-size financial statements,   page 638

compliance with loan covenants,   page 613

corporate financial planning,   page 584

direct forecasting method,   page 607

extremely conservative strategy,   page 618

financial control,   page 615

financial plan,   page 585

financial restructuring,   page 656

float,   page 603

forecasting,   page 587

indexed balance sheet,   page 638

information asymmetry,   page 657

inventory conversion period,   page 601

liquidity buffer,   page 618

liquidity risk,   page 613

maturity-matching strategy,   page 618

minimum operating cash balance,   page 613

net working capital,   page 603

nominal-terms approach,   page 592

operating cycle,   page 602

operating plan,   page 584

payables deferral period,   page 602

payment pattern method,   page 610

permanent current assets,   page 617

precautionary motive,   page 613

Important Equations

Balance sheet equation

$$\text{Assets} = \text{liabilities} + \text{shareholders' equity} \qquad \text{(Equation 10-1)}$$

Inventory conversion period

$$\text{Inventory conversion period} = \frac{\text{average inventory}}{\left(\dfrac{\text{cost of goods sold}}{365}\right)} \qquad \text{(Equation 10-2)}$$

Receivables conversion period

$$\text{Receivables conversion period} = \frac{\text{average accounts receivable}}{\left(\dfrac{\text{annual credit sales}}{365}\right)} \qquad \text{(Equation 10-3)}$$

Payables deferral period

$$\frac{\text{Payables deferral}}{\text{period}} = \frac{\text{average accounts payable} + \text{average accruals}}{\left(\dfrac{\text{cost of goods sold}}{365}\right)} \qquad \text{(Equation 10-4)}$$

Cash conversion period

$$\begin{matrix} \text{Cash} \\ \text{conversion} \\ \text{period} \end{matrix} = \begin{matrix} \text{inventory} \\ \text{conversion} \\ \text{period} \end{matrix} + \begin{matrix} \text{receivables} \\ \text{conversion} \\ \text{period} \end{matrix} - \begin{matrix} \text{payables} \\ \text{deferral} \\ \text{period} \end{matrix} \qquad \text{(Equation 10-5)}$$

Net working capital as a function of credit sales

$$\text{NWC} = \left[(\text{IC} - \text{PD}) \times \frac{\text{COGS}}{365}\right]$$
$$+ \left(\text{RC} \times \frac{\text{CS}}{365}\right) + \text{AC} - \text{ANP} - \text{CPLD} \qquad \text{(Equation 10-6)}$$

where

$\quad$ NWC = net working capital

IC = inventory conversion period

PD = payables deferral period

$COGS$ = cost of goods sold

RC = receivables conversion period

CS = yearly credit sales

AC = average cash level

ANP = average notes payable

$CPLD$ = current portion of long-term debt

Return on equity (ROE)

$$ROE = \frac{\text{net income}}{\text{average shareholders' equity}} \qquad \textbf{(Equation 10-7)}$$

Return on equity as a function of total assets

$$ROE = \frac{\text{net income}}{\text{average total assets}} \times \frac{\text{average total assets}}{\text{average shareholders' equity}} \qquad \textbf{(Equation 10-8)}$$

Return on equity as a function of the equity multiplier

$$ROE - ROA \times EM \qquad \textbf{(Equation 10-9)}$$

where

ROA = return on assets

EM = equity multiplier, which is a measure of financial leverage

Return on assets

$$ROA = \frac{\text{net income}}{\text{average total assets}} \qquad \textbf{(Equation 10-10)}$$

Return on assets as a function of net profit margin

$$ROA = \frac{\text{net income}}{\text{net sales}} \times \frac{\text{net sales}}{\text{average total assets}} \qquad \textbf{(Equation 10-11)}$$

$$ROA = NPM \times TAT \qquad \textbf{(Equation 10-12)}$$

where

NPM = net profit margin

TAT = total asset turnover

Net profit margin

$$NPM = 1 - \frac{\text{direct operating expenses}}{\text{net sales}} - \frac{\text{fixed operating expenses}}{\text{net sales}} - \frac{\text{taxes}}{\text{net sales}}$$

$$\textbf{(Equation 10-13)}$$

Web Links

Canada Deposit Insurance Corporation (CDIC)

■ http://www.cdic.ca/ The CDIC is a federal Crown corporation that insures the savings of Canadians. You can check its Web site to confirm that a bank or institution is a member of the CDIC.

Code of Ethics and Professional Responsibility

■ http://www.cfpboard.org/learn/ethics.asp The Certified Financial Planner Board of Standards is a certification standard for financial planners.

Financial Planners Standards Council

■ http://www.cfp-ca.org/ The FPSC is a not-for-profit organization that promotes competency, ethics, and the development and regulation of standards in financial planning.

Financial Planning Perspectives Internet Radio Show

■ http://www.fpanet.org/public/tools/fppshow.cfm A 13-part online radio show that discussed various aspects of personal financial planning, from estate planning to year-round tax strategies.

Income Security Programs

■ http://www.hrsdc.gc.ca/en/gateways/nav/top_nav/program/isp.shtml Provides information about the Canada Pension Plan and Old Age Security as well as a link to international benefits.

Journal of Financial Planning

■ http://www.fpanet.org/journal/?WT.svl=0 Read selected articles online from the official publications of the Financial Planning Association.

Ratio Calculators

■ http://www.bdc.ca/en/business_tools/calculators/overview.htm?cookie%5Ftest=1 This section of the Business Development Bank of Canada's Web site provides links to some commonly used ratios for financial analysis.

BOOK SUMMARY

This text is a comprehensive, self-contained guide to the principles and practices of financial management. The background information, theories, and practical applications of capital investment, financing, risk analysis and management, and financial planning have been presented in a logical sequence to emphasize the interrelationships among the roles and diverse functions of the financial manager.

The book has extended your knowledge in two ways. First, it has provided additional insight into some of the basic issues of finance, such as forces that affect the financial system, basic securities, evaluation of securities, making strategic choices, capital budgeting, and capital management. Second, it has pointed out new financial management problems and given you practice in solving them. In particular, you learned skills to assist you in solving advanced issues in capital budgeting, capital structure decisions, dividend policy, special financing and investment decisions, option pricing, treasury-risk management, cash management, and financial planning.

Following is a summary of the basic skills and knowledge presented in this book, which are designed to prepare you for the role and duties of a financial manager.

■ Chapters 1 and 2 focused on capital investment decisions under the assumption that the financing decisions have already been made.

- Chapters 3, 4, and 5 assumed that the investment decisions have been made and covered the financing problems faced by a financial manager.

- Chapter 6 considered several investment and financing alternatives that have special features, specifically project financing and leasing. The chapter covered the special tools and techniques that the financial manager needs to use to evaluate these investment decisions.

- Chapter 7 provided a comprehensive analysis of treasury-risk management, complementing the previous sections on investment and financing. Up to Chapter 7, investing and financing decisions were considered *assuming* a given level of risk and assuming that diversification was the only way to manage this risk. Chapter 7 highlighted the basic knowledge and techniques used in actively managing risk.

- Chapter 8 considered the features and valuation techniques of futures and forwards derivative securities.

- Chapter 9 looked at the features and valuation techniques of options and swaps. The chapter pointed out that the investment projects undertaken by a firm and the securities used to raise funds often contain embedded options. These options are often ignored in the traditional techniques of analysis. A framework for estimating the values of these options was provided, thereby taking the investment and financing decisions one step further in dealing with practical problems.

- Chapter 10 covered the relationships among a firm's investment, financing, and risk management decisions. The chapter introduced short-term financial planning and emphasized the role of cash budgeting as the main tool for short-term financial management. Also, it addressed the relationship between the firm's liquidity and its long-term financing decisions. Chapter 10 then developed the long-term financial planning model as a tool to test the consistency of the firm's financial, operating, and investment decisions.

Self-Test Questions

Qualitative Questions

Answer each of the following questions in point form:

1. What is corporate financial planning?
2. What are the objectives of financial planning?
3. What is the role of forecasting in financial planning?
4. What are the difficulties in forecasting the various variables needed in the financial planning model?
5. What are the sources of cash and cash equivalents for a firm?
6. How can the cash flow statement facilitate an analysis of the interaction of the firm's policies?
7. What are short-term financial plans?
8. What are the purposes of cash budgeting?
9. How can financial analysts forecast the various cash outflows?
10. Why must firms choose between short-term and long-term financing?
11. What are the management choices with respect to short-term and long-term financing?

12. How is ratio analysis used to determine the weaknesses and strengths of a firm?

13. What are the advantages of using a spreadsheet to develop financial planning models?

14. How is the financial planning model used to identify the likely weaknesses of a firm's plans?

15. How is long-term planning used to assess the impact of changing opportunities?

16. How can financial planning provide strategic advantages to the firm?

17. Identify the ethical issues that may arise from strategic decisions.

18. Identify approaches to correcting potential ethical problems.

Qualitative Multiple Choice Questions

1. Which of the following statements about the cash conversion period is true?
   i) The cash conversion period is the time between when goods are sold and when payment is received from the customer.
   ii) The cash conversion period is the time between the purchase of raw materials and the time when goods are sold.
   iii) The cash conversion period is the time between when accounts payable are paid and when payment is received from the customer.
   iv) The cash conversion period is the time between when accounts payable are established and when accounts payable are paid.

2. Which of the following is *not* spontaneous financing?
   i) Accounts payable
   ii) Notes payable
   iii) Accrued liabilities
   iv) Accrued taxes payable

3. Which of the following financing approaches would lead to the lowest current ratio?
   i) Risk management approach
   ii) Conservative strategy
   iii) Maturity matching
   iv) Aggressive strategy

4. Which of the following statements *best* describes the relationship between short-term and long-term financial plans?
   i) Long-term financial plans are more accurate than short-term plans.
   ii) Long-term financial plans generally reflect seasonal factors, while short-term plans ignore these factors.
   iii) A long-term financial plan involves preparing a detailed cash budget.
   iv) Short-term financial plans detail the coming fiscal year's results projected by long-term financial planning.

5. Which of the following financial ratios is used to measure corporate liquidity?
   i) Debt to assets
   ii) Average collection period
   iii) Inventory turnover
   iv) Quick ratio

6. During a major holiday shopping season, what will a retailer following a strict risk management approach to financing current assets *most likely* do?
   i) The owner will divest marketable securities.
   ii) The owner will invest in marketable securities.

iii) The owner will borrow short-term financing.

iv) The owner will borrow long-term financing.

7. Which of the following statements correctly describes the process of corporate financial planning?

   i) The firm formulates a set of business and financial plans consistent with its business and financial objectives.

   ii) Management identifies where it would like to lead the firm in the future by focusing only on the long-term horizon.

   iii) Management decides the optimal way of using resources over the next several years.

   iv) Management uses financial planning to eliminate the need to formulate contingency plans.

8. Which of the following statements regarding the cash flow statement is true?

   i) It indicates how the cash position of the firm has changed prior to the period covered by the income statement and the balance sheet.

   ii) It lists the amount of cash involved in operating activities, investing activities, and financing activities.

   iii) It indicates that an increase in the firm's cash account should be equal to the amount of external financing.

   iv) It is useful to determine a firm's cash flows from operations, which are operating profits plus interest payments less capital cost allowances.

9. The managers of a firm decide to finance assets with short-term liabilities. Which of the following circumstances is consistent with the decision?

   i) The firm's owners are risk averse.

   ii) The yield curve (term structure of interest rates) is inverted (downward sloping).

   iii) The firm's assets are highly liquid because they consist mainly of a storage facility in a booming industrial area and canned food inventory.

   iv) A firm's liquidity risk decreases as a firm relies more and more on short-term financing.

10. Which of the following ratios correctly describes what can be used to measure management's ability to efficiently manage a firm's assets?

    i) The equity multiplier

    ii) Earnings per share

    iii) The return-on-assets ratio, because it measures the profit produced by one dollar of assets

    iv) The total debt ratio, because it measures the amount of debt as a percentage of total assets

11. Which of the following strategies correctly describes how financial planning can provide the firm with strategic advantages?

    i) Providing management with a decision-making tool that ensures highly accurate results

    ii) Providing optimal solutions to complicated problems related to financial leverage, dividend policy, and operating strategies

    iii) Allowing management to identify the strengths to be magnified and publicized for the purpose of temporarily increasing share price before a major share offering

    iv) Identifying the weaknesses and providing data to help management in eliminating or avoiding them

12. Which of the following statements regarding unethical behaviour is correct?

   i) Judicial costs are really the only significant cost incurred by a firm when lawsuits are instigated for unethical behaviour.

   ii) Agency relationships are not a factor when explaining unethical behaviour.

   iii) It occurs when a manager reports the discovery that a newly drilled oil well is dry before the company concludes a new share issue.

   iv) It occurs when a finance professional breaches the fiduciary relationship with the client by telling a friend, who is a stock promoter, how much money the client has to invest.

Quantitative Multiple Choice Questions

The following data apply to the next two questions:

Ottawa Inc. is currently operating at only 85% of fixed-asset capacity. Current sales are $425,000.

1. How fast can sales grow before any new fixed assets are needed?

   i) 8.50%

   ii) 13.45%

   iii) 15.65%

   iv) 17.65%

2. Suppose fixed assets are $385,000 and sales are $500,000 and are projected to grow to $520,000. How much in new fixed assets is required to support this growth in sales?

   i) $15,400

   ii) $16,800

   iii) $18,350

   iv) $20,500

Quantitative Problems

Problem 1

Your firm is considering three different financing policies: aggressive, matching, and conservative.

	Aggressive	**Matching**	**Conservative**
Accounts receivable	$ 120,000	$ 160,000	$ 240,000
Inventory	150,000	200,000	300,000
Other current assets	30,000	40,000	60,000
Long-term assets	700,000	600,000	400,000
Total	$1,000,000	$1,000,000	$1,000,000
Accruals and accounts payable	$ 300,000	$ 200,000	$ 100,000
Short-term borrowing	200,000	150,000	100,000
Long-term debt	100,000	250,000	400,000
Common equity	400,000	400,000	400,000
Total	$1,000,000	$1,000,000	$1,000,000

Selected income data are as follows:

	Aggressive	Matching	Conservative
Sales	$1,800,000	$1,800,000	$1,800,000
Cost of goods sold	1,260,000	1,280,000	1,300,000
General, selling, and administrative	300,000	300,000	300,000

The sales are all on credit. Your firm has a tax rate of 30% and the short-term and long-term interest rates are 10% and 12%, respectively.

As a financial analyst, write a brief memorandum to the V.P. of Finance discussing each of the three financing policies, supported by your calculations of net income, cash conversion cycle, current ratio (current assets/current liabilities) and net working capital (current assets less current liabilities) for each policy. Be sure to address the advantages and disadvantages of each policy.

EXAM

Problem 2

James is the cash manager for Precision Heating Systems (PHS). He is in the process of preparing the cash budget for PHS over the coming year.

The firm's customer base consists mainly of hardware stores. About 50% of PHS's sales occur during the months of August, September, and October. Net working capital doubles throughout this high sales season.

Credit sales are high, with only 20% of customers paying in cash. Sales for the year are $9.25 million. The cost of goods sold is normally 60% of sales, and it is not expected to change. Last year's administrative, selling, and other expenses were $1.8 million. The firm's balance sheet at September 30, 20X1, is displayed below.

a) Estimate the seasonal portion of net working capital.
b) What policy is the firm following regarding the financing of its net working capital needs?
c) Calculate the cash conversion period.
d) Using Equation 10-6, estimate PHS's net working capital needs over the 20X1 fiscal year.

Precision Heating Systems Balance Sheet
September 30, 20X1 ($ Thousands)

Assets		Liabilities	
Current assets		**Current liabilities**	
Cash	$ 100	Accounts payable	$ 332
Accounts receivable	750	Accrued expenses	84
Inventory	1,020	Notes payable	140
	1,870	Current portion of long-term debt	50
Capital assets	1,850		606
Total assets	$3,720	**Long-term liabilities**	
		Long-term debt	960
		Shareholders' equity	2,154
		Total liabilities and shareholders' equity	$3,720

Problem 3

The sales of a retail business have two cyclical peaks per year. One peak occurs during the month of June, while the other occurs during November. The firm's fiscal year ends April 30. You are assigned the task of analyzing the firm's financial ratios.

a) What impact might this seasonality have on the current ratio, inventory turnover ratio, and return on assets? Why?

b) What would you do to minimize the bias, if any?

Problem 4

A company made a major investment in new plant and equipment about ten years ago. Because of amortization, the book value of these capital assets is far below their market values. You are given the task of analyzing the firm's total-asset turnover, return on assets, and times interest earned ratios.

a) What impact, if any, will the book value of the older plant and equipment have on the ratios? Why?

b) What special adjustments should you make, if any, before you calculate these ratios?

Problem 5

Well to Pump Gas (WPG) is a vertically integrated oil and gas company with headquarters in western Canada and operations in all provinces. The company's income statements and balance sheets for the past three years are provided below. Industry averages for a select group of ratios are also provided. Suppose that all sales are made on credit.

Well to Pump Gas Income Statements Years Ended December 31 ($ Thousands, Except Per-Share Data)			
	20X2	**20X1**	**20X0**
Sales	$3,834.00	$3,723.00	$3,109.00
Cost of sales			
Raw material	1,895.00	1,695.00	1,243.00
Labour	415.00	415.00	385.00
Expenses	2,310.00	2,110.00	1,628.00
Amortization	362.00	362.00	362.00
Selling and administrative	479.00	479.00	479.00
Income (loss) from operations	683.00	772.00	640.00
Other income	56.00	0.00	0.00
Income before interest and taxes	739.00	772.00	640.00
Interest expense	375.00	375.00	375.00
Taxable income (loss)	364.00	397.00	265.00
Income taxes at 25%	91.00	99.25	66.25
Net income (loss)	$ 273.00	$ 297.75	$ 198.75

Continued >

Preferred dividends	$ 64.00	$ 64.00	$ 64.00
Common share income (loss)	209.00	233.75	134.75
Common dividends	156.50	156.50	156.50
Retained earnings	$ 52.50	$ 77.25	$ (21.75)
Common shares outstanding	313.00	313.00	313.00
Earnings (loss) per share	$ 0.67	$ 0.75	$ 0.43
Dividend per share	$ 0.50	$ 0.50	$ 0.50

Well to Pump Gas Balance Sheets
December 31 ($ Thousands)

Assets	20X2	20X1	20X0
Current assets			
Cash	$ 25.51	$ 125.20	$ 2.84
Accounts receivable	783.12	775.00	767.00
Inventory	491.23	265.00	260.00
	1,299.86	1,165.20	1,029.84
Capital assets			
Equipment	2,254.12	2,458.23	2,662.34
Plant and property	1,812.88	1,970.77	2,128.66
	4,067.00	4,429.00	4,791.00
Total assets	$5,366.86	$5,594.20	$5,820.84
Liabilities			
Current liabilities			
Accounts payable	$ 508.12	$ 490.25	$ 485.11
Accrued liabilities	26.34	22.75	20.41
Bank loans	47.27	73.32	285.69
	581.73	586.32	791.21
Long-term liabilities			
Long-term debt	2,756.65	3,056.65	3,056.65
Shareholders' equity			
Preferred shares	189.87	189.87	189.87
Common equity	1,466.63	1,466.63	1,466.63
Retained earnings	371.98	294.73	316.48
Total liabilities and shareholders' equity	$5,366.86	$5,594.20	$5,820.84

Average Values of Selected Ratios for a Group of Representative Companies			
Current ratio	1.24	Net profit margin (%)	6.50
Acid test ratio	0.84	Debt ratio (%)	57.50
Inventory turnover	10.50	Long-term debt ratio (%)	52.00
Days sales outstanding	52.52	Times interest earned	2.00
Capital-asset turnover	1.00	Earnings per share	$ 0.75
Total-asset turnover	0.95	Dividends per share	$ 0.40

a) Calculate for WPG the sample of ratios suggested in the final table. Calculate the ratios for all three years if data are available.

b) Analyze WPG's working capital management.

c) Comment on management's effectiveness in managing the firm's assets.

d) Describe the firm's financial policy.

e) Comment on the firm's dividend policy.

f) What suggestions would you make to WPG?

Cases

Case 1: Miller Manufacturing

As cash manager of Miller Manufacturing, you are planning your cash budget for the next quarter. It is now April 1, 20X3. Summary financial statements for the year ended December 31, 20X2, are shown in Case Exhibits 10-1 and 10-2. Actual sales for the first quarter of 20X3, and projected sales for the coming quarter, are provided in Case Exhibit 10-3. Credit sales represent 80% of total revenues, and credit terms are net 30. Half of the credit customers pay exactly on time, while the remainder take 60 days to pay. No penalty is charged for late payment. Miller Manufacturing purchases materials on terms of net 30 and always pays on time on day 30. Actual and projected cash expenses and purchases for the first 6 months of 20X3 are provided in Case Exhibit 10-4. Credit purchases represent 40% of the total projected cash expenses and purchases.

Miller Manufacturing has no plans for capital expenditures at this time. Miller Manufacturing generally pays quarterly cash dividends, and the next dividend payment is due to be paid on July 1, 20X3. There are 1,000,000 shares outstanding, and the company has been paying a constant dollar dividend of $1.50 a year per share. The April 1, 20X3, cash balance is $670,000, and the minimum precautionary cash balance of Miller Manufacturing is $500,000. The income taxes for 20X2 are due on May 1, 20X3. A portion of the long-term debt is due for renewal or renegotiation as of July 1, 20X3, in the amount of $750,000.

Required

a) Define each of the following motives for holding cash balances:
   i) speculative
   ii) precautionary
   iii) transaction

b) Using year-end balances, identify and calculate one financial ratio to measure each of the following characteristics of Miller Manufacturing:
   i) liquidity
   ii) solvency
   iii) profitability
   iv) activity

c) Using year-end balances, calculate the cash conversion period for Miller Manufacturing, and identify each component of the calculation:

   i) inventory conversion period

   ii) receivables conversion period

   iii) payables deferral period

   iv) cash conversion period

d) **i)** Prepare a monthly cash budget for Miller Manufacturing for the end of April, May, and June 20X3. For each month, calculate the impact of cash sales and receivables collections, and cash expenses and payables payments, on the cash balance.

   ii) Explain what your results indicate about whether Miller Manufacturing will have sufficient cash to pay its planned dividend on July 1, 20X3. State what recommendations your results suggest for this firm's cash, dividend, and credit policies.

NO CASH BUDGET ON EXAM

Case Exhibit 10-1
Miller Manufacturing Income Statement Year Ended
December 31, 20X2 ($ Thousands)

Sales	$ 78,480
Cost of goods sold	51,074
Operating expenses	10,211
Operating earnings	17,195
Interest expense	6,800
Earnings before income tax	10,395
Income tax expense	4,158
Net earnings	$ 6,237

Case Exhibit 10-2
Miller Manufacturing Balance Sheet
December 31, 20X2 ($ Thousands)

Cash	$ 9,300
Accounts receivable	8,600
Inventory	8,210
Total current assets	26,110
Plant, building, and equipment	42,220
Total assets	$ 68,330
Accounts payable	$ 5,800
Long-term debt	27,000
Common shares	10,000
Retained earnings	25,530
Total liabilities and equity	$ 68,330

Case Exhibit 10-3
Miller Manufacturing Sales, Actual and Projected 20X3 ($ Thousands)

	Actual	Projected
January	$8,200	
February	10,400	
March	9,800	
April		$8,000
May		6,000
June		5,500

Case Exhibit 10-4
Miller Manufacturing Cash Expenses and Purchases, Actual and Projected 20X3 ($ Thousands)

	Actual	Projected
January	$6,400	
February	7,500	
March	5,800	
April		$6,000
May		5,000
June		4,500

Case 2: Super Soft Inc.

Super Soft Inc. has steady sales throughout the year and a stable client base. Half of its sales are made on credit. Its balance sheet (reporting the average sizes of accounts) and its income statement as at December 31, 20X1, are displayed in Case Exhibits 10-5 and 10-6 below:

Case Exhibit 10-5
Super Soft Inc. Balance Sheet December 31, 20X1

Assets		Liabilities and equity	
Current assets		**Current liabilities**	
Cash	$ 400,000	Accounts payable	$ 1,600,000
Accounts receivable	2,000,000	Accrued liabilities	320,000
Inventory	2,800,000	Notes payable	1,800,000
	5,200,000	Current portion	
		of long-term debt	200,000
			3,920,000
Capital assets	5,000,000	Long-term debt	3,080,000
		Shareholders' equity	3,200,000
Total assets	$10,200,000	Total liabilities	
		and shareholders' equity	$10,200,000

Case Exhibit 10-6
Super Soft Inc. Income Statement Year Ended
December 31, 20X1

Sales	$41,000,000
Cost of sales	25,000,000
Selling and administration expenses	6,480,000
Fixed operating expenses	6,800,000
Income from operations	2,720,000
Interest expense	320,000
Taxable income	2,400,000
Income taxes	960,000
Net income	$ 1,440,000

Required

a) Define the term "cash conversion period" and calculate the cash conversion period for Super Soft Inc. Show calculations for each of the *three* components of the cash conversion period (inventory conversion period, receivables conversion period, and payables deferral period). Also calculate the amount of net working capital as at year end 20X1.

b) Everything else remaining constant, how would the net working capital needs of Super Soft change if it changed its receivables conversion period to 20 days?

c) Everything else remaining constant, how would the net working capital needs of Super Soft change if it extended its payables deferral period to 40 days?

d) For each of the following financial characteristics of Super Soft, identify and calculate *one* ratio to assess the characteristic:

  i) liquidity
  ii) activity
  iii) profitability

Glossary

acquisition buying control of either of a target company's shares or of its assets

adjusted present value (APV) method a valuation method that separates the cash flows of a project into (1) the cash flows obtained assuming the project will be financed with all equity, and (2) the incremental cash flows obtained if the firm uses a source other than equity to finance the project

agency costs costs to an organization in the event that management violates the principal-agent relationship and commences decision making toward objectives other than maximizing shareholder wealth

aggressive strategy financial strategy that relies on long-term debt to finance only a portion of the long-term assets and the permanent net working capital; the other portion, as well as the seasonal portion of net working capital, is financed with short-term borrowing such as bank loans and commercial paper

American option an option that can be exercised *on or before* the expiry date

announcement date (dividend) the date on which the amount of dividends per share, the record date, and the payment date are announced, after approval of a dividend by the company's board of directors

announcement date (rights offering) the date on which the company announces a rights offering

anti-takeover measure an action taken by management to fend off a hostile takeover

arbitrage the purchase of one security and the immediate or simultaneous sale of the same or a related security, the result being a risk-free profit

asset risk *see* business risk (1)

asymmetric information information available to some but not other investors

at the money an option whose market and exercise prices are equal

average rate of return on book value measures the profitability of a project as the ratio of the average annual incremental after-tax cash flows from operations to the average book value of the investment

balloon loan a type of loan that involves a balloon payment

balloon payment the balance remaining at the end of the term when the principal portion of an instalment is less than the amount needed to amortize the loan over the agreed term

bankers' acceptances written demands, accepted and approved by a bank, stipulating a commitment to pay a certain amount at a given point in time

bankruptcy may occur if a firm's cash flows from operations do not meet payments of interest or principal in full and on time

basis the difference between the futures or forward price and the spot price

basis risk the inherent risk that the rates on both sides of a hedge do not move in such a way as to satisfy the original purposes of the hedge

best-efforts underwriting arrangement arrangement in which securities dealers do not purchase shares for sale, but use their best efforts to sell the issue on behalf of the issuer at the highest possible price

bill of exchange *see* draft arrangement

bill of lading a formal document that substantiates the nature of, ownership of, and responsibility for goods from point of loading to destination

"bird-in-hand" view the view that shareholders prefer to have cash dividends paid to them now rather than wait for potential payments in the future

Black-Scholes option-pricing model one of the pioneering models of option valuation, developed in 1973 for pricing common share options; later modified for use in pricing options on futures contracts or on physical or real assets

bond a debt contract in which the borrower receives a fixed amount, the principal, at time 0 and promises to pay the interest periodically and the principal at maturity

bond indenture or **deed of trust** the formal agreement between the issuer of a bond and the bondholders

bond rating an assessment of the possible risk of default prepared by independent private companies that specialize in bond rating, known as bond rating agencies

bond refinancing or **refunding** the process of recalling a bond issue, paying the call premium, and refunding the issue at a new lower rate

breadth a market in which outstanding orders for securities are numerous and come from diverse and unrelated sources

broker a financial intermediary who facilitates the buying and selling of securities for investors

bullet loan a type of loan in which instalments only pay the interest on the loan, with no allowance for principal repayment; the entire principal will be due at the end of the loan term

business risk (1) or **asset risk** measures the total risk generated by the nature of the firm's assets and business

business risk (2) the uncertainty regarding a firm's operating income before interest and taxes

buyer credit credit in which the buyer finances the transaction, either internally or externally with its bank

call option gives the holder the right but not the obligation to *buy* an asset at a fixed exercise (strike) price within a specified period or on a specified date

call premium the extra amount that will be paid to the bondholders if a callable bond is called; typically set as a fraction of one year's interest

call provision enables a bond issuer to reserve the right to pay off the entire bond issue before maturity

callable or **redeemable bond** a bond with a call provision

callable or **redeemable preferred shares** preferred shares giving the issuer the right to call the shares for redemption

cap a type of interest-rate option that protects against rising rates

capital asset pricing model (CAPM) describes the relationship between a security's expected return and its systematic risk

capital budgeting the process by which the financial manager decides whether to invest in specific capital assets or projects

capital cost allowance (CCA) tax shield that can be claimed over the useful life of an asset

capital or **financial lease** a lease contract that generally encompasses the entire life of the asset

capital market line (CML) represents any desirable combination of expected return and risk

capital rationing occurs when a firm does not invest in all its positive net present value projects because of a constraint imposed voluntarily or involuntarily on the total amount of funds to be used on capital projects

capital risk the fluctuation in the market values of financial or other assets resulting from changes in interest rates

cash budget a planning schedule that summarizes cash receipts and cash disbursements over time

cash conversion period the average period of time elapsing between the payment of a supplier and the actual point that payment from sales is received

cash flow guarantee arrangement a method of project financing in which one or more of the sponsors are required to make up any deficiency in cash flows required to service the debt, thus reducing the risk of the project

cash management the procedures, tools, and techniques that financial managers use to manage cash

cash or **spot price** the price at which an asset can be purchased today

cash settled for futures on stock indexes, this means that when the futures contract expires, the seller delivers to the buyer the current cash value of the index rather than the assets that make up the index

characteristic line provides a given security's return based on the security's systematic risk

clearing house acts as seller to the buyer and as buyer to the seller of a derivative

clientele effect the effect whereby different groups of shareholders prefer different dividend payout policies

coefficient of variation measures the relative variation (or risk) of a project in relation to the mean or expected return

collar a type of interest-rate option that combines caps and floors to form another customized instrument; involves the purchase of a cap with the sale of a floor

commodity option an option written on a commodity

commodity-price risk the fluctuation in the profit or market value of a firm's shares that results from changes in commodity prices

common-size financial statements financial statements expressed on a basis that eliminates the effect of a firm's size on performance evaluation and allows a firm-to-firm comparison

compensating balance the average minimum cash balance that a borrower is required to keep on deposit with the lending institution

competitive offering a process in which the issuer invites securities firms to submit bids to purchase the entire issue for resale to the public

compliance with loan covenants loan agreements which may require compensating balances

compromise approach risk-management approach in which a firm develops a complete hedging strategy to minimize its risk exposure and follows it with some exceptions

congeneric merger a merger that combines companies selling different but related products in the same market

conglomerate merger a combination of two (or more) firms that operate in entirely unrelated markets and/or industries and have no particular relationships or similarities

constant dividend payout ratio policy used by firms that wish to pay out a constant percentage of earnings in dividends on a regular and predictable basis

constant-dollar dividend policy used by firms that wish to pay out a fixed-dollar amount on a regular and predictable basis

consumption preferences line a graphic representation of optimal investment strategies

continuous equilibrium occurs if all security prices equal their intrinsic values

convertible bond a bond carrying the additional option of being exchanged for common shares

convertible preferred shares preferred shares are similar to convertible bonds in that they enable the holder to convert the preferred shares into some other class of shares (usually common) at a predetermined price

corporate financial planning the process by which a firm formulates a set of consistent business and financial objectives and identifies how they can be achieved

correlation coefficient statistic that measures the degree of association between two variables

covenant a provision or provisions placed by the lender on the borrower in order to protect the lender against possible default of a loan

cross hedge an arrangement in which the asset underlying a futures or forward contract is different from the asset being hedged

cumulative preferred shares preferred shares requiring that unpaid dividends on them accumulate until the company is able to make full payment

cumulative voting a voting method designed to enable minority shareholders to have a voice in the control of the company by permitting shareholders to cast their available votes for one candidate or many candidates at their discretion

currency swap an arrangement in which two parties agree to exchange currency payments at certain points in the future at agreed prices

daily price limits specify a range of prices around the opening price within which trading can take place

debenture an unsecured bond; the only protection to the buyer is the good faith of the issuer

deed of trust *see* bond indenture

default risk (1) the possibility that some borrowers may not return the money fully or on time

default risk (2) the expected losses due to the possibility of default

defence costs the costs of actions taken by managers in an attempt to ward off bankruptcy

defensive approach risk-management approach in which the manager takes action in the financial market to insure against major risks, which threaten substantial losses that may lead to bankruptcy

degree of operating leverage the percentage change in earnings before interest and taxes divided by the percentage change in sales

depth the existence in a market of many independent buyers and sellers who are ready to trade securities above and below the current quoted price

derivative a contract whose value is derived from the value of an underlying asset

derivative securities futures, options, swaps, and other securities that derive their values from other assets

direct costs of bankruptcy the result of default or actual bankruptcy; they include notification costs, court costs, lawyers' fees, and the loss from the forced sale of assets below market prices or the deterioration of property through negligence or lack of maintenance

direct forecasting method forecasts cash by dividing the forecast period into equal time periods and estimating receipts and disbursements on a category-by-category basis for each period

direct hedge an arrangement in which the asset underlying a futures or forward contract is the same as the asset being hedged

direct lease entails acquiring the right to use a new asset through a lease

discount interest loan a type of loan in which the bank deducts the interest from the loan amount in advance

discounted payback period similar to payback period, except that future cash flows are discounted as part of the evaluation

diversifiable risk *see* unsystematic risk

diversification an investment strategy to reduce total risk whereby the investor acquires many securities from different industries with different risks

dividend distributions of earnings to shareholders paid primarily in cash or shares

dividend-on date the last day that an investor can buy shares in time to be entitled to the dividend declared on those shares

dividend policy a firm's long-term policy toward the distribution of earnings

dividend reinvestment plan an arrangement whereby a firm directs dividends of participating shareholders to the purchase of additional shares

domestic bond a bond denominated in the currency of the issuer's country and sold in the issuer's domestic market

draft arrangement an agreement in which an importer promises to pay the exporter the amount of the draft either at a specified future date or on presentation

duration a measure of the average maturity of a stream of payments generated by a financial security

duration-based or **price sensitivity hedge ratio** hedging model in which the number of futures contracts used should be set in such a way that the change in value of the futures position will offset the change in value of the spot position, given a small change in interest rates

Dutch auction tender offer repurchase method whereby the firm specifies the maximum and minimum purchase prices it is willing to accept and the maximum and minimum number of shares that it is willing to buy

economic value *see* intrinsic value

economic value added (EVA) a popular measure used by many firms to determine whether an investment positively contributes to the owners' wealth; calculated by subtracting the cost of funds used to finance an investment from its after-tax operating profits

effective annual rate (EAR) the amount of annual interest divided by the amount of the outstanding balance

efficient market occurs when prices of securities traded regularly in the market fully reflect all publicly available information related to their valuation and adjust quickly to new information

efficient set the set of portfolios within the investment opportunity set that offers investors both maximum expected return for varying levels of risk and minimum risk for varying levels of expected return

election period the specified time within which preferred shares can be redeemed

equity residual method a valuation method that first determines the cash flows that can be distributed to shareholders after paying operating costs, financing costs, and debt repayments, and then calculates the present value of these cash flows

equivalent loan the loan that would commit the firm to exactly the same cash outflows as a lease

ethics standards of conduct or moral judgment

Eurobond a bond denominated in a currency foreign to the country in which it is sold

European option an option that can be exercised *only* on the expiry date

ex-dividend date the day after the dividend-on date

exercise price or **strike price** the price specified in the contract at which the underlying asset will be traded on exercise of the option

expectations view of dividend policy the view that the share-price reaction to a dividend announcement is not entirely governed by dividend policy

exercise date *see* expiry date

expiration date the date on which rights in an offering expire

expiry date or **exercise date** the last day on which an option holder can demand delivery

ex-rights date the date set two business days before the record date for a rights offering

extendible bond a bond issued with a short term to maturity, typically five years, plus an option for the holder to exchange the debt for an identical amount of longer-term debt at the same or a slightly higher interest rate

externally efficient a market in which, given a set of information, the prices of securities in the market fully and immediately reflect that information

extra or **special dividend** a dividend over and above the regular dividend

extremely conservative strategy financial strategy that relies on long-term debt to finance not only all long-term assets but also the permanent and the seasonal portions of net working capital

factoring a financing agreement in which a firm sells its accounts receivable, usually at a discount to the lender, without recourse

financial control the practice of monitoring the firm's progress in relationship to the overall financial plan and cash budget

financial flexibility a firm's ability to raise funds quickly at reasonable costs

financial lease *see* capital lease

financial option an option written on a financial asset such as bankers' acceptances, currencies, or Treasury bills

financial plan consists of both strategic and operating plans, which forecast possible outcomes and results

financial restructuring managerial actions that are primarily intended to change the capital structure of the firm

financial risk the additional risk placed on common shareholders as a result of using debt (or preferred-share) financing in the firm's capital structure

first or **senior mortgage bond** a type of bond that ranks ahead of any other bonds secured by the same asset

float the time that elapses between the time the payor forwards a cheque and the time the payee receives the cash

floating-rate preferred shares *see* variable preferred shares

floor a type of interest-rate option that protects against falling rates

floor trader buys and sells futures for his or her own account or on behalf of others

flotation costs costs incurred by a firm when issuing new securities

forecasting process of estimating the effects or results of future financial events

foreign bond a bond issued in a country other than the country of the issuer

foreign-exchange risk risk due to changes in the foreign exchange rate

forfeiting a financing agreement similar to factoring except that the receivables are longer term and have higher values

forward contract a derivative traded directly between buyer and seller in the over-the-counter market; all aspects of the contract are governed by the parties to it, one of which is usually a bank or financial institution

forward price *see* futures price

friendly takeover a business combination of two (or more) firms through cordial and structured negotiations, supported by the board of directors and management of the firm being acquired

futures contract a derivative transacted on an organized exchange; all aspects of the contract and trading in it are governed by the exchange and its clearing house

futures option an option written on a futures contact

futures or **forward contract** an agreement to trade an asset on a specified future date at a specified price

futures or **forward price** the price at which an asset is to be delivered at a specified future date

gap analysis a measure of interest rate-risk, derived from the difference between the values of interest-rate-sensitive assets and interest-rate-sensitive liabilities

hard rationing a situation in which a firm is not able to finance all its positive NPV projects because of a lack of funds

hedge ratio the number of futures contracts that need to be purchased or sold in order to hedge and cover all risk safely

hedger a person or firm that has a direct interest in the actual commodity or asset underlying a futures contract

hedging the use of futures, options, or other means to manage an existing risk; involves the initiation of a position in the futures or options market that is intended as a temporary substitute for the purchase or sale of the actual commodity or asset at a later date

holder the party who buys the option

homemade dividend the ability of shareholders to sell portions of their investments to generate their desired pattern of cash flows

homemade leverage lending or borrowing to establish the investor's preferred expected return and risk

horizontal merger a merger that combines two or more firms that are direct competitors in the same product lines and markets

hostile takeover a combination of two (or more) firms in which the firm being acquired opposes the bid

income risk the fluctuation in net income resulting from changes in interest rates

indexed balance sheet a statement that reports assets and liabilities in terms of the same assets and liabilities measured at the end of a base year

industry norms effect whereby the degrees of financial leverage of firms in an industry tend to cluster in a narrow band around the mean for the industry

initial margin the collateral required when a derivative contract is signed

instalment loan a type of term loan that specifies that the borrower will pay equal periodic payments

interest-rate risk the fluctuation in a firm's income or expenses or in the market value of its assets, liabilities, or shares that results from changes in interest rates

interest-rate swap an arrangement in which two parties agree to exchange the payments of a debt obligation

internal rate of return (IRR) the rate of return from acquiring an asset that discounts the future cash flows to equate them to the acquisition price of the asset

internally efficient a market that has depth, breadth, and resiliency

in the money a call option whose current market price is above the exercise price, or a put option whose exercise price is above the underlying asset's market price

intrinsic value the present value of all expected future cash flows from the security

inventory conversion period the average period of time that elapses between the purchase of raw materials and the sales of finished goods to a customer

investment banker serves as an intermediary between the issuer and the purchasers of the securities, providing advice regarding the type and terms of the securities to be issued and the market in which the securities are to be sold

investment opportunity set a selection of potential investments that represent appropriate degrees of risk and efficiency for investors

investment schedule used to show available investment alternatives

irrevocable letter of credit a letter of credit that cannot be altered or terminated without the approval of the beneficiary

January effect anomaly by which Canadian shares, particularly those of small companies, tend to fall two to three percentage points late in December and rise early in January

junior mortgage bond *see* second mortgage bond

law of one price states that the futures price of an asset is determined from the spot price of the same asset or the cash price of any product related to the asset

lease an arrangement in which the lessor makes an asset available to the lessee in return for periodic lease payments

lessee the entity or individual who will have full use of a leased asset

lessor the entity or individual who owns a leased asset

letter of credit a document that effectively commits a bank to the creditworthiness of its client in order to substantiate the client's future business dealings with a third party

level principal repayment loan an instalment loan that requires equal periodic principal payments to amortize the loan over the agreed term; the interest portion of each payment is the interest on the outstanding balance over the instalment period

leverage-indifference EBIT level the EBIT (earnings before income tax) level at which the return on assets, return to shareholders, and interest cost of debt are equal

leveraged buyout (LBO) the acquisition of a company by using little capital and large amounts of debt

leveraged lease a form of capital lease in which the lessor finances the cost of the asset with debt secured by the same asset

levered firm a firm that is partially or wholly financed with debt

liquidity buffer the portion of long-term debt used to finance seasonal assets

liquidity risk the risk of failing to pay creditors, suppliers, or employees as payments come due

long hedge gives the hedger the obligation to *buy* an asset at a future date at an agreed price, effectively locking in a purchase price

long position the purchase of a futures or forward contract on a security or commodity

macro approach measures risk exposure by examining an entire set of transactions that the firm may undertake over a given period of time

maintenance margin or **maintenance performance bond** the minimum balance that a brokerage firm will permit commodity futures traders to keep in their margin accounts

majority voting *see* non-cumulative voting

margin call or **performance-bond call** a request to add cash to the clearing-house margin account to bring the total back to the initial margin

margin requirement represents cash or securities provided by a futures exchange trader as collateral

marginal return the return on the last dollar invested

market price of risk *see* market risk premium

market price the amount of money at which a security can be bought or sold in the market

market risk premium or **market price of risk** the difference between the expected return on the market portfolio and the risk-free rate; the premium anticipated by investors for taking the risk of investing in the market portfolio

market risk *see* systematic risk

marking to market the process of updating margin accounts on a daily basis to reflect the market value of a trader's position

maturity-matching strategy financial strategy that matches the maturities of assets and liabilities

merger a combination of two or more companies in which ownership interests are joined

micro approach measures risk exposure by examining risks on a transaction- by-transaction basis

minimum operating cash balance the minimum level of cash that a firm holds under normal circumstances

mortgage bond a bond in which a mortgage against a corporation's property is deposited with a trustee, usually a trust company, which sees that the terms of the loan contract are followed

mutually exclusive a state in which projects cannot be undertaken simultaneously

naive or **1:1 hedge** hedge in which the position in the futures market is equivalent to the position in the spot market

negative gap when a firm has more rate-sensitive liabilities than assets

negotiated offering a sale of a security whereby the issuer negotiates the offering price and gross underwriting margin with the underwriting syndicate

negotiated purchase a share repurchase that takes the form of acquiring a large block of shares from one or more holders, negotiating the price in the process

net present value (NPV) the present value of the future incremental operating cash inflows of an asset, less the present value of all future incremental operating cash outflows, less the value of the initial investment

net value to leasing (NVL) method a method of evaluating a lease based on whether the NVL is positive

net value to leasing (NVL) the difference between the initial investment outlay saved under the lease and the value of the equivalent loan

net working capital the difference between current assets and current liabilities, can be estimated from the accounts of both the balance sheet and the income statement

nominal interest rate the stated or contracted interest rate on a bank loan

nominal method both the discount rate and the cash flows for a project are adjusted to reflect the impact of inflation

nominal-terms approach approach to inflation that involves forecasting all the variables, including sales, operating costs, fixed financial obligations, and capital expenditures, in nominal dollars

non-cumulative or **majority voting** a voting method that requires one vote per share for each director up for election

non-discounted equivalent rate the equivalent interest that would be paid at year end to the nominal interest rate paid up front on a one-year discount interest loan

non-diversifiable risk *see* systematic risk

normal-course issuer bid *see* open-market purchase

odd lot a stock transaction that is not an exact multiple of 100 shares

odd-lot order costs additional costs that may be incurred when selling securities in odd lots

offer to purchase repurchase method whereby the firm states a price at which it will repurchase shares and offers that price to existing shareholders

offering memorandum provides detailed information on a bond indenture and is part of the package used by investors in making decisions

open interest the number of outstanding contracts held by traders at a particular point in time

open-market purchase repurchase method whereby the firm acquires the shares from stockbrokers at the going market price

operating cycle the sum of the inventory conversion period and the receivables conversion period

operating lease contract that entitles a lessee to the right to use an asset for a specified period in exchange for specified payments on a regular basis

operating leverage the extent to which a company's costs are fixed as opposed to variable

operating plan a detailed schedule of activities used to accomplish the firm's strategic objectives

opportunistic approach risk-management approach in which management has superior ability to forecast financial or commodity prices; decisions are made based on the forecast to benefit from changes in these prices

opportunity cost of capital the return forgone by investing in real assets rather than investing in securities offered by the financial markets

optimal capital structure a combination of long-term sources of financing that maximizes firm value and minimizes the WACC

optimal investment strategy the aggregation of investments offering the highest NPV

optimal set of projects the combination of projects that maximizes the total NPV

option the right (but not the obligation) to buy or sell an asset at a specified exercise price within a specified period or on a specified date

option premium the price that the holder pays to acquire the option

options exchange an organized market in which traders buy or sell options

out of the money a call option whose exercise price is above the underlying asset's market price, or a put option whose current market price is above the exercise price

participating preferred shares preferred shares entitling the holder to share in the earnings of the company over and above the specified dividend rate

passive approach risk-management approach that ignores risk and relies on the ability of the company to ride the fluctuations; the manager assumes that over the long run any gains or losses will balance out

payables deferral period the average period of time elapsing between a credit purchase from a supplier and the issuance of the payment for that account

payback period the time (usually in years) that it takes a project to pay back its initial cash outlays

payback technique accepting projects with a payback period equal to or less than a target payback period; requires assessing a capital project by estimating its initial cash outflows and comparing them to the operating and terminal cash inflows

payment date the date on which the dividend is paid to all shareholders who are entitled to receive the dividend

payment pattern method forecasts cash receipts based on an analysis of historical customer payment patterns

payout ratio the percentage of earnings a company pays as dividends

pecking order theory the order by which various sources of funds are selected, reflecting a firm's preferences for funding

performance-bond call *see* margin call

permanent current assets the minimum level of current assets required to maintain the firm's operations regardless of the level of sales

perpetual bond a bond that has no maturity

pledging a financing agreement in which accounts receivable are used as security for a credit extended by a lender

portfolio immunization hedging against changes in the values of securities due to changes in interest rates, by balancing the duration of a firm's assets with the duration of its liabilities

positive gap when a firm has more rate-sensitive assets than liabilities

precautionary motive the need for a financial reserve to meet contingent cash needs as they arise; cash reserves insure the firm against liquidity risk

pre-emptive rights rights giving existing shareholders the privilege of buying from any new share issue an amount proportionate to their current degree of ownership

preferred shares with warrants preferred shares entitling the holder to purchase common shares of the issuer at a stated price without commission

preferred shares combine some characteristics of equity, as they entitle owners to periodic dividend payments and have no specified maturity date, and some characteristics of debt, as the payments are specified in the firm's charter and do not change in amount over time

prime rate the interest rate that banks charge their most favoured and creditworthy clients

price sensitivity hedge ratio *see* duration-based hedge ratio

private placement a share issue is sold to a group of institutional investors such as insurance companies, pension plans, or mutual funds

product-extension merger *see* congeneric merger

profitability index the present value of the incremental after-tax cash inflows for a project, divided by the initial investment outlay

project beta measures the sensitivity of a project's expected return relative to the return on the market portfolio

project financing financing of a large project on a stand-alone basis

promissory note a written promise that commits the borrower to pay the lender a specified sum of money either on demand or at a fixed future date, with or without interest

Prompt Offering Prospectus (POP) a short prospectus approved by the Ontario Securities Commission (OSC) for large corporations that file regular annual and interim financial statements with the OSC for at least 12 months and comply with the continuous disclosure requirements, regardless of whether they are issuing new securities

protective covenant or **protective provision** designed to safeguard the position of the preferred shareholders against any actions that may dilute the dividends of the security

public offering a sale of securities to the general public

purchase arrangement a method of project financing in which one or more sponsors guarantee to purchase part or all of the output or services produced by a project

purchase fund set up to retire, through purchases in the market, a specified amount of outstanding bonds or debentures only if purchases can be made at or below a stipulated price

put option gives the holder the right but not the obligation to *sell* an asset at a fixed exercise (strike) price within a specified period or on a specified date

put-call parity the central relationship between the value of a call option and the value of a put option when the two have the same underlying asset and exercise price

rate-insensitive an asset or liability that will not be assigned a new rate if interest rates change

rate-sensitive an asset or liability that is repriced when the interest rate changes

real method estimates the cash flows for a project based on present-day dollars and uses the real (nominal less inflation adjustment) rate to discount the cash flows

real-terms approach approach to inflation that involves forecasting all the variables that enter the financial planning model in real terms

recaptured depreciation a situation in which an asset is sold for an amount greater than its UCC at the time of sale

receivables conversion period the average period of time elapsing between credit sales to a customer and the receipt of cash from that customer in payment of the customer's account

record date (dividend) the cut-off point that determines who is entitled to receive the declared dividend

record date (rights offering) the date on which the company distributes to its current shareholders of record one right in an offering for each common share held

redeemable bond *see* callable bond

redeemable preferred shares *see* callable preferred shares

regression analysis an analytical technique used to estimate linear relationships between the value of a firm and various sources of risk

reinvestment rate risk the risk that borrowers may return the money early when interest rates have dropped, so that the lender is forced to reinvest the money at a lower rate

residual dividend policy used by firms that wish to pay dividends only if earnings and cash flows exceed the amount of funds needed to finance all investment projects that have zero or positive NPV

resiliency a market in which a price change will activate a wave of new trading orders below and above the quoted price

restricted shares common shares that do not entitle shareholders to full voting rights

retractable bond a bond issued with a long term to maturity plus an option for the holder to redeem the bond at par several years sooner

retractable preferred shares preferred shares for which the holder can retract the maturity by tendering the shares to the issuer for redemption

reverse stock split an action taken by a firm to decrease the number of shares outstanding without repurchasing shares

revocable letter of credit a letter of credit that may be modified or cancelled at any time without informing the beneficiary

revolving line of credit a variant on a straight loan in which the firm negotiates a line of credit, at a predetermined interest rate, and the lender advances funds as required to cover the firm's cash outlays

rights offering a type of offering in which the company distributes certificates to its current shareholders, giving them the rights to subscribe to additional shares of the company at a specified price

rights-on period the time between the announcement date and the ex-rights date in a rights offering

risk-adjusted indicates a rate that contains a premium to account for uncertainty

risk-adjusted discount (or required) rate captures the portfolio (or covariance) effects of a project; compensates the investor for committing the funds and accepting the risk to undertake the investment

risk-free rate the rate that compensates lenders for giving borrowers the right to use the lenders' money and for any expected losses to lenders that may occur because of inflation

risk management the reduction or elimination of risk arising from market factors such as interest rates, foreign exchange rates, or commodity prices

risk premium the additional interest demanded by investors as compensation against various types of risk

S&P/TSX Composite Index an index made up of a selection of stocks from the Toronto Stock Exchange that meet certain minimum price, liquidity, and index weighting requirements

sale and leaseback arrangement a form of lease in which a company sells an asset that it owns to another party for cash and then contracts to lease the asset back for a specified term

scenario analysis measures risk exposure by changing sets of variables to create alternative scenarios and provide a better understanding of the overall most likely, best, and worst scenarios

seasonal temporary current assets the level of current assets needed above permanent current assets

second or junior mortgage bond a type of bond that is junior in priority to the claims of first or senior mortgage bonds

secured bond a bond backed by a pledge of specific assets

security market line (SML) a graphic representation of the relationship between a security's expected return and its systematic risk

semi-strong form of market efficiency a market in which prices reflect all publicly available information, past and present

senior mortgage bond *see* first mortgage bond

sensitivity analysis the process by which the financial manager studies the sensitivity of a project's net present value to changes in one of the variables used in determining the cash flows or the discount rate

service lease an operating lease that requires the lessor to handle all maintenance and servicing

share repurchase an action whereby a company reacquires its shares by paying cash to shareholders in return for their share rights

short hedge gives the hedger the obligation to *sell* an asset at a future date at an agreed price, effectively locking in a selling price

short position in a derivative contract, agreeing to sell an asset one does not own

short-term financial plan a detailed forecast of the income statement, cash flow statement, and balance sheet over the coming fiscal year

sight draft a draft arrangement with payment on presentation

signalling the process of conveying information through a firm's actions

signalling event in one view, an event such as the issue of new securities to the public that provides information regarding the future projects planned by a firm

signalling hypothesis the view that changes in dividends are considered to be useful information to investors concerning a company's future prospects

sinking fund money set aside by the bond issuer to provide for the repayment of all or part of a debt issue before maturity

soft rationing management's decision to limit the capital spending budget available for some or all divisions

solvency a firm's ability to pay its liabilities after the dividend payment

special dividend *see* extra dividend

speculative motive the need to take advantage of bargain opportunities such as discount sales, attractive interest rates, and favourable foreign exchange rate fluctuations

speculator a person or firm that purchases and sells futures or forward contracts with the sole intention of making a profit by closing out the position at a price that is higher than the initial price

spontaneous current liabilities current liabilities that result from operations over which management has no influence

spontaneous financing short-term financing that a firm obtains from accrued liabilities and accounts payable

spontaneous permanent current liabilities the minimum level of accounts payable, accrued liabilities, and accrued taxes payable that arises regardless of the sales level

spontaneous seasonal current liabilities the difference between the total spontaneous current liabilities and the spontaneous permanent current liabilities

spot market a market for trading assets where there is an immediate exchange of the asset for cash

spot price *see* cash price

standby agreement requires that the underwriter purchase unsold shares at the subscription price of the offering (in the case of a rights offering) or at an agreed price (in the case of a public issue)

statutory amalgamation *see* merger

stock dividend additional shares distributed to existing shareholders

stock split an action taken by a firm to increase the number of shares outstanding without issuing new shares and selling them in the market

straight preferred shares preferred shares that rank in priority ahead of common shares and behind debt, have a fixed dividend rate and trade in the market on a yield basis, have no voting privileges and no potential for appreciation, and normally have no maturity

strategic plan lays out the general direction for a firm's future

strike price *see* exercise price

strip or **zero coupon bond** a bond that does not promise any cash flows to the owner until maturity, when the face value is paid back to the owner

strong form of market efficiency a market in which all securities prices quickly reflect all information available to investors

subordinated debenture a debenture that is junior to other securities issued by the company

supplier credit credit in which the supplier funds the entire trade

systematic, non-diversifiable, or **market risk** the contribution of a particular security to the overall risk of the market portfolio

tax shield method used to calculate after-tax cash flows using tax shields

tax-differential view of dividend policy the view that the difference in the tax treatment of dividend income and capital gains should make dividend policy important in determining the value of a firm

term loan a loan for a specified amount to be repaid over a specified period of time

terminal cash flows cash flows at the end of a project that may include the net cash generated from the sale of the asset, tax effects from the termination of the project, and the release of net working capital

terminal loss occurs when an asset is sold, there are no other assets in the asset class, and the asset is sold for an amount less than its UCC at the time of sale

time draft a draft arrangement with payment at a specified future date

total return the growth rate of the initial investment over an investment horizon of one year

total risk measured by the standard deviation of returns on a security

trading costs the transaction costs of buying and selling securities

traditional view of capital structure view that under perfect market conditions and in the absence of taxes, a large proportion of debt in the capital structure is desirable

transaction costs the attendant costs of conducting securities transactions

transaction motive the need to have cash on hand to pay specific bills or is the result of the non-voluntary holding of cash because of the timing of collections

Treasury bill short-term debt instruments issued by the federal government that mature within three months

treasury risk risks that arise from changes in interest rates, foreign exchange rates, or commodity prices

treasury shares repurchased shares that are held in the company treasury as opposed to being immediately re-sold

undepreciated capital cost (UCC) cost of capital assets before deducting the net proceeds from the sale of the assets

underlying asset the asset specified in the contract to be traded on exercise of the option

underwriting spread the difference between the sale price and purchase price of a share issue; comprises the management, underwriting, and selling fees

unique risk *see* unsystematic risk

unlevered firm a firm financed through means other than debt

unsecured bond a bond only by the earning power of the borrower and a claim against residual assets

unsystematic, diversifiable, or **unique risk** the portion of total risk that can be eliminated by combining the security with others

variable or **floating-rate preferred shares** preferred shares paying dividends that fluctuate to reflect changes in interest rates

vertical merger a merger that combines a company anId its direct customer or a company and its direct supplier

volatility a measure of the sensitivity of a security's market value to changes in interest rates

warrant a certificate giving the holder the right to purchase additional securities at a stipulated price within a specified time limit

weak form of market efficiency a market in which the historical price and volume data for securities contain no information that can be used to earn higher trading profits than would be obtained with a simple buy-and-hold strategy

weighted average cost of capital (WACC) the expected return on a portfolio of all the firm's securities and its retained earnings

weighted average cost of capital (WACC) method a valuation method that adjusts the weighted average cost of capital, which is used to discount the cash flows

writer the party who sells the option

yield curve the graphical relationship between interest rates for different maturities

zero coupon bond *see* strip bond

Index